Municipal Management Series

Local Government Police Management

**International
City
Management
Association**

The International City Management Association is the professional and educational organization for chief appointed management executives in local government. The purposes of ICMA are to strengthen the quality of urban government through professional management and to develop and disseminate new approaches to management through training programs, information services, and publications.

Managers, carrying a wide range of titles, serve cities, towns, counties, and councils of governments in all parts of the United States and Canada. These managers serve at the direction of elected councils and governing boards. ICMA serves these managers and local governments through many programs that aim at improving the manager's professional competence and strengthening the quality of all local governments.

The International City Management Association was founded in 1914; adopted its City Management Code of Ethics in 1924; and established its Institute for Training in Municipal Administration in 1934. The Institute, in turn, provided the basis for the Municipal Management Series, generally termed the "ICMA Green Books." ICMA's interests and activities include public management education; standards of ethics for members; the *Municipal Year Book* and other data services; urban research; and newsletters, a monthly magazine, *Public Management,* and other publications. ICMA's efforts for the improvement of local government management—as represented by this book —are offered for all local governments and educational institutions.

Municipal Management Series

Local Government Police Management

Second Edition

Editor
Bernard L. Garmire

Published for the
Institute for Training
in Municipal Administration

By the
International
City
Management
Association

Municipal Management Series

David S. Arnold Editor

Local Government Police Management

Community Health Services

Developing the Municipal Organization

Effective Supervisory Practices

The Essential Community:
  Local Government in the Year 2000

Management Policies in Local Government Finance

Managing Fire Services

Managing Human Services

Managing the Modern City

Managing Municipal Leisure Services

The Practice of Local Government Planning

Public Relations in Local Government

Small Cities Management Training Program

Urban Public Works Administration

Library of Congress Cataloging in Publication Data

Main entry under title:
Local government police management.

  (Municipal management series)
  Bibliography: p.
  Includes index.
  1. Police administration—United States. I. Garmire,
Bernard L. II. Series.
HV7991.L6 1982   352.2'0973   81-7174
ISBN 0-87326-024-4   AACR2

Printed in the United States of America   2345 · 89888786858483

Foreword

Modern police executives, of necessity, are confronted with changing management and operational methods. Most law enforcement agencies are faced with diminishing resources and a burgeoning crime rate. To have an impact on an ever increasing crime problem with fewer personnel, less equipment, and reduced support from the state and federal levels is a continuing challenge. To do more with less is the burden borne by today's police manager.

In the pages that follow, many nationally and internationally recognized police leaders address this changing image of law enforcement management. Within their respective areas of expertise, these contributing authors have provided the guideposts by which we, as police administrators, may advance the arts and sciences of our chosen profession. To be sure, we are currently in a state of transition. The material presented here reflects the dynamic nature of police work in all of its phases and offers the student of criminal justice valuable insight into the emerging role of tomorrow's law enforcement official.

By contrast, the major emphasis of earlier American policing was reactive and repressive. Police responded to incidents after the fact and most often operated to preserve the dominance of the political structure then in power. Reaching well into the fifties, the use of police to enforce the separation of races in public accommodation and transportation facilities is a clear example of such repression. Through a series of civil rights movements and antiwar protests, the birth of a federal agency devoted to assisting state and local law enforcement, and a number of social reforms by the courts and Congress (many of which were instigated by the police themselves), the nature of policing began to change.

Today more than ever, American policing has solidified its position as an integral part of the community it serves. It has shed the mantle of police "force" in favor of the more appropriate role of police "service." Law enforcement initiatives of reaching out to the public with police–community relations programs and upgraded testing, selection, training, promotion, and retention processes have helped identify policing as one of the most responsive, responsible, and representative agencies of government. From the chaos of the sixties, police became the focal point of massive studies. And, to the surprise of many, they emerged with a better report card than expected. Modern public confidence polls rate police among our most highly regarded professionals, in spite of the fact that the title of "professional" still eludes the police practitioner.

The most contemporary technology available has been adapted to the police service throughout the country. Automated data capability has been incorporated into police information systems as a matter of routine. Forensic sciences have made great advances in police laboratories. Computers have been coupled with helicopters, power boats, automobiles, and other response equipment. College educated officers at the entry level are more common today than at any other time in our history. And, following the democratic ideal, policing has moved away from the quasi-military mode of administration toward a sharing of the decision-making process through labor–management negotiations.

It has long been argued that the lack of standards by which to measure police performance transcending jurisdictional lines stands in the way of professionalizing the service. This, too, is currently being addressed by the nation's leading police research organizations under a federal grant to accredit law enforcement agencies that meet or exceed field-tested standards that are accepted by the Commission on Accreditation of Law Enforcement Agencies. The professionalization of the police service is also stymied by ancient misconceptions that use the absence of crime as the primary measure of police effectiveness and efficiency. Crime causation theory considers environments over which police have little or no control. Poverty, unemployment, lack of education, poor housing, and other conditions all contribute to crime. Other theorists hold that the commonly accepted age of majority constrains police too long from invoking the criminal justice system when the home, school, church, and social services have failed to adequately address the factors that predispose to crime. Finally, police represent one-third of a criminal justice system badly in need of a balance among its parts.

Continuing research is vitally needed in these areas. The proper role for law enforcement will always be a subject of debate and controversy. It is to their credit that police have functioned so well in the absence of a universally acceptable definition of their place in society. This book becomes all the more important to the philosophers, teachers, researchers, writers, practitioners, and administrators who toil so earnestly to formalize the relationships of government services into a meaningful and understandable model within the complexities of our social order.

Norman Darwick
Executive Director

International Association
of Chiefs of Police, Inc.

Gaithersburg, Maryland

Preface

The principal purposes of the second edition of *Local Government Police Management* are to provide police chiefs and other command officers with information on contemporary principles and practices for police management and to set forth the latest methods for police department operations. Management problems are approached from the point of view of the police chief, command officers, and the chief administrator. This book therefore is designed both to serve police officers and to meet the educational and training needs of police instructors and students.

Local Government Police Management has been published by the International City Management Association to replace the first edition, which was issued in 1977. The first edition, in turn, replaced *Municipal Police Administration,* which was published in seven editions between 1938 and 1971.

This and other titles in the Municipal Management Series have been prepared especially for the Institute for Training in Municipal Administration, which offers a wide variety of in-service training courses, workshops, and seminars for local government employees. ICMA has sponsored the institute since 1934.

Reflecting the evolving nature of police service, this second edition contains substantial revisions. A new chapter, "Emerging Police Issues," has been added to provide an informed commentary on mandates, discretion, and the boundaries of police responsibility. Other chapters have been revised and rewritten on the police environment and the governmental setting, police organization and management, police patrol administration, crime prevention and the community, personnel management and labor relations, and research and planning.

Like the first edition of *Local Government Police Management,* this volume stresses the shift in emphasis from the traditional areas of law enforcement to broader concerns of police organization and management, productivity, community relations, labor–management relations, and other subjects that show how the police are a part of a much wider community.

Over the years the predecessor editions of *Municipal Police Administration* reflected the changing and expanding needs of the police service. The first edition (1938) dealt with the traditional subjects of crime prevention, traffic, patrol, investigation, communications and records, and property and equipment, as well as such management areas as organization, personnel, and training. The second edition in 1943 added coverage of police and wartime responsibilities. Subsequent editions in the 1950s and 1960s added coverage of delinquency prevention, control of vice conditions, community relations, and planning and budgeting. The 1969 and 1971 editions expanded the coverage to include internal controls, intelligence, criminalistics, law enforcement planning, and a generally broader management orientation.

It is a pleasure to acknowledge the work of the chapter authors, reviewers, and others who participated in the preparation of *Local Government Police Management*. These persons are recognized individually in the "Acknowledgments" section.

The police mission today encompasses a wider range of services than ever before. It is hoped that this book—building on the work of predecessor volumes going back more than forty years—will help police administrators apply their talents for social ends as well as professional goals.

Bernard L. Garmire

Phoenix, Arizona

Contents

1 Emerging police issues

In the past fifteen years police departments in the United States have undergone a remarkable transformation. While the past has been a period of abundant resources and optimism, the present and probably the immediate future will be marked by a more conservative mood. Thus, it is likely that police departments will have less freewheeling experimentation, less exploration in new areas of activity, and probably a great deal less freedom in the use of resources. In some ways the change of mood constitutes a setback; a cutback atmosphere seldom is a reform atmosphere. On the other hand, the new situation offers an opportunity for taking stock. Those who have been active in the police field over the decade of the seventies can now catch up with one another; the value of their endeavors can be assessed; and programs can be put into some sort of order. This means that now is the time for synthesis; it is necessary to explore what the whole complex of policing, the old and the new parts of it, adds up to.

In the past, the nature and necessity of policing were implicitly understood. In the 1960s these implicit understandings came under severe attack. But even the demolition of old myths has not led to a notable clarification of the police mandate. Instead, the changes that have taken place usually have been responses to situational demands of all sorts. It may have been fortunate that the recent past has seen numerous poorly coordinated and inadequately justified projects. We learned more from this, and probably accomplished more, than we would have by implementing a rigorously formulated plan of action that left no room for mistakes or waste. But while expansion and growth benefit when enterprising innovators are given a free hand, consolidation is possible only when basic principles are understood. To make something lean and strong it is necessary to know what is fat and what is muscle. In the absence of a clear definition of the basic purpose of the police, the activities of police departments will be determined solely by political expediency. Determinations whether to cut back a given program will follow the sentiments of the moment. Alliances with citizens' groups, with various institutions, and with other units of government will be formed, cultivated, or neglected depending on what seem to be the balances of momentary advantage and disadvantage. And in all this the gains of the past decade and a half are sure to be lost.[1]

The formulation of the terms in which all parts of the vast complex we call policing could be assessed for their value and necessity is an essentially theoretical task. Not surprisingly, practitioners are rarely thrilled by theoretical analyses. They may allow that such efforts bring some spiritual comfort, but they do not find them immediately helpful in dealing with day-to-day problems. Police officers are not alone in this attitude. Practitioners of all vocations prefer dealing with questions that arise spontaneously and that must be answered without delay. In well-established professions such as teaching, the ministry, or medicine such neglect is relatively harmless. In a profession like policing, which has just passed through a period of beneficial but uncoordinated growth and is facing either a rational consolidation or a disorganized retreat, such neglect is very harmful indeed.

Some people think that it is quite enough that no one believes any longer that policing is a rather unsophisticated game of cops and robbers. These people need to be reminded that such revised beliefs will not be given full credit until the statement of what policing *is not* is accompanied by a strong and clear statement of what it *is*. None of the major questions about the conduct of policing in the years to come can be answered rationally without such definitional clarity. One cannot expect urban governments to underwrite programs for which only inchoate and ad hoc justifications are available. Nor will city hall accept empirical data of success, knowing how rarely such success is repeated. And while city hall will refuse to give in to demands, it will be in a good position to make demands of its own. After all, police departments traditionally have been available for assignments for which no other resources seem to exist.

The lack of clarity about the definition of its mandate not only hampers the police department in its dealing with urban government but also prevents the formation of any long-range cooperative understandings between police departments and citizens. The vagueness with which citizens perceive what they may expect of the police and the uncertainty with which the police respond to such expectations have created a situation in which even the best-organized efforts at cooperation disintegrate after the emergency that has led to their formation has passed. It must not be assumed that knowing exactly what the police provide to a community can solve all police–community relations problems. How can there be trust and reliance when the police convey to the people, directly or by implication, that they themselves are not entirely certain what can be expected of them?

Although uncertainties about the nature of the mandate clearly affect the external relations of the police, their effects are even more devastating internally. The following three illustrations of this impact all involve matters about which some decisions will have to be made in the near future.

First, as long as it can be maintained more or less legitimately that policing is done in an inchoate way and that it defies all efforts at conceptual formulation, the vocation of policing will be perceived as a low-grade occupation. It does not matter that policing properly done is most demanding, and it does not matter that a surprisingly large number of officers do a good job of it. The assumption that police officers do not need a firm intellectual grasp of their vocation leads to a staffing pattern in which bright and prudent officers may have only marginally competent co-workers.

Second, with no good way of specifying basic work responsibilities, there can be no justifiable way of discriminating between good and bad performance. In the absence of clear standards of workmanship, rewards must go either to those who follow orders and stay out of trouble or to those whose activities are highly visible. In either case, there are few incentives for resolute and skilled work.

Third, when officers are unsure which parts of policing are necessary and must assume that this is decided by rule of thumb, then job assignments, especially changes in job assignments, tend to be perceived as arbitrary. It is quite possible, therefore, that the notorious resistance of police officers to change results from the perception that so-called reforms are based primarily on managerial expediency.

One could easily extend this litany, but these examples should suffice to make the point that none of the problems facing policing today can be addressed properly, let alone dealt with effectively, without settling the question of what sort of activity policing essentially is. Instead, solutions to problems will have to be merely ad hoc, and police departments will continue to be buffeted by the tides of urban politics.

This chapter presents a definition of the mandate of the police, not in the abstract but in terms of concrete objectives, responsibilities, procedures, and capacities. The formulation is descriptive rather than prescriptive. It is based on observation of all kinds of police work, observation focused on discovering what police officers themselves consider to be serious and important police work well done. Thus the proposed formulation is no more than a way of offering suggestions about the possible definition of the police mandate and about approaches to investigating these matters further. In any case, the definition of the function of the police will have to come from within the institution, in dialogue with society. Everything else is preparatory.

Because the explicit formulation of the police mandate is practical—even though the task itself is theoretical—it will be allowed to emerge in the discussion of four prominent problems that face police institutions today in the United States. None of these problems is of recent origin. All of them have become critical because the current shift from expansive growth to consolidation will force some decisions about the direction of future development. The four problems are (1) the specific significance of criminal law enforcement in the total universe of police activity; (2) the determination of the outer boundaries of police responsibility; (3) relations between the police and members of disadvantaged segments of society; and (4) the nature of police work viewed as a vocation with special regard for educational and training expectations, the internal organization of police departments, and unionization. These matters are in various ways related and deserve a unified approach in preference to the kinds of tinkering adjustments they ordinarily receive.

The police and criminal law enforcement

The question of what the police do—both what they *actually do* and what they are *supposed to do*—is often answered by giving lists of their activities. For example, in an excellent review of police functions in Western Europe and North America, one author identifies no less than twenty fields of activity, each comprising its own complexities.[2] With one or two possible exceptions, all these activities are encountered in most police departments in the United States. Such lists are practically endless, and their content and priorities would vary with departments and with particular ideological positions. In all such lists, however, criminal law enforcement would appear either as the highest or as a very high priority.

Conditional versus unconditional responsibilities

While there may be some police officials who consider the settling of domestic disputes to be as important as catching criminals, it is unlikely that any of them would regard it as more important. Moreover, it is certain that police officials consider the obligations arising out of the provisions of the criminal law as unconditional and would quote the penal codes to support this belief. But duties connected with such problems as domestic disputes tend to be viewed as conditional, though it is not quite clear what is meant by the term. If one asks whether an officer has a duty to intervene in a domestic dispute, the answer is likely to start with some form of "it depends." But if one asks whether an officer has a duty to arrest an offender, the answer is affirmative without qualification, even though in practice various unstated considerations are known to play a part in the decision to make an arrest, even in cases where probable cause evidently exists.[3]

Saying that police officers might properly become involved in domestic disputes under certain conditions draws attention to some contingent features; if such features are present, the duty to intervene is unconditional. That is, obligations not connected with criminal law enforcement can be regarded as conditional only because the relevant situations are not sufficiently specified. For example, the mere fact that two or more family members are quarreling is not, in and of itself, a sufficient reason for police intervention; but if the dispute implies a threat of serious harm, injury, or loss, then it must be stopped. The perception of this threat involves the exercise of informed judgment and is therefore complicated.

Discretion in law enforcement

It is well known that police officers do not invoke the law mechanically. This is so in part because they must assess the value of their information relative to certain standards of proof. Accordingly, an officer cannot act on an inner sense of certainty if this certainty cannot be converted into admissible evidence. In addition, officers are expected to consider some general policy interests in deciding whether or not to invoke the law. For example, it is commonly understood that the law is not to be invoked against citizens with unblemished records who are suspected of technical and relatively trivial breaches of the law. The extent to which discretionary latitude exists and is regarded as legitimate and desirable varies considerably with the type of crime and the type of suspect. Almost certainly any police officer would arrest a homicide suspect regardless of circumstances or the identity of the suspect. It is equally certain that four elderly women caught playing penny-ante poker in the church basement will not be arrested and charged with violating the state's gambling laws.

Ever since this fact became openly acknowledged, people have worried about the extent of discretion and urged that it be restricted by additional rules of procedure.[4] But this is easier said than done. If, for example, it were determined that arrests must be made in all felony cases, but judgment could be exercised for misdemeanors, then judgment could merely be exercised in a different way —it is not difficult to justify referring to the same set of facts as either felonious auto theft or misdemeanor joyriding. By defining the case as one or the other, the officer complies with the rule that was supposed to reduce the scope of discretionary freedom without actually losing any of it. Thus, criminal law enforcement is in practice conditional, even though it is commonly regarded as unconditional.

Common versus white collar crimes

Police duties relative to crime are also conditional in another way that is neglected in the literature, even though the facts are well known. Police officers are expected and expect to be involved in the control of certain crimes, especially common crimes (burglary, robbery, assault, and prostitution, for example), but they usually do not feel called upon to be involved in other crimes, especially white collar crimes. The decision whether or not to invoke the law in cases involving common crimes is made by the individual officer or sometimes by departmental policy. But questions of whether or not to intervene in cases from the large complex of white collar crime ordinarily do not even come up in police work. This fact raises additional questions about police discretion and about class bias in enforcement.

The designations *common crime* and *white collar crime* are imprecise, and it is hard to separate the two. Embezzlement is a good example of this difficulty, for it seems to be both a common and a white collar crime. Still, at the extremes the distinction is fairly clear. That is, there is general agreement that a police officer has a duty to move against a suspected mugger, assuming that conditions of probable cause are met. But a police officer is not expected to act in a case involving a state banking statute violation that is punishable by fine and/or imprisonment, regardless of the strength of probable cause. Police noninvolvement in most crimes committed in connection with the conduct of business, in the practice of a profession, or in politics seems to be based on a policy choice that, even though not always clearly articulated, is commonly understood among police agencies. According to this understanding, the police have refrained from developing enforcement capacities in these areas of criminal conduct because special enforcement agencies were created when the various crimes were defined in legislation.

Not surprisingly, there is ambiguity and overlap here, but it would be extraordinary indeed if a patrol officer initiated the prosecution of a group of steel manufacturing companies on charges involving price-fixing; it is not certain whether the officer would arrest a physician suspected of performing an illegal abortion; but it is virtually assured that he or she would nab the assistant manager of a supermarket loading pilfered merchandise into a car after closing hours, even though that too might be regarded as a white collar crime. The fact that price-fixing may involve a federal crime does not seem to be decisive, because the same officer would surely move against a person hijacking a U.S. Postal Service truck, even though this too is a federal crime. Nor can it be argued that the police have responsibilities only if the acts in question have been regarded as criminal from time immemorial. So-called victimless crimes are virtually all of recent origin, while the crime of bribery is of great antiquity. The former are a routine target of police interest; the latter rarely is.

The possible need for force

In addition to explicit or implicit conventions in the way the criminal law enforcement pie is divided, another principle also appears to explain who does what and why. In general, the people who commit common crimes are likely to try to evade arrest and may have to be caught and brought to face justice forcibly, while people who commit white collar crimes are likely to appear in court in response to a written court order. This is so, common sense suggests, because the former have nothing to lose in trying to evade prosecution illegally, while the latter might thereby risk a business, a profession, or a career. By and large it is assumed that burglars, rapists, robbers, and prostitutes, for example, act as if their cases are won or lost in a contest of wits, strength, or speed between themselves and the police officers who are trying to nab them. But congressmen charged with accepting bribes, brokers suspected of investment fraud, or lawyers accused of misapplying entrusted funds win or lose their cases only when the last judicial appeals are exhausted. On the other hand, of course, not all persons accused of common crimes actually try to flee even if they can; and some South American countries are said to be havens for fugitive white collar offenders.

The police maintain a special readiness and capacity to act in cases where by common assumption force may have to be used, and in maintaining this readiness and capacity they reduce the likelihood of opposition and of the need for the actual use of force. Naturally, readiness is not limited to giving chase and subduing suspects. Readiness also involves the use of investigative techniques appropriate to the crime in question, although the kind of detective work romanticized in the figure of Sherlock Holmes is the exception rather than the rule.[5]

Thus, the responsibilities of the police in criminal law enforcement also are conditional. Officers are not expected to act wherever and whenever any kind of crime has taken place. Instead, the mandate restricts them to dealing with those crimes whose clearance *may* require force. When this is the case, then the duty becomes unconditional. This is not to say that officers always or even often have to use force in clearing crimes. Yet there is a sphere of criminal conduct, a group of crimes, in which it is commonly assumed that force may have to be used. The absence of the assumption about the possible need for force identifies the alternative sphere of criminality, with which the police have no business to be involved.

The boundaries of the sphere of common crimes cannot be drawn sharply, but the area is very large and most of it is quite clear. Moreover, it becomes even clearer when one considers the types of criminality that are excluded. The decisive characteristic of the excluded kind of criminal conduct—that is, white collar crime—is that it can be committed only by taking advantage of one's position in business, in the professions, or in public life. Ordinarily such positions rank high on scales of wealth, power, and prestige, and the people occupying them are quite resourceful. Without access to such positions one cannot commit white collar crimes. Common crimes, on the other hand, are equally accessible to all kinds of people, without regard to wealth, power, or prestige. But it is common knowledge that the vast majority of common crimes are committed by people on the bottom of the social heap. As far as the police are concerned, it makes not a whit of difference whether a mugger is a prominent person or a ne'er-do-well. That is, we do not have two police forces, one for the poor and one for the well off. We only have a police force that addresses its concerns to those crimes in which poor people happen to specialize and that leaves other crimes to the care of other law enforcement agencies. If the urban police are portrayed as society's strike force against crime generally, however, it becomes difficult to avoid the impression that this struggle is permeated by a strong class bias.

The outer boundaries of police responsibility

Thus far it has been argued that criminal law enforcement by the police is limited to types of crime in which it is safe, or at least safest, to assume that the alleged culprit will not submit voluntarily to arrest. The tools of the police officer's trade—handcuffs, nightsticks, guns, high-speed vehicles—all imply the threat of force. Criminal law enforcement is assumed to deal with crimes against persons and property such as homicide, assault, armed robbery, and burglary. Through long experience, the police have developed procedures, skills, and resources to deal with such actions against individuals and society. In dealing with such crimes, police officers are empowered and required to use force, if necessary, to resolve the situation. This police power, especially the use of force, extends to other kinds of problems that are unrelated to criminal law enforcement.

Peacekeeping functions

It is well known that the majority of police actions are unrelated to criminal law enforcement.[6] At times these actions are referred to as peacekeeping, order maintenance, or simply service. But none of these designations helps identify the domain of a police officer's proper business. Some informed observers believe the domain outside of criminal law enforcement is beyond the ken of police officers and that, indeed, the demands that seemingly could be made of a police officer exceed ordinary human capacities. Many police officials are especially alarmed about the possibility that police work may become swamped with demands for services that are ordinarily provided by social workers.

These apprehensions, however realistic they may seem at first glance, are based on conceptual confusion. Police activities involving peacekeeping, order maintenance, or service are not a recent development at all. They did not begin as a result of recommendations of commissions or academic researchers. Policing always has included a great number of activities through which people in trouble have been helped, troublesome people have been controlled, critical situations have been handled, and conflicts have been resolved. All of this has been done informally, without any records being kept and, in fact, without anyone's taking notice. That is, to put it colloquially, people have always called the cops, and the cops have come and taken care of whatever needed to be taken care of and left without taking any "official action." Thus, it is simply not the case that the police were suddenly burdened in the 1960s by a vast increase in duties of a social service nature. What did happen was that all these activities began receiving the attention, within and outside police departments, that was denied them in the past.[7]

As it became known—more precisely, as it became acknowledged—that police officers maintained a form of unofficial control of unruly youth, extended protection to disoriented and incompetent persons, attempted to prevent suicide, and otherwise dealt with crises, emergencies, disasters, dangers, accidents, and other unusual situations, certain of the therapeutic professions felt called upon to come to the rescue of the police. They did this partly on their own initiative and partly in response to invitation from the police establishment. Perhaps it was the invasion of professional advice and instruction from psychiatrists, psychologists, social workers, sociologists, and so on that created the impression in the minds of some police officials that police work was on the verge of turning into social work. This was a misperception, however, due no doubt to the fact that there was no conceptual clarity about the inherent purposes of police work. As there was nothing to which to relate these professional teachings, they had to be perceived either as irrelevant to police work or as subverting it. Of course, the instructors too were confused and often seemed to think that they were training police officers to be family counselors. In fact, however, police officers needed instruction in clinical psychology not to be practicing clinical psychologists but to do better police work.

An example will help clarify the point. Assume that it is in the public interest to prevent suicides. Two approaches are possible. The first calls for eliminating causes leading to suicide, a task associated with the practice of clinical psychology or psychiatry. The second calls for stopping all incipient suicides. The latter task is police work. It would seem reasonable that a police officer who has the duty of preventing suicide would benefit from knowing something about its psychodynamics and about therapeutic techniques applicable to it. Still, the officer's duty would be confined to taking potential victims off roofs, disarming them, getting them to the hospital to have their stomachs pumped, and so on, all of which are provisional solutions to long-range problems.

What the officer learned of the psychodynamics of suicide had to be useful in doing this part of police work; otherwise it was irrelevant. Psychiatric instructors, however, may neglect the officer's special task—to prevent the suicide from taking place—and emphasize psychiatric concerns, thus preventing the needed adaptation of psychodynamic knowledge to police work. Therapists tend to convey their belief that preventing suicides without getting at the causes of suicide attempts is of little use. In fact, of course, preventing suicides is a serious, important, and complex task, even if it does not get at the root causes. Officers who may have to do it need to be prepared for it. The only way they can be prepared is to adapt what is known about suicide to their own concerns with it. Anyone who thinks that social work principles are taught to police officers in order to have them do social work simply misunderstands the purpose of the instruction. The purpose is to make available to the police the knowledge and skill that will be useful in police work.

The specific police mandate

Suicides are a good example because intervention is likely to be resisted, even when the victim hopes to be saved. It illustrates that what the police officer has to do may involve opposition, and here the obligation of the officer differs from that of other professionals concerned with suicide. The officer, and the officer alone, is empowered and required not to retreat in the face of opposition but to overcome it, with force if necessary. It is the thesis of this section that *all such situations, where something has to be done immediately, possibly against opposition, are the specific targets of police intervention.* The situation may involve catching a mugger who resists or tries to elude arrest, making peace between two fighting neighbors who are about to harm each other, forcing a landlord to let an emergency crew work on his property to stave off imminent tragedy, taking a mentally ill person to a hospital, or dealing with any other of an endless variety of unforeseeable problems that must be handled without delay.

In all such cases the police officer is empowered and required to use force if force is required to prevent a feared outcome or to cause the necessary to happen. The principle that gives specificity to police competence in the area of peacekeeping, order maintenance, and service is exactly the same one that identifies the specific role of the police in criminal law enforcement. Police officers are expected to deal with all problems in which force may have to be used to arrive at a provisional solution, in the expectation that others will deal with the underlying causes. As the next section will show, provisional solutions often have lasting consequences—a most troublesome matter that poses serious problems and should not be neglected.

It has been proposed here that the mandate of the police is to deal with all problems in which force may have to be used, regardless of whether the problems arise out of the criminal law or some other context. It does *not* follow that police work consists of using force to obtain certain desired results. Most skills and resources that are used in police work must be devoted to succeeding without recourse to force, but officers also must have skills and resources to use force as a last resort. This might be called the lean definition of the police mandate. No one can expect police work to be limited to matters that could be subsumed under the proposed definition. Teachers, clergymen, and nurses do many things that have nothing to do with education, the ministry, or nursing, respectively. And it seems only reasonable to expect that police officers will do many things that are not policing in its narrow sense.

Two other important reasons why police work should not be defined narrowly involve the *essential* nature of police work. First, police officers must be available when and where their specific skills are needed. This includes not only those critical situations where force may be required but also many police calls that turn out to be trivial. Second, police officers are the only helping hand available twenty-four hours a day, seven days a week, fifty-two weeks a year. One needs no appointment to see them and they make house calls in every part of the city. But it is not merely the fact that they are there that counts; it is also that they are viewed by most people as a trusted source of help.

It is essential that the specific police mandate be the governing criterion for judging the appropriateness of all police activities. Moreover, while there is nothing intrinsically wrong in having a police officer ease the movement of traffic at the county fair, it is crucial that police work not be understood to be this kind of job. By the same token, a person who might be regarded as capable of living up to the demands of this kind of job must not be judged capable of living up to all the other occupational demands of police work. The mandate must be clearly and explicitly defined not in terms of things police officers might do, often or rarely, because they happen to be available, but in terms of those activities in which they alone are competent and those that make the greatest demands on their skill and judgment.

The police and the urban poor

The duty to intervene—with force if need be—is connected with signs of impending disaster. At times these signs are clear enough. More often, however, the interpretation of signs is a difficult and elusive art. How do officers know whether a particular gathering is dangerous and should be dispersed? How do they know whether a party is disturbingly noisy and should be quieted? How do they know whether a quarrel between two persons has reached the point where one must be ordered to leave? Moreover, how do they know when the time has come to use force to take care of a problem?

Intervention among the poor

In present-day police work in United States cities the answers to the questions of whether or not to intervene and whether or not the time has come to resort to force exhibit a certain pattern. Specifically, observations of police practice suggest that officers find occasion to intervene much more readily in the lives of poor people than in the lives of other members of society and that they resort to force in these encounters more readily than in other encounters. Just as criminal law enforcement by the police focuses on those crimes in which the poor specialize, so do the other activities of the police focus on poor people. Although it may appear otherwise, there is a certain peculiar impartiality in this.[8] The police direct their attention to risk, danger, violence, impending chaos, tension, uncertainty, despair; and the lives of the poor happen to be far more densely textured with these than are other lives. As a result, one is less likely to notice these problems in parts of the city inhabited by the well-to-do. This perception is justified by the knowledge that the rich, the powerful, and the prestigious have an abundance of remedial help and social strength to maintain order spontaneously. But among the poor one is inclined to expect the worst. Experience indicates that even a trivial provocation can trigger a major disaster in the blighted section of a city. Further, since violence is more prevalent among the poor it seems natural to fall back on violence early. Police officers feel that they must gain an initial advantage; they do this by acting forcefully, from which it is only a short step to acting forcibly. Finally, the lives of the poor, although rich in their own self-help mechanisms, are virtually devoid of such formal remedial resources as lawyers, psychiatrists, and marriage counselors, many of whom serve only those who can afford their services. Thus, there are objective reasons for the frequency of police interventions in the lives of the poor, and the perceptual distortion that causes greater readiness to keep the lid on does not seem unreasonable for officers acting under conditions of uncertainty, ambiguity, and possible danger.

Still, an apparent bias emerges. An officer will readily disperse a group of youths congregating noisily in front of a business and interfering with its operation, but he will do nothing when business activity inconveniences, annoys, or otherwise disrupts the lives of the poor. In fact, it seems unfair even to bring up this kind of comparison. Given society's structure and values, the police officer has a duty to do the former, while the latter is within the jurisdiction of a zoning board or some other regulatory agency. But this is precisely the point, and officers who are unwilling or unable to confront these realities from the perspective of those who are oppressed by them are not really conscious of the complexity of their jobs.

Racial prejudice

One might infer from all this that urban police forces are in some simple sense an instrument of the ruling elites to keep the proletariat down, much like the English police in the nineteenth century.[9] But as Bruce Johnson has demonstrated, American police forces have not played this role, at least not in this century.[10] In fact, American police of the last several generations have been conscious of their origin in, and social ties to, the working class of white ethnic groups.

Unfortunately, those same ethnic groups have been and remain a source of racial prejudice, directed primarily toward blacks and Spanish-speaking people. Police practices reflect these attitudes to an extent that is a constant source of provocation to minority groups. The racist officer may feel empowered to express contempt and often to act brutally. Even in departments in which such conduct is not condoned, there is little control over it. Since such misconduct is often addressed to troublesome individuals, it is justified as aggressive police work. Of course, it is also often directed to persons who deserve courtesy and consideration. Officers often explain that in policing dangerous districts it is not always possible to act with kid gloves on. Moreover, it is argued, because police work is inherently provisional in nature, there is no permanent harm in (for example) a mistaken arrest. Unfortunately, formal provisional action does have lasting effects. An arrest record, even one entirely without convictions, does not open doors. But the most devastating effect of casual mistreatment of poor minority group members is their lasting hostility toward the police. Thus, while it is wrong to attribute the heavy presence of the police in the ghettos to their racism (they were sent there by all of us), the problem that cries for recognition is that even a little racism in police work does more harm than a great deal of responsible policing can repair.

All this leads to the following conclusion. Urban policing in the United States is set up to control forms of conduct that are considerably more prevalent among the poor than among other members of society. Some hold that this involves an unwarranted imposition of middle-class standards on people whose culture dictates a different kind of morality and that the burden of police control ought to be lifted entirely. Though this view is based on a desire to avoid casting aspersion on the poor and on minorities, it is biased in its own way. It is not fair to forgive a black mugger who has robbed another person of a welfare check, regardless of whether the victim was white or black. It is one thing to understand why so many minority youths become muggers; it is quite another to let it go at that.[11] Tolerance and prejudice walk hand in hand. Mugging is inexcusable, and it deserves unqualified and forceful condemnation. But the officer who thinks that mugging and other common crimes are the only evil in society, and who thinks it either is not true or does not matter that common criminals are themselves often victims of criminal exploitation, is just too simple-minded for the complicated job of policing.

There is a great risk in the police mandate. Because the mandate concentrates police activity on the poor, and because the majority of minority group members live in poverty, policing provides the racist with virtually unchecked opportunities to express racism in word and action. It is by no means necessary to assume that all, or even many, police officers are prejudiced to explain the notorious tension, anger, and distrust known to exist between the police and minority communities; it is quite sufficient that some such officers exist. It is illegal for public servants, including police officers, to be prejudicial or discriminatory in their actions. But in police work racist attitudes do more than violate the law and ideals of justice; they run counter to considerations of common sense and expediency. Considering what the police must try to accomplish, sending a racist out on the beat is not unlike letting a disease carrier do public health work.

The elimination of every vestige of racism and other forms of bigotry is only the first step in putting the relations between the police and the urban poor in good order. Beyond that must come the realization that the poor need competent police services to a far greater extent than people in the rest of society. People living in poverty are vastly more likely to be victims of common crime than are others, and they are considerably more likely to need help. The police mandate must be viewed in light of these considerations. It is, indeed, capable of being a provisional solution to some of the consequences of injustice and inequality in society.

Police work as a vocation

It is well established that policing is *not* a simple ministerial function that can be performed with virtually no training by anyone with an above-average physical constitution and more or less average intelligence. But it is not yet clear what kind of occupation it *is*. Educational requirements and training standards have been raised considerably, and performance expectations have risen accordingly. But this change has not been guided by clearly formulated ideas of purpose and direction. Such unplanned outreach is not necessarily bad (in any case it is inevitable in periods of rapid change), but it produces stress in coordinating the demands of police work with personal and career aspirations of officers. The character and value of policing as a person's lifework will be influenced significantly by the way these tensions are dealt with now.

However beneficial the recent years of change may have been, they have created more uncertainty than police personnel should have to endure. Under these circumstances it is only natural that police officers should organize to protect their interests. Recent increases in police unionization demonstrate this tendency. Though one cannot generalize, it is probably fair to say that police unions are opposed to change. Further, it is not difficult to understand the reason for this opposition. Change or reform is, after all, something that comes down from the top, and it is the business of unions to negotiate the price of compliance. It is still not customary in police departments for the rank and file to participate in decisions regarding changes in organization and practice. Even where honest efforts are made to establish open consultation, the absence of experience with participatory management prevents the process from being effective. So it probably is not fair to think that police union representatives are simply stubborn in refusing to accept every proposed change enthusiastically. Instead, it seems more reasonable to conclude that efforts to make policing more socially responsible require that this be done in a socially responsible manner from within as well. There is a certain irony in the fact that line personnel in police departments have as much reason to be skeptical of police management as members of minority communities have to be skeptical of the police generally.

Given that understanding policing as an occupation must begin with a fair and practical recognition of where the occupation is now, what is the ideal for a person whose lifework is police service? Following are some observations about the nature of police work, appropriate preparation for it, and the organizational context conducive to optimum work.

First, policing is a complex occupation addressing serious problems. It calls for knowledge and skill. More important, however, its practitioners are entrusted with the very considerable power to use force when necessary. In a culture in which force seldom has the sanction of legitimacy, this trust has special significance.

Second, policing is not technical in the sense in which engineering is. Instead, it makes great demands on experience and judgment. Experience is accumulated knowledge on which is based the understanding of practical necessities and possibilities. This understanding guides judgment.

Third, in their day-to-day work police officers often deal with matters to which other people respond with fear, anger, or loathing. One could say that police work consists of proceeding methodically where an impulsive reaction would be the norm.

Fourth, the preponderance of police work is done by individual officers or pairs of officers. Thus, police officers depend primarily on their own knowledge, skill, and judgment, and they must be prepared to finish what they start by themselves.

Fifth, more than almost any other occupation, policing offers opportunities for sloth, abuse, and corruption. This risk applies to individuals and also to the institution as a whole. The police can be—and often have been—used as an instrument of oppression.

This list is incomplete, but it is enough to make a person wonder how anyone could be adequately prepared for so demanding an occupation. Detailed discussion of preparation for policing is beyond the scope of this chapter, but two points can be made. First, it makes no sense to recruit police officers on the basis of an antiquated conception of what the work entails. Having learned that officers are required to make serious decisions, it seems absurd to accept candidates who have demonstrated only that they are capable of following simple commands. The quality of officers is being addressed by raising educational requirements and rewarding officers who increase their educational qualifications. But this is at best a stop-gap measure that often creates as many problems as it solves.[12] In the long run it will be necessary to convince the most talented and aspiring young people that policing offers a satisfying career.

Second, even though the preparation of police officers ought to involve an adequate general educational background, and even though other helping professions can provide auxiliary instruction, the invention and administration of the police training curriculum will have to come from the police themselves.

In light of all this, it hardly seems appropriate for policing to remain organized in its present form. It is scarcely imaginable that future police officers, fully aware of the nature of their mandate, would accept positions in a quasi-military hierarchy of command, the only conceivable purpose of which could be to make their work more difficult. Saying this strikes some people as suggesting the abandonment of organizational discipline. What actually is at issue, however, is the invention of an appropriate discipline that would function to control the risk of abuse and to enhance the effectiveness of the service.

1 For a review of recent change in the field of policing, see: Ruben G. Rumbaut and Egon Bittner, "Changing Conception of the Police Role: A Sociological View," in *Crime and Justice: An Annual Review of Research*, vol. 1, ed. Norval Morris and Michael Tonry (Chicago: University of Chicago Press, 1979), pp. 239–88. For an argument demonstrating that the time has come to rethink the direction of reform, see: Herman Goldstein, "Improving Policing: A Problem-Oriented Approach," *Crime and Delinquency*, April 1979, pp. 236–58.

2 David H. Bayley, "Police Function, Structure, and Control in Western Europe and North America: Comparative and Historical Studies," in *Crime and Justice: An Annual Review of Research*, ed. Morris and Tonry, pp. 109–43.

3 The richest collection of information about, and the most careful analysis of, discretionary law enforcement is contained in: Wayne R. LaFave, *Arrest: The Decision to Take a Suspect into Custody* (Boston: Little, Brown & Company, 1965).

4 The whole question of discretion in invoking the law was first analyzed with exemplary precision by: Joseph Goldstein, "Police Discretion Not to Invoke the Criminal Process: Low Visibility Decisions in the Administration of Justice," *Yale Law Journal* 69 (1960): 543–49. A veritable flood of literature followed.

5 Jan M. Chaiken, Peter W. Greenwood, and Joan Petersilia, "The Criminal Investigation Process: A Summary Report," *Policy Analysis* 3 (spring 1977): 187–217.

6 I have tried to summarize and interpret the evidence concerning this matter in: Egon Bittner, "Florence Nightingale in Pursuit of Willie Sutton:

A Theory of the Police," in *The Potential for Reform of Criminal Justice*, ed. Herbert Jacob (Beverly Hills, Calif.: Sage Publications, 1974), pp. 17–44.

7 One of the earliest statements about this came from an English scholar who observed police practices in the United States. See: Michael Banton, *The Policeman in the Community* (New York: Basic Books, 1964).

8 This impartiality has an analogue in the formal properties of law in the Western tradition; see: Isaac D. Balbus, "Commodity Form and Legal Form: An Essay on the 'Relative Autonomy' of Law," *Law and Society Review* 11 (winter 1977): 571–88.

9 Allan Silver, "The Demand for Order in Civil Society: A Review of Some Themes in the History of Urban Crime, Police, and Riot," in *The Police: Six Sociological Essays*, ed. David J. Bordua (New York: John Wiley & Sons, 1967), pp. 1–24; Robert D. Storch, "The Policeman as Domestic Missionary: Urban Discipline and Popular Culture in Northern England, 1850–1880," *Journal of Social History* 9 (1976): 481–509.

10 Bruce Johnson, "Taking Care of Labor: The Police in American Politics," *Theory and Society* 3 (1976): 89–117.

11 This whole troublesome topic is treated with remarkable fairness in: Charles E. Silberman, *Criminal Violence, Criminal Justice* (New York: Random House, 1978).

12 Lawrence W. Sherman and the National Advisory Commission on Higher Education for Police Officers, *The Quality of Police Education* (San Francisco: Jossey-Bass Publishers, 1978).

2 The evolution of contemporary police service

In introducing a discussion on almost any topic in contemporary American society—from aviation to zoological park planning—it has become commonplace to speak of the momentous changes that have occurred in recent years. The discussion that will be found in this book is no exception. The present volume, now in its second edition, is the successor to *Municipal Police Administration,* first published in 1938, which went into its seventh and last edition in 1971. Indeed, it is of more than passing significance that this latter book was revised twice in its last three years. That in itself is one indication of the torrent of new policy considerations, operational strategies, technological devices, court decisions, federal guidelines, and local pressures that has engulfed the thousands of police service administrators today.

It would be difficult to point to another public institution in American society that has been subject to as many major policy shifts and operational realignments as has the modern police service. For some, there have been far too many changes; for others, there have been far too few. Change in policing, however, has undeniably occurred: dramatically in some areas, almost unnoticeably in others. The net effect, however, has been sufficient to enable us to describe the modern police organization today as, in certain respects, a fundamentally different type of institution from the police operations that existed only forty or so years ago.

Eight years before *Municipal Police Administration* first appeared, in 1930, there were less than a thousand police patrol cars in use in the entire United States; today patrol cars are as much a part of standard police equipment as are uniforms, revolvers, and nightsticks. In those earlier days only one city had radio-equipped patrol cars—and these were equipped only for the transmission of messages from the station to the patrol car. Today police services possess a two-way communications system of such sophistication that thousands of police departments across the nation are linked with and have access to a national, computerized data bank that provides almost instantaneous responses on stolen property, wanted persons, criminal histories, and similar information.

The first well-equipped police laboratory in the United States was not established until 1929; however, owing to the skepticism of police officials concerning the value of such scientific procedures, this laboratory was established by private interests and was located at a university. Today the indispensability of a good police crime laboratory would be acknowledged by every police chief in the nation.

Four decades ago police personnel ranks were almost exclusively white and male; today the recruitment of minorities and the assignment of women to patrol duties are considered feasible by most police administrators and desirable by many, and in an increasing number of communities are regarded by police administrators as a priority departmental policy objective.

Although police unions can be traced back to the post–Civil War period, in the 1930s police unions were still virtually nonexistent and a police strike, in spite of the infamous Boston episode, was considered an organizational contradiction in terms. Today police unions and collective bargaining are a fact of life for police administrators in both large cities and small towns, and police chiefs are increasingly confronting actual or possible police strikes.

The list of specific changes in policing over the past fifty years is virtually endless. As stated above, there have been mixed reactions. Some administrators applaud the technological developments but are appalled by the prospect of a woman on patrol assignments and by the rise of police unionism. Some critics praise these developments but have profound misgivings about the current infatuation with technology.

Whatever the priorities, the fact of change is inescapable. Understanding that change—what is occurring, the pressures, developments, and events that have brought it about and will continue to stimulate its occurrence, and how the police organization can be most effectively adapted to it—is a hallmark of enlightened, professional police leadership. In practical terms, learning to cope with change, rather than being overwhelmed and outdated by it, is an essential strategy for administrative survival in the fast-paced, continually changing world of the contemporary police administrator.

The effects of social change

It is sometimes thought that the problems of change—of changing societal attitudes and values, of changing expectations of public institutions, of changing responses institutions must make to new expectations—are new problems arising from the turbulence in American society in the last generation. The police service, in particular, felt the brunt of the shifts in American society during that time. What today have become household words in policing—*Gideon* v. *Wainwright* (372 U.S. 335 [1963]), *Escobedo* v. *Illinois* (378 U.S. 478 [1964]), *Miranda* v. *Arizona* (384 U.S. 436 [1966])—were landmark court decisions of that time. Encounters with civil rights marches, with anti-Vietnam war protests, with college campus upheavals, and with the "long, hot summers" were features of that time for urban police. Even small town police chiefs and county sheriffs had their share of the upheavals. *Miranda* had the same impact on policing in rural Nebraska and in urban Newark, while rock music festivals brought problems to a number of rural police agencies that their administrators had always associated with the "big cities."

Law enforcement was the subject of three federal commissions in the late 1960s. The first, the President's Commission on Law Enforcement and Administration of Justice, issued its carefully measured recommendations in 1967,[1] but police and public attention to that report were virtually eclipsed by the civil disorders which seemed to reach a fiery peak that same year. Two subsequent commissions were established—one to examine the civil disorders themselves, the other to look at the larger question of the causes and prevention of violence.[2] Both reports offered sobering insights into the turmoil in American society, but because their recommendations—some of which were critical of the way in which police handled the disorders—differed from public perceptions of the nature of the problem, these reports were largely ignored. Brief summaries of these three reports and two other reports of that period appear in Appendix A of this book.

The 1960s were the period during which researchers "discovered" the fields of law enforcement and the police service. Publications on police attitudes and practices were few, and random, in the early years of the decade. Then came the civil disorders of 1964–68. By the end of the decade a flood tide of publications, reports, and research findings was pouring forth from university faculty offices and private research firms. Many of these studies were seen by some police administrators as lacking understanding of the plight and the problems of modern policing.

Such events tended to bring about a great nostalgia, as most turbulent periods in history do, for what police officers remembered as "the good old days." In both the chief's office and the locker room veteran officers spoke of the days when "everyone loved and respected a cop," when the courts "left police matters to policemen," when "kids went to college to study," and their professors minded their own, nonpolice, business.

Right to counsel In the 1960s the United States Supreme Court handed down three decisions that have been extremely influential in stating clearly the rights of citizens to legal counsel. In *Gideon* v. *Wainwright,* 372 U.S. 335 (1963), the Court held that the right to counsel is a fundamental right in state, and therefore local, courts as well as in federal courts and that an indigent felony defendant should have such assistance.

The Supreme Court next held in 1964, in *Escobedo* v. *Illinois,* 378 U.S. 478, that the right to counsel also applies when the accused wishes to consult with legal counsel during the time of accusation—that is, prior to any indictment—so that he or she can be advised of his or her privilege against self-incrimination.

In *Miranda* v. *State of Arizona,* 384 U.S. 436 (1966), the Supreme Court further extended the right to counsel to the initial point of custody when a person is picked up by the police. One of the reasons again was to protect a person from possible involuntary self-incrimination.

In actual fact, such recollections are not very accurate reflections of the realities of the police world—in the pre-1960 era or at any other period in the history of American police service. A look at that history indicates that the decade of the 1960s was neither different nor unique. History also shows us how, and perhaps offers some clues as to why, the world of the police service has always been one of learning to cope with change.

The historical background

What, then, can we learn about contemporary dilemmas in policing from the history of the police service? We can profitably begin with the obvious statement that (to parody Gilbert and Sullivan) "a police chief's lot is not an easy one!" That in itself says nothing new, but what may come as a surprise is the discovery that even in the days of Sir Robert Peel and the organization of the London Metropolitan Police (the forerunner and model of the American police system) the lot of police administrators was not easy.

The London Metropolitan Police

It is well known that Sir Robert Peel, as Britain's Home Secretary, implemented in 1829 plans which had been developed almost a half century earlier for the reorganization and centralization of London's police force. Prior to this period, policing in London had been carried out for centuries by some variant of the watch and ward system in which each sector or ward of the city appointed constables to "maintain the King's Peace" and to take suspicious or rambunctious persons into custody. Watchmen were also appointed whose primary tasks were to maintain a fire watch, enforce England's version of our Sunday blue laws, and confiscate smuggled goods.

An important element of the reorganization which followed passage of the Metropolitan Police Act of 1829 called for consolidation of the crime prevention and law enforcement powers of constables and watchmen and required that the entire city be patrolled both night and day by men who were assigned to regular sectors or "beats." These tasks were then centralized under the authority of the Metropolitan Police of London, which took its organizational model from the highly successful British military system in the hope that emulating the latter would instill discipline, loyalty, and efficiency into the ragged ranks of London's first patrolmen–constables.

Sir Robert and his first commissioner of police, Colonel Charles Rowan, took great pains to see that the first group of a thousand London "bobbies"—as they came to be called in dubious honor of Sir Robert—were a model crew. Months were spent in selecting the first recruits. It is said that Colonel Rowan and Sir Robert personally interviewed over twelve thousand men. Sir Robert himself designed a distinctive uniform, and the men were put through an extensive training program. However, on the rainy day on which the new force was to be commissioned, many of the officers-to-be arrived at the ceremony carrying umbrellas; some, having celebrated the occasion on the previous night, were too drunk to stand at attention. Over a third of the force was fired annually during the first few years, before the London Metropolitan Police finally managed to develop a reliable, stable force.

American beginnings

"Police" conditions in America up until the mid-nineteenth century were strikingly similar to those which preceded the inauguration of the London Metropolitan Police. In the colonial towns during the seventeenth century the tasks of public safety and "law enforcement" were carried out by constables and by a night watch in which each citizen was assigned to take his turn at watching for fires and for unruly persons. In some towns, citizens on night watch were required to call out the time of night and the weather conditions, but for the most part citizens were simply required, as Boston ordered its watchmen, "to walk their rounds slowly and silently and now and then stand still and listen." Most towns also selected a constable who, in addition to serving as jailer, frequently performed the duties of land surveyor, keeper of weights and measures, and announcer of forthcoming marriages. By the beginning of the nineteenth century most citizens who could afford to do so had begun to pay someone else to take their assignments at night watch, thus marking the initial stage of a paid policing force of sorts, although, for all practical purposes, this policing force was still a night watch.

Boston instituted a night watch in 1636; Philadelphia became the first city to establish a separate daytime force in 1833. In that year Philadelphia was the beneficiary of an estate left to the city by one of its wealthy merchants, whose will stipulated that the city should "provide more effectually than they now do for the security of the persons and property of the inhabitants of the said city by a competent police force."[3] Boston inaugurated a separate day watch (of six men) in 1838. New York followed suit a few years later, while in 1850 Cincinnati provided by city charter for the election of six day watchmen from each ward.

The emergence of police organizations
in the United States

The first significant step toward the reorganization of these rudimentary police services and the emergence of a centralized police organization came in 1844 when, following the British model, New York consolidated its separate day and night watches into a single law enforcement unit under the control of an appointed chief of police. Chicago adopted the same system in 1851, followed by New Orleans and Cincinnati in 1852, Boston and Philadelphia in 1854, and Baltimore and Newark in 1857. This major development also marked the beginning of enormous problems for the nation's first police administrators.

What those first chiefs of police found in their newly consolidated forces was a motley, undisciplined crew composed, as one commentator on the era described it, principally of "the shiftless, the incompetent, and the ignorant."[4] Tales abounded of police officers in the 1850s who assaulted their superior officers, who released prisoners from the custody of other officers, who were found sleeping or drunk on duty, or who could be bribed for almost anything. The nation's first top police administrators, therefore, faced the task not only of imposing organizational order on what had previously been two separate and independent operations, but of doing so with a personnel force that, by anyone's estimation, left a great deal to be desired.

Ever since that time, the American police service has faced a dual role—that of constantly refashioning the machinery of policing to meet the problems of public safety and social order in a rapidly changing society, and that of reshaping the attitudes, perceptions, and skills of the men and women who must carry out this vital social responsibility. This remains as important a challenge for police administrators today as it was almost a hundred and fifty years ago.

Issues and social values

A return to the history of the police service makes another fact abundantly clear—namely, that many of today's most controversial issues in policing have been hotly debated *for the past century.*

Strange as it may seem, such topics as community control of the police, respect and support for police officers, the problem of drugs and crime, police corruption, and maintaining independence from political interference are only a few of the current issues in American policing that have been discussed and debated since the mid-nineteenth century—often far more vehemently than they are today, as newspapers, journals, and records would indicate.

For example, long before the idea of civilian review boards gained currency in this country the citizenry were insisting on the most rigorous control over police operations and personnel by making the jobs of police supervisors and, in some instances, of police officers, subject to popular vote. In a number of cities in the 1850s police chiefs were elected by popular vote for specific terms of office, often for no more than a year; other cities appointed the entire force for a similar brief term. Some cities took community control of policing with a rugged seriousness: Cincinnati elected its entire police force, while Brooklyn elected its chief and its police captains.

Similarly, the issue of respect and support for the police was as much a matter of controversy a century ago as it is today. A commentator in 1853 lamented that "hardly a day passes but the thief or felon turns round and attacks the policeman. They inspire no respect, they create no fear."[5] As for drugs and crime, the police chief of Newark, in an address in 1915 to the International Association of Chiefs of Police convention, noted that "men and women who ordinarily commit no crime, when under the influence of their favorite 'dope' will hesitate at none."[6]

The problems of "political interference" and of police corruption are also as old as the practice of policing itself. Hardly a decade passed in the nineteenth century without some major debate on the former or some major exposé of the latter.

Even an issue such as that of assigning women to patrol duties is not as recent as one might think. In a footnote to his classic study, *American Police Systems,* Raymond Fosdick reports with some concern that "in too many departments women police have been installed with no clear idea as to what functions they were to perform. Thus, in some cities they have been used merely as police matrons; in others they have been uniformed and assigned to ordinary patrol duties.'' Fosdick then adds, with an obvious note of alarm, ''In one large city at the time of my visit, the women police who had been recently appointed had been taught to shoot and were then given pistols and blackjacks and assigned to precinct stations!''[7] Fosdick undertook the research for his book, including the visit to the unknown large city, just prior to World War I.

Suffice it to say, then, that the view held by some police administrators to the effect that their current ''troubles'' are the legacy of the 1960s, when a group of ''militant left-wingers'' and a handful of ''liberals''—some of whom managed to sit on the bench of the United States Supreme Court—combined (a few might even wish to say conspired) to make life miserable for the police service, does not fit the facts. Instead, what emerges when we look at a century and a quarter of American law enforcement is the tumultuous record of a nation that built cities and amassed large concentrations of diverse peoples so rapidly that its machinery of public security and order maintenance could not keep up. How that order should be maintained in the face of rapid social change, what authority would be granted its agents of enforcement, how those agents themselves would be held accountable—these issues have been at the heart of some of the great debates of past years.

The history of American law enforcement, then, is inseparable from the history of the United States itself—a nation that has always had a particular concept of and commitment to the principles of a free and democratic society. What such a nation does about the tasks of order maintenance, and with those who are given the authority to perform them, is never an easy question to resolve. The countless debates and experiments with various forms of police organization and administration in the past, and their continuation in our own era, are part of the inevitable tension that arises from the need to preserve individual freedom on the one hand, and the need to maintain social order on the other. Thus, today's police administrator stands in the middle of an uncomfortable but time-honored debate and tradition concerning what values this society will uphold and what mechanisms, liberties, and constraints are necessary to their protection and preservation.

The historical resistance to change

History may also help us understand that police administrators have continually encountered *both internal and external resistance to change.*

Subsequent chapters in this book will document many of the immense changes that have occurred in recent years in personnel policies, patrol strategies, management methods, investigative procedures, internal controls, external relations, and other facets of policing. In part, these changes are symbolized by the new vocabulary in law enforcement. ''Productivity,'' ''criminalistics,'' ''crisis intervention,'' and ''conflict management'' are only a few of the new terms found in police literature today. These terms may deal with problems that have long been familiar to the police administrator, but they represent new ways of approaching police service problems.

Ignoring change and experimentation or, even worse, denouncing them can be of short-lived value for the modern police administrator. What may be gained in immediate popularity can mean loss of reputation for astuteness and for ability to provide leadership. Many police administrators who have been in the forefront of resistance to change have been swept aside for more progressive successors when a new policy or an innovative strategy has become widely accepted. However, even an administrator committed to staying current with developments in the field will frequently find that a proposed change in police policy or operational strategy will face resistance from the ranks, from command staff, or from the general public.

Police chiefs are accustomed to public resistance to change: it is said that a mob greeted Sir Robert Peel's newly commissioned officers with the evident intent of clubbing them off the streets. In the United States, and more recently, there has been public outcry in the many cities when police departments, in order to conserve manpower and better utilize patrol forces, have requested that citizens fill out reports of stolen bicycles at precinct stations.

Internal resistance to change in police practices has been equally dramatic. It was well over a decade after the formation of the first American police forces that attempts were made to require police officers to wear uniforms. The rank-and-file reaction was instantaneous and most uncooperative: cries of "militarism," "un-American," and "a badge of degradation and servitude" were the responses. In Philadelphia police officers even objected to wearing badges on their coats; it was a bitter four-year struggle before they were finally persuaded to wear a complete uniform. New York decided in 1856 to require its officers to be uniformed but the style of dress was left to the decision of each local ward. The results, according to Fosdick, were that in some sections of the city police officers wore straw hats while in others they wore felt. Summer uniforms in some wards were white duck suits; in other wards they were multicolored outfits.[8] A writer of the period complained, "If the police were mustered together, they would look like Falstaff's regiment."[9]

Similar internal opposition has occurred with nearly every major change in policing since the turn of the century. Today, police academy training, civil service merit systems for promotion and advancement, and telecommunications systems are taken for granted as indispensable to a modern police force, but each of these "innovations" was accepted only after a hard-fought battle.

The public responsibility for police services

Having discussed the continuing complexities of police administration, the persistence of many police issues, and the resistance to change in the police field, we would do well to remember that *the problems of policing are issues for both the police and the public to resolve*.

Public attention to the problems of law enforcement has been welcomed by many police administrators who feel that greater citizen awareness will eventually result in greater understanding of and support for the difficult tasks of crime

Training is now regarded as indispensable for all police officers. Shown here, a class at the Education and Training Division, Baltimore (Maryland) Police Department.

control and public safety. Other police officials have been wary of any outside interest, especially when such interest takes the form of citizen commissions, public boards, or investigative bodies.

Crime and law enforcement have become popular, and in some instances profitable, preoccupations of our society. Given impetus in part by a seemingly irreversible rise in the rate of reported crime, by growing public expressions of career frustration on the part of many rank-and-file police officers, by dramatic and often controversial encounters between police agents and various segments of the public, and by periodic widely publicized accounts of police officer or police agency misfeasance, the American public seems to have taken a special interest in the issues of police change and reform.

Commissions to study police services Five national commissions during the 1960s and the early 1970s studied various aspects of police services and the criminal justice process. Some of their work has been quite influential. Perhaps the best known was the Kerner Commission which issued its report in 1968 under the official title of the *Report of the National Advisory Commission on Civil Disorders.* The report was the aftermath of riots and other disorders in many American cities in the summer of 1967.

One of the most influential groups for the police service was the President's Commission on Law Enforcement and Administration of Justice which issued a principal report and various task force reports in 1967. The work of this commission resulted in the adoption of the Safe Streets Act in 1968, the establishment of the Law Enforcement

Assistance Administration, and the subsequent allocation of millions of dollars in grants to states and municipalities for police training and other purposes.

The National Commission on the Causes and Prevention of Violence was established after the assassinations of Robert Kennedy and Martin Luther King in 1968, and the President's Commission on Campus Unrest was established following student deaths at Kent State and Jackson State in 1970.

The National Advisory Commission on Criminal Justice Standards and Goals issued six reports in 1973 with standards and recommendations that are keyed to a national strategy for criminal justice administration and police service.

These commissions and their reports are further described in Appendix A.

To a considerable extent, American law enforcement is currently a victim of its success at garnering increased public support in the 1960s. Rising crime rates and the civil disorders of the mid-1960s led to unprecedented shifts in resources at the federal and local levels into the law enforcement area. The federal Law Enforcement Assistance Administration (LEAA) alone dispensed billions of dollars, while city coffers were tapped extensively to increase police salaries and to recruit and place more officers on the streets. Many a city mayor won office on the pledge to "do something about the crime problem"; tax increases were taken in stride by city dwellers as long as they were earmarked for crime control.

Today disillusion has set in among the taxpaying public. The general apathy if not downright hostility toward government in general is widely apparent, but the changing attitude of the public toward law enforcement should also not escape notice. In general, that attitude is one of cynicism—a growing conviction that all the increases in salary, manpower, new equipment, and operational strategies have not produced as promised, and a vague suspicion that the crime problem may be beyond the ability of normal police operations to handle.

It may be of little reassurance to observe that this swing of the pendulum in public attitudes toward the police is not new, that Americans have historically altered between championing the cause of law and order and demanding the tightest possible restraints on policing. What is more important to note is that the current era is one in which the public will demand honesty and candor from law enforcement. This is obviously not the time for police administrators, for example, to advocate the "add on" theory of crime control—to plead that with a 10 or 15 percent increase in departmental budget and manpower the crime problem could be solved. Police productivity has become a public as well as an administrative concern that should be taken seriously by every enlightened police official.

Candid discussions about the limits as well as the potential of effective efforts on the part of police agencies to control crime can provide an opportunity to bring the public back into the task of public safety and order maintenance. Organized municipal law enforcement efforts were relatively late in developing in this country, in large part because the basic task of crime control was considered a responsibility of the entire community. The formally constituted law enforcement efforts of the past were considered a supplement to, not a substitute for, fundamental community responsibility. The vastness and complexity of the current problems of the police service, together with the growing tendency to leave such matters to professionals and the still prevalent attitude of "not wishing to get involved," combine to make many citizens feel that crime control is an exclusive police responsibility. Police administrators do themselves and their problems a service when they encourage public debate on police issues as well as the recognition that maintaining a peaceful and ordered society is a task in which every citizen must share.

Distinctions between urban and rural police

The historic distinctions between urban and rural police services *are rapidly disappearing*.

Little has been said thus far about the county sheriff. In discussions of municipal police administration the sheriff's office is frequently overlooked, not out of disregard for its importance but because, historically, the tasks and roles of sheriffs and police chiefs have been fundamentally different. Much of the difference, of course, remains. Sheriffs are generally responsible for jurisdictions that include large, sparsely populated areas. Sheriffs are elected rather than appointed; as elected officials, they normally have a significant political as well as policing role in their jurisdictions, and custody of criminal offenders or of persons awaiting trial is still a much larger part of their responsibilities than is the case with police administrators in municipal police agencies.

These differences, while important, tend to become secondary in light of the challenges that both sheriffs and urban police administrators share. The nature of these challenges is such that the tasks that sheriffs and police chiefs have in common are rapidly becoming far more significant than the historic differences. Certainly, from the standpoint of professional police administration, there is little that divides the two offices.

The office of sheriff, the older police function, is almost a direct import from seventeenth century England and in several ways is in fact more compatible with the demands of a democratic society than is the police chief function. As an elected official, the sheriff has been more subject to the popular will than has the appointed police chief. At the same time, and again from a professional police perspective, the elective nature of the sheriff's office has posed some of its principal problems: sheriffs with no police service experience or training have been common, and tenure in office has frequently demanded political skills at the expense of professional commitment.

With the spread of urbanism, however, especially after World War II, the concept of sheriffs as "rural" peace officers and city police administrators as "urban" law enforcement officials, or of sheriffs primarily as jailers and municipal chiefs as those with the "real" police problems, has become meaningless. The growth of suburbs and the development of metropolitan regions, many areas of which are policed by county sheriffs, have brought "big city" problems to formerly rural areas. The mobility of criminal offenders, made possible by freeways and automobiles, and the numbers of people who may live twenty-five miles from the heart of a city, make the diversity of tasks and the demands on many county sheriffs just as great as for their urban counterparts. County sheriffs and their deputies may face the same problems with robbery, burglary, and homicide investigations, organized crime, and fraud as police officers in central cities. The sheriff of San Joaquin County in California—a predominantly agricultural region—may encounter the same dilemmas stemming from labor–management confrontations as do police commissioners in major union cities such as Detroit, Gary, and Birmingham.

The fact that the lines of distinction between these two principal police service positions are diminishing has its special implications for police work. Both sheriffs and police chiefs must give the same attention to personnel recruitment and training, to selection of supervisors, to development of innovative approaches to patrol and investigative techniques, and to use of technology. There has been discussion for decades in police service circles concerning the need to develop a police system that will more adequately address the needs and problems of metropolitan regions. Some experiments along this line have been developed in several areas of the United States. The organizational and political problems that such a development entails are immense, but the continuing growth of metropolitan areas, with their peculiar combination of rural and urban components, will continue to present police service problems that demand creative solutions.

Criminal justice, citizen involvement, and the rule of law

At least three essential aspects of modern police management emerge from this brief historical view of the evolution of the police service in the United States: (1) the place of the police service in the larger flow of the criminal justice process; (2) the role of citizen involvement in the police service; and (3) the framework provided by the rule of law in a democratic society.

The criminal justice process

Police service at all levels—urban, suburban, county, state, and federal—is part of a larger mechanism for public safety and order maintenance that is now termed "the criminal justice process." Perhaps police officers, more than anyone else, realize how disordered and fragmented this process is—a fact which prevents most students of the phenomenon from describing it as a "criminal justice system." In spite of its seeming disarray, however, the criminal justice process represents a discernible, reasonably well defined and consistent procedure by means of which communities across the country formally deal with those who violate the law, a procedure within which law enforcement functions as the first, vital, step.

In the criminal justice process it is the task of the police to receive reports of, or on their own initiative to detect, law violations, to apprehend those reasonably believed to be responsible for such violations, and to present those apprehended before a court of law for a determination of guilt or innocence. The court, through a time-honored procedure, weighs the charge and the evidence as presented both by an officer of the court who represents the people of the community and by an officer of the court who represents the person accused. If found to be guilty of the charge, the accused either is sentenced by the court to a term of confinement in a county or state (or, in the case of violations of federal statutes, a federal) facility or is permitted to return to the community under close, formal supervision. Persons confined for a designated period may, if their behavior seems to warrant it, be permitted to return to the community before the term of their confinement period has formally expired, in which case such persons are also kept under close, formal supervision until the full period of their sentence has been completed.

Contained within this criminal justice process are all the terms and concepts that are of such widespread controversy in contemporary American society. Hardly a single issue of discussion and debate in the criminal justice field today—from "diversion" to "plea bargaining" to "rehabilitation" and a dozen other matters—is not in some fashion related to the effect and effectiveness of this procedure. These issues cannot be addressed within the limits of this chapter, but there are two critically important observations which it is vital that police officers and administrators understand.

First, as disorganized as the process might appear to be, it is a carefully contrived procedure of *checks and balances,* designed to ensure that no person is accused of a crime and subsequently deprived of freedom of movement without every reasonable step being taken to guarantee fairness and equity in the process. For the working police officer, who deals with crimes of all sorts and descriptions and who is continuously exposed to the more sordid aspects of human behavior, this is often difficult to understand and even more difficult to accept. Police officers, therefore, may denounce the actions of defense attorneys who, from the police perspective, manage to get out of the criminal justice process those whom the police have worked diligently to put into it. Also, police officers through their associations sometimes offer public ratings of judges who are candidates for reelection on the basis of whether the police agree or disagree with their courtroom procedures and/or sentencing practices.

What the police overlook in such instances is that, while law enforcement is a vital part of the criminal justice process, it is only a part—it is not the entire procedure. If it could be assumed that every person apprehended by the police was in fact guilty of the crime for which he or she was arrested, we could dispense with prosecutors and courts and could merely truck apprehended persons directly from the precinct station to the county jail or state prison. Justice, however, is a vital, inextricable, and indispensable part of the criminal justice process in our society; it is not included in the formulation by accident or to make the entire procedure *appear* fair. Rather, it is the bottom line in the entire matter. As discomforting as its demands may be to many police officials and to many segments of the public, it remains one of the cornerstones of a free, civilized, and humane society.

The second critically important observation is that the criminal justice process is an adversarial one—not just in the courtroom setting between the prosecutor and defense counsel but at *every* step along the way. A police officer who makes an arrest must request that formal charges be brought against the accused by a public prosecutor who, in turn, has the power to dismiss the charges completely or to reduce them to a lesser offense. In some states the prosecutor must submit evidence to a grand jury composed of ordinary citizens who then make the determination whether the accused should be brought to trial. At the other end of the process, a person technically eligible for parole is not simply released by prison officials who are reasonably satisfied with that person's behavior while in confinement. The parolee must be examined, by a panel of appointed citizens who have the authority to determine whether that person should be released.

While none of these procedures may work perfectly (or, in many instances,

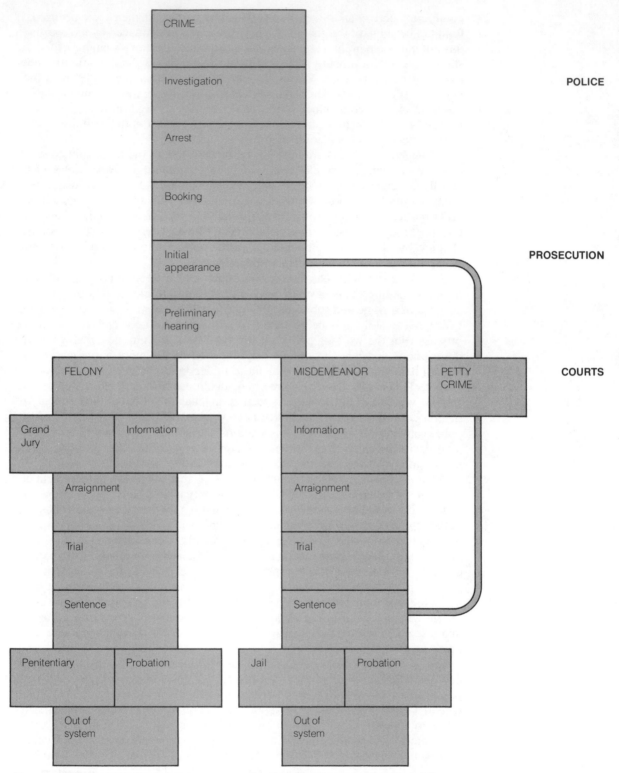

The criminal justice process is much more complex than this diagram suggests, but the major steps are shown. What is not shown are the many safeguards for the suspect or the accused, including various kinds of informal hearings, the right of the police to release without booking, the right of the prosecutor to decide whether evidence justifies seeking indictment, etc. Recommended reference: U.S. Advisory Commission on Intergovernmental Relations, *State–Local Relations in the Criminal Justice System,* especially pp. 66–145 (Washington, D.C.: Government Printing Office, 1971).

even well), the critical matter to note is that the criminal justice process is not a legal assembly line consisting of all the institutional forces of the law—police, prosecutor, courts, prisons, probation, and parole—on which accused persons are placed. It is a process from which a person may emerge at any time. Too cozy a relationship between police and prosecutors, between judges and prison officials, or between others in the process destroys the justice in the criminal justice process; it may appear to improve "efficiency" but it does so at a terrible cost to the principles of a society based upon the rule of law.

Citizen involvement

The formal components of the criminal justice process are buttressed and, in fact, preceded by an informal but nevertheless vitally essential ingredient—that of citizen involvement. The attempt to maintain social order exclusively through the pressures of community disapproval of law violators broke down early in American society. John Winthrop, first governor of Massachusetts, lamented in the 1630s that as people increased in the colony so did the amount of sin! In passing, it may be recorded that ever since Winthrop's day Americans have persisted in confusing sin with crime, but more important is the fact that a strong, cohesive community of citizens who are sensitive to and actively engaged in the day-to-day tasks of preserving the public order is the first and most essential factor in effective crime control.

Police administrators have always given some recognition to this fact, but at the same time they have insisted on dealing with citizens on their own (i.e., police) terms. Police administrators appear to be torn between the idea that it is important to have citizens "on our side" and the desire to preserve the complexity and secrecy within which police agencies traditionally operate.

In attempts to encourage interaction with citizens in the 1960s, it became fashionable for police departments to establish citizen complaint bureaus or police–community relations units and, in the more progressive departments, to create police–community precinct groups which might meet monthly with the precinct captain in the station house. Most of these meetings were characterized by one way communication: the police captain would appear in full uniform, set the agenda for discussion, chair the meeting, tell the citizens what was expected or needed from them, and, perhaps (if the captain were so inclined), entertain a few questions about traffic or juvenile problems in the neighborhood. The citizens who attended were usually those already "on the side of the police," and, consequently, little was achieved in overcoming the enormous gap between the police and the public or in bringing about a genuine police–public partnership.

However, these citizen complaint bureaus, police–community relations units, and police–community precinct meetings were a breakthrough of sorts in the area of citizen involvement. They did manage to open up policing somewhat to the community and to provide at least a formal, internal mechanism for receiving citizen grievances. But they were only a first step.

A more viable program of citizen involvement would need to begin with the recognition on the part of police officers and administrators that they are supplements to, not substitutes for, the mechanisms of social control which the community itself represents. Citizen involvement is not an adjunct to effective policing; effective policing depends on genuine community participation in the planning, implementation, and evaluation of programs and strategies to reduce crime. Or, to state the matter in more stark but direct terms: if there are no effective forces of community social control at work, there is little if anything the police can do to deal with crime and lawlessness.

This fundamental fact of social order is being recognized increasingly by police officials in suburban and rural, as well as urban, areas. As long as suburbs were primarily bedroom communities and rural areas consisted of small towns and family farms, their police officials could count on community cohesiveness and the infrequency of major crimes to make their policing tasks fairly simple. Urbanization has changed the face of suburbia and the small town, and it is changing the face of policing and police–community relations in these areas as well. The sheriff or small town police chief who is not as genuinely committed as his urban counterpart to the authentic involvement of citizens in the tasks of crime control and effective policing will not be able to meet the professional demands of today's police world.

The rule of law

If policing is only one part—albeit an essential one—of the criminal justice process, and if the involvement of an active citizenry in crime prevention and control is also essential to the total community effort, then it must be recognized that the entire process operates well in our society only when it operates under the rule of law. The heightened degree of public concern over the crime problem in American society and the increasing frustration of police officers in coping with its increase tempt both the police and the public to forget this essential fact of the American democratic experience. Accordingly, there have been repeated attempts by both police and citizens, in various periods in American history, to "take the law into their own hands." Currently there are periodic reports of vigilante-style citizen groups operating in various sections of the country, and almost all police departments are plagued by those officers who occasionally decide to mete out "justice" in the alley, the back of the patrol car, or the lockup.

Police administrators must continually remind themselves and the personnel under their command that this is a nation of laws, not of men and women—even when the men and women wear the uniform and badge of the police service. Acting "under the color of law" or exercising illegal direction under the guise of official authority has always been a particularly odious practice wherever it occurs, but in no sphere of public life is it more repugnant than in policing.

This represents a matter of acute importance precisely because of the wide discretionary powers which must be granted to those in the police service if they are to accomplish their tasks with any reasonable effectiveness. For police officers go about their daily rounds with a great deal of latitude in making judgments and decisions, in spite of all the external statutes and ordinances which they are sworn to enforce and the internal rules and regulations designed to govern their conduct. Countless times during the course of a watch the individual police officer faces the choices of whether to arrest or to warn, of how much force to use in effecting an arrest or if any force is required, of whether to take a law violation more seriously in one section of the city than in another, and of innumerable other situations which call for an independent assessment and a weighing of alternatives. The police officer thus becomes the first "interpreter" of the law in the criminal justice process; the person who carries this enormous responsibility must both recognize and be continually reminded of the fact that he or she stands under that law which it is his or her responsibility to interpret and enforce.

The initial judgments which a police officer makes on the street, often in extreme and stressful situations and without the luxury of time for reflection, will, in the course of the criminal justice process, often be subject to repeated review by supervisory officers, by the public prosecutor, by defense counsel, and by the court. It can be irritiating at best and dispiriting at worst to police officers to have their judgments and decisions questioned or criticized, or, in many instances, overturned. But it is precisely this process of review and examination, of sorting and weighing, of assessment under the most deliberately adversary of circumstances possible, that constitutes the rule of law and distinguishes it from a rule of men and women in the street. It is fidelity to this principle that permits us to speak of a criminal justice process. Without this process there is questionable effectiveness in our crime control efforts and certainly no justice at all.

New directions in American policing

The decade of the 1960s was a turning point in law enforcement in the United States. Two developments helped set the stage for present and future directions in American policing. The first was the creation in 1965 of the President's Commission on Law Enforcement and Administration of Justice. The commission's report, issued in February 1967 and entitled *The Challenge of Crime in a Free Society,* represented the most comprehensive examination of the problems, needs, and dilemmas of the criminal justice process since the famed Wickersham Commission report of 1931. The title of the President's commission report is suggestive of its major thrust, that the nation must establish new policies and mobilize new resources in order to deal with the critical problem of crime in America and that such efforts must be undertaken within the framework and principles of a free and democratic society.

The report is remarkable for its understanding of problems faced by American law enforcement, for its anticipation of the tremendous scientific and technological resources that would be utilized in improving police operations, for its sensitivity to the demands on policing in a multiethnic society. Most especially, the report emphasizes throughout that any new developments in law enforcement must take place within the constraints of those traditional American democratic values that call for a maximum amount of attention to individual liberties.

A year after the President's commission report was issued, Congress passed the massive Omnibus Crime Control and Safe Streets Act (1968). In one sense this act was a direct outcome of the President's commission, which noted that

local communities today are hard-pressed just to improve their agencies of justice and other facilities at a rate that will meet increases in population and in crime. They cannot spare funds for experimental or innovative programs or plan beyond the emergencies of the day. Federal collaboration can give State and local agencies an opportunity to gain on crime rather than barely stay abreast of it, by making funds, research, and technical assistance available and thereby encouraging changes that in time may make criminal administration more effective and more fair.[10]

The title of this act, too, had its significance. It indicated a priority concern for the types of crime which make the streets unsafe, and thus directed most of its attention and resources to the problems of urban crime in general and crimes against persons and property in particular. The act gave comparatively little attention to the special problems and needs of rural law enforcement, sheriff's departments, and state law enforcement agencies. Until subsequently amended, its major emphasis was on the upgrading of law enforcement operations, with comparatively little concern for the two other major components of the criminal justice process—the courts (including prosecutors' offices) and corrections. Perhaps of greatest significance was the creation of a new network of federal, regional, state, and city–county administrative agencies that, in principle, have been designed to bring about better coordination and cooperation between local, state, and federal criminal justice agencies.

Taken together, the President's commission report and the Omnibus Crime Control and Safe Streets Act provide two essential ingredients for contemporary American policing. The commission report still serves effectively as a charter for progressive, enlightened law enforcement policy; it identifies most of the major problems and pinpoints most of the principal alternatives that confront the modern law enforcement agency and administrator. The Omnibus

Crime Control Act, in addition, provided significantly increased fiscal resources for upgrading police operations. With careful planning and with clear organizational goals in mind, there is no reason why police administrators and their agencies cannot continue to press for substantive improvements in the quality and effectiveness of policing.

To a considerable extent, however, the expectation expressed in the President's commission report (quoted above) that the availability of federal funds would lead to experimentation and innovation in police methods and strategies has not been realized. A major portion of the federal funds has been used by police agencies to reinforce and expand traditional police approaches to crime control—even in some instances in which the evidence suggests that such approaches have limited or no value. Those few experiments which have been undertaken and which suggest possibilities for improvement in patrol and criminal investigation strategies, in training, and in corruption control have not been widely adopted.

It is perhaps in the area of law enforcement technology that the greatest change has occurred and the most serious problems are posed for the police administrator. The amount and diversity of police hardware currently on the market is almost overwhelming; the availability of federal funds for its purchase has resulted, in far too many instances, in an indiscriminate technological buying spree that has left many police agencies with expensive equipment which no one is adequately trained to utilize, or with equipment of questionable usefulness in the first place. American police agencies currently have an unsurpassed technological capacity for crime control; the problem is that technology cannot control crime. Police hardware, after all, consists only of tools; their utility (or abuse) is directly related to and dependent on the skills and values of the police personnel who employ them.

An overreliance on technological devices on the part of a police administrator to the neglect of an equal emphasis on the quality of personnel recruitment, training, and management can lead to a severely imbalanced and ineffective police agency. An assumption that change in policing is primarily measured by the amount of hardware a department can amass confuses improvement with gadgetry; the latter may aid the former but it does not automatically guarantee it. Finally, the cost-effectiveness of the new police technology must be weighed by the police administrator not only in economic terms but also for its impact on the principles and values of a democratic society. The police administrator who fails to undertake this complex task only invites the curbs and restraints on technological utilization which a concerned public will impose.

Technology, in a sense, poses the ultimate dilemma for today's police administrator. There is little question but that our technical capacity to develop and utilize devices that would reduce crime and make our streets safer can be greatly expanded. If we were to combine our technological know-how with the principles of a police state in which the daily activities of every citizen were subjected to close scrutiny and criminal suspects as well as criminal offenders were summarily arrested and imprisoned, if we dispensed with the time-consuming details of due process and imposed the harshest possible penalties for the maximum number of offenses, we could greatly reduce the volume of crime in American society. It is appropriate to remind ourselves, however, that the United States chose a deliberate course two hundred years ago. That course called for an unremitting commitment to the principles of a free and open society. Maintaining social order and the public peace within the constraints of that commitment is no easy task, and there is probably no single profession upon which that task rests more heavily than on the police service. For this very reason, there is probably no profession other than that of police administrator in which the understanding of the nature of that national commitment, and the professional loyalty to it, are so vital to the nation's present and future.

Conclusion

This chapter has traced the historical development of policing, both in London and in the United States, the effects of social change on police service, particularly the significant changes that occurred during the last generation, and the continuing debate over the role of the police and police services in society—an issue that goes back more than a hundred years. The gradual obliteration of urban and rural lines in police services has then been discussed. This has been followed by a section outlining the broad framework of criminal justice as a process, citizen involvement in that process, and the overall framework provided by the rule of law. This overview has concluded with a discussion of recent new directions in American policing and of some of the problems and possibilities posed by the future.

1 President's Commission on Law Enforcement and Administration of Justice, *The Challenge of Crime in a Free Society* (Washington, D.C.: Government Printing Office, 1967).

2 National Advisory Commission on Civil Disorders, *Report of the National Advisory Commission on Civil Disorders* (New York: E. P. Dutton & Co., Inc., 1968; Bantam Books, 1968); National Commission on the Causes and Prevention of Violence, *To Establish Justice, To Insure Domestic Tranquility* (Washington, D.C.: Government Printing Office, 1969).

3 Raymond B. Fosdick, *American Police Systems* (New York: The Century Co., 1920), pp. 63–64.

4 Bruce Smith, *Police Systems in the United States* (New York: Harper & Brothers, Publishers, 1940), p. 127.

5 Fosdick, *American Police Systems,* p. 71.

6 Ibid., p. 358.

7 Ibid., p. 376.

8 Ibid., p. 71.

9 Ibid.

10 President's Commission on Law Enforcement and Administration of Justice, *The Challenge of Crime in a Free Society,* p. 284.

3 The governmental setting

The modern police service is a part of the governmental process that provides public safety through a number of divergent activities: the protection of persons and property; the prevention of crime; firefighting and fire prevention; maintenance of the structural safety of buildings through code enforcement; traffic engineering; safety education programs; and enforcement of a range of environmental protection regulations aimed at protecting the public health. A number of agencies undertake these activities as part of the governmental public safety function. The police service is the most visible of these agencies, performing a range of activities far broader than law enforcement.

This chapter discusses the place of the police service in the broader governmental setting by describing the environment and the historical development of American policing, followed by a discussion of important jurisdictional issues affecting police agencies. Next is a review of the changing role of the police service and the importance of policy development as a guide: the definition of police objectives and priorities, methods for goal achievement, and administrative procedures. The remainder of the chapter is concerned with the role of the police agency and the roles of the two key executives who most directly affect the delivery of police services: the mayor, city manager, or other local government administrator and the police chief. For the municipal administrator, the discussion focuses on the crucial questions surrounding the selection of a new chief of police, management relationships between the government executive and the police chief, and the political questions involved. For the police chief, the discussion touches on issues that are broader than those of simply being a manager, including policy development and implementation.

The environment of policing

Police effectiveness and perceptions about the quality of police service are heavily influenced by the complex nature of the environment in which policing occurs. The political process in each community, whether urban or rural, obviously varies with local priorities and needs. Even among the smallest communities, economic and social variables often produce greatly different service needs and citizen expectations.

Local government itself is the common link among these often diverse and sometimes competing pressures to provide such services as sewers, water, police protection, fire protection, and street maintenance. Priorities and service levels must be determined for each of these services as the basis for the municipal budget. These priorities are most often set by the local legislative body.

In the public safety area, municipalities, communities, and even neighborhoods often do not agree on what police priorities or actions should be. Just as many communities experience major disagreements about school location, school curricula, welfare benefits, or protection of housing patterns, so there are frequently major disagreements about what the police should be doing and how it should be done. Sometimes these conflicts reflect police methods; other times they reflect utilization of scarce resources. With the rapid rise of inflation during the 1970s and 1980s, the competition for police resources has been increasing, and the debate over police priorities has become more intense.

The debate over police priorities has increased the visibility of police operations after a period of relatively little public concern. During the 1960s substantial attention was focused on police practices in urban neighborhoods (and police actions in dealing with riots), but during the 1970s the public seemed less concerned, and attention shifted to other areas of government.

The increase in crime during the early 1980s, coupled with reduced municipal expenditures in real dollars, has again made levels of police protection an important, visible public issue; but the concern goes far beyond financial questions.

Police practices are also being reexamined. Watergate abuses and more recent exposure of the abuse of police powers at the federal, state, and local levels have increased public consciousness of several important policing issues, such as investigative methods and use of force. Police agencies are expected to abide by rules that reflect a basic public morality. While police "review boards" and other methods of external control are again being proposed by disaffected community groups, it is through the governmental process that most communities expect to maintain control over their police. Commissions and other political bodies are becoming much more active in overseeing police matters in direct reaction to this increased community concern.

The continually changing environment places great demands on both the police administrator and the municipal or county chief executive. No longer is it acceptable for police chiefs to remain isolated from the social and political forces of their communities. Today, police administrators must accept a number of important responsibilities, including interacting constructively with political representatives of the community. Local government administrators must also fully understand the complexities of modern policing so that they can serve as the link between the police agency and the political structure, as the latter is represented formally by the council or similar body. The police can no longer exist as an independent body of government, handling incident after incident and pretending that their only job is law enforcement. Police service delivery is an integral part of the quality of community life. Police actions and perceived priorities directly affect numerous community problems. Thus, three factors are especially important in determining the quality of police service delivery in an urban environment: accountability and control of the police force, the role of the police, and development and implementation of policy.

Accountability and control: the historical development

To understand the context in which policing occurs, it is useful to consider the historical stages of development through which policing has come. While many police issues reflect current national concerns, the structure of police service within the governmental setting is based on a number of important historical developments. Policing in the United States has traditionally been a strictly local matter providing for local accountability and control.

The early years

Originally police in this country were elected. The constable in eastern areas and the sheriff in the Midwest were selected by their constituents to deal primarily with matters of public order and to see that the public peace was not disturbed. As the country became more urbanized and government more formalized, control of police power was often vested in elected legislative bodies such as city councils. To run the first formal police forces, chiefs were often elected.

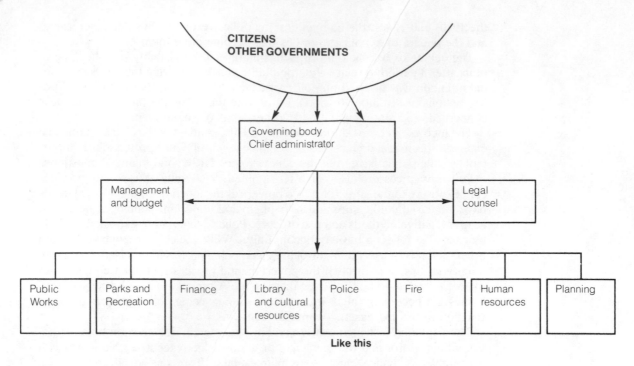

Like this

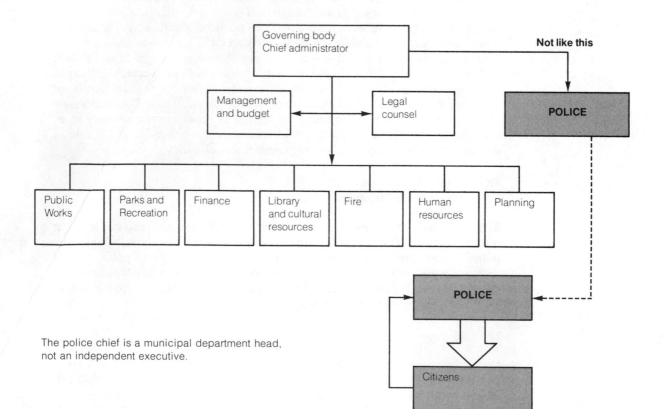

Not like this

The police chief is a municipal department head, not an independent executive.

Elected police chiefs faced a multitude of political pressures, because their reelection usually depended on their responsiveness to various power groups in the community. Enforcement of the law (or the lack thereof) often depended on the desires of a dominant political group. Indeed, in some large cities the police were direct agents of the political machine, enforcing the party's dictates as their primary function and giving little attention to matters of street crime and safety. As this political abuse of police power became more widespread, there were two responses: one was the creation of independent boards or commissions to control police activities and the other was state control of the policing mechanism.

Independent boards and commissions

The creation of independent boards and commissions had little effect on eliminating partisan considerations from policing, because members were usually appointed by the dominant political party. Even where the boards were bipartisan, members tended to view themselves as the representatives of a particular party obliged to protect the party's interests. While some of these police boards still exist, their number has greatly declined as the movement toward municipal reform has gathered momentum.

State control

State control of police has been no more successful than independent boards and commissions. The use of boards and commissions, widespread in such cities as New York and Boston in the late nineteenth and early twentieth centuries, has decreased. Only a limited number of such arrangements remain today—for example, in Kansas City and St. Louis, Missouri. Citizens have tended to resent outside control of local policing activities, especially when issues of policy and procedure have focused local concern on police operations. And state control has rarely eliminated partisan considerations from policing. Rather, the political priorities of the state have simply replaced those that existed at the local level. In addition, there is growing resentment in some cities that the state has control over what are considered local priorities.

Government reform and police control

Municipal government reform resulted in major changes in police control during the early twentieth century. Initially, the reform movement had encouraged broad adoption of the commission form of government, but since commissions tended to foster factionalism and generally proved ineffective, they were soon replaced by mayor-council and council-manager forms of government. In both forms, the police chief was made directly responsible to the chief executive (mayor or manager). The chief executive was vested with broad powers of administration, based on the belief that accountability and control for government operations should be clearly placed. Within such a system the heads of municipal departments reported to the chief executive, who had ultimate responsibility for delivering services. These systems are the most common ones in operation today.

Two other historical movements have directly affected the environment of policing: civil service and the development of a "professional" orientation for policing.

Civil service

Civil service developed as a means of providing protection for employees from partisan considerations when political parties changed. Numerous cities established civil service structures to provide tenure to a broad range of employees and to provide a mechanism for selection and promotion insulated from partisan politics.

Some civil service systems were developed on a statewide basis, and so exist today. State systems were begun in the belief that they would further insulate the system from what was viewed as the spoils of partisan politics. In such instances testing, certification, and even recruitment were undertaken on a statewide basis for every municipality. While numerous state and local civil service systems exist today, there remain a substantial number of agencies without such a system.

"Professional" policing

The development of "professional" policing went hand in hand with the emergence of civil service. The professionalization movement encouraged police independence from local political concerns while supporting the concept of neutrality in enforcing the law and in dealing with community conflicts. This role definition contrasted sharply with the obviously partisan conduct of many police forces at the time and was viewed as the best method for ensuring the existence of a nonpolitical police in the future.

As protection against improper political interference in police matters, the traditional professional school strongly advocated equal enforcement of the law, internal mechanisms for handling police misconduct, and isolation of the police from local political pressures. The strength of the professionalization movement was such that many local government executives began to have second thoughts about any involvement in police affairs—whether they concerned matters of overall policy or such issues as budget or priority setting. In this sense, the original "professional" movement was successful in protecting the police from political considerations by creating and then supporting the belief that all police department operations were dictated by some aspect of the law. The movement failed to acknowledge that the police exercised discretion in dealing with many matters that came to their attention. The police function was viewed in absolute terms solely as the enforcement of the law.

The 1960s

The development of civil service protection and the growth of the "professional" movement decreased the concern with partisan political influence. At the same time, policing gradually became both a field of study and a recognized professional competency. The President's Commission on Law Enforcement and Administration of Justice was formed in the mid-1960s to focus on police issues and nationally perceived problems resulting from a disorganized criminal justice system. The work of the commission quickly became adopted as the standard for police professionalism and provided guidance for local police improvement efforts. The disorders and urban conflict of the late 1960s placed new emphasis on police responsiveness to emerging community social concerns. However, the political insulation of the police resulting from their "traditional professionalism" made it difficult for the community to influence police actions and priorities. With community social disorder and conflict increasing, the role of the police in the community was acknowledged to encompass more than law enforcement.

Since the police function had been narrowly defined according to a sterile professionalism, discretion continued to be a major factor in actual field procedures. There existed a considerable gulf between the formal definition of the function by the police themselves on one hand and actual practice on the other; it was apparent that the police did more than simply enforce the law. In many communities it was perceived that the police selectively enforced the law according to the racial or ethnic composition of each neighborhood.

During this period it was widely believed that there were few political channels through which citizens could address these concerns. In many instances the police were in fact practically an independent agency operating under few governmental controls. It was often unclear exactly who was accountable for specific police practices. As conflict escalated, both citizens' groups and the police responded.

The primary response by police was to implement police–community relations programs, which they hoped would provide a direct link to the community. While some of these programs were only public relations activities, many of them concentrated on providing the opportunity for concerned citizens to have input into some levels of the police agency. However, these programs normally bypassed the local government political structure and thus did not provide for accountability for police actions.

In a number of cities community groups pressed for the establishment of formal mechanisms to provide influence over police procedures and conduct. In Rochester, New York, and New York City, for example, civilian boards were formed to review police conduct. In Berkeley, California, a proposal for community control of the police was placed on the ballot. None of these proposals was ultimately successful, but their existence indicated the seriousness with which community groups regarded the need for a mechanism through which police policy and operations could be made more responsive to changing neighborhood concerns.

The 1970s

During the 1970s, a period of decreased community conflict, less attention was given to police accountability issues. Police reform in the United States focused on management issues, control of corruption, and police effectiveness. Several important research activities were undertaken with support of the Police Foundation and the Law Enforcement Assistance Administration: the Kansas City preventive patrol experiment, Response Time Studies, and the Managing Criminal Investigations experiments in Rochester, New York, and other cities. Few of these dealt with police policy, role, or accountability, since the pressure was for increased technical progress in policing.

By the end of the 1970s, however, new issues had begun to surface, including neighborhood responsiveness and concern over the use of force by police. Inflationary pressures resulting from economic stagnation caused government and community members to renew their interest in important policing issues.

Dealing with these issues has often been difficult because of differing conceptions about the true nature of the police role. Local government administrators, political leaders, and police chiefs often have difficulty establishing an environment conducive to constructive police–political process interaction unless the dynamics of the police role and the impact of discretion on that role are fully understood.

Jurisdictional issues

The governmental setting within which the police agency operates and policy decisions are made is reflected by the jurisdiction of the police service. Jurisdiction refers to the area served by the agency. Over the last ten years there has been pressure for consolidation of police jurisdictions, and these pressures will continue as budget constraints limit the ability of local governments to maintain existing service levels.[1]

As previously noted, policing in the United States has traditionally been a local affair. Each local unit of government has had its own police force, resulting in a multitude of mostly small police agencies throughout the country. In many areas ten or more police agencies may have concurrent jurisdiction, reflecting overlapping government jurisdictions (township, city, village, state, county, and special district, for example). Because our mobile society allows criminals to move freely among jurisdictions, recommendations for the unification or consolidation of police services in these jurisdictions have increased. But several important issues have limited such unification. Most of these issues relate to the governmental setting of the police agency and affect the ability of any jurisdiction to carry out unification of services.

One important issue relates to the political structure of government. Since American policing is based on local control of police power, there is usually resistance by local political leaders to giving up this control.

A second issue, linked to political power, is the responsiveness of the police to neighborhood concerns. Especially in urban centers, the police often are perceived by segments of the community as unresponsive to local priorities, in terms of enforcement of minor ordinances and quality of service delivery. As larger police agencies have decentralized to deal with this issue, they believe that unification would be incompatible with increased responsiveness.

Both of these issues focus on the community's perception that the police are operating under their control and responsive to their priorities. Smaller police units usually are perceived by the community as being more reflective of local priorities.

There are three types of consolidation or unification of police service:

1. A merger of governmental units into a single larger unit covering a broad jurisdiction (or creation of a new unit to serve the jurisdiction)
2. An arrangement by which one jurisdiction contracts with another for services
3. A cooperative provision of selected functions but maintenance of the separate agencies serving the local jurisdiction (see the accompanying model local inter-governmental mutual aid agreement).

Most consolidation of police service in the United States has focused on cooperative provision of selected functions, such as training (at regional police academies) and technical assistance (at regional crime labs). In some areas the state has begun to provide some of these functions, thus cutting costs for all jurisdictions.

When governmental units consider consolidation or unification of police service, they must analyze the proposal in terms of cost and financing, impact on labor agreements, impact on perceived and actual neighborhood responsiveness, and method of political control responsive to a community's own priorities. Several tests can be made to assess whether there is a receptive climate for a unified services program and, if so, to what extent it exists.

One test is to determine whether there is a willingness among existing local government services to alter traditional methods of doing things. Do unified service approaches exist in other local service areas? Does one local government provide services for another even though both, or more, could potentially provide the same service? Are existing unified services stable economically and politically? To the extent that these and similar questions can be answered in the affirmative, there is a strong chance that some joint police service venture would be successful. If, on the other hand, a police service venture will be

Model local inter-governmental mutual aid agreement

This agreement, made and entered into this ＿＿＿ day of ＿＿＿＿＿ 1973, by and between the political subdivisions of the State of ＿＿＿＿＿, who are signatories hereto.

Whereas, the political subdivisions of the State of ＿＿＿＿＿＿＿＿＿ have determined that the provision of law enforcement mutual aid across jurisdictional lines in emergencies will increase their ability to preserve the safety and welfare of the entire area; and

Whereas, the political subdivisions of the State of ＿＿＿＿＿ are authorized by Public Law ＿＿＿＿＿ (or other statutory designation) to provide law enforcement mutual aid.

Now, therefore, the parties hereto do agree as follows:

1. When a state of emergency involving conditions of extreme peril to the safety of persons and property exists within the boundaries of any of the parties hereto, the party or parties shall notify the other party or parties to this agreement of such emergency and its need for law enforcement assistance. Such assistance shall be rendered according to the procedures established in the operational plans developed and agreed to by all of the parties to this agreement pursuant to the provisions in paragraph 2 herein. Each party shall designate an appropriate official within its jurisdiction who is empowered to request assistance under this agreement.

2. The mutual assistance to be rendered under this agreement shall be available upon the development and approval by the parties hereto of an operational plan. The plan shall outline the exact procedure to be followed in responding to a request for assistance. Upon execution of this agreement, the parties hereto shall designate an appropriate official in each jurisdiction to participate in the development of the operational plan. The parties shall meet at least annually to review and, if necessary, to propose amendments to the operational plan. Any proposed amendments shall not be effective until approved in writing by all the parties to this agreement.

3. The services performed and expenditures made under this agreement shall be deemed for public and governmental purposes. All immunities from liability enjoyed by the local political subdivision within its boundaries shall extend to its participation in rendering mutual aid under this agreement outside its boundaries unless otherwise provided by law.

Each party to this agreement shall waive any and all claims against all the other parties hereto which may arise out of their activities outside their respective jurisdictions while rendering aid under this agreement.

Each party shall indemnify and save harmless the other parties to this agreement from all claims by third parties for property damage or personal injury which may arise out of the activities of the other parties of this agreement outside their respective jurisdictions while rendering aid under this agreement.

4. All the immunities from liability and exemptions from laws, ordinances and regulations which law enforcement officers employed by the various parties hereto have in their own jurisdictions shall be effective in the jurisdiction in which they are giving assistance unless otherwise prohibited by law.

All compensation and other benefits enjoyed by law enforcement officers in their own jurisdictions shall extend to the services they perform under this agreement.

5. Law enforcement officers rendering assistance under this agreement shall do so under the direction and control of the appropriate official designated by the jurisdiction requesting the aid.

The parties shall notify each other of the name, address and telephone number of the official authorized to direct mutual aid activities within their jurisdiction.

6. This agreement shall remain in effect until terminated by all the parties hereto upon written notice setting forth the date of such termination. Withdrawal from this agreement by any one party hereto shall be made by thirty days' written notice to all parties but shall not terminate this agreement among the remaining parties.

In *witness whereof,* the parties hereto have executed this agreement as of the date first above written.

(To be signed by the Mayor, County Manager or other appropriate official having government-wide jurisdiction in each political subdivision.)

among the first joint service programs in the area, the potential for an effective program may well be diminished.

A second and perhaps more important test is to assess what types of service programs are currently operated jointly. Are the existing joint programs in service areas remote from direct daily contact with people (e.g., sewer and water)? Are the existing joint programs in personal service areas of activity (e.g., transportation, libraries), or are such programs found in areas that involve police powers (e.g., planning and zoning, building inspection)? The more unified service programs there are in a personal service or police power area, the greater is the likelihood for joint police service ventures. However, if the existing joint service efforts are found in such areas as water and sewer, there is less likelihood of success.

A third test might be to evaluate the total number of local governmental units serving essentially the same geographic area. The greater the number of units providing full services, or attempting to do so, the less is the potential for joint ventures in the police service area. In contrast, where a single large city is situated within a particular county and only a few very small cities are located in that county, there is a strong possibility that the city and the county can effect some cooperative police service programs more easily. The reason seems clear. The greater the number of local units, the more diverse will be the styles of managing conflict. In such cases, the opportunity for success in joint police service efforts will be smaller than in areas with only a few governmental institutions.

The police role

As mentioned earlier, the police traditionally view their role as little more than enforcing the law. This view disregards the important decision-making process that is a major part of policing today.

The police enjoy great discretion in virtually all their functions, from management decisions (such as how to allocate resources) to operational decisions (such as whether to intervene in a family fight or what action will best resolve a neighborhood dispute). Unlike many other organizations, the police service provides for the greatest amount of discretion at the bottom of the structure. It is the patrol officer who has the widest range of alternatives in handling the functions of his or her duty. In most of the situations with which the police officer must deal, there are a number of alternatives for action. These range from taking no action at all to full application of the law.

Because of the existence of this discretion and the power inherent in the police role, many regard the police as the most important decision makers in society today. The actions they take, or the absence thereof, can seriously affect the lives of many citizens.

The police role is influenced as much by the power it holds as by the discretion that is a part of it. The power inherent in the police function that differentiates it from other governmental functions is the ability to use force. There is widespread recognition of the police capacity to use force properly in the enforcement of the criminal law; yet some observers have noted that the use of force by the police is the basis of their authority in providing general service responses in the community. As Bittner notes,

Whatever the substance of the task at hand, whether it involves protection against an undesired imposition, caring for those who cannot care for themselves, attempting to solve a crime, helping to save a life, abating a nuisance, or settling an explosive dispute, police intervention means above all making use of the capacity and authority to overpower resistance to an attempted solution in the native habitat of the problem.[2]

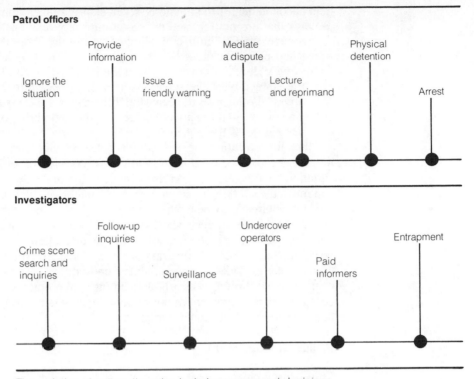

Patrol officers

Ignore the situation | Provide information | Issue a friendly warning | Mediate a dispute | Lecture and reprimand | Physical detention | Arrest

Investigators

Crime scene search and inquiries | Follow-up inquiries | Surveillance | Undercover operators | Paid informers | Entrapment

The varieties of police discretion include management decisions, enforcement priorities, service allocations, and others. Two of the most frequent decisions are those involving patrol officers and investigators.

The potential use of force and the fact that there can be no appeal from police use of fatal force provide the police with great influence over citizens in determining what citizens can and cannot do. Since police functions are an extension of political authority, it is intended for the police to have the power to regulate many aspects of public behavior.

A majority of the public respects and follows police authority. Indeed, while the police officer can use force to overcome resistance by a single member of the community, this is only because a majority of the citizenry accepts police authority and ability to use force. Were a majority of the community not willing to respect this authority, the police would be ineffective in maintaining order. Indeed, in city after city when major civil disorders have occurred, military force has had to be used because the political authority of the police was not recognized by a sufficiently large segment of the population.

The ability of the police to use force and the fact that the police represent public authority make it important that there be clearly defined mechanisms to ensure accountability and control. If the police begin to lose touch with public expectations, there is the potential that they will misdirect their authority.

Paradoxically, many police administrators—citing the principle of "laws, not men"—do not perceive the range of alternatives available to the officer on the beat or the power inherent in the police function.

The existence of so much discretion among officers on the beat poses a critical problem for both the police administrator and the local government chief executive. The actions of individual officers—often invisible to their superiors and therefore unreviewable—do much to determine a community's feelings about whether a police agency is responsive to local priorities. Officers who are overaggressive, who harass individuals, or who exercise poor judgment not only harm that relationship but do so with relative certainty that they will not be held accountable for their actions. Even skillful officers may not always behave in ways that promote a good police–community relationship.

It is impossible, of course, to eliminate discretion from the police role. Laws, rules, and policies cannot be written with sufficient breadth and precision to cover every situation in which police are required to act. The vagueness of the law, the ambiguity of the situations in which police intervene, the isolation of the individual officer on the beat, the difficulty of supervising people who work essentially alone—these are the sources of discretionary power, and they rest in the very nature of the police role.

Thus, justice cannot be served by a police service that attempts to eliminate judgment and force officers to follow rigid codes. The officer responding to a situation must be able to exercise judgment and make decisions. Only he or she can make the subtle connection between what he or she is confronting and what the law requires; only he or she can decide whether legal force should be applied or whether some sanction short of the law would be more effective. But such decisions cannot be made in a vacuum. The discretion of the police officer must be acknowledged, but, at the same time, the local government and political leadership must provide for accountability and control of police activities. This is best achieved through a clearly defined intragovernmental process. In this process it is the development of police policy that sets the framework in which police operational decisions are made.

Policy development

Through the development of policy, a police agency can define its role in the community and control its practices in light of community expectations. Guidelines can be set for police operations and practices that will make them responsive to community priorities. Policy indicates to the community where the police agency stands on major issues and at the same time provides the police agency with a set of standards for which it can be held accountable. Policy also permits some limits to be placed on the great amount of discretion that is part of the police function.

It has been common for police chiefs and local government administrators to be unwilling to engage in the type of discussion necessary to develop meaningful policy. Even when such discussions are held, there is often reluctance to commit the policy to writing for fear that future events will cause critical comment to the effect that policy was not followed.

In fact, quite the opposite is commonly true. When written policy statements are not available (or not well disseminated), the police agency and the administration run considerable risk that some police actions will be completely alien to a segment of the community. The result can be aggravated conflict between police and the community, resulting in political demands for major measures to ensure accountability on the part of the police organization. Citizens may even file lawsuits charging discriminatory practices.

Policy is best developed before such incidents have a chance to occur. The community may well regard the entire governmental process as unresponsive if preventive policy is not implemented. In this climate tensions will inevitably rise, and their resolution through legitimate channels becomes difficult. Policy is not immutable; it must be constantly revised to reflect changing social conditions.

Policy development is appropriate in the following three areas, each of which is important in placing the police function in its proper perspective within the governmental setting: (1) definition of police objectives and priorities; (2) definition of methods for goal achievement; and (3) administrative procedures.[3] In these areas, policy that structures police discretion can be provided through administrative rule making.[4]

Definition of police objectives and priorities

The police perform such a wide variety of tasks that there is often little direction as to what they should and should not do. The American Bar Association's *Standards Relating to the Urban Police Function* (the ABA Standards) note that there are five factors accounting for the responsibilities given to the police:

1. Broad legislative mandates to the police;
2. The authority of the police to use force lawfully;
3. The investigative ability of the police;
4. The twenty-four-hour availability of the police, and;
5. Community pressures on the police.[5]

They note that without policy decisions as to what will and will not be done, ad hoc judgments will be made by the police on the basis of their own priorities and objectives.[6]

If police objectives are not thoroughly understood, then a course of action selected by police may not be the one that is most acceptable to the community and its political leadership. In dealing with juveniles, for example, police action can be aimed either at protecting the welfare of the youth or at strict enforcement of the law. In matters of maintaining public order, there is frequently a choice between strict application of the law and actions to avoid the escalation of disorder. These difficult decisions are an inherent part of the discretionary nature of the police function. The community, the government, and each officer must understand what the police agency is seeking to achieve, and these objectives must be responsive to the needs and desires of the community.

The police can undertake a wide variety of activities. The number of services they can offer is almost unlimited. For the past ten years the police and government in general have continually expanded the scope of such services—with the greatest increases being in the social service category.

These increases in services, however, have been accompanied by rapidly escalating costs, primarily for personnel. Rarely have old services been discontinued when new services were implemented, even if serious questions arose regarding service effectiveness.

In the late 1970s municipal revenues began to decrease in many cities while municipal expenses continued to escalate. As a result, a number of cities have recently discovered that they cannot finance their present level of services. Police agencies in numerous large cities have been faced with dual pressures— fewer employees and continually increasing demands for services. Few police agencies have established a mechanism for assigning priorities to the various aspects of their function. And those agencies that have considered priorities have rarely regarded priority setting as a matter of public discussion.

Now, in the 1980s, inflationary pressures prevent many communities from providing an unlimited range of services. But the law, community expectation, and priorities of police agencies remain unchanged, necessitating important choices among alternatives for police service.

For their own protection as well as for effective management of increasingly scarce resources, police agencies must engage in priority setting. Service demands on the police will continue to far exceed available resources, and the public will continue to expect the police to make their individual needs a high priority unless publicly stated policy indicates higher priorities. In addition, competing demands for police resources require internal administrative guidelines for direction of personnel in responding to these demands.

The ABA Standards commentary raises the following questions relevant to the setting of objectives and priorities for services:

1. What problems in the community should become matters of governmental concern?

2. If recognized as a matter of appropriate government concern, what should the response be?
3. Should the police be the agency to implement the agreed-upon response?
4. And if the police are to be the responsible agency, what priority should they attach to meeting one obligation as related to others for which they are also responsible?[7]

These priority decisions must be made jointly by the police chief and the government administrator. Public discussion of proposals for priorities can begin to provide a community understanding of why priorities are being established and can also provide for valuable community input. Once established, priorities should be widely communicated.

Definition of methods for goal achievement

The police have wide latitude in selecting the methods by which they achieve their goals and objectives. As noted earlier, discretion increases toward the bottom of the police organization, among patrol and investigative personnel, because there is little visibility in the decision-making process at these levels.

The variety of alternative methods for goal achievement available to the police is extensive. Despite the common belief that police always "enforce the law," they in fact ignore violations as often as they enforce the law. Indeed, the police primarily provide a government response to a variety of community needs. In providing this response, enforcement of the law is merely one option they have available for achieving their objectives; it is not an objective in itself. Utilizing warnings, educating minor violators, referring family dispute participants to social service agencies, and bringing intoxicated people to detoxification facilities are among the common options used by police officers in the field. In dealing with crime, police methods can include potentially illegal or questionable practices—wiretapping or searching homes without a warrant, for example.

With such a wide variety of methods available, police administration must provide guidance to personnel as to which methods are acceptable. This guidance is required on three levels: policy, rules, and procedures are of equal importance. Policy indicates the values to be applied to the area of concern. Rules provide absolute limitations on police action by stating clearly what actions or methods are required or prohibited. Procedural guidelines provide direction for action within those absolute limits—action that must be consistent with the values articulated through the policy statement.

The importance of providing guidance in the selection of methods increases when the police agency serves a multiracial or multiethnic community. When decisions on matters of discretion, such as when the criminal process is to be invoked, are not defined through policy, there is a substantial chance that those affected negatively by these decisions will challenge them on the basis of discrimination. When visible guidance is lacking, individual differences in treatment by the police may appear to be—or may actually be—based on the personal bias of the individual police officer. The potential for this public belief, whether accurate or not, mandates clear definition of acceptable methods and options for police action.

Administrative procedures

The police agency's use of administrative procedures is the third important area appropriate for policy making. Police administrators have substantial discretion in the use of resources and in the selection of the administrative procedures to which the department adheres. In the past ten years a number of these administrative decisions have come under public scrutiny and criticism.

Administrative procedures cover a variety of management matters; for example, the types of records kept by the police agency, how they are used, and how they can be sealed are often matters of public concern. Promotional procedures, labor–management relations activities, use of technical equipment, and types of training are other examples of administrative actions of potential public concern. While these decisions traditionally have been the responsibility of the chief of police alone, community concern has increasingly made them matters of public discussion and objects of political action. Many of them are no longer decisions that can be made out of the public view. The results of federal court suits during the past several years have indicated that, as mentioned earlier, agencies without documented policies are open to the charge that they have discriminatory practices and that application of procedures varies according to an individual's social status. The now common freedom of information procedures make issues such as record and file content of more concern.

The development of policy concerning administrative procedures need not limit the police administrator's discretion or flexibility. Instead the discretion of lower level employees will be decreased, and the chance for discriminatory treatment of citizens through the bureaucratic process will be limited—changes that can only strengthen the accountability of the police agency.

The role of the police agency

Policy decisions of the types described earlier are made at three levels: by elected officials (the council and the mayor), by the chief local government administrator, and by the police administrator. The interrelationship of these levels constitutes the governmental setting for police services, and it is the ability to create a constructive relationship among these levels that determines the quality of policing in the community. In addition, the police agency, the municipal administrator, and the police administrator all have significant roles in this complex.

Because of the detrimental influence of partisan politics on many police agencies in the past, and because of the development of the "professional" model of an independent police, many chief municipal executives have maintained a stance of noninvolvement in police matters. Local government managers and mayors often have felt that visibly exercising control over the police agency could be viewed as interference in the police organization and that politically noninvolvement was the safest course of action. Indeed, in many places, when the mayor or manager has expressed concern about police operations, the tenured police administrator has publicly complained of "interference."

The lack of a relationship between the municipal executive and the police executive can make it increasingly difficult for citizens to use what are termed "legitimate channels" to influence police policy affecting issues of priorities, methods, and service. Yet there has remained a real need for clearly established mechanisms of accountability and control within the political system.

Political leadership has an important responsibility in providing direction and policy guidance—serving as the link between the police administrator and the electorate. But the limits of political responsibility and involvement need to be clearly defined. A number of principles can be applied in setting these limits. Foremost among them are the following:

1. The police are not an independent agency.
2. The police agency should be isolated from political pressures.
3. Police administrators should have flexibility in their role.
4. The police should be supported in protecting individual rights.

The police are not an independent agency

While some police activity centers on the enforcement of state law, the police function is primarily concerned with a broad range of order maintenance and community service activities. The latter are clearly local, often neighborhood, concerns requiring responsiveness and accountability to community priorities.

There is little guidance in the law about how police should handle these concerns. At the most, the law provides the police with limits on their potential responses, but the discretion inherent in the police function permits wide variation. The acceptable limits of response to such matters as juvenile disturbances, traffic problems, domestic disputes, drunkenness, and vice, for example, vary greatly from one community to another; therefore, it is necessary to have a structure and process to ensure responsiveness of the police to the desires of the local community.

Local government, through the political process, organizes to provide services responsive to community needs. Coordination of services, development of priorities, and maintenance of a balance between the services offered and the financial resources of the community require that the agencies delivering the services be responsible to the electorate through the political process. The determination of police services, priorities, and responses properly rests with the political leadership of a community.

The police agency should be isolated from political pressures

Responsiveness and accountability will help assure that police actions reflect the needs of the community; protection of the police agency from partisan political pressures will help assure that police services are provided equitably. The three most common areas in which political leaders have tended to exert discriminatory pressures are: (1) enforcement of the law against individuals or particular groups; (2) protection of special interest groups or individuals; and (3) control of internal police department personnel matters.

Pressures employed against individuals or groups Historically, it has been common for police agencies to be used by political figures to bring pressure to bear on individuals or groups opposing the political party in office. Strict enforcement of particular ordinances against specified people or groups and other forms of harassment have been carried out with a minimum of public visibility owing to the discretion that is a part of the police function. Often a subtle form of political use of the police, such as discriminatory enforcement, leaves the agency open to other misuses of its power. In a number of cities today, these pressures still exist.

Special protection Political influence in police matters also has taken the form of granting special exemptions from enforcement to particular groups or individuals. There are two levels at which such influence occurs. At the lowest levels of the organization, among the patrol officers, there is often a tendency to overlook minor violations by their friends or by influential individuals. On a broader scale, some departments have an unwritten policy that instructs officers not to enforce laws against certain politically favored groups. For example, in one city a large taxi fleet owned by a prominent political figure was never inspected. In another city certain liquor establishments were permitted to stay open after legal closing hours.

Although police services and priorities are rightful decisions of the political leadership of a community, the application of police power cannot be permitted to assist politically favored groups.

Internal control As with all other city services, the police must not be subject to political pressures related to matters of internal management. Historically, political interference in police matters began with selection, promotions, and assignments within the agency. This type of control has tended to make police officials beholden to local political figures, thus laying the groundwork for control of actual police operations. This is why civil service systems have grown so rapidly throughout the country. In recent years we have seen a move toward more sophisticated merit systems, well documented to protect against undue political influence.

Police administrators should have flexibility in their role

If police administrators are to be held accountable for their actions and the operation of the police agency, they must be provided with substantial flexibility and discretion in the use of their resources to achieve policy objectives.

In recent years the discretion of the police administrator has been greatly reduced. The broad application of civil service has provided employees with job protection, but it has often made it difficult for the administrator to provide positive or negative sanctions to employees on the basis of performance. The growth of police unions in many communities—often in response to past management abuses—has made it difficult for police administrators to experiment with potentially productive service delivery improvements even when these changes do not affect employee rights or benefits. And the action of state and local legislative bodies has often mandated that the administrator implement procedures that have the effect of inhibiting police effectiveness and efficiency.

Accountability cannot be achieved if the police administrator does not have freedom to control all aspects of the organization's operations. Public policy can effectively provide the administrator with direction concerning objectives, but the administrator must have sufficient resource flexibility to respond effectively to the uneven nature of police service demands.

The police should be supported in protecting individual rights

Every resident of the community has the same rights, and these rights are protected by the Constitution. It is a primary police responsibility to ensure that the degree of protection of these rights is equal throughout the community. In recent years, such as during civil rights demonstrations or during court-ordered school desegregation activities, the police often have found themselves responsible for protecting the rights of individuals who are a distinct minority in the community. Only through strong political support of the police responsibility to protect all people's rights will the police be able to deal with what are often intense community pressures to support only majority desires.

Political and police leadership also must recognize that the equal protection of individual rights by the police is a far different matter from the conception of the police function as being solely the enforcement of the law. When individual rights are involved, the police have a constitutional mandate to provide every resident with equal protection. This responsibility forms the basic fabric of the police function.

The role of the chief local government administrator

Most of the involvement of political and administrative leadership in police affairs flows through the chief local government administrator. Whether manager or mayor, this administrator is ultimately responsible for the operation of the police agency and other local services. Even in communities where the police are responsible to an independent board or commission, the municipal administrator should be knowledgeable about police affairs and should be involved in the development of police policy.

Municipal administrators often have found it difficult to establish productive relationships with their police chiefs for a number of reasons. Police chiefs may resist administrative views of their agencies—mistaking proper executive accountability for political interference. Many municipal administrators are cautious about involvement in police matters, believing that in some sense the police agency is different from other agencies of government. And sometimes government executives fail to explain their concerns and priorities to the police chief, making it difficult for the chief to be responsive.

Municipal administrators will find that their role vis-à-vis the police department will reflect their performance in three critical areas. One is the selection of the police administrator; the second is the management relationship between the municipal administrator and the police chief; and the third is the political role of the municipal administrator when dealing with police issues. All three areas must be addressed by the chief administrator within the context of the governmental setting.

The role of the chief municipal administrator

Selection of the police chief
Broad perspective, commitment to openness in policy making, sensitivity to community needs, ability to manage, professional qualifications

Management relationships
Police chief as department head, not an independent executive; team work in planning, budgeting, training, as part of management team

Political role of the chief municipal administrator
Major link between council and police chief; buffer for partisan political influences; helps coordinate police services with other departments and other governments

Three major roles of the chief administrator and the police chief: selection of the police chief, continuing management relationship between the two officials, and political role of the chief administrator.

Selection of the police chief

Since policing is one of the most visible and important services of municipal government, it follows that the position of police chief is one of the most important municipal appointments. Since incompetence on the part of the police chief can affect the tenure of the chief administrator, and since the quality of police service delivery directly affects the quality of life in the community, it is important that the municipal administrator select a police chief who is fully capable of both managing the police organization and interacting positively with the community.

Michael Kelly, in his excellent work on selection of a police chief, notes that there are seven special problems in choosing a police chief.

(1) *Contemporary policing is at the center of some of the most profound sources of friction in American life.* These include racial tensions and hostilities, activist protest movements of various kinds, restlessness of young people, widespread distrust of government at all levels, and public expectation of virtually perfect personal and official conduct on the part of public officials. . . .

(2) *Policing is perhaps the most important function of local government.* . . . The powers of police to arrest citizens and to affect the moral complexion of the community, as well as the duties of police to maintain public order and protect constitutional liberties, are the most fundamental public functions. . . .

(3) *Internal politics within the police department can cause difficulties.* Many police departments have traditions by which top management personnel work up through the ranks. These traditions are often backed up by laws requiring civil service procedures for promotion or limiting eligibility to "inside" personnel. High-level police officials may also have close working relationships with business and other community groups and may view a city manager or mayor as a relative newcomer. These police officials, and police unions in some departments, as well as their allies and opponents within the community, will carefully scrutinize the choice of a new chief. As a result, many constituencies within the department have significant and sometimes powerful personal and ideological interests at stake in the selection.

(4) *There are few rules to go by in judging a police official.* Police management is an amorphous body of knowledge, best learned through experience. It is difficult to assess a police official's talent by using widely accepted standards of educational credentials, training, or position. . . .

(5) *The quality of leadership is probably more important to the performance of police than of any other municipal service.* Police departments are generally organized in a quasi-military structure that puts a high degree of responsibility and control at the top. No other method of affecting police behavior—lawsuits against officers, "exclusionary" rules of the courts, or citizen review boards—is as effective as discipline and leadership by the chief. . . .

(6) *Because of the tight organizational structure of police departments, it may be difficult to obtain accurate information about candidates.* Police departments are often isolated as an organization so that a recruiter may find it hard to penetrate the barriers to ask about a candidate. . . .

(7) *There are deep divisions within the police profession over where a contemporary police force should place its priorities.* One commentator describes three competing concepts of police professionalism in the United States today: a union-oriented "guild professionalism" concept; a "military bureaucratic model" calling for a highly structured organization to improve police services; and a "therapeutic model" giving emphasis to social concerns and community relationships [Harold Richard Wilde, Jr., "The Process of Change in a Police Bureaucracy" (Ph.D. dissertation, Harvard University, 1972)]. In any case, it is clear that different police professionals may have widely divergent ideas on the directions in which policing should be headed. Those involved in a search process must at least be aware of these differences and may wish to define their own goals for policing in their community.[8]

In selecting a police chief the municipal administrator must ensure that the criteria applied to potential candidates reflect the real concerns of the community and its political leadership about the police function and its administration. It is impossible to delineate exact, universal selection standards, since each community will look for candidate skills and abilities most suitable to local priorities. Several characteristics can, however, be identified as criteria for application to potential candidates. These characteristics, which reflect issues also of importance to the chief administrator, include understanding the nature of the police function, openness and responsiveness in policy making, and management ability and experience.

The first characteristic, an understanding of the true nature of the police function in a democracy, requires a broadly defined perspective on the police role based on a firm commitment to the equal protection of the individual rights of all citizens. The personal integrity of the candidate must be beyond question, reflecting a commitment to adherence to the law in both professional and personal matters. Also required is sensitivity to and understanding of the governmental system, including a perspective on the police service within local government.

The second characteristic is a commitment to openness in the process of policy making and recognition of the necessity for responsiveness to local priorities and needs. Equally important is a sensitivity to the dynamics of the community and of social problems that are strongly affected by police actions. The perspective required is an understanding of police power and police discretion.

The third important criterion for a police administrator is the ability to manage and head a major unit of government. However, it should be kept in mind that management ability differs from command ability. Leadership qualities, often so difficult to define adequately but so obvious when present, include the ability to motivate an employee of the agency toward accomplishment of the agency's goals while representing the agency to the community in an open and constructive manner. In this sense leadership requires the ability to accept proper political accountability and to lead the agency toward change and improvement. Management ability includes the ability to perform in a complex series of leadership roles—for example, as community leader and as professional executive.

There are numerous modern devices that can assist the chief administrator in making a selection. For example, the assessment center, which utilizes job-related exercises to assess a candidate's skill, is one increasingly popular method for selection (see Chapter 13). The oral interview is important for assessing the candidate's views on and understanding of the complexities of the police function.

As a part of the selection process, the chief administrator should thoroughly review the quality of the police department, since it is important that a candidate's strengths complement any weaknesses of the department. For example, if it is found that the administrative procedures utilized by the department are ineffective, the candidate selected should have skills necessary for upgrading the administrative process. Or if there are concerns about the department's integrity, the candidate selected should have a clearly demonstrated capability to deal with problems of police corruption.

The general areas for the city administrator to review in the police agency in preparation for the selection of a chief reflect those areas in which the chief should have knowledge and concern on a regular basis. They are: (1) the clarity of the department's objectives; (2) the internal quality of management in the department; (3) the organization's integrity; (4) the relationship of the department to the community; (5) the relationship of the department's administration to labor organizations; and (6) the degree to which the department is responsive to the legitimate concerns of democratic government.

The final consideration in the selection of a police chief is the candidate's ability to assume the new position. Whether selected from within or from outside the department, the new police chief must understand the basic strategies of organizational change. The new chief must understand how to take over the job, how to build support within the organization, and how to assess the costs and benefits—financially and politically—of every proposed action. A number of new police chiefs have not had these skills, and though well intentioned, they have alienated the police agency and the community with their initial management actions.

The management relationship

The management relationship between the chief administrator and the police chief is the second area in which the role of the chief administrator is significant.

This relationship depends heavily on many of the concerns described in the previous section. But equally important is the management style of the chief administrator (see Chapter 5).

Municipal administrators should work with their police chiefs as municipal department heads, not as independent executives. Although the relationship of the chief administrator with the police chief may differ somewhat from that with other executives owing to the sensitivity of the police function, the police chief must have equal "cabinet" status with other agency heads. That is to say, the police chief should attend all staff meetings for department heads, provide the same management reports, respond to the same budget requirements, and be held to the same standards of accountability. The chief administrator who exempts the police chief from these management responsibilities will find that the accountability of the police chief is greatly lessened.

It has been common for police chiefs to be considered "different" from other government executives. In one East Coast city, for example, for years the police chief was not required to attend the meetings of the city's department heads with the mayor because of the police chief's fixed independent tenure. This resulted in eventual conflict between the police chief and city administrator, as the administrator's priorities and concerns were not communicated. Unless regular interaction occurs as a part of the governmental process, the relationship will be based solely on crisis responses. The negative or critical nature of such a relationship cannot facilitate sound management interaction.

Constructive relationships between chief administrators and police chiefs often are made more difficult by lack of management experience and training on the part of most chiefs of police. Many police chiefs have had limited opportunities to develop their management skills. The chief administrator should recognize this and should be supportive of the chief's attending seminars and courses on modern management concepts and current governmental issues.

Finally, the management effectiveness of the chief of police in medium-sized or large departments can be increased if the chief is permitted to have a highly skilled administrative assistant. It is fruitless for a chief administrator to make certain management demands on the police chief if the chief has no staff to call on for assistance in meeting executive requirements. The investment in a staff assistant can help ensure that the chief of police has the needed resources and data on which to base management decisions.

The political role

The political role of the municipal administrator has great bearing on the effectiveness of the police agency. A community can achieve police responsiveness and accountability only if the chief administrator accepts the role of the major link between the council and the police chief. The political role of the administrator requires that he or she accept a number of important responsibilities.

One of these responsibilities is to ensure that partisan political influences are kept apart from the police agency. The political pressures described earlier in this chapter will rarely occur if the municipal administrator is strongly supportive of maintaining police neutrality. To accomplish this, the chief administrator must fully comprehend the difference between partisan political pressures and accountability through the political process.

The municipal administrator must demand accountability from the chief of police and also must see that the police chief actively participates in a highly visible policy-making process. To ensure that accountability is established, the municipal administrator must fully understand the most important aspects of the police function, police objectives, and the permissible limits of discretion. Unless the chief administrator requires the development of policy and procedural guidelines for the police force, he or she will have difficulty establishing that agency's accountability.

In order to achieve accountability, the municipal administrator must provide the required administrative flexibility for effective management of the police organization. When issues affecting the delivery of police services are under discussion, the chief administrator has the responsibility to see that the police chief is properly involved in the decision-making process. The administrator must also work to prevent constraints from being imposed on management flexibility through labor contracts and related means.

Most important, the municipal administrator must maintain an activist orientation toward the police agency. He or she must care enough about the quality of police service delivery to keep informed on major agency developments. He or she should consider the chief of police a public safety professional and should rely on the advice of the chief of police, especially when dealing with the political leadership. Overall, however, the chief administrator should understand that police priorities and policies should reflect the priorities of the community itself.

The role of the police administrator

As we have seen, the complexities of the police function and the environment in which policing occurs place great pressures on the police administrator to maintain a balance between professional competence and responsiveness to legitimate political pressures reflective of the needs of the community. The position is clearly one of the most difficult within local government and requires performance in a number of different roles.

An important role of the police administrator, and certainly the most traditional one, is that of organizational manager. Being a good manager is not the same thing as being a competent field operations commander. It requires leadership qualities that are not found in all persons. It also requires the ability to manage time, resources, and events, molding them all into police services within the framework of public policy. To motivate even a small group of public employees is often a complex undertaking.

But the role of the police administrator is far more than simply that of manager. The chief of police must assume the role of community leader as well, for the demands of policing today will not permit police executives to be reactive solely to crime and other negative community incidents. Failure to adopt a proactive posture in leading the police agency will result in an increase in the division between police and community. This leadership role requires that the police chief be open and honest about police operations and available to the total community. In order to fulfill this role, certain guidelines should be borne in mind.

The police chief must have a basic commitment to maintaining a position of neutrality when partisan political issues are involved and must ensure that partisan interests are separated from community priorities.

A second requirement is openness when responding to community criticism. The defensive posture adopted by some police officials is a not-so-subtle suggestion that citizens and community groups have no right to express their concerns. The effective and responsive chief will always be open to criticism, recognizing that the chief and the agency are accountable to the community through the political process. When a mistake is made, it should be admitted. If one has not been made, the reasons for a police action should be fully explained.

Since policing so directly affects the quality of life in the community, the police chief must be willing to speak out on matters that affect it. When a police executive has a commitment to democratic principles and the protection of individual rights, he or she must be willing to speak out in public when those rights or principles are violated. Issue-oriented commentary by the police chief, directed away from persons, can help a community better understand social change and deal with it. In this way the community can also be encouraged to accept more responsibility for order maintenance activities.

Public comment by the police executive, and the development of police policy in the public view, can greatly increase a community's feelings that their police agency is responsive. The police administrator should not be afraid to be visible in times of community crisis. Time and again police chiefs have maintained low visibility during community tensions directly affected by their agency's activities. The result has been public distrust of the agency and public feeling that there is something to hide.

Finally, the police leadership role requires acknowledgment of police discretion. A police claim of neutrality loses credibility when the facts show discretionary application of the law. The police chief who fully understands the police function, recognizing that police have other choices besides application of the law in order maintenance situations, will have a solid basis on which to control police behavior. Only by publicly recognizing that discretion exists can the police administrator pave the way for the development of meaningful policy.

Conclusion

This chapter has reviewed the governmental setting for police work, giving particular attention to the development of policy and the work of the police agency in carrying out its program in relation to other departments and agencies of the local government of which it is a part. Discussions of the historical development and the environmental concerns of policing have shown how police administrators depend on the electoral process to provide both legislative and administrative support for their work on a permanent basis. It is not necessarily stating the obvious to point out that the police service is part of the total governmental process just as it is a part of the criminal justice process.

From a management point of view, the most important participants in this governmental setting are the chief administrator of the local government and the police chief. These are the persons who help establish policy and who provide the leadership, develop the budget, make the decisions, accept the responsibilities, and are held accountable. These are the persons who must work with the city council or other legislative body and who are most visible to the public.

1 Standards for combined police services are presented in: National Advisory Commission on Criminal Justice Standards and Goals, *Police [Report on Police]* (Washington, D.C.: Government Printing Office, 1973), pp. 108–116.

2 Egon Bittner, *The Functions of the Police in Modern Society* (Chevy Chase, Md.: Center for Studies of Crime and Delinquency, National Institute of Mental Health, 1970), p. 40.

3 A more detailed description of these areas is provided in: American Bar Association Project on Standards for Criminal Justice, *Standards Relating to the Urban Police Function* (Chicago: American Bar Association, 1974).

4 An excellent discussion of these issues can be found

in: Herman Goldstein, *Policing a Free Society* (Cambridge, Mass.: Ballinger Publishing Company, 1977).

5 American Bar Association Project on Standards for Criminal Justice, p. 3.

6 The development of policies and supplemental procedures and rules is described in a later chapter of the present volume.

7 American Bar Association, *Standards for the Urban Police Function* (Chicago: American Bar Association, 1973), p. 72.

8 Michael J. Kelly, *Police Chief Selection: A Handbook for Local Government* (Washington, D.C.: Police Foundation and International City Management Association, 1975), pp. 5–6.

4 Corruptive influences

An encouraging development in the police service during the past few years has been a significant and open acknowledgment of one of the service's chief problems—police corruption. There are many signs of this change in attitude. Twenty years ago many police departments did not have internal affairs bureaus to fight corruption. Today it is hard to find a large department without one. Articles on police corruption have begun to appear in police and related journals. Authors dealing with police corruption have begun to receive informed attention instead of antagonism from the police. And at the forums at which police administrators talk about common problems, the mention of police corruption is no longer taboo.

This new willingness to bring police corruption into the open has not come easily, however, and it is still far from universal. The reason is not hard to find. Those who belong to police departments know, either from personal experience or the experience of other departments, that open attempts to discuss and to deal with corruption almost invariably have a negative effect. They tarnish the reputation of the entire department. This is a direct consequence of the comparatively low status still accorded to the police despite the broad range and the social importance of their duties. When a doctor, lawyer, or teacher is expelled from his or her profession for unethical conduct, few people conclude that all members of the profession are blameworthy, but many people do conclude from police scandals that all police are corrupt.

Lumping the honest police officers with the corrupt is obviously an injustice. Because this is usually the case, however, police chiefs have traditionally taken the attitude that the less said about corruption the better. In addition to remaining silent, many police officials are resentful if asked about the possibility of corruption and feel compelled to deny its existence. Even worse, many chiefs fail to correct corrupt practices, whether minor or major, or to keep up the constant vigilance that is needed to maintain integrity. They assume, without looking for evidence to the contrary, that every member of the department is honest. This naive approach is a mistake for police administrators.

The police work in a world in which corruption is found in all walks of life. To suppose that all police officers will remain honest despite continuous exposure to such an environment is to suppose the impossible.

Any attempt to deal with police corruption must begin with a willingness to confront it, to see things as they are. Police corruption is a reality whose existence has been revealed time and again in various communities.

Police corruption, of course, is far more serious in some departments than in others. A few departments may be so corrupt that police connive in burglary and other hard core crimes. Other departments are basically clean except for the vice squad. In some departments high ranking officers are in on graft; in others they are honest, but this does not prevent the rank and file, whose freedom of action is great, from continuing on the take. So, too, the climates within departments range from integrity (officers report corrupt behavior on the part of their colleagues unhesitatingly) to corruption (a code of silence prevails concerning corruption), with various gradations in between.

As a rule, serious police corruption is more likely to be centered in the big cities, with their concentrations of prostitution, narcotics, gambling, and organized crime. However, there are notable exceptions to this generalization. Some big city departments are honest, and some suburban and small town departments are notoriously corrupt.

On the whole, there is less police corruption today than there was a generation ago, but the improvement is not so much the result of reforms within police departments themselves as of external changes which have reduced corruptive influences on the police.

There is less political pressure on police departments and individual officers than in the past. The day of machine politics, when powerful and corrupt political organizations ruled city hall, has diminished appreciably, and today's politicians are less likely to try to influence police performance of their duties.

In addition, more and more police departments have been placed under civil service. Fewer police officers are hired or promoted as a result of political favors or outright payoffs. The integrity of a department's recruitment practices has a lot to do with determining the ethical climate in the department.

Another but less important change is financial. Partly as a result of unionization, police officers are paid more adequately today than in the past, which has made bribery less enticing.

While police corruption is less common today, it still remains a serious problem in many departments. The temptations facing police officers are still considerable, as is the difficulty of controlling what goes on in a large police department. The recent establishment of permanent internal affairs bureaus in many departments testifies to the fact that police corruption is something which must continually be controlled.

The long history of police corruption has led pessimists to conclude that nothing can be done about the problem. Positive steps can be taken, however, by the police administrator. This chapter[1] opens with a description of the damage done by corruption, and then discusses the factors influencing reform. The degrees and types of police corruption are then outlined, followed by a review of the various complex factors that contribute to corruption. The chapter continues with specific and practical steps that police chiefs can take to combat corruption in their department. Next, there is a section on sources of help outside the department. The chapter ends with an evaluative conclusion.

The damage done by corruption

Police corruption does particular damage in the following ways: (1) it undermines the confidence of the public; (2) it destroys respect for the law; (3) it undermines departmental discipline; and (4) it harms police morale.

Public confidence

First, police corruption does considerable damage in that it undermines public confidence in the police. Because police agencies are given the job of enforcing the law, they frequently define their actions in moral terms: they say they are protecting the law-abiding citizen and bringing the criminal to justice. Frequently, too, the police urge the public to obey the law and to cooperate with them. Messages such as these are important, among other reasons, for their psychological value. Police agencies must reassure the public that they will not abuse the power with which they are endowed by society.

But when police corruption is exposed these messages lose much of their impact. Unexposed police corruption is just as harmful, particularly in city neighborhoods in which the police can be bribed to ignore certain crimes. These neighborhoods are typically poor ones, often mainly inhabited by minorities.

The coexistence of police corruption and such crimes as gambling and drug peddling has in some cases virtually destroyed the confidence of citizens in these neighborhoods in the police and in public authority generally.

Respect for the law

Second, police corruption destroys respect for the law itself. Corruption indicates that the police themselves, who are sworn to uphold the law, hold it in contempt. Citizens ask why they should obey the law when it is clear that some police officers do not.

Departmental discipline

Third, police corruption undermines departmental discipline in ways that seriously impair effectiveness and efficiency. Police officers who spend their working hours pursuing payoffs have little time and less inclination to perform their assigned duties. They will attempt to subvert or sabotage reorganizations or changes of assignment that threaten to curtail their corrupt activities, and will see directives from the chief's office intended to promote more enlightened law enforcement—for example, an order not to enforce Sunday blue laws except upon citizen complaint and with supervisory approval—as directly opposed to their corrupt interests.

Disciplinary problems are compounded, of course, when supervisory personnel are also corrupt. The corrupt commanding officer lacks the moral authority to compel obedience, even if he or she wanted to. In departments in which a climate of corruption prevails, commanding officers are unlikely to achieve satisfactory levels of either discipline or productivity. In corrupt departments sergeants and those higher in rank may get the lion's share of the graft. Patrol officers may learn that as long as they don't "rock the boat" they need not worry about discipline. Their main reward in the corruption process is being allowed to take their duties lightly. They know that if they want to find a cozy spot to take a nap on duty, or decide to stop for a long cup of coffee, they don't have to worry about being called on the carpet.

Police morale

Fourth and last, police corruption has a bad effect on police morale. Distrust is common between those who are trying to be honest and effective and those who participate in either minor or major graft. Exposure of the problem, unfortunately, does not always help the situation. The honest officer will be angered by those whose involvement in corruption has incurred public wrath. But frequently such exposure will tend to make his or her life more difficult, because the public so often takes the attitude that corruption is not limited to those who got caught. The honest police officer frequently winds up resenting not only corrupt officers but also the news media (if they exposed the corruption) and the public as well.

What often happens after a scandal is that the department establishes new procedures and regulations intended to prevent future problems. These new rules usually arouse skepticism among the rank and file about the intelligence or intentions of the agency leadership, since new rules alone rarely have any effect on corruption. To the ordinary officer they look like attempts to make the public believe that something is being done. Over time, anticorruption rules simply accumulate. Their worst defect is that they fail to provide positive guidance on how to stay honest. Instead, they are negatively phrased, a storehouse of "thou shalt nots." As Herman Goldstein points out, "This emphasis upon negative guidance creates an atmosphere of distrust that is demoralizing to honest and well-intentioned police officers."[2]

The factors influencing reform

For all these reasons, and others, police corruption must be taken seriously by police administrators everywhere. It is a problem that must be faced as openly and courageously as circumstances will permit. That is, a wise administrator will understand the importance of timing and will appreciate the limits of what is possible. He will avoid an overreach that could be suicidal. Some reform is better than none.

Reform may be easier in the future than it is now. While recent national political scandals have aroused an unprecedented distrust of governmental institutions at all levels, that is not the whole story. Perhaps never before have the American people looked so eagerly for a restoration of character, honesty, and integrity among all those entrusted with public responsibilities. The time is ripe for the police, as well as other public institutions, to set their houses in order.

In recent years it has become evident that there are many important steps that police departments can take to control police corruption. They are outlined later in this chapter, under the heading What the Police Chief Can Do about Corruption.

Taken alone, however, these steps are not enough. Ultimately, control of police corruption will also depend heavily on action by mayors, city managers, city councils, local district attorneys, the news media, businessmen, and many other citizens. For that reason a section of this chapter headed Outside Help is devoted to a discussion of the major sources of support for reform outside the area of policing.

But in any scheme of things, solutions come last. First, it is necessary to take a good look at the many activities that come under the heading of police corruption and then discuss the reasons why police corruption has remained an insoluble problem for so long.

Degrees of corruption

One of the problems in talking about police corruption is defining it. The words *police corruption* mean different things to different people. Indeed, some citizens use the term loosely to mean any and all kinds of wrongful police activities—from taking payoffs to brutality, racial discrimination, and general arbitrariness. A precise and practical definition of the term is misuse of police authority for mercenary purposes—that is, to get money, services, or material goods. It confuses the issue to include other evils. Even political interference and favoritism, while they often exist side by side with corruption and contribute to it, are different problems.

Two generalizations need to be made about the many forms of police corruption. First, there is an enormous range in the amount of the financial gain. For obvious reasons, it is the spectacular corruption that wins the greatest public attention—the payoffs amounting to many thousands of dollars received by police officers in return for not arresting those involved in gambling or narcotics, for example. But it is important to remember that payoffs range all the way down to a bottle of liquor or a five dollar bill for permitting illegal parking, or less for ignoring an ordinance violation.

Second, just as the payoffs cover a vast range, so does the effort involved in obtaining the payoff. In any police department in which corruption exists the largest part of it is probably what might be called passive graft. That is, much of it does not involve active pursuit of payoffs by police officers. The payoff is initiated by a citizen; the officer simply accepts it—a bottle of liquor, for example. It is preceded by little, if any, discussion about the size of the bribe, often because there is some sort of informal understanding between the officer and the citizen as to what the size of the bribe should be, depending on what law has been or is being violated.

Another kind of graft, usually somewhat less common in terms of the percentage of officers involved, might be called negotiable graft. It is here that we get into the realm of serious crime. Since there is less in the way of informal understanding, the officer and the criminal engage in a kind of bargaining. A burglar, for instance, may carry so-called insurance money to buy off the police officer who catches him in the act. The burglar, of course, knows how much he is carrying, and the police officer may find it more prudent to negotiate a payoff rather than search the suspect to find out how much more he can get.

Finally, there are a small percentage of officers in any corrupt department who engage in hard-nosed extortion, or what might be called active graft. These are officers determined to make as much money as possible through the misuse of authority, and very little will deter them.

To distinguish payoffs according to size and the amount of effort expended by police officers in getting them is not to excuse any of them. But it is critical to an understanding of the problem in realistic terms. Police corruption is not simply a matter of dishonest individual police officers. The real problem is the climate in a police department which permits corruption of all kinds or any kind to exist. At the same time, the fact that the majority of corrupt police officers engage solely or primarily in passive graft suggests that the task of controlling police corruption is far from hopeless.

Types of corruption

In addition to understanding degrees of corruption, it is important to understand the various kinds of corruption. Of all of them, none is more common than the acceptance of bribes from those who deal in the vices—gambling, prostitution, illegal drinking, and illegal use of drugs.

Ignoring vice

Because vice is so profitable, the vice laws provide enormous opportunities for police corruption. Human nature is hard to change. Despite the laws, millions of citizens want to indulge in the vices. And there are many other citizens willing to provide this ready market with the opportunity to do so. Just as there are groups willing to provide legal goods and services—groups that are called industrial and commercial firms—so there are groups willing to take the risks of offering illegal goods and services. These groups, which collectively are frequently referred to as organized crime, have many things in common with legitimate businesses. They are more or less permanent, they have hierarchies and branch offices, they compete with each other (sometimes in murderous ways), and so on. They continue to exist because the rewards are simply too large for some people to forgo. (Chapter 10 outlines the special problems of organized crime and the departmental approaches, including intelligence operations, that are required to combat it.)

The very nature of policing means that those who enter it soon become realists. No one sees or comes into contact with a wider range of human behavior than the police officer. The officer knows that no matter how many gambling operators or prostitutes or drug pushers he or she arrests, the vice itself will continue to exist. No one is better aware than the police officer of the comparative lack of social concern regarding the so-called "victimless crimes." The social consensus which supports the police in apprehending those guilty of such crimes as rape, murder, assault, and robbery often does not exist when it comes to vice.

Thus, all the conditions favorable to police corruption are present. The public generally is not bothered by the vices, particularly if they are kept within certain geographical boundaries or are kept more or less out of sight. The actual crimes are carried out by permanent organizations with money to offer as bribes, and the police have the task of enforcing laws which lack widespread public support.

In connection with gambling, in particular, police corruption is a perennial threat. Gambling rings often make regular monthly payments that are divided up among all officers who might constitute a threat. The highest ranking officers may get the largest amounts and patrol officers the smallest. Or vice squads may receive graft while patrol officers are excluded. Thirty years ago, in Boston, police officers called it the "union wage." More recently, it was referred to as the "pad" in New York and the "steady note" in Philadelphia.

No one sees a wider range of human behavior than the police officer.

Drug trafficking goes on more covertly than gambling. Dealers change locations frequently and use all the other well-known devices to elude capture. Generally, payoffs to the police by those involved in the drug trade are not regular. Most frequently the payoff occurs when the opportunity presents itself. Drug dealers are engaged in a crime that frequently involves much larger sums of money in individual transactions than do gambling and prostitution. As a result, dealers carry large sums of cash and unscrupulous police do not hesitate to make them part with it in return for nonarrest.

Fixing traffic tickets

In addition to the vice laws, other laws and regulations provide a variety of opportunities for graft.

At the one end of the scale is the motorist apprehended after committing a moving traffic violation (e.g., speeding or ignoring a red light). The motorist does not want a summons, which means a fine, the inconvenience of a court appearance, or, even worse, the possibility of a substantial increase in his or her auto insurance premium. If he or she accumulates enough violations, it may mean loss of license or required attendance at a police or traffic court driving school. It seems much simpler to offer the police officer a small bribe. The police officer knows it. In some cities this petty bribery has been so much a fact of life that drivers have made a habit of folding money into their driver's or owner's license. No need to embarrass the officer, to make it obvious to any passerby that the officer is taking a bribe. Just pass the officer a license with a bit of the bill showing.

Bargaining with the criminal

At the other end of the scale is the professional criminal who does not want to be charged if caught. A bribe is offered. The offer may be made to the arresting officer or it may be made to the detective investigating the case. The briber is not fussy; he or she knows that freedom can often be purchased.

One professional safecracker reportedly was arrested 300 times over a period of forty years. He was able to avoid prosecution on all but five occasions, usually by corrupting the investigators.

This type of corruption has many variations. The unscrupulous police officer may suspect, with good reason, that the professional criminal will increase the offer as his or her court appearance gets closer. Or the criminal may think he or she can bluff his or her way through and does not offer a bribe immediately but waits until the last possible moment. The case may already be under way in court when the criminal's lawyer passes along the bribe offer in return for perjured testimony by the officer or the disappearance of important evidence. The dishonest officer can play the same game.

Accepting small gratuities

There is also the minor corruption that almost everyone knows about and that many people do not think of as corruption at all: the free cup of coffee; the free meal; the discount "police price" on merchandise; the Christmas present; the weekly $10 bill from the jeweler for patroling his street frequently; the reward from the insurance company representative for recovering stolen property.

Most of the time the police officer doesn't even have to put out a hand to gather these small additions to his or her paycheck. That doesn't mean that the officer may not expect them, however. They are such a tradition in some departments that most police officers think of them as "perks," or perquisites—something to which the police have a right.

The citizens who hand out these small favors also may not regard them as acts of corruption. Some do it simply because they like the police, but most see it as a small "investment." When the Knapp Commission in New York City asked businessmen why they handed out such favors, most of them made it clear that they "expected to receive either extra or better service than that given to the general public, and many expected the police to overlook minor illegal acts or conditions."[3] Often police officers oblige. How can it be corruption when it's so small, when it comes from perfectly respectable citizens?

And some police departments do not really frown on it. Departmental rules may prohibit it, but to many departments other problems seem far more important. If the officer is doing his or her job satisfactorily, if the citizen doesn't offer his or her gift in too blatant a manner, no one in authority worries about it. Some police managers rationalize as follows: if officers are prohibited from accepting these small rewards, which may be a long-standing benefit of working for the department, they will be less productive.

Taking kickbacks and similar "rewards"

The officer accustomed to accepting small rewards is going to find ways in which to justify accepting larger ones. So the acceptance of small gratuities gradually shades into accepting kickbacks. In kickback situations the police officer actively helps the businessman, particularly the small businessman whose business is street-oriented. Tow truck operators may reward police officers who help them get the business of motorists who need a tow. The towing fee itself may be of small consequence to the tow truck driver, because in some areas the fees are regulated. What the driver wants is the opportunity to take the damaged car to his garage in order to get the repair job. The police officer is a figure of authority and can steer citizens to a particular garage.

Such working relationships are also often established between police officers and certain "substantial" citizens to whom the public turns in crises, such as undertakers, bondsmen, criminal lawyers, and even doctors.

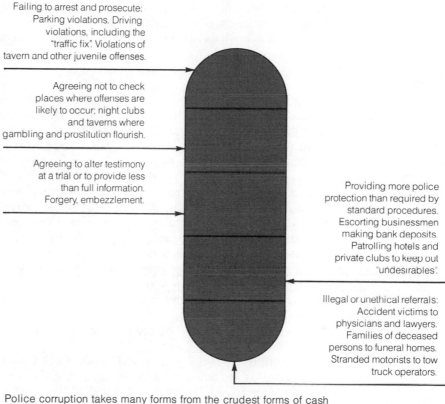

Failing to arrest and prosecute: Parking violations. Driving violations, including the "traffic fix". Violations of tavern and other juvenile offenses.

Agreeing not to check places where offenses are likely to occur; night clubs and taverns where gambling and prostitution flourish.

Agreeing to alter testimony at a trial or to provide less than full information. Forgery, embezzlement.

Providing more police protection than required by standard procedures. Escorting businessmen making bank deposits. Patrolling hotels and private clubs to keep out "undesirables".

Illegal or unethical referrals: Accident victims to physicians and lawyers. Families of deceased persons to funeral homes. Stranded motorists to tow truck operators.

Police corruption takes many forms from the crudest forms of cash bribes to the most subtle forms of influence. Some of the most insidious kinds, shown here, require direct connivance by respectable members of the public.

Another common type of police corruption arises from the fact that the police are given the task of enforcing municipal ordinances, conducting investigations, and in some jurisdictions issuing licenses for many activities which have little to do with crime. Thus, the police enforce Sunday blue laws and issue permits to owners of pistols. Such tasks involve ample opportunities for petty bribery.

Of course, sometimes enforcement of municipal ordinances, conduct of investigations, and issuance of permits are related to crime. For example, there are states in which the state liquor control board issues liquor licenses but lacks the personnel to conduct background investigations of applicants. The job of investigating falls on the local police. Some applicants are known to have unsavory backgrounds. These may arrange with the investigating officer, for a fee, to omit such information from the report. Who would know it except the applicant and the investigator? The investigator's supervisor? There may be something in it for the supervisor as well.

Stealing

Another form of corruption has been described as "opportunistic theft." It is clearly criminal as well as corrupt. It takes place during the course of a police officer's regular duties. The officer called upon to assist in cases of citizens who are drunk or injured, or in the case of a death, has obvious opportunities to commit theft with very little chance of discovery. In some cities police officers have been known to accompany a dying person or a corpse to the hospital, take their house key, and return to the house and ransack it. Commercial establishments may present similar opportunities. The patrol officer may find a store unlocked or broken into. It may be 3 A.M., when no one else is around. The officer thus has a marvelous opportunity to help himself or herself.

Taking a bribe from another officer

All the varieties of police corruption discussed up to this point have involved bribes passing between citizens and police officers. Another type involves payments between one officer and another for any of a whole range of favors. Goldstein reports that investigations in several large cities "have described such practices as street officers paying inside men for falsifying attendance records, influencing the choice of vacations and days off, reporting them on duty when they are not, providing them with records faster than usual, arranging for them to be called at the beginning of a court session, and giving them passing grades in training programs."[4] Or the payoff may be in exchange for being assigned to an area with ample opportunities for graft. Internal payoffs thus are also a way in which illegal gains of the police on the street are shared with those who work inside and therefore have fewer opportunities for corruption. Wherever there is widespread corruption involving police and citizens, there may be payoffs *among* police officers as well.

Factors contributing to police corruption

Police corruption does not occur just because a few dishonest people join a department. Its roots are much broader and deeper. Little can be done about police corruption unless its sources are understood. Five can be singled out: (1) community standards; (2) police chief attitudes; (3) attitudes of the rank and file; (4) police discretion; and (5) prosecutors and court actions.

Community standards

The preceding recital of the many varieties of police corruption should have made one thing clear: namely, that police corruption does not take place in isolation. Without corrupt citizens there would be far less police corruption. The fact is that police corruption is one reflection of the ethics of a larger community in which the police carry out their duties. This is not said to excuse corrupt police officers. The point is that police officers are human. No police department can remain an island of integrity in a sea of corruption.

The current era has been notable for its revelations of corrupt behavior among people of far higher ostensible social standing than the police. The Watergate affair, of course, is the first that comes to mind, but corruption has not been confined to the White House. It has been found among a number of corporation executives, willing to make illegal political contributions and to bribe foreign buyers of American goods. Corruption has also surfaced in the Congress and in some of the hitherto most prestigious federal agencies.

But this is not the first era in which high level corruption has been uncovered. The path of political corruption at all levels of government winds through American history. Inevitably, what has happened in government has spilled over into policing, because our entire criminal justice process is heavily influenced by the wishes of mayors, city council members, prosecuting attorneys, and judges. However frequently it is asserted that politics and law enforcement do not mix, frequently they are forced to.

Given this environment, it is not surprising that police should become cynical about their work and should feel that "nothing is on the level." In every walk of life there are citizens who will pay the police officer to overlook the law—the citizen who wants to avoid a traffic ticket, the businessman who wants to get the jump on competitors, the criminal who wants to be free to carry on his or her operation. The temptation before the police officer is enormous, particularly when he or she knows that within the community impartial law enforcement is difficult to achieve. When the police become accustomed to seeing assignments made on the basis of political considerations and promotions made on the basis of favoritism, integrity can easily be damaged. When it is apparent that everyone else is out to take care of personal concerns, the police officer committed to honest and objective law enforcement can only see himself or herself, as Jonathan Rubinstein says, as "operating in a world where 'notes' are constantly floating about, and only the stupid, the naive, and the fainthearted are unwilling to allow some of them to stick to their fingers."[5]

Attitude of the police chief

As mentioned early in this chapter, police chiefs as a group have always been reluctant to deal with corruption, unwilling to discuss it, and horrified at the thought of squarely facing it. Barker and Roebuck point out that "personally honest police chiefs will go to extraordinary lengths—even to the point of making fools or suspects of themselves in public—in efforts to shield from exposure crooks and incompetents within the ranks."[6]

One reason for this attitude has already been cited—the fear that any corruption which is brought to light will be blown out of all proportion by a public only too willing to believe that the whole department is corrupt. For police chiefs, such a situation can mean that their jobs are at stake. In baseball, you don't fire the team, you fire the manager. This applies to policing as well. Therefore the police chief may try to minimize corruption, to declare that it involves only a few "bad apples."

But there is more to this than the chief's wish to preserve the department's reputation and his or her job. Various influences dull the chief's sensitivity to corruption. Why not ignore a problem which seems so intractable? What can chiefs do when their officers go out to work in a corrupt environment every day? History gives them reason to believe that regardless of what the chief does, police corruption will continue. Well-meaning people say to them, in effect, that police corruption is inevitable and action against it is more or less futile. (However, public opinion may swing suddenly to a demand to wipe out corruption. The public and the news media are fickle. And a chief cannot anticipate events which overnight may cause indifference to turn into insistence.)

The experience of most police chiefs tends to destroy their perspective and erode their conscience. In most departments the chief and the top administrators, as well as many older officers still in the ranks, all began their careers as patrol officers in that department. They know each other well. Police officers are bound by close personal ties. And the chief is part of this. When police officers are charged with corruption, those involved are frequently people the police chief knows, people the chief has worked with for years. They are the chief's friends, and friendship means looking tolerantly on faults. Even in large departments where chiefs do not know personally some or any of those charged with corruption, they are still likely to be tolerant. Either the chiefs did the same things themselves at one time, or they knew police officers who did. In many cases the chiefs have seen corruption for so long that they are unable or unwilling to take it seriously.

Because of this, police chiefs have seldom given much thought to how police corruption can be combated internally. The limited time spent on the subject of corruption in police academies illustrates the point. The Pennsylvania Crime Commission found in 1974 that police recruits in the nation's nine largest cities received from 480 to 910 hours of training, but, except for one academy which devoted 30 hours to integrity in policing, none offered more than 4 hours of such instruction. This lack of interest in this subject is not limited to the nine largest cities.

The Knapp Commission Charges of corruption in the city administration and the police department brought about the Knapp Commission, headed by Whitman Knapp, New York attorney, and composed of thirty people with investigative and legal backgrounds.

In New York City, the Knapp Commission found corruption to be widespread among plainclothesmen, narcotics officers, detectives, and uniformed officers. Two terms were used in the commission's report to describe the nature of police corruption: "meat-eaters" and "grass-eaters." A meat-eater was defined as an officer who aggressively misused his police powers to seek huge payoffs, while a grass-eater was defined as an officer who did not seek payoffs but who would accept them if they happened to come his way. The commission found the majority of officers were grass-eaters.

At the conclusion of two years of investigations the Knapp Commission recommended that the governor of New York appoint a special deputy attorney with authority to investigate and prosecute all crimes of corruption within the criminal justice process, that existing laws against gambling, prostitution, and the conduct of certain businesses be changed to reduce the occurrence of payoffs and bribes, that the powers of the police commissioner be enlarged for taking action against officers found guilty of misconduct, and that changes in personnel practices and managerial procedures be made to limit opportunities for corruption.

Source: Harry W. More, Jr., *Critical Issues in Law Enforcement* (Cincinnati: The W. H. Anderson Co., 1975), pp. 357–74.

Also, little effort goes into departmental efforts to expose and deal with police corruption. Most departments have an internal affairs bureau or a similar organizational unit to deal with corruption, but these bureaus are rarely effective. They lack personnel, they lack prestige, and members are not trained in how corruption can be fought successfully.

Internal affairs bureaus often react instead of taking the initiative. They do not actively seek to uncover corruption; they wait for word of corruption to come to them. This passive method of operation can be disastrous, particularly if these bureaus employ the only personnel in a department assigned to corruption control. Relying exclusively on internal affairs bureaus, some departments fail to hold precinct and division commanders accountable for corruption in their commands. (This may be the ultimate failing of chiefs in deeply corrupt departments, who, however honest themselves, have survival as their main goal.) This, in turn, encourages commanders to pass the buck on corruption control to the bureau.

Tolerance among the rank and file

One of the most significant moments in any police officer's life comes when he or she first puts on a uniform and a gun. From then on the officer realizes that he or she has been given a very special role, a role that inevitably has a socially isolating effect. He or she has been given a unique form of power in order to carry out many of society's most dangerous, unpleasant, and often unrewarding tasks. As a result, it is natural that police officers develop among themselves a special kind of comradeship to compensate for the isolation inherent in their work.

Unlike those of most citizens, the working hours of many police officers change constantly. These hours make it difficult for the officer to retain the friends he or she made in civilian life. They also have an effect on the officer's family, who learn that the police officer's lot is different from that of most other people.

The social isolation of police officers is often reinforced by the situations in which they carry out their duties. Their attempts to enforce the law, maintain order, and even provide help to those in distress are frequently met with scorn or derision, if not outright hostility and physical resistance. Both the psychological strain of the job and the frequent danger in which police officers are placed compel them to look for support among their fellow officers. They are the only ones who know what the work is really like. Police officers are encouraged by circumstances to accept their peers and to seek their acceptance, both professionally and socially. They come to depend strongly on the group that they belong to.

In departments in which corruption is rife, officers frequently must show that they are willing to engage in illegal conduct in order to be accepted by the group. An officer must demonstrate that he or she can be trusted, and the first corrupt act is a kind of initiation. It proves the officer's solidarity with the group. The officer's peers will breathe more easily once they know that he or she can be "trusted." If the officer declines to act illegally, he or she becomes suspect in the eyes of the others. In such departments, then, officers are confronted from the beginning with tremendous pressures to accept bribes, to do what so many other officers are already doing. Most corrupt officers were honest at the start. In a climate of corruption reinforced by tremendous peer pressure, they succumbed.

Typically, the corrupting of a new police officer is a gradual, insidious thing. It begins with little things—a free drink, a free meal, a "tip" for good service. Other officers on the shift encourage the officer to accept. This leads to more substantial favors. The officer begins to do his or her "friends" favors in return, cutting corners on his or her duties in the process. The officer rationalizes this: Why not? No one is hurt. Other officers do it. After all, that's the way the whole world is.

As time passes, rationalization frequently becomes easier. The officer discovers that most police officers stay on patrol throughout their careers. Their ambitions are frustrated and the pay on patrol is only moderately attractive. Yet police officers are required to perform tasks that in a perfect world would be performed by social workers, psychiatrists, physicians, and lawyers. Under these circumstances the illegal gains come to be seen as part of what society owes the police officer for handling society's troubles. Police officers come to depend on corrupt rewards. They provide officers and their families with things they could not have otherwise, and the officers ultimately find themselves in the position of fighting to keep these rewards. Police officers learn to make untenable distinctions between "good" and "bad" (meaning unacceptable) "notes" (bribes). They say to themselves that taking a bribe from a gambling operator or a prostitute doesn't matter, since the corrupter is providing services demanded by otherwise "law-abiding" citizens.

Tolerance of corruption extends even to the honest police officer. Even though he or she may refuse corrupt rewards, he or she will keep silent and pretend not to see the corruption of others. After all, the honest officer has to work with them.

The corrupt officer, if caught, often takes much the same attitude, refusing to implicate other police officers, not so much out of fear as out of a perverted sense of loyalty. To inform would be a sign of weakness and would be regarded as the act of a "coward."

Police discretion

Few police chiefs are willing to admit that the members of their department exercise discretion in carrying out their duties. As Goldstein notes, "To acknowledge the exercise of discretion belies the very image in which he [the chief] takes such pride and which he strives so hard to achieve. This is the image of total objectivity—of impartiality—and of enforcement without fear or favor."[7] But it is more, of course, than just a matter of image, important though that may be. Most police chiefs and most police officers, if questioned about the matter, will argue that they *cannot* exercise discretion, that "the law," meaning, in general, the government, forbids them.

Yet the obvious fact is that the police do exercise discretion, from the highest ranks downward. Almost every policy determination that the chief makes involves discretion. The number of men put on each shift, the functions to which personnel and equipment are assigned, the kinds of crimes on which stress is placed—all are exercises in discretion.

Even more obvious is the discretion of individual police officers. Their job would be impossible without discretion. They know that they are expected to carry out their duties with the best judgment they can muster. Many of the laws they are supposed to enforce are obsolete, and others are ambiguous. Still others were passed merely to assuage the community's conscience, and everyone knows that their enforcement is a fiction.

The use of discretion by the police is indispensable for other reasons as well. In most communities the number of major and minor violations that occur each day are far more than the police can attend to. Police officers must pick and choose, partly for the sake of their own effectiveness and efficiency and partly because crime is more important than the violation of regulations and major crime is more important than minor crime.

Good relations with the community also require discretion. The police who arrest every inebriate, who charge every juvenile offender, who ticket every driver they observe breaking the law, are laying a foundation of deep community resentment. Most police know better. They want the community on their side. Therefore, they exercise discretion.

The problem with discretion is not that it exists, but that it is a two-edged sword. Placed in the hands of corrupt police officers, it becomes a weapon for extracting payoffs. Working alone or with a partner, rarely supervised for any length of time, the officer is called upon to make decisions as to when to arrest, why to arrest, and whom to arrest. In the wrong hands discretion becomes a hunting license. The corrupt officer can use his or her enormous powers to threaten arrest or summons unless a bribe is forthcoming.

Actions of prosecutors and courts

Police officers charge, but they do not prosecute or convict. Prosecution is the province of the prosecuting attorney and conviction the province of the courts. Thus, an effective criminal justice system demands close cooperation among the police, prosecutors, and judges. What one often finds instead is antagonism and backbiting. And in a very real sense prosecutors and judges sit in review on the activities of the police.

Whichever side may be at fault is immaterial. The fact is that the police often believe that their good faith efforts to enforce the law and control crime are thwarted by prosecutors, courts, or both. The arrests that police make may be held defective by prosecutors. When they do prosecute, many cases are quashed because the judge disagrees with the police and the prosecutor.

Convictions, from the standpoint of the police, all too often result in insignificant fines or short sentences, particularly when the charges are morals violations. The police complain time after time that the courts are sending offenders back onto the street faster than the police can arrest them.

When police officers know, or suspect, that prosecutors and judges are corrupt, police contempt for prosecutors and judges grows. In other words, the police officer who believes court action often leads to unjust disposition of crimes may decide that he or she might as well get a payoff rather than make an arrest or provide the opportunity for a prosecutor or judge to obtain a bribe.

What the police chief can do about corruption

The task of combating corruption falls on the chief of police. But no chief intent on dealing with corruption will find the task an easy one. And certain circumstances will tend to be inhibiting factors.

The web of corruption: what the chief can do; outside help.

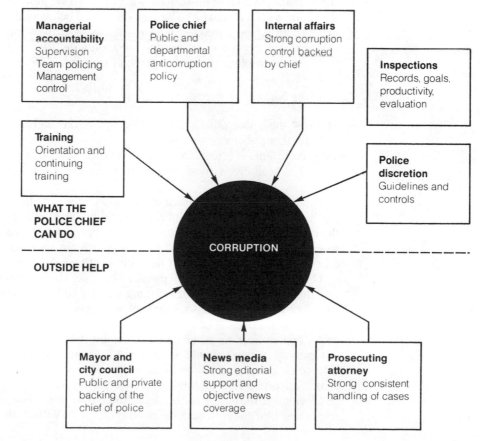

Managerial accountability
Supervision
Team policing
Management control

Police chief
Public and departmental anticorruption policy

Internal affairs
Strong corruption control backed by chief

Inspections
Records, goals, productivity, evaluation

Training
Orientation and continuing training

Police discretion
Guidelines and controls

WHAT THE POLICE CHIEF CAN DO

CORRUPTION

OUTSIDE HELP

Mayor and city council
Public and private backing of the chief of police

News media
Strong editorial support and objective news coverage

Prosecuting attorney
Strong consistent handling of cases

66 *Local Government Police Management*

Take the chief who is promoted from within the department. As previously noted, the chief's whole life is bound up with the organization. He cannot attack corruption without, in some sense, disassociating himself from his own past, from the friendships and alliances made over the years. This is a terribly difficult thing to do. It is even harder if the chief has waited until he reached the top before doing anything about corruption.

As a result, the main hope for cleaning up corrupt departments may lie with chiefs recruited from the outside. However, those chiefs hired from outside have their own handicaps. They will know very little about their new department apart from its reputation. Its particular style of policing, the quality of its personnel, who can be depended on, and the ways in which corrupt activities are carried on must all be learned gradually and, sometimes, painfully. Such chiefs will also have to learn a good deal about the community; that, too, will take time.

Suppose, nonetheless, that a chief takes over a corrupt department with the aim of eliminating or at least minimizing corruption. Whether promoted from within or appointed from without, to have a chance of success the chief must possess three attributes. First, his authority as chief must give him the power to carry out wholesale reforms. Second, he must possess political as well as administrative skills, not least the ability to communicate and to listen, in order to deal effectively with police personnel, police unions, the chief administrator for the city, the prosecutor's office, and the public. Third, if the elected officials of the city or county the chief serves will not provide effective support for corruption control, the chief must be willing to take on city hall or the county courthouse. The risks of the third attribute are obvious, but the choices are few when the governing body is not working with the chief.

In a large department a new chief, if he is wise, will have in mind a plan for reforming the department gradually and with great patience (anyone who expects quick results in a large bureaucracy is in the wrong job). What should the main elements of such a plan be? They are discussed below under the following headings: speaking out; making internal affairs effective; improving inspections; seeing that everyone in authority is accountable; improving the use of discretion; and controlling corruption through training.

Speaking out

The first thing that chiefs should do is speak out and make their policy clear: namely, that police corruption is wrong and will not be tolerated. Obvious as it may sound, this is one of the most significant steps that an anticorruption chief can take. Nothing is more important in determining the climate of a police agency.

This message should be sent to two audiences. The first, of course, is the department itself. A good deal of care should be taken in phrasing the message for the rank and file in such a way that it does not appear to be an attack on all personnel. The chief's statements to the department should condemn the corrupt officers while offering support to the honest and dedicated ones.

The second audience is the public. The chief should point out that the briber and the officer who takes the bribe are equally guilty. This point should be made in talks by the chief to associations of local businessmen, to civic organizations, and to other groups. The same point can be made to the public at large through press conferences or other appearances by the chief before the news media.

One way to give new life to this point is to enforce laws against the bribery or attempted bribery of police officers. In addition, the public should be warned that if anyone offers a bribe to a police officer he or she will be arrested.

Obviously, messages to the department and the public are not enough. It is important that they be accompanied by actions within the department. In the past the approach of most police departments has been to track down and punish individual offenders. This approach misses the heart of the problem. Police corruption is an institutional problem. The principal strategy must be the revision or elimination of the many arrangements, practices, and traditions that provide the breeding ground for corruption within police departments. You cannot eliminate mosquitoes by killing them one by one, and you cannot control corruption by concentrating on individual officers. The emphasis must be on structural and psychological change.

Making internal affairs effective

An obvious area for change is the conduct of internal affairs units. The weaknesses frequently found in internal affairs units are understaffing, poorly trained personnel, lack of prestige, and little incentive to take action. Members of these units need to be motivated, rewarded, and supported in ways that will make them effective.

First, the unit commander, in addition to directing his or her own personnel, should have staff responsibility for the corruption control programs of all of the other units.

Second, some point should be designated beyond which officers cannot be promoted until they have served in internal affairs and demonstrated a willingness to "bite the bullet." In too many departments the "cop catchers" are pariahs. A policy of mandatory previous internal affairs experience for all high ranking officers would go a long way toward eliminating such a climate.

Third, personnel in internal affairs should be trained to recognize patterns of corruption and should be trained to unearth evidence of it. Available means of securing evidence of corruption are not always used. One of the myths that has circulated in police departments is that it is impossible or wrong to "turn" corrupt officers. That is, impossible to make a corrupt officer incriminate others after he himself is exposed. Supposedly, the "code of silence" among police officers is an unbreakable barrier.

We now know this is not true. The Knapp Commission investigators, the New York police department, and Pennsylvania Crime Commission investigators in Philadelphia were able, with a good deal of effort, of course, to persuade corrupt officers to point a finger at others. Those who had been caught were given the chance to cooperate with investigators or prosecutors and possibly benefit. "Turning" is especially defensible when it leads to higher ranking offenders.

Another tactic which internal affairs bureaus can use is that of having their own investigators or other handpicked officers assigned to an undercover role in vice squads, detective squads, or precincts. These officers report on the corruption in these units. Some may find this tactic objectionable, but it can be justified where police corruption is of serious proportions.

Improving inspections

Inspections are an essential tool of management in large organizations. It is not an investigation function as internal affairs is. The inspection unit should be separate from internal affairs.

Most of the work of an inspection unit is accomplished openly, reviewing with the commander and other personnel of a unit their records, policies, goals, controls, problems, and productivity. Performance is evaluated for the information of the chief. Suggestions for improvement are discussed and future goals agreed on.

Some covert observations may be conducted to accurately determine whether policies are conformed with and procedures followed. Failure to comply with procedures designed to prevent corruption is evidence of weakness in management. Failure of management to correct weaknesses pointed out after inspections indicates the chief should remove commanders who cannot meet reasonable standards.

Determining that officers who stop motorists for traffic violations comply with a requirement that a written record be made if a violation notice is not served is an example of the kind of covert activity in which inspection units engage. (Inspections and internal affairs are further discussed in Chapter 14.)

Seeing that everyone in authority is accountable

No matter how large or how competent they may be, the internal affairs and inspections bureaus can do only so much. Their task of policing the police is just as difficult as the department's task of policing the community. A large department with serious corruption can be reformed only when a chief makes every manager and supervisor answerable for the misconduct of his or her subordinates. Accountability at every level is the key to fighting corruption.

Nothing is perhaps more frustrating to the police administrator than the problem of fixing responsibility for what happens or does not happen in the many squads, units, divisions, and bureaus that comprise city police departments. Police supervision in general is fragmented, for obvious reasons. The bulk of the department's personnel, those in patrol and detective work, operate independently most of the time. In addition, policing is a twenty-four-hour-a-day job. There are different supervisors on the three shifts, and substitute supervisors fill in when the regulars are out sick, on vacation, or in court. The difficulty of trying to determine what happened and how and why it happened should be evident. By the same token, the looseness of the organization lends itself to those who want to conceal corrupt acts.

To control corruption, it is not enough to have honest people at the top. A chief must hold those at the top accountable, and the accountability must be extended throughout the agency. An honest chief needs to delegate responsibility for fighting corruption. This is the only way to achieve accountability. He cannot do the job alone. Nor can a few people in headquarters do it. Every manager or supervisor must participate. None can be permitted to pass the buck.

The chief needs to monitor continually the work of principal assistants as they attempt to deal with corruption and take various other steps described later in this chapter. Responsibility for corruption control is shared throughout the department, but final authority and responsibility reside with the chief.

Delegating responsibility means that the chief makes each top administrator responsible for certain parts of a corruption prevention and control program. They, in turn, place responsibility on their subordinates. This is carried down the line to the sergeants, who become responsible for any misconduct by the patrol officers under them.

Good supervision involves taking a new psychological approach to the question of corruption. In many departments there has been a kind of ritual. The chief calls in the commanders one by one and asks if they have had any problems with corruption. The reply would be some variation of the stock answer, "Not a bit of it in my command, chief." And there the matter ends.

This is the wrong approach and the wrong question. Personnel should be made to think and talk about corruption as a real problem requiring solution.

A chief should be frank with his top subordinates about what he is doing about corruption. He should tell the assistant chiefs and deputy chiefs, "I've tried to get the monkey off my back, gentlemen. I've assigned responsibility to each of you, and I will continue to check on how you're carrying it out. If corruption is found in your command, *you* are responsible. If it is found, I'll use whatever power I have to take your job away. I'll force your retirement, demote you, even dismiss you. I'm making you responsible. If you're smart, you'll figure out how to make the echelon below you responsible. And you'll do it right down to the level of sergeant. So, if six months from now you learn one of your officers is corrupt, you'll call his sergeant on the carpet and demand to know how he's supervising him."

A chief should not stop there, however. He can't call in his assistants, give them a speech, make a record of their new responsibilities, put it on file, and forget about it. Some chiefs do leave it at that. They go through the motions to show the department is combating corruption, and then some officers are left to do more or less as they please. But should corruption in the department be exposed to the public, a chief will never survive the accusation of having given some subordinates responsibility for corruption on paper and then having ignored the problem.

After delegating responsibility for corruption to certain administrators, it is important that the chief supervise them on a continuing basis. That means continuing communication, discussion, and overseeing. Regular interviews may be helpful. In larger departments questionnaires may be useful. In addition, inspection teams, both overt and covert, should be sent into the precinct periodically to determine compliance with policy, to detect evidence of corruption, and to see how the police deal with situations which could lead to corruption.

Four specific suggestions for improving accountability within the department are discussed immediately below.

Focusing on high ranking officers   A chief should make it his business to hold not only top administrators but every officer at the rank of captain and above personally accountable. They are the key links in the chain of accountability. One way of doing this would be to penalize them when it is clear that their efforts to combat corruption are weak. Another is to take a close look at those seeking promotion to the highest levels. Exemplary personal behavior should not be enough. An officer should have demonstrated successful, active efforts to expose and discipline corrupt subordinates or to prevent corruption.

One of the complaints voiced most frequently by police chiefs—at least in private discussions—is the weaknesses in top and middle managers. Their police experience and lack of management training fail to prepare them for their positions, and the promotion process does not adequately measure their qualifications. The problem is complicated when high ranking officers enjoy tenure, depriving the chief of flexibility in dealing with them. In this situation a chief should shift anticorruption and other important responsibilities to other managers and see that they carry these responsibilities out. An adept chief can change a bad situation into a productive one.

Adding sergeants   There are other ways of improving accountability. One of the simplest is to increase the number of first-line supervisors—meaning sergeants—if the number currently results in an excessive span of control. Beyond that, every officer must be under a single sergeant for continuing evaluation. Their duty schedules should coincide as much as possible.

Utilizing team policing   Another way of improving accountability is to initiate or improve a neighborhood style of team policing. Under team policing a team composed of supervisors and patrol officers is given almost total responsibility for policing a specific geographical area on a twenty-four-hour basis. (Infrequent crimes, such as homicide, remain the responsibility of centralized detective squads.) With teams, personnel shuffling, delegation of responsibility to other units, and the resulting anonymity and lack of accountability common in standard police operations are minimized. The team is held accountable for what happens within its territory at all times. As a result, both supervisors and officers become much more aware of what everyone on the team is doing, including misconduct of any sort.

An important feature of this system is that citizens become more familiar with officers and their work. Officers are much more accountable to residents and those employed in an area under the "friendly" style of urban policing than under the traditional "stranger" style.

This approach, of course, flies in the face of the anticorruption strategy popularized years ago whereby officers were rotated by both beat and working hours. The theory has been that this "stranger style" reduces opportunities for corrupt alliances. The theory is no longer valid, if it ever was. The cost is too high in reduced effectiveness, and urban anonymity facilitates corruption as it does crime.

Strengthening accountability of detectives   Accountability is particularly lacking within detective units and can be strengthened substantially. In most departments detectives work largely on their own, whether as generalists or specialists. This freewheeling can be curbed, and opportunities for taking payoffs reduced, by strengthening management controls, including much closer direction of detective work, and giving less discretion to individual detectives and more to supervisors and managers.

Improving the use of discretion

Among other things, improved accountability leads to improvement in the use of discretion. They are two sides of the same coin. The police cannot do without discretion, but it may be used poorly or with corrupt intent. The aim, then, is to make police officers, supervisors, and managers more accountable for the way in which discretion is exercised.

Supervisors cannot, however, hold their subordinates accountable when guidelines concerning the use of discretion are vague or absent. A chief must define and limit discretion in ways that reduce the opportunities for graft. That is, the chief must stipulate police priorities and make certain that discretion is exercised at the highest appropriate level, according to the importance of the matter at hand.

One method of limiting discretion, for example, is to eliminate arrest quotas, formal or understood, particularly in such fields as gambling and narcotics. Police departments under pressure to curb gambling and drug abuse have traditionally tried to take the easy way out by stressing quantity of arrests over quality. Thirty numbers writers, for example, might be arrested to show that the police were on the job. But in the course of fulfilling quotas, police officers find numerous opportunities to extort payoffs from small-change operators.

A change in focus is needed. Law enforcement must be redirected to those at the top of the crime pyramid who perpetuate and make the greatest profit from gambling and drug abuse. In the conduct of these investigations as little discretion as possible should be left at the level of operations. Supervisors and managers should make all important decisions and should be held strictly accountable for them.

Another way of limiting discretion is for higher authority to control the enforcement of municipal regulations. Municipal statute books are filled with regulations, many of them vague, archaic, unenforceable, or unnecessary except to the police officer who uses the threat of enforcing them to extort payoffs. Instead of enjoying a free hand in their enforcement, officers should be required to obtain approval from a supervisor or manager before acting.

Controlling corruption through training

Finally, a word must be said about training. If corruption is to be controlled, both recruit and in-service training must devote substantial time and effort to it. Like those at supervisory levels, those in the ranks must be taught what corruption is, why it must be avoided, and how it can be avoided. To make a lasting impression, instruction must be realistic, not moralistic.

Recruit and in-service training are reviewed in some detail in Chapter 13. The principal requirements of such training are: that it should be concerned with people; that it should anticipate problems and requirements; and that it should be a continuous process. From this point of view training is a permanent part of every job, a lifelong developmental process that meets and anticipates change. The control of corruption (itself a part of everyday life) lends itself well to training. Corruption can be categorized and explained, and examples of it can be found everywhere.

Outside help

Police chiefs determined to root out corruption in their departments cannot do it alone. They must have help. Public support is important. Until the public stops offering bribes, stops making corruption easy, the chief will be waging an uphill battle. Also important is support from local elected officials, the chief administrator, the local prosecutor, and the news media.

Local officials

The mayor and the chief of police cannot fight the political wars alone; they need legislative and administrative support. If they do not have political support from the city council, or at least a majority of the council, it is likely that the cause is lost. The city council, either openly or behind the scenes, has too many ways of undercutting the police department by the adoption of ordinances and the appropriation of funds, and by working with constituent groups. And it does not have to violate a single law to do this. Political support is not merely public speeches and public relations gestures. It is genuine commitment. The police chief will quickly know the difference.

Administrative support is equally important in cities with the council-manager form of government or in which a full-time professional administrator reports to the mayor. The chief administrator has important resources at his or her command in terms of personnel, equipment, and money as well as information and a host of intangibles that can help police chiefs contend with corruption. Particularly significant and often underestimated is the information that the chief administrator can draw on from other municipal departments and agencies concerning land use, codes, motor equipment, assignment and reassignment of personnel, and other operating data. In addition, the chief administrator has his or her own network of information leads into the community that can supplement and complement the information network that the chief of police has developed. Each person needs the other.

The media

Equally important are the news media. If they believe the chief is right, the press and broadcasters can be an invaluable source of support. But if they take the view that the chief is exaggerating a problem or hunting for scapegoats they can cripple an anticorruption campaign. Then, too, in a community where corruption has existed for years, where it has become a fact of life, some editors may not find corruption among the police particularly outrageous.

It may be more than a matter of simply overcoming the media's apathy, however. Like politicians and much of the public, the media may be tolerant of police corruption for a reason. In a community where vice is common there may be a tacit understanding not to disturb the status quo because many people profit from it. Editors may avoid "rocking the boat" at almost any cost. Like some businessmen and politicians, they may feel that an "open town" is good for business.

For example, a town built on convention business knows that the availability of liquor, sex, and gambling is essential to attract conventions. The powers that be in such a town may well prevent the appointment of a reform-minded police chief. If such a chief were selected, that chief undoubtedly would find the press hostile to a campaign against police corruption.

The prosecuting attorney

Great power is wielded by the prosecuting attorney by virtue of his or her discretion over corruption cases brought to his or her office for prosecution. The police must put themselves in the prosecutor's hands on criminal matters. The prosecutor may have to drop the charges on technical grounds (e.g., because an illegal search or seizure was used in making the arrest). If the prosecutor refuses to prosecute corrupt officers he or she may force the department to try to involve the state government through special procedures or to settle for pressing administrative charges only. The prosecutor may thus hamstring the department's investigation.

A prosecuting attorney may provide minimal cooperation with or may actually impede a corruption investigation for any of several reasons. Often an elected official, the prosecutor may fear that prosecution will embarrass his or her party or the mayor. He or she may be unwilling to risk alienating members of the police department on whose cooperation his or her work heavily depends. And the prosecutor may be corrupt.

But one day the same prosecuting attorney may decide to run for governor. And to everyone's surprise, including those who profit from illegal activities and who have contributed money to his or her last campaign to protect their interests, the prosecutor may undertake his or her own investigation of police corruption.

Political ambition may not be the reason in every case, but, in any event, a well-publicized investigation by the prosecutor's office can have far-reaching effects. It can cause a dishonest or incompetent police chief's early retirement or resignation. Or it can greatly strengthen the hand of a chief bent on cleaning up the department.

Conclusion

The problems, factors, degrees, and types of police corruption have been described in considerable detail in this chapter, and the dreary history is available for those who want to read crime commission reports going back over almost fifty years. As has been pointed out, police corruption is, in large measure, a community problem as well as a police department problem. It is less likely to be encountered in an upper middle income community than in the city with a high ratio of low income residents with the familiar problems of unemployment and bad housing. But generalizations are always susceptible to exception, as this chapter carefully notes. In other words, no community or police department has any guarantee of being corruption free. No police administrator can, therefore, sit back and assume that corruption "can't happen here."

This chapter has outlined the problem and the complex forces that bring the problem to the fore, the degrees and types of corruption, and the factors contributing to corruption. Of particular use to the police administrator have been the concluding sections on what the chief can do about the corruption that may be encountered, the practical steps that can be taken from the management point of view to control and eliminate corruption within the department, and the sources from which help can be sought outside the department.

Clearly, outside forces can help, hinder, or even make or break an investigation of police corruption. What this means is that a police chief bent on rooting out entrenched corruption should be realistic about what is politically possible in the situation. It may be that the chief cannot quickly turn the department upside down (if that is necessary), that only incremental improvements can be made. In some agencies several years of well-planned, carefully phased change are required.

Some chiefs push too far too quickly and are strongly opposed by those in the community with an interest in letting police corruption continue. If a chief recognizes that what can be done about corruption is limited, the chief is likely to be more successful than one who undertakes more reform than political circumstances permit. The political difficulties of a situation, however, are no excuse for doing nothing. If a chief is skillful, wise, and willing to take risks, changes can be made.

Chiefs must understand that the degree of reform they may achieve will depend on their leadership and management as well as on the integrity of the members of the department. Too many chiefs believe that if they fire all the dishonest officers under their command and hire only honest ones they will automatically have an honest department. It is not that simple. A climate of corruption can infect large segments of a department, so that even the "honest" officers tolerate graft on the part of others. Such a climate will turn new officers into dishonest officers, for people in an organization tend to act according to the norms of that organization.

The most effective way to instill integrity into a department is through leadership and a system of accountability at all levels that motivates officers to be honest (i.e., that encourages honest officers to perform their duties as they deem right and discourages other officers from resorting to corruption).

Careful selection and hiring of recruits is an important part of integrity control. The most critical factor is effective management practices that maintain a healthy climate.

1 Portions of this chapter draw on the following publication: Herman Goldstein, *Police Corruption: A Perspective on Its Nature and Control* (Washington, D.C.: Police Foundation, 1975).
2 Ibid., p. 12.
3 Knapp Commission, *Report on Police Corruption* (New York: George Braziller, 1973), p. 180.
4 Goldstein, *Police Corruption*, p. 21.
5 Jonathan Rubinstein, "The Dilemmas of Vice Work," in *Police Corruption: A Sociological Per-*

spective, ed. Lawrence W. Sherman (Garden City, N.Y.: Anchor Books, 1974), p. 189.
6 Thomas Barker and Julian Roebuck, *An Empirical Typology of Police Corruption* (Springfield, Ill.: Charles C Thomas, 1973), p. 13.
7 Herman Goldstein, "Police Discretion: The Ideal versus the Real," in *Police in America*, ed. Jerome H. Skolnick and Thomas C. Gray (Boston: Little, Brown and Company, 1975), p. 101.

5 Police organization and management

Discussions of organization and management in police administration have defined organization as the structural aspects of the police enterprise, while management has been considered the processes of planning, coordination, and control. Various principles of organization, such as unity of command, chain of command, and span of control, reappear constantly. They are frequently merged into a view of management reflected in the acronym POSDCORB (planning, organizing, staffing, directing, coordinating, reporting, and budgeting). These perspectives can be traced largely to the organizational theorists of the first half of this century, particularly to such scholars as Henri Fayol and to Luther Gulick and Lyndall Urwick.[1]

Definitions, characteristics, and concerns

Organization

Organizations have been described by Amitai Etzioni as

. . . social units (or human groupings) deliberately constructed and reconstructed to seek specific goals . . . characterized by: (1) divisions of labor, power, and communication responsibilities, divisions which are not random or traditionally patterned, but deliberately planned to enhance the realization of specific goals; (2) the presence of one or more power centers which control the concerted efforts of the organization and direct them toward its goals; these power centers also must review continuously the organization's performance and re-pattern its structure, where necessary, to increase its efficiency; (3) substitution of personnel, i.e., unsatisfactory persons can be removed and others assigned to their tasks. The organization can also recombine its personnel through transfer and promotion.[2]

The definition and characteristics of an organization highlight three key aspects that should be of primary concern to the police organization:

1. The goals or purposes for which the organization was intentionally created and which it continues to seek
2. The continual process of organizational review and rearrangement that allows the organization to better achieve its purposes and, given the nature of society as a whole as well as the identifiable segments the organization serves, to respond creatively and effectively to changing environmental conditions
3. The overall social setting of the organization.

These concerns require contemporary police organizations and management to establish organizational climates that foster challenge, inquiry, and creativity on one hand and rapid, effective implementation and feedback on the other. This requirement becomes increasingly vital as one considers the vast changes in social mores, public service costs, and management–employee relations that have occurred during the past two decades.

Management

Management is more difficult to define than organization. If a survey of all executive level managers were conducted, it is questionable whether a universally acceptable definition could be developed. Management is a process—"the process of *planning, organizing, leading, and controlling* the efforts of organizational . . . resources in order to achieve *stated organizational goals*."[3] Management is also an art—a practiced art in which knowledge and skill are acquired through a balanced combination of experience, education, and observation, which are then systematically applied in an effort to realize a desired result. Today's police administrators, except in the smallest of agencies where the chief executive also has to perform line functions, have to achieve their personal and organizational goals by relying on the efforts of others. Modern police administration can, therefore, be defined as the managerial application of the process and art of getting things done through and with human and material resources.

There are three central concerns of management that police administrators must address and solve if they are to achieve a high level of effectiveness:

1. They must create an atmosphere in which members of the organization will comprehend, be stimulated by, and commit themselves to the goals of the organization. This includes the integration of employee and organizational needs and clear-cut acknowledgment of the employee as a vital part of the organization.
2. They must establish and maintain a visible degree of stability in the organization's internal environment and develop a workable degree of predictability in the organization's work processes.
3. They must minimize the intrusion of disruptive influences on the organization from within and without. To do this, administrators need a good working relationship with the governing political body.

The organization–management dilemma

The concerns relating to the organization and to management initially appear to place the administrator in a dilemma. The organization requires ongoing review and rearrangement—a continuing process of change—in order to meet the changing needs of society and its many groups. On the other hand, the central concerns of management require the establishment and maintenance of organizational stability and predictability in work processes.

The dilemma can be resolved and the simultaneous requirements can be made to complement each other if the administrator can do the following: (1) maintain stability in internal management–employee relations and avoid erratic or oversensitive management behavior; (2) fully analyze and identify the dimensions of the organization's human energy, not by overtaxing it, but by channeling it toward constructive ends consistent with change and by minimizing disruptions; and (3) demonstrate true concern for those affected by a change and, whenever possible, include them in the planning and discussion.

The hallmark of successful police administration, particularly as it relates to the organization–management dilemma, is the ability to establish a climate and conditions that meet the legitimate expectations of organization members in ways that will encourage them to contribute to the mission of the organization. It is not the pitting of formal authority against the power of individuals or work groups.

This managerial orientation also should prevail in dealings with individuals and groups outside the police organization, such as local executive officers, elected officials, community groups, and the general public.[4] Such orientation is vital if external disruptions are to be minimized.

Purposes, functions, and roles

Organization

Purposes of the police organization were fairly easy to define during the early 1960s. Police organizations and officers were viewed largely as agents of a political entity and as having the primary functions of law enforcement and maintenance of the peace. These functions were carried out under the authority and definitions of an assortment of state and municipal statutes and ordinances. The defined purposes (or goals) of police organizations emphasized crime control and other regulatory tasks.[5]

Many social changes have occurred since the 1960s. Public attention has been directed toward police practices and the degree of discretion practiced by the police organization and its members. Theorists have openly questioned the compatibility of the dominant or paramilitary mode of police organization with the multitude of demands society now places on the police service. Police are now, for example, expected to perform many services that were once considered to be strictly within the realm of social service agencies. In the early 1970s the American Bar Association Project provided an overview of police responsibilities, which was subsequently updated by its author, Herman Goldstein:

1. To prevent and control conduct widely recognized as threatening to life and property (serious crime).
2. To aid individuals who are in danger of physical harm, such as the victim of a criminal attack.
3. To protect constitutional guarantees, such as the right of free speech and assembly.
4. To facilitate the movement of people and vehicles.
5. To assist those who cannot care for themselves: the intoxicated, the addicted, the mentally ill, the physically disabled, the old, and the young.
6. To resolve conflict, whether it be between individuals, groups of individuals, or individuals and their government.
7. To identify problems that have the potential for becoming more serious problems for the individual citizen, for the police, or for government.
8. To create and maintain a feeling of security in the community.[6]

The revised purposes for police organizations clearly reflect the input of the citizenry and their local governments into the responsibilities and priorities of police service. The emphasis on the service and assistance aspects of the police organization as compared with arrest and regulation is unmistakable (the terms *arrest, suppress, repress,* and *regulate* do not appear). It is emphasized, however, that the defined purposes of police organizations, while applicable to the social attitudes of the 1970s, may or may not be representative of society's needs in the 1980s. As this chapter is being written, the public and the communications media are expressing a renewed concern about rising violent crime rates, terrorist activity, and increasing disregard of individual property rights. Researchers are studying the direct and residual impact of crime on the national economy. If these concerns continue to increase and permeate the various levels of the political community, it is not unlikely that the purposes of police organizations in the 1980s will be redirected toward crime fighting.

The philosophical redirection of police purposes in the 1970s, combined with the possibility of further revision in the 1980s, illustrates the need for police organizations to be aware of and responsive to changing social climates. The police organization is no longer (if it ever truly was) a self-styled independent agency operating autonomously and under a myriad of laws, housed in a community rather than being responsive to it. Like all other local government agencies, the police service has its goals set through a political process involving the input of elected officials and their appointees, special interest groups, and individuals; the opinions and judgment of police and other public administrators; and the perceptions, attitudes, and influences of police employees and their unions or associations.[7]

Management

A review of the definitions of organization and management and their respective characteristics and concerns affirms a synonymity of purposes between them. The organization is constructed to seek specific goals, and management steers the organization toward them. The organization has to undergo continual reexamination, and management provides the examination. The organization requires an open-minded and progressive atmosphere, and management is the primary contributor to that climate. The functions and roles of management are interwoven with the purposes and goals of the organization.

This blending of organizational purposes and managerial functions is especially visible in police organizations. The police administrator often is faced with organizational goals or purposes developed primarily by external sources— goals or purposes sometimes lacking a foundation in reality and unaccompanied by necessary monetary resources. Such demands may require a modification of operations and priorities and a shifting of work processes. It is immaterial, however, whether long-established or new goals and purposes are comparatively easy to reach, unrealistic and difficult, or (most likely) a mixture of the two. The application of certain administrative functions and roles is critical to success or failure.

Planning Planning is generally considered to be the key process of police administration. It is an ongoing routine that comprises: (1) identification of immediate and potential needs; (2) determination of available resources and alternatives; and (3) formulation of a course of action likely to achieve the desired outcome. It is essentially the road map for the administrator and the organization.

Planning may be complicated and formal, involving a major overhaul of the organization, or it may be simple and informal, a slight adjustment in a particular phase of an operation. A plan may occur and be carried out in minutes, or it may take years to develop and implement. The police administrator can be assured that planning, whatever its nature, will affect the entire police organization and should therefore never minimize its importance.

Organizing Organizing is the process of dividing and rearranging labor, power, and communication responsibilities. When used effectively, it provides a powerful stimulus for stability, reduction of conflict, and development of a climate for change. It is the outgrowth of planning and includes the structural and actual phases needed to supplement planning.

Coordinating Defined in the administrative and organizational sense, coordinating is the orderly arrangement of group effort to provide unity of action in pursuit of a common purpose. Lawrence and Lorsch identified four types of differences in attitude and working style that arise among the various individuals and units in organizations: First is differences in goal orientation; members of different units develop their own views about "what is really needed" to achieve organizational goals. Second is differences in time orientation, an imbalance between members concerned with short-range solutions and members who preoccupy themselves with problems that will take years to solve. Third is differences in interpersonal orientation: the "this is the way it is so let's get on with it" attitude as compared to a more easygoing, participative style. This difference is highly visible in police organizations, because different units and activities can require both types of people. Fourth is differences in formality of structure, the varying methods and standards used for measuring work progress and rewarding employees.[8] Here again, this difference is prevalent in police organizations.

To achieve coordination, the police administrator would have to resolve these four differences; yet the variety of activities performed in a police organization and the variety of units involved cause this task to be realistically impossible. The chief executive and management staff can, however, neutralize the differences and direct them toward serving, rather than hampering, organizational goals.

Planning may be the most important function of a police administrator, but coordinating is the most difficult.

Controlling   Controlling is the function of ensuring quality in the organization. It is an ongoing inspections process designed to measure individual and group compliance with the organization's goals, policies, and procedures, and to evaluate the use of available resources. Controlling is a vital function of every organizational unit and, depending on the size of the agency, may be assigned to a separate staff inspections group.

Controlling is a component of effective and efficient management of an organization. It is also a management tool that can increase stress levels among the members of the organization and should, therefore, be exercised judiciously and with full awareness of its positive and negative aspects.

For years, the responsibilities of planning, organizing, coordinating, and controlling have been described as the primary functions of management. Other functions also exist and are given different emphasis by theorists and practicing police managers. The fulfillment of the four functions discussed here, however, should give the police administrator a sound managerial base from which to develop and direct the organization and exercise three additional key management roles—leadership, liaison, and resource allocation.

The roles of police administrators have been expanded recently in response to various internal and external changes. Increased community and political involvement in police goals and practices, the evolution of multilevel participative management rather than the ruler or patriarch system, and the inclusion of the police union or association as a voice in certain working practices have all necessitated this expansion or redefinition of roles.

The role of *leadership* is essential for the contemporary police administrator, not only in the traditional sense as boss of the police organization, but also in the sense of one who subtly and informally exerts control over the behavior of others over a period of time.[9] The leader has to exemplify and instill the ethics of professionalism in the police organization, ensure adequate communication of organizational goals, and direct, stimulate, and motivate others toward goal achievement. The effectiveness of the administrator's performance of the leadership role ultimately determines the effectiveness of the organization.

The role of *liaison* is critical to the organization and actually supplements the leadership role. The police organization continually interacts with numerous other organizations or groups both inside and outside the police and municipal organizational structures and needs to establish relationships with them. Service clubs, the business and political communities, the judicial system, mental health organizations, police unions, and so on all can affect the working practices and goals of the police organization. The leader must establish liaison with these groups so that these liaisons can be extended throughout the department. The liaison role includes the functions of spokesman and negotiator. It is necessary for the leader to speak out and be heard regarding the department and its needs and to negotiate with formal and informal groups in order to fulfill these needs if the police agency is to achieve its goals.

A third role, *resource allocation,* is linked with liaison and leadership. The human and material resources obtained through leadership and liaison have to be put to good use. Efficient and effective allocation of resources is increasing in importance as more and more citizens, either individually or collectively, focus their democratic microscope on the rising costs of public services. Moreover, municipal organizations directly involved in public safety are invariably brought to the forefront of such discussions. The police administrator can be assured that allocation of resources in the police organization will be subjected to close scrutiny.

The dynamics of organizational change

A recurrent theme in discussions of organization and management is the need for a process of organizational change or innovation. This does not mean innovation merely for its own sake. Rather, it means innovation predicated on the changing needs or goals of the groups the organization serves and the changes that occur in the overall environment.

Drucker defines innovation (change) as "the task of endowing human and material resources with new and greater [production] capacity."[10] He also notes that "the measure of innovation is the impact on the environment," including the marketplace.[11] Application of this definition to the police organization simply means that change should fulfill the following conditions:

1. Meet the needs of the community and the police organization
2. Have an impact on community and organization environments
3. Improve the use of resources and provide a greater service return for tax dollars spent.

Resistance to change

Assuming that a proposed change fulfills these conditions, why is it so difficult and traumatic to introduce change and innovation into a police organization?

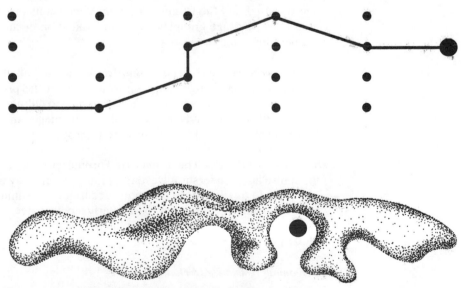

The process of organizational change more closely resembles . . . biological evolution than . . . a technological breakthrough in the hard sciences or engineering.

This difficulty is discussed intensely whenever police administrators get together. Many executive and management seminars are devoted to the subject. Some chief executives have been removed from their positions because of the organizational resistance and chaos that resulted when beneficial and necessary change was introduced.

It is not unusual for the rank and file to resist innovation and change even though its implementation would improve working conditions, community reputation, and/or salary. Why? Perhaps it is the threat of change in a service that is perceived as being steeped in tradition. Perhaps it is the perceived threat to the economic or personal security and role of those affected by the change. Perhaps it is the management–employee atmosphere, the "we–they" syndrome that is becoming more prevalent in some organizations with the growth and power of police unions. Perhaps it is a mutual lack of understanding of the roles and stresses of management and employees: "They don't know what a chief goes through" versus "They don't know what the street is like anymore." Perhaps it is a combination of all these things.

Examining change in the organizational context

One "perhaps," and possibly the most important one, was omitted from the preceding paragraph. Perhaps the major cause of resistance is the methodology used or not used by the administrator when introducing change. While there is no formula that will guarantee successful, well-received implementation of change, there is a series of steps the police administrator can take to plan a strategy for reducing negative reaction. The first is to make sure the change or innovation is necessary and meets the three previously suggested conditions of change. The second is to answer four questions about the organization:

Where have we been?　The administrator should review the overall history of the organization; its systems, philosophies, method of service delivery, culture, traditions, and folklore; the development of personnel and their exposure to and interaction with external sources; and their reaction to changes in the past.

Where are we now?　This question involves an examination of the answers to the preceding question in the context of the present; informal changes that already have occurred and the reaction to them; dimensions of personnel, their educational levels and age groupings; and an evaluation of the likely response to or readiness for change.

Where do we want to go?　The administrator should look at the physical, tactical, and philosophical changes required to implement the proposal; who and what the change will affect and how; the traditions and cultures to be affected and to what extent; and the advantages and disadvantages of present levels of employee development and what must be improved.

How do we get there?　The answer is: Through planning, organizing, coordinating, controlling, leadership, liaison, and allocation of available resources.

In order to answer these questions accurately or stimulate others to answer them, the police administrator, particularly a newcomer to the organization, will have to be aware of organizational philosophies, cultures, and traditions. These will be discussed shortly.

Overcoming resistance to change

Once the administrator understands the implications of change and the reasons for resistance in the organization, a strategy must be devised for overcoming the

The elements of change In planning and directing change within the organization the police administrator must be somewhat like the conductor of an orchestra, blending the various elements of change in a manner that equips the total organization to perform more effectively. He will err if, for example, he becomes totally preoccupied with mechanical improvements to the point that substantive issues are ignored. But, likewise, even if new commitments and new orientations are the heart of his program, he will have to devote considerable time to technical areas that he may consider mundane. He must develop an atmosphere of change that permeates the entire organization, but which is managed in such a way that it is not disorienting or overly threatening. Change tends to be self-generating, with forward movement and evidence of progress in one area stimulating and supporting movement in others. . . .

Rank-and-file police personnel whose functioning is to be changed must themselves be involved in the process of change. The administrator must, as a minimum, keep his personnel informed of the nature of contemplated change and provide them with the information on which management bases its key decisions. Ideally they should participate in the actual planning of change, for it is the rank and file of the organization who must actually carry out the procedures and policies that are altered. Their lives are often most directly affected by change. And their support is essential if the changes are to work and to endure.

Source: This material is excerpted from Herman Goldstein, *Policing a Free Society* (Cambridge, Mass.: Ballinger Publishing Company, 1977), pp. 309–10.

---

resistance.[12] It is often suggested that administrators communicate with personnel about impending changes, telling them what to expect in order to allay fears that may be generated by the "rumor mill." In addition, personnel should be invited to ask questions and provide feedback.

Employees may accept change more readily if they feel involved, either formally or informally, in planning and decision making prior to the change. Attempts to involve personnel must be genuine, however, or employees will soon come to mistrust management and resent the upcoming change even more.

If personnel will experience changes in wages or working conditions, it is often best to face and discuss such changes openly and directly. For example, a threatened personnel cutback will make some officers fear for their jobs, while others foresee an increased workload. If such fears are realistic, nothing will be gained by denying them.

Whatever methods are employed, they will be most effective if personnel have trust in and respect for the organization. Further, the administrator must take care not to destroy that trust and respect in attempting to overcome resistance to change.

Philosophy

Organization

Police organizational structures will vary from one agency to another depending on available resources, needs of the community being served, and the need-related goals of the organization. Division of labor, power, and communication responsibilities may be determined by hour of day, geographical sector, function, or any combination of the three. Power centers can be distributed equally among the organization's divisions or purposely imbalanced because of management and/or political philosophy and emphasis regarding certain operational

Historical perspective on organizations Forms of organization developed historically from the military and the church. With the rise of industrialism the classical approach to organization first developed. In industry it was based on the assumption that workers were motivated almost entirely by economic incentives. The classical approach settled then and now such management concepts as hierarchy, authority and responsibility, span of control, and other aspects of a mechanical-rational approach to work.

The human relations approach, generally dated from influential studies conducted at the Western Electric Company almost one-half century ago, focuses much more on meeting the needs of people in the organization. The human relations approach stresses the psychology of the worker,

participative management, group dynamics, democratic decision making, and other aspects of motivating people.

An emerging trend has arisen in an effort to reconcile obvious extremes of the classical and the human relations approaches. Known generally as organization development, this approach attempts to look at the organization by motivating management and workers over a long period of time to undertake their own management development. It tries to build on the best of the past, recognizing that both structural and psychological elements are needed and that motivation comes from within. One of its major characteristics is a process to facilitate change while respecting the needs and values of individual employees.

---

or support tasks. Each organization's method for selection, transfer, and promotion of personnel will vary depending on state and local personnel practices, desires of management, and influence generated by the police union or association. There are, however, three distinct organizational philosophies into which the majority of police organizations can be categorized: the watchman style, the legalistic model, and the service model.

The *watchman style* is a term used to describe the mission of police during the formative years of the United States police service. This style emphasizes use of the law as a means of maintaining order rather than regulating conduct by enforcing laws fairly. It judges the requirements of order differently within the community depending on the character and socioeconomic composition of identifiable groups.[13] The watchman style can be expected to degenerate into a policing system in which the degree of enforcement or nonenforcement of laws, particularly laws regulating prostitution, gambling, liquor, and minor disturbances, is determined by the special interests of a political system and the police administrator. The watchman style is seldom evident in modern police organizations and is, therefore, not discussed further in this chapter.

The other two philosophies—the legalistic (formal) and service (informal) models—are those most often encountered in today's police organizations. They are totally separate in their delivery of police service to the public and also in the development of internal organizational relationships. Each model has distinct characteristics, as shown in the accompanying figure.

Either the legalistic or the service model can provide a satisfactory and effective level of police service, provided the model used is compatible with the social setting—the interaction of the organization with its members and with the community. Interaction with the community is probably the primary consideration when determining organizational style.

It is not uncommon for the police organization or any of its internal divisions to fluctuate between the two models as it undergoes review and change. The interdependency of the eight characteristics of each model is not, however, conducive to an intermingling of the two. The overall characteristics and methodology of the organization will eventually conform to one model or the other.

Management

Just as the style of the organization must meet the needs of the community and organizational goals, the style of management must meet the needs of the organization and facilitate achievement of its goals. There are two general philosophies or styles into which the majority of police management practices can be categorized—centralized and decentralized.

Centralized management The centralized style may also be referred to as the autocratic, authoritarian, or dominant boss type. It is a rigid management philosophy characterized by a seldom-violated chain of command; emphasis on written rules, regulations, policies, and procedures accompanied by strict application; and a task orientation. The decision-making process normally centers on the police administrator and members of the management staff who occupy power positions. Delegation of authority is practiced but is usually applied within the framework of written directives among the central power group and tends to diminish as it moves downward through the organization.

The main advantages of a centralized philosophy are that work processes are rigidly identified, employees know exactly what is expected of them, and the dimensions of individual authority and discretion are clear-cut.

A major disadvantage is the lack of opportunity for development of lower level employees (the managers of the future) and their subsequent frustration because they are seldom included in power center decision making and therefore cannot supplement their education and experience with observation. A second problem frequently occurs when the primary power center, the police administrator, leaves the organization. The replacement often is recruited from outside the organization because insiders aren't prepared.

Decentralized management Decentralized management is also called the participative, democratic, or humanistic philosophy. It is a softer managerial approach than the centralized style and is more flexible in its application. In the decentralized style, chain of command is tempered with recognition of the need for open communications and interpersonal relationships among all levels. Written direc-

---

Legalistic and service models for police organizations.

Legalistic model

1. Highly specialized with great division of labor and a centralized style of command.
2. Stresses rules, policies, and procedures and obedience thereto.
3. Primary operational thrust is reactive—suppression and apprehension.
4. Impersonal attitude toward public and its problems.
5. Selection of personnel based *solely* on achievement and criteria: tests, education, and past accomplishments.
6. Stresses influence of authority to accomplish tasks.
7. Narrowing of role of employees.
8. Exemplary conduct of employees based on threat, external control, and enforcement of rules.

Service model

1. Generalized approach with less division of labor and a decentralized style of command.
2. Stresses individual discretion and trust of individual decision making.
3. Primary operational thrust is proactive—prevention and deterrence.
4. Personally involved with public and its problems.
5. Selection of personnel based on tests, achievement, and ascriptive criteria with voluntary recognition of need to recruit minorities and different types of people.
6. Stresses influence of persuasion with subtle use of authority to accomplish tasks.
7. Expansion of role of employees.
8. Exemplary conduct of employees based on training, self-control, and individual responsibility.

tives and task orientation are accompanied by consideration for the human element of the organization. Decision making is participative and includes as many levels and members as possible and practical, particularly those most directly affected by the decision; and the scope of authority and discretion is expanded throughout the organization.

The main advantages of decentralized management include the personal development opportunities offered to lower level employees and the creation of an organizational environment that fosters beneficial change.

The primary disadvantage is the difficulty experienced by the chief executive and management staff in coordinating the efforts of individuals and units that tend to become somewhat autonomous in a decentralized atmosphere. The police administrator also encounters a no-win situation in the decentralized management style. The system itself will quickly identify the competency levels of middle managers, and, in turn, the administrator must correct the deficiencies of the incompetents or remove them. This becomes a delicate problem when an incompetent is a veteran of the organization or has acquired a following.

Either the centralized or the decentralized philosophy can provide a satisfactory and effective degree of management to the organization as long as it meets the managerial needs of the organization and propels it toward the achievement of its goals. What is important is the awareness that a change from one style to the other, unaccompanied by adequate planning and gradual transition, will most likely cause organizational chaos. The dynamics of the organization and its internal power structures dictate the approach of the administrator, not the other way around. Until the dynamics are altered and redirected by the administrator, a changeover is extremely difficult to implement.

The police administrator who, for example, forcibly and without concern for the organization's dynamics imposes a centralized style on an organization with a history of decentralized management will frustrate and alienate most members. Similarly, the administrator who fails to prepare the organization for a centralized-to-decentralized changeover runs the risk of nothing getting done. This risk inherent in a decentralized approach is often perceived as threatening by management personnel whose experience is with the centralized model.

The philosophy and characteristics discussed in this section reaffirm the synonymity, or at least the inseparability, of organization and management. Either organizational model (legalistic or service) and either management approach (centralized or decentralized) can work if they are consistent with the goals, needs, and dynamics of the organization. A properly planned and implemented changeover from one to the other can be accomplished without extensive disruption or trauma. The police administrator has to recognize, however, the need for compatibility between organization and management philosophies. The service model of policing will work best with a decentralized style of management. The characteristics of a legalistic model require a more centralized management philosophy.

Administrators who, for whatever reason, are about to rearrange the operational systems of a police organization should study the existing philosophies of the organization and its management. Their suitability to each other, to the present operation, and to future organizational plans should be scrutinized and then followed by identification of the philosophical changes required to accommodate the upcoming changes.

Culture

The culture of an organization is its character, formal or informal traditions, and overall environment. Culture can be influenced by regional considerations, the culture of the governing political body, past administrations, and the nature and attitudes of the community. The culture of a police organization is most often manifested in such areas as management–employee relationships; interaction with the public; and overall officer attitudes toward the community, the police organization, and policing in general.

Characteristics of an organizational culture

The unique culture of each police organization is difficult to define and measure. Certain elements can be clarified, however, and the police administrator can learn to recognize them and use them as tools to help achieve organizational goals and/or change. Anthony Jay defined nine characteristics of organizational culture.[14] These have been modified here to apply more directly to police organizations.

External identity   External identity is the reputation of the organization and the degree of its interaction with other organizations, groups, or individuals. It has the potential to influence the quality of police applicants, the quality of employees who remain or go elsewhere, and the implementation of change.

Introduction of change into an organization that enjoys a healthy external identity may be resisted from both inside and outside the police organization. Change may be more readily acceptable if the organization has a questionable or poor external identity.

Internal status system   The internal status system provides for differential treatment of the police organization's members, units, or functions and establishes a recognition system for personal qualities and achievements. It goes hand in hand with various status symbols such as titles or rank, differences in apparel, office size and furnishings, equipment, assignments, and the degree of regulation of working hours.

The internal status system influences employee motivation, performance, and aspirations and the overall internal values of the organization. The administrator should be aware that the introduction of change that threatens the existing status system or symbols may generate hostility or bitterness.

Leadership operation   The means by which the leadership operates in a police organization determines who will do what and how, defines internal control systems, establishes a style or philosophy of command (centralized or decentralized), and sets the limits of individual discretion. Leadership operation is a powerful organizational force that quickly becomes evident to the newcomer. It is capable of influencing the entire organization and all of its cultural and operational elements.

Police administrators must identify the types of leadership authority in each division, particularly if they intend to implement change. Planned changes should be preceded by thorough orientation if the changes affect management style. A sudden change without proper preparation can result in a breakdown of the leadership operation which, in turn, will affect the entire organization.

Central faith   Central faith involves the perceptions widely shared by the police organization's members regarding the organization, its work, and its ethics. Articles of faith also focus on the role of the police—whether they consider themselves to be crime fighters (most popular), social workers (least popular), or something in between (most realistic). Most such perceptions tend to ignore the wide range of police responsibilities and the realities of the job.

Central faith influences the way in which police services are delivered to the community. It is necessary for police administrators to understand the articles of faith within the organization and how they affect the members' acceptance of responsibilities, responsiveness to citizen needs, and safeguard of individual constitutional rights. Interestingly, change that alters the role of the organization's members can be implemented with minimal disruption if the change does not overtly disturb members' self-perceptions.

Doctrine   Doctrine is the operational integration of central faith into the real world. Whereas central faith is unquestioned by the majority of the police organization's members, doctrine can be argued and periodically reshaped to fulfill changing environmental needs and expectations.

The central faith precept under which officers regard themselves as crime fighters, for example, is merged with the real world organizational doctrine of allocating considerable resources to non-crime-related activities.

Ritual   Ritual describes long-standing and routine activities performed mechanically by members of a police organization. Such activities may actually persist long after the reason for their creation has been forgotten. Ritual is reflected in procedures, forms, and various types of maintenance and inspection activities. It may accomplish useful and beneficial services or be a waste of time and effort.

Rituals can be identified by three characteristics: (1) their routine nature causes them to remain unexamined even when more effective techniques are available and readily evident to anyone not immersed in the organization's culture; (2) they provide security, stability, and unity to those who perform them; and (3) resistance to change of a ritual is inevitable, even after the reasons and benefits of the change are explained.

Rituals are affected by change and can affect it in turn. It is advisable for police administrators, particularly newcomers, to understand the rituals of the organization and move carefully when they find it necessary to change them. The quickest way to stimulate resentment and negative reaction to change is to display disrespect and disregard for an organization's rituals.

Proper behavior   Proper behavior delineates right and wrong ways to act and defines patterns for interaction between management and employees, members of different groups, and peers. It defines fair and unfair behavior, introduces standards of conduct, and provides for a high degree of stability in the police organization. Agreement on proper behavior is the nucleus of an organization's informal communication network and defines the dimensions of loyalty among peers.

Officers' commitment to departmental standards of behavior is often the stimulus for the initial resistance or suspicion that greets an incoming administrator. The newcomer is perceived as one who will introduce uncertainty into previously understood patterns of behavior.

Internal communication system   A police organization's internal communication system is built up around shared perceptions about leadership, proper behavior, personnel, doctrine, and articles of central faith. This system provides a valuable shorthand and channels for the rapid transmission of large volumes of significant information. It permits the transference of performance expectations without elaborate detail, and it imparts significant meaning to statements that might appear neutral to an outsider. This system can transmit vital information required for the completion of tasks in separate areas of responsibility. Similarly, it can alert organization members to surprise inquiries, covert investigations, and assorted organizational intrigues. Most important, the internal communication system provides a self-regulatory mechanism that transmits such information as the status ranking of individuals, whose opinion counts, what are acceptable production rates for the "good" worker, and what innovations should be given a fair opportunity to prove themselves.

Memory and folklore   The last cultural component is the organization's memory and folklore—the body of events, experiences, stories, and jokes frequently referred to by older members and passed on to new members. This element transmits the organizational culture to successive generations. The factual accuracy of these transmissions is not important. Their significance lies in the perceptions conveyed of the organization and its environment, particularly the values and behaviors that are praised or derided.

The culture and change

The causes of individual and collective resistance to organizational change are most often embodied in the components of the organizational culture. This does not mean that the culture is to be regarded negatively. Indeed, it is the vehicle by means of which the operating ethics of successful and effective organizations are maintained and transmitted even when formal management may have significantly weakened. The culture also provides a means through which many routine tasks are performed properly with little or no imposed direction. It permits the rapid and effective transmission of vital information for successful work performance.

The organizational culture is clearly a force to be reckoned with, especially when the administrator is introducing needed change. This is particularly true when the administrator is a newcomer. The organizational culture and the administrator's sensitivity to it are capable of tipping the scales for or against change.

Subsystems

The line operations in the police organization are composed of a variety of activities and tasks that provide direct services to the public. They form the primary system of the police organization. This nucleus of police service determines how the police agency is perceived by those it serves; it is capable of affecting the police administrator's credibility with the community and the administrator's overall reputation and tenure. Line operations are continually in the forefront of discussions regarding organizational changes, goals, priorities, and allocation of resources.

Line operations are supplemented and supported by internal subsystems, also called staff units. Although the designations or titles of these subsystems will vary from one police agency to another, they are easily identified by the nature of their activities: they provide services to the line operations. It is true that some staff units provide direct services to the public, such as handling incoming phone requests for information or service, processing records, and carrying out community relations programs, but by and large the primary purposes are to serve the line operations and assist them in their efforts to achieve organizational goals.

Depending on the size of the organization, a subsystem may be a unit of the line operations, or it may be a separate bureau or division. Whenever the size of the organization dictates a separation of subsystems into two or more units, one will generally concentrate on the human resources of the organization, while the rest center on material resources and other line-related activities such as communications and records. The human resources aspect includes recruitment and training, planning and research, and other personnel functions. The material resources aspect involves budgeting and the procurement, distribution, and maintenance of equipment.

The establishment of balance between the primary line operations and the support subsystems is critical to long-range goal achievement. There has to be a conscious consideration of cause-and-effect relationships throughout the continual process of organizational reevaluation, planning, and change. Any significant imbalance is likely to result in goal displacement or distortion and an overemphasis on one phase at the expense of the other. Two common examples illustrate this potential problem:

A combination of community and political forces pressures the police administrator to put more officers on the street, decrease response time to emergencies, and reduce crime frequency. This pressure does not, unfortunately, provide funds for additional personnel and equipment. The organizational reaction is to strip personnel from the subsystems and transfer them to line operations. This may temporarily solve the problem, but, as vacancies occur and equipment breaks down due to overuse, the subsystems will not have the personnel to recruit, process, and train replacements adequately or to provide for replacement and/or maintenance of equipment. The end result is either a diminishing supply of human and material resources and an inability on the part of the subsystems to meet the demands, or a periodic shuffling back and forth of personnel, which obviously disrupts the organization's continuity.

Following the civil unrest of the late 1960s, many organizations created community relations units as part of the subsystem. The initial intent was for community relations to plan and coordinate community resources and public relations programs with full participation of line operations personnel. Gradually, however, the full scope of community relations programs gravitated to the subsystem unit, and participation of line personnel was reduced or eliminated. The frequent result was a drawing of funds and/or manpower from line operations to a subsystem. This, in turn, led to an uncomfortable situation in which a subsystem unit was advising the public of what line operations would accomplish, when line operations did not have the resources to do it.

The police administrator must avoid tendencies toward either of these extremes. It is accepted that occasional situations will arise where emphasis must be placed temporarily on a line operation or on a subsystem. A long-range imbalance, however, will damage the entire organization and its efforts. One way for the police administrator to avoid this imbalance is to identify the management staff as a managerial subsystem. Regardless of their individual commands and responsibilities, their collective overriding responsibilities toward the organization must be clearly understood.

Organizational forces

Earlier in this chapter, it was stated that the dynamics of the organization can dictate the approach of the manager, and, until the dynamics are redirected, they have the capability to inhibit change regardless of the police administrator's philosophy and desires. Dynamics are all the forces and energy within the organization—the culture, style of policing, management attitudes, subsystems, and so on.

Dynamics and management orientation

Three dynamic forces must be considered when determining, identifying, and changing management orientation: (1) forces in the manager; (2) forces in the subordinates; and (3) forces in the situation.[15] The components of these forces most directly related to management approach include decision-making latitude, delegation practices, acceptance of responsibility, and employee development. The intent to redirect these forces must be preceded by their examination, an examination that not only views the dynamics collectively—that is, as they relate to groupings of employees by rank, position, assignment, and so on—but also on an individual basis within each group. The view of the individual is a must for managerial personnel.

Decision-making latitude   The term *decision-making* as used here refers to decisions affecting the organization as a whole, not the routine decisions made daily. The question of latitude involves how organizational decisions are made and by whom, the extent of employee participation, and the extent to which the organization and management encourage or discourage independent action and discretion.

Delegation practices   Delegation practices include the extent of delegation and the levels to which authority is delegated, the degree of confidence each level has for a subordinate level, risk taking versus playing it safe or "checking with the top" before doing anything.

Acceptance of responsibility   Questions concerning acceptance of responsibility include its perception as a tribute to ability or as a troublesome, risky burden; preferences for a high degree of flexibility or limited responsibilities with clear-cut directions or limitations imposed by others; and willingness of members of the organization to take risks.

Employee development   Employee development involves the extent of development fostered by the organization for employees at all levels, the degree to which personnel exhibit independent thinking and initiative versus waiting to be told what to do (or having to wait as per written directives), and the dimensions of employee preparation for the next step on the promotional ladder.

The identification and analysis of the forces at work in an organization are not necessarily difficult, even for a newcomer. The great majority of police administrators did not attain their positions by being fools; they have the ability to perceive, analyze, and evaluate organizational processes quickly. The next step also is relatively easy. It is merely to compare the dynamics of the organization with the characteristics of the management philosophy of the chief executive. If similar, little or no change is necessary. If different, the administrator must determine the extent of the differences and initiate changes.

Redirecting organizational forces

Redirecting the forces at work in an organization is a difficult task. The administrator's goals for redirection may be immediately attainable, gradually attainable (with time, patience, and guidance), or nearly impossible.

Goals for redirection may be *immediately attainable* when the existing dynamics have been perpetuated by past administrators and/or upper levels of management, while personnel at lower levels want a change and are fully prepared to expand their abilities to accommodate it. Redirection measures will vary depending on the circumstances, but they will usually involve opening lines of interlevel communications, modifying written directives to encourage a change, and neutralizing those who cannot alter their attitudes. Risk to the police administrator rests in the neutralization of those who cannot accept redirection measures. Care must be exercised not to alienate their followers any more than necessary and to neutralize the individuals, not their positions.

Redirection may be *gradually attainable* when there is a division in the dynamics of the organization without regard to levels or job assignments, and when employee development and orientation will be required prior to completion of the changeover. The administrator will perceive an organizational wait-and-see posture rather than overt positive or negative reactions. In addition to employee development efforts, opening lines of communication, and modifying written directives, administrators should consider the possibility and practicality of job matching. Job matching is moving key personnel to job environments in which they will work best—placing risk takers and flexible personnel in less structured units and functions, and putting the inflexible in routine jobs with a high degree of predictability. The primary risk to the administrator is that the change may not occur within the time that has been established for its completion.

Redirection is *nearly impossible* when dynamics are stable and employee values and perceptions are commonly held. In this case, the administrator has less-than-satisfactory choices: either relinquish the desired changes and conform with the existing dynamics (highly unlikely), or literally force-feed the organization and remove those in key positions by retirement or termination and replace them with outsiders. Either course poses a high risk to the organization and the administrator.

Budgeting

Budgeting, one of the management functions included in the acronym POSDCORB, is the process of developing and managing the organization's financial resources. It is also a management tool and, when used effectively, will assist the police administrator and management staff in carrying out their functions of coordination and control. Budgeting takes place twelve months a year, not just a few months prior to the beginning of a fiscal year. The demands on the chief executive to fulfill the obligation as a business manager are very difficult, now more than ever. As local government spending is subjected to increased scrutiny and limitation, the police administrator must compete with other department managers. Because mayors, managers, and councils must allocate limited resources according to perceived public needs, the police executive must carefully develop the police budget with adequate justification of all major items and programs.

Quite often the task of fiscal management is delegated to subordinates; however, accountability for all aspects of the department's fiscal policies and practices rests with the chief executive.

Concepts and practices of government budgeting have changed in the past

---

Taxing and spending limits

Indicative of the public mood for limiting taxing and spending of state and local governments are the actions taken by many state governments during the first nine months of 1979.

Six states imposed spending limitations. In three states specific lids were imposed on tax and expenditure growth; in the other three states formulas were enacted to control the magnitude of allowable increases. Usually the lid was rather moderate—providing in effect that state spending should not grow faster than the overall economy of the state.

Twenty-three states either initiated or expanded tax relief measures for home owners and renters.

Twenty-five states reduced state income taxes—nineteen by reductions in the tax base and six by rate reductions.

Four states—Iowa, Minnesota, Oregon, and Wisconsin—partially indexed their state income taxes.

Fifteen states reduced the general sales tax, twelve by reductions in the tax base and three by rate reductions.

Source: John Shannon and Chris Cooper, "The Tax Revolt—It Has Hurried History Along," paper delivered to the Public Securities Association, Colorado Springs, Colorado, October 8, 1979.

few decades. Historically, budgeting has been control-oriented, and this is the essence of the line item budget. A new concept of management needs resulted in performance-oriented budgeting in the mid-1950s. Another planning-oriented concept was recognized when the President ordered adoption of a planning-programming-budgeting system (PPBS) in federal civilian agencies in 1965.[16]

Budget preparation

Budget preparation in police organizations is generally practiced as either an independent administrative process or a multilevel participative system. As an administrative process, budgeting proceeds from top to bottom. The administrator and top-level management develop and prepare budget requests, determine organizational goals, and define measurable objectives for all parts of the organization. There is little consultation with lower level managers and supervisors and, when consultation does occur, it is usually limited to opportunities for countermeasures that may or may not be considered.[17]

The multilevel participative method is a bottom-to-top approach. Initial budget requests and preparation are performed by lower level managers and supervisors based on guidelines set by the administrator and top management staff. These guidelines normally include a statement of organizational goals, the management or supervisory levels to which initial budget preparation will be assigned, estimates of available dollars, and deadlines for completion. As each level completes its budget requests, they are thoroughly discussed, negotiated, modified, and/or approved with the next higher level of management. This process is repeated up the chain of command until all budget packages are submitted to the top management level and the administrator.

The participative method has several advantages over the independent administrative process. It provides opportunities for employees at several levels to "buy in" to the budget itself as well as to the objectives they have helped establish for the unit. It helps avoid budget oversights or problems for each unit—lower level managers and supervisors have a more intimate knowledge of their units and a more realistic view of its work processes and needs. Its primary disadvantage is time. Discussing and negotiating budget requests at each level of the organization is time-consuming.

The following conditions must be met if participative budgeting is to work:

1. Guidelines set by top levels must be broad enough to allow a reasonable degree of flexibility; otherwise, budgeting is nothing more than an administrative process with lower level personnel doing the paperwork.
2. Initial preparation responsibilities should be assigned to the lowest practical level, considering the size and structure of the organization. This level is usually the unit supervisor or section manager.
3. Each unit must specifically identify what it will accomplish (its measurable objectives) during the budget term if its initial requests are approved. If budget requests are modified, the unit's stated objectives must be changed accordingly.
4. Level-to-level discussions require an open-minded, give-and-take attitude. Each discussion at every level must relate unit requests and objectives to organizational goals.
5. Completion deadlines must be enforced.

Budgeting problems

Regardless of the budgetary process used (line item, performance, PPBS, or zero-base budgeting), police administrators can expect certain internal problems to occur periodically as budget preparation gets under way. Among them are padding, manipulation of supportive data, and organizational dramatics.

Padding   Persons submitting budgets often overstate needs and expense estimates in order to provide a cushion against anticipated budget cuts prior to final approval and to allow a safety margin for unplanned developments during the budget term.

Manipulation of supportive data   Akin to padding is the manipulation of data, usually statistical information, in support of budget requests. Manipulation can be for legitimate purposes, such as to justify a truly necessary budget request, or for questionable purposes, such as padding or empire building.

Organizational dramatics   Organizational dramatics is the withholding or premature release of information or services until the action will have the most dramatic impact on those who make final budget decisions. It can occur internally in unit-to-unit relationships or externally in daily public–police–political interactions.

Setting personal and organizational ethics aside, the use of padding, manipulation, and dramatics as part of the budget process is risky to the administrator and the organization. It sets the stage for allocation of resources based on who best accomplishes the three questionable practices rather than the actual needs and goals of the organization and its parts. It creates an internal and external facade that, when exposed, can have serious consequences. Most important, however, budget padding, manipulation of supportive data, and organizational dramatics are indicative of poor management.

Budgeting approaches

Four major approaches to budgeting are line item budgeting, performance budgeting, planning-programming-budgeting systems, and zero-base budgeting.

Line item budgeting   Line item budgeting is a very simple form of expenditure accountability based on control. In small organizations it may well be the only practical way to budget.

Line item budgeting is essentially cyclical budgeting. It focuses on the next fiscal year, and it is largely based on the current or previous year's budget. It provides great detail on the objects of expenditure and simplifies the comparison of one year's recommendations with the prior year's expenditures. Its use results in discrete additions to particular line items from year to year. It is neither performance- nor program-oriented. Its cyclical nature is both its key advantage and its key disadvantage. It does force—perhaps not too objectively—an annual review of expenditures with reasonable attention to functions, activities, and policies.[18]

Sole reliance on line item budgeting discourages long-range planning. Too often the result is "getting by for another year" without consideration of, or action on, important expenditure and revenue needs of ensuing years.

Other problems face the user of the line item budget, especially in large jurisdictions. Line item budgeting has no provision, for example, for integrating planning, budgeting, and control. It is difficult to relate budgeting to objectives, and expenditures to accomplishments. Objective evaluation of alternative means of gaining prescribed objectives is impractical. Line item budgeting, used alone, provides neither a sound basis for resource allocation nor a means of measuring the impact of current budget decisions on subsequent budgets. Finally, inherent in line item budgeting is a restriction on administrative flexibility with regard to ongoing activities; the police chief executive has little freedom to make even nominal changes in expenditure patterns and trends.

While line item budgeting remains common, particularly in small cities, it fails to further the concept of budgeting as a management process.[19]

Performance budgeting A performance budget, in contrast to one based solely on objects of expenditure, is oriented toward major functions and activities to which money (input) is directly related; it is predicated on objective, quantitative measures of achievement (output) in relation to resources allocated or used in particular functions.

The performance budget relies on work units and cost per unit as the basis for budgeting and subsequent evaluation of services. It is management-performance-oriented. Under performance budgeting, management works with broader appropriations and greater flexibility in moving or shifting resources so that they serve program ends. The performance budget is characterized as an input-oriented budget, but less so than the line item budget.[20]

The person or office developing a performance budget for a given fiscal year will be expected to define the agency's objectives for the year, the specific activities or programs needed to achieve those objectives, and the cost. Pure performance budgeting, as described here, has limited application in police agencies and should be used initially in areas of work where quantification is clearly feasible. It requires careful attention to sound, effective, and efficient management records systems, and it depends on sophisticated programs of cost accounting.[21]

PPBS (planning-programming-budgeting system) A planning-programming-budgeting system is a program-oriented budget system designed to integrate the organization's activities, resources, and goals. It is intended to provide a systematic approach to (1) planning (identifying and evaluating the costs of objectives); (2) programming or organizing (translating the objectives into human and material resources); and (3) budgeting (translating the resources into costs).[22] There are five basic steps to PPBS:[23]

1. *"Specify and analyze basic objectives in each major area of activity."* This first step forces the organization to examine what it is trying to accomplish. Then it can analyze the various elements of programs to see which ones will most efficiently and effectively accomplish these objectives. If overall organizational goals are not kept in mind, programs and systems are difficult to compare directly.
2. *"Analyze the output of a given program in the light of the specified objectives."* Next, the agency determines how well a given program achieves its objectives. The measure of a program's effectiveness would *not* necessarily be the quantity of service but the quality and objectives achieved.
3. *"Measure the total cost of the program for several years ahead."* Agencies often begin programs on the basis of cost estimates for the first year or two. But most programs—particularly government programs—increase in cost over time. Projecting costs into the future enables managers to make more realistic budget decisions.
4. *"Analyze the alternatives."* Next, managers analyze the alternatives available and determine which will most effectively and efficiently achieve the stated objectives. This step is basic to the entire PPBS approach.
5. *"Make the approach an integral part of the budgetary process.* The PPBS approach would only be a theoretical exercise if it did not become a basis for making budget decisions."

PPBS makes it possible to select alternative programs designed to accomplish similar ends and to select alternative functions and activities to support those programs. It also assists in assigning priorities to competing activities and in resolving apparent conflicts among activities. Thus, resources can be allocated on a rational basis within integrated systems or among disparate subsystems. Within PPBS, systematic analysis is applied to processes in use to ensure their efficacy and to make adjustments when necessary. Very important, PPBS is a multiyear approach to departmental budgeting.

PPBS causes organizations and their components to plan, establish goals and objectives, and continually analyze the results of their services. It makes it easier to compare the program costs of one organization with the similar program costs of another and requires the organization and legislative body to set priorities.

The primary problem encountered with PPBS in the police service is the rapid changes that can occur in a community with respect to political attitudes, needs, and demands for service. The problems of decision making in a complex government organization and its intense political environment inhibits long-range effective use of PPBS.[24] Many police organizations and municipalities that use PPBS have modified it and combined some of its principles with other systems.

Zero-base budgeting   Zero-base budgeting requires organizations to review their entire operation each budget year and literally reevaluate, redefine, and rejustify each goal, objective, and activity. The process involves three major steps:

1. Breaking down the activities of the organization into "decision packages"—that is, the information that will allow managers to evaluate that activity and compare its costs and benefits with those of other activities. A decision package might include "the activity's purpose, costs, and estimated benefits, *plus* the consequences expected if the activity is not approved and the alternative activities that are available to meet the same purpose."[25]
2. Evaluating activities and ranking them in order of benefit to the organization. Ranking may be done at several levels of the organization, then reviewed and selected by top managers.
3. Allocating resources. "The organization's resources are budgeted according to the final ranking that has been established. Generally, funds for top-priority activities will be allocated fairly quickly; lower-priority items will be scrutinized much more carefully.[26]

The primary difficulty of zero-base budgeting is the lack of available data in many programs during its initial implementation. This hampers a realistic and accurate analysis. Use of this budget system should be preceded by training of management personnel to show them how and what their analysis is intended to accomplish and to acquaint them with present as well as potential sources of data.

Control and coordination in budgeting

The control aspect of budgeting involves a comparison of actual performance with budget objectives and estimates. Dollar figures are a convenient unit of measure for a wide variety of organizational activities and can serve as a basis for comparing revenue income with service output from one budget term to the next.[27] The entire budgetary process, from preparation through retrospective review and evaluation, offers an insight into the extent of each manager's and supervisor's knowledge of responsibilities and their effectiveness in carrying them out.

The interaction required among all levels and units and the exchange of information that occurs during budget preparation provides an opportunity for organizational coordination. As each unit defines and strives to achieve its objectives, it tends to recognize and acknowledge the contributions of others. Separate activities and individuals tend to unite in an atmosphere of a common organizational cause.

Budgeting is a process, but it is also a valid management tool. This fact should never be overlooked or minimized.

Conclusion

This chapter has brought together two topics that frequently are addressed separately—organization and management. The two are inseparable, however, for the style of the manager or administrator and the dynamics of the organization go hand in hand.

The police organization, like all others, has a certain resistance to change. At the same time, it is subject to diverse and changing pressures from citizens and local government officials. The successful administrator must examine the static and dynamic elements of the organization, including its purposes, goals, philosophy, culture, and subsystems, and determine how best to implement changes as they become necessary or desirable. Methods of implementation will depend on whether the organization is based on a legalistic (formal) or a service (informal) model and whether the management style is centralized or decentralized.

There is probably no greater challenge facing the police administrator today than attempting to address increased demands for service with fewer dollars. Understanding budgeting strategies can help, and this chapter has included alternative means of approaching the budgeting task.

In sum, there is no single best way to organize and manage a police agency. Perhaps the most important fact for the administrator to bear in mind is that organization and management are dynamic. Changes occur spontaneously from within and are imposed from without, and the administrator must understand the choices available and be able to respond to or initiate change flexibly and creatively.

1 Luther Gulick, "Notes on a Theory of Organization," in *Papers on the Science of Administration,* ed. Luther Gulick and Lyndall Urwick (New York: Institute of Public Administration, 1937).
2 Amitai Etzioni, *Modern Organizations* (Englewood Cliffs, N.J.: Prentice-Hall, Inc., 1964), p. 3.
3 James A. F. Stoner, *Management* (Englewood Cliffs, N.J.: Prentice-Hall, Inc., 1978), p. 7.
4 Harry Levinson, *The Exceptional Executive* (Cambridge, Mass.: Harvard University Press, 1968), pp. 3–7.
5 Egon Bittner, *The Functions of the Police in Modern Society* (Chevy Chase, Md.: Center for Studies of Crime and Delinquency, National Institute of Mental Health, 1970), pp. 52–62.
6 Herman Goldstein, *Policing a Free Society* (Cambridge, Mass.: Ballinger Publishing Company, 1977), p. 35.
7 F. Gerald Brown, "The Municipal Organization as a System," in *Developing the Municipal Organization,* ed. Stanley Piazza Powers, F. Gerald Brown, and David S. Arnold (Washington, D.C.: International City Management Association, 1974), pp. 51–64.
8 Paul R. Lawrence and Jay W. Lorsch, *Organization and Environment: Managing Differentiation and Integration* (Homewood, Ill.: Richard D. Irwin, 1967), pp. 9–10.
9 James M. Banovetz et al., "Leadership Styles and Strategies," in *Managing the Modern City,* ed. James M. Banovetz (Washington, D.C.: International City Management Association, 1971), p. 109. See also: F. Gerald Brown, "Management Styles and Working with People," in *Developing the Municipal Organization,* ed. Powers, Brown, and Arnold, pp. 70–74.
10 Peter F. Drucker, *Management: Tasks, Responsibilities, Practices* (New York: Harper & Row, 1974), p. 67.
11 Ibid., p. 788.
12 The following discussion is adapted from: William B. Eddy, "The Management of Change," in *Developing the Municipal Organization,* ed. Powers, Brown, and Arnold, pp. 151–52.
13 James Q. Wilson, *Varieties of Police Behavior: The Management of Law and Order in Eight Communities* (Cambridge, Mass.: Harvard University Press, 1968), pp. 140–43.
14 Anthony Jay, *Corporation Man* (New York: Random House, 1971), pp. 174–92.
15 Robert Tannenbaum and Warren H. Schmidt, "How To Choose a Leadership Pattern," in *Management: A Book of Readings,* ed. Harold Koontz and Cyril O'Donnell (New York: McGraw-Hill Book Company, 1976), pp. 502–4. (This chapter is an update of an article of the same title appearing in the *Harvard Business Review* 36 [March–April 1958]: 95–101.)
16 V. A. Leonard and Harry W. More, *Police Organization and Management,* 4th ed. (Mineola, N.Y.: The Foundation Press, Inc., 1974), p. 306.
17 Stoner, *Management,* p. 597.
18 Leonard and More, *Police Organization and Management,* p. 307.
19 Ibid.
20 Ibid., p. 307.
21 Ibid., p. 308.
22 Peter A. Pyhrr, *Zero-Base Budgeting* (New York: John Wiley & Sons, 1973), pp. 140–57.
23 Partly quoted and partly adapted from: Stoner, *Management,* p. 607.
24 Jack W. Carlson, "The Status and Next Steps for Planning, Programming, and Budgeting," in U.S. Congress, Joint Economic Committee, *The Analysis and Evaluation of Police Expenditures: The PPB System* (91st Cong., 1st Sess., May 1969), pp. 613–34.
25 Stoner, *Management,* p. 608.
26 Ibid.
27 Ibid., p. 593.

Police productivity

Increasing police productivity means improving current police practices to the best level known, to get better performance without a proportionate increase in cost. In its simplest form, this means doing the things that are considered to be a necessary part of good police work, but doing them as well or efficiently as the best current practices permit. . . .

Increasing police productivity [also] means allocating resources to activities which give the highest return for each additional dollar spent. A police department carries out a range of activities, many of which are non-crime-related and most of which are necessary to its overall mission and its responsibility to the public. Beyond a given scale, however, expanding certain activities will give the force less value than initiating or expanding others. . . .

[Finally,] increasing productivity in police work means making the most of the talents of police personnel.[1]

These productivity benefits have assumed so much importance today, especially because of increased manpower restrictions and budgetary constraints and the widespread relentless pressure to make the most of limited resources in police departments, that the subject merits a chapter of its own.

Apart from the rather narrow gratification of getting the most out of a dollar, the police administrator can derive a great deal of satisfaction out of taking every step possible to simplify work, to develop better procedures, to enlarge training opportunities, and to provide other measures of job enlargement and work improvement that will give satisfaction to as many members of the work force as possible. In this sense, productivity can become a positive force in which all can participate.

This chapter deals with the subject of productivity from several perspectives. It first discusses the framework of productivity with respect to the following: the benefits and concepts of productivity; the basics of effectiveness and efficiency; and the systems approach to productivity. Next, the following subjects are discussed: the productivity process, including work analysis and supportive actions; specific targets for productivity improvement, including functions and activities that can be studied for the development of work units; measurement methods; innovative approaches to productivity; labor relations and productivity; and the human aspects of productivity. A concluding checklist on productivity for self-evaluation, and an evaluative summary, conclude the chapter.

The police productivity framework

When the Boston police were faced with a busing situation in the 1970s, they had to maintain the peace "at any cost." Naturally, after they had accomplished this mission they faced the fact that they had just so many dollars with which to carry out their overall responsibilities to the community.

"At any cost" situations will continue to confront local and even state agencies throughout the country. However, the economic crunch that has enveloped municipalities in recent years has resulted in a belt tightening that in turn has resulted in unfilled vacancies in some police agencies and the elimination of positions in others. This situation has stunned the police ranks from chief to patrol officer, since public concern about crime for many years assured the police of the need for their services. It would appear that elected and appointed officials now feel it is politically feasible to ask the police to justify that one extra beat that, if covered round-the-clock, could mean between $130,000 and $170,000 when one considers salaries, fringe benefits, uniforms, training, and other essential costs for the five officers necessary for the task. Cover that beat with two officers in a patrol car and the cost could possibly exceed $300,000. How might a city spend $300,000 other than for an extra beat and still provide protection for its citizens? This is the type of question that faces officials today. The answer lies in an examination of productivity and its application to police work.

The productivity ratio

Productivity means working smarter, not harder. It is a yardstick which gauges how effectively the resources are used that go into making an output of goods and services. In general, productivity can be considered a ratio of results attained (outputs) to resources utilized (inputs). Output includes consideration of the quality, and thus the effectiveness, of the service. Without quality control, output would mean merely a work measure (the relation of some phase of an entity's output to the labor time required to complete that phase). Productivity measures require a broader comparison of the quality of services and goods produced to the quantity of resources employed in producing them. Developing a productivity program would also include "throughputs," "activities," and standards. Thus, the procedure would follow the sequence: inputs (resources), to throughputs (policies, procedures, etc.), to activities (reports, investigations, etc.), to outputs (arrests, cases cleared, etc.) *measured against standards* (e.g., arrests that survive the first judicial process). An example of this process is given immediately below.

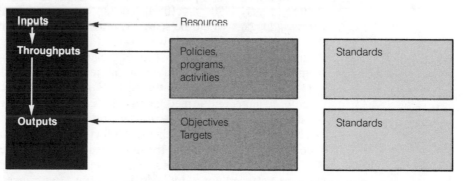

The productivity process is a sequence of inputs, throughputs, and outputs, desirably measured against standards.

A crisis intervention program is started in a police department because of the large number of arrests (which, in turn, have increased attacks on police officers and/or reduced citizen cooperation with the police) generated as a result of disturbance calls. Officers (inputs, or resources) are selected and made aware of departmental desires concerning interventions in family disturbance calls (throughputs). They then receive training in crisis intervention (activity). A goal is set concerning a specific *reduction* in the number of arrests for this type of call (standard), and the actual number of arrests made on such calls (output) is recorded and compared with the standard.

Productivity can be increased by obtaining greater output with less input. In the example given, as the officers perfect their intervention techniques they will probably reduce even further their numbers of arrests (in this case, an increase in their output). Eventually, fewer officers (smaller input) will probably be able to maintain the desired low level of arrests attained.

If a program were aimed at increasing arrests (e.g., New York City's Street Crime Unit), then comparing arrests ("controlled" by conviction standards) per officer (and for the unit) with similar activities of other officers in other units would enable one to make a determination as to the increased productivity possible through special units of this type.

Thus, in these times of economic necessity it behooves the police manager to embrace the concept of productivity and utilize the measurements that accompany it as an in-house management tool. It makes more sense to measure the effectiveness and efficiency of a police department by its ability to meet the standards it sets rather than by a comparison of crime rates with those of another city that happens to have approximately the same number of residents.

Effectiveness and efficiency

The interaction of effectiveness and efficiency is essential if there is to be any significant productivity improvement. Effectiveness has already been identified as the ability of an individual unit, or organization, to achieve an objective—sometimes at any cost. Efficiency considers that cost. Stating that productivity must be increased "at any cost" would be a tautology, since productivity must consider cost. There are agencies that can achieve fantastic results—at astronomical costs; there are others that are so cost conscious that they can get nothing done; and there are some that spend more money carrying out an efficiency project than they can expect to save.

Because of the emergency nature of police work, it might sometimes be desirable to concentrate first on making operations effective; then efforts could be directed later at making the operation efficient. The ultimate goal would still be productivity improvement.

When the hijacking problem was at its height in the United States in the late 1960s and early 1970s, an official decision was made that all passengers and their carry-on luggage would be searched prior to boarding any commercial flight in the country. In addition, it was decreed that an armed guard must be present during such searches (in most cases the guard was, and still is, a sworn officer from the municipality having territorial jurisdiction over the airport).

During the early stages of this security program, searching stations, made up of both civilians and armed guards and containing electronic screening equipment, were normally located at every boarding gate.

The results of this comprehensive effort to stop hijacking (the goal) were very successful. However, could the same results be accomplished more efficiently? The answer (stimulated by economic considerations) was yes. Today, passengers are screened not at individual gates but at entrances to boarding areas. In some cases this has eliminated up to 50 percent of the manpower and equipment needed.

The results (outputs) of this later approach are the same—elimination of hijackings—but the resources expended (inputs) have been reduced.

A systems approach

Even if the basic concept of productivity is understood and accepted, agencies can make a mistake if they institute a program to increase productivity in one function without looking at the overall effect on the other parts of the organization. Thus a systems approach, recognizing entities and their interrelationships, is necessary so that productivity can be embraced as a total approach rather than a one-shot effort.

If the installation of burglar alarms in all the downtown commercial establishments in a city results in an increase in arrests and convictions for burglary (the goal), the possibility still exists that this effort is not as productive as it appears. What must also be considered is the time police spend answering false alarms set off by faulty equipment or careless employees. The favorable picture in the burglary prevention function might become clouded if it were achieved at the expense of time and effort wasted by police in this way, which in turn would result in an increase in response time to genuine emergency calls. Thus, it can be seen that the effect of a program on the total objective of a police department must be considered—not just its impact on a particular function. And this systems approach should not be limited merely to internal considerations.

A good deal of time, effort, and money have been expended in recent years on programs designed to decrease response time. Delays are usually classified as follows: (1) dispatch delay (the time from the receipt of a call to the time the dispatcher is ready to assign a unit); (2) queue delay (the time a dispatcher must wait before a unit is available for dispatch); and (3) travel delay (the time from the actual dispatch of a unit to its arrival at the scene). As each of these delays is minimized, so is the response time. This, in turn, supposedly increases the likelihood of the apprehension of the criminal. Police managers have had to ask themselves (and their staffs): At what point will all the resources expended (inputs) to reduce response time really pay off in the form of increased arrests and convictions (outputs—including quality control)? Now it appears that police officials may have been misdirecting their efforts.

Gerald M. Caplan, then director of the National Institute of Law Enforcement and Criminal Justice, reported the following preliminary findings of a project by his agency:

Many victims fail to report crimes immediately, and this delay dwarfs any delay in police response. For example, an assault is not reported to police until more than an hour after it has occurred, on the average, while the police car responds in a little more than three minutes. The average delay in reporting a robbery is nearly 23 minutes, but the police arrive at the scene within three and a half minutes after the car receives the call. Burglaries aren't reported for more than a half hour after they are discovered—and perhaps hours after they are actually committed—but the police officer responds to the dispatcher's call in six minutes. Nearly three quarters of an hour elapses before larcenies are reported, while the police are on the scene within five minutes after the call is received. Reports of auto theft are made 31 minutes after discovery; the police respond within five minutes of receipt of the dispatcher's call.[2]

It is obvious, then, that a portion of the dollars expended on reducing response time should be directed into programs that reduce the delay in reporting crimes.

The productivity process[3]

The concept of productivity is enhanced by certain management approaches, such as participatory management and management by objectives (MBO). The necessity for these companion management methods can be seen from the review, given immediately below, of the process of productivity improvement. This process includes: (1) commitment and support from the top; (2) participation from all ranks; (3) policies that are directed toward productivity improvements; (4) identification of objectives; (5) analysis and evaluation; and (6) supportive action.

Commitment and support

Without commitment and support, not only from the top staff of the police department but also from city hall, efforts toward productivity improvements will be doomed to failure. This support must be declared and must be communicated to the "troops," and those uttering it must become actively involved in developing policies, objectives, incentives, and other aspects of the process.

In 1976 the city of Boise, Idaho, decided to pursue productivity improvements for all the city departments, beginning with the police department. The mayor communicated his feelings on the project to all police department personnel in the following message:

I'm sure you are all aware of the project now underway in the Police Department to develop and implement a productivity improvement program. I want to stress again my interest in and commitment to this project, which eventually will involve all of you.

I want to point out that you are not being used as "guinea pigs" so to speak. It's because of your willingness to look for new and improved ways to do your jobs that it seemed logical to start a pilot program like this in your department. What you are doing, in addition to looking for better ways to do *your* jobs, is to test ideas, concepts, and methods that can be utilized in *all other* City departments.

The City is really committed to finding better ways of budgeting and allocating resources, based on factual, performance-oriented information. Your efforts in this direction will certainly help pave the way to development of methods to do this and offset the growing budget squeeze we face each year.

I'm happy and encouraged that the Police Department is taking the initiative with a project that will, in the long run, benefit the entire City. My thanks to you . . . and keep up the good work![4]

In addition to this correspondence, the mayor reinforced the commitment of his office by assigning the director of city finance to participate in all meetings and workshops held in conjunction with the police department's productivity program.

Time lag in reporting crimes

Robbery		23 minutes
Burglaries		30 minutes
Larcenies		45 minutes
Auto thefts		31 minutes
Assault		60 minutes

Average time lag in reporting crimes defeats typical police response time of three to six minutes.

Productivity improvement implies criticism of past and present methods of operation. Thus the leadership of top management is indispensable to initiating the productivity process.

Participation

Since all ranks are normally involved in carrying out the productivity program, they should also be involved in the planning process—particularly in setting objectives. Employees are more likely to strive to meet objectives that they themselves have set rather than objectives established by others.

If the individual talents of the rank and file are overlooked or are stifled by antiquated organizational structures and procedures, productivity improvements at best will be short term and marginal; at worst they could be sabotaged.

Policies

One way in which management can formalize its support for productivity programs is through the issuance of explicit policies on productivity improvement.

Policies, when formulated concerning productivity, legitimize such programs and allow them to take their place as an integral part of management's plans and actions. This guarantees a degree of continuity for such programs, even when there is a change in management or in political leadership.

Identifying objectives

The defining of objectives, by all ranks, provides specific direction for productivity programs and forms the basis for action planning. This should not present a problem for those agencies familiar with management by objectives. Other agencies, however, will have to realize that, whereas policies provide organizational guidelines, objectives provide specific direction for what is to be accomplished. Some characteristics of objectives are that they are: specific as to what is to be accomplished, when, and by whom; attainable, but allow for some "stretching" of employee talents; related to either inputs or outputs; quantifiable; and flexible.

Analysis and evaluation

Measurements are needed if management is to know where it is now, what objectives are to be achieved, and if these objectives are eventually reached. This subject is covered in some detail in the section on Measurements, later in this chapter.

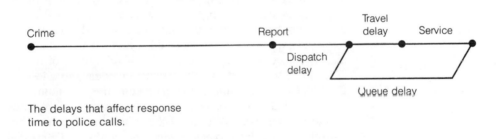

The delays that affect response time to police calls.

Supportive action

There are three principal means through which support can be obtained for the productivity process. These are incentives, training, and technical assistance.

Incentives[5] Broadly speaking, an incentive is anything offered to obtain desired performance or behavior from an employee. It may be a reward, such as pay tied to performance, or more responsibility, or more free time. Some people also consider penalties, such as a reduction in pay, loss of benefits, or even dismissal, as a type of incentive.

This concept of an incentive goes beyond the definition of an incentive as simply meaning more money, either in pay or fringe benefits, because experience shows that the objectives served by incentives—increased productivity and/or better morale through improved motivation—can also be achieved by contributing to a wide range of other employee needs. These include job security, equitable distribution of rewards, personal growth, opportunities to exercise craftsmanship, and desires for increased autonomy (i.e., an improvement in the individual's ability to influence and in some measure control his work methods, job assignments, working hours, and various other conditions of the work environment).

Moreover, nonmonetary incentives may be particularly effective with government workers, whose economic drives are often counterbalanced or outweighed by the desire to perform useful public service. In addition, nonmonetary incentives have an obvious appeal for cost-conscious public administrators.

No incentive scheme is universally applicable. Jobs differ; employees differ. Some governments are unionized; others are not. Laws differ from one jurisdiction to the next and often preclude some types of incentive arrangements. Incentive plans must therefore be adapted to fit or change these conditions.

Training The traditional police hierarchy, moving, as it does, from the bottom up, has resulted in the fact that very few police managers acquire any significant expertise in developing system-wide productivity improvements. The same applies to the rank and file who must also participate in the process. True, the influx of college educated officers and the acquisition of degrees by some managers may have exposed some police personnel to the general concept of productivity, but few have had the opportunity to develop it to any degree within their agencies. Therefore, it is necessary to present carefully designed productivity training programs to police agencies before and during the introduction of any productivity process.

Technical assistance The type and amount of technical assistance required by a police department during the productivity process will vary with the department's in-house capabilities. There are limits to the amount of assistance that should be expended for the process. Acquiring a staff more costly than the anticipated savings is the antithesis of productivity improvement.

A key figure in the productivity team is the analyst. Whether he or she is in-house or from outside, this individual should have academic training and professional experience that will enable him or her (or them) to analyze tasks, help identify objectives, and assist in the development of measurements.

In addition to that of productivity manager (an additional responsibility for the chief or an administrative assistant) the remaining positions on the team would probably be those of project coordinators. Whatever his or her rank within the department, each of these individuals would be assigned to coordinate that particular project in which he or she had a special interest and/or expertise. Normally this responsibility could be handled on a part-time basis, which would allow the coordinators to continue their customary police duties.

Incentives, training, and technical assistance, then, constitute the type of supportive action necessary for a successful productivity improvement process and program. Since these actions involve the expenditure of funds, they tie in with the first step of the productivity process—top management commitment and support. In one way or another, the entire productivity process revolves around commitment and support from the top which, in turn, stimulates the interrelations necessary for the success of the process.

Targets for productivity improvements

Certain areas seem particularly susceptible to productivity. Four of these have been identified as follows: (1) operations involving large numbers of employees performing routine tasks; (2) functions consuming large numbers of man-hours; (3) functions normally resulting in a backlog of work; and (4) areas with high unit costs.[6]

In each of these areas the key to successful analysis lies in challenging assumptions. The easiest way to accomplish this is to ask the following questions:

Why is this done? Why is it done this way? If the answer to one or both of these questions starts out with the words: "Because we have always . . . ," there is a good chance that productivity improvements are in order. The text that follows will deal with each of these four areas.

Large numbers of employees performing routine tasks

This is an area in which police agencies have made real progress, especially in the traffic area. Meter maids, school crossing guards, and traffic aides who handle minor traffic accidents are the kinds of paraprofessionals who are able to produce the same amount of outputs as those produced by sworn officers (in some cases, the output may be even greater). The costs of their services in salaries, fringe benefits, training, etc. (inputs), are less than those of professionals, and thus there is an increase in productivity. In accordance with the systems approach, the dollar savings should be "significant" if such a program is to produce overall improvements. If the net savings involved in utilizing a meter maid for a downtown commercial district are less than $500 a year, this substitution could be questioned—especially if the beat officer replaced has been removed from a potentially high crime area. This and other types of on-street substitutions can also cut down on available backups for dangerous types of situations to be handled by sworn officers.

Other types of "civilianization" programs also have the potential for improving productivity in this target area, provided the net results are closely monitored. For example, if a $9,000-a-year typist could produce the same quality and quantity of work (outputs) as an $18,000-a-year patrol officer assigned to typing duties, use of the former for typing duties would mean a decrease in resources (inputs) and thus an increase in productivity. If, however, it took two typists at $9,000 each to replace the sworn officer, there would be little reduction in the area of inputs. On the other hand, if these two civilians were able to increase the output by 20 percent over that of the patrol officer, there would be an increase in productivity, provided the quality of work remained the same.

Functions consuming many man-hours

Patrol operations, with all their functions, obviously fall into this category. It is in this general area that many police managers have exercised a very basic productivity maneuver (without calling it such). The use of differential manning by police managers, which acknowledges the variations in manpower needs at different times of the day, is a testimony to their awareness of the importance of getting the maximum return from available resources. But what else might be done to further improve productivity?

For years, police officials, as a rule of thumb, have anticipated the expenditure of patrol manpower in the following manner: one third of the time expended answering calls for service; another third spent on administrative matters (report writing, court appearances, etc.); and the remaining third spent on what has been termed preventive or random patrol. The last third was the nondirected time that officers spent driving around (or parking) between calls. It was assumed that the mere presence of a marked police unit was preventing crime and giving citizens a feeling of security. In Kansas City, Missouri, this assumption was, in fact, challenged as a result of their preventive patrol experiment (for details see Chapter 7). Other cities are also beginning to look at this "one-third" portion of patrol time with an eye toward better utilizing this "available" time for such functions as crime prevention security checks, directed patrol, and even some investigative duties.

Other time-consuming procedures that could be challenged are:

1. The belief that a uniformed patrol officer must automatically be dispatched every time a citizen calls. ("Screening" calls can result in referrals to other agencies, and, in some cases, reports can even be taken over the phone by specially trained employees.)
2. The belief that every arrest must result in the incarceration of the subject. (Misdemeanor summonses have been successfully utilized by many police departments.)
3. The belief that the arresting officer must be physically present in court during most of the procedures. (Some courts have accepted sworn affidavits or complaints at arraignments in lieu of the officer's presence. Some cities have their subpoenaed officers patrol the area around court until they are actually needed to testify.)

Functions normally resulting in a backlog of work

The paper war that faces police departments is typical of that facing most bureaucratic agencies. However, there are ways of winning a battle or two.

Reports   A review of the types of reports (and the numbers of copies) produced by a police department followed by the simple question: Why do you need this? directed at the individual designated to receive it, could uncover some good opportunities for eliminating a certain amount of work and thus reducing some backlogs. One of the first discoveries is likely to be that police employees are producing some reports that are used almost exclusively by insurance companies. Another revelation might be that reports are being generated by staff members who want to keep in touch with the activities of divisions or units they formerly commanded. One can probably find some reports that are being made "because we always have made them—that's why."

Letters   In spite of the typical backlog in the word processing center—a modern version of the typing pool—it is almost impossible to identify a police department that has any restrictions on the number of outgoing letters or even their length, although almost every police agency has some type of procedure that severely restricts the placing of long distance calls. And most police departments would be unable to identify the cost of a "long distance" letter to compare it with the cost of a long distance telephone call—which is easily retrieved from a statement. While few would dispute the value of a live conversation over a letter, the cost of a long distance phone call is usually considered prohibitive, while the costs of the letter are mostly hidden.

Clerical work   Clerical procedures, too, have great potential for productivity improvement if police departments make an effort to overcome the inertia that has built up over the years in this time-consuming function.

The investigative function   Another activity that generates large backlogs of work, at least on paper, is the investigative function. A study conducted by the Rand Corporation[7] has challenged the effectiveness of those normally assigned this function. (This study is discussed in Chapter 9.) Even before the Rand study results appeared, it was obvious that there were some nonproductive aspects, or, rather, wasted efforts, associated with the investigative function as practiced by some police departments.

A police department places one beat officer on foot in an area and asks him to prevent crime, arrest violators, and be ready to take any action necessary to accomplish his mission. After the commission of a major crime, however, *two* detectives arrive at the scene. In most cases these detectives are paid more money than the beat officer, are backed up by an evidence technician, and ask the same questions of the victim already asked (with answers recorded) by the beat officer who arrived at the scene shortly after the crime was reported.[8] This "two platoon" system is a waste of manpower.

There has been a misconception on the part of both the police and the public to the effect that every crime committed must be assigned to a detective for investigation and that when an investigation does take place it must be undertaken by a specialist. Gradually, it is being acknowledged that some cases, because of lapse in time between the perpetration of the crime and its discovery (therefore, no fresh leads), or because of the nature of the case (e.g., some prosecutors refuse to take certain types of cases), do not call for an active investigation involving expenditures of time and resources. There has also been a realization, as a result of the successes of several cities, that patrol officers can investigate some cases with better results (based on closure rates) than detectives can when the officers have beat or area stability.

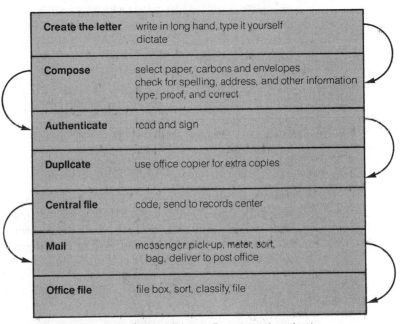

Create the letter	write in long hand, type it yourself dictate
Compose	select paper, carbons and envelopes check for spelling, address, and other information type, proof, and correct
Authenticate	read and sign
Duplicate	use office copier for extra copies
Central file	code, send to records center
Mail	messenger pick-up, meter, sort, bag, deliver to post office
Office file	file box, sort, classify, file

The cost of a "long distance" letter. Even a rough estimate of the personnel costs for a letter often will show that a long distance phone call is less expensive.

Since many police executives have served in the detective division in the course of their career and have many friends still serving there, productivity improvements in the investigative function will probably become a reality only incrementally, and very slowly at that.

Areas with high unit costs

Apart from personnel costs, the most expensive regular budget item for a police department is probably the vehicles purchased for its officers. Automobiles should be chosen with an eye to their actual use. Every officer does not need a police "pursuit" car. (There may be occasions when a scooter, a jeep, or even a horse is more practical than a gas-eating, four-barrel, eight-cylinder, four-door sedan.) However, a decision to purchase a compact car just because it will save on gas may not represent much of a saving if the severity of injuries to officers involved in accidents is greatly increased, if officers develop bad backs and retire for medical reasons, or if officers feel they are getting second class treatment and therefore cut corners in the delivery of their services.

Two other areas for potential savings are given below:

A fully staffed and equipped photography lab may be a prestige asset to a police department, and a police administrator may contend that police photographs have to be handled confidentially, but isn't it perhaps possible that an outside laboratory could both meet the confidentiality requirements and do the job more cheaply?

Spending $2,000 to send an officer to a training program offered by a prestige institution when approximately the same program is offered locally for $200 is a high price to pay for a fancy lapel pin. What is even worse is that the $2,000-officer often becomes the sole custodian of the knowledge acquired at the training program. A formal system for diffusing the knowledge acquired at a training program can greatly increase the output produced from the time and money invested.[9]

After various targets for productivity improvements have been identified, methods should be established that will enable the police executive to measure whether progress is being made.

Measurements

Since the concept of productivity was developed in industry, where goods such as automobiles, refrigerators, and television sets are produced, it has been slow in moving into the service areas, where the results are less tangible and thus far more difficult to quantify.

Crime statistics versus productivity measurement

The most utilized "measurements" in the police field have been the Uniform Crime Reports (UCR) of the FBI. The regular dissemination of the UCR (quarterly and annually) has made the series very popular with those outside the police community. The UCR is an official document that can be used by laymen to rate and compare various police agencies.

Recent victimization studies have demonstrated that the UCR, which lists only reported crimes, reflects only a fraction of the crimes committed. This comes as no surprise to police officials, but the absence of other measures has elevated crime statistics to a level of importance far beyond their actual worth.

And, in addition, these crime statistics result from numerous and various conditions over which the police have little or no control. Among these conditions are the proportion of low income families in the community, the ratio of youths to the total population, the number of unemployed, the population density, and the effectiveness of courts and correctional programs.

Other important factors that affect the usefulness of crime statistics are the methods by which they are collected and recorded and the consistency with which they are interpreted. Any of these factors, or several of them taken together, may have more to do with changes in crime rates than anything the police department may do.

The frustrations that accompany the statistical UCR game are highlighted when a chief promises to reduce crime just when a program has been introduced to increase the community's confidence in their police. If this program takes hold, there could be a surge in crime reporting by enthusiastic citizens and thus an *increase* in crime rates.

Even as the expenditure of police time and resources becomes better identified—namely 80 to 90 percent on order maintenance activities and only 10 to 20 percent on law and order situations—the use of crime rates as evaluators still hangs like an albatross around the neck of police administrators. To shed this bird, police agencies will need to identify categories within their order maintenance function for evaluation and shift some emphasis from the law enforcement function. (In an effort to judge police agencies on their ability to keep the peace, perhaps an evaluation ratio could be developed, like that established for crisis intervention programs, whereby for certain crimes calls for service resulting in arrests would be held against the responding officer. Such action would be based on the concept that in some cases police "arrest their mistakes" in much the same context that it is alleged that doctors "bury theirs.")

If the community information program is successful, more crime will be reported which will mean an increase in crime rates!

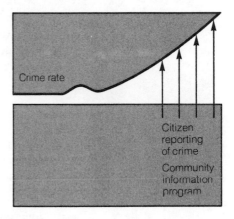

Productivity measurement used for management evaluation (not for comparing figures with those of cities of similar size, as is done with crime rates) offers police administrators the opportunity to have their departments evaluated by standards set internally.

Such productivity measurement is not easy, since police work deals mostly with service rather than products. In some cases indicators will have to be substituted for actual measurements. The Advisory Group on Productivity in Law Enforcement in its report on improving police productivity[10] suggested both measurements and indicators. Some are developed in the section immediately below. They should be modified and expanded to meet the specific needs of individual departments. However, police managers should not wait for a report, nor should they act solely on the basis of one. Concern for productivity stemming from a defensive managerial response will not have the same impact as programs developed through positive action.

Measuring police productivity

It would be wrong to develop overall standards for police productivity in view of the wide range of activities performed by police and the degree to which these activities vary from community to community. This would negate the internal role suggested for productivity measurements. Even if such diversifications from department to department were not present, developing measurements would be difficult, since many police objectives cannot be quantified. It is possible, however, to use partial measures, or to break activities down into segments which can be more precisely measured, in order to give police managers a better idea of their progress as well as their problems.

The following are examples of how this might be done for the patrol force:

1. When the objective is to make a greater proportion of police officers available for active (street) patrol work (up to a reasonable limit)
   Measure:

   $$\frac{\text{Police officers assigned to active patrol}}{\text{Total police officers}}$$

2. When the objective is to increase the "real patrol time" of those who are assigned to active patrol
   Measure:

   $$\frac{\begin{array}{c}\text{Man-hours spent on actual ("real") patrol}\\ \text{(time-servicing demands for police services)}\end{array}}{\text{Total patrol man-hours}}$$

3. When the objective is to utilize patrol time to best advantage (this is broken down into three principal objectives of patrol)
   a) Crime deterrence, as a result of response time
   Measure:

   $$\frac{\begin{array}{c}\text{Number of calls of a particular type}\\ \text{responded to in less than } x \text{ minutes}\end{array}}{\text{Total calls of that type}}$$

   b) Apprehension
   Measure:

   $$\frac{\text{Patrol-related arrests surviving first judicial screening}}{\text{Total patrol man-years}}$$

   c) Noncrime services
   Measures:

   $$\frac{\text{Noncrime calls responded to satisfactorily}}{\text{Total noncrime calls}}$$

   $$\frac{\text{Disturbance calls requiring no further attention}}{\text{Total disturbance calls.}}[11]$$

The above measures, and others, are discussed in detail in the report of the Advisory Group on Productivity in Law Enforcement. Most of these measures are relatively new and need to be further tested. However, the advisory group found that most of the police departments they surveyed had the data available to apply such measures or could get the data without great difficulty.

It remains for departments to begin testing these and other measures developed by the advisory group, to develop measures of their own, and, in general, to develop the capacity to analyze more precisely the results and costs of their activities. The purpose of all such measurements is to provide the information that will assist managers in obtaining quality results from the resources at their command.

Innovative approaches

Once a police department embraces productivity as a philosophy, develops an implementation process, identifies targets of opportunity, and develops measurements to evaluate progress, it might wish to seek out even bolder productivity programs. The economic and political restraints placed on municipal agencies create an environment that is not conducive to radical departures from traditional procedures. That leaves a great deal of responsibility for experimentation to outside agencies—who will need the cooperation of one or more local agencies—(such a partnership is, indeed, essential).

Innovation requires first of all a police administrator who sees the opportunity for significant improvements in the delivery of services yet is also aware of the limitations of departmental resources and the political realities of the local scene. The other requirement is an external organization with the funds and talent to develop new ideas, formalize ideas of the chief, and test both.

The Police Foundation, a privately funded, independent, nonprofit organization established by the Ford Foundation in 1970, is dedicated to supporting innovation and improvement in policing. The Kansas City preventive patrol experiment, mentioned earlier in this chapter, was financed by the Police Foundation. In this case a progressive department, that of Kansas City, under the leadership of a professional police chief, Clarence Kelley, teamed up with a funding agency to challenge a long-standing tradition—the value of preventive patrol.

The Rand Corporation is an example of a research organization that receives funding in order to pursue studies that have system-wide implications. The breadth of their inquiries is such that they could only be pursued by such an independent agency. The work of the Rand Corporation is described in some detail in Chapter 9.

Another agency that has helped police departments eliminate some nonproductive, traditional approaches to the delivery of services is the National Institute of Law Enforcement and Criminal Justice, the research arm of the Law Enforcement Assistance Administration (LEAA).[12]

Changes have been suggested by other outside agencies which, while they do not have the resources of those already mentioned, still have the potential for significant improvements in productivity. For example, the Institute for Local Self-Government (ILSG), a nonprofit research organization, under a grant from the Lilly Endowment Corporation, embarked on an eighteen-month study of various public safety service delivery systems. Acknowledging that consolidation, contracting, and civilianization are obvious areas for possible, practical, and political implementation, their executive director urged additional exploration, saying:

There is a consensus among concerned public administrators that the traditional, conventional methods of delivering public safety services are overdue for examinations as to their cost effectiveness/efficiency and that, in fact, the present system may be obsolete, even counter productive.[13]

One of the areas the institute has explored is an alternative to the traditional pension systems that can "lock in" a nonproductive worker. Although it is only in the exploration stage, a "Public Safety Employment Contractual System" is being developed by the institute.[14] It proposes the replacing of early tenure (e.g., nine or twelve months), which occurs under present systems, with a series of three contracts—one for four years and two for three years each. Thus, "tenured" positions would occur only after ten years of service. The plan calls for lump sum severance payment to those not offered a new contract and "reenlistment" bonuses for those invited to continue their service.

The National Clearinghouse for Criminal Justice Planning and Architecture has identified a method by which communities can save on police buildings. Stated very simply, police departments can lease these buildings instead of buying them.

In most cases, ownership of property provides no advantage to a police agency that could not be realized by leasing the property. In fact, in some instances ownership of property could be considered a definite liability. By using various leasing arrangements a municipality can significantly reduce the amount of capital needed for the acquisition of adequate new facilities.[15]

All of the above possibilities reflect the new concern for fiscal responsibility—a concern that can be met in part by productivity improvements.

Labor relations and productivity

Productivity programs can take on a negative quality if employees see productivity as a euphemism for the old fashioned "efficiency expert"—for time and motion studies and speedups. If, under the guise of productivity, changes are made by management which affect working hours, scheduling, and methods of payment, they will be resisted by employee associations and unions.

Strikes, slowdowns, and court actions against the imposition of productivity measures have already occurred in the public sector and elected officials—conscious of the need to maintain services as well as the political consequences for failing to do so—have been reluctant to take the lead in instituting major productivity programs. This is especially true when they do not have sufficient background in or appreciation of the productivity concept and those methods of implementation and measurement that can be successfully employed, for when it is handled properly, the productivity improvement approach can generate public acceptance and can activate and achieve employee participation and support.

Productivity bargaining in the police field is relatively new. It has been met with some skepticism but no major objections. The limited literature available on police labor contracts that contain productivity programs reflects the fact that labor has not been hurt and, in fact, has done quite well.[16]

Problems occur when productivity programs are placed on the bargaining table. They are then subject to alterations by the other party, and, once placed in a contract, they become subject to grievance procedures. A better alternative to bargaining over specific inputs and outputs is to acknowledge the concept of productivity in the contract at the very outset by using language along the following lines:

Delivery of municipal services in the most efficient, effective, and courteous manner is of paramount importance to the city and the union. Such achievement is recognized to be a mutual obligation of both parties within their respective roles and responsibilities. . . .

The union recognizes the city's right to establish and/or revise performance standards or norms notwithstanding the existence of prior performance levels, norms, or standards. Such standards, developed by usual work measurement procedures, may be used to determine acceptable performance levels, prepare work schedules and to measure the performance of each employee or group of employees.[17]

Labor–management cooperation in the area of productivity can be facilitated by labor–management committees. These present a viable alternative to formalized productivity bargaining. Some general principles have been developed to enhance the success of such committees.

A committee should be authorized by a collective bargaining agreement or memorandum of understanding between a public employer and public union or employee association, where they exist, to attain greater stability and prestige. However, it is important that committee members steer clear of contract interpretation matters and not turn committee sessions into extensions of the negotiating process. Each has its own purpose, place, and time.

As a first step, it may be desirable to make the committee recommendations advisory in nature to help overcome management concern that somehow the committee will trespass on its traditional prerogatives.

Probably more for symbolic than operational reasons, committees should have equal numbers from labor and management and it may be desirable to alternate the chairmanship from one side to the other at each meeting.

Meetings should be scheduled on a regular basis, rather than on call. It is likely that the imminence of a meeting will invite discussion of an issue rather than direct it into less conciliatory channels.

Agendas should be planned with both sides in a position to add items. A follow-up mechanism, such as posting of results and review of minutes of the preceding meeting, can be helpful.[18]

The success of productivity programs in the labor–management arena depends on both sides. Management must invest in developing the analytical capacity necessary to develop, monitor, and constantly improve programs aimed at increasing productivity. Organized labor must take positive positions on productivity that can be accepted by a volatile and sometimes suspicious membership. The types of programs that will probably be palatable to both sides include: job enrichment, enlarged promotional opportunities for productive employees, and greater flexibility in lateral and horizontal transfer. Success will require outstanding leadership on both sides.

The human aspects of productivity

Because of the necessary concentration on measurements and systematic analysis which they entail, productivity improvements might seem to suggest a return to scientific management, with the individual taking second place to the organization. That is not, in fact, the case. Productivity improvements, in addition to dealing with inputs and outputs, are also involved in improving the morale and the professionalism of individual officers and their departments.

Police managers who can accomplish the goals of their departments through their staffs and at the same time help these staffs achieve their own personal needs will have fulfilled the definition of their position—they will have meshed individual objectives with those of the organization. Contrary to the belief of some, productivity can play a part in this meshing process since productivity does not necessarily mean working harder or faster. In the police field it should mean working better.

Although the introduction and implementation of most productivity programs can be accomplished unilaterally under the guise of management rights, managers should reach out for employee and union involvement and cooperation in improving productivity. If productivity improvement programs are explained to employees and if employees are allowed and encouraged to participate in their formulation, these programs stand a better chance of succeeding.

The goals for the patrol force that were set out earlier in this chapter, in the section on Measurements, provide a good conclusion to this present section.

Making patrol officers available

The goal is to make a greater proportion of police officers available for active (street) patrol. If a young man or woman wanted an eight to four desk job, he or she would have chosen a career other than police work. Those entering police work do so for various reasons including the excitement and challenge of the job. This is found on the street, not behind a desk. The more sworn officers that can be assigned to street duty, the better the chances for increased service to the community (departmental goal) and the more opportunities for employees to fulfill their needs.

Increasing patrol time

The goal is to increase the "real patrol time" of those who are assigned to active patrol. If time spent in court, writing reports, responding to each and every call, etc., is cut down, those officers assigned to street duty will be able to devote more time to "real" police work. This should increase the quality of service to citizens with serious police problems and at the same time serve as a safeguard against boredom and apathy on the part of police officers. The handling of mostly quality cases can also serve as a motivator for the officer as he or she grows both in skill and in sense of accomplishment in handling the more difficult calls for service.

Utilizing patrol time

The goal is to utilize patrol time to best advantage. Increasing the ability of officers to perform their job by better training, by placing them where crime is most likely to occur, and by making available technical equipment to assist them will help them achieve the personal satisfaction that comes with completing a job and solving problems. Multiply these personal successes by a large percentage of employees, and in most cases the goals of the organization will also be met. The goals of the police department, its managers, and the men and women on the street can all be integrated in well-run productivity programs.

Checklist on productivity

The following "yes and no" questions can serve as a checklist to the subjects covered in this chapter, and then, it is hoped, to productivity improvements in the individual department or agency. It is suggested that this be used as a self-evaluation.

1. Is the addition of more police officers the response to increasing crime rates in your community?
2. Are your officers evaluated primarily on the number of arrests they make?
3. Do you restrict the discretion of patrol officers by the imposition of inflexible rules concerning their every action?
4. Are you content with one program that has proved successful?
5. Would you involve all ranks in improving productivity in your agency?
6. Would you legitimize productivity programs through policy statements?
7. Does defining of objectives assist in productivity improvements?
8. Are most of your police officers on duty when calls for police service are heaviest?
9. Does your agency train your officers for the real problems they will encounter?
10. Are there any tasks presently performed by sworn officers that could be done better or more cheaply by civilians?
11. Do your detectives handle every investigation?
12. Do detectives keep every case active until they make an arrest?
13. Do you know the total cost of sending a letter?
14. Do you have a photo lab? If so, do you know the cost of producing one picture?
15. Do you have data available to develop measurements?

If any of your answers to 1 through 4 are yes, you have the opportunity of improving the productivity of your agency. A positive response would indicate that you are approaching your crime problem from a very narrow perspective, evaluating your officers on a similar plane, disregarding the potential of your personnel, or failing to recognize the potential of the systems approach to productivity improvements.

If your answers to 5 through 7 are yes, you understand the concept of productivity and, therefore, are in a position to make improvements.

A negative answer to 8 and 9 and positive responses to 10, 11, and 12 identify specific targets for productivity improvement.

Negative answers to 13, 14, or 15 would indicate that you could well do some homework—not only if you wish to introduce productivity improvements, but also if you wish to continue as chief of police.

Conclusion

This chapter has presented the framework for productivity in police services, briefly described the process, indicated targets for productivity improvement, given some simple methods of measurement, touched on a few innovative approaches, discussed the human aspects of labor relations and employee involvement, and provided a checklist for self-evaluation so that the reader—whether police administrator, district commander, or other police officer—can judge where his or her own department stands on productivity.

Although the word productivity may be relatively new to police jargon, the approach and methods have been embraced over the years by many progressive police officials by choice. Now they must be accepted by many others because of economic necessity. Productivity programs offer the police manager the opportunity to assure maximum utilization of tax dollars.

Since the key element in such programs is the development of measurements, the police field has the opportunity to introduce means of evaluating their department other than the UCR. It has long been recognized that there is no one method of judging a police agency. However, no alternative methods of evaluating police effectiveness have been developed because it was assumed that relevant measures were either not available or were too difficult to develop. The concept of productivity and its reliance on measurement might well be the stimuli that cause police officials to become better managers and to develop an analytical approach to their jobs.

As long as productivity programs are meaningful and allow for participation by all ranks, not only in their implementation but also in their formulation, such programs should not be feared by the rank and file. Naturally, the application of sound administrative techniques by management is still a key consideration in productivity improvement. With the caliber of individuals attracted to police work today, it behooves managers to be well prepared to assume such a responsibility or else their weaknesses might be called to their attention.

Since most productivity improvements are in the best interests of all members of a police department, such programs present the opportunity of integrating the individual and the organization, with the ultimate benefit accruing with the community.

1 Advisory Group on Productivity in Law Enforcement, *Opportunities for Improving Productivity in Police Services* (Washington, D.C.: National Commission on Productivity, 1973), pp. 2–3.

2 Gerald M. Caplan, in an address delivered at the Police Foundation's Executive Forum on Upgrading the Police, Washington, D.C., 13 April 1976.

3 Some of the material in this section is adapted from: Boise Center for Urban Research, *Enhancing Productivity in Local Government: A Primer for Citizen Interest Groups* (Boise, Idaho: Boise Center for Urban Research, 1975).

4 Dick Eardley, mayor of the city of Boise, Idaho, interdepartmental correspondence to all police department personnel, Boise, Idaho, 20 February 1976.

5 This section on Incentives has been excerpted from: National Commission on Productivity and Work Quality, *Employee Incentives To Improve State and Local Government Productivity* (Washington, D.C.: National Commission on Productivity and Work Quality, 1975), p. 9.

6 James P. Morgan, Jr., "Planning and Implementing a Productivity Program," in *Readings on Productivity in Policing*, ed. Joan L. Wolfle and John F. Heaphy (Washington, D.C.: Police Foundation, 1975), pp. 135–37.

7 Originally published in 1975 as a three volume Rand Corporation report, the latest version is: Peter W. Greenwood, Jan M. Chaiken, and Joan Petersilia, *The Criminal Investigation Process* (Lexington, Mass.: D. C. Heath & Company, 1977).

8 A 1975 study of the Raleigh, North Carolina, police department by the Public Safety Research Institute acknowledged the role of the beat officer and recommended that the recruit work his way up to police agent and his own beat by first serving in specialized units, such as the detective division, that do not require the broad conceptual skills of a beat officer. See: Public Safety Research Institute, *Management Study of the Raleigh Police Department* (St. Petersburg, Fla.: Public Safety Research Institute, 1976).

9 Morgan, "Planning and Implementing a Productivity Program," pp. 136–37.

10 Advisory Group on Productivity in Law Enforcement, *Opportunities for Improving Productivity in Police Services*.

11 Ibid., pp. 15–28.

12 U.S., Department of Justice, Law Enforcement Assistance Administration, *The Law Enforcement Assistance Administration: A Partnership for Crime Control* (Washington, D.C.: Law Enforcement Assistance Administration, [1976?]), p. 17.

13 John C. Houlihan, "Can We Still Afford the Traditional Public Safety System?" *Western Cities,* June 1976, p. 7.

14 Patrick Gallagher, Director, Public Safety Delivery Systems Project for the Institute for Local Self-Government, in an interview, 20 April 1976, Washington, D.C.

15 Brian N. Nagle, "An Alternative to Municipal Ownership of Police Facilities," *The Police Chief,* April 1976, p. 48.

16 See: Raymond D. Horton, *Municipal Labor Relations in New York City: Lessons of the Lindsay–Wagner Years* (New York: Praeger Publishers, 1973); Edward K. Hamilton, "Productivity: The New York City Approach," *Public Administration Review* 32 (November/December, 1972): 784–95; John M. Greiner, "Tying City Pay to Performance," *LMRS Special Report,* December 1974.

17 Sam Zagoria, "Productivity Bargaining," *Public Management,* July 1973, p. 16.

18 National Commission on Productivity and Work Quality, *Labor–Management Committees in the Public Sector* (Washington, D.C.: National Committee on Productivity and Work Quality, 1975), pp. 2–3. Labor–management relations are also discussed in Chapter 13 of the present book.

7 Patrol administration

Patrol is the essence of the police mission. The patrol force is the primary instrument through which the police mission is accomplished. The patrol officer is the most visible symbol of local government, and public attitudes toward government in general and toward the police in particular are often formed on the basis of the actions of the uniformed patrol officer.

Despite the fact that the patrol force is the most important, and usually the largest, element of any police organization, relatively little is known about patrol effectiveness and efficiency. Indeed, many aspects of police patrol have been taken for granted. For example, it was always assumed that there was a direct correlation between the number of uniformed officers patrolling a city and the level of crime. The Kansas City preventive patrol experiment, however, has caused many to question the validity of such assumptions.

Police patrol methods have evolved dramatically over the years. In earlier days, the foot patrol officer was a common sight to most residents of a city, but today the automobile has largely taken over as the dominant patrol method. Interestingly, there is renewed interest in foot patrol today. As the police patrol mission becomes more complex, and as the problems confronting patrol officers become more difficult, alternative methods and strategies are being developed. Now more than ever before, modern methods of operations analysis and planning are being applied to the patrol mission.

The role of the police patrol officer is undergoing change as well. Despite considerable rhetoric concerning the importance of the patrol force as the "thin blue line" guarding a peaceful society from the lawless elements that would prey upon it, the image and status of the patrol officer in many police agencies have suffered considerably due to technological advances and increased specialization. This situation, too, is receiving considerable attention.

In summary, the police patrol function is rapidly evolving into one of the most exciting fields of police endeavor. This chapter discusses some of the issues surrounding the patrol function and attempts to explain what is known, and what is not, about police patrol today.

The police patrol mission

The police in the United States have been delegated a number of important responsibilities, such as enforcing the law, investigating crimes, and preserving the public peace. These responsibilities are discharged largely through the efforts of the uniformed patrol force, supplemented by plainclothes investigators, radio dispatchers, record clerks, and a host of other staff and support personnel. Thus, the police mission in society is synonymous with the role of the patrol force.

A great deal of debate and controversy has surrounded the issue of the police role. The essence of the dilemma lies in the fact that the duties and responsibilities of the police are often in conflict with one another. There is little consensus among informed authorities concerning the proper and accepted definition of the police mission. As Goldstein has observed:

The police function is incredibly complex. The total range of police responsibilities is extraordinarily broad. Many tasks are so entangled that separation appears impossible. And the numerous conflicts among different aspects of the function cannot be easily reconciled. Anyone attempting to construct a workable definition of the police role will typically come away with old images shattered and with a new-found appreciation for the intricacies of police work.[1]

There are those who argue that if policing is ever to attain the status of a true profession, the police function must become more uniform and standardized, and the confusion surrounding the police role must somehow be eliminated. For example, some would argue that many of the service functions of the police should be transferred to other local government agencies, thereby freeing the police to concentrate on the more important and accepted tasks of crime prevention and law enforcement. In many communities, however, these service functions play an important role in the police service delivery system, and the manner in which they are performed has a great effect on citizen satisfaction with the police. It is difficult to predict the impact on police–community relations if these duties were arbitrarily eliminated from the police mission.

In light of present efforts to economize in government and to eliminate waste and duplication, it may be necessary for police administrators to examine the total range of services provided by the police and to determine which of those services, if any, can be either eliminated altogether or substantially modified in some way. Indeed, some police agencies have taken steps in this direction. In some departments, for example, police officers no longer respond to minor complaints of theft or vandalism. These calls are routed instead to trained operators who take the necessary information over the telephone, thus eliminating the need for response by a uniformed patrol officer. In still other departments, nonsworn personnel are being employed to handle many duties needing less training, experience, and authority, such as traffic control, parking enforcement, local code enforcement, and similar functions previously performed by uniformed patrol officers.

However, any radical change in the police mission should be undertaken only after serious consideration of its possible implications. This point was made very well in 1967 by the President's Commission on Law Enforcement and Administration of Justice:

In the absence of conclusive proof to the contrary, the Commission believes that the performance of many of the nonenforcement duties by the police helps them to control crime, and that radically changing the traditional police role would create more problems than it would solve—including the problem of finding other people to perform the indispensable services the police would be excused from performing.[2]

It must be remembered that the power of the police in any community is ultimately vested in the people of that community and is exercised through their legally elected and appointed representatives. Thus, the people themselves have the power to choose the form of policing they desire, the level of policing that they believe is best for them, and the style of police behavior that is most suited to their needs. The police must ultimately be a reflection of community values and expectations. Just as no two communities are exactly the same, no two styles of police operation can be identical.

In some communities, for example, the enforcement of traffic regulations may be regarded as a very important police function, while in others this may not be the case. Some cities may, through their elected and appointed representatives, place a heavy emphasis on maintenance of public order, or on the provision of community services, while in other cities these functions may be regarded as substantially less important than, say, crime prevention or law enforcement. Thus, what the police do, and the priorities they assign to their various responsibilities, depends ultimately on what the public expects of them.

This lack of uniformity in the police role should not be regarded as a failure to achieve professional status, but rather as a recognition of the fundamental principle of community-oriented policing. What is needed is not a uniform definition of the police role that will apply equally to all communities, but rather the development and application of uniform standards of conduct by which the police mission is performed.

Important issues in police patrol

The police patrol function can no longer be taken for granted. Increased public concern about the economy and efficiency of governmental services, coupled with a growing demand for the police to be more responsive to sensitive community issues, makes it more important than ever before that all police functions, including patrol, be subjected to greater scrutiny and analysis in order to maximize their impact and effectiveness. A number of crucial issues surrounding the police patrol function must be considered when evaluating the overall performance of patrol efforts. Among them are the value of preventive patrol, active versus passive patrol, the use of field interviews, and police response time.

The value of preventive patrol

One of the greatest controversies surrounding the police patrol function in recent years concerns the value of routine preventive patrol. It has traditionally been assumed that criminal conduct can be deterred through the mobilization of a highly visible uniformed patrol force and a prevailing sense of police "omnipresence." This is the underlying principle of preventive patrol.

Police administrators in years past have justified increases in police staffing on the basis of rising crime rates, believing that increased police visibility would have a suppressant effect on criminal activity. The validity of this assumption was not challenged until a major study designed to evaluate the effectiveness of routine preventive patrol was conducted in the Kansas City, Missouri, police department under the auspices of the Police Foundation.

The Kansas City preventive patrol experiment was intended to determine whether varying levels of patrol intensity would produce differences in criminal activity, in citizen satisfaction with the police, and in perceptions of safety and security. The study was conducted over a period of twelve months (October 1972 to September 1973) and involved two experimental areas and one control area. In one experimental area (proactive), the level of preventive patrol was increased significantly beyond normal levels, while in another experimental area (reactive), routine patrol was discontinued altogether. In the control area, preventive patrol remained unchanged.[3] The study produced some interesting and surprising findings.

Among other things, the Kansas City study revealed that neither the level of criminal activity nor citizens' satisfaction with the police was significantly affected by variations in patrol activity. As might be expected, the study results met with mixed reactions. Some persons criticized the study on methodological grounds and implored public officials to place no credence in the implications of the study's conclusions.[4]

Notwithstanding its apparent imperfections, the Kansas City preventive patrol experiment marks a significant contribution to the field of police administration. It was, for example, the first time that actual police operations had been critically examined under carefully controlled conditions. In addition, it suggested that variations in the level of police patrol—but not the elimination of patrol altogether—can be undertaken without serious implications. More important, the study stimulated an interest in the development of alternative patrol strategies, an interest that continues today.

While the Kansas City preventive patrol experiment may have raised many more questions than it answered, its most important contribution was a realization that routine, undirected, random patrol is not a sufficient deterrent to crime and is not a productive use of patrol resources.

Active versus passive patrol

If routine preventive patrol is not a deterrent to crime, then what is? There are no clear-cut answers to this question, but evidence suggests that highly proactive patrol behavior may have a direct impact on certain types of serious crimes. In highly proactive patrol, officers make a maximum number of citizen contacts and situational interventions. In passive patrol, on the other hand, the patrol officer simply roves from one part of the beat to another, waiting to be directed to calls by the police dispatcher. Proactive patrol officers, for example, maximize their available patrol time by making a high number of pedestrian and vehicle checks, by inspecting premises on their beats for possible criminal attack, and by employing both low-visibility and high-visibility surveillance techniques in selected areas.

Researchers for the Urban Institute completed a study for the National Institute of Law Enforcement and Criminal Justice in which they examined the effect of police practices on robbery rates in some thirty-five large American cities.[5] Entitled *The Effect of the Police on Crime,* the report concluded that an active patrol strategy can affect the rate of robbery simply by increasing the probability of arrest. The authors of the report went on to say that if the police are known to actively stop suspicious persons for field checks, or if they have a reputation for issuing a large number of traffic citations or warnings, or if they have a high rate of visibility in high crime areas, criminals may conclude that their chances for success in committing robbery are diminished. This perception, according to the authors of the report, will have the effect of decreasing crime rates.

The conclusion to be drawn from this report is that the number of patrol officers assigned to an area is probably less important than what those officers do while on patrol. Officers who simply patrol their areas and take little affirmative action to thwart crime probably have very little deterrent value. On the other hand, officers who maximize their available patrol time as suggested above are making a much more valuable contribution to the attack on crime.

It should be noted, however, that proactive patrol is not intended to include intimidation or harassment of law-abiding citizens. Proactive patrol should be conducted in a carefully planned, rather than an indiscriminate, fashion. Officers who employ proactive patrol tactics indiscriminately, or who do so only as a means of harassment or intimidation, may deter crime at the cost of injuring police–community relations. While proactive patrol may be a valuable crime deterrent, it must be conducted in a reasonable and intelligent manner.

The use of field interviews

An excellent example of a proactive patrol tactic is the field interview, or field interrogation (FI), as it is sometimes called. The field interview is a contact initiated by a patrol officer who stops and questions a person the officer has reason to believe has committed, or may be about to commit, a crime. The field interview is a valuable investigative and deterrent tool. For investigative purposes, the field interview report (FIR) may lead investigators to the solution of one or more crimes. As a patrol tactic, the field interview can, if properly conducted, serve as a deterrent to those who may be contemplating some kind of criminal action.

Since field interviews are usually conducted in the absence of any clear-cut evidence of criminal conduct, it is important that the police department have policies indicating under what circumstances, and in what manner, field interviews should be conducted. It is important also that police administrators make it clear to their personnel that field interviews are not to be conducted as a method of harassment or intimidation. In addition, field interviews should be conducted in a professional and courteous manner.

The need for clear, concise policy guidelines concerning field interviews was underscored in Washington, D.C., where a federal judge told District police officers that they can no longer arbitrarily stop persons on the street and question them unless an officer has reason to believe that the individual is involved in, or may have committed, a criminal act. If this ruling is eventually applied to all police agencies, it would mean that a police officer must be able to show some justification beyond mere "suspicious behavior" before initiating a field contact.[6] This same principle, it would seem, could be applied to police stopping motorists in the absence of some clear violation of the law.

Until recently, there was very little hard evidence concerning the utility of field interviews. In 1973, however, the Police Foundation awarded a grant to the San Diego police department to conduct an experiment to test the value of the field interview. The research design called for three levels of field interviewing. In a control area, field interviews were conducted as before. In a second area, field interviews were conducted only by officers given special training in interview techniques. This training focused on methods of reducing conflict between the patrol officer and the person being interviewed. In a third area, field interviews were suspended for the nine-month study period.[7]

Several important findings emerged from the study. First, the suspension of field interviews was found to be associated with an increase in the frequency of suppressible crimes, including robbery, assault, burglary, and auto theft. Second, the frequency of suppressible crimes did not change substantially in those areas in which field interviews were continued. Third, persons subjected to field interviews reacted more favorably when interviewed by officers who had received special training in field interview techniques.

The key findings that emerge from this study are that (1) an active policy of field interviews, conducted under carefully controlled conditions, can have a positive impact on crime suppression; and (2) patrol officers should be given special training in conducting field interviews.

Police response time

It has long been assumed by police authorities that a rapid response by the police to a citizen's call for service was important, not only in terms of apprehending a suspect involved in the commission of a crime, but also in assuring citizen satisfaction with the police. Consequently, a great deal of effort has been devoted to providing prompt police response to calls for service, and police response time continues to serve as an indication of individual and organizational performance. Like many other aspects of policing, the real value of rapid response has only recently been subjected to critical analysis.

As a by-product of the Kansas City preventive patrol experiment, researchers collected data on police response times and related variables. Although the study of response time was secondary to the central issue of the study, an examination of the data was considered worthwhile in view of the scarcity of scientific information concerning police response time and its effect.

An analysis of the data generated during the study produced several interesting findings, including the fact that response time was not a significant predictor of the outcome of an encounter, of citizen satisfaction, or of attitudes toward the police in general. In addition, it was discovered that police assurances of rapid response may lead to public dissatisfaction if response is slow. On the other hand, in nonemergency cases, if citizens are told to expect a delayed police response, they will be satisfied with such a response.[8]

These findings suggest the need for police agencies to reevaluate their methods of handling and dispatching calls for service and to establish call priorities when the volume of calls exceeds police response capability. For example, it may be desirable to establish three or more call priority classifications, such as the following:[9]

Priority 1: Time critical; immediate response required.

Priority 2: Time not critical; delayed response permitted.

Priority 3: Mobile response not required; call deferred.

In addition, when such priority classifications are employed, it is important at the outset that citizens be advised of the probable response time of the patrol unit. It is only when they are led to expect an immediate patrol response and do not receive it that citizens become dissatisfied.

Maximizing patrol resources

In the face of shrinking tax resources and increased demands for police service, police administrators must be constantly alert for ways to maximize the limited resources available to them. This can be done in several ways. One is through the careful planning and deployment of patrol personnel. Another is through the use of alternative personnel resources, such as community service officers (CSOs) and police reserves. The use of civilians in police work is increasing rapidly. Civilian personnel represent between 25 and 35 percent of the total authorized strength of some police agencies. In addition to the traditional duties of record keeping and dispatching, civilian personnel are being used in key staff positions, such as personnel and training, planning and research, crime scene investigation, and evidence and property control. In some departments, for example, nonsworn personnel are used as investigative aides who assist detectives in such routine duties as interviewing suspects and victims, collecting physical evidence, and preparing cases for prosecution.

Community service officers, as they are sometimes called, are usually young persons between the ages of eighteen and twenty-one who are seeking a career in police work and who attend college in conjunction with their police duties. CSOs usually handle a variety of functions that would otherwise occupy a great deal of a patrol officer's time. These functions may include, for example, parking and local ordinance enforcement, traffic control, bicycle licensing, and routine public service complaints. CSOs can be a valuable supplement to the regular patrol force. In Worcester, Massachusetts, for example, it was reported that up to 40 percent of all calls for service were handled by such personnel.[10]

Another valuable supplement to the regular patrol force is the police reserve program. Some police agencies make good use of reserve programs, but others do not. The principal objection to reserves is that they are not capable, in terms of initial training or individual qualifications, of performing the same duties as patrol officers. In addition, their availability is rather limited, since they perform as reserve officers in conjunction with full-time jobs.

A properly organized and well-trained reserve force, however, can substantially increase the effectiveness of patrol operations. Several conditions should be placed on the reserve program. First, the persons selected to participate in the program must be carefully screened and evaluated in terms of mental and emotional maturity. While it is not necessary that reserve officers have the same qualifications as regular officers, minimum standards should be established for their selection.

Second, a regular program of pre-service and in-service training for reserve personnel must be established. In California, for example, there is a three-stage reserve training program, with each level of training corresponding to the types of duties the reserve officer may perform. In addition, regular in-service training sessions, usually under the direction of the department training officer, should be scheduled, and participation in such sessions should be a requirement of the program.

Finally, the duties reserve officers are allowed to perform should be carefully set out in written policy statements. The reserve program should be coordinated by a senior staff member, usually the commander of the patrol force or a subordinate officer. Although police reserves can never take the place of regular officers, they can, if properly managed and controlled, provide a valuable supplement to the regular patrol force.

Improving patrol efficiency

When police patrol is conducted in a strictly random fashion, with little thought given to identifying specific objectives or to measuring patrol effectiveness, it can be very wasteful and inefficient. There are, however, several steps that can be taken to reduce waste and to improve the efficiency of patrol operations. For the most part, these steps can be taken at any level (e.g., squad, district, precinct) in the patrol organization. Moreover, they can be applied in small forces as well as large ones.

Implementation of these measures does not require a great deal of sophistication, but it should not be undertaken hastily or without sufficient planning. In addition, an attempt should be made to collect baseline data before implementation in order that the real value and impact of the measures may be determined by comparison with data collected later. For example, if smaller patrol cars are utilized, such data as operating costs, roadability, and repair frequency should be recorded and compared with the same information for larger vehicles. Following is a description of efficiency measures that have been successfully implemented in several police agencies.

Reduced vehicle/engine size

A number of police agencies in the country have experimented quite successfully with utilizing smaller cars and/or engine sizes for patrol and administrative purposes. The Los Angeles sheriff's department has conducted a series of exhaustive tests on various types and sizes of police cars and has made the results of its tests available to law enforcement agencies.[11]

Police agencies that have adopted smaller cars for police patrol use have reported a number of encouraging results, including reduced operating costs, greater officer satisfaction, and good vehicle performance. With fuel costs rising steadily, these fuel-efficient cars can have a very favorable impact on police department budgets.

Any police agency considering a conversion to smaller cars should first attempt to collect detailed information on the cost and performance of existing fleet vehicles for comparison purposes. In addition, the agency should consider the limitations that smaller cars impose in terms of storing auxiliary equipment, such as accident investigation gear, fire extinguishers, protective vests, and so forth. Some departments have had difficulty finding adequate storage space in smaller cars, thus limiting their utility.

In addition, the safety and comfort of the individual patrol officer must be considered. While many small cars will easily accommodate officers of considerable bulk and height, others may not. If possible, several different models should be obtained on loan, and as many officers as possible should be allowed to drive them for the purpose of comparing their overall comfort and suitability.

Conversion to alternative fuels

A few police departments have converted their patrol fleets to butane fuel as an alternative to gasoline. While overall fuel consumption is somewhat higher for butane, the cost per gallon is considerably less. Such factors as overall performance and engine maintenance costs have not yet been determined. In the future, however, it can be expected that greater attention will be given to finding alternative fuel sources for motorized fleets at all levels of government.

Combination automobile/foot patrol

Despite the fact that a majority of police agencies rely almost exclusively on automobile patrol, the use of foot patrol in combination with automobile patrol is being employed successfully in many departments. There are several reasons for employing foot patrol in conjunction with automobile patrol.

First, police administrators recognize that exclusive reliance on automobile patrol tends to isolate the patrol officer, both physically and emotionally, from the public. This isolation has been identified as a major stumbling block in efforts to foster favorable police–community relations. An officer on foot patrol is able to make many more favorable citizen contacts and come to grips much better with the problems of the citizens on his or her beat.

Second, despite the many obvious advantages of automobile patrol, it inhibits the ability of officers to detect subtle signs of criminal activity. The scrape of metal against wood, a furtive movement in the darkened shadows of a doorway, the creaking of a door or window being forced open—all are difficult to detect by a patrol officer driving by a location at twenty-five or thirty miles an hour. They are much easier to detect by an officer who is approaching on foot and whose senses are alerted to such telltale indicators.

Finally, routine undirected automobile patrol can be a waste of fuel and should be curtailed as much as possible. Some police agencies, for example, have established written procedures that call for officers to stop and park their vehicles at conspicuous locations periodically during each shift and to patrol on foot for brief periods of time. This can be particularly effective in areas where automobile patrol is not possible, such as shopping centers, downtown malls, parks and playgrounds, and similar areas.

Other departments have established policies that limit the number of miles a patrol officer should log each shift. Of course, any such attempt to limit patrol mileage should take several things into consideration, including the size and population density of the patrol beat, the number of calls for service received, and the level of criminal activity. Nevertheless, the concept of limiting patrol mileage is a good management tool and should be carefully considered.

Efficient patrol beat design

The primary purpose of assigning members of the patrol force to individual patrol beats or sectors is to equalize workload. A secondary purpose is to provide uniform patrol coverage throughout the entire community. An additional factor, not always considered, is the increased efficiency resulting from properly designed patrol beats. Obviously, it is not as efficient to drive fifteen miles to answer a call as it is to drive only three. In rural areas, such as those patrolled by county sheriff's departments, distances may be even greater.

In cities, however, it is necessary that patrol beats be designed to minimize as much as possible the distance a patrol officer must travel from one call to the next. Periodic analyses should be conducted to measure average response times and distances traveled in responding to calls for service in all patrol beats in order to determine whether beat boundaries should be adjusted. In addition, it may be necessary to have several beat plans to correspond with varying patrol staffing levels as well as a different beat plan for each patrol shift, since patrol activity levels often vary with the time of day.

One-officer versus two-officer patrol units

One question that continues to plague police executives in determining the most effective and efficient method of patrol deployment is whether to use one-officer or two-officer patrol units. In many cities, of course, limited resources demand that single-officer units be used almost exclusively. In large cities, however, particularly those with serious crime problems and those in which officer safety is a daily problem, two-officer patrol units are used much more frequently.

The arguments for and against two-officer units are both practical and emotional. On the practical side, there is no question that two-officer patrol units are less economical than single-officer units. From an emotional point of view, however, proponents of two-officer units argue that reasons of officer safety and the ability to respond with sufficient force to critical situations dictate in favor of two-officer units.

For many years prominent police authorities have argued in favor of single-officer patrol units simply on the basis of overall efficiency. It is obvious that nearly twice as many single-officer units as two-officer units can be fielded, thus increasing the overall mobility and visibility of the patrol force. In addition, a great many calls require the presence of only one officer. Calls that require more than one officer, such as alarms or crimes in progress, can be handled just as effectively by assigning two or more single-officer cars. Finally, a single officer is often much more attentive than two officers in the same patrol vehicle.

Until recently, however, little empirical evidence existed to demonstrate the validity of the arguments for and against single-officer patrol units. In 1975 the Police Foundation's Evaluation Advisory Group approved funding for a study of two-officer and one-officer patrol units in San Diego, California. The study involved the deployment and evaluation of patrol units in four experimental groups:

Group I: One-officer units deployed in areas previously served by one-officer units.

Group II: One-officer units used in areas previously patrolled by two-officer units.

Group III: Two-officer units deployed in areas previously patrolled by one-officer units.

Group IV: Two-officer units deployed in areas previously patrolled by two-officer units.

This deployment plan allowed for several important comparisons. For example, a comparison of Groups I and III was used to determine differences in performance between one-officer and two-officer units in areas of the city defined as low-risk areas, while comparison of Groups II and IV determined whether there were any significant differences in areas of the city defined as high-risk areas.

Several measures were used to compare the outcomes of the one-officer and two-officer patrol methods, including:

1. Unit performance: the type, quality, and quantity of services performed
2. Unit efficiency: The unit time and cost associated with comparable levels of performance
3. Officer safety: The rates of assaults on officers, resisting arrest situations,

vehicle accidents, and officer injuries resulting from comparable levels of unit exposure

4. Officer attitudes: The preferences and opinions of officers assigned to single units and two-officer cars.

The findings of the study indicated that the overall performance of patrol units in terms of frequency and types of calls for service and officer-initiated activity were about equal for single-officer and two-officer units. Interestingly, calls serviced primarily by one-officer units were more likely to result in arrests and formal crime reports than those serviced by two-officer units. In addition, there were fewer citizen complaints resulting from incidents handled by single-officer units than from those handled by two-officer units.[12]

Despite the fact that one-officer units required more backup support, the overall efficiency of these units clearly exceeded that of two-officer units. One reason was that two-officer units were frequently assigned to calls that could have been handled by single-officer units. In addition, officers reported that some 50 percent of the backup assistance they received on calls was not necessary.

On the issue of officer safety, one-officer units were shown to have an advantage over two-officer units. With an equivalent amount of estimated exposure, one-officer units encountered fewer situations involving resisting arrest and an equal number of situations involving assaults on officers and injuries sustained by officers. Single-officer units that had a lower estimated exposure to potential hazards also had significantly fewer assaults on officers and fewer situations in which suspects resisted arrest.

Overall, the San Diego study concluded that two-officer patrol units could not be justified on the basis of cost, performance, or safety in San Diego. The study pointed out also that eighteen one-officer units could be fielded for the same approximate cost of ten two-officer units, thus increasing the staffing and deployment advantages of one-officer units. While the results of the San Diego study may not be applicable to all communities, it is clear that exclusive reliance on two-officer patrol units is, in many cases, not warranted and substantially decreases patrol efficiency.

Evaluating patrol performance

Increased productivity has become a common goal of police and other public agencies in recent years (see Chapter 6). Toward this goal, definite steps have been taken to define productivity and to develop some means for measuring it. Measuring the productivity of police patrol is a difficult task, however, since the ultimate goal of preventive patrol is the absence of crime, and it is difficult to measure a nonevent. In addition, other variables, such as the economy, also affect the incidence of crime.

Nevertheless, it is important that some means be used to measure the overall performance of the patrol force and of individual officers. For example, one key indicator of patrol effort is the number of officer-initiated contacts, such as vehicle checks, pedestrian checks, and premise inspections recorded by patrol officers. Anyone interested in evaluating patrol performance would want to know, for every unit of effort (e.g., patrol hour), how many police-initiated activities were recorded. As pointed out earlier in this chapter, such activities may have an inhibiting effect on specific types of criminal activity.

Another good indication of patrol performance is the amount of time devoted to particular functions or types of activities. For example, it would be useful to know how much time during a given shift, day, or week is devoted to crime-related functions, public service, and administrative duties. If this information is available, it is relatively simple to determine, based on departmental averages, which officers are the "low" and "high" producers on a particular shift or watch.

Each police agency should have an information system capable of determining the performance of the patrol force and of individual officers in key areas. The accompanying figure shows typical performance indicators that can be used for this purpose. As those examples show, there is no single or best measure of patrol performance. In addition, what may be considered a good measure of patrol performance in one department may be entirely unsuitable in another. Whatever measures are used, however, it is important that some means be devised to gauge patrol performance and to monitor it closely. Without this capability, it is impossible to know with any degree of certainty whether the patrol force is performing effectively and whether it is accomplishing its intended purpose.

Performance indicators for police patrol.		
Response time indicators	Sum of response time for all calls ÷ total calls Sum of response times for emergency calls ÷ number of emergency calls Sum of response times for nonemergency calls ÷ number of nonemergency calls	
Consumed time indicators	Patrol hours devoted to calls ÷ total calls handled Patrol hours devoted to X-type calls ÷ total X-type calls handled	
Directed patrol indicators	Patrol hours committed to directed patrol ÷ total patrol hours Directed patrol incidents ÷ total patrol incidents	
Enforcement Indicators	Felony arrests by patrol (by type) ÷ total felony arrests (by type) Misdemeanor arrests by patrol (by type) ÷ total misdemeanor arrests (by type) "On view" arrests (by type) ÷ total arrests (by type)	
Effectiveness indicators	Felony arrests surviving first screening ÷ total felony arrests Misdemeanor arrests resulting in conviction ÷ total misdemeanor arrests	

Improving the status of police patrol

One of the greatest challenges facing the police administrator is improving the status and image of the patrol officer. Despite the fact that police executives are often heard to say that the patrol officer is the most important member of the police organization, this is not always the case.

Over the years, a number of things have occurred to diminish the status of the police patrol officer. For example, the increasing reliance on specialists for criminal investigation, traffic enforcement, community relations, and crime prevention has served to narrow the duties and responsibilities of the patrol officer. In some communities, patrol officers are expected merely to patrol their assigned area, handle routine calls for service, and refer more serious or complex incidents to specialists.

In addition, very few police agencies offer any kind of incentive for officers to remain in patrol. Instead, they provide incentives, such as increased salaries or more attractive duty schedules, for officers assigned to specialist positions. Police officers who choose to remain in patrol and in nonsupervisory positions are often regarded as lacking motivation and are often looked down upon by their superior officers.

In recent years, however, there has emerged a trend toward greater recognition of the patrol function, and attempts have been made to increase the status and prestige of patrol personnel. This has come about in several ways. Some departments, for example, have begun to stress the involvement of the patrol officer in community relations, crime prevention, and other areas once reserved for specialists. In addition, the role of the patrol officer in conducting preliminary and follow-up investigations has been expanded. In some departments, for example, the patrol officer is expected to carry an investigation through to its logical conclusion rather than merely taking the initial report and turning the case over to an investigator. Thus, the concept of the patrol officer as a generalist, trained and equipped to handle a variety of problems and to perform more functions than before, has contributed to an expansion of patrol responsibilities and increased officer job satisfaction.

Also, a number of police agencies have begun to implement career development programs, different rank structures, new assignment policies, and various kinds of incentive plans that allow patrol officers to advance their careers and financial rewards without relying on the traditional means of promotion in rank. These new systems recognize that a patrol officer should be able to develop professionally without leaving patrol and that a failure to advance through promotion is not necessarily an indication of poor performance.

If patrol officers are to be expected to perform ably the difficult tasks assigned to them, they must receive the total support of police administrators. They must be given the necessary training and equipment to do the job expected of them, and they must be given the latitude to do the job in the manner they consider best. Finally, they must be given due recognition for their efforts in order to convince them of their importance in the police organization.

The Integrated Criminal Apprehension Program

The Integrated Criminal Apprehension Program (ICAP) was developed by the Law Enforcement Assistance Administration in the late 1970s on the basis of a series of projects that demonstrated the importance of crime analysis and practical planning techniques in the allocation and deployment of police patrol forces. Crime analysis is the key concept in the ICAP methodology. Simply stated, crime analysis is the collection, analysis, and dissemination of information concerning crime and offender traits for the purpose of better deployment of the patrol force. In addition to crime analysis, ICAP incorporates the following concepts:

1. Proportional scheduling and deployment of the patrol force on the basis of service demands
2. Call screening techniques by which nonessential service calls are diverted to other response methods
3. Increased emphasis on follow-up investigation by patrol officers as opposed to referring all cases to detectives for investigation
4. Use of solvability factors (pertinent bits of investigative information) for the purpose of determining systematically which cases will be referred for follow-up investigation and which ones will be administratively closed.

The key word in ICAP is *integrated,* since ICAP provides a logical structure and process for providing police services as opposed to the rather fragmented approach common in many police agencies today. ICAP is fully operational in some fifty police agencies in the United States; and some states, such as California, have developed state programs based on the ICAP model.

The basic ingredients of the ICAP concept—crime analysis, proportional scheduling of the patrol force, and increased emphasis on the investigative skills of patrol officers—are not new or revolutionary, but when incorporated into a total, integrated plan of action they represent a logical and systematic approach to the improved delivery of police services. The ICAP concept is an excellent example of the contribution that careful study and analysis can make in the continuing effort to improve the efficiency and effectiveness of police operations.

Community-oriented policing

It has become obvious in recent years that if police operations are to be successful, they must be sensitive to community needs and expectations. The prevention of crime is a good example of one major police objective that requires a strong partnership between the police and the public. It has long been recognized that the police, without strong support and involvement from community elements, can do little to control crime. Thus, there is an increasing emphasis today on the development of programs to bring police operations closer to the mainstream of community affairs.

Team policing, community relations and community crime prevention programs, and similar methods have been developed for this purpose. Other police departments have tried still different approaches. The Santa Ana, California, police department attempted to develop a community-oriented style of policing in a somewhat unusual manner. In 1974 the Santa Ana city council established a Citizens' Crime Prevention Commission to examine the city's crime problem and offer recommendations for a community-based strategy to reduce crime. The commission met on a regular basis with police representatives and city officials for the purpose of gaining a better understanding of the scope and complexity of the crime problem and the efforts of the police department to combat crime.[13]

The commission also reviewed large quantities of statistical data provided by the police department, studied various reference materials, visited nearby police agencies, and sought input from various community groups. After several weeks of intensive study, the commission prepared its final report to the city council, recommending a number of long-term and short-range solutions, including the following:

1. An increase in the authorized strength of the police department
2. The adoption of a community-wide team policing program
3. The establishment of a youth services unit
4. A strengthening of the department's research and planning capability
5. The adoption of a comprehensive police–community relations program.

The Santa Ana experience is but one example of what can be achieved when police officials and community leaders join forces to attack common problems. Furthermore, this approach demonstrates an acknowledgment that policing must be sensitive and responsive to local community interests. Chief Ray Davis of the Santa Ana police department stressed the underlying principle of the commission's work in these words:

A community evaluation of . . . the Santa Ana Police Department is extremely important. It does not guarantee success, but without community support, community evaluation, and community input we do invite failure. We must establish standards and goals to enable the City and its citizens to know where the Police Department is heading, what it is trying to achieve, and what—in fact—is being achieved.[14]

The example set by the Santa Ana police department is a good model for other law enforcement agencies facing similar problems. (Police–community relations are discussed further in Chapter 11.)

Patrol staffing and allocation

Two problems that continually plague police administrators are (1) determining the proper size of the patrol force and (2) allocating the patrol force in the most effective manner. With regard to the first problem, there are no universal standards that can be employed to determine a proper staffing level. The second problem is less complicated. Both problems, however, need to be given serious consideration by police administrators if they hope to achieve optimum patrol effectiveness and efficiency.

Determining staffing requirements

When determining the optimum size of the patrol force, consideration must be given to the duties the patrol force is expected to perform. Basically, these duties can be described as follows: (1) responding to calls for service; (2) conducting preventive patrol; and (3) performing miscellaneous administrative tasks.

Of these three broad classifications, the first and the third can usually be measured reliably through the use of radio logs, dispatch cards, or patrol activity logs of some type. Through these logs, for example, it is usually possible to determine on an annual basis what portion of an officer's time is devoted to responding to calls for service and performing administrative duties. The balance of an officer's time can then be said to be devoted to preventive patrol.

The amount of time that should be devoted to each of these three broad areas is largely a policy decision that should be made locally, based on past experience. As a general rule, it has been stated that "uncommitted" patrol time should range between 25 and 35 percent of the total time of the patrol force. The remaining 65 to 75 percent, then, can be apportioned between responding to calls for service and performing administrative duties, such as servicing the patrol unit, transporting prisoners, and so forth.

In determining how much time should be allocated to responding to calls for service, it is necessary to consider the time needed to respond to the initial call, plus any additional time required for follow-up investigation, report preparation, prisoner processing, and related duties. It should be noted, however, that when determining patrol staffing requirements, only actual calls for service, and not officer-initiated incidents, should be counted. The reason is that officer-initiated incidents are a direct result of patrol staffing, while calls for service are independent of staffing levels.

Once the total required patrol time has been determined, it is necessary to convert this to patrol positions on the basis of the average number of days or hours a patrol officer can be expected to work in a given year. This can be calculated by reviewing a sample of personnel time sheets for a one-year period. For example, after accounting for time lost due to vacations, holidays, training, and other absences, it may be found that the average patrol officer can be expected to work 1,890 hours during a twelve-month period. This figure can then be divided into the total number of patrol hours required to provide the necessary staffing level.

Assume that a police agency determined on the basis of past experience that a patrol officer's time should hypothetically be allocated as follows:

1. One-third responding to calls for service
2. One-third performing preventive patrol
3. One-third performing administrative duties.

Hypothetical incident levels and time requirements.

Activity	Number of incidents	Average time per incident (hours)	Total required time (hours)
Investigation of crimes and arrests	8,350	1.5	12,525
Investigation of traffic accidents	1,950	1.0	1,950
Miscellaneous services	6,330	0.5	3,165
Total	16,630	. . .	17,640

Assume further that analysis of patrol activities for a twelve-month period had indicated incident levels as shown in the accompanying table.

In order to provide additional time for preventive patrol and handling administrative duties, the total required time (17,640 hours) must be multiplied by 3, resulting in a total of 52,920 hours required to provide an adequate patrol staffing level. This figure is then divided by the number of hours a single officer can be expected to work in a year (1,890) to produce the actual number of personnel that must be assigned to the patrol force: 28.

It must be emphasized that the figures in this example are merely hypothetical and are not intended to represent actual time estimates. Actual figures and time allocations will vary from one department to the next. The most important requirement, however, is the ability to collect and analyze patrol activity data in order that these calculations can be made.

Patrol force distribution

Once an acceptable patrol staffing level has been determined, it is necessary to devise a plan that will provide for the temporal and geographic distribution of the patrol force. Once again, reliable activity data are needed as a basis for these decisions.

Using the figure of 28 patrol officers, again assume that a department employs three eight-hour shifts that run from 8:00 A.M. to 4:00 P.M., 4:00 P.M. to 12:00 midnight, and 12:00 midnight to 8:00 A.M. Assume that an analysis of patrol incident data reveals the following distribution of activities in each of these three shifts:

1. 8:00 A.M. to 4:00 P.M.: 32 percent
2. 4:00 P.M. to 12:00 midnight: 43 percent
3. 12:00 midnight to 8:00 A.M.: 25 percent.

Applying these percentages to the patrol staffing level would indicate a desired staffing of nine officers from 8:00 A.M. to 4:00 P.M., twelve officers from 4:00 P.M. to 12:00 midnight, and seven officers from 12:00 midnight to 8:00 A.M. In most cases, of course, the percentages will not come out as precisely as in this example, but the principle is the same. In addition, unusual variations in patrol workload may indicate the need for an overlap or power shift during periods when patrol activity is unusually heavy.

Once the desired distribution of the patrol force to each shift has been determined, it is necessary to devise a work schedule that will accommodate variations in patrol workload by day of the week. The simplest method for this purpose is the five-day, eight-hour work schedule, with fixed days off. Using this method, it is relatively easy to stagger individual shift and days-off assignments to correspond with typical fluctuations in workload from day to day. By using five-day, eight-hour shifts, the following work schedule might be developed based on the shift assignments outlined above. The first figure under each day indicates the number of officers on duty and the second figure is the number off duty:

Shift	Sun.	Mon.	Tues.	Wed.	Thurs.	Fri.	Sat.
12 midnight–8:00 A.M.	4–3	5–2	6–1	5–2	4–3	5–2	6–1
8:00 A.M.–4:00 P.M.	6–3	7–2	6–3	6–3	6–3	7–2	7–2
4:00 P.M.–12 midnight	8–4	9–3	9–3	9–3	8–4	8–4	9–3
Total	18–10	21–7	21–7	20–8	18–10	20–8	22–6

It can be seen that the number of officers on duty varies on each shift from day to day. While it will not be possible in all cases to match exactly the number of patrol personnel on duty with workload levels, it is possible to schedule the patrol force in a manner that closely approximates workload fluctuations.[15]

Developing patrol strategies

It should be obvious by now that a great deal of planning and thought should go into developing patrol methods and strategies. Patrol is too important a function to be simply taken for granted. Unfortunately, little is known about the most effective patrol strategies to employ in specific instances, but our knowledge of the subject is expanding rapidly. In recent years several alternative patrol methods, such as split-force patrol, directed deterrent patrol, and decoy patrol have been developed and successfully implemented in several police agencies. Of these alternative methods, the two that appear to be the most promising for the small and medium-sized police departments are directed deterrent patrol and split-force patrol.

Directed deterrent patrol

The directed deterrent patrol (DDP) concept was developed and implemented in the police department in New Haven, Connecticut (population 126,100), in 1974 and 1975 under a grant from the Law Enforcement Assistance Administration.[16] Unlike traditional preventive patrol, which is largely random and unplanned, DDP directs limited patrol resources to those places and times at which deterrent runs (called D-runs) can have the greatest impact on an identified crime problem.

For planning purposes, the city of New Haven is divided into twenty-one neighborhoods, and D-run planning and evaluation are conducted on a neighborhood rather than a citywide basis. The selection of target crimes is limited to those that can most likely be deterred by visible patrol activities. Selected target crimes may vary by season and by neighborhood characteristics. Those that are commonly targeted for D-runs are commercial and residential burglary, vandalism, auto theft, purse snatching, and theft from auto.

Patrol officers are provided with written instructions on deterrent patrol strategies for each deterrent patrol area in the city. Using these instructions as a guideline, officers may choose the tactics they deem appropriate. Specific information contained in biweekly crime analysis summaries details current information for appropriate D-run areas.

The instructions for D-runs, the biweekly crime analysis summaries, and the scheduling of D-runs to be dispatched are prepared by the crime analysis unit on the basis of crime incident analysis. The crime analysis unit acts on information contained in case incident reports completed by field personnel and subsequent information contained in the automated Case Incident Reporting System (CIRS).

The directed deterrent patrol program has met with a great deal of success in New Haven and has since been implemented in the New Castle, Delaware, Department of Public Safety. Directed deterrent patrol is but one example of the manner in which advanced planning techniques, crime analysis, and crime prevention technology can be applied in an integrated approach to the deterrence of criminal activity. While directed deterrent patrol may not be the ultimate solution to the crime problem, it offers substantial advantages over traditional patrol methods.

Split-force patrol

The concept of split-force patrol is based on the assumption that a patrol officer's time is divided into two distinct functions, responding to calls for service and performing preventive patrol, and that these functions can be performed more effectively if carried out by two separate elements of the patrol force. By splitting the patrol force into two elements, this method allows each one to concentrate primarily on one function or the other.

It is not uncommon is some police agencies for some patrol officers to do a very superficial job of handling a citizen's complaint or conducting a routine investigation because of the pressure to resume normal preventive patrol duties. On the other hand, officers in some departments have difficulty conducting thorough preventive patrol efforts because of periodic interruptions by calls for service. As a result, neither function can be performed satisfactorily. It is the intent of the split-force patrol method to allow sufficient time for both of these functions to be performed well.

The split-force patrol concept was implemented in the Wilmington, Delaware, Bureau of Police in 1975–76 under a grant from the National Institute of Law Enforcement and Criminal Justice. In Wilmington, the patrol force was divided into two basic elements. The basic patrol force (BPF) was assigned to handle calls for service, while the structured patrol force (SPF) was assigned to carry out carefully designed preventive patrol activities. Twenty-seven patrol units were assigned to the BPF, and sixteen to the SPF. BPF units were assigned to duty periods consistent with service demands, with varying numbers of units on duty during each of six four-hour periods. The sixteen SPF units were assigned to either the 10:00 A.M. to 6:00 P.M. period (seven units) or the 6:00 P.M. to 2:00 A.M. period (nine units). The assignments were developed after a careful analysis of frequency of calls for service and crime incident data.

An evaluation of the split-force patrol method in Wilmington produced several interesting findings:[17]

1. Both violent and property crimes decreased during the experimental period, with violent crimes showing the most significant decrease.
2. Clearance rates for both property and violent crimes decreased during the experimental period, apparently because of decreased investigative efficiency resulting from decreased communication and coordination with members of the Structured Patrol Force.
3. Both nonindex (Part II) offenses and calls for service declined during the study period.
4. A majority of officers in the department *disliked* the split-force patrol concept, although members of the structured patrol force expressed considerably more satisfaction with the program than did other personnel. Detectives proved to be the strongest opponents of the program.

Police officials in Wilmington have reacted favorably to the split-force patrol program and have decided to continue it because of the favorable results achieved, including increased productivity in calls for service and in arrests.

There are, however, several preconditions that must be met before implementing the split-force concept. First, top command officers must fully understand and support it. Second, the department as a whole must be receptive to the basic changes required to adopt the program. Third, program implementation must be undertaken only after careful planning, analysis, and program design.

Like directed deterrent patrol, split-force patrol is not the ultimate solution to rising crime rates; nor is it applicable to all police agencies. It does represent, however, a significant improvement over traditional patrol methods and indicates what can be achieved when advanced research and planning techniques are applied to police patrol operations.

The home fleet plan

Several police agencies in the United States, including those in Indianapolis, Indiana; Elyria, Ohio; and Lexington–Fayette County, Kentucky, have adopted what is known as the home fleet plan as a way of reducing vehicle operating costs, improving police response capability, and increasing visible police presence in the community. For example, in Lexington–Fayette County, which has a combined city–county law enforcement agency, marked police cars were assigned to each member of the patrol section, the crime prevention unit, the community relations unit, and the training unit.[18]

Officers assigned to these units drive their patrol cars to and from work and also use them for personal activities while off duty. Officers are required to have the police radio on at all times while they are in the vehicle in order to be able to respond to calls from the police dispatcher. In addition, off-duty officers are expected to initiate law enforcement activities while driving the patrol car. This results in considerably more on-the-street patrol time with reduced personal services costs. In Prince George's County, Maryland, where the home fleet plan is also used, it was found that off-duty officers driving home fleet cars were involved in 6,084 incidents in one twelve-month period.[19]

There are several advantages of the home fleet plan. Since home fleet cars are used on a more limited basis than pool cars, they tend to last longer before they must be traded in. Because individual officers are responsible for care and maintenance of the vehicles assigned to them, overall maintenance and repair costs are lower than for pool cars. Finally, the presence of more police cars in the community is intended to contribute to an increased sense of community safety and security, although this aspect of the program has not been fully evaluated.

Due to the increased start-up costs involved in the home fleet plan, some cities may be reluctant to implement this plan. In addition, in areas where officers may live a considerable distance from the jurisdiction boundary, it may not be possible to assign individual patrol cars to all officers, since the intent is to increase police visibility within police jurisdiction, not in other areas. Nevertheless, the home fleet plan has been found to be a successful alternative to the pool car plan, and it is one additional method of increasing the effectiveness of preventive patrol.

Conclusion

Police patrol is in a period of rapid change and development. Traditional patrol methods are being replaced or supplemented by alternative techniques, many of which have real promise in terms of improving patrol effectiveness and efficiency. More research is needed to test new theories of police patrol and to increase the growing body of knowledge concerning police patrol operations. It is clear, however, that routine patrol can no longer be taken for granted by police administrators.

1 Herman Goldstein, *Policing a Free Society* (Cambridge, Mass.: Ballinger Publishing Company, 1977), p. 21.

2 President's Commission on Law Enforcement and Administration of Justice, *The Challenge of Crime in a Free Society* (Washington, D.C.: Government Printing Office, 1967), p. 98.

3 George L. Kelling et al., *The Kansas City Preventive Patrol Experiment: A Summary Report* (Washington, D.C.: Police Foundation, 1974).

4 Edward M. Davis and Lyle Knowles, "A Critique of the Report: An Evaluation of the Kansas City Preventive Patrol Experiment," *The Police Chief*, June 1975, pp. 22–27.

5 James Q. Wilson and Barbara Boland, *The Effect of the Police on Crime* (Washington, D.C.: Law Enforcement Assistance Administration, National Institute of Law Enforcement and Criminal Justice, 1979).

6 Laura A. Kiernan, "Judge Curbs Power of District Police to Stop Pedestrians," *Washington Post*, May 14, 1981, p. C1.

7 John E. Boydstun, *San Diego Field Interrogation: Final Report* (Washington, D.C.: Police Foundation, 1975).

8 Tony Pate et al., *Police Response Time: Its Determinants and Effects* (Washington, D.C.: Police Foundation, 1976).

9 Charles D. Hale, *Police Patrol: Operations and Management* (New York: John Wiley & Sons, 1981), p. 191.

10 Theodore H. Schell et al., *Traditional Preventive Patrol*, National Evaluation Program, Phase I Summary Report (Washington, D.C.: Government Printing Office, 1976), p. 60.

11 Peter J. Pitchess, "Los Angeles County's Vehicle Evaluation Test Results," *The Police Chief*, July 1978, pp. 55–57.

12 John E. Boydstun et al., *Patrol Staffing in San Diego: One- or Two-Officer Units* (Washington, D.C.: Police Foundation, 1977).

13 Santa Ana Citizens' Crime Prevention Commission, *Report*, February 1975.

14 Ibid., p. 1.

15 For further information on work scheduling, see: U.S., Department of Housing and Urban Development, *Work Schedule Design Handbook: Methods for Assigning Employees' Work Shifts and Days Off* (Washington, D.C.: Government Printing Office, 1978).

16 See: *Directed Deterrent Patrol: An Innovative Method of Preventive Patrol* (New Haven, Conn.: Department of Police Service, n.d.).

17 James M. Tien et al., *An Evaluation Report of an Alternative in Police Patrol: The Wilmington Split-Force Patrol Experiment* (Cambridge, Mass.: Public Systems Evaluation, Inc., 1977).

18 *A Comparative Analysis of the Lexington–Fayette Urban County Police Division's Home Fleet Program Versus the All Pool Plan* (Lexington–Fayette Urban County Division of Police, 1977).

19 Ibid.

8 Traffic supervision

When people talk about the traffic problem they are generally referring to the automobile traffic problem and usually to the problem of driving to work. The "problem" includes many other elements—motorcycles, bicycles, streets, highways, pedestrians, air pollution, street and highway construction and maintenance, land use and access, buses and other forms of public transportation, and, the principal subject of this chapter, police traffic supervision.

The police have operational responsibilities to help keep vehicle traffic moving safely and expeditiously along a network of expressways, arterial roads, and various categories of lesser streets and roads, by monitoring and enforcing various state and local laws and ordinances that are usually in the form of a vehicle code. Equally important responsibilities are carried out by public works, state highway, and engineering departments that plan, design, build, and maintain streets, roads, and highways—and by regional, county, and local planning agencies that make highly significant land use decisions which not only determine the location of new streets and highways but also have an enormous impact on the generation of traffic.

This chapter opens with a perspective of highway transportation as a system, touches briefly on management responsibilities of the police and other agencies in transportation and engineering planning, and then describes the police functions in traffic supervision. Subsequently, the chapter covers planning for traffic law enforcement in considerable detail with respect to methods and police service responsibilities. The chapter then discusses vehicle collision reporting, alcohol-related traffic offenses, parking supervision, bicycle traffic, traffic records, and traffic laws and ordinances. There is a concluding section on decriminalization and the administrative adjudication of traffic offenses. At several points in this chapter the text notes that the police must handle the seemingly contradictory tasks of unpopular enforcement on the one hand and upholding traffic safety and service on the other.

A perspective

Highway[1] transportation as a system

Vehicular movement on streets and highways may be characterized as a "system" with interacting components. A primary objective of the system is to move people and goods from one place to another. There are numerous constraints that hamper its effectiveness (e.g., safety, comfort, time, convenience, and cost). Safe movement and efficient movement, however, are not thoroughly compatible objectives. As the President's Task Force on Highway Safety has stated, "Highway transportation is a very complex phenomenon that pervades our entire society. Responsibility for those elements that deal with highway safety rests with many levels of government and in different departments, as well as many components of the private sector."[2]

Police officials have been slow to realize that motor vehicles—individually owned, designed and sold by a for-profit agency, and operated over a publicly

In the 1930s a relatively simple street system could handle auto traffic, and on-street parking was available and free. Police patrol was concerned largely with speeding and with parking violations.

owned and maintained road network under a variety of regulatory guides consisting of both requirements and prohibitions for vehicle and roadway use and user—constitute a transportation system. In the system concept, police perform as operational level staff. They are expected to gather and record as much pertinent information as possible about each element (driver, vehicle, roadway, and controls) for use and analysis for their needs and those of others.

The need for a comprehensive management program

In communities of all sizes the need has never been greater for comprehensive management of the highway transportation system. Conditions for vehicle movement and storage have become more complex and are interwoven with problems resulting from urban change and growth. The traditional police efforts of traffic supervision, operations, and control represent a less than adequate approach to achieving a desired level of transportation. Traffic improvements of lasting and beneficial value require high levels of technical skill and must be based on a continuing and comprehensive program.

In the past the primary objective of highway transportation management has been to achieve the safe and efficient movement of traffic. This objective by itself is no longer sufficient to the transportation needs of today's society. Public needs and expectations require that transportation alternatives provide an improved environment in which to work, live, and travel. This requires not only improving the efficiency and safety of passenger vehicle and truck transportation, but also emphasizing other modes of travel, including pedestrian and bicycle traffic and public transportation vehicles and facilities.

Highway transportation system management includes many functions, only one of which is police traffic supervision. Numerous departments of local government may have an interest in and responsibility for the management of the highway transportation system. These may include the police department, the traffic or transportation engineering department, the public works or public service department, the planning department and planning and zoning commissions, the traffic commission, and the court hearing traffic cases. Emphasis in this chapter will be primarily on the police traffic supervision aspects of highway transportation management and transportation engineering.

Police traffic regulation and surveillance

The objective of traffic regulation is to provide road use information to drivers, pedestrians, and bicyclists, so that each can properly comply with traffic laws and regulations. In this respect it is necessary to indicate to drivers and pedestrians what is desired and expected of them, especially under conditions of unusual congestion and hazards. Police occasionally must take emergency action to direct traffic flow when the usual traffic regulations or control devices prove to be inadequate.

Since they are constantly surveying the street transportation system, police must be the eyes, ears, and voice that report—that make recommendations on inadequacies of traffic regulations, traffic control devices, physical features of the roadway system, and other special hazards. The interchange of information between police and engineering agencies cannot be effectively communicated without specific and clearly defined working relationships. This requires that appropriate liaison personnel be established in both departments and that direct lines of communication be established. In emergency situations such as traffic signal malfunctions or stop signs that have come down, radio communications should be employed with follow-up by written memorandum. For other reports and recommendations written communications should be used, but the report preparation time of the officer should be kept to a minimum. This can be done with a prepared form which lists many of the standard roadway and traffic control device deficiencies so that the officer can check the appropriate box or write a brief message. If the officer is to continue to have an interest in filing this type of report, it is essential that he or she receive at least a brief reply from the engineer as to the type of action taken or the reason action was not taken. In addition, lines of communication must be simple and direct so that reports on defects do not get lost in the chain of command.

Police responsibility in the traffic regulation and surveillance area involves several functions. The most important are (1) informing drivers and pedestrians as to what to do at congested points or where hazards make roadways dangerous and difficult to use, and (2) providing information on how to find a route, on restrictions on roadway use such as "no parking," on clearance limits of underpasses, etc.

In addition, a variety of other tasks are performed within the context of traffic regulation and control. Included are school crossing protection; crowd control during parades and special events; facilitation of movement around street openings or construction sites that affect traffic; and operation of inspection points to check for auto licensing and equipment violations.

Coordination of police and engineering functions

The police and transportation engineers need the assistance of one another in executing their responsibilities in the management of the street transportation system. To adequately describe the police traffic supervision function and responsibilities, it is desirable to first summarize the functions and responsibilities of transportation engineering.

Titles and functional assignments of engineering departments vary with the structure and size of the community. In larger communities transportation departments may have the responsibility for all transportation functions; in medium-sized cities traffic engineering departments may have responsibilities for the street management functions; in smaller communities a public works department or a city engineer's office may have responsibilities for some of the engineering and management functions relating to the street transportation system.

The street transportation management functions of the transportation or traffic engineering department could include: surveys and studies; traffic control device installation; consultation on traffic regulations and ordinances; planning and design of streets; and the master street plan.

Surveys and studies This includes the collection and analysis of data on high accident locations, movement delay studies, speed studies, vehicle and pedestrian counts, parking studies, observance of traffic control devices, and physical characteristics of the street transportation system. Additional surveys could include vehicle and street classification studies, origin and destination surveys, travel time studies, area parking supply and demand studies, accident evaluation studies, and inventory of the street system, as well as its traffic carrying capabilities.

Traffic control device installation This includes the recommendations and plans for the installation of traffic signals and the supervision of the installation, operation, timing, and maintenance of these devices or systems. It also includes recommendations for and supervision of the installation of street lighting, traffic signs and pavement markings, and traffic flow improvement techniques (such as speed zones, turning restrictions, one-way streets, and pedestrian protection and control and other traffic regulatory, warning, or directional devices). In the performance of these functions, cooperation with the police department on the

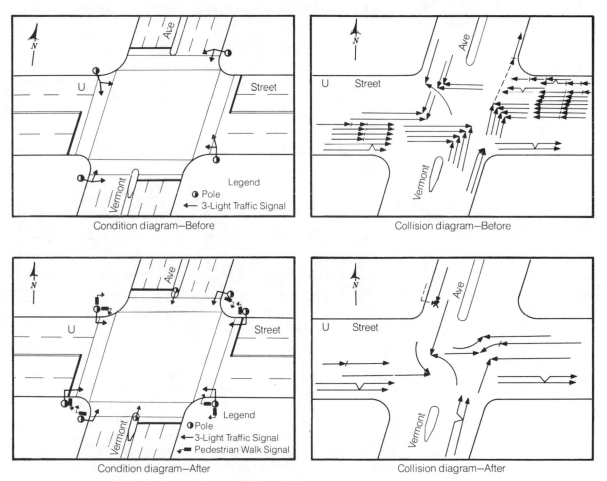

Condition diagram—Before

Collision diagram—Before

Condition diagram—After

Collision diagram—After

This example from Washington, D.C., illustrates how traffic engineering can make police traffic regulation more effective. The "before and after" sets of condition and collision diagrams for a busy intersection show a situation that was hazardous to both motorists and pedestrians, primarily because of poor visibility of primary and supplementary signals and inadequate yellow clearance interval time. The lower diagrams show the vehicle and pedestrian control measures adopted to improve the situation and the resulting improvement in traffic movement.

part of engineers is essential, since police are knowledgeable in traffic operations problems and have the direct responsibility for the supervision and enforcement of traffic regulations in the street system.

Consultation on traffic regulations and ordinances   Although responsibility for the enactment of traffic ordinances and codes, as well as for special ordinances and regulations necessary for the installation of special countermeasures, may be invested in the city administrator or the legal department, the development of adequate traffic ordinances and the updating of existing ordinances should come through consultation with all interested and involved agencies and persons throughout the community. In some areas of the country, the state has preempted authority for the promulgation and revision of traffic regulations.

Planning and design of streets   Achieving safe and efficient use of new and existing streets often requires the help of an engineer knowledgeable in the effect of design features on traffic operations. Street standards and roadway design elements should be based on analysis of traffic data as well as established design policies. Representatives of the police department should be consulted during the planning and preliminary design phases of all street and roadway facilities.

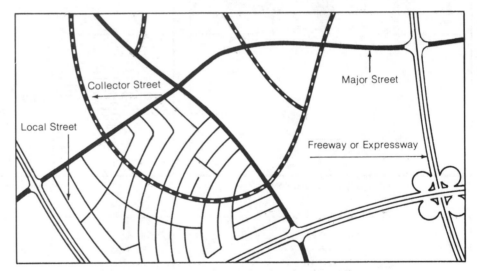

The police department should be consulted during the planning and preliminary design stages of all freeway and street facilities.

The master street plan   The existence of a master street plan, the classification of the street system, the designation of through streets, and the planning of the street system as it relates to the overall planning and development objectives of the city all contribute to effective traffic law supervision. New land developments, subdivision plans, and zoning changes which may affect traffic operations and street design should be reviewed by engineers and police. Such review always should be with representatives of the city planning agencies and, where appropriate, with representatives of transportation study groups and county and state highway departments. Police departments review all such plans and designs to assure that provisions are made to facilitate traffic supervision, crime prevention, and emergency and driver services.

Closely related to this planning is the need to control special uses of the street system. This control would include issuance of permits and authorizations regarding movement of overweight and oversize vehicles, use of streets for special events, street closures, vacating of alleys, erection of sidewalk structures, curb openings, street openings for utility work, etc.

Police functions in traffic supervision

General obligation for conduct

In every state, requirements and restrictions have been placed on the conduct of persons authorized to operate a motor vehicle on a public way. These are codified in a uniform vehicle code and model traffic ordinance. Failure to comply with the restrictions subjects a driver to a penalty. The police are authorized as part of such a traffic code to take such action against violators as may be necessary to deter them from continuing illegal behavior. A function of police traffic supervision, therefore, is to observe the user and use of motor vehicles to detect and deter driving behavior which is controlled by state codes or municipal ordinances.

Under the Federal Highway Safety Act of 1966 the National Highway Traffic Safety Administration, U.S. Department of Transportation, has issued eighteen program standards for the states to follow. Among these standards are standard 7 on police traffic services and standard 10 on traffic records. Every administrator should be aware of these program standards, since the expenditure of federal highway safety monies is controlled thereby. Forty percent of federal grant monies to a state must be distributed to cities and counties of the state to support their efforts at meeting the various standards.

The police traffic services standard requires the following:

Every state in cooperation with its political subdivisions shall have a program to insure efficient and effective police services utilizing traffic controls:

> To enforce traffic laws
> To prevent accidents
> To aid the injured
> To document the particulars of individual accidents
> To supervise accident cleanup and to restore safe and orderly traffic movement.

The program shall provide as a minimum:

> For the training of police in vehicular and pedestrian traffic operations
> To allocate police resources commensurate with the magnitude of the traffic problem
> For the selective assignment of trained police personnel for investigation, recording and reporting accidents
> For recognizing and reporting hazardous driver, roadway and vehicle defects.[3]

The obligation to maintain traffic records is the subject of the traffic records standard, which requires that:

Each state, as part of its highway safety program, promulgate a uniform report form with a schedule for recording all appropriate data available on traffic accidents, driver, motor vehicles and roadways to provide:

> A reliable indication of the magnitude and nature of the highway traffic accident problem on a national, state and local level
> A means for identifying short term changes and long term trends in the number and nature of traffic accidents
> A valid basis for:
>
>> The detection of high or potentially high accident locations and causes
>> The detection of health, behavioral and related factors contributing to accident causation
>> The design of accident, fatality and injury countermeasures

Developing means for evaluating the cost effectiveness of these measures
The planning and implementation of selected enforcement and other
operational programs.[4]

The politics of police traffic supervision

The success of a police traffic supervision program will be influenced by the
ability of police management to develop and maintain the cooperation of many
other agencies, both official and nonofficial.

Officials and legislators   Police management relationships with the principal
elected or appointed official and the legislative body of the jurisdiction are most
important. It is a fact of life that a police administrator needs the informed support of the mayor, city manager, county supervisor, and members of the council
or the board of commissioners to obtain the resources for an effective traffic
supervision program. The police manager must be sensitive to the political considerations inherent in so many department requirements and activities. Such
awareness should be reflected in all traffic program development, and, once
recognized by elected and appointed officials, will aid their understanding of
the police objectives. A technique of proved value is a willingness to pursue
the selection of acceptable alternatives.

The prosecutor   Another official relationship involves the prosecutor. The police
role in initiating the prosecution of traffic offenses and assisting in case preparation and giving testimony is facilitated when police leadership has established a
harmonious relationship with the prosecutor and his or her assistants. A clear
understanding of the needs of each agency is then possible and the probability of
"personality" or "philosophy" conflicts is lessened considerably.

The courts   Of equal importance is the department's relationship with the
courts. In those jurisdictions where a special "traffic court" is utilized, the matters of liaison and cross-communication of objectives are relatively easy. Most
"traffic court" judges understand both the attitude of the offender and the police role. In a judicial system where the hearing of traffic offenses is joined with
other law violations, it becomes imperative that the police management group
establish a method of communications with the court to ensure a two-way understanding of their special aims and objectives.

Nonofficial agencies   Many nonofficial agencies in the community can aid the
police traffic services program if the administrator provides an opportunity for
them to participate in the formulation of police programs. Examples of such
groups are local safety councils, chambers of commerce, business groups, and
the various service clubs such as the Rotary and Lions Clubs. Effort to gain support of ethnic and religious groups or of senior citizens for selected traffic accident programs is often productive.

Probably the most important nonofficial "agency" in a community is the
news media (the press, radio, and television). The police administrator must
provide clear-cut informational guidelines for police–media relationships. Increased mobility and more sophisticated recording and broadcast capabilities
highlight the need for a definite understanding of the rights and responsibilities
of citizens, the news media, and the police. Arriving at such an understanding
will permit the administrator to issue clear written statements which will facilitate media cooperation in publicizing the role of the police in highway safety.[5]

Planning for traffic law enforcement

The objectives of police traffic law enforcement are generally agreed to include the following:

1. Development, through a program of supervision and enforcement action, of avoidance by drivers of dangerous or prohibited behavior
2. Detection and removal of impaired drivers from the highway transportation system
3. Informing and educating drivers (pedestrians, cyclists), through direct contact or observations of enforcement action against others, about conduct in traffic that differs from that prescribed by law or ordinance
4. Inducement of a high level of voluntary compliance with traffic laws and ordinances by drivers through creation of a belief that detection and apprehension of violators is a reality and penalty is a certainty.

Guides to planning

The manager for police traffic services has available a wide range of guides for the design and evaluation of programs. These guides range from recommended policies to detailed and proven procedures.[6] Each guide is intended to assist in the development of a program which meets a high standard of quality and uniformity.

Among the various available guides, some consist of "should do" statements, such as the material quoted immediately below, while other guides are more precise and consist of specific recommendations.[7] Among the "should do" statements are the following:

Traffic laws should be enforced at a substantial level with uniform interpretation in all jurisdictions. The quantity of enforcement should be sufficient to produce maximum safety in each locality.

Equally as important as the amount of traffic law enforcement is the quality of enforcement. To be effective, enforcement must be directed at the violations known to be accident causative. In addition, it must be applied in those places and at those times shown by experience to have a disproportionately high percentage of accidents. There will probably never be enough policemen to apprehend all violators for every violation, therefore, enforcement personnel and enforcement effort must be used to the best possible advantage.

Every police officer on the streets and highways—regardless of his specific assignment—should, when he observes a traffic violation or nontraffic offense, take appropriate enforcement action.

The enforcement of traffic laws solely for revenue purposes is as abhorrent to the police as it is to the public. The practice should be eliminated wherever it exists.

The enforcement of traffic laws for the sole purpose of building a record of police activity is as repugnant as enforcement for revenue purposes.

There should be one enforcement policy for all street and highway users and not one that gives preference to either local residents or nonresidents.

Traffic law enforcement is affected by the "community climate." Public understanding and support is essential for success of this function of police service. An effective state or local public support organization such as a Safety Council can help create needed public understanding and support. Police agencies should provide leadership in the development of a solid public safety education program.

The police are also responsible to a substantial degree for public attitude toward traffic law enforcement. Traffic law enforcement and traffic direction must be performed in a uniform manner to be understood and acceptable. But even more important, this must be done in an efficient and courteous manner.

The police are definitely and unequivocally opposed to the "fixing" of traffic cases in any manner by an agency official, or person. It should be eliminated if and wherever it exists.

The enforcement of traffic laws by the police should not be regarded as a contest between police and drivers. Such an attitude has no place in modern-day traffic flow on public streets and highways. The police are committed to a policy of traffic patrol which normally will be conducted by uniformed officers using easily identifiable vehicles, supplemented when necessary by officers using equipment not readily identifiable as police equipment. The IACP also believes concealment for traffic law enforcement is justifiable when necessary to bring under control a situation that cannot be controlled by usual methods.

The use of scientific devices such as mechanical, electronic, photographic, and chemical test for alcohol equipment is justifiable when required to enhance the lawful efforts of the police. Limits to the use of such supplemental equipment by the police should be determined by its legality and scientific soundness.[8]

Roles of the chief and command personnel

The police administrator and the command and supervisory personnel (the management group) should see that traffic supervision and law enforcement work effort by patrol personnel will be planned and directed by management, as opposed to effort that is merely the product of occasional action by individual officers.

A planned and directed program implies the existence and use of reliable traffic data identifying the current level of driver obedience for requirements or prohibitions in existing codes, identifying major contributing causes to vehicle collisions for a three-year period, and containing a consideration of needed ease and convenience of vehicle movement. Data of this kind should be the base for formulating a departmental objective.

Extent of police responsibility

For a street transportation system to operate with a degree of safety, regular, consistent enforcement of the vehicle code is essential. Included are: detection of defects in individual behavior or condition, in vehicle equipment or condition, or in highway condition; implementation of appropriate action to prevent such defects from causing accidents or delay; remedy of defects where possible; and discouragement of the repetition of dangerous and prohibited acts through apprehension of violators. When less than appropriate enforcement action is taken, the full value of many engineering improvements cannot be achieved. On the other hand, there are conditions within traffic operation that cannot be improved through traffic law enforcement. Deficiencies or defects in the design of the roadway system or in the design, placement, or operation of traffic control devices may create erratic or improper driver behavior which can be corrected only by remedial engineering. It is, therefore, important that police have an understanding of basic street design principles and traffic operations techniques so that they can call on engineering assistance when it can be an effective alternative to police enforcement.

One issue in planning a program of police traffic law enforcement is the amount of uncommitted time available to patrol personnel. If the majority of time for preventive patrol is committed by responding to radio-transmitted complaints, then traffic law supervision will receive little time or attention. If the activity of personnel on patrol is not directed, then the individual work interest or energy level of each patrol officer is likely to dictate the kind and amount of police work performed. Such a situation is unacceptable. The traffic objectives stated previously cannot be accomplished by casual enforcement of traffic laws on the part of the police.

Management of police traffic functions

The organization for police traffic supervision and the prominence given the function in a police agency are a reflection of the management group's attitude toward traffic. It is a characteristic of police management that when command level personnel are enthusiastically involved in a specific function the overall quality of that function is noticeably enhanced. It has been stated that, "when upper management, particularly the chief, was aware of traffic activity, knew the level of enforcement and accidents, and demonstrated specific interest in police traffic services, this attitude was reflected throughout the department."[9]

Police supervision and traffic law enforcement alone will not provide a community with the level of safe and efficient highway transportation that most citizens desire. Required is a sound, realistic, and balanced program consisting of traffic laws; highway, automotive, and traffic engineering; driver licensing and driver improvement; traffic courts and prosecutors; driver education and training; analysis and use of traffic data; coordination of effort in a community by all agencies with traffic responsibilities; and a climate of support resulting from public understanding.

Pending development of such a balanced approach, a carefully designed and continuing program of police traffic supervision, directed toward those needs as revealed through an analysis of traffic data, is a community's most effective control over losses from vehicle collisions.

There is a wide range of options by which a program of police traffic supervision can be achieved. These options include the following:

1. Enforcement by any uniformed officer when a violation occurs in his or her view
2. Enforcement by specially trained and assigned personnel whose effort is directed toward a special class of violators—speeders, drivers operating while driver's license is suspended, drivers operating while under the influence of alcohol or other drugs
3. Enforcement at collision scenes for violations found to be a contributing cause of the collision
4. Detection and enforcement of traffic offenses by uniformed personnel in clearly marked patrol vehicles or on motorcycles who are assigned to a specific area, intersection, or roadway
5. Detection and enforcement by uniformed personnel but in unidentified patrol vehicles
6. Enforcement of speed restrictions by uniformed personnel using mechanical or electronic speed measuring devices.

Separation of traffic enforcement from general police functions

In recent years there has been much discussion about the feasibility of relieving regular uniformed police of responsibility for traffic law enforcement and traffic services. Underlying the discussion are the beliefs that traffic supervision is primarily a regulatory activity; that, as "crimes" go, traffic violations are fairly minor; that the volume of traffic offenses requires an inordinate amount of police time; that much hostility toward police is generated in traffic enforcement situations; and that it is not an effective use of resources to use full authority, highly paid and trained police officers to enforce traffic laws. Various proposals have been made that some traffic enforcement and supervision functions be transferred to some group or agency other than regular police.

Some limited efforts have been made to implement these proposals. For example, the use of civilians as school crossing guards and for parking meter supervision is widespread. At least one city is using nonsworn personnel to report and investigate traffic accidents. Such limited transfers of traffic responsibilities have generally been effective and satisfactory.

However, little has been done to implement the concept in its broader aspects because of the lack of adequate solutions to several anticipated problems. For example, it is clear that regular police could never be entirely relieved of the responsibility for directing some of their attention to vehicles. Much serious criminal activity involves the use of vehicles as a means of escaping the scene of a crime and transporting fruits of a crime. Also, vehicles are frequently targets of serious crimes such as theft. Routine traffic law enforcement often leads to discovery of more serious offenses and apprehension of felons and other wanted persons. It is unlikely that the police would be willing to relinquish the authority to use traffic code violations as a tool in fighting more serious criminal activity, and it is far from clear that they should be required to do so.

Accident investigators In Fort Lauderdale, Florida, sworn police officers were replaced with civilian traffic safety aides who investigate traffic accidents and are authorized to issue citations. Sixteen men and women traffic aides patrol areas with cars marked "Accident Investigation Unit." The Selective Traffic Enforcement Program (STEP), which has operated the Accident Investigation Unit (AIU) for over ten years, releases police officers to perform activities more closely related to police patrol.

It is true that in some jurisdictions there are separate enforcement agencies, such as a highway patrol, with primary responsibility for enforcement of traffic violations within a defined geographical area, such as on state highways. However, as yet no adequate proposal has been made as to how to delineate separate *functional* responsibilities within a given jurisdiction between regular police and some other agency. Until problems such as this are resolved, it appears impractical to attempt to remove traffic enforcement from the general police responsibility.

The selectivity principle

Several decades ago it was recognized that the police cannot enforce all traffic violations. This recognition led to the development of a method of enforcement based on the concept that resources should be directed at violations which are frequently a contributing cause of vehicle collisions. Thus, the concept of selective enforcement[10] was applied to traffic laws. The term selective traffic law enforcement first appeared in the early 1930s. It is associated with the efforts of Franklin M. Kreml, then a lieutenant in the Evanston, Illinois, police department, to reduce traffic accidents. It is a technique wherein trained personnel direct their observations to selected moving traffic offenses at times when and at locations where a high number of vehicle collisions occur. The technique is part of a planned allocation of specially trained and equipped personnel. The enforcement effort is guided by a study of those driver actions and roadway conditions which investigators have previously identified as factors contributing to the occurrence of a vehicle collision.

The logic and simplicity of this basic concept have made it very attractive. There is difficulty, however, with implementation of the concept. Clearly, the application of the theory requires an identification of the behavior which has proved dangerous; then this information must be given to the enforcement personnel. Availability of the data must then be followed by appropriate action to deter similar offenses.

The type of enforcement action taken by selective enforcement units often differs from the activity of general patrol units. The general patrol units are dealing with a larger geographical area and normally a greater density of traffic. The immediate tendency for general patrol personnel is to take action on the obvious and serious violations. Normally, there are a sufficient number of these violations to occupy the available enforcement time. The selective enforcement unit is faced with a different situation. It is usually assigned to a relatively small area, sometimes a group of intersections. This results in a far more detailed observation of the traffic flow. Thus, it is easily understood why such units make more arrests for the less obvious violations.

Many police have believed for too long that an application of selective enforcement is the one and complete answer to the control of traffic law violators. Selective enforcement must be thought of as an administrative mechanism for meeting a special need. The principle can be applied to the enforcement of criminal or traffic offenses.

Selective traffic law enforcement was the subject of a federally funded study undertaken by the Highway Safety Division, International Association of Chiefs of Police (IACP). It resulted in a publication[11] intended to aid police personnel and others to understand the principle of selective enforcement and to promote the use of improved technical and operational practices based on that principle.

A small select and specialized operational group for traffic law supervision was an effective approach when the country had 25 million licensed drivers. Today, with more than 143 million drivers, the principles of selectivity are still sound. The form of implementation, however, must be different. Today, responsibility for program development and for coordination of effort and evaluation of results is likely to be assigned to a trained person in smaller departments or a special staff group in larger departments.

Most police engage in traffic law enforcement and other traffic services. Few do so, however, in support of prestated goals or objectives. The need for managers of police services to develop and follow such guides is reflected in recommendations found in a growing number of prestigious reports and studies produced during the past several years.

Supervisors and patrol personnel engaged in traffic law supervision need "direction" when performing their respective jobs. One such form of "direction" is the use of an enforcement bulletin. Traffic data compiled from collision reports and investigations and offenses for which citations are issued are analyzed and a plan is developed to guide supervision and enforcement effort. The content of an enforcement bulletin may cover the accident and citation experience for the previous one-month period or for one quarter. The purpose is to provide a review of past accident and enforcement data, and guidance for directing future enforcement effort.

The bulletin should provide guidance as to the nature of enforcement attention to be given. For example, "following too closely" is a violation that has been reported as a contributing cause in some 12.2 percent of all collisions investigated, and it has received practically no enforcement. Officers should be instructed to enforce regulations, using as a uniform guide one car length for every ten miles of speed. Improper lane change is another unsafe practice. Increased enforcement is warranted against drivers who cut in and out of traffic lanes without due regard for other traffic.

Speed enforcement

Law enforcement has as its general objective the maintenance and protection of public order, safety, and welfare. Excessive speed is hazardous to both drivers and pedestrians.

Speed limit enforcement has several general objectives. These include:

1. Increasing obedience to existing traffic regulations
2. Apprehending drivers whose speed endangers themselves and others
3. Conserving energy—enforcing the congressional mandate which restricts the speed on all highways in the United States to a maximum of fifty-five miles an hour
4. Creating a safer environment for driving by narrowing the extremes in vehicle speeds.

Most municipal law enforcement personnel hold that substantial compliance with speed regulations produces a safer driving environment. Police enforcement of speed limits is seen as an effort that contributes primarily to improved highway safety. This is so even though the police enforcement effort is seen by motorists as an unneeded regulation or an undeserved punishment. There can be little doubt that collisions at lower speeds tend to produce less severe personal injuries and property damages than do those involving higher speeds.

Methods of enforcement

A variety of instruments and techniques are used by police for control of speed. Most departments routinely rely on some form of electronic speed determining instrument.

Electronic devices A number of speed measuring devices, improved in design and reliability, are available for use by police. Pacing a suspected violator or following him or her in a distinctly marked police vehicle is still a widely used technique. So is the motorcycle, particularly where vehicle density is high. Radar units have largely replaced the motorcycle for speed control in smaller cities. Patrol vehicles used for pacing are usually equipped with calibrated speedometers. Motor vehicle department use of driver records as a means for driver control, point systems which reflect citations received for hazardous moving violations, and point systems for determining insurability of a driver result in a greater number of contested traffic cases. As a result, police give greater attention today to accuracy of speed measurement, whether by patrol vehicle pacing or by use of a radar or other type of instrument.

Speed enforcement by local government police ranges from a low of 10 percent of all traffic law citations issued to a high of 70 percent. An average is 25 percent of all traffic citations written.

A planned mixture of open and concealed enforcement by marked patrol vehicles, the selected use of some form of electronic speed measurement device and the use of unmarked cars in areas of high accidents (where speed contributed to severity of personal injury or property damage) is the typical pattern of deployment in all but the small (under 10,000) and the larger (over 100,000) departments.

Authorities are in agreement that, while speed control seldom reduces accidents in a known area of high accident occurrence, such enforcement pressure does reduce accident severity.

Issuance of a high number of speed citations under high volume traffic conditions would suggest that the speed limit is too low. In such a case, the police administrator should work with the traffic engineer and seek an increase in the allowed maximum speed. Such action would help increase the degree of voluntary obedience by drivers and reduce the need for enforcement.[12]

Situational enforcement Police managers and students of police operations have made a number of observations about the behavior of patrol personnel confronted with a specific traffic offense. An examination of traffic arrest data in a community, for example, might reveal that all arrests for driving while under the influence of alcohol involved a driver blood alcohol concentration of 0.18 percent or above. This is so even when the state vehicle code sets 0.08 or 0.10 percent blood alcohol as the presumptive level of impairment. An examination of traffic activity for a department frequently will indicate that some officers issue citations for speed violations only when speeds exceed the permitted limit by twenty or more miles per hour.

In many enforcement situations in which a police officer could enforce the law, he or she may conclude that it would be wiser not to do so. One study, Project STAR,[13] introduced the term "situational enforcement" to describe the way in which a police officer deals with this condition. This concept is discussed in detail in the publication cited in this paragraph.

Enforcement action The reduction of collisions, both to decrease their number and severity and to facilitate vehicle movement, is one objective toward which traffic supervision is directed. To accomplish this goal the principal tool is enforcement action. It is a well-documented fact that when the quality and quantity of citations are increased in a given area, the number and severity of collisions will tend to decrease.[14] More drivers voluntarily comply with required or prohibited traffic conduct when they believe that detection is likely. An informative report on the impact of various enforcement techniques on traffic accidents is found in a study conducted by the Tacoma, Washington, police department.[15]

Unnecessary tickets

The necessity for police efforts to bring about driver and pedestrian compliance with traffic laws is not understood by the public, nor are the efforts widely accepted. Many motorists, in particular, believe that traffic officers operate under a quota system in issuing citations. Some police supervisors believe that patrol officers are indifferent in their work if they do not issue a certain number of citations every day. There *are* indifferent officers. Some, when prodded by a supervisor, do issue citations when the better action would be to inform a driver of his or her error. As the city of Tacoma, Washington, has stated, "A concern for revenue and/or for the evaluation of traffic officers by citation production has often appeared to obscure the primary enforcement objective—accident prevention."[16]

Civil versus criminal aspects of traffic law enforcement

Those who enforce, prosecute, and hear traffic violations must remember that traffic laws are made to prevent collisions and to promote a safe and orderly flow of traffic on the roadway. This means that traffic law enforcement must create deterrents to violation by bringing to justice those who jeopardize the safety of others by violating the rules of the road—which are nothing more than safe driving rules. Many hazardous violations do not result in accidents—a fortunate circumstance. Many such violations, however, do cause or contribute to a collision which too often results in death, personal injury, or property damage. In any case, the purpose of enforcement is the same: to create deterrents to unsafe conduct by users of the roadway.

Unfortunately, police, prosecutors, judges, and others too often direct the inquiry away from the importance of society protecting itself from those who violate safe driving rules. Some judges refuse to hear violations arising out of accident cases, insisting instead that the parties should settle their damage claims between themselves, without realizing the public interest in enforcing the traffic laws. A prosecution is a proceeding brought by *all the people* against *one who has violated the law.*

Another failure is that of looking upon the *result* of the violation as the controlling factor. If no one is hurt or no property damaged as a result of someone running a stop sign, then it is considered a "minor" offense. But if, by chance, another road user happens to be on the cross street and there is death or personal injury, or if there is property damage, then it becomes a "serious" offense. Those with this attitude do not realize that driving is largely done by habit—that it is learned behavior that to a large extent takes place without conscious thought. Consequently, enforcement must control habitual patterns of driving and it is vital that a *climate* of safe driving be created in the community. Extra attention for only those violations which actually kill, injure, or destroy property focuses only on the end product—not on the importance of prevention.

Collisions can result in a charge of violating the traffic laws as well as in a civil negligence case for damages arising out of the incident. These two purposes must be kept separate.[17] However, during the investigation of accidents police officers many times consider whose *fault* it was rather than who *violated* the law. Determining *fault* is the function of the civil courts in the negligence lawsuit, and the investigating officer has a duty to record the facts so that this issue can be settled objectively. But just as important is the need for the public interest in enforcing the traffic laws to be carried out by charging and bringing to justice those who violate the law. Police officers should not confuse these separate purposes of accident investigation and traffic law enforcement.

Selection and training

To be effective, the specialized traffic group must be staffed with personnel who have been selected for their interest in traffic. Assignment of personnel to this important police function must not be based on any other criteria, such as temporary or extended inability to perform other police functions.

Specialized traffic work demands that sufficient training be devoted to traffic subjects, so that all personnel assigned will be well grounded in both the requirements and the techniques of the job. The amount of time required for training will depend on the previous training and work experience of the personnel. The training should combine classroom instruction with supervised active experience. The following topics should be included in the training course:

1. Basic philosophy of police traffic supervision
2. Department goals in traffic safety and accident prevention
3. Policy rules and procedures relative to police traffic supervision
4. Laws and ordinances as applied to traffic, and pertinent court interpretations and constraints
5. Techniques for the traffic patrol, for traffic law enforcement, and for traffic direction, and the procedure for investigation of collisions involving motor vehicles, pedestrians, or cyclists, including compilation of required reports
6. Specific procedures to be followed to assure court acceptance of breath test results, radar speed measurement, etc.
7. Case preparation and court testimony
8. Officer–violator relations.

In addition, retraining, or in-service training, should be conducted on a planned basis to reinforce essentials and provide an opportunity to communicate new ideas and techniques. In-service training should be ongoing to help correct problems and/or deficiencies revealed through supervisory and command evaluation of the traffic program.

In the operation of the specialized traffic division it is important that the administrator provide for the advanced training of those individuals whose functions are critical to an effective program. This applies not only to data analysts and similar specialists but also to supervisory and command personnel. Departments lacking the resources to carry out their own training should explore the availability of traffic training courses offered through regional or area facilities. The Traffic Institute, Northwestern University, upon request will develop and present on-site traffic training programs designed to meet the specific needs of a department or a group of departments. Funds for such special training in traffic sometimes are available to local departments through the U.S. Department of Transportation's National Highway Traffic Safety Administration (NHTSA) and other federal and state agencies.

Courses of one to five weeks devoted to a single facet of police traffic services such as on-scene or technical accident investigation, analysis and use of police data, traffic law enforcement, management, and other related subjects are offered by the Traffic Institute, Northwestern University.

In many communities an automobile club or traffic safety association has provided funds to assist one or more representatives of the police department to obtain special training in an area of police traffic supervision.

Traffic safety education

Although responsibility for educating a community in requirements for traffic safety should not rest solely with the police, experience has shown that police cooperation and participation in traffic safety education programs is necessary to the success of these programs. Many police agencies, recognizing a public relations value, will designate a traffic safety officer or establish a traffic safety education unit. Their efforts are mostly with educators in elementary schools and junior and senior high schools. However, the trend today is to consider this function as a part of an overall community relations program.

Authorities in traffic safety generally agree that public education in matters of traffic safety should consist of three separate and distinct phases: (1) education of the beginning school group; (2) continuing education aimed at improvement of safe driving and pedestrian practices; and (3) remedial education to correct specific individual defects.

The police role in the first phase is one of cooperation with school personnel, of assistance to them in identifying problem areas, and of communicating police objectives, the accomplishment of which can be aided through knowledge and skill.

In the continuing phase, the police can make a significant contribution when their efforts are supportive of a community-wide program carried out by a local safety council or traffic safety association. A good example is the defensive driving course developed by the National Safety Council.

Police participation in the third phase emerges from their responsibility to maintain records which will indicate those drivers who need improvement and to transmit such information to the appropriate authority. Examples are the driver improvement schools frequently mandated by ordinance or state law which function as an "alternative sentence" in court disposition following a guilty finding.

Vehicle collision reporting and investigation

It is essential for police to understand the significance of vehicle collision[18] investigation and the uses of the information obtained therefrom. Data from the police reporting or investigation of vehicle collisions are the prime source of information for accident prevention programs. Only through adequate and reliable accident data can effective police and engineering countermeasures be developed and their effectiveness evaluated.

Traffic accident (vehicle collision) investigation is not defined adequately by law, either by professional associations or by a uniform operational standard. In practice, vehicle collision investigation, which begins with basic reporting, may be carried as far, for a particular collision, as special interest by the officer or limitations on his or her availability dictate. To the extent that such practices occur, information which is vital to meeting the objectives of the department and needs of drivers and others is often lost. Correction of this situation demands administrative guidance in the form of policy and procedures to assure uniform and appropriate emphasis on the various aspects of collision reporting and investigation. Noted authority J. Stannard Baker has stated that "laws relating to traffic accident investigations are brief and vague. In general they provide neither guidance nor constraints to the investigator or administrator."[19] The principal basis for traffic accident investigation is administrative policy.

The National Highway Traffic Safety Administration has included a standard on accident investigation and reporting—standard 18—in its series of traffic safety program requirements for state and local government. The standard states:

The purpose of this standard is to establish a uniform, comprehensive motor vehicle traffic accident investigation program for gathering information—who, what, when, where, why, and how—on motor vehicle traffic accidents and associated deaths, injuries, and property damage; and entering the information into the traffic records system for use in planning, evaluating, and furthering highway safety program goals.[20]

Police objectives

The objectives for police responding to the scene of a collision should include the following:

1. Providing emergency services, usually noninvestigative, at the scene of each motor vehicle collision occurring within the jurisdiction consistent with the availability of uniformed police personnel, the expectation of the community for these services, and the need to identify and request additional services from others in order to reduce the emergency
2. Systematically providing an officer who records contributed information, or a trained investigator, at the scene of each motor vehicle collision involving personal injuries and/or vehicle disablement in order to obtain and record basic collision data and data that could be quickly obliterated by clearing of debris at the scene, by traffic, or by weather conditions
3. Obtaining data about the vehicle, roadway, driver (or pedestrian) and the result of the collision in a manner which permits tabulation of such data according to standard classifications and in amounts needed to support planning and coordinated programs of motor vehicle accident countermeasures on the part of the department and by other agencies, as required
4. Protecting persons and property involved in, or in the vicinity of, the accident
5. Taking enforcement action (verbal, written warning, citation, arrest) when, in the opinion of the attending officer, there is evidence to support a prosecution
6. Engaging in special temporary in-depth investigation programs, to gather additional selected data regarding the driver (pedestrian), vehicle, roadway controls, or such related collision information as may be required for special research studies of the highway transportation system.[21]

Police practices in general

In theory, police personnel investigate every motor vehicle traffic accident in their jurisdiction reported to them. In reality, however, the presence of police personnel at a collision scene, the extent of emergency and investigative services provided, the amount of information recorded, and the time spent will vary greatly from department to department.

In practice, the extent of police involvement and resulting information gathering depends mainly on the seriousness of personal injuries or extensiveness of vehicle damage resulting from the collision. Few departments have established administrative guidelines delineating the extent of emergency services or investigation and information gathering to be performed. Judgments in these areas are usually made by individual officers directed to the scene. Each officer may decide how much and what kind of information is useful or may be wanted. Attitudes and practices existing within a police department about motor vehicle accidents influence these judgments. A wide range of practices by individual investigators further modifies such services. Some investigators are motivated to assist with the personal problems of the driver or passenger, others are motivated by the investigative challenge found at the scene. This makes it difficult to define exactly what is meant by "investigate" and to determine when an "investigation" is complete.

Two traditional guides for the police officer at the scene of a collision are available. The first is the report form (usually provided by a state agency) for recording data about the collision. When the form is completed, the officer's work at the scene is completed. But no single police traffic accident report form can provide for all the selected data required by the special requirements of motor vehicle accident research and related groups. To obtain the special data desired, use of a temporary special data collection system, as required by objectives, is recommended.

The second guide is the discretionary authority of a supervisor or prosecutor to require that additional information be obtained. This is done to assist in presenting evidence to support a criminal charge arising from a motor vehicle collision.

As a guide to establishing police (emergency or investigative) service, vehicle collisions can be grouped by such methods as severity of personal injury, extent of property damage, extent of vehicle disablement, or extent of traffic interruption resulting from the collision.

Every reported occurrence of a motor vehicle collision does not justify the dispatching of highly trained investigative personnel to observe and record information about various elements contributing to the collision, such as the driver, vehicle, road, environment, or controls. Departments should assign patrol personnel, if available, to the scene of every motor vehicle traffic accident reported to them. Upon arrival, officers should provide emergency assistance as required and determine whether additional investigative skill is needed. A record should be made of every motor vehicle traffic accident reported to the police. The form used may be an incident report or it may be a state-provided uniform traffic accident report form.

When personnel are not available and a number of collisions are reported and awaiting service, a policy and procedure are needed to help allocate police resources and to meet the expectations of the public for some form of service. The policy should identify priorities and reflect the need for police services at the scene. Alternative reporting procedures must be identified when police cannot respond at the scene.

A guide for police managers on when to send trained accident investigators might include an approach such as the following:

1. A trained investigator is needed when at least one vehicle[22] is disabled or one person is disabled[23] and, in addition, at least one of the following circumstances exists:

   a) A person is dead at the scene or appears likely to die soon as a result of the vehicle collision.

   b) A disabling injury occurs in a public passenger-carrying vehicle.

   c) A government owned vehicle is involved and there are disabling injuries to others than occupants of that vehicle.

   d) More than one vehicle with three or more axles is disabled and there is also an incapacitating injury.

   e) There is destructive damage to major structures, such as bridge collapse, fire, high tension wires grounded, etc. All such collisions would warrant investigation by a trained investigator. Photographs, tire and lamp examinations, and measurements of vehicle movement and final position taken at the scene and useful for later reconstruction of the accident scene would be completed.

2. A trained investigator is not needed when the collision involves no disabled vehicle and no disabled person, traffic is not blocked, and no assistance is needed to clear the scene of the accident. A report would be completed for all such collisions known to the police.

Alcohol-related traffic offenses

The growing awareness that drinking and driving is a major contributor to the number of deaths and injuries resulting from traffic collisions has led to the development of a variety of countermeasure programs, each having the object of seeking to reduce the incidence of alcohol-related traffic offenses. Prominent among the countermeasures are federally funded research studies which range from factors which influence police in their arrest/no arrest decision for alcohol-related traffic violations[24] to special enforcement efforts through alcohol safety action projects (ASAPs). Research findings have helped to better define the various facets of the problem and to design programs for improved enforcement efforts by police.

An explicit police management commitment to a high level of enforcement against alcohol-related traffic offenses is an essential prerequisite for improved effort. More departments must provide clear direction to patrol personnel through various forms of administrative guidance, such as policy statements and written procedures, before enforcement of alcohol-related traffic law violations will receive the attention it deserves.

Policy and procedures, however, can do little more than remove some potential impediments to enforcement. Police managers, supervisors, and patrol personnel must understand what is expected of them and must possess the knowledge and skill required to meet these expectations. One element that has been common to nearly all countermeasure programs is stepped up police enforcement of the drinking–driving statutes. One study has documented the fact that there is a relatively low level of police enforcement against alcohol-related driving offenses. For example, roadside surveys conducted prior to the funding of ASAP programs showed that nearly one out of twenty drivers on the road on weekend nights exhibited a blood alcohol concentration (BAC) at or above the statutory presumption.[25]

Factors that positively or negatively affect the arrest/no arrest decision in alcohol-related traffic violations were found to include:

1. The existence of written administrative guidance as to a department's expectation in the detection of alcohol-related traffic offenses,

supported by action of supervisors to assure that guidelines are being followed and that expectations are being achieved

2. Specific enforcement plans as to patrol locations and schedules, procedures for the processing of those cited, the use of specialized squads, and the use of investigative techniques or equipment to aid the officer in his or her arrest/no arrest judgment

3. Training which develops skill in the detection of borderline suspects, belief in the fairness of blood alcohol concentration, and awareness of the amount of alcohol that must be consumed to produce a particular blood alcohol concentration

4. Active communication between police and judicial personnel on such issues as scheduling court dates, admissibility of evidence, plea bargaining, and the development of an understanding of the needs and problems of each agency.

Recommendations for legislative changes to facilitate enforcement of alcohol-related traffic offenses without harm to the rights of the suspect frequently emerge from such studies. Proposed changes include establishment of an absolute (per se) statutory blood alcohol concentration, providing for the use of preliminary breath tests, use of portable breath testing apparatus, and revision of statutory penalties to permit greater judicial discretion in imposition of innovative approaches designed to decrease recidivism.

There should be available in the community alcoholic rehabilitation programs for drinking drivers. Such programs should be part of the court's dispositional alternatives after an adjudication of guilt. The primary objective of such rehabilitation programs should be the modification of a problem driver's attitude toward drinking and driving with the hope of eliminating the driver as a recidivist. Participation in such programs should be under court supervision.

In some communities a program of diverting drinking drivers out of the court system into rehabilitation programs is being tested. However, such programs raise questions of due process of law for those persons found not guilty of the charge.

Supervision of parking

Supervision of street parking and enforcement of parking regulations are often assigned to municipal police. The purpose of parking control is to provide adequate road space for the movement of traffic and to ensure equitable use of curb space when on-street parking is permitted.

The use of a trained, uniformed police officer to enforce time and place restrictions on curb lane parking is a questionable practice. This is particularly so when the activity is clearly regarded as a revenue operation with little or no concern for the objective of providing a regular turnover of curb parking spaces. The use of civilian employees for this function should be considered. When civilians are used, a job classification which distinguishes the work from tasks performed by uniformed officers must be established.

Motor vehicles abandoned on the public way are a growing problem in many communities. As a minimum activity, police should initiate the legal process for removal of such vehicles. In some communities, depending upon the action of local officials, police may be required to perform the complete process of removal, including final disposition of those vehicles not claimed by registered owners.

The cost of removal can be high; therefore, the administrator who decides to perform this service or is forced to accept this responsibility must be prepared to identify the personnel and equipment needed and to give a cost estimate for carrying out the service.

Requests for driver services are a growing problem for police when vehicles are disabled on an interstate route which goes through a city. Drivers of such vehicles expect local police to provide them with a number of services.

Initially, there is a need for a clear understanding between local police administrators and state officials as to jurisdiction and the fixing of responsibility for specific functions such as investigation of collisions, extent of assisting disabled motorists, etc. Agreement reached must be communicated clearly and fully to all command, supervisory, and operating personnel. If the local police administrator accepts full responsibility for total police traffic service on an interstate, he or she must decide the extent or level of that service (i.e., from merely communicating the need for assistance to actually transporting the motorist to a point where assistance is available). In many jurisdictions local automobile clubs assist the police in providing this service.

Bicycle traffic

There is renewed interest in the use of bicycles by adults, for purposes of commuting as well as for recreation. As a result of the energy crisis, plus other urban problems such as air and noise pollution and traffic and vehicle parking congestion, the bicycle has in recent years come to be looked upon as a means of alleviating these problems and contributing to the physical health of the nation's citizens. The bicycle is being used increasingly as a commuter vehicle, especially where the distances from home to work are no more than a few miles. The interest in the bicycle as a vehicle for adult and family recreation is reflected also in federal and state legislation providing for assistance to states and municipalities for bike paths in their community.

While at least one federal agency[26] is encouraging the use of research funds to explore and develop effective methods of integrating instruction for bicycle operation and automobile driving, police at the local level are confronted with other forms of the bicycle problem, for example, the need for effective laws[27] and community-accepted enforcement practices, the prevalence of bicycle theft, and the need for a comprehensive community program of bicycle rider control and safety. A California study[28] on actions of bicyclists prior to collision showed that 77 percent of all collisions resulted when the cyclist was joining or intersecting the pathway of vehicle or pedestrian flow, riding against traffic on the left side of the roadway, riding with traffic on the far right side of the roadway, or disregarding traffic signs and signals.

A number of law enforcement agencies actively engaged in bicycle safety and enforcement against unsafe operation have documented their activity. Most successful efforts[29] involve an ongoing program of public information on bicycle rider responsibilities in traffic, a requirement for inspection, licensing and registration of bicycles, establishment of bike routes and paths, and police enforcement of bicycle regulations with appearance in a special bicycle violators' court for offenders sixteen years of age and under.

During the past decade the United States has experienced a marked upsurge in the ownership and use of bicycles. Over one-third of all Americans own bicycles.[30] In some recent years the number of bicycles sold has exceeded the number of automobiles sold. As a result of such increased interest, local government agencies have been besieged by requests for provisions to be made for bicycling.

With the increase in bicycle use has come an increase in associated problems. These problems may be categorized generally as personal safety, access to roadways, and security.

Personal safety is perhaps the most serious problem for the rider, the police, and other users of the roadway. The National Safety Council estimates that there are at least 50,000 bicycle/motor vehicle accidents nationally on an annual basis and 1,000 fatalities.

There is significant evidence to suggest that many accidents are not being officially reported. A Seattle survey[31] shows a ratio of ten nonreported accidents to every one reported. On the basis of accident statistics alone, a sound argument can be established for local police agencies to act to improve bicycle rider safety.

Little has been written about police supervision of nonmotorized transportation. Innovative concepts and procedures are needed. The pressure for police to "do something" will continue to meet with resistance, owing in part to preconceived police attitudes and in part to the lack of knowledge of how to deal with these new problems. Police agencies that have developed effective approaches to bicycle rider safety are urged to submit detailed information about their programs to state and national police and safety journals.

Traffic records and summaries

Police are expected to maintain records and compile summaries on their traffic activity. These include files of traffic accident reports and investigations, enforcement records (citations, arrests, and court dispositions), roadway hazard reports, traffic safety education efforts, and traffic personnel activity. It must be stressed that the collection and compilation of traffic data is justified only when they are used to identify problems, to demonstrate the effectiveness of solutions, and to provide direction to police efforts in motor vehicle accident prevention and traffic safety in general. These records and summaries should be made available to other official departments having responsibilities in street traffic management. Police cooperative effort with engineers, educators, courts and prosecutors, licensing agencies, and nonofficial agencies can find needed direction through analysis of traffic data. Such analysis is facilitated when the data are available through a computer printout.

Traffic laws and ordinances

Traffic laws permit wide discretion in their application by police officers. It is essential, therefore, that police managers provide their supervisors and personnel with a uniform interpretation of traffic laws and of when enforcement action is warranted. This is essential in any form of selective enforcement program. In addition to such management direction, special training in traffic law is necessary to permit quick and certain recognition by police personnel of those elements which constitute a traffic offense and justify officer action.

One of the principal purposes of traffic laws is to provide a single uniform guide in which a driver finds guidance for driving behavior and the police find standards for assessing vehicle use and roadway actions of all drivers.

It is especially important that those engaged in traffic law supervision and enforcement fully realize that the modern approach to the reduction of traffic injuries and property damage stresses *prevention*. Recognition of this principle, belated though it has been, has brought substantial results. It has encouraged responsible authorities to give close attention to the various laws and city ordinances, many of which require extensive overhauling and revision to be effective tools in the preventive approach. It has prompted police authorities to attend to the qualifications and training of their officers who enforce these laws.

An effective approach to police traffic supervision begins with realistic laws, designed to prevent collisions and congestion, enforced by police officers specially trained in vehicle traffic law, and administered and adjudicated by courts functioning according to modern standards for the administration of justice in traffic cases.

Safety of the roadways requires that each driver and pedestrian know what is expected of him or her as well as what he or she may expect from other road users. Therefore, uniformity of traffic laws is vital both within a state and among states. The goal of the federal highway safety program standard on codes and laws is stated as follows:

> To eliminate all major variations in traffic codes, laws, and ordinances on given aspects of highway safety among political subdivisions in a State, to increase the compatibility of these ordinances with a unified overall State policy on traffic safety codes and laws, and to further the adoption of appropriate aspects of the Rules of the Road section of the *Uniform Vehicle Code.*[32]

It should be noted that the *Uniform Vehicle Code*[33] is cited as the document to be used in achieving uniformity. This code recommends that there should be one comprehensive traffic code of statewide application and that local ordinances should not conflict with, duplicate, or cover any matter adequately covered in the statewide vehicle code provisions. To achieve this it may be required that all charges be filed under the state code or, if that is not legally possible, that the state legislature grant authority to local governments to adopt the state provisions by reference.

By this means, uniform rules of the road can be achieved on a statewide basis with a minimum of effort. The *Model Traffic Ordinance,* which is the companion document to the *Uniform Vehicle Code,* now contains only additional provisions and does not have the rules of the road.

It is important that administrators recognize the need for uniform traffic ordinances for their communities and move to implement them. The responsibility for drafting would normally fall to the city attorney or corporation counsel. However, there must be close coordination and consultation with the police, traffic engineer, firemen, planning and zoning commission, street department, and any other local agency which has responsibility for or interest in the use of the roadways. The *Model Traffic Ordinance* recommends a permanent traffic commission to coordinate traffic activities. Such a commission should be composed of all the local agencies which have responsibility for or interest in the use of the roadway. This would be the proper forum for assisting the city attorney in drafting traffic ordinances.[34]

Uniform Vehicle Code and Model Traffic Ordinance   First published in 1926 and 1928, respectively, the code and ordinance have been revised and republished at intervals of two to six years since then to serve as comprehensive standards for state and local laws. They cover highways, streets, motor vehicles, registrations, driver licensing, dealer registrations, financial responsibility, civil liability, accidents and accident reports, motor vehicle equipment, and related subjects.

Based on actual experience, the code and ordinance are revised by the National Committee on Uniform Traffic Laws and Ordinances. The committee, representing federal, state, and local governments as well as insurance companies, automobile manufacturers, safety councils, unions, and others with an interest in transportation, operates through studies and reports in various fields of transportation engineering, planning, safety, and law.

Supplements are issued to accompany the 1968 revised edition of the *Uniform Vehicle Code and Model Traffic Ordinance* which can be obtained from the National Committee, First and Merchants Bank Building, 801 North Glebe Road, Suite 400, Arlington, Virginia 22203. A supplement was issued in 1979.

After the ordinances of a community are well drafted and uniform, it is equally important to train law enforcement officers in the elements of these ordinances so that enforcement can be effective. Furthermore, officers should be trained to charge the most specific offense. General charges such as careless driving or reckless driving too often tend to be catchall charges. It is important that education of the road user be as clear as possible. Many motorists do not understand what they did wrong when charged with careless or negligent driving in contrast to a charge of running a stop sign or going the wrong way on a one-way street. Thus, for educational purposes, officers should file specific charges whenever possible and avoid catchall charges such as careless or negligent driving.[35]

Decriminalization and administrative adjudication of traffic offenses

Traditionally, state traffic offenses are classified as misdemeanors and are tried in the criminal court system.[36] Today, several states are experimenting with alternative methods of processing and hearing traffic cases.

There are several reasons for trying these alternative methods. The main one is probably that the large volume of traffic cases in metropolitan areas has placed a heavy load on the criminal court system. Another reason is the decision of the United States Supreme Court in *Argersinger* v. *Hamlin*, 407 U.S. 25 (1972), which requires the appointment of counsel for indigent persons in misdemeanor cases in which a jail penalty is imposed. The appointment of counsel for defendants in traffic cases is beyond the resources of many jurisdictions. A third reason is that the right to a jury in some jurisdictions extends to every traffic offense, including parking violations. Holding a jury trial is expensive and time-consuming and, because of the large volume of cases, it has been felt that limited resources require that this right be restricted in some manner.

The alternative methods have taken several forms. Frequently, the first step is to "decriminalize" most traffic offenses. In states in which this has been done it usually means that traffic offenses are classified as *noncriminal* and are then called "infractions," "civil forfeitures," or something else other than crimes. This decriminalization has usually been applied to all traffic offenses except driving under the influence of alcohol or other drugs, motor vehicle homicide, hit-and-run incidents, reckless driving, and driving under suspension or revocation. The intent of decriminalization is to eliminate the need for a jury trial, to reduce the burden of proof on the prosecution from "proof beyond a reasonable doubt" (the required burden in criminal cases) to a lesser burden of "a preponderance of the evidence" or "clear and convincing evidence," and, since decriminalization normally eliminates the possibility for the imposition of a jail penalty, to eliminate the need to appoint an attorney for indigent defendants. Thus, the speedy disposition of cases is facilitated. At least twenty states have changed the classification of traffic offenses in recent years.[37]

After decriminalization of traffic cases, an additional step that can be taken is to continue to *hear* traffic cases in the criminal court system. In some states, however, this has included a hearing officer or referee under the supervision of a court. The SAFE Project in Seattle, Washington, is an example.

New York City, Buffalo, Rochester, and Suffolk County (New York) and the state of Rhode Island have adopted what is called "administrative adjudication." This involves removing traffic case hearings from the criminal court system and holding them before a hearing officer of an administrative agency in the executive branch of government. In New York this agency is the Department of Motor Vehicles.

Since law enforcement officers continue to appear and testify in traffic cases in these states, it does not appear that much police time is saved by decriminalization or administrative adjudication. The benefits largely flow to the hearing process and the speedier disposition of cases.

Critics of decriminalization or administrative adjudication acknowledge that the processes may improve the disposition of cases but they express concern about taking away the rights of defendants. In an era of increased efforts to protect citizens from abuses of power by the government, such concerns must be balanced against the benefits to the larger society of expeditious determination of individual cases.[38]

Conclusion

Perhaps no other police role is as unpopular as that of traffic law enforcer. The National Safety Council and other independent sources have, however, demonstrated that traffic accident prevention and control programs of a comprehensive nature, of which police traffic supervision is a significant part, do bring about a significant reduction in the number and severity of motor vehicle accidents. The organizational arrangements and degree of commitment will vary, obviously, from one community to another, but this chapter has provided the framework for police services and has shown where the work fits in with respect to engineering and planning services.

The chapter has provided a perspective of highway transportation, engineering, and planning in their relationship to police traffic supervision, and has described the police functions in traffic control and planning for traffic law enforcement (including the police responsibility, selective enforcement, speed enforcement, and other methods of enforcement). The chapter has then discussed vehicle collision reporting and investigation and has covered alcohol-related traffic offenses and the supervision of parking. Next, the chapter has reviewed bicycle traffic control and analyzed traffic records and summaries. The chapter has concluded with a legal review of traffic laws and ordinances and a discussion of the question of decriminalization of traffic offenses.

1 As used in this chapter, the term highway includes all roadways used by vehicles in urban, suburban, and rural areas.
2 President's Task Force on Highway Safety, *Mobility without Mayhem* (Washington, D.C.: Government Printing Office, 1970), p. 1.
3 U.S., National Highway Traffic Safety Administration, *Highway Safety Program Standards,* standard 7: Police Traffic Services, 1968, p. 29.
4 Ibid., standard 10: Traffic Records, p. 19.
5 For further details on such relationships, see: International Association of Chiefs of Police, *Police Traffic Responsibilities* (Gaithersburg, Md.: International Association of Chiefs of Police, 1976.)
6 See the following publications of the U.S., National Highway Traffic Safety Administration: *NHTSA Model Police Traffic Services: Policies,* 1974; *NHTSA Model Police Traffic Services: Procedures,* 1975; *NHTSA Model Police Traffic Services: Rules,* 1976 (all Washington, D.C.: National Highway Traffic Safety Administration).
7 National Advisory Commission on Criminal Justice Standards and Goals, *Police [Report on Police]* (Washington, D.C.: Government Printing Office, 1973), standard 9.6, pp. 225–32.
8 International Association of Chiefs of Police, Highway Safety Committee, *A Position Statement on Police Traffic Management* (Gaithersburg, Md.: International Association of Chiefs of Police, 1964), pp. 1–2.
9 Edward F. Fennessy, Jr., *The Technical Content of State and Community Police Traffic Services* (Hartford, Conn.: Travelers Research Center, Inc., 1968), p. 41. On the pivotal role of the chief in

establishing and executing departmental policy on traffic law enforcement, see also: John A. Gardiner, *Traffic and the Police: Variations in Law-Enforcement Policy* (Cambridge, Mass.: Harvard University Press, 1969).
10 Franklin M. Kreml, *Traffic Law Enforcement: An Address,* Beecroft Award Lectures, National Safety Congress, Chicago, 1952.
11 International Association of Chiefs of Police, Highway Safety Division, *Selective Traffic Law Enforcement Manual* (Gaithersburg, Md.: International Association of Chiefs of Police, 1972).
12 Eno Foundation for Transportation, *Speed Enforcement Policies and Practices* (Saugatuck, Conn.: Eno Foundation for Transportation, 1970), p. 65.
13 See: California Commission on Peace Officers Standards and Training, *System and Training Analysis of Requirements for Criminal Justice Participants* (Sacramento: California Commission on Peace Officers Standards and Training, 1974).
14 Franklin M. Kreml, *Traffic Law Enforcement.*
15 City of Tacoma (Washington), *Selective Traffic Enforcement Program (STEP),* Contract DOT-HS-225-2-385 (Washington, D.C.: Government Printing Office, 1976); available through National Technical Information Service, Springfield, Virginia 22161.
16 Ibid., p. 4.
17 A more detailed discussion of this matter is found in Robert H. Reeder, *Civil versus Criminal Aspects of Traffic Accident Cases,* Student Reference SN 2157 (Evanston, Ill.: Traffic Institute, Northwestern University, 1975).

18 Collision investigation and accident investigation are used interchangeably.

19 J. Stannard Baker, *Traffic Accident Investigation Manual* (Evanston, Ill.: Traffic Institute, Northwestern University, 1975), p. 8.

20 U.S., National Highway Traffic Safety Administration, *Highway Safety Program Standards,* standard 18: Accident Investigation and Reporting.

21 Northwestern University, Traffic Institute, "Traffic Accident Investigation Policy," staff paper prepared by the Traffic Institute, July 1974.

22 Disablement of vehicles is described as: "Any damage to a motor vehicle such that it cannot be driven, or in the case of trailers, towed from the scene of the accident, in the usual manner by daylight after simple repairs," in National Safety Council, *Manual on Classification of Motor Vehicle Accidents,* 2nd ed. (Chicago: National Safety Council, 1970), pp. 24–25.

23 Disablement of persons is defined as: "Any injury other than fatal, which prevents the injured person from walking, driving, or normally continuing activities which he was capable of performing prior to the motor vehicle traffic accident," in ibid., pp. 28–29.

24 John F. Dunlap & Associates, Inc., *Factors Influencing Arrests for Alcohol-Related Traffic Violations,* Report HS–801–230 NHTSA DOT –HS–4–00837 (Washington, D.C.: National Highway Traffic Safety Administration, 1974); Arthur Young & Company, *Factors Influencing Alcohol Safety Action Project—Police Officers' DWI Arrests,* DOT–HS–801–151, (Washington, D.C.: National Highway Traffic Safety Administration, 1974). For a discussion of "the condition of the driver," see Chapter 14, "Driving under the Influence of Alcohol or Other Drugs," in Edward C. Fisher and Robert H. Reeder, *Vehicle Traffic Law* (Evanston, Ill.: Traffic Institute, Northwestern University, 1974), pp. 171–82.

25 U.S. National Highway Traffic Safety Administration, *Alcohol Safety Action Projects: Evaluation of Operations: 1972,* vol. 1, Summary (Washington, D.C., National Highway Traffic Safety Administration, 1972), p. 22.

26 U.S., Department of Transportation, National Transportation Safety Board, *Bicycle Use as a Highway Safety Problem* (Washington, D.C.: Government Printing Office, 1972).

27 National Committee on Uniform Traffic Laws and Ordinances, *Uniform Vehicle Code and Model Traffic Ordinance,* article 11: Regulations for Bicycles (Washington, D.C.: National Committee on Uniform Traffic Laws and Ordinances, rev. 1968, with current supplement).

28 Automobile Club of Southern California, Public Safety Department, *Special Survey on Bicycling and Bicycle Accident Records* (Los Angeles: Automobile Club of Southern California, 1972).

29 Des Plaines (Illinois) Police Department, 1973; State of Wisconsin, Office of Highway Safety Coordinator, *Model Programs in Pedestrian and Bicycle Safety for Wisconsin Communities* (Madison: State of Wisconsin, Office of Highway Safety Coordinator, rev. 1976); Santa Barbara City Transportation Engineer, *A Balanced Approach to Bicycle Safety* (Santa Barbara, Calif.: Office of the City Transportation Engineer, 1974).

30 Seattle, Washington, Engineering Department, *Bikeway System Planning and Design Manual* (Seattle: Engineering Department, 1975).

31 Ibid.

32 U.S., National Highway Traffic Safety Administration, *Highway Safety Program Standards,* standard 6: Codes and Laws, 1967, p. 11.

33 The *Uniform Vehicle Code and Model Traffic Ordinance* (1968), with Supplement III (1979), is published and kept current by the National Committee on Uniform Traffic Laws and Ordinances, First and Merchants Bank Building, 801 North Glebe Road, Suite 400, Arlington, Virginia 22203. This committee is a private organization composed of about 60 percent representative public officials from all levels of government and about 40 percent officials from organizations in the private sector having an interest in highway safety and use. The committee meets, on the average, every four years to revise and update the code and ordinance.

34 See Sec. 2-12, *Model Traffic Ordinance* (1968), for further information on a traffic commission.

35 For further discussion of the elements of traffic offenses, the power to regulate traffic, federal powers, and other aspects of traffic law, see: Fisher and Reeder, *Vehicle Traffic Law.*

36 For further discussion of the classification of traffic offenses, see ibid., pp. 56–57.

37 See: U.S., National Highway Traffic Safety Administration, *New Trends in Advanced Traffic Adjudication Techniques* (Washington, D.C.: National Highway Traffic Safety Administration, 1976), Appendix A, pp. 22–29, and Fisher and Reeder, *Vehicle Traffic Law,* pp. 56–57.

38 For a more detailed discussion of decriminalization and administrative adjudication, selected references are: U.S., Department of Transportation, *Final Report of the Ad Hoc Task Force on Adjudication of the National Highway Safety Advisory Committee* (Washington, D.C.: Department of Transportation, 1973); U.S., National Highway Traffic Safety Administration, *A Report of the Status and Potential Implications of Decriminalization of Moving Traffic Violations* (Washington, D.C.: National Highway Traffic Safety Administration, 1973); U.S., National Highway Traffic Safety Administration, *Report on Symposium on Effective Highway Safety Adjudication* (Washington, D.C.: National Highway Traffic Safety Administration, 1975), vols. 1 and 2; U.S., Department of Justice, Law Enforcement Assistance Administration, *Administrative Adjudication Bureau of the New York State Department of Motor Vehicles* (Washington, D.C.: Law Enforcement Assistance Administration, 1976); American Bar Association, Committee on the Traffic Court Program, *Standards for Traffic Justice* (Chicago: American Bar Association, 1975).

9 Criminal investigation

The process of criminal investigation, probably the most glamorous aspect of the police service to the general public, has been a tradition-bound operation since the nineteenth century. For every major crime it has been assumed that a "follow-up" investigation is required, even if the chances of apprehending a suspect are almost nonexistent. The evaluation of performance has been casual, and the work has often been routine.

As this chapter shows, however, significant change can be undertaken by the progressive police administrator who will look critically at the criminal investigation process and raise questions about why the process is undertaken, the methods employed, the manpower assigned to the function, and the results obtained.

The chapter opens with a discussion of the setting for the investigation process and the questions that have been raised as to the efficacy of investigation on the basis of studies that have been undertaken by the Rand Corporation. Investigation is then discussed on the basis of the importance of solvability factors. Next, the investigative process is described in some detail. Subsequent portions of the chapter deal with referral points in the investigative process: relationships with the prosecutor; relationships with the victim; juvenile investigations; and the career criminal. A discussion of the management of investigations, including selection and training of investigators, evaluation, and organizational performance, follows. A brief evaluative summary concludes the chapter.

The investigative setting

The criminal investigation process is one of the most important police responses to the problem of crime. The success of criminal investigation has a direct impact on the amount of crime in a given community. While an effective criminal investigative process involves a coordinated effort among many units in the police agency, primary responsibility rests with the patrol and investigative units.

It is amazing how little is known about the criminal investigation process. Detectives have often operated under a shroud of secrecy commonly referred to as the "detective mystique." Police administrators, lacking much substantive knowledge about what a detective actually does, have been hard pressed to evaluate their performance. And yet tradition has provided the impetus for police agencies to respond to every report of a crime with a standard follow-up investigation. Thus, as reported crime has increased so have the number of police department employees assigned to investigation.

Largely because of the detective mystique, the major means for evaluating investigative results has been assessment of clearance rates. In many major police agencies in the United States such rates show that less than 20 percent of major crimes are cleared by arrest. Observers of investigative procedures have noted that a great deal of an investigator's time is spent on unproductive activities, such as redundant reinvestigation, trivial paperwork, and information processing. For many crimes, follow-up investigation appears to have little relationship to crime clearance; most of the cases solved are those in which suspect identity was known at the time of the crime.

Criminal investigation is not solely the responsibility of detectives. Likewise, crime control is not necessarily primarily an investigative responsibility. It is the patrol force that must assume major responsibility for the police response to crime. The rapidity of response to crimes in progress, the proactive nature of patrol strategies, and a thorough preliminary investigation have a greater total impact on criminal apprehension than do follow-up investigative activities.

Clearly, improvements in the criminal investigation process can be made. But the task of investigative improvements requires an accurate understanding of investigative objectives and their limitations. It also requires sensitivity to the types of resource pressures now affecting many police agencies, as well as a willingness to reallocate investigative resources.

The single-handed investigations of Sherlock Holmes are as remote from the reality of criminal investigation today as they were in the nineteenth century. The detective mystique is confined to short stories, novels, movies, and television.

Improvements in the criminal investigation process can only be effective if a police agency adopts a creative patrol strategy followed by a responsive criminal investigation process that directs resources into those areas with the greatest potential for success. The resources available for carrying out these strategies are directly affected by external pressures.

Current resource pressures

Since the mid-1960s, increasing legal and financial pressures have been placed upon police administrators. Many of these pressures have had an effect on the entire scope of police operations, and several have had their greatest impact on investigation. These resource pressures fall into two broad areas: pressures on personnel due to fiscal constraints, and pressures on investigative procedures due to increased emphasis by the courts on the protection of individual rights.

Beginning in the 1960s and continuing through the early 1970s, the fiscal and personnel resources available to police agencies increased dramatically. The birth of the strong police movement coupled with collective bargaining forced many cities to drastically raise police salaries which, historically, had been low. During this period little attention was focused on productivity and resource utilization. Since the mid-1970s many cities have found it increasingly difficult to adequately fund the broad range of services developed during the previous fifteen years. Even though calls for police service, and crime, have continued to increase, most cities have been unable to continue to fund increased police operations. Indeed, a number of large police forces throughout the country have made significant reductions in police personnel.

These fiscal pressures have directly affected police operations. The emphasis has shifted from increased resources to increased productivity. Attention has also focused on measures of productivity, resource utilization, and performance evaluation. Since crime can be expected to increase in the near future, administrators need to ensure that those personnel available for the investigative function adopt procedures reflective of this resource scarcity and that yardsticks within a department are developed to evaluate their performance. (Productivity improvement is discussed in detail in Chapter 6 of the present volume.)

The second area of pressure has come from the continued emphasis on individual rights. In former years investigative operations were judged solely by the result—that is, whether the criminal was apprehended. There was little concern with the operational procedures followed or with whether police adhered to the procedural rules of law. As a result of a series of Supreme Court decisions in the 1960s, it is now generally accepted that, regardless of investigative objectives, police must adhere to certain measures concerning individual rights.

Indeed, the methods of crime solution are now as important as the outcomes, as convictions are increasingly difficult to obtain when the proper procedural rules have not been followed. This has placed severe pressures on the investigative function.

Successful investigative operations require that specific procedural guidelines be provided to investigative personnel. A thorough investigation requires that investigators direct their attention throughout toward providing supportive documentation for their activities. It is obvious, then, that today's administrators must continually review policies and practices to ensure that existing methods of preliminary investigation, case assignment, and follow-up are achieving maximum results and citizen satisfaction.

In this setting, police administrators have had to cope with the fact that past practices are not able to provide maximum productivity and that there is a lack of substantial knowledge and research on which investigative improvements can be based. It is only relatively recently that a limited number of analyses and experiments have been undertaken that are aimed at providing a base for the improvement of investigative effectiveness.

The Rand analysis

One of the more comprehensive analyses of the investigative function was undertaken by the Rand Corporation[1] with funding from the Law Enforcement Assistance Administration (LEAA). The analysis, which was based on a review in detail of the investigative operations of twenty-five police agencies and a questionnaire completed by 153 jurisdictions, provided several findings:

1. On investigative effectiveness: Department-wide arrest and clearance rates are unreliable measures of the effectiveness of investigative operations. The vast majority of clearances are produced by activities of patrol officers, by the availability of identification of the perpetrator at the scene of the crime, or by routine police procedures.
2. Department-wide arrest and clearance statistics vary primarily according to the size of the department, the region of the country in which it is located, and the crime workload (number of reported crimes per police officer). Variations with investigative training, staffing, procedures, and organization are small and do not provide much guidance for policy decisions.

3. On the use of investigators' time: While serious crimes are invariably investigated, many reported felonies receive no more than superficial attention from investigators. Most minor crimes are not investigated.
4. On the use of investigators' time: An investigator's time spent on casework is preponderantly consumed in reviewing reports, documenting files, and attempting to locate and interview victims. For cases that are solved (i.e., a suspect has been identified), an investigator's average time in post-clearance processing is longer than the time spent in identifying the perpetrator. A substantial fraction of time is spent on noncasework activities.
5. On collecting and processing physical evidence: Many police departments collect more physical evidence than can be productively processed. Allocating more resources to increasing the processing capabilities of the department is likely to lead to more identifications than some other investigative actions.
6. On investigative thoroughness: In many large departments, investigators do not consistently and thoroughly document the key evidentiary facts that reasonably assure that the prosecutor can obtain a conviction on the most serious applicable charges.
7. On relations between victims and police: Crime victims in general strongly desire to be notified officially as to whether or not the police have solved their case, and what progress has been made toward convicting the suspect after his arrest.
8. On proactive investigation methods: Investigative strike forces have a significant potential to increase arrest rates for a few difficult target offenses, provided they remain concentrated on activities for which they are uniquely qualified; in practice, however, they are frequently diverted elsewhere.[2]

On the basis of these findings, the study made the following substantive recommendations for reform of the criminal investigation process:

1. Postarrest investigative activity is not only important for prosecution but it is also one of the major activities now performed by investigators. This activity can perhaps be performed in a less costly and more effective manner. Police and prosecutors should make explicit the types of information that are appropriate to collect and document for each type of crime. Above and beyond merely improving coordination between police and prosecutors, it is worthy of experimentation to assign the prosecutor responsibility for postarrest investigations.
2. Assigning all apprehensions of known suspects to investigators does not appear to be cost effective. Certain patrol officers, whom we call generalist-investigators, should be trained to handle this function. Only when apprehension proves difficult should investigative units become involved.
3. Any steps a police department can take to convert investigative tasks into routine actions will increase the number of crimes solved. Information systems and well-organized manual files help produce routine clearances. We believe an experiment should be conducted to determine the cost and effectiveness of lower-paid personnel performing these routine tasks.
4. A significant reduction in investigative efforts on crimes without known suspects would be appropriate for all but the most serious offenses.
5. Establish a Major Offenses Unit to investigate serious crimes.
6. Assign investigations of serious offenses to closely supervised teams rather than individual investigators.
7. Police departments should employ strike forces selectively and judiciously. The advantages of strike force operations are unlikely to persist over a long period of time. Departments must accustom themselves to creating and then terminating strike forces.
8. Evidence-processing capabilities should be strengthened.
9. Police departments should initiate programs to increase the victim's desire to cooperate with the police and to impress upon citizens the crucial role they play in crime solution.[3]

In an overall commentary on the policy implications of the above recommendations, Rand suggested that patrol practices and citizen response and cooperation are more important determinants of criminal apprehension than refinements in the investigative process. The "ultimate implication of our work," they stated, "would be a substantial shift of police resources from investigative units to other units."[4]

While many police administrators agree with a majority of the Rand recommendations, there has been little concurrence on the suggestion to reduce investigative efforts. Most police administrators, while admitting that much present investigative effort is wasted, believe that investigative process reform should aim at maximizing investigative productivity. The clearance rate is only about 20 percent in many major crime categories; the present investigative resources should be redirected toward increasing this rate and the equally low conviction rate. Once clearances approach 50 percent (or more), consideration can be given to reallocation of investigative resources.

Despite this basic disagreement, the Rand analysis does provide an important overview of present investigative practices and their productivity and does tend to point to the fact that the detective mystique impedes productivity improvement and investigative effectiveness.

Early case closure: solvability factors

Even before the Rand analysis, some administrators were concerned with improving the allocation of investigative resources. For example, there was concern about the common practice of automatically following each preliminary investigation with a more detailed follow-up by experienced detectives. Often these follow-up investigations duplicated the work of the preliminary investigator or provided no additional information that was useful for solving the case.

In many instances investigative supervisors assigned only those cases that appeared most productive (solvable) to their investigators. In those cases in which there were no leads provided by the preliminary investigation, one of the three actions was taken: the case was not investigated further (and was thus held in a "pending status"); the victim was reinterviewed by telephone; or the assigned investigators simply reinterviewed the witnesses and victim in the field to see if something had been left out of the preliminary investigation. In all three instances, these investigative efforts were of minimal productivity, and investigative resources available for assignment to potentially productive cases were diminished.

Early case closure was seen as a method for dealing with these cases in which the preliminary investigation had provided no leads. Could not a system be devised to identify during the preliminary investigation those cases having little chance of solution? If those cases were administratively filed, would not more investigative time be available for cases in which leads were present? Administrators and researchers considering these questions believed that focusing follow-up investigative effort on solvable cases would provide improved productivity in terms of case clearance and arrest.

Police resources are limited: therefore, it makes sense that the effectiveness of police investigations will be increased if resources are allocated only to those crimes that have a chance of solution. To direct investigative resources into crimes that have little chance of solution is both wasteful and generally unproductive. Solvability factors are so important, then, because they can provide a valid guide to the allocation of scarce resources. It is suggested that an early case closure system be considered for stolen vehicles, larcenies, and most burglaries, robberies, and assaults.

A solvability factor is information about a crime which can provide the basis for determining who committed that crime. In simple terms, the solvability factor is a lead—a clue—to who the criminal is. Without a solvability factor the chances for solution are small; when a solvability factor is present there is a reasonable chance for solution.

A number of efforts were undertaken to deal with these issues. In California a Stanford Research Institute team designed a system to quantitatively evaluate "leads" discovered through the preliminary investigation.[5] At the conclusion of the preliminary investigation, the patrol officer assigned a weight to the existence of any of a series of factors or leads.

These were considered solvability factors. By totaling the weights, a determination could be made as to whether the probability of case solution at a later time was sufficient to warrant continuation of investigation.

A different system was designed and implemented by the Rochester, New York, police department. A sample of 500 solved criminal cases was analyzed to determine what factors had led to their solution. From this analysis, twelve factors were identified, one or more of which was present in every case cleared through investigation. These solvability factors were as follows:

1. The suspect could be named
2. The suspect could be identified
3. The address of the suspect was known
4. The suspect could be located
5. The vehicle plate number used in the crime was known
6. The vehicle could be identified
7. There was traceable property
8. There were identifiable latent fingerprints
9. A significant modus operandi could be developed
10. It was reasonably suspected that there was a limited opportunity to commit the crime
11. There was reason to believe that the crime would arouse such public interest that public assistance would lead to crime solution
12. There were reasons to believe that further investigative effort would lead to the solving of the crime.

Rochester then redefined its preliminary investigation objectives from data gathering for a crime report to search for and identification of solvability factors. If none of the above solvability factors was found in the crimes previously listed, the case was not further investigated. If one or more solvability factors were found, a follow-up investigation was conducted.

In the Rochester system, cases not expected to be resolved through arrest were not assigned to a follow-up investigator; thus the plan of early case closure was developed. The evaluation of the Rochester system has shown an increase in clearance rates. The system, then, can serve as an example of improvement in the investigative process as suggested by the Rand analysis, and can be of value to police administrators reviewing the effectiveness of their investigative organizations.

The investigative process

Classification of investigations

Criminal investigations can be classified into three broad areas: preliminary investigations, follow-up investigations, and special subject investigations.

Preliminary investigations The preliminary investigation is that initial action by the police agency in response to a report that a crime has occurred. It is aimed at determining who the offender is, what happened, who witnessed it, and what physical evidence is present. The basic facts about the crime are collected during the preliminary investigation. In some jurisdictions this state of the investigative process is aimed at identifying whether leads or solvability factors exist.

Follow-up investigations   The follow-up investigation continues much of the work begun during the preliminary investigation. The overall objectives are the same—identification and apprehension of the offender. Leads are followed up, evidence is collected, and attempts are made to link the crime with others which are similar in the hope of identifying a common perpetrator.

Special subject investigations   Special subject investigations are efforts concentrated on particularly sensitive areas of criminal activity, such as vice, narcotics, and organized crime. Their sensitivity and potential for influence by corruptive practices requires close supervision by the chief of police or a senior command officer of unquestioned integrity. While the objective of special subject investigations is apprehension of criminal offenders, attention is often focused on building an information base about criminal activity patterns toward later apprehension of organized criminal groups. Intelligence (or criminal information) gathering is often an important objective of this type of investigation.

The structure for investigations

There are a great many options in placement of the investigative function within the organization. The decision as to whether to have a centralized or a decentralized detective function, the need for specialized investigative units, and the placement within the organizational structure of these units depend on department size and local priorities. However, the following considerations should be borne in mind in determining organizational placement.

The first consideration is that responsibility for case closure for certain crimes should be pinpointed with the patrol force. When responsibility is divided between the patrol units and a centralized investigative unit, the role of the patrol force is lessened. The Rochester study has shown that the initial response to the criminal event must be rapid if criminal apprehension is to be maximized. Centralized investigative units with responsibility for the actual investigation of crimes (except for serious crimes such as homicide and rape) limit the potential for rapid response. Investigative effectiveness is therefore diminished. Smaller departments, however, should resist the temptation to staff separate investigative units, since the cost to the patrol force is usually excessive and investigative effectiveness is rarely improved.

The second consideration is that specialized investigative units should be formed only when there is sufficient criminal activity of a "crime-specific" nature that intensive follow-up of cases with solvability factors is necessary. As specialized investigative units expand, they tend to diminish the responsibility placed on the patrol force during the preliminary investigation process. Experience has shown that the greater the number of investigative specialists, the greater the duplication of effort.

Centralization versus decentralization   The major issue to be considered concerning investigative organization is that of centralization versus decentralization. The experience of a number of cities indicates that departments with clearly delineated patrol areas (or sections being policed by a number of patrol officers) would do well to decentralize that portion of their investigative operations concentrating on stolen vehicles, larcenies, burglaries, assaults, and robberies. Decentralization of investigators does not mean the elimination of the investigative function; it is simply the placement of supervisory responsibility for most follow-up investigations on the patrol commanders. This provides pinpointing of case closure responsibility for most cases at the lowest operational level—with the patrol force.

Specialized investigative units Even when most of the investigative function is decentralized, there may be a need for specialized centralized investigative units. There are a number of options for assigning responsibilities to such units. The specialized units can be divided according to broad crime classification (crimes against the person, crimes against property, etc.) or by specific crime type in larger cities (homicide, rape, fraud, etc.). Highly specialized crime units can assume total responsibility for crime investigation or else can engage only in follow-up of those crimes in which the preliminary investigation has provided leads or solvability factors.

There are several investigative activities that require a specialized unit for purposes of coordination, investigative sensitivity, and control. Major vice and intelligence investigations should be under the direct supervision of the chief of police. Even where some of these responsibilities are left to the patrol commander, it is necessary to have a unit directly responsible to the chief to see that investigative policies and actions are of a high level of integrity and responsive to the chief's direction. In the same way, when a police officer is suspected of criminal activity the investigation of that officer should be supervised by a unit with direct responsibility to the chief.

Intelligence gathering activities should also be coordinated by a unit reporting to the chief or an immediate subordinate. It is important that intelligence activities be separated from the criminal investigation function and that intelligence officers not be permitted to close cases, make arrests, or assist in prosecution. If this does occur, the value of the intelligence operation is greatly diminished, as sources of information will dry up.

The preliminary investigation process

Thousands of preliminary investigations are conducted every day by police officers across the country. Only a small portion of these investigations result in an arrest or in a crime being cleared. The research and resulting experiments in Rochester indicate, however, that the success of criminal investigations is largely dependent on the strategy of the preliminary investigation, the rapidity of police responses, and the quality of the initial police investigation into a report that a crime has occurred. The preliminary investigation is clearly the important first link in a police department's total investigative effort. The quality of that initial effort will determine the police department's overall success in crime solution.

The primary objective in the preliminary investigation is to determine who committed the crime and to apprehend the criminal. This includes collection of data about the crime which will solidly support eventual court action when an arrest is made.

As simple as this overall objective may appear, it is often completely forgotten as preliminary investigators conduct their work. All too often the investigating officers see their role as merely that of report takers—although the report itself is the instrument for reporting the results of the preliminary investigation, and, in this sense, the preliminary investigator is *the* investigator. It is at this early stage of an investigation that a majority of the usable information about a given case will be found.

The framework for the preliminary investigation is the undertaking of three major tasks:

1. Verification that an offense has actually occurred, and identification of the victim, the place of the crime, and when the crime occurred

2. Identification of solvability factors (or leads)
3. Communication of the circumstances of the crime, and identification of completed investigative tasks and of those yet to be done.

While there is no definitive order of priority in which these actions must be completed, generally the best investigative strategy dictates that the officer should initially determine whether a crime has occurred, since this will affect all other actions.

Crime occurrence is usually a fairly easy thing to document in the abstract, but the police officer has to relate the occurrence to the criminal law with its varying degrees and limitations. It is best for the officer to initially consider, in a broad sense, what crime has occurred and then, later, after other facets of the investigation are complete, to consider the exact definition of the crime, such as degree of offense. The determination that an offense has not occurred normally stops the investigation and places the officer in the role of reporter of facts and adviser on what the complainant can do to resolve his or her problem.

Definition of crime A crime is an act committed or omitted, in violation of a public law forbidding or commanding it. It can also be defined as any social harm made punishable by law.

Society outlaws certain acts for a number of reasons: to protect life and property, protect individual freedoms, preserve the system of government, and maintain the morality of the community. Ideally the goal of the law is to regulate people so that they can live within their society without chaos and under the best possible circumstances.

Source: This material is excerpted from Georgetown University Law Center, the D.C. Project, *Street Law: A Course in Practical Law* (St. Paul, Minn.: West Publishing Co., 1975), p. 19.

If a crime has occurred, the preliminary investigator must next direct attention toward identification of solvability factors. Whether an early case closure system exists or not, by identifying solvability factors the preliminary investigator can systematically ensure that all important areas are covered in a logical manner. The objective of the solvability factor search, of course, is to determine who the criminal offender is and where he or she can be found. Thus, most police agencies will find that their solvability factors (however they may be described) center on collecting witness information and other identifiers such as vehicle description, suspect data, and property information.

Once solvability factors have been thoroughly searched out, the preliminary investigator must communicate his or her findings to the follow-up investigator, whether or not a continuation of the investigation is proposed under an early case closure system. This communication should be based on a report form that covers solvability factors and includes identifying information on the victim, the suspect, witnesses, stolen property, the modus operandi, and physical evidence, together with a brief narrative report. Such a report forces the officer to systematically categorize information for every reported crime on a prenumbered report form which is then transmitted to the follow-up investigator. However complete the preliminary investigation, if the report on activities does not reflect the actual effort undertaken, follow-up investigators will repeat much of the preliminary work.

Since crimes have little chance of solution unless solvability factors have been identified, it should be clear why the initial investigator's work is so important. If the initial investigative work is competently done and reported, a police agency can assign follow-up investigators only to those cases where success is considered possible (or probable, depending on case circumstances). The initial investigator must convince the follow-up investigator that all potential solvability factors have been explored. If the follow-up investigator is not convinced, again there will be duplication of much of the preliminary work.

Finally, the preliminary investigator must communicate case status to the victim at the very least and to important witnesses if possible. The victim should receive a copy of the preliminary investigation report (perhaps even at the conclusion of the preliminary investigation) for two reasons. First, it provides a good statement of the police action that has been taken. Second, it places some responsibility on the victim to consider—over the following days—what additional information may exist that would be useful to the police. This placement of responsibility can be helpful in getting citizens to accept early case closure.

Some police agencies have the preliminary investigator give each person interviewed (witness, victim, reporting person) a small business card containing the officer's name, the complaint number, and a suggestion to call the police if any additional information becomes available. Such a system can be very useful in maximizing investigative information from a neighborhood when a crime has occurred.

The preliminary investigation, then, is clearly the most important part of the criminal investigation process. In smaller police agencies the preliminary investigation will often be the entire investigative effort. And, in larger agencies, a good preliminary investigation can and should eliminate the need for duplicative follow-up investigation activities.

The follow-up investigation process

Where the preliminary investigation indicates the existence of substantive leads or solvability factors, there is a need for a follow-up investigation. It is in this stage that analytical and substantive crime specialists may be brought into the case.

Whether the investigative function is decentralized or not, the follow-up investigator (1) checks to see that the preliminary investigation was thoroughly done; (2) continues investigation of those leads which have surfaced; (3) works to link the crime with others of a similar type; (4) if an arrest is made, prepares the case for prosecution.

The investigator ensures that the preliminary investigation was thoroughly done so that important leads will not be overlooked. This is not to say that any duplication of preliminary investigative effort should occur. Indeed, if weaknesses in the preliminary investigation are found, the investigator would be wise to have them corrected by the patrol unit involved so that they will not happen again. Through the process of reviewing the preliminary investigation, the investigator familiarizes himself or herself with all aspects of the case and avoids the need to undertake activities which have already been completed.

Once leads have been identified, the criminal investigator proceeds to follow those leads as far as possible toward apprehension of the criminal. The tendency to search for additional leads must be resisted, since it is clear that a majority of such effort is wasteful and ineffective. Once a lead has been followed up as far as possible, the investigator should decide whether the case status is to be changed to inactive.

As part of the follow-up investigation process, the investigator should compare the case with others which are similar in the hope of linking together like crimes. Since the leads available from each crime vary, and since career criminals commit a majority of the serious crimes, developing linkages between similar crimes is an effective way for the investigator to increase the chances of identifying the perpetrator. Indeed, the process is often akin to puzzle-making, in which a total picture is made from independent parts. Some departments with a decentralized investigative structure have limited the role of the remaining centralized investigators to that of a specific crime specialist piecing together the parts of individual crimes. This activity of puzzle-making can effectively be linked with the crime analysis function which should be able to provide pattern and trend analysis useful in establishing linkages. Throughout this entire process, the investigator tries to determine whether one individual committed a series of similar crimes.

Importance of the crime scene search   It should be borne in mind when the case is being prepared that a thorough crime scene search and the subsequent hard evidence that can be obtained are becoming more critical as confessions, admissions, and search warrants become more fragile in court. The problems facing administrators are what crime scenes or how many crime scenes can be processed, and what proportion of manpower should be assigned to this function. Sufficient manpower must also be available to process the evidence so that crime scene searches are not conducted for publicity purposes.

The degree of intensity of a crime scene search will naturally vary. A department cannot process every larceny in the same manner as a homicide. At major crime scenes the trained technicians along with the criminal investigator in charge must be sure that every item possibly connected with the scene is carefully gathered and processed and that this is accomplished in a manner that provides for the minimum chain of evidence. It would be well to process all burglaries at least to the extent of photographing and dusting for fingerprints for the points of entry and exit and for the location of the crime within. For the lesser crimes, such as larceny and stolen cars, departments may consider processing only those crimes in which a suspect can be named and the processing of fingerprints is realistic. Fiscal constraints may mandate that an administrator give serious consideration to the number of personnel assigned to the function to ensure that all serious crimes are processed and that some consideration is given to other crimes with a realistic potential for solvability.

The structure of the evidence technician unit will vary with the size of the department. The small department may be so structured that every officer is his own technician, or, on the other hand, the services of a larger nearby department may be utilized. Large departments may have separate evidence technician units within major divisions. For medium-sized departments, consideration should be given to having a small evidence technician unit to process major crime scenes. These departments should equip some officers on each shift or in each section with modest cameras and fingerprint kits, so that certain crime scenes (larcenies, burglaries) may be readily photographed and a limited effort made to check for fingerprints.

Concluding cases

The final responsibility of the follow-up investigator is the preparation of the case for prosecution. The quality of the investigative effort will directly affect the ability of the department to successfully conclude the case with a conviction.

The good street police officer is most often well aware of all of the techniques and strategies which lead up to what the public generally believes is the successful conclusion of a case: the arrest of the perpetrator. (It is the time period from the preliminary investigation through the arrest in which most of the "exciting" activity in fact occurs.) In reality, however, the arrest is often only the halfway mark of a successful investigation. It is at the point of arrest that a competent trained supervisor or an investigator with administrative skills must begin to take over and pull together a case that will stand up in court some time in the (often distant) future.

To help assure future prosecution success, the arresting officer seeking such advice in the collection and presentation of case materials will ensure that quality control is maintained. At the same time, efforts should be made to enhance the quality of the case. For example, an investigator should never rely on an oral admission of participation in a crime but should secure a written, witnessed, notorized statement from the suspect. While an investigation is being processed, every effort should be made to obtain additional supportive witnesses who, when questioned, should be kept apart so that investigators can obtain additional independent identifications. And a review of all statements from suspects must be made to ascertain that the suspect was advised of his or her rights during the processing of the investigation. Care must be exercised to make certain that no constitutional rights were violated by an improper lineup or returning of a suspect to the scene. Even when a suspect has acknowledged the location of fruits of a crime, or contraband, if time permits a search warrant should be obtained that will subsequently ensure the admission of the evidence into court.

In cases involving larceny, burglary, or street robbery, the apprehended individual may well have been involved in many other "like" crimes and may well admit to additional crimes through interrogation. Departments should make two uses of such data. First, they can enhance their overall clearance rate with admissions that will lead to multiple clearances. Second, in instances where multiple clearances occur departments should strongly consider the preparation of a second arrest and a supporting case, if sufficient evidence is available to present a companion case in court. In many instances it is common for the victim or witness to either refuse to testify or to be unavailable to testify when the first case is ready for the grand jury or the trial. The investigator who has spent a few more hours developing a companion case may then be able to successfully prosecute that second case in court instead of letting the suspect be released. This can give the department a higher chance of conviction, in addition to the benefit of increased clearance rates.

Referral points in the investigative process

Criminal investigation involves much more than the deductive processes of verification, identification, and other tasks connected with solving a crime. It also entails helping the prosecuting attorney develop the best possible case for presentation to a grand jury and for trial; providing information to the victims of crime and soliciting their help; dealing with the special problems of juvenile cases; and working out improved investigative methods for dealing with career criminals. Each of these tasks will be discussed in the section that follows.

Investigator–prosecutor relationship

To support an effective case conclusion effort, police departments should develop a close working relationship with the prosecuting attorney's office on several levels.

The highest level of coordination requires periodic meetings by the prosecutor or the prosecutor's chief assistant with the chief of police to establish guidelines for both agencies. These meetings will help clarify any differences of opinion or differences in procedures between the departments. At the operational level, if the prosecuting attorney is not a part of the arrest process by routine, then procedures should be developed whereby the prosecutor or his or her assistant should be on call on an as needed basis to assist the police in the development of major cases. In addition, procedures should be developed whereby the prosecutor or his or her assistant should review, on a daily basis, all felony arrests and grand jury "packages" to ensure that cases are completely prepared for prosecution.

Procedures should also be developed for a review of cases following court disposition. When cases have been dismissed, either by no bill of the grand jury or following trial, the police administrator and the criminal investigators will be advised of the outcome and of whether poor investigation or incomplete cases were the cause of the dismissal. Only through such feedback can future mistakes be prevented and investigators made aware of the faulty case in a constructive manner so that the faults will not be repeated. A combination of the prosecuting attorney's assistance in case preparation and his or her critique of both successful and faulty cases in court should be utilized by every department as the basis for training programs to improve the department's investigative ability.

Investigator–victim relationship

An important part of the total criminal investigative process is the police relationship with victims of crime. It has been too common in the past for victims to be forgotten after the crime, until they are needed to assist in the prosecution of the offender in court. Then, in many cases, the victim either cannot be found or is unwilling to appear.

The police have a responsibility to help the victim understand his or her options and to keep the victim informed as to the status of the case. Several larger police agencies now have victim assistance programs aimed at meeting this dual need. Every police agency, regardless of size, has a responsibility to develop a positive relationship with victims of crime. Such a relationship, too, is important to the outcome of any subsequent court case.

The most important victim contact, of course, is that made at the time of the preliminary investigation. When this phase is completed, the patrol officer should give the victim a realistic assessment of what he or she can expect in the future. If the police agency has an early case closure system, the officer should advise the complainant that nothing further can be done without additional information. At this time the victim should be given a copy of the preliminary investigation report and an identification card with a telephone number to call if additional information becomes available. Providing honest and accurate information to the victim can build up important respect between police and client. Failure to provide such information can create expectations among victims which cannot be met and can greatly harm the police–community relationship.

Immediately following a crime, the police agency should provide the victim with information about the types of assistance which may be available. For example, rape victims should be informed about rape crisis center assistance, if such is available. Burglary victims should be reminded to contact their insurance companies. And victims of serious assault or robbery should be directed toward counseling, medical, or psychiatric services if they appear to be appropriate. Where victim's compensation benefits are available, the procedure of application should be fully explained. In order to provide such advice, the police agency needs to see that patrol officers are well informed on such services; also, a follow-up contact with the victim might well be made by a specially trained officer.

Legal advice is also needed by many victims. It is common for victims of crimes to be without a regular attorney. In these instances, legal aid offices can provide legal counseling to the victim who is unsure of his or her rights. The police agency should direct the victim to such assistance.

Since the victim is usually an important part of the prosecution if the offender is apprehended, it is desirable for the police agency to maintain contact with him or her over the course of any productive investigation. This requires periodic reports to the victim on the status of the investigation. If property is recovered, the victim should be advised on how its return can be facilitated. If court action is scheduled, the victim should be briefed as to courtroom procedure, when to appear, and how to get there. Once a trial has begun, the victim must be kept informed as to its progress. If a case is disposed of by a guilty plea or plea bargaining, the victim must be notified.

A police agency can provide these positive responses to victims in ways which can enhance the overall effectiveness of the criminal investigation. A formal victim's assistance program in the police agency can be established with full-time staff; or the responsibility can be assumed by another city agency. In either case, the police agency should still provide a copy of the original crime report to the victim and should send a follow-up letter to the victim informing him or her of case status.

Victim Aid The Victim Information Bureau of Suffolk (VIBS) offers a twenty-four-hour hotline service and a short- and long-term counseling center to any of the 1.25 million Suffolk County [Long Island, New York] residents who are victims of rape and family violence.

About 85 percent of VIBS clients are victims of family violence. Although the term "family violence" includes any confrontation within the family unit which leads to a violent act, most VIBS clients are married couples. The project has been successful in persuading either husband or wife to call the hotline just before an argument escalates into violence. For their own safety, however, counselors never travel to the scene while a family dispute is in progress. They will meet the caller in a restaurant, telephone booth, or any other place requested.

Source: *Target,* October 1976.

Crime has a traumatic effect on those it strikes. When the police appear unsympathetic or unresponsive, citizens will be less willing to assist in later phases of an investigation in which their participation may be required for successful case closure.

Juvenile investigations

The juvenile offender creates special problems for the police administrator, the police investigator, and the community. The role of the police officer as a juvenile officer or youth worker has varied over the years. At one time, in the 1950s, a great deal of police manpower was diverted to juvenile crime prevention programs, such as Police Athletic League programs, where the police engaged in work normally performed by recreation workers and social workers. In most jurisdictions today, this type of police responsibility has been reduced or almost completely eliminated as other community agencies have developed capabilities in these areas and police manpower pressures have meant redirection of resources.

The young offender continues to pose severe problems to most jurisdictions. When a juvenile offender first becomes involved in criminal activity, he or she generally comes to the attention of the uniformed patrol officer through involvement in minor nuisance, harassment, or gang activities. This first involvement with the criminal justice system is a critical time, since it is either the beginning of the recidivist or the diversion of the juvenile from a future of deviant behavior. If the police are a failure at this stage, they can conceivably look toward hundreds of crimes perpetrated by this one person in future years. Because juvenile activity is most often neighborhood based, it is wise for most juvenile offense investigations to be the primary responsibility of the neighborhood beat or patrol officers. Their contacts in the neighborhood and knowledge of the area's juveniles put them in a position to deal with offenders positively.

There are no simple answers or clearly effective procedures to follow with the juvenile, but experience suggests that communities consider alternatives to arrest if they are available through other agencies. In those cases where it has been the practice to effect a juvenile arrest, or where alternative systems are not available, departments should consider developing juvenile diversion programs whereby a reasonable number of police officers can be trained as specialists in relating with juveniles in their neighborhood setting.

When an arrest normally would appear appropriate, diversion should always be considered where it is practical and where the victim, investigating police officer, and juvenile officer concur that such diversion may be productive. The diversion may be simply an agreement whereby the juvenile agrees to pay back the victim or work off the damages through some acceptable program. Referral of the juvenile and his or her family to counseling services is also an option.

Regardless of options available, however, the police administrator should be aware that involvement in a program of juvenile offender diversion may alter arrest statistics. Departments that analyze the work load of investigators may encounter resistance to a diversion program which, while continuing investigative efforts, reduces the number of arrests. (Juvenile programs are discussed in detail in Chapter 12 of this book.)

Career criminals

Special attention should be given to the career criminal as a part of a police agency's total investigative effort. While it is difficult to state exactly how much crime can be attributed directly to the career criminal, most police administrators feel that about 10 percent of the criminals are committing a majority of the crimes. Career criminal activity is most common in robberies, burglaries, larcenies, stolen cars, forgeries, and frauds.

Often the career criminal is thought of as a member of organized crime—an invisible figure, highly sophisticated, possessing cunning and cleverness. Such is not, in fact, the case. The career criminal is often known to the police from prior offenses; he or she is most often an opportunist who will commit whatever crime is convenient. Often the career criminal is highly talented in one speciality, such as fraud, passing bad checks, or burglary. A single arrest is not sufficient to alter his or her pattern of crime.

There are a number of ways in which a police agency can improve its effectiveness in dealing with the career criminal; the most common are improvements in crime-specific apprehension capabilities, concentrated warrant service follow-up, specific individual criminal surveillance, and special major case preparation.

Certain types of crimes lend themselves to rapid apprehension of the criminal offender. For example, passers of bad checks can be apprehended if early response is made to a report of such an incident. It is important that police departments work closely with local banks and respond immediately to silent alarms when an individual is attempting to pass a bad check. While some administrators may feel bank alarms should be used only for robberies, passing bad checks and bank frauds are far more common and when alarm systems are used in such cases an increased number of apprehensions will probably be made and the criminals apprehended will often be wanted for other crimes.

Attention should also be focused on indictment warrants. If someone served a warrant fails to appear at an indictment (especially in cases of robbery, burglary, larceny, and bad checks), it probably follows that that person is a career criminal. A concentrated effort by a warrant squad to find such persons can be highly productive.

Another method serving the same purpose is to place a task force or strike force in a small high crime area to concentrate on the activities of known criminals. This force can be given data regarding the types of crimes occurring in the area as well as information on and descriptions of known and suspected criminals and information on outstanding warrants of individuals living or thought to be living in the area.

Surveillance teams are a fourth such method. Usually, a group of senior investigators, the surveillance team, concentrates on a known criminal, giving attention to his or her activities, the locations that he or she visits, and the people with whom he or she associates. Surveillance of this type may require the combined activities of more than one police agency, especially if the criminal leaves the city on a regular basis. The use of surveillance teams has two potential outcomes. The investigators can come to thoroughly understand the criminal, his or her movements, and his or her associates so that if a major crime occurs they will find it easier to make the required connection between the criminal and the crime. Second, there is a good chance that the investigators will intercept the criminal in the commission of a crime.

The fifth strategy is major case preparation. When a major offender or career criminal is apprehended, investigators, with the assistance of the prosecutor, should concentrate on preparing the strongest possible case by making an effort to produce hard evidence such as fingerprints, additional witnesses, and an admission. At this point, it is also wise to concentrate on the preparation of a second strong case so that if the first case is flawed there will still be a conviction. Multiple clearances are the basis for making the second case; they must be more than simply enhancement of the clearance record of the department. Admissions by career criminals to numerous crimes can be used by the department to improve its conviction rate by concentrating on prosecution of these companion cases. For this strategy to be effective, however, lines of communication must be developed between the police agency and the prosecuting attorney's office so that the case preparation is a joint effort. Larger departments may want to form a special career criminal or major violator's unit to take over major cases immediately after arrest has been made.

Managing the investigative process

It is all too common for police administrators to focus on the day-to-day operations of the investigative function while ignoring the management aspects upon which so much of investigation success is based. There are four areas of management upon which the investigative process is built: coordination and communication; supervision of the investigative process; selection and training of investigators; and assessment of investigative results.

Coordination and communication

Effective management of the investigative process requires a system for coordinating the parts of the process. A generation ago it was typical for detectives to keep investigative information to themselves. Patrol officers were never involved in an investigation for fear that the information would not be kept confidential. And information was not shared with other investigators for fear that the detective would lose his "pinch." Today, the spiraling crime rate and the apparent trend toward a small number of professional criminals committing a large number of crimes mandate open and rapid communication between patrol and investigative personnel.

The need for communication begins during the preliminary investigation by patrol personnel. As soon as information is developed that first identifies a suspect, that information must be relayed to all concerned officers and, in some cases, to adjacent police agencies as well. When a positive identification is made of a suspect, that information must be rapidly disseminated again to all personnel and affected agencies. One means of disseminating this information is through a "wanted" flier, containing a picture or mug shot and a description of the subject, and his or her known "hangouts" and last known address. The flier can be disseminated on a routine basis, but it is critical that there be a recall system to ensure that when the suspect is either apprehended or cleared of the offense officers are so notified. It is also important to segregate persons actually wanted on a warrant or indictment from those wanted for investigation only. In larger departments, where the volume of "wanted" fliers would make such a system impractical, some means should be developed on a division or precinct level that will permit all uniformed officers and investigators to have this information at hand about the section of the city they police.

Regardless of how the investigative function is organized, it is critical that there be strong coordination of all investigative activities in the police agency. Information dissemination to and among patrol units is one part of meeting the need for coordination, but equally important is coordination of actual investigative and patrol activities among patrol officers within units, among investigative personnel within a unit, and between patrol and investigative units. The objective is to make all concerned personnel knowledgeable as to crime patterns and the status of criminal investigations, and as to who suspected or wanted criminals are. With this information patrol officers, for example, can direct their patrol time on expected locations of criminal activities. And investigators can make use of information obtained by patrol officers who are regular observers of suspects' activities.

The method used to achieve patrol–detective coordination is largely dependent on organization size and structure. Small police agencies can best achieve the required level of coordination through regular roll call meetings of patrol officers with representatives of the investigative units during which information can be exchanged. In addition, a list of crime clearances and arrests should be made available to patrol and investigative personnel on an almost daily basis. To encourage information exchange, it is important that when information received results in an eventual arrest or crime clearance the officer providing the information receive full or partial credit.

Larger police agencies, especially those with a decentralized patrol structure, should consider the assignment of an officer in each patrol unit as an investigative coordinator. This officer would serve as a link between investigative units and patrol personnel, identifying criminal patterns in the patrol sectors, assisting in the design of patrol strategies and priorities responsive to criminal activity, and supervising investigators working in that patrol area.

Supervision of the investigative process

Much of the success of the investigative process depends on first-line supervision. While many of the responsibilities of the first-line supervisor of patrol officers are substantially the same as those of the investigative supervisor, some responsibilities differ if the department uses an early case closure system. It is important that these responsibilities be clearly defined and regularly evaluated by police management.

One of the primary responsibilities of first-line supervisors in investigation is certification of the completion and accuracy of preliminary investigative reports by patrol officers. Since most of these reports provide the data on which follow-up investigations will be based, their completeness is essential if investigators are to avoid duplication of the information gathering process. The supervision of the preliminary investigation process will be strengthened if supervisors are thoroughly trained in their responsibilities and have an understanding of investigative procedures and requirements, especially at the follow-up inves-

tigative level. Special training in investigative procedure is particularly important because many supervisors have never served as investigators.

Police agencies that use the early case closure system have additional first-
line supervision requirements. Since the preliminary investigation in these
departments serves as the basis for a decision as to whether or not a follow-up
investigation is desirable, the supervisor must understand what constitutes sufficient information upon which such a decision should be based. This requires
full understanding of and ability to evaluate early case closure, solvability
factors, and investigative recommendations based on supportive facts.

Departments should consider assignment of newly promoted supervisors to
an investigative unit as a part of their promotional training. Also, the police administrator should require that evaluation of the completeness of preliminary investigations be carried out as a routine. When incomplete investigations are discovered, or when the evaluation indicates a pattern of incomplete reports, the
first-line supervisor should be held accountable for the performance deficiency.

Investigative supervisors should ensure that cases are properly prepared, that
follow-up investigative effort does not duplicate preliminary investigation, and
that individual investigative efforts are directed toward following through on
leads rather than on "fishing" for new information. Investigative supervisors
should not use their time for conducting individual investigations. They are supervisors first and investigators second: their responsibility is to coordinate
follow-up investigations to achieve maximum productivity.

Selection and training of investigators

Supervisory effectiveness will be limited unless investigative personnel are
properly selected and adequately trained. Few issues in the investigative
process are more important. All police employees do not have the natural ability
to be effective investigators, and those officers who have the required ability
must have their skills developed through an effective training program. It has
been the practice in many police agencies for investigators to be assigned on the
basis of external or internal departmental politics. Investigative assignments are
generally considered highly desirable positions having a great deal of status. It
has been difficult for police administrators to develop meaningful selection processes for investigators when little has been known about the actual substance
of an effective investigative process.

Selection   A few cities have developed task analyses of investigative positions
that have identified the knowledges and abilities needed for the position of investigator. The most common of these are as follows:

1. Decisiveness: readiness to make decisions or to render judgments
2. Judgment: ability to reach logical conclusions on the basis of the
   evidence at hand
3. Planning and organization: effectiveness in planning and organizing
   own activities and those of a group
4. Problem analysis: effectiveness in seeking out pertinent data and in
   determining the source of the problem
5. Impact: ability to create a good first impression, to command attention
   and respect, to show confidence, and to achieve personal recognition
6. Initiative: actively influencing events rather than passively accepting;
   self-starting.

These attributes provide a starting point in the selection process for investigators. With this information as a base, police administrators can go on to implement effective selection processes for investigative assignments.

Some police departments have begun to utilize the assessment center as a means of making that selection. (See Chapter 13 for a further discussion of the assessment center as a part of personnel management.) The assessment center consists of a series of job-related exercises performed in a controlled environment by applicants. While applicants are performing the exercises, they are observed by a small group of assessors who rate the performance against prestructured scales. Exercises most commonly used are the in-basket test, the fact finding exercise, the leaderless group discussion (to assess qualities of leadership and persuasion), and the case file (in which the applicant is provided with a half-completed investigative file on which recommendations are made for future investigative steps).

While the design of investigative assessment center activities can be expensive and their administration is time-consuming, the center is an effective means by which a police agency can select the most skilled personnel for investigative assignments. If properly designed, the examination process is considered unbiased and job-related.

Other important factors to be considered in selecting investigators are: the initiative shown by an applicant while assigned to the patrol function; the quality of preliminary investigations undertaken while the applicant has been a patrol officer; and the applicant's general motivation toward engaging in criminal investigation activities.

Training   Once selected, investigators must be provided with training which will include both classroom exercises and field experience. In addition to the standard classroom lecture, the training options include, for example, temporary assignment to specialist investigations; fact finding exercises; case preparation for court; courtroom procedure; and several kinds of group discussion.

Many assessment center activities are also effective as training devices; from the critique of a new investigator's performance in these activities, skills which need improvement can be identified. As a part of the training process investigators should be closely supervised and should be provided with regular feedback so that they may work toward self-improvement. Training should also include material on case preparation, courtroom procedure, and effective court prosecution. The ability of the investigator to successfully conclude cases through prosecution is as important as the success of the investigation itself.

To ensure that investigative personnel maintain maximum productivity, it is important that the department regularly evaluate investigative performance. This review should be carried out annually, at least. Those investigators who are not performing at an acceptable level should be counseled and their deficiencies discussed. A follow-up evaluation should then be conducted after an additional six months. If an investigator's performance has not improved, he or she should be reassigned to the patrol function and replaced with a new, more productive, investigator.

Assessment of investigative results

Investigative effectiveness and productivity should be measured both by individual performance and by organizational performance.

The individual investigator   Two kinds of performance analysis must be considered. The first is the comparison of the individual investigator's efforts at the lowest unit level. The police administrator must be careful not to place primary emphasis on a comparison of number of arrests. To develop an effective evaluation system, a comprehensive analysis must be made of the total number of cases assigned to an individual investigator. A comparison must be made of cases eventually cleared by arrest with the total number of cases assigned, and of cases cleared by arrest in which the investigator developed solvability factors over and above those initially listed by the preliminary investigator.

The second kind of performance analysis involves the quality of final case preparation. For example, in those instances where the preliminary investigator has named a suspect or has described thoroughly the identity of a suspect, the assessment should determine whether the follow-up investigator obtained stolen property, obtained an admission, obtained the names of additional accomplices, or obtained additional witnesses and supporting affidavits. Factors such as these indicate the competence of an investigator who has enlarged the case beyond the preliminary investigation.

In addition, it is important to analyze how many additional cases were developed by the investigator from the original information. The importance of these multiple factors beyond the arrest itself as an indicator of performance is supported by studies which have indicated that if a crime is not cleared at the original contact, or if evidence is not obtained at that time, the crime will probably never be solved.

Organizational performance The second area of investigative effectiveness, organizational performance, is best evaluated through a monitoring system. Such a system effects periodic review of selected aspects of investigative performance by providing the administrator with data on both individual investigator performance (as previously described) and unit performance.

A system is needed for data collection to obtain the required input to the monitoring system. This requires crime and investigative follow-up reports which provide substantive input on the crime and the status of the investigation. There must be a structure for data analysis so that the data collected can be placed in a format responsive to management needs. A reporting mechanism needs to be developed that will present the results of the data analysis in a useful format: computer or hand tabulated reports are most common. There should be a system for data validation to ensure that the statistics reported are indeed an accurate representation of actual data, and evaluation criteria must be developed and tested. These criteria are the basis of value judgments the administrator makes about performance.

The measures which are selected for a monitoring system could include the following:

1. Number of offenses—citywide or in each district
2. Differences in offenses between present and past reporting periods
3. Number (and percentage) of cases closed after (a) preliminary investigation, and (b) follow-up investigation
4. Number of cases closed without follow-up investigation and comparison of resulting clearance rates for these cases and those receiving further investigation
5. Number of convictions versus arrests
6. Number of cases cleared by individual investigators versus number of cases assigned.

Numerous other measures can be identified. They should be based on the requirements that system users place on the monitoring system. Common requirements of the police chief, for example, may be personnel performance evaluation, resource allocation, case status, procedural effectiveness, and investigative outcome analysis. The monitoring system is the best method by which the police administrator can receive data on which these assessments can be based.

Evaluative summary

This chapter has described the criminal investigation process, including the investigative setting; the questions raised in current police work with respect to the efficacy of automatically assigning an investigator to every major crime; the process of early case closure; the use of solvability factors; the importance of preliminary investigation as a part of police patrol; the importance of concluding cases successfully; the use and value of referral forms in the investigative process; and the four areas of investigative management: coordination and communication, supervision, selection and training of investigators, and assessment of results.

The requirements and the process of criminal investigation will continue to change during the next few years. Technology will improve while personnel resources remain static. Police administrators will increasingly be required to assess present investigative practices and to design new and improved investigative strategies. Additional experimental and research efforts, such as the Rand analysis and the Rochester experiments, should be undertaken and supported by police administrators. Most important, the mystique surrounding investigative operations must be totally eliminated and the process based on well-evaluated procedures and strategies.

1 Originally published in 1975 as a three volume Rand Corporation report, the latest version is Peter W. Greenwood, Jan M. Chaiken, and Joan Petersilia, *The Criminal Investigation Process* (Lexington, Mass.: D. C. Heath & Company, 1977).

2 ©1977 The Rand Corporation. Reprinted with permission from ibid., Chapter 14.

3 Ibid., Chapter 15 (excerpted).

4 Ibid., p. 243

5 Bernard Greenberg, Oliver S. Yu, and Karen I. Lang, *Enhancement of the Investigative Function*, vol. 4 (Menlo Park, Calif.: Stanford Research Institute, 1972).

10 Organized crime

The police in America are expected to deal effectively with diverse responsibilities.[1] Loosely categorized, these responsibilities are divided into crime control and noncrime services. Certain responsibilities are so clear that they require no elaboration beyond the mere statement of the mandate—for example, "to promote and preserve civil order."[2]

At first glance it would appear that the duty to identify and apprehend criminals is equally simple. After all, individual criminal incidents such as a homicide or a theft are obvious acts which represent violations of the criminal law. It also follows that one or more persons are responsible for such acts. While identifying the particular violator may present difficulties to the investigator, the objectives of police action are nevertheless clear. A citizen has been victimized and the event has been reported to the police. The appropriate response is not as clear, however, when the police are confronted with a mandate to suppress, prevent, or control the phenomenon which is commonly termed organized crime.

There has been and probably will continue to be much disagreement over the police role in dealing with organized crime. The professional administrator can begin to move more effectively against this problem only after it is explained in terms befitting a problem of such enormous complexity and such magnitude.

One of the major purposes of this chapter is to clarify terminology and provide ways of identifying organized crime through the four municipal indicators: people, organization, enterprises, and acts. Organization and crime syndicates are given particular attention with respect to the linkages, both real and alleged, between legal and illegal businesses. The chapter then goes on to show the harmful effects of organized crime and the special situations in vice, narcotics, and the white collar area. Discussions of intelligence and of privacy and security are next presented, and are followed by a brief summary.

Definition of "organized crime"

Each time there is a heightened concern over what is called organized crime, this concern begins with a dedicated and sincere, but usually unsuccessful, attempt to arrive at a single definition. When these efforts do manage to produce a definition, it is usually after the opinions of experts from diverse fields have been solicited. Unfortunately, this results in the disagreements that almost inevitably accompany interdisciplinary efforts. The resulting definitions produce as much dissent as agreement, and the term organized crime has become a buzz-word in criminal justice with its own special meaning for each official who uses it.

Depending on which expert is consulted, organized crime refers—at various times and in different contexts—to: (1) a collection of criminals, (2) a type of structure and hierarchy, (3) legal and illegal businesses, and (4) a variety of criminal acts. This kind of collective term that identifies people, organizations, businesses, and actions will cause confusion as it shifts from one of these areas (e.g., people) to another (e.g., crimes). Because the term "organized crime" is so comprehensive it often fails to exclude activities and people that are not the subjects of consideration. Most professionals have stopped explaining what they mean when they use the term. Consequently, many officials—including, for example, police chiefs from two different departments—may talk past each other, using the same term but actually meaning different things.

How to identify organized crime

Before moving to the question of what to do about organized crime, it is first necessary to try to better understand what is being talked about. An approach that promises to reduce confusion is to *describe* rather than *define* organized crime. The President's Commission on Law Enforcement and Administration of Justice (known as the President's Crime Commission) approached the issue in this way:

Organized crime is a society that seeks to operate outside the control of the American people and their governments. It involves thousands of criminals, working within structures as complex as those of any large corporation, subject to laws more rigidly enforced than those of legitimate governments. Its actions are not impulsive but rather the result of intricate conspiracies, carried on over many years and aimed at gaining control over whole fields of activity in order to amass huge profits.[3]

A secondary noteworthy attempt to reach a broader understanding of the problem was at a conference of prominent experts from the entire range of criminal justice held at Oyster Bay, New York, in 1967. These experts emphasized still other factors that coincide with the existence of organized crime:

Organized crime is the product of a self-perpetuating criminal conspiracy to wring exorbitant profits from our society by any means—fair and foul, legal and illegal. . . . It survives on fear and corruption. By one or another means, it obtains a high degree of immunity from the law. It is totalitarian in organization. A way of life, it imposes rigid discipline on underlings who do the dirty work while the top men of organized crime are generally insulated from the criminal acts and the consequent danger of prosecution.[4]

Although the above two efforts increased the understanding of organized crime, they neglected to include all of the features that are present where organized crime exists. It is possible to increase the ability to identify organized crime where it exists, and to determine how extensive it is, by isolating a set of indicators or attributes that together signal the presence of organized crime groups and their operations. Sometimes only a few of the indicators can be seen (like the tip of an iceberg), but on close inspection of intelligence information the rest of the attributes can be identified. In other cases, most or all of the indicators are visible because of the extent of organized crime in that community.

Indicators of the existence of organized crime

The indicators of the existence of organized crime can be identified in the following four areas: people; organization; enterprises; acts. These are outlined in the figure on page 183.

The approach presented here allows police administrators to look at each of the four principal criteria to determine whether enough of the factors are present to qualify criminal activity in their city or town as organized crime. Clearly, vice operations where prostitutes work alone or where there is scattered but unorganized bookmaking would not meet the criteria. At the other extreme are large crime syndicates with a boss, captains, enforcers, and hundreds or thousands of employees in different enterprises.

The problem for the typical police administrator, however, is not the scattered incidence of vice activity at one extreme or a crime syndicate with national ties at the other. The problem is organized crime in the middle range of

The people	**Career criminals** with records and histories of offenses in the categories of providing illegal goods and services (e.g., gambling, loan sharking) and	maintaining discipline and eliminating competition (e.g., extortion, assault, homicide).
The organization	**Crime syndicate** hierarchical structure beginning with street level service, first-line supervisors, mid-level managers, and a top level leader, or boss.	**Entrance requirements** membership criteria based on such factors as racial or ethnic background, prior criminal history, commission of a significant crime to gain membership, and membership for life.
The enterprises	**Ongoing illegal businesses** to provide illegal goods (stolen food and clothing, precious metals) and services (gambling, loan sharking, prostitution).	**Legitimate business** acquired through a pattern of illegal activity (default on illegal loan, extortion) or with the proceeds from an illegal business.
The acts	**Pyramid arrangement of crimes** to guarantee maximum return on investments or to disguise the commission of an earlier crime. **Continuous conspiracies** committed because of the ongoing nature of the illegal businesses and for the purpose of establishing, managing, maintaining, and protecting illegal enterprises from competition or official intervention. **Coercion and violence** committed to eliminate competition or to discipline employees or actual or potential witnesses in government proceedings.	**Corruption** of public officials in criminal justice and other agencies in order to neutralize their interference in the conduct of illegal businesses; to assure that investments in legitimate businesses bring a maximum return on investments; and to develop political influence as a service made available to others for a fee. **Monopolistic control** over an illegal good or service in a defined geographic area in order to maximize profits.

Indicators of the existence of organized crime.

the spectrum—the organization that runs a numbers bank, a bookmaking operation, a prostitution ring, etc. If upon examining the list of indicators the police administrator determines that several of the indicators clearly exist in the community, but most do not, then he or she has the task of investigating whether the other indicators exist but are hard to document (a common problem) or whether they really do not exist. The absence of one or two of the factors is no reason to deny the existence of organized crime activity or influence. The police administrator should look at the number of other dangerous factors that are present, and should act resolutely to combat them.

Unfortunately, the public has a picture of organized crime as a group of criminals always displaying the most sinister and violent behavior. The reality is that organized crime leaders and their syndicates adjust remarkably well to local conditions. If they must keep their illegal operations as inconspicuous as possible, they will usually succeed unless vigorous police action identifies them and their actual threat to the community. It is important that police administrators remember that factors such as the relative size of the syndicate in their community and the most efficient means of providing illegal services will determine how organized crime appears—both to the police department and to the general public. Administrators who recognize the fact that organized crime exists in their community but wonder whether the existence alone constitutes a problem should read the next section closely.

How organized is organized crime?

Police administrators who examine the vast range of criminal activity in their city or town recognize the fact that each type of crime-for-profit is organized in its own distinctive way. There is much crime that is unorganized—where criminals in pairs or lone offenders commit muggings, for example. Moving toward crimes noted for some degree of planning and specialization, there are small groups involved in car theft, burglary, and bank robbery. Moving toward higher degrees of organization, where planning and specialization are further developed, there are larger groups with a hierarchy of leaders, managers, and street level workers. Examples of this level of organization are narcotics distribution systems, numbers banks, and hijacking–fencing operations. Still further along, at the greatest level of organization, planning, hierarchy, and specialization, is the organized crime syndicate. Its main, distinguishing feature is the claim that it controls who can and cannot operate within the boundaries that it identifies as its territory. In the list of organized crime indicators appearing in the figure accompanying this text, the crime syndicate is in the business of monopolizing organized crime-for-profit in its territory.[5]

Because crime syndicates seek to extract as much profit and tribute from illegal enterprises as possible, they try to control all highly organized crime, much large group crime, some small group crime, and almost no crime committed by pairs or lone offenders. Why does organized crime follow this path of control? Because the larger and more permanent criminal enterprises usually realize larger and more predictable profits. Consequently, the larger the illegal enterprise, the more revenue there is for the crime syndicate to tap as the tribute it demands to allow the enterprise to operate in its territory. Also, the larger criminal enterprises have offices that can be located (at least by racketeers), and they keep books. These records can be examined for purposes of computing the amount of tribute that is owed to the syndicate.

The point to remember is that the feature of monopoly control, practiced through various forms of extortion and violence, is at the core of organized crime. The police administrator who searches for these signs of violence and coercion as evidence of monopoly control may not find them and may therefore conclude that there is no organized crime in the jurisdiction. The administrator may not be aware that certain rackets long ago adjusted to the payment of syndicate tribute and that the cost is now treated as just another business expense. Organized crime may exist in this type of situation, then, even though its coercive influence is invisible.[6]

Membership in organized crime syndicates

There have been as many disagreements over who controls organized crime as over the definition of the problem. For decades the popular image of the racketeer has been that of a Sicilian- or Italian-American. For a number of historical reasons, the identification of the leadership of organized crime with a small minority of Sicilians and Italians was accurate. The Sicilian Mafia and later the Sicilian–Italian Cosa Nostra had perhaps the most formal structure of hierarchy, policies, and rituals of any sizable criminal groups.[7]

However, there is and has been for over a century a rich mixture of ethnic groups of all types active in the hierarchies of organized crime across the nation. Most of these groups came from eastern and southern Europe, where historical conditions created career ladders in organized crime. In recent decades, as social and economic opportunity in America has improved, the dominance of racketeers hailing from ethnic groups once at the bottom of the social and economic ladder has declined somewhat. While the older groups have never completely loosened their grip on syndicate structures and individual enterprises, the new racketeers have elbowed, fought, and in a variety of other ways have maneuvered their way into control of organized crime in many communities.

Today it is common to find organized criminal groups of blacks and Hispanic-Americans in many urban centers where those groups form a sizable minority of the population. Many of their organizations manifest the same styles of management, discipline, and alliances between competing crime groups that brought wealth and power to their earlier counterparts. Like their predecessors, the syndicates composed of newer ethnic and racial minorities are often bound together by blood and marital ties.

Organized crime has always provided the underprivileged in our society with folk heroes who stand as symbols of the short route to money, fame, and power. So long as crime syndicates continue to reinforce that path to success, the ranks of underprivileged urban youth will continue to be a breeding ground for criminals of all types. And where the older organized crime syndicates adopt a color-blind approach to investments and stand ready to support and occasionally bankroll new groups in their illegal ventures, the wealth and power of crime syndicates will continue to grow.

The organization and structure of crime syndicates

A crime syndicate is a management apparatus that controls a diverse collection of legal and illegal enterprises. The larger syndicates operate as a board of directors led by an autocratic chairman, or boss. The holdings of some syndicates are small and very limited (for example, a numbers bank, a vending machine company, and perhaps a bar). Others control a variety of enterprises that may total in the hundreds. As the size and diversity increase, so do problems for police in controlling these activities. The most important concerns of the police administrator should be whether a crime syndicate exists in the community and what types of criminal activities it encourages and supports. The more prominent features of crime syndicates and how they are organized are discussed in this section. An understanding of these features is an important factor in determining what countermeasures the police should take.

Ranks and responsibilities The criminals who fill the rosters of crime syndicates are ranked according to the importance of their positions. Each member contributes either to the management of the syndicate from within the management structure or to the operation of a particular enterprise. A very important position in a syndicate is that of the "money mover." This person assists in the flow of cash from an illegal operation into a legitimate business front. Often he lacks a criminal record, and this eases his movement between the criminal and business worlds. Other members serve as advisers because of the expertise they have developed over the years in managing conflict within the syndicate. Some members serve as enforcers of discipline within the organization, others as collectors of outstanding debts for loan shark operations, and still others as executioners of anyone unfortunate enough to incur the wrath of the syndicate's leaders.

Because the syndicate engages in so much crime on a day-to-day basis, it is vital that the boss be protected from any connection with individual criminal acts. Therefore, most syndicates maintain a position of "buffer" to the boss. This person conveys the orders of the boss without allowing any of the orders or acts to be traced back to the source.

As in any other organization, some members are aggressive and hard working and strive to move upward in the organization. Others seem content to remain at the lower levels, performing routine, illegal, and often mundane tasks. In other words, there is a differentiation of responsibilities within a syndicate: some members spend their days running a numbers bank, others spend their

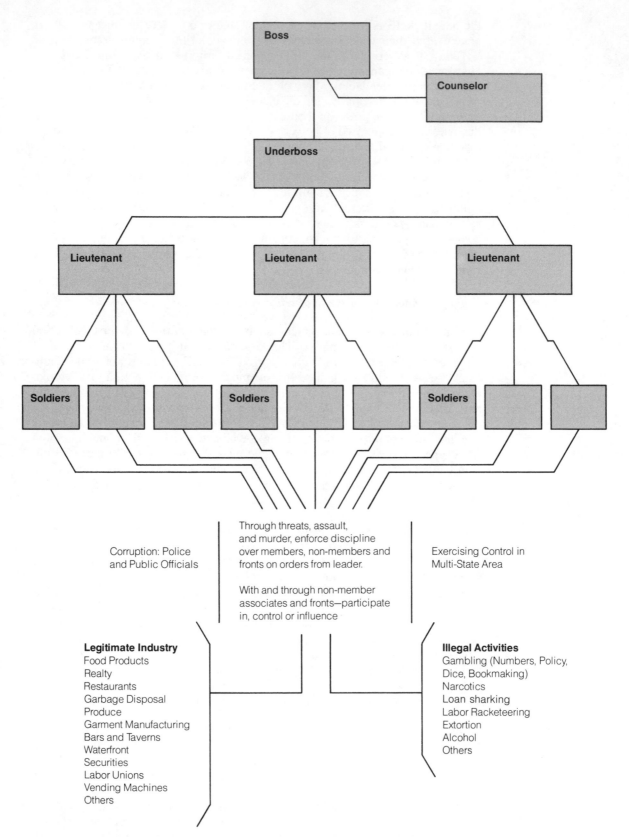

An organized crime family. Note how legitimate and illegal activities can be commingled through intricate, hidden networks.

days logging bets in a bank office, and still others devise illegal schemes for investing the money generated from the bank in legitimate businesses. Police administrators need to develop a strategy whereby their limited manpower can combat as much of this organized criminal activity as possible.

Enterprises   Where a crime syndicate exists, regardless of its size, it has one or more of three types of relationships with individual enterprises or rackets within its territory.

First there is the *syndicate run* operation, such as a numbers bank, where the mob's own employees and capital are used. Members of the syndicate are usually installed in the top managerial positions of the operation, and underlings man the offices.

The second arrangement is the syndicate *franchise,* whereby a distinct geographic area, such as a neighborhood or an entire city, is ceded to an independent operator for the purpose of running an illegal business. Here the syndicate attaches a price to the franchise, which operates as a tax on the business. The tax can be paid by requiring the independent operator to subscribe to a syndicate run operation such as a race wire or gambling layoff service. The fee for the use of the service adds up to a considerable sum over a period of time.

The third arrangement may be termed a *joint venture*. Unlike the syndicate run or franchised arrangement, this joint venture does not occur between a powerful syndicate leader and an independent of lesser rank. Syndicates often encounter other criminal organizations that are roughly equal in size, wealth, power, and the ability and readiness to employ violence. In such a situation a syndicate may enter into a joint venture with the other party. Here equals deal with equals and both parties stand to make a considerable profit, given the many short cuts that racketeers employ to maximize their profits. Such mutual arrangements promote friendship and stability, and thus tend to decrease the chance that a rivalry over territory or control of a new enterprise will lead to conflict and bloodshed.

Are syndicate leaders always notorious?

Much has been said about the organization of crime syndicates along lines of strict authority and raw power. The most formal and rigid systems of command and supervision are found in the Cosa Nostra families. Other syndicate organizations vary in structure from tightly to loosely knit, often depending on where they are located and the extent of competition they have to contend with in that locality.

Whatever the ethnic background of a syndicate or the operator of an illegal business, the leaders will choose their own styles of handling outside competition, internal disputes, and relationships with public officials. Some leaders consciously choose a low profile that is consistent with the claim—usually traceable directly to them—that there is no organized crime in their community because no racketeers can be identified. Others seem to enjoy the public spotlight for the influence and prestige that attach to a position noted for the cold, calculating exercise of power.

The personal style of a syndicate leader—and often that of his lieutenants—is important in determining whether there is public perception that organized crime exists in the community; in this way it is a law enforcement problem. The police administrator who mounts an attack on organized crime without first succeeding in convincing community leaders that the problem is a real one often faces a challenge that can range from mild static to unbending opposition.

Once again, it should be stressed that a police administrator would be wise to invest considerable time and effort in gauging whether there is an organized crime problem and, if so, to what extent it exists. If some or most of the indicators are visible to the administrator but not to the public, the administrator may have to document the existence of the syndicate—to sharpen its profile in the public eye—before sufficient support and adequate resources to combat the problem can be forthcoming. Means of accomplishing this are discussed later in this chapter under the role of intelligence.

Where it appears that there is gambling and other vice, but they are not organized to the extent that a syndicate (however small) controls them, police efforts to combat the apparently unorganized victimless crimes are scaled down. However, where organized crime maintains control the threat to the public welfare is a real one, whether or not the existence of a crime syndicate ever makes the headlines.

Is organized crime harmful?

At the beginning of this chapter it was noted that the police in America discharge certain major responsibilities. These responsibilities are usually discussed in terms of a crime, a disorderly situation, or an emergency reported to the police through normal channels of communication. In other words, they are discussed in terms of police reaction to a crime report or to the observation of a crime in progress. The situation is different with organized crime: patrons of its services seldom report such activities. Therefore, the police administrator who wants to combat organized crime cannot wait for reports of gambling or prostitution but must select investigative targets and proceed to build cases. This is called proactive enforcement. However, this enforcement approach is difficult to adopt because of manpower and budgetary pressures and because of local priorities that emphasize violent crimes and property crime taking place in the streets.

Victimless crimes   A concise definition for victimless crimes would be "situations in which one person obtains from another in a fairly direct exchange, a commodity or personal service which is socially disapproved and legally proscribed." [E. M. Schur, *Crimes without Victims* (Englewood Cliffs, N.J.: Prentice-Hall, Inc., 1965), p. 170.]

The most common victimless crimes are gambling, prostitution, and narcotics. They may also include the following, which are defined by some state laws and local ordinances as crimes: certain types of sexual acts, pornography, homosexual acts. . . .

Four distinguishing characteristics of victimless crimes are: (1) the accused does something which the victim wants the person to do, and the victim frequently is willing to pay for the commodity or service; (2) the offense usually does not generate complaints to the police; (3) the offense tends to be carried on in private; and (4) there is an absence of direct and immediate injury to the victim.

Source: William J. Chambliss and Robert B. Seidman, *Law, Order, and Power* (Reading, Mass.: Addison-Wesley Publishing Co., 1971), p. 231.

As a result, many honest and dedicated police administrators have made a conscious choice not to combat organized crime. The reason given most frequently is that there are no real victims of organized crime and that the police should not assume the role of complainant where there would otherwise be no complaints. This line of reasoning rests on the assumption that organized crime is harmless because it involves victimless crimes. It may be true that the services of most syndicate operations (gambling, prostitution, and pornography) do not produce immediate victims. However, the most serious damage done by organized crime does not surface immediately. The citizens of a community and its institutions are the collective victims of organized crime, and certain patrons of organized crime enterprises where extortion and violence are used are the individual victims.

The pyramid effect

The best illustration of the harmful effects of organized crime is the way in which the operation of an illegal enterprise forces its managers to commit other crimes. The objective of these other crimes is to ensure maximum profit from the original enterprise, to disguise and protect it from competition and from law enforcement, and to parlay the profits from that enterprise into investments in still other legal and illegal businesses. This growth or accumulation of crimes has a pyramid effect—one of the indicators of the existence of organized crime discussed earlier in this chapter.

The crime pyramid begins with a large-grossing illegal enterprise such as a numbers bank. To run the bank, its managers and employees must violate state lottery and perhaps other gambling laws, as well as state conspiracy, federal wagering tax, and probably federal income tax laws. If interstate communications facilities are used to lay off heavy bets, or if the bank's personnel travel interstate to and from work, federal antiracketeering laws are violated each day that the bank operates.

Up to this point it may appear that the syndrome of victimless crime has not been broken and that neither society nor the individual bettors who patronize the bank, or citizens who live in the neighborhood, have been hurt. However, a closer look reveals that the profits from the numbers operation are invested in other lucrative businesses and ventures. These include real estate and loan sharking. Occasionally, a businessman who falls deeply into debt to the bank watches helplessly as the syndicate moves in and takes over his business, installing racketeers in key positions. These racketeers may choose to strip all of the assets of the firm until only a shell of the former business is left. In other cases gambling profits are plowed into real estate ventures that do not produce the return projected for the original investment. Without compunction, the racketeers arrange to have the property burned in arson-for-profit schemes to collect fraudulent insurance claims. However, the most vivid examples of the victimization of citizens come from documented cases of loan shark operations.

Crime syndicates place enormous pressure on loan sharks to move money on the street and collect installment payments on time, so that the money can be reinvested. The pressures are so intense that the loan sharks frequently resort to threats and the actual use of violence to effect their collections. The result is that those citizens who are loan shark customers live with a degree of fear and face coercion usually unknown in most democratic societies. A case that demonstrates this is given below:

In Philadelphia, a jeweler with a penchant for gambling was the valued client of a local usurer because he repaid his loans punctually. The jeweler introduced two of his friends to the usurer, not knowing that he thereby was automatically guaranteeing their interest payments. But the friends missed a few payments and took off for California, leaving the jeweler liable for their debts and interest. Four goons showed up at the jeweler's store and glared at him. The jeweler even cashed bad checks to pay his friends' loans, but he couldn't make it. He was invited to visit the local usurer, and he accepted the invitation. Upon his arrival, the four goons—"one looked like King Kong"—put him in his own car, drove him through an alley, beat him on the head with a club, stopped the car, took him to the back room of a restaurant, beat him with a blackjack, returned him to the car and knocked out two of his teeth with a whiskey bottle. Then they put him in the trunk of his car and drove around for about a half-hour. After more beating with the blackjack, he was again taken to the basement of the restaurant, handcuffed to an overhead pipe in a walk-in refrigerator, and punched in the stomach by all four men, working in a relay. Then he was released, but without his car. He took a taxi to a hospital where he was informed, the next day, that the $2,000 car would pay $500 worth of the debts, and that if he didn't sign over the title, he would owe the usurer $100 a week interest. When he went home that night, he called his girl friend, who told him she had received two threatening telephone calls, one of them saying, "If [the borrower] don't pay the loan we'll cut off your teats and send them to him in a box."[8]

The corruption of public institutions

The second type of harm caused by organized crime is the corruption of public institutions. All taxpayers suffer from the corruption that organized crime requires in order to operate without official interference. Where there are dishonest public servants, especially the police at the front lines of public protection, they are paid one salary to uphold the common good and public welfare and a second one to pursue personal gain and selfish ends. The employee's loyalty is transferred from the public agency to the private interest group or individual making the bribe payment. It follows that the corrupt employee becomes enmeshed in a system of private rewards, and this incentive system is reinforced as bribe payments continue.

Where organized crime groups—or other interests—corrupt police officers, serious consequences can follow for the protection of life and property in a community. Herman Goldstein states that

the corrupt police officer is not likely to do the kinds of things that he should be doing. The officer who spends his time in corrupt activities does little police work. He is unlikely to take seriously requirements that he check the security of various premises . . . or that he respond speedily to calls for assistance. In extreme cases, he may even see such requirements as intrusions on his time. If his supervisors are also corrupt, it becomes even more likely that he will ignore these responsibilities.[9]

The above observations also hold true for employees of licensing, regulatory, and other public agencies (such as health and zoning boards) where bribe payments neutralize the enforcement of laws, ordinances, and codes designed to protect the life and property of the general public. It follows that when more and more public agencies are nullified through corruption the community finds itself less able to meet urban problems and crises of every type. However difficult it may be for a public official such as a police administrator to define and then uphold the common good, corrupt relationships will guarantee that it will never be served.

Vice, narcotics, and white collar crime

Vice control

Police use the term vice to mean a variety of illegal services: prostitution, gambling, pornography, liquor, and, occasionally, narcotics.[10] When typical police administrators speak of vice control, they usually have one objective in mind: to reduce the ability of vice operators to conduct their trade in open view (i.e., in direct or close contact with the public). This is difficult because gamblers and prostitutes must remain available to their clientele in order to complete enough transactions to make their business profitable. Since there are normally more vice operators than there are police to remove them from the streets, finding and deploying enough police officers is a major problem of police resource allocation.

Administrators who define their mission as the suppression of open vice conditions should examine the consequences of that position. Frequently, the operational objective of the police is to drive the vice operators off the streets and into locations where their reduced visibility will make it difficult for critics to determine how much vice activity there really is. Therefore, the administrator's operational objective is met when the prostitute and gambler begin to operate secretly, using the telephone or a courier. Because so many police administrators are resigned to the existence of vice as a fact of life, they are relieved when vice operations move from the street to the back room or the penthouse.

Police administrators who accept this view usually do so after examining a number of alternatives. They conclude that the benefits of reducing vice to an irreducible minimum do not outweigh the costs in terms of manpower diverted from other duties and the lack of police visibility in meeting other crime control objectives. Therefore, this approach relies on suppression and on the displacement of vice activities, and often this approach becomes an end in itself.

Before accepting this approach to vice control, the professional administrator should consider two consequences that follow from the failure to treat the displaced but still thriving vice problem as an equally serious matter.

First, vice operators who have gone underground cause different types of problems. One of these is corruption. When administrators believe that the problem has disappeared, they tend to lose interest and often will not require—and may even choke off the flow of—information on the extent of vice activities. By doing this they are allowing (and even tacitly encouraging) corruption to enter vice enforcement in the community or to grow much worse if it is already there.

Second, when the police relax their enforcement of vice laws organized crime groups may establish or enlarge their foothold in these lucrative rackets. In fact, one of the strongest arguments for enforcing vice laws is to dry up the huge revenues that would flow to organized crime groups.

The special case of narcotics control

The control of hard narcotics in a community is a problem that falls somewhere between street level vice and syndicated crime. The main reason for the special status of narcotics control is that, while street sales to addicts create a type of vice problem, the large quantities of money required to bankroll large purchases, and the presence of higher level distributors, require the type of attention usually devoted to syndicate operations.

Most police departments of moderate size have a special narcotics unit. Because of limitations of manpower and funds with which to buy information and evidence, most police departments have made a practice of concentrating on the smaller retail dealer—usually the pusher and his source of supply. However, because of the fantastic profits that can be made in the narcotics trade, organized crime syndicates in many areas have entered this field.

Today it is common to find syndicate members and, occasionally, top level leaders financing large shipments of hard drugs, particularly of heroin and cocaine. They are usually far removed from the actual exchange of the drugs for money, but many large-scale transactions could not take place without their backing. When police administrators learn that this type of organized crime occurs in their community, their first option is to develop a capability to make conspiracy cases against the wholesale dealers and financiers. A sustained attack at those levels can make it costly for drug wholesalers to deal in the larger quantities. Consequently, other dealers are reluctant to move into the vacancies created by their conviction and imprisonment. Where well-organized narcotics dealers, but not syndicate racketeers, occupy the higher levels in the distribution system, the police administrator will want to maintain this same capability.

The gray area between organized and white collar crime

As suggested earlier in this chapter, the difficulty of defining organized crime has both bedeviled and retarded police department efforts to deal with the problem. To some extent the same difficulty has confronted police concerned with white collar crime. Fortunately, however, in recent years a consensus has formed around the definition of white collar crime presented by Herbert Edelhertz in his monograph, *The Nature, Impact, and Prosecution of White-Collar Crime*. In that paper white collar crime is defined as:

An illegal act or series of illegal acts committed by non-physical means or by concealment or guile, to obtain money or property, to avoid payment or loss of money or property, or to obtain business or personal advantage.[11]

Although much of today's white collar crime is totally unrelated to or uncontrolled by organized crime, some of it may be an enterprise or venture of an organized crime syndicate. An example is fraudulent bankruptcy. Typically, syndicate members secure operating control of a retail business that enjoys an excellent credit reputation with its suppliers. Control is often secured in response to the demand for payment of gambling or loan shark debts. Once the syndicate is in charge of the business, orders for merchandise are steadily and substantially increased while the time for payment of bills is extended on the basis of the preexisting good credit rating. The new merchandise is sold for cash, frequently at prices below cost. After substantial cash has been generated and looted from the business, the business is bankrupted or "busted out." Victimized suppliers rarely recover much, if anything, from the bankrupted business, and criminal investigations usually do not reach syndicate members who engineer the schemes.

Another traditional area of white collar crime by criminal syndicates is the theft and disposition of stolen securities. After arranging the theft of securities from brokerage houses, syndicate members also provide distribution channels for the stolen property. Frequently the stolen certificates are pledged as collateral for bank loans. These loans are negotiated through corrupt or negligent loan officers and provide substantial profits. After a short time the loans are defaulted and the lending institution discovers for the first time that the collateral it holds is stolen property. The loss burden ultimately falls on the lender's insurance carrier and contributes to increased premiums for insurance coverage.

Even when criminal syndicates are not engaged in white collar crime schemes as profit making ventures, such groups cannot operate effectively without committing some white collar crimes. Most obvious in this context is tax fraud. Income obtained from illegal activities such as loan sharking, hijacking, and trafficking in narcotics is concealed with the preparation of fraudulent income tax returns at federal, state, and (in some jurisdictions) local levels. Similarly, to avoid tax liabilities and to conceal the fact of prior criminal activities, false returns are submitted in connection with requirements to pay sales, excise, and gross business taxes. False documentation is frequently used to obtain or renew licenses of various kinds. Liquor licenses are typical. When syndicate members own and control bars, nightclubs, or retail liquor outlets, their ownership is usually secret. Consequently, application and other forms are inevitably falsified. If not, regulatory agencies will refuse to grant, or will revoke, operating authority because of the ineligibility of the real owners.

Unlike the commission of street crimes such as assault or robbery, the commission of white collar crimes almost invariably requires the use of documents of various kinds: invoices, tax forms, correspondence, and so on. Thus, a complicated but real paper trail exists for a knowledgeable investigator to follow. Such paper trails, however, frequently require investigative skills not always found among detectives who are effective in the solution of street crimes. The relevant skills are those of investigative accountants, and such persons are in short supply in municipal, county, and state law enforcement agencies.

By all indications, crimes that fall under the white collar headings are increasing. Because many types of white collar crime, such as land fraud, have become enormously profitable, they have attracted the interest and active involvement of crime syndicates. Police administrators should be concerned with maintaining efforts against independent and syndicate-affiliated white collar fraud. They should distinguish a campaign aimed at using a particular fraud offense to apprehend syndicate criminals from the need to maintain a capability to combat white collar fraud wherever it victimizes investors.

Police administrators should remember that as individual fraud schemes succeed in their community they will increase in number and size. Syndicate racketeers may be attracted by the easy environment. They will try to organize it, and by the time the police department begins a counteroffensive the defrauders may be so deeply entrenched that neither the police nor the prosecutor can oust them. Early identification and resolute action are the only safeguards against this type of problem, which is getting out of control in many sections of the country.

Opportunities for training in white collar crime investigative techniques have increased in recent years,[12] but the pool of trained investigators must be substantially expanded.

The role of intelligence

A police department that maintains an effective intelligence program should be able to answer any one of the following questions on organized crime:

1. Does it exist in this community, and how extensive is it?
2. Who controls it?
3. Are leadership positions changing and are new groups entering?
4. What illegal enterprises and legitimate businesses does it control or have an interest in?
5. What section of the population is most directly victimized—drug addicts, loan shark borrowers, businessmen in certain industries?
6. What is the extent of public corruption?

Gathering, analyzing, and acting upon information about criminal activity has always been an essential and legitimate police function. However, intelligence is a special class of information because it is cultivated either to identify crimes that otherwise would not be identified (owing to their hidden nature) or to identify offenses that are likely to occur at a prearranged time in the future (e.g., hijacking).

Intelligence is used most productively in selecting targets for special investigative attention. In the course of gathering information in pursuit of that objective, extensive background information is collected that may or may not be relevant to the ultimate development of a criminal case. As the intelligence process begins, much information is developed concerning people whose associations with organized crime figures may be coincidental and unrelated to criminal acts.

Because the intelligence process demands a major commitment of time and manpower, police must invest in a considerable effort before any useful information is developed. Frequently the productivity of an intelligence program is called into question—not only by civil libertarians but by police administrators themselves. As a result, many police administrators do not feel justified in supporting an intelligence effort in their department.

The most common complaint is that after a long time has been spent reducing raw intelligence to a few quality kernels of information, city officials or prosecutors remain uninterested in combating organized crime. There is no better way to destroy the morale of police intelligence personnel than to have them spend months developing good information only to see their product grow stale. Since this is not a rare event, the police administrator should consider the following two steps to assure that intelligence is put to productive uses: (1) collecting the appropriate types of information, and (2) improving the quality and use of information.

Types of information to be collected

Intelligence information is divided into *strategic* and *tactical*. Strategic intelligence identifies patterns and trends of activity, including activity in which organized crime is engaged, in such areas as the leadership structure, legal and illegal enterprises, and destinations of illegal profits. Tactical intelligence in its most useful form provides the police with information with which to make a criminal case. Therefore, good strategic intelligence should identify the leaders and managers of the syndicate, their legal and illegal enterprises (such as a numbers bank and its office and layoff structure), and where the gambling profits are invested. Good tactical intelligence should give the police probable cause to raid the bank, each of its offices, and the layoff center, and develop evidence to build conspiracy cases against the higher echelons in the syndicate.

Police often make the mistake of investing little time in strategic intelligence, spending most of their time gathering tactical intelligence. The result is that they line up raid after raid and try in this way to drive illegal operations out of business. However, a good strategic picture would have enabled police to target the key managers and layoff men in an operation, and move much higher in the structure of that operation.

All too often, a lopsided investment in tactical intelligence merely serves the arrest quota syndrome and gives the appearance that police are attacking organized crime. Such efforts may result in merely forcing racketeers to shuffle numbers writers and lower level office locations around. As in most enterprises, low level employees and storefront offices can be replaced with relative ease. The most honest and industrious police efforts aimed at street level targets barely make a dent in syndicate operations.

Improving the quality and use of information

The first task in improving the quality and use of information is to establish an analytical capability to extract as much meaning as possible from the raw information collected. The administrator who wants the department to produce quality intelligence will need to invest in specialized training for his analysts.[13] Experience in many departments has shown that a mixture of uniformed and civilian analysts can work well, with the civilians bringing into the unit their backgrounds of accounting and economic analysis to trace cash flow and the impact of a business or racket on the population of consumers. However, the department whose resources must limit it to uniformed personnel will find that basic training in intelligence analysis can in fact make good police officers into good analysts.

The second task is to disseminate the strategic intelligence where it will have its greatest impact. The first destination is the department's organized crime tactical unit, which may use the information to set priorities and select enforcement targets. It may also be productive to disseminate the information to the local prosecutor so that he or she may use it to proceed with a special investigative campaign. Where the local prosecutor or state attorney general is authorized to impanel a special grand jury, seek grants of immunity for witnesses, and use an arsenal of other legal tools to combat organized crime, it is essential that police make their information available to that official. One of the most powerful investigative weapons against organized crime is the investigative grand jury. In most jurisdictions, however, it can be impaneled only with a strong showing that organized crime is a problem in that jurisdiction. Strategic intelligence is critical in documenting the nature and extent of organized crime in such a situation.

The above recommendation assumes that other units in the department and local agencies such as the prosecutor's office actively seek out and welcome the intelligence that the department produces. However, there are many cases in which the police administrator finds that he does not have sufficient manpower to act on information that his own department develops and the prosecutor—for whatever reason—in unconcerned. In that environment, the normal reaction is not to supply intelligence where it is not requested. Files begin to grow fat and stale with old and useless information. Soon the department may call a halt to its intelligence effort. Before a police administrator considers the alternative of disbanding the unit, he should examine some options for dealing with the problem of lethargy and inaction.

The first such option is to supply the information, on a restricted and need-to-know basis, to state and federal authorities who have the capability and the commitment to act against organized crime. The state police, the FBI, and federal organized crime strike forces are among the more prominent examples. If nothing else, the offer to provide information assures the other agencies that the inaction of the police administrator is not a policy of his own choosing. The second option is to continue a vigorous collection and analysis effort, and to wait and hope that a new municipal administration or a new county prosecutor will select organized crime for priority attention and give the administrator the manpower, support, and other resources needed.

The point to be made is that the supply of organized crime intelligence is often viewed as a function of the demand for it. A high quality supply of strategic intelligence can help stimulate its own demands—if not locally, then at the state or federal level. Although this approach does not guarantee that a vigorous, sustained, and comprehensive attack on organized crime will follow, it goes a long way toward breaking the cycle of lack of interest and inaction that many administrators confront and that is an unfortunate tradition in many police departments throughout the United States.

Privacy and security considerations

No discussion of the use of intelligence in controlling organized crime would be complete without some words of caution. Public concern over the indiscriminate collection and distribution of information is mounting. In some cases this reaction is understandable; whether this general concern is exaggerated or not, the collection of information on the activities and associations of citizens is a serious issue. Police administrators who take precautionary steps to assure the fairness and integrity of their intelligence effort can avoid demands to abandon it.

The basic safeguards include: collection of information that is limited to criminal conduct; development of standards for data that are to be included in the system; collation and analysis in a secure environment; purging of information or leads that are unfounded or out-of-date; and dissemination only to criminal justice agencies with a clear need to receive the information.[14] While these safeguards are not difficult for a single department to adopt and abide by, they become complicated in regional and other multijurisdictional intelligence sharing arrangements. For this reason a formal compact that sets forth explicit criteria and due process safeguards should precede the implementation of any intelligence sharing arrangement.[15]

Conclusion

This chapter begins with a discussion of the confusion over what organized crime really is. A simplistic definition is carefully avoided, because organized crime is a complex of people, organization, enterprises, and a pattern of illegal acts. It often involves a mesh of legal and illegal enterprises that has been built over several decades. Indicators of the existence of organized crime in a community are described, and the structure of organized crime is discussed at some length. The harm caused by organized crime is outlined, as are the problems of vice, narcotics, and white collar crime.

The characteristics of organized crime outlined in this chapter provide guidelines for the police administrator for dealing with a situation that can arise in any community. Particularly significant is the closing discussion of intelligence, which holds the key to ending the confusion about what organized crime really is.

1 Eleven major police responsibilities are identified in American Bar Association Project on Standards for Criminal Justice, *Standards Relating to the Urban Police Function* (Chicago: American Bar Association, 1974), pp. 3–4; they are as follows: "(1) to identify criminal offenders and criminal activity and, where appropriate, to apprehend offenders and participate in subsequent court proceedings; (2) to reduce the opportunities for the commission of some crimes through preventive patrol and other measures; (3) to aid individuals who are in danger of physical harm; (4) to protect constitutional guarantees; (5) to facilitate the movement of people and vehicles; (6) to assist those who cannot care for themselves; (7) to resolve conflict; (8) to identify problems that are potentially serious law enforcement or governmental problems; (9) to create and maintain a feeling of security in the community; (10) to promote and preserve civil order; and (11) to provide other services on an emergency basis."

2 Ibid., p. 4.

3 President's Commission on Law Enforcement and Administration of Justice, *Task Force Report: Organized Crime* (Washington, D.C.: Government Printing Office, 1967), p. 1.

4 Counsel to the Governor of New York, *Combating Organized Crime* (Albany, N.Y.: Office of the Governor, 1965), p. 19.

5 The concept of syndicate control of crime as crime increases in complexity was presented by Donald R. Cressey at the Third Organized Crime Law Enforcement Training Conference, sponsored by the Law Enforcement Assistance Administration and held at the University of Oklahoma in Norman, 4 March 1970.

6 See: Thomas C. Schelling, "What Is the Business of Organized Crime?" *Journal of Public Law* 20, no. 1 (1971): 71–84.

7 Donald R. Cressey, "The Functions and Structure

of Criminal Syndicates," in *Task Force Report: Organized Crime,* ed. President's Commission on Law Enforcement and Administration of Justice, Appendix A, pp. 25–60.

8 Example cited in Donald R. Cressey, *Theft of the Nation: The Structure and Operations of Organized Crime in America* (New York: Harper & Row, Publishers, 1969), p. 83.

9 Herman Goldstein, *Police Corruption: A Perspective on Its Nature and Control* (Washington, D.C.: Police Foundation, 1975), p. 11.

10 Treating narcotics as a vice control issue creates problems, mainly because narcotics control is often assigned to a separate unit. Because narcotics distribution systems are always well organized, this problem is discussed separately in this section.

11 Herbert Edelhertz, *The Nature, Impact, and Prosecution of White-Collar Crime* (Washington, D.C.: Government Printing Office, 1970), p. 3. For a detailed discussion and guide to the investigation of white collar crime, see: Herbert Edelhertz et al., *The Investigation of White-Collar Crime: A Manual for Law Enforcement Agencies* (Washington, D.C.: Government Printing Office, 1977).

12 Illustrative are training programs conducted by the Federal Bureau of Investigation and programs of the National Center on White Collar Crime of the Batelle Law and Justice Study Center in Seattle, Washington.

13 For a thorough discussion of training, see E. Drexel Godfrey and Don R. Harris, *Basic Elements of Intelligence* (Washington, D.C.: Government Printing Office, 1971), pp. 73–91.

14 See ibid., Appendix A, pp. 107–14.

15 A good example of a statewide intelligence system that publishes its objectives, methods of collection, and safeguards, is: New Jersey Department of Law and Public Safety, *New Jersey State Police Intelligence Manual* (West Trenton: New Jersey Department of Law and Public Safety, 1975).

11 Crime prevention and the community

No matter how dedicated, efficient, or well-intentioned, the police alone, whether as an institution or as individuals, cannot hope to resolve all the community problems with which they are faced in ever-increasing numbers and ever-changing forms. More often than not, when a conflict, crisis, or question affecting the community arises, the police are the first, and usually the only, representatives of the government to respond. In the case of crime, their role is particularly visible.

Crime, however, is not solely a police problem; it is also a community problem.[1] The solutions must evolve from a cooperative relationship involving the police, the local government, and the community.

Because utopian relationships do not exist, discord and misunderstanding all too frequently disturb what should be a harmonious interaction of police and citizens. Accordingly, the public may distrust or fear the police because they do not understand the police role, methods of operation, and priorities. In turn, the police may contribute to this alienation by being inadequately prepared to deal effectively with grievances, concerns, and special needs of the community.

Thus does the concept of police community service come into being, with the objective of resolving, or ideally preventing, these problems through the joint efforts of the police and the people with whom they work.

A well-planned community relations–crime prevention program will ultimately provide great rewards for police and citizens alike. A well-executed community relations effort not only will foster an improved public attitude toward the police but will almost certainly lead to a reduction in crime and an increase in arrested offenders. A sound crime prevention program will achieve similar results and will strengthen police–community ties.

This chapter will discuss a total approach to community service. It will propose programs designed to encourage community participation in police efforts and strengthen the bonds of mutual respect and cooperation that can lead to the solution of mutual problems.

Definitions

Before examining the interaction between the police and the community, it is necessary to define the concepts involved.

Following some fifteen years of work, the National Center on Police and Community Relations, Michigan State University, developed a concise and comprehensive definition of the term police–community relations:

Police–community relations in its general sense means the variety of ways in which it may be emphasized that the police are indeed an important *part of,* and not *apart from,* the communities they serve. Properly understood, police–community relations is a concept for total orientation, not merely the preoccupation of a special unit or bureau within the department. It bears upon administrative policy, it bears upon line service through the uniformed patrol division. In short, police–community relations ideally is an emphasis on attitude, a way of viewing police responsibilities that ought to permeate the entire organization.[2]

The components of the concept of community relations are drawn from the allied fields of social and behavioral sciences.

Human relations is a field of the behavioral sciences that addresses itself to determining what people do and how they do it. The ultimate aim of human relations is to improve human behavior via intergroup and interpersonal relationships.

Intergroup relations is a part of human relations and concerns itself with conflicts between groups. Understanding conflict, resolving it, and using it creatively are all the concern of intergroup relations.

Interpersonal relations concerns itself with conflict between individuals belonging to different groups. Some writers treat the terms intergroup and interpersonal relations as though they were different. Both, however, involve the understanding of conflict, which in turn provides a foundation for developing effective police–community relations.

In Baltimore the community service function of the police has been extended to the area of crime prevention through the Crime Resistance Unit. The following definition of crime resistance has been adopted by that police department: "An attitude on the part of citizens that manifests itself when they take measures to avoid becoming victims of crimes and when they join with those in law enforcement in reacting against criminal activity."[3]

Thus by definition these two facets of community service—community relations and crime resistance—appear to have different orientations. In community relations it is incumbent on the police to initiate measures that address the concerns of the community. Crime resistance, on the other hand, places the onus on the citizen as the prime if not the sole mover in the quest to prevent crime. However, a common thread binds the two functions—the willingness of the police to go into the community to seek a dialogue with the citizen in order to strengthen the police–community relationship. Because of this interaction in each instance, both functions are included under the umbrella of community service. Indeed both concepts depend on a bilateral flow of information and cooperation between the community and the police. A partnership is formed between the police and the community as they work together to solve community problems and combat crime.

Police–community relations propositions

In order to examine the police and the community, it is necessary to consider some propositions describing their interrelationship. The following propositions are offered as guidelines:

1. Police departments are service organizations. Law enforcement is only one (though a very important) service rendered by the police.
2. Public cooperation is essential for the successful execution of the police mission.
3. What the police do and how they do it will influence the public's attitude and determine the level of public cooperation.
4. Public cooperation must be the superordinate goal of all police activities.
5. Police–community relations should not be viewed as a mere program. Rather, it must be both a policy and a process permeating all aspects of police work.

The achievement of public–police cooperation is paramount, and a large part of the police effort must be targeted at garnering that cooperation.

Levels of police–community relations

Police–community relations are promoted on three basic levels. The first is the manner in which the police, both individually and collectively, carry out their functions. This is obviously important, because the real police relationship with the public is established at this level. Consequently, personal attitudes, mannerisms, dress codes, and appearance are of concern.

The second level is the development of specific programs to increase public awareness of police policies, operations, and procedures. This can be viewed as a public education effort. However, responses from the public relative to policies, operations, and procedures must be solicited and analyzed. If it is determined that a police operation is a source of friction between the police and the public, the department must consider changing the operation in an effort to achieve the same goal in a less antagonistic manner. Examples of activities that can be undertaken at this level include talks, school programs, and crime prevention programs.

The third level involves the police officer as a private citizen and may include the PTA, civic clubs, churches, community councils, and other educational, civic, religious, and service organizations. Such involvement has a dual impact. First, it demonstrates to the public that police officers are indeed citizens who accept their community responsibilities. This should go a long way toward lowering barriers between the police and the public. Second, it provides the individual officer with opportunities to relate to people on an unofficial basis.

Policy

Over the past two decades the nation has witnessed an alarming escalation of violence. A dramatic change in mores and attitudes has been influenced by a number of events that appear to have decreased individual appreciation of the traditional values placed on life and property. For a period of about ten years, the American public watched the destruction and suffering of the Vietnam War on television. During the same period cities were burned, and the attendant devastation and looting of private property was viewed by millions. Overlaying this violence were the activities of war protesters who challenged laws, attacked peace officers, and bombed or damaged government, college, and private installations. These decades of violence and counterculture changed the course of events in the United States.

Violence begets violence, and the change in attitude toward established institutions, especially the police, was soon evident. Statistics began to show dramatic increases in serious or fatal physical assaults on police officers. In order to deal with this mounting threat, law enforcement officials were forced to initiate safety measures. The number of one-person motorized units assigned to patrol duties was sometimes reduced, while the number of two-person motorized units was increased to afford the patrol officer greater protection. In some instances police budgets were strained to provide soft body armor for officers, a measure unheard of twenty-five years ago. The personal safety of officers was further protected through new training programs dealing with barricades, sniper attacks, and the use of special weapons.

Unfortunately, the police can do little to redirect the attitude of the community, but the police chief can and must initiate procedures to regulate the conduct of personnel, especially in the use of force and discretion. The police have accepted this challenge and have adopted measures designed to ensure the exercise of legitimate authority within democratic and legal limits.

Discretion It is a major responsibility of police management to establish rules governing the actions of officers and guidelines controlling the exercise of discretion. In its prescriptive package on improving police–community relations, the Law Enforcement Assistance Administration (LEAA) outlined the following principles of policy making:

1. The department should acknowledge and discuss the role of discretion in police work
2. All policies should embody a commitment to democratic values, to the legitimacy and appropriateness of constitutional limitations, and to the fundamental goals of community service and responsiveness
3. The department should use the policy-making process as a framework in which to examine or establish its basic goals and priorities
4. The department should use the policy-making process to explore new roles and areas of service which traditionally have not been considered business of the police
5. The issues to be addressed in the policy-making process should be carefully selected, especially during early efforts at establishing policy in the department
6. The department should develop and enforce strict policy governing the use of force
7. The department should involve beat officers in policy development
8. The department should experiment with community participation in policy making
9. The department should circulate policy to its members in a form which makes it useful, comprehensible, and credible
10. The department should use the policy-making process to eliminate petty rules
11. The department should take advantage of the policy-making experienced by other cities
12. The department should adopt a process of regular, automatic policy review so that outdated, inappropriate policy is eliminated or replaced.[4]

Use of force and firearms   The unwarranted application of force, especially the shooting of a citizen, may severely damage the trust that may have taken years to build between the police and the community. Resentment is especially high if the police chief in the face of such action fails to discipline the offending officers. It follows that the issue of force, especially deadly force, has become a major concern of the police chief. Unless clear guidelines are developed to help officers exercise judgment, and unless procedures for accountability are established, police use of force will continue to present problems.

A policy on deadly force should outline the circumstances under which an officer is justified to use a weapon. A number of agencies have adopted a firearms policy that is similar to the FBI guidelines, which state: "Agents are not to shoot any person except as necessary in self-defense, where they reasonably believe they or another are in danger of death or grievous bodily harm."[5]

The Baltimore police department is guided by a definitive firearms policy that has been in effect for fifteen years. The guidelines state in part:

No member shall use firearms in the discharge of his duty, except:

a. In self-defense, or to defend another person (unlawfully attacked) from death or serious injury.
b. To effect the arrest or to prevent the escape when other means are insufficient, of a person convicted of a felony of the dangerous type, or of a person who has committed a felony of the dangerous type in the presence of the member.
c. To kill a dangerous animal, or an animal so badly injured that humanity requires its relief from further suffering.
d. To give an alarm or to call for assistance when no other means can be used.
e. When used in practice on the range.[6]

This order also prohibits officers from firing at a fleeing misdemeanant; warns that when in doubt, officers do not fire; and provides for a means to monitor the use of deadly force by members of the department.

**Resolution on
police use of deadly force**

WHEREAS, legitimate circumstances exist in which police officers must use their weapons, and

WHEREAS, it is the sworn duty of police and other law enforcement agencies to uphold the United States Constitution and to protect the lives and general welfare of the public, and

WHEREAS, the police misuse of deadly force has often sparked tension between police departments and the communities they serve and, in some communities, has undermined the effectiveness of the police, and

WHEREAS, many police departments do not have clear-cut policies on the use of firearms and thus fail to provide adequate direction to officers in life-and-death situations, and

WHEREAS, the absence of these guidelines is unfair to communities, individual police officers, and their agencies, now therefore be it

RESOLVED, the membership of the National Organization of Black Law Enforcement Executives call upon all of the nation; police departments and other law enforcement agencies to formulate strict policy guidelines governing the use of firearms, and be it

FURTHER RESOLVED, that these policy guidelines be based on the principle that officers may not discharge their weapons except to protect their lives or the lives of innocent citizens from imminent danger, and be it

FURTHER RESOLVED, that police departments design and enforce sanctions against officers who unwarrantedly discharge their firearms, and be it

FURTHER RESOLVED, that police departments adopt recordkeeping systems to document all firearm discharges by their officers, and be it

FURTHER RESOLVED, that police departments establish mechanisms to ensure proper investigation of all instances of the use of deadly force.

Source: National Organization of Black Law Enforcement Executives (NOBLE), 8401 Corporate Drive, Suite 360, Landover, Maryland 20785. This resolution was adopted unanimously on 26 June 1980 at NOBLE's fourth annual conference in Inglewood, California.

A resolution enacted at the national conference of the National Organization of Black Law Enforcement Executives (NOBLE) in June 1980 represents the feelings of many police executives. This resolution is reprinted in the accompanying sidebar.

Any firearms policy that is developed to control the use of deadly force must explicitly recognize that the use of deadly force must be not only legally authorized but also socially and morally warranted and in keeping with the ideals of a democratic society. Such a policy must be easily understood by all officers, must be easy to enforce, and must hold those officers that use deadly force strictly accountable for their actions.

The police role and responsibility

The police exist to preserve the peace. This objective is attained through the law enforcement function, the order maintenance function, and the service function. All three of these functions are given equal weight in our society. Thus, the omission of one will cause an imbalance in the total concept of professional policing.

Traditionally, the police have placed major emphasis on law enforcement and less on order maintenance and service. In the past, the crime control functions were the only responsibilities most police officers recognized. Consequently, police departments were generally organized into two major components—a patrol division and a criminal investigation division. Because of this emphasis, the performance evaluation of a police department was limited to such things as the number of criminal investigations, arrests, and convictions. Little if any attention was given to the total effect of police attitudes, behavior, and practices on the community.[7]

As a result of the social upheavals of the 1960s, however, greater emphasis is now placed on order maintenance and community service. This change has been realized in a variety of ways, such as the implementation of police training programs that deal with human relations, social issues, crisis intervention, and juvenile delinquency, and increased emphasis on establishing lines of communication with all segments of the community in order to identify problems and develop broad-based support for resolving them.

Focus also has shifted to police professionalism founded on scientific knowledge, technical knowledge, and careful observance of legal procedures. Such professionalism is intended to reduce simplistic action orientation, improve police–community relations, promote reliance on other agencies instead of the police alone, and encourage additional crime prevention measures. In short, the police are becoming more proactive rather than reactive in their mission of preserving the peace.

The following principles are representative of the role and responsibilities of police in contemporary society:

1. The most important responsibility of the police is the preservation of human life.
2. The police responsibility for the maintenance of social order is conditioned by a responsibility for protecting individual rights and ensuring social justice. . . .
3. Police organizations are in a unique position to support other governmental agencies with information about citizens' problems and needs. . . .
4. Law enforcement is an important function of the police; however, physical arrest is only one strategy that is used to enforce laws. The state law requires police to "enforce" the criminal code, but it does not specifically direct police to "arrest" every person who violates the law. Therefore, police officers can legitimately exercise discretion. . . .
5. Police must work with and for citizens as much as they serve the government. Police must strive to assist citizens in developing communities that are livable places where citizens do not have to be afraid of being abused, attacked, placed in jeopardy of injury, or denied fair treatment. Police methods must stress cooperation with citizens based upon trust rather than fear, and they must emphasize prevention of crime rather than suppression. Police should be more concerned about obtaining voluntary rather than forced compliance with laws.
6. The existence and authority of the police depend on public approval of police actions and behavior and in general on the police ability to secure and maintain public respect.[8]

These principles reflect a need for the police to become more involved in the problems confronting the community. Only when such a partnership exists can both parties deal effectively and constructively with issues.

The role of the patrol officer

From the viewpoint of public relations and police effectiveness, the patrol officer is extremely important. This officer usually has more contacts with citizens than any other person in a police department, and the resulting interrelationship influences public opinion toward the department. Consequently, the officer's behavior, demeanor, helpfulness, and display of respect or lack of respect for individuals and groups will have a direct impact on citizen attitudes.

In a study completed by the International Association of Chiefs of Police, a group of young officers were asked to enumerate the qualities they regarded as most necessary to their jobs. These officers consistently rated such qualities as "honesty," "loyalty," and certain job-related skills as most important. A survey of city residents made during an earlier study, however, showed that the public had consistently listed such descriptions as "helpful," "friendly," and "understanding" as being more important for a police officer. In other words, the police and the public see the police role quite differently. The public regards human relations attributes as far more important than abstract virtues or general abilities, although police officers usually evaluate their needs in a way that places human relations attributes very low on their list of priorities. An awareness of these differing points of view is essential to a successful police–community relations program.[9]

The police–community service role may be fulfilled only if individual officers represent the department's official attitude in their dealings with the public. The patrol officer's feelings about his or her position in society must be both positive and healthy. It is imperative that the officer view the job of policing as that of a service to the community. In short, management must establish a climate that motivates the individual to adopt a service orientation.

Showing an intense interest in the problems of the public is the job of the patrol officer, who must take an active role in resolving these problems. This officer must have the ability to work effectively with others in building a cooperative spirit. To develop this ability, patrol officers must understand the different cultures and value structures of the people with whom they will be working and must be constantly aware of the need for fairness in dealing with the public.

The patrol officer must have self-respect. This attitude is reflected in his or her dress, personal hygiene, vocabulary, firmness and resoluteness, and above all courtesy. The patrol officer who has self-respect will have little trouble gaining the confidence and respect of others.

As a crime prevention generalist, the patrol officer should be able to help members of the community protect themselves and their property from criminal injury. The officer can educate citizens in methods to prevent or minimize injury and loss resulting from assaults and robberies and methods to safeguard homes or apartments against theft and business establishments against burglaries and robberies. Such efforts should not overlook small merchants or the elderly, both of whom are frequent targets of crime.

The patrol officer should know about public and private resource agencies in the community. A few of the major resources an officer may develop are agencies dealing with domestic problems, abused spouses and children, and alcoholics. The department should provide an up-to-date listing of such agencies and their telephone numbers. Having this information, the officer in the field can respond to the needs of individuals seeking assistance, even though the final resolution of their problems may not be within police power.

One of the more important functions of the patrol officer in the area of community relations is the role of liaison between the community and the police department. Although most difficulties can be effectively and tactfully resolved as they arise or as they are brought to the attention of the beat officers, any major, complex problems confronting the community should be referred to the community service unit in the police department for attention. This "feedback" process is essential to alert the department to potential crime and other community problems so that preventive or remedial measures may be implemented.

The role of other operational units

The criminal investigator, too, is in a good position to generate positive attitudes toward the department. Communication with a detective may be a witness's only contact with the police, and the manner in which that witness is treated will largely determine his or her attitudes toward the department. In addition, such experiences are sure to be shared with friends and relatives.

Traffic officers also are important agents in community relations, because they are constantly in contact with the public. Their courtesy, integrity, and exemplary bearing go a long way to foster compliance with the rules of the road and respect for the police.

The role of the chief of police

The public expects the chief of police not only to exercise firm control over the agency but also to deal effectively with crime. Consequently, the chief often is placed in the role of an educator to both the public and elected officials.

In the quest for public support, the chief must be able to deal effectively with the entire community. The seriously conflicting viewpoints of groups and individuals will severely test the chief's ability to keep all segments of the public informed on departmental programs. Quite frequently, the chief will need to enlist the support of public interest groups during the planning and development of particular programs. Public-spirited citizens or groups committed in favor of programs designed to reduce the opportunities to violate the law can strengthen the support required to adopt these programs.

Public support is based primarily on a general understanding of the department's goals and programs. The chief may increase this understanding through public appearances and the release of statements to the news media or through informal personal contacts with the decision makers of the community and government.

Public support for police programs is more likely when (1) the community has confidence in the chief; (2) the chief encourages citizen cooperation; (3) the chief recognizes the fundamental importance of developing positive community relationships to achieve crime reduction objectives; and (4) the members of the police department demonstrate an interest in their community.

Managing the community service program

Over the years the United States has experienced a continuing increase in reported crime. Concurrently, there has been a growing public demand for the police to demonstrate a greater awareness of community needs and to establish an open forum in which the police and citizens can meet to discuss common problems and plan coordinated remedies. The police in general have responded through the institution of community relations units, specialized training in this area, and the implementation of crime prevention programs that have become an integral part of the community service function. Although this function does require some specialization to plan, develop, and coordinate, the patrol force should be expected to conduct most of the department's crime prevention activities.

Utilizing existing functions

A department does not need to develop a new specialization in order to maintain an effective community service program. In dealing with changing social attitudes over the last decade, police organizations have developed talents and channels necessary to communicate and maintain liaison with the community, and the general expertise that has been achieved throughout the ranks should be fully utilized. The objective of the community relations unit has been to seek support for the department and to alert the police to changes in community needs and attitudes, as well as to prevent or resolve conflicts that might arise out of blind misunderstanding. The tasks associated with the administration of crime prevention programs lend themselves to incorporation as community relations functions.

Community service programs should be coordinated from one central point. In small agencies this responsibility will fall on the chief of police. In medium-sized agencies the job may be assigned to a community service officer. In large departments a community service division should coordinate all departmental and community-based activities whether they pertain to community relations or crime prevention.

However it is coordinated, the community service program should be responsible for giving staff assistance and staff supervision to all community-related projects and programs within the department and for ensuring that all policies and programs are implemented, coordinated, and directed toward departmental goals. Specifically, the coordinating unit should (1) help field commanders establish new programs and improve ongoing programs; (2) provide staff supervision and assistance for all community-based programs within the department; (3) coordinate the efforts of patrol personnel to conduct community programs; (4) formulate and recommend department-wide policies and programs; and (5) coordinate and establish liaison with community-based agencies conducting crime prevention programs.

The community service officer

Merging crime prevention activities with community relations functions will necessarily expand the role of the community relations officer. In major agencies, the community relations officer assigned to the police district or precinct would assume new responsibilities for community-based crime prevention activities. The old job description could then be revised and the title changed to community service officer.

As the principal staff coordinator of crime resistance programs, the community service officer should have duties consisting of, but not limited to, the following:

1. Recommending programs for implementation and expansion utilizing existing community-based and departmental resources.
2. Maintaining liaison with crime resistance programs of other governmental agencies.
3. Maintaining multimedia research and reference data concerning crime resistance. This information should be distributed throughout the department as appropriate and should be made available to all personnel on request.
4. Ensuring that individual department members and citizens are recognized individually or collectively for their contributions to crime resistance efforts.
5. Ensuring that programs are reinforced, but without duplication of effort.
6. Maintaining accurate historical records of the department's crime resistance programs, with evaluation where appropriate.
7. Recommending discontinuation of programs determined to be ineffective.

The community service officer must be very sensitive to informal social control. Where little or no informal social control exists, the officer needs to bring to bear a variety of community organizational skills, primarily through other people who are able to influence the collective behavior and attitude of a group.

Police–citizen councils

Some departments have an advisory council to inform the district or precinct commander, the chief of patrol, or the chief of police on community relations. The citizen council offers ready-made lines of communication to the community and should be used to generate community interest and participation in crime prevention projects.

Each police district or precinct in a major city can establish a council to advise its commander of conditions and feelings in the community and of particular crime problems. Smaller agencies can organize a similar council on a citywide basis. A council should be composed of a cross section of the community, possibly five to seven interested citizens. It should operate in a purely advisory capacity to establish communication between the police and all sections of the community, especially neighborhood groups.

Council members should elect officers as soon as possible and should form committees on such subjects as juvenile delinquency, street crime, burglary, and narcotics and drug abuse.

The Baltimore police department has developed the following proposition as goals for the police–community councils that operate in each patrol district:

1. To create understanding and cooperation between the police and citizens
2. To provide opportunities for citizens to suggest improvements in police service
3. To acquaint police officers with the citizens they protect and to consider the ideas of these citizens on police matters
4. To acquaint citizens with the professional operation of police activities
5. To promote increased cooperation between the police and other local government agencies
6. To assist in crime prevention activities through education and information dissemination
7. To consult with police department district personnel on problems of law enforcement in the district.[10]

The councils meet monthly, and membership is open to all citizens residing or working in the community.

A monthly newsletter is published containing community news programs, crime prevention procedures, and police–community functions. The council is an excellent vehicle for promoting information exchange and instituting community-based crime resistance programs.

Training

Training plays a vital role in determining the effectiveness of a department's community service efforts. Officer preparation for law enforcement should stress not only operational techniques but also the way in which police officers deal with the public in the role of maintaining social order and preventing crime.

Community service training

A great amount of a police officer's workload, whether that officer is a member of a small agency or a major city department, consists of calls for service regarding noncriminal matters. Examples are: (1) assisting the aged and the mentally ill; (2) locating missing persons; (3) providing emergency medical assistance; (4) mediating and dealing with domestic, landlord–tenant, merchant–customer, and neighborhood disputes; (5) dealing with dependent and neglected children; (6) providing information; (7) regulating traffic; (8) investigating accidents; and (9) assuring the rights of citizens.

Each of these areas provides fertile grounds for developing programs emphasizing the community service responsibility of the police officer, and to this end officer preparation should include extensive training in interpersonal relations.

An effective police training program prepares an officer to think. It provides the officer with an understanding of self, society, and the criminal justice system. At the entrance level, it is important that the officer understand the role of the criminal justice system as a means of social control, giving special attention to the role of the police in society.

From the very outset, "service to the public" should be the theme of the police training program for both recruits and in-service officers. Police officers should receive thorough exposure to cultural awareness, human and group behavior, conflict management, causes of crime, and the changing role of the police. Courses in sociology and psychology should be given to develop an understanding of human behavior and to enhance the officer's ability to work effectively with others in the community.

The trainer should not assume that all officers have the attitude necessary to deal with citizens. Considerable effort should be devoted to preparing officers for the various human relations tasks they will be performing. Attitudinal training is essential in that a conflict may exist between the officer's and the public's perceptions of law enforcement. Members of the force should have no doubts that their profession works with people and not against them. They must be attuned to the fact that the underlying principle of police work is respect for human dignity.

Communications skills, including body language, should be made an important part of the training curriculum. Training should also increase the police officer's listening skills. The ability to listen is essential, and it is often overlooked. Instruction in telephone courtesy, effective interviewing, and proper means of addressing citizens should also be incorporated.

Constant training in the application of force, particularly the proper use of firearms, is of utmost importance, and policy should be reviewed periodically to make certain the rules are in keeping with contemporary standards.

The department should seek out instructors that include not only police personnel but also college and university faculty members, community organizers, welfare workers, chamber of commerce representatives, clergymen, and others, depending on the nature of the community. Social service agencies should be invited to tell police training groups about their referral services and functions. Members of minority groups should be invited to discuss problems and to help dispel misunderstandings and myths.

To find a common ground for understanding, training programs should expose police officers to community organizations serving the physically and mentally handicapped, for police officers must understand disabled persons and their disabilities and have some knowledge of available community resources. The handicapped include people impaired or disabled by mental retardation, physical disability, or visual or hearing difficulties. Whenever possible, handicapped citizens should be invited to address police classes. Training courses in sign language are given as part of entrance level and in-service training in the Baltimore police department.

Finally, officers should learn the historical, demographic, and geographic characteristics of their jurisdiction through a course on "Knowing Your City." Included should be historical background, political status, important physical characteristics, ethnic and cultural makeup, community associations, current events, and the major institutions that make up the character of the city.

Crime resistance training

Community oriented crime resistance training should be implemented at both entrance and in-service levels. At the entrance level this training should be integrated into the regular course on patrol procedures and should stress the police officer's role as an educator. Two units of instruction are of special importance.

The first, methods of community crime control, helps develop a better understanding of community dynamics and the structure and functioning of community organizations. The second, residential and commercial security inspection techniques, covers building security inspection and target hardening techniques. Relatively inexpensive countermeasures that citizens can employ to deter crime are stressed (elimination of obstacles to vision at entrances and store windows, choice of proper locks, and use of television cameras).

Training in crime and the elderly, juvenile delinquency and crime, crisis intervention, and dealing with death should be required for police officers.

Juvenile diversion program

A two-week juvenile diversion program implemented by the Baltimore police department is designed to provide an understanding of juvenile diversion through a series of courses in the topics outlined below. Lectures, demonstrations, role playing, situational problem solving, and field trips are combined. This program was offered to carefully selected members of the patrol division to prepare them for juvenile delinquency prevention through redirection of the activities of juvenile offenders. Emphasis is placed on referral to community-based agencies. The course content is as follows:

1. *Orientation.* General introduction; purpose and goals of the diversion program.
2. *The police role.* Societal demands placed on law enforcement; redefinitions of the police role in contemporary society.
3. *Departmental juvenile procedures.* Departmental procedures in the diversion program.
4. *The family in contemporary society.* The institution of the family and its function in the socialization process; the impact of family disorganization on society.
5. *The history and philosophy of juvenile justice.* History of the juvenile court movement with emphasis on legal foundations.
6. *Police discretion.* Issues of police discretion, with specific reference to its role in diversion.
7. *The diversion process.* Background and philosophy of diversion and its objectives; factors in adjustment and referral.
8. *Understanding juvenile delinquency.* Survey defining juvenile delinquency and indicating relationships between the problem and the social setting in which it occurs.
9. *Juveniles and the law.* Legal definitions of juvenile delinquency; jurisdiction of the juvenile court; legal basis for diversion programs; related laws.
10. *Principles of interviewing and counseling.* Interviewing techniques; interviewing minority group members.
11. *Community resources.* Panel discussion by representatives of community agencies to which youthful offenders are to be referred.
12. *Case study workshop and practicum.* Practice in analyzing case histories, making referral decisions, and completing departmental forms.
13. *Adolescent growth and development.* Analysis of the physical, psychological, and social stages of adolescence and how they relate to behavior.
14. *Field trip.* Visits to area diagnostic and group home facilities.
15. *Examination.* Comprehensive examination upon completion of the course.

Crisis intervention course

The Baltimore police department, employing the generalist approach, has developed a thirty-two-hour course consisting of lectures, demonstrations, and practice designed to provide an understanding of the dynamics of crisis situations and expertise in employing the techniques of controlling, interviewing, negotiating, and referring. The course also covers cultural and legal issues that are germane to the dispute situations encountered in crisis intervention. (Crisis intervention will be discussed further in the latter part of this chapter.)

Planning

Planning must precede the implementation of community-based programs and projects designed to prevent crime. Planning involves an examination of the extent of crime and community problems, a review of the applicable facts, and formulations of acceptable solutions and alternatives.

In general, planning for community service programs should cover identification of the problem, the resources, and alternative methods of obtaining public support; development of programs; continuation of countermeasures to crime; and an evaluation component.

Costs

The cost of a proposed program should be considered in the early stages of planning. This cost will determine the agency's ability to support such a project financially over an extended period of time. Costs are particularly important in a program involving an increase in authorized strength through the hiring of specialized personnel. Failure to consider the financial implications of a program may well result in the abandonment of worthwhile efforts following the expiration of an initial grant.

Too often, police administrators and local officials have been tempted by the availability of outside funding and have implemented programs that could not be sustained following its severance. Consequently, intended remedies have become mere palliatives, and problems have remained unsolved. Planning efforts, then, should address long-term goals rather than stopgap measures.

Crime and problem analysis

Before a program can be developed or implemented, the extent of crime and other problems in the community needs to be known. The initial planning stages should present a thorough analysis of crime data and information on other serious community problems. Frequently crime conditions and community problems are found together. Thus, in order to identify a particular problem, the department needs accurate field reporting and record keeping systems along with reliable lines of communication with the community.

The crime data should include such basic information as types and patterns of crime; location, date, and time; offender information; victim characteristics; target characteristics; and description of difficulties experienced by the community.

Members of the community should be encouraged to report incidents to the police. The police, in turn, should make more than a superficial attempt at complainant satisfaction; they should conduct a thorough preliminary investigation. Confidence is reinforced by positive follow-up action.

Reports resulting from completed preliminary and follow-up investigations become the working source documents from which police departments can determine the significance, the nature, and the particulars of a problem. With this information, a department can evaluate realistically the temporal, geographic, and social factors that will permit the development of effective strategies. In larger police departments an in-house data processing capability will be needed to deal with the enormous volume of reported information.

Police management should transmit to the field forces a clear and concise picture of the problems existing within their specific areas. The information should be arranged by time frames to facilitate planning and should be prominently displayed to members in the field by means of pin maps or charts if the data relate to criminal activities. Thus personnel can familiarize themselves with the type and frequency of criminal activity on each beat or shift.

Crime analysis data should be reviewed by patrol command and supervisory personnel and should be used to develop preventive patrol strategies that are responsive to situations of concern to the community. These data should be published daily if the department has the computer capability to do so. Efforts then can be concentrated in specific areas at the time of day when they are likely to be most effective. (Information management will be discussed further in Chapter 16.)

Community support and program planning

The objectives of planning at the community level are to stimulate citizen support and participation in community-based programs, to develop new programs, and to coordinate and provide staff supervision to departmental efforts that apply to such programs. Methods of opening lines of communication with the community need to be considered and developed during the planning process. Police–citizen councils provide this necessary link.

Planning efforts should next address the types of programs to be developed and the manner in which citizens should be made aware of them. The plans may call for the use of media time, for pamphlets or handbills, and for personal contacts by members of the police–citizen council. Issues pertaining to communications should be resolved before any program is completed, since total community participation is essential to success. For example, an antiburglary campaign designed to increase home security would be virtually useless if only a small portion of the homes in the community were involved.

Finally, planners should consider the cyclical nature of crime so that continuing crime control programs can be implemented. In many instances agencies have limited their consideration to the Christmas shopping season, when various property crimes tend to increase. However, criminal activity is ongoing and requires a continuing application of countermeasures. (Planning is discussed further in Chapter 15.)

Programs

Eliminating the desire and the opportunity to commit crime is not easy, and neither task will be even marginally successful in the absence of some progress in the other. Chiefs of police have become increasingly aware that progress in crime prevention cannot advance very far without the informed efforts of both local government and society at large.

However, police chiefs cannot wait for overtures from local government and community leaders. It is their responsibility as crime experts to become movers. Police chiefs should open the doors to cooperation, should provide information and direction, and should constantly encourage participation. If the chiefs fail to act, if they regard crime control and prevention as a personal fiefdom to be jealously protected, they will program themselves for failure.

The National Advisory Commission on Criminal Justice Standards and Goals established the following guidelines regarding police involvement in preventive activities:

Every police agency should immediately establish programs that encourage members of the public to take an active role in preventing crime, that provide information leading to the arrest and conviction of criminal offenders, that facilitate the identification and recovery of stolen property, and that increase liaison with private industry in security efforts.

1. Every police agency should assist actively in the establishment of volunteer neighborhood security programs that involve the public in neighborhood crime prevention and reduction.
   a) The police agency should provide the community with information and assistance regarding means to avoid being victimized by crime and should make every effort to inform neighborhoods of developing çrime trends that may affect their area.
   b) The police agency should instruct neighborhood volunteers to telephone the police concerning suspicious situations and to identify themselves as volunteers and provide necessary information.
   c) Participating volunteers should not take enforcement action themselves.
   d) Police units should respond directly to the incident rather than to the reporting volunteer.
   e) If further information is required from the volunteer, the police agency should contact him by telephone.
   f) If an arrest results from the volunteer's information, the police agency should immediately notify him by telephone.
   g) The police agency should acknowledge through personal contact, telephone call, or letter, every person who provides information.
2. Every police agency should establish or assist programs that involve trade, business, industry, and community participation in preventing and reducing commercial crimes.
3. Every police agency should seek the enactment of local ordinances that establish minimum security standards for all new construction and for existing commercial structures. Once regulated buildings are constructed, ordinances should be enforced through inspection by operational police personnel.
4. Every police agency should conduct, upon request, security inspections of businesses and residences and recommend measures to avoid being victimized by crime.
5. Every police agency having more than 75 personnel should establish a specialized unit to provide support services to and jurisdictionwide coordination of the agency's crime prevention programs; however such programs should be operationally decentralized whenever possible.[11]

The formation of a viable working relationship between police and the communities they serve is essential to crime prevention.

Crime prevention programs: reducing the opportunity to commit crimes

While community councils are effective, they are composed primarily of community members who are strongly motivated. The majority of citizens, through apathy, lack of information, or frustration, do not generally participate formally. It is up to the police to attempt to reach the majority of the citizens. In order to be effective, such contacts are best made at the grass roots level—that is, by police officers on the beat. "Police public relations units or similar divisions can serve well-defined purposes, but they should not be used as substitutes for regular patrol police contact."[12] In the course of those contacts, the patrol officer should provide the citizen with crime prevention information and solicit assistance and cooperation. The nature of this information should be proactive— that is, aimed at forestalling offenses.

Operationally, police need to apply the most effective methods of patrol and deployment to maximize crime prevention efforts. Police techniques depend on the types of crime occurring, the modi operandi of criminals, and the locations of occurrences. The more frequently employed prevention methods consist of saturation and tactical patrol deployment. Newer approaches such as team policing also have been devised. Team policing is designed to decentralize police decision making by distributing authority to individual law enforcement teams assigned to target neighborhoods. This method of deployment seeks to improve police service and community responsiveness by creating "neighborhood police departments."

Target hardening　The opportunity to commit a crime may be reduced by placing obstacles in the way of the criminal. In other words, potential targets may be made more resistant to attack. This process, known as target hardening, will be discussed below in connection with burglary, automobile security, bicycle larceny, various types of robbery, commercial theft, and vandalism.

Burglary　One method of reducing the threat of burglary is through police-initiated premises inspections. Here, the police identify security deficiencies within premises and make corrective recommendations. The police collect significant data through their offense reporting system and can identify methods of operation, points of entry and exit, time frames, types of structures, and other pieces of information necessary to conduct a thorough premises examination. Equipped with such data, the police can identify vulnerable areas and effect target hardening. A door-to-door premises examination by the beat officer in vulnerable areas can make the occupants aware of security measures they can take.

The National Institute of Law Enforcement and Criminal Justice states that "for homes or apartments, security recommendations range from the [little] things a citizen can do (such as leaving lights on when going out for the evening . . .) to installation of hardware (such as deadbolt locks on doors). For commercial establishments, security recommendations usually pertain to hardware (such as locks, alarms) and keeping windows clear of display and signs so that intruders [could be] visible to police and passersby."[13]

The California Council on Criminal Justice identified two problem areas in premises survey programs. First, residents may not be able to correct security deficiencies because of lack of expertise in installing the hardware. Second, low income residents may not be able to afford such hardware. In this case the police could explore the possibility that lock companies might provide quality locks at cost for low income residents while installation could be provided by service clubs.[14] Also, inquiries could be made to determine the availability of a government subsidy for the purchase and installation of the necessary hardware. Such resources need to be identified by the police in planning any security inspection program. By these direct efforts police officers are able not only to provide technical assistance to reduce the opportunity for burglary, but also to allay the fear produced by the threat of crime.

A great variety of burglary prevention programs have been designed to meet the particular needs of individual communities. The National Institute of Law Enforcement and Criminal Justice says that "the burglary threat is far from uniform among cities or within a city among all household or commercial establishments, and police departments have profited by taking variations into account when developing a prevention program."[15]

The National Neighborhood Watch Program, initiated by the National Sheriffs' Association, recommends that local law enforcement agencies provide leadership to stimulate citizen and community involvement in reducing opportunities to commit crime. The program is designed to disseminate information to the public that will aid them in reducing the threat of burglary.[16] The National

Sheriffs' Association encourages police to use the mass media in addition to such personal efforts as door-to-door contacts to deliver these services. The mass media provide advertising space and air time without cost for public service information.

A survey conducted by the Law Enforcement Assistance Administration (LEAA) identified numerous effective programs. In Monterey and Oakland, California, police officers were specially trained to conduct premises security examinations and provide corrective recommendations to occupants. Police officers in Huntington, West Virginia, made residential and business inspections upon request. Law enforcement agencies that find the use of police officers in premises examination campaigns to be costly might use the service of auxiliary police, student interns, and volunteer community groups to provide a door-to-door inspection service in selected neighborhoods. In St. Paul, Minnesota, Marine Corps reservists were used to encourage residents to participate in the Neighborhood Crime Watch program.[17]

Such programs are usually supplemented with property identification programs. Items of value are marked and decals advertise the fact. "Operation Identification attempts to: discourage burglaries, deter fencing operations, assist in the apprehension of offenders and in the return of stolen property."[18]

The Montgomery County, Maryland, police department has devised and implemented a program aimed at reducing residential burglaries. The program is called Shield of Confidence and is aimed at encouraging residents and residential builders to take steps to upgrade security standards.[19] A stringent examination encompassing doors, locks, and windows is requested by the resident or builder and carried out by crime prevention personnel. If all requirements are met (they are many and exacting) the dwelling is given a Shield of Confidence sticker and a letter verifying compliance. Adding to incentives to participate is the offer by a major local insurer of substantial discounts on home and dwelling insurance rates to those who qualify for Shield of Confidence certification.

Automobile security   To most Americans the purchase of an automobile represents a major income expenditure. Simple methods can be employed to protect the car and its contents against theft. Several practices for increasing the security of automobiles are:

1. Removing the key from the ignition
2. Locking the auto
3. Never leaving the car unattended with the engine running
4. Parking in well-lighted areas
5. Removing valuables
6. Recording the serial numbers of such accessories as citizens' band radios and stereo tape decks
7. Marking all accessories with an identifiable number traceable to the owner (i.e., driver's license or registration number)
8. Installing alarms.

The police have a responsibility to employ various means to communicate this type of information to the public. Many departments use the media for this purpose by producing public service announcements and having officers make personal appearances on television shows.

Private automobile clubs and television stations can play a major role in helping reduce auto thefts. A special antitheft system that has been proven effective in reducing auto theft in major cities is the H.O.T. Car program. This program originated in Boston, Massachusetts, where it has proven successful. In Baltimore, the program is sponsored by the Montgomery Ward Auto Club and WMAR-TV.

Essentially, the program is designed to discourage thieves from stealing and tampering with automobiles registered in the program. Program participants receive a bumper sticker indicating that a $1,000 reward is offered by the sponsor of the H.O.T. Car program for information leading to the arrest and conviction of anyone who steals the car. If one is stolen, a description of the car and the tag number are aired over local participating television and radio stations. The program also offers special devices to discourage theft. Examples are tapered door lock buttons, vehicle identification number strips, and a handbook containing measures to further protect the car.

Police agencies should consider involving insurance companies, automobile associations, city councils, new and used car dealers, and automobile rental agencies in a united campaign against auto thefts and larcenies from autos. Coupling this program with concentrated patrol efforts can significantly reduce the opportunity for such thefts.

Bicycle larceny   The popularity of the bicycle as a method of transportation and recreation has made it an inviting target for theft. Local police can help cyclists reduce the opportunity for theft and also increase the recovery rate of stolen bicycles.

The Los Angeles County sheriff's department prepared a bicycle security pamphlet describing various theft prevention methods. Chaining and padlocking the bike when not in use, recording serial numbers, and marking the driver's license number on the frame of the bicycle are measures the police can encourage to increase bicycle security.[20] Enlisting the aid of the media, schools, businesses, recreation centers, and cycling clubs in the prevention effort will maximize the dissemination of security information.

The need for more stringent security controls may inspire the enactment of legislation requiring the registration and licensing of all bicycles. The state of California has enacted this type of legislation, which can significantly assist police agencies in preventing thefts and apprehending offenders.[21]

Robbery   Robbery, unlike burglary, auto theft, and bicycle larceny, requires a confrontation between the victim and the assailant. The potential for violence in robberies is high and causes a great deal of concern and fear within the community.

Although some street robberies are well planned, most are indiscriminate occurrences precipitated by immediate opportunities. Saturation patrols and the use of decoy techniques in high-frequency areas may reduce steet robberies. In South Bend, Indiana, hand-picked uniformed officers were employed outside normal working hours to walk in teams in high crime areas. Known as "stake-out squads," these teams were to concentrate on "muggings, purse-snatchings, and related street crimes."[22]

Target hardening in this area requires educating citizens in ways to avoid victimization and steps to take if they are robbed:

1. Avoid going out at night alone.
2. Stay in well-lighted areas and avoid strangers.
3. Carry a sound device such as a whistle, and sound it if danger is anticipated.
4. Avoid cashing public assistance or social security checks on the day of delivery.
5. Periodically alter your route to grocery stores and check cashing establishments.
6. Report the actions and locations of suspicious persons to the police.

Police in Daytona Beach, Florida, instituted a program of audiovisual lectures on robbery prevention for members of civic groups and fraternal organizations. Other components of the program included handout material and robbery pre-

Empty streets are a somber symbol of the fear
that plagues many communities—large and small.

vention displays in shopping centers, central business districts, retirement centers, and schools.[23]

Commercial robbery commonly involves planning and the use of a weapon. The National Institute of Law Enforcement and Criminal Justice states that "most commercial robberies are of small businesses and stores, particularly chain stores and gas stations open late at night." Moreover, "stores in out-of-the-way places, run by a lone or elderly shopkeeper are more prone to robbery attempts."[24] Effective target hardening in this area involves a variety of operational tactics combined with the individual business owner's responsiveness to robbery prevention efforts.

In Denver the Special Crime Attack Team (SCAT) is responsible for implementing antirobbery tactics. This unit, in addition to disseminating crime prevention information, also makes inspections of businesses and recommends security improvements.[25] The Washington, D.C., metropolitan police department has initiated a robbery prevention program involving a silent alarm system developed by an electronics firm. This device consists of a foot treadle that, when depressed, transmits a radio signal to the police. This system is reported to have two strong points. It results in quick response and saves manpower.[26] Other examples of physical and psychological barriers the business owner can employ are decals in show windows advertising the use of detection devices, and shielding of customer counters.

As part of its Robbery Reduction Program, the Minneapolis police department places a 35-millimeter camera in selected stores having a high robbery incidence. The camera is activated when a bait bill is removed from the cash register.[27]

Brochures such as the Description Sheet published by the Traveler's Insurance Company entitled *What Did the Robber Look Like?* and the pamphlet produced by the Los Angeles police department, *Will You Be His Next Customer?*, contain helpful tips for the business owner. The Los Angeles police department disseminates helpful information to the local business community in the form of pamphlets with suggestions on the handling and storing of cash receipts and the implementation of safety measures that are designed to reduce the would-be robber's opportunity to commit a crime.[28]

Police robbery control An effort has been made by the Law Enforcement Assistance Administration to develop a systematic approach to robbery control by preparing a "prescriptive package" entitled the *Police Robbery Control Manual.* The manual is intended as a practical guide for police departments, provides a step-by-step process of analyzing the pattern of robberies in a community, and shows how to set up a plan of action.

Published in 1975 and available from the Government Printing Office, the

manual shows how to develop a robbery control project by developing objectives, designing the program, and carrying through several kinds of projects. The manual also covers organization, training methods, and possible funding sources. Appendices provide synopses of robbery programs in selected cities, an illustration of robbery analysis, and examples of public information materials on robbery prevention.

The police agency is the local information repository for measures the business community can employ to prevent robbery. An asset to any police department's robbery prevention effort is public support and understanding. For this reason, departments should consider conducting seminars and instructional programs for the general public. Police departments in Concord, California; Washington, D.C.; and Charlotte, North Carolina, have instituted on-site classroom and seminar training sessions with merchants on how to cooperate with the police in preventing robberies and apprehending offenders.[29]

Commercial theft Retail merchants lose billions of dollars every year through shoplifting, bad checks, and credit card fraud. These crimes result in inventory shortages, lower profits, and higher prices. Cooperative deterrent and prevention efforts between the police and the business community will depend on the scope of the problem, the availability of resources, and the physical design of the premises. Police liaison with local affiliates of the National Retail Merchants Association, the National Federation of Independent Business, the Chamber of Commerce of the United States, and other organizations can be invaluable in developing effective programs to combat commercial crime. Efforts should focus on (1) making the community aware of the seriousness of the crime and its impact on the consumer; (2) training employees to recognize theft techniques; and (3) installing detection and prevention hardware.

Philadelphia developed a program, STEM (Shoplifters Take Everybody's Money), to emphasize the fact that shoplifting is indeed everyone's problem. Cooperation among merchants, business organizations, local government officials, and law enforcement authorities produced a broad media campaign against shoplifting.[30]

When a department store in Toronto trained its sales personnel to detect various shoplifting techniques, a significant reduction of the problem resulted. Similar training efforts were made by the San Diego police department in cooperation with the local chamber of commerce in establishing a shoplifting prevention clinic.[31]

Many businesses are equipped with protective systems employing security personnel and utilizing various types of security hardware designed to reduce the opportunity for shoplifting. The hardware ranges from sophisticated electronic merchandise tags and closed circuit television to the placement of convex and one-way mirrors in strategic locations.

Police can assist business proprietors in efforts to minimize losses due to fraudulent checks and credit cards by distributing stolen check and credit information, plus helpful guidelines for the recognition and deterrence of passers.

Merchants can minimize fraudulent check losses through the following practices:

1. Limiting the cash amount of checks
2. Limiting checks to the amount of the purchase
3. Requiring adequate identification
4. Comparing signatures with identification cards
5. Writing down physical description and other identifying information on backs of checks
6. Photographing each person who cashes a check.

Merchants can minimize credit card losses through the following practices:

1. Comparing account numbers with lists of stolen, lost, or suspended cards
2. Matching the signatures on cards and merchandise bills
3. Checking expiration dates on cards
4. Verifying by phone any charge amounts that exceed the card plan floor limit.

Police also can assist businesses in training employees. Merchants and business owners interested in setting up loss reduction programs can obtain booklets, motion pictures, and other aids for the prevention of business crimes from the Chamber of Commerce of the United States and various trade associations.

Vandalism   Vandalism is a major problem in this country, with much of the destruction aimed at schools. A conservative estimate of the annual cost of vandalism to the public schools is $600 million.[32] Setting fires, breaking windows, and other acts of property damage are all too common. One writer on the problem tells of a suburban school administrator who spends more on glass replacement than on textbooks.[33]

Police effectiveness in this area may well be increased by working in cooperation with school officials and community councils or associations. The police can aid school officials by recommending improvements in both internal and external security. Such programs as "Officer Friendly" and Police Explorer troops can help build rapport between youngsters and police and alert juveniles to their roles and responsibilities in society. Working through police–community councils, police and school officials can meet with parents of school age youngsters and impress on them that the damage done to schools and other buildings lowers the quality of education and life in general in their community.

In addition, police departments, with the cooperation of school personnel, should institute in-service training programs on school violence and vandalism. Working closely with school officials and members of parent–teacher associations is a must if any benefit is to be derived from such programs. School officials should be invited as guest speakers for police in-service training programs and, in turn, police officers should participate in teacher in-service programs.

Community involvement   Authorities believe that the success of any crime prevention program depends on placing much greater responsibility with citizens in the neighborhood.[34] The police service has a responsibility to mobilize and direct the energies of communities to reduce their vulnerability to crime. Communities have scores of indigenous resources that have gone unrecognized as viable sources of crime prevention.

Existing community organizations, such as churches, schools, and civic groups, provide the means by which police may disseminate information and suggestions on particular crime problems and steps for control, and a complete inventory of these resources is essential to any crime prevention effort. Opening lines of communication and establishing a foundation of mutual understanding with working community organizations may prove to be invaluable in developing an interdependent relationship between the police and the public. Among the cooperative techniques that can be employed are block associations, community walks, radio watch, and tenant patrols.

Block associations The seriousness and extent of the crime problem in a community will sometimes act as a catalyst for the creation of volunteer crime prevention groups. The concerned citizens who form these groups often look to their local police department for leadership. Efforts can be made to form block associations of neighborhood residents and local business owners who, through their collective efforts, may attempt to reduce the opportunity for crimes. The goals of these block associations are to increase the cooperation between citizens and law enforcement agencies, to prevent the occurrence of crimes, and to reduce the fear of crime.[35]

Citizen involvement with the police Police efforts to achieve a higher degree of citizen involvement may be the single most important means the police have available to them for coping with crime. A 5 or 10 percent increase in the involvement of all citizens in a community could possibly prove of much greater value in combating crime than a 50 or 60 percent increase in the number of police officers or an equally large investment in technical equipment. . . .

In some cities community groups have begun to take a more active role in stressing the need for a sense of personal responsibility in combating crime. The police can aid this movement in three ways. They can take the initiative, at every opportunity, to impress on a community the responsibility citizens have for dealing with crime and to inform them of the limited potential of the police. They can offer specific advice to citizens on how they can aid in protecting themselves and their property from criminal attack. And they can cultivate their relationship with the community so that the community will freely turn to the police for support in those situations in which the police are uniquely equipped to be of assistance.

Source: This material is excerpted from Herman Goldstein, *Policing a Free Society* (Cambridge, Mass.: Ballinger Publishing Company, 1977), pp. 62–63.

A significant problem with volunteer citizens' groups, however, is the maintenance of enthusiasm and active participation. Assertive police leadership in this area will have a positive effect on maintaining group solidarity and purpose. Official recognition by the police department and local government, formalized training, and awards for exemplary work all help sustain citizen involvement. It must be borne in mind, however, that the police must never let their legal powers be used by persons outside the law. Citizens' associations can be a hazard if allowed to usurp legitimate police authority.

Block associations can be organized to assist in such community crime prevention programs as crime walks, mobile radio patrols, tenant patrols, and home security operations. The nature of these programs and their geographic distribution in a community require that staff supervision and liaison with the department be administered by the community service officer rather than by the beat officer.

Community walks Neighborhood volunteer walk programs are designed to minimize street crime by supplementing police patrols. Walkers can assist the police by giving special attention to abandoned houses and the homes of vacationers, by providing escort services to elderly people and others late at night, and by disseminating crime prevention literature. Equipped with devices such as whistles and air horns, walkers patrol in groups of two or three. When they observe a situation requiring police service they are instructed to notify the police immediately and not become personally involved. West Philadelphia has a block program in which volunteers walk a two-hour shift each month. Two shifts operate each evening between 7:00 and 11:00 P.M.[36] This type of walk program allows community residents to take an active interest in their neighbors' welfare. By demonstrating a sense of community, such a program can create an environment of neighbor interdependence and can encourage further participation in community crime prevention efforts.

Radio watch The growing popularity of the citizens' band two-way radio has presented the police agency with an opportunity to promote citizen involvement in crime control and to expand patrol capabilities. Community residents with citizens' band radios in their automobiles can be organized into neighborhood mobile radio patrols. These patrols can notify the police of situations requiring official attention. Existing programs incorporate several methods for notifying the police. In some jurisdictions the police monitor the citizens' band and are in direct contact with the mobile operator. In other areas the radio patrols report to a citizens' band base station whose operator in turn notifies the police.

Businesses using vehicles equipped with two-way radios can be enlisted to cooperate with the police by instructing their drivers to notify the dispatch office when observing suspicious activities or criminal acts. For example, Baltimore has enlisted the cooperation of taxi drivers who, in addition to reporting suspected criminal activity, display conspicuous decals identifying their taxicabs as "crime watch vehicles," thus increasing their deterrent effect.

The Los Angeles police department issued a *Radio Watch Driver's Booklet* describing the appropriate action to be taken by drivers observing criminal situations.[37] Departments organizing similar efforts should be sure drivers understand the types of incidents to be reported and should emphasize to participants that they should never become directly involved in any situation.

Tenant patrols The high-rise public housing environment seems to provide a growth medium for all types of crime. In many public housing projects there is a pervasive fear that makes residents barricade themselves in their apartments after dark, thus making lobbies, hallways, and elevators virtual no man's lands. The lack of defensible space, ease of penetrability, and lack of surveillance personnel and hardware seem to present insurmountable problems to effective crime prevention.

In Oakland, California, public housing authorities organized a Home Alert program. Meetings were called and police lectured on personal safety.[38] The housing authority in Baltimore employs residents of high-rise public housing as housing security aides. These tenants are furnished with uniforms and local communications devices. Their function is to patrol hallways, handle minor tenant complaints, report criminal incidents to the police, provide escort service to elderly residents, and help tenants mark property for identification. These security aides receive a minimum of forty hours of training from the Baltimore police department. Apartment residents have adopted many of the crime prevention techniques used in public housing.

Police and the elderly The elderly can be considered the hidden victims of crime. All too often they are trapped alone in their dwellings, fearing to venture out lest they fall prey to those who would choose them as easy targets for street crime, burglary, and confidence schemes.

Police departments working in conjunction with senior citizens' centers, social agencies, and local government can educate the elderly to help them avoid victimization. Some of the communities that have such programs are Kansas

City, Missouri; Montgomery County, Maryland; Wilmington, Delaware; Jersey City, New Jersey; and Mansfield, Ohio. These programs generally include referrals to social service agencies and instruction in target hardening, personal safety, avoiding confidence schemes, and traveling in groups to the bank, stores, or other locations. The Baltimore police department has implemented a program called BASE (Business Assisting Seniors in Emergencies). BASE attempts to foster a feeling of security among the elderly by displaying highly visible placards in a variety of places where they can seek help. Churches, businesses, libraries, and schools stand ready to aid and assist older persons in coping with a variety of problems.

Crime prevention programs: reducing the desire to commit crimes

The police can apply short-term corrective treatment to persons who find themselves in situations that may lead to criminal acts. Programs dealing with conflict management, domestic crisis intervention, and juvenile diversion attempt to render effective first aid to people by referring them to the appropriate sources of help.

Conflict management   The social upheavals of the 1960s placed the police in the tenuous and unfamiliar position of dealing with new types of conflicts. Unprepared and ill-equipped to resolve these seemingly endless conflicts, the police often provided the catalyst that precipitated violence. A hard lesson on the nature and management of conflict emerged from those experiences. To identify conflict within the community before it reaches dangerous limits, close contact and communication should be developed with the individuals, groups, or communities involved.

To recognize and name potential sources of conflict within the community, the Dayton, Ohio, police department created a conflict intervention team to seek out, identify, and intervene in areas of the community displaying symptoms of potential conflict before they became serious disruptions. Possible neighbor disputes, racial conflicts, labor–management problems, and civil demonstrations are all volatile areas requiring police attention. Any such police effort requires that officers spend considerable time in the community, talk with people, and build the sincere and honest relationship that is necessary to effective police–community interaction.[39]

Domestic crisis intervention   Police spend an overwhelming amount of time performing order maintenance and service functions. Domestic disturbances represent perhaps the most significant and time-consuming of all requests for service. Often a domestic situation does not involve any illegal behavior but does create an atmosphere in which violence could occur.

An examination of homicides and serious assaults indicates that a significant number of the victims have had some form of interpersonal contact with the assailant. Many of these crimes are a direct result of domestic disturbances. The volatile nature of these conflicts has resulted in a significant number of assaults on police officers. The FBI Uniform Crime Reports have consistently emphasized the danger inherent in these situations. Yet with proper training the police can generally manage these conflicts and prevent their escalation into violence.

A preliminary assessment of a conflict and an appropriate referral may render invaluable aid to the people involved and reduce the possibility of violence. To deal effectively and safely with domestic disturbances requires the application of various defusing and mediating skills.

There are two approaches to developing the most appropriate police response to domestic crises. Morton Bard proposes a specialist approach as indicated by his work with the New York City police department. Specially selected and trained officers in the Thirty-ninth Precinct were organized into a Family Crisis Intervention Unit. This team of specialists patrolled a regularly assigned sector, but were dispatched to any sector of the precinct when a family disturbance occurred.[40]

A generalist approach to domestic crisis intervention was implemented in Richmond, California. Specialized training was given to all members of the patrol division. The critical factors considered in reaching this decision were (1) a desire to avoid elitism; (2) awareness that officers occasionally will handle family fights even if specialists have been trained; (3) unwillingness to "lock in" specialists; and (4) recognition that the tone of community relations often is shaped by the crucial role that police play when intervening in family fights, thereby indicating a need for all uniformed officers to be skilled in this area.[41]

Crisis intervention techniques are easily adaptable to other areas in which police encounter significant problems. Handling mentally disturbed persons who may be threatening violence to themselves or others is an area in which police often feel unprepared. Victims of rape and sexual molestation also should be recognized as persons in crisis who require proper treatment.

Police and the young person   The rise in the number and types of crimes committed by juveniles has been staggering. In searching for a way to reach out to young people, to acquaint youngsters with the police role and their role as responsible citizens, the Norfolk, Virginia, police department implemented the Officer Friendly program. The goals of the program are:

1. To alert young children to their rights, responsibilities, and obligations
2. To provide them with a realistic understanding of the police role
3. To establish rapport between the elementary student and the uniformed police officer
4. To create a positive attitude in children toward their own welfare and that of others.

In three forty-five-minute visits, uniformed officers talked about the police role, safety, and crime prevention. Results showed that children who participated in the program had more positive attitudes toward and better feelings about relating to police.[42]

Many departments sponsor law enforcement Explorer troops through their local Boy Scout organization. The Suffolk County, New York, police department, the Los Angeles County sheriff's department, and the Tillamook County, Oregon, sheriff's department all have sponsored such groups. Explorer troops give teen-age youths a serious look at police and their function. The concepts of public service, responsibility, and good citizenship are stressed as in all scout endeavors.

Programs aimed at young people also include athletic teams, police-sponsored bus trips, youth clubs, and summer camps. Such activities staffed by police officers help young people see police as active community helpers, not adversaries. While still quite young, participants are given a foundation for good citizenship and responsibility that may bear a welcome harvest in future years.

Juvenile diversion   The growing involvement of youth in violent crime has made juvenile delinquency an important social issue, and much attention is directed toward combating this problem. Delinquency prevention efforts are focused on recognizing early warning signs of possible problems and employing methods that will prevent this early behavior from developing into violent criminal activity.

Pretrial diversion permits offenders who meet certain established criteria to be channeled away from the criminal justice system and into appropriate social service or rehabilitation programs. Pretrial diversion for adult offenders has caused certain groups to question whether such systems represent a denial of due process to the accused. However, such questions lose much of their force when applied to juvenile offenders, since the prevailing judicial philosophy is that, generally, juveniles are not criminals but children in need of guidance.

Pretrial diversion is of particular benefit to the youthful first offender. Rather than being identified as a delinquent, the offender receives help from agencies experienced in addressing the problems and needs of youth.

The police chief who wants to institute a juvenile pretrial diversion program must obtain court sanction and should then institute a training program for police personnel.

The Limited Adjustment Program (LAP) of the Baltimore police department is an attempt to divert certain juvenile offenders from the court. The program seeks to identify juveniles who may be precariously near the threshold of a criminal career and to adjust their behavior prior to the commission of delinquent acts. Rehabilitative counseling and community referral are used to induce socially acceptable behavior and thus reduce or prevent criminal behavior.

The LAP is designed to involve the complainant, the juvenile, and the juvenile's family in determining the applicability of "diversionary" processing. Resources in the community form a referral reservoir that can effectively address the needs of the juvenile offender and help change his or her behavior without increasing the expenditure of public funds.

Specially screened and trained patrol officers coordinate the diversion activities. These Youth Service Officers (YSOs) were formed into teams and assigned to individual patrol districts. The YSO serves as a district level screening agent for the program by identifying the immediate needs of the juvenile and implementing one or more of the discretionary alternatives, which include warning and releasing, diversion to community resource agencies, personal counseling, and diversion to a work program or referral to court for "system processing." Juvenile programs are further discussed in Chapter 12.

Special problems

The areas in which police and citizens can work together are expanding yearly. For example, in an attempt to deal with the problem of child abuse, the Pomona, California, police department developed a pilot program that provided intensive in-service training on the subject, coupled with a series of community awareness sessions stressing prevention, recognition, and reporting of abuse cases. Another community-based project that cooperates with the police is the Women's Haven in Fort Worth and Tarrant, Texas. The Haven was incorporated to provide shelter for women victimized by spousal assaults. Police refer such cases to the shelter and provide additional support working with shelter personnel.

Such projects as these not only can improve the quality and expand the scope of police service but also can demonstrate to the public that police services are community-oriented and aimed at helping those in need.

Conclusion

In policing a complex and changing society, crime prevention is one of the many tasks expected of a police officer. While traditional methods of crime control are still used, today's police agency must make use of community resources if it hopes to be effective.

Crime prevention and community relations go hand in hand in today's police department. As the police establish lines of communication in the community, citizens become increasingly willing to cooperate in crime suppression efforts. In building sound community relations, the patrol officer has a primary role. The officer on the beat is in constant contact with citizens, and it is largely through those contacts that public attitudes toward the department are formed. The chief of police must reinforce the impressions made by patrol and other officers by public appearances, statements to the media, personal contacts with community leaders, and formulation and implementation of policy.

The police and the community can work together through a great variety of programs designed to reduce both the opportunity and the desire to commit crime. For police service agencies, such cooperative efforts will undoubtedly be increasingly prevalent in the future.

1 Portions of this chapter are taken from: Lee P. Brown, "Community Relations," in *Local Government Police Management*, ed. Bernard L. Garmire (Washington, D.C.: International City Management Association, 1977), pp. 349–66.

2 A. F. Brandstatter and Louis A. Radelet, *Police and Community Relations: A Source Book* (Beverly Hills, Calif.: Glencoe Press, 1968), p. 17.

3 "Crime Resistance: An Alternative to Victimization," *FBI Law Enforcement Bulletin* 46, no. 6 (June 1977): 5.

4 Robert Wasserman, Michael Paul Gardner, and Alana S. Cohen, *Improving Police–Community Relations*, Prescriptive Package, LEAA (Washington, D.C.: Government Printing Office, 1973), p. 15.

5 James J. Fyfe, "Deadly Force," *FBI Law Enforcement Bulletin* 48, no. 12 (December 1979): 7–9.

6 Donald Pomerleau, *General Order 23–78*, "Rule 3 —Firearms" (Baltimore, Md.: Baltimore Police Department), revised June 1978.

7 *Police–Community Relations*, Training Key No. 175 (Gaithersburg, Md.: International Association of Chiefs of Police, 1972).

8 John Angell, "Summary Report: Police Consolidation Project," unpublished report distributed by the Portland–Multnomah County (Oregon) Bureau of Central Services, 1974, p. 18.

9 *Police–Community Relations*, p. 37.

10 *Police Community Relations Handbook* (Baltimore, Md.: Baltimore Police Department, 1973), p. 6.

11 National Advisory Commission on Criminal Justice Standards and Goals, *Police [Report on Police]* (Washington, D.C.: Government Printing Office, 1973), p. 66. This and other landmark reports are described in Appendix A.

12 George J. Washnis, *Citizen Involvement in Crime Prevention* (Lexington, Mass.: Lexington Books, 1976), p. 12.

13 National Institute of Law Enforcement and Criminal Justice, *Police Burglary Prevention Programs* (Washington, D.C.: Government Printing Office, 1975), p. 22.

14 California Council on Criminal Justice, *Selected Crime Prevention Programs in California* (Sacramento: California Council on Criminal Justice, 1973), p. 41.

15 National Institute of Law Enforcement and Criminal Justice, *Police Burglary Prevention Programs*, p. 3.

16 National Sheriffs' Association, *National Neighborhood Watch Program: Phase 3*, Information Packet (Washington, D.C.: National Sheriffs' Association, 1975), p. 1.

17 National Institute of Law Enforcement and Criminal Justice, *Police Burglary Prevention Programs*, p. 19.

18 Ibid., p. 26.

19 Montgomery County (Maryland) Police Department, *The Shield of Confidence Program*, March 1977, pp. 1–7.

20 California Council on Criminal Justice, *Selected Crime Prevention Programs in California*, pp. 82–89.

21 Ibid., pp. 87–89.

22 National Institute of Law Enforcement and Criminal Justice, *Police Robbery Control Manual* (Washington, D.C.: Government Printing Office, 1975), p. 48.

23 Ibid., p. 46.

24 Ibid., p. 7.

25 Ibid., p. 44.

26 Ibid., p. 46.

27 Ibid., p. 50.

28 California Council on Criminal Justice, *Selected Crime Prevention Programs in California*, pp. 61–63.

29 National Institute of Law Enforcement and Criminal Justice, *Police Robbery Control Manual*, pp. 42, 46, 52.

30 U.S., Department of Commerce, Bureau of Domestic Commerce, Office of Business Research and Analysis, Consumer Goods and Services Division, *Crime in Retailing* (Washington, D.C.: Government Printing Office, 1975), p. 14.

31 National Advisory Commission on Criminal Justice Standards and Goals, *Community Crime Prevention* (Washington, D.C.: Government Printing Office, 1973), p. 200.

32 John R. Ban and Lewis M. Ciminillo, *Violence and Vandalism in Public Education: Problems and Prospects* (Danville, Ill.: Interstate Printers and Publishers, 1977), p. 2.

33 Jerry J. Tobias, "Suburban School Vandalism—A Growing Concern," *Journal of Police Science and Administration* 5, no. 1 (March 1977): 112–14.

34 National Advisory Commission on Criminal Justice Standards and Goals, *Community Crime Prevention*, p. 2.

35 Washnis, *Citizen Involvement in Crime Prevention*, p. 7.

36 Ibid., p. 21.

37 California Council on Criminal Justice, *Selected Crime Prevention Programs in California*, p. 76.

38 Washnis, *Citizen Involvement in Crime Prevention,* p. 23.
39 Tyree Broomfield, "Conflict Management: The Dayton, Ohio, Experience," in *Community Relations and the Administration of Justice,* ed. D. P. Geary (New York: John Wiley & Sons, 1975), p. 352.
40 Morton Bard, *Training Police as Specialists in Family Crisis Intervention* (Washington, D.C.: National Institute of Law Enforcement and Criminal Justice, 1970).

41 Lourn G. Phelps, Jeffrey A. Schwartz, and Donald A. Liebman, "Training an Entire Patrol Division in Domestic Crisis Intervention Techniques," *The Police Chief,* July 1971, p. 180.
42 Nancy K. Eberhardt, James R. K. Heinen, and Valerian Derlega, "Teaching Crime Prevention in Elementary Schools: The Officer Friendly Program," article submitted to the *Virginia Police Journal,* April 1978, p. 5.

12 Juvenile programs

Few police functions engender more debate among adherents to competing viewpoints than do those which focus on juvenile delinquency. People between the ages of eleven and seventeen commit a disproportionate share of the crime in the United States. Together with their older counterparts—to the age of twenty-five—these young people make up the largest client group of most police service agencies.

The police cannot deal with juveniles in the way they would deal with adults. Neither the law nor prevailing community values will allow this. Therefore, the police administrator must balance the competing demands of delinquency prevention, delinquency control, service to young people, protection of the community, protection of basic human rights, and enforcement of the law.

It is not a new dilemma for the administrator. Nor are these competing demands necessarily categorical; but they do involve questions of values and priorities for which there are no universally accepted answers. In recent years, police work with juveniles has come increasingly under the scrutiny of the courts, lawmakers, community groups, and all parts of the criminal justice system. The results have been far from definitive, but changes have been wrought that have considerable import for what the police service role in the juvenile justice system is and what it is likely to become.

It is the purpose of this chapter to show how some of the changes have affected police juvenile services as regards both the internally focused and externally focused activities. The chapter opens with outlines of the historical background of juvenile services and the pressures for change that have had a profound effect on juvenile programs. Following a discussion of the emergent police role, internal activities are described from the standpoint of youth offenses, disposition decisions, policies and procedures, training, and internal consultation. Externally focused activities are then discussed in terms of systemic policies, training, consultation, and leadership. The chapter closes with a discussion of programmatic efforts, followed by a conclusion.

Historical considerations

Historically, juveniles have created special problems for those charged by society with enforcing laws and rules of conduct. Just as Socrates decried the unruliness of adolescents in his day, commentators portray youthful unruliness as a major problem of our time. In the interim, each generation has identified unacceptable behavior, hypothesized causes, and mounted efforts to control it. Despite these efforts, these problem behaviors have persisted.

Early reactions

In the United States, early law enforcement efforts to control delinquent behavior arose in response to conditions of poverty over which the police had little or no control. Juvenile crime was a condition of the inner city. Delinquent youth were treated in the main just as adult offenders. There were no specialized services available to children in trouble, and, since the prevailing value was to view children's behavior as the responsibility of the family, there was no emphasis placed on developing such services. When a child committed an act which brought him within the purview of the police, the officer had few options. He could attempt street corner adjustment, or he could arrest and jail the young-ster. The latter course, taken when the offense was of such severity that it could not be handled less formally or when a pattern of behavior had emerged that was not susceptible of correction on the street, was the police agency's last resort.

This limited repertory of police responses led to the first articulation of a public policy that children should be treated differently from adults in the arms of the law. Prompted by social reform women's groups, the New York State legislature passed a law in 1877 to restrict police from commingling any child under the age of sixteen years with adult offenders. Additional measures followed a few years later which provided options for the placement in other than traditional penitentiary settings of children convicted of crimes.[1]

These first moves to provide specialized treatment of juveniles by the agencies of justice were reactive in nature and were procedurally oriented. They were explicit in what was prohibited but often ambiguous in what could be done. In many respects these characteristics reflect the history of the development of the contemporary juvenile justice system and do much to explain why such great emphasis is placed on the police officer's discretion in dealing with juvenile offenders. It has been much easier to react to and to define what should not be done than to identify in specific terms what should be done.

Just as there were early efforts to prohibit certain police practices, reformers also focused on the judicial handling of youthful offenders. Reacting against court practices which treated children like adults in criminal matters, Illinois reformers masterminded the Act To Regulate the Treatment and Control of Dependent, Neglected, and Delinquent Children, which was implemented by the nation's first juvenile court in Cook County in 1899. This act extended the doctrine of *parens patriae* to children who had committed delinquent acts; prior to that time the doctrine had covered only those children who had been abandoned, neglected, or were otherwise dependent. In essence, the Illinois act charged the juvenile court with the rehabilitation of youngsters, holding that their age militated against their being held fully responsible for their acts.

These early reactions against what was considered to be grossly improper treatment of children by the agencies of justice set the stage for subsequent developments in law enforcement, court, and correctional operations. In brief, these developments stressed specialized police procedures for dealing with youthful offenders; informal, nonadversary court proceedings oriented toward fact finding and identification of appropriate rehabilitative services for the child; and correctional services based on rehabilitation.

The rehabilitative philosophy

The result was to create a "nonsystem" of juvenile justice in which the law enforcement role was significantly separate from those of the court and correctional components. The police were relatively free to exercise broad discretionary powers, unrestricted by the more stringent procedural requirements that applied in matters involving adults. Police administrators recognized the rehabilitative philosophy underlying the juvenile court process and responded organizationally by defining police work with juveniles as including reasonable efforts to correct a young person's unacceptable behavior short of referral to the court. The latter action would be taken only when other efforts appeared to have failed or when the offense was of such a serious nature that unofficial police action was impractical.

This basic approach has prevailed throughout the history of modern law enforcement, although the specifics of putting it into operation have varied considerably. Primary causes of this variation have included the state-of-the-art in police administration (largely a factor of time), the size of the agency, the socioeconomic characteristics of the community, the prevailing view of delinquency causation and appropriate corrective methodology, and the availability of treatment resources.

Thus, the past three-quarters of a century have seen a variety of organizational arrangements and operating methods applied to police work with juveniles. These have ranged from a single officer assigned to specialized juvenile duties on a full-time or part-time basis (common in smaller agencies), to juvenile bureaus with internal specialization according to type of offense or other criteria, to no specialization whatsoever.

External pressures have provided the impetus for the establishment of formal juvenile operations, while prevailing professional standards of police administration have determined organizational placement and, to a considerable degree, techniques to be applied when processing offenders. Many of the early police efforts which resulted from pressure by reform groups were conducted in units created especially for them, since they bore little resemblance to traditional police functions. The assignment of police officers to work as probation officers and the establishment of women's and children's bureaus typified early efforts to respond effectively to the rehabilitative philosophy embodied in various juvenile court acts.

As the rehabilitative philosophy became firmly entrenched nationally, and as police administration itself came to resemble a discipline, further refinements were made in the police service approach to dealing with children in trouble. For example, in the 1930s many larger agencies regarded work with juveniles as equivalent to crime prevention and created departmental units which were charged with juvenile work. Their activities were predicated on the belief that when a young offender was set straight his or her wrongdoing as an adult would be prevented.

Recent changes

Subsequent changes in police administrative theory have continued to affect juvenile operations. For many years it was strongly recommended that juvenile officers (or the responsibility for dealing with offenses committed by or against juveniles) be included within the arm of the agency charged with criminal investigation. The rationale was simple: the responsibility of the police agency was to investigate the alleged offense and to provide necessary input to the juvenile court. Since investigative techniques were considered essentially the same regardless of suspect or victim, it was believed that the responsibility for their effective accomplishment should be assigned to a single departmental entity.

In recent years changes in theory have resulted in the belief that the police role with juveniles is significant enough to require separate organizational status and, further, that it should extend to active efforts to mobilize community resources in combating both the causes and the effects of juvenile misbehavior. It is no longer sufficient to investigate, to counsel, and to refer. A more proactive stance is required if the full potential of the police presence in the community is to be realized.

Pressures for change

Since juveniles have historically comprised a significant portion of the police clientele, shifts in philosophy over the years have not occurred without considerable debate and, often, tension. Sheer weight of numbers usually precludes assigning responsibility for all juvenile contacts to specialists: most contacts are made in the field by uniformed officers. Also, juveniles account for many of the crimes being investigated by generalist detectives. Thus, there is a widely shared investment in the methods established by the agency for dealing with those juveniles for whom an initial field contact is not sufficient.

The substance of the internal debate over how best to process juvenile offenders has focused on three primary issues: (1) the extent to which cases involving juveniles should be handled by specialists as opposed to generalists; (2) the extent to which police officers should engage in what might be termed "social work" activities as opposed to investigative activities; and (3) the extent to which the police have a responsibility toward rehabilitative goals as opposed to prosecutorial goals. While it is often tempting to state these three issues in either/or terms, the nature of the juvenile justice process precludes such a simplistic approach. Rather, they are most usefully noted as points on a continuum, and the location at which a particular agency finds itself in regard to the three issues goes far to describe that agency's approach to dealing with youthful wrongdoers.

The specialist–generalist issue

Of the three issues mentioned above, the first has come closest to resolution so far as current administrative theory and practice are concerned. For example, a 1970 study conducted by the International Association of Chiefs of Police (IACP) indicated that of 1,399 police agencies responding more than 72 percent had designated an individual or an organizational unit to specialize in juvenile matters. The larger the agency, the more likely it was that a specialist unit had been formed.[2]

Pressure for specialization has come from four primary sources. First, public interest groups with a special concern for juveniles who come into contact with the law have been most forceful—and successful—in promoting the advantages of having an empathetic, trained juvenile specialist available to deal with the problems of young people. Second, other professionals in the juvenile justice system have long stressed the advantages of having counterparts within the police agency who are cognizant of the requirements of the juvenile code and the policies and procedures of the juvenile court and with whom they can establish regular communications. Third, there is often pressure from other officers—especially in patrol—for an internal resource to which juveniles may be referred. The impact of this pressure is heightened by the fact that many field officers are relatively unfamiliar with the requirements of the juvenile court process. Fourth, some pressure has undoubtedly been generated by the recognition granted specialization by professionals in the field, most notably the International Association of Chiefs of Police, which has made the following recommendations:

It is recommended that all police departments in medium to larger cities establish specialized juvenile units; in smaller cities, it is recommended that at least one officer be assigned specifically to the police–juvenile functions in addition to his regular patrol duties.[3]

The "social approach"

In many respects the specialist–generalist issue has been the easiest to resolve, for it involves only the acceptance of the fact that juveniles require different treatment from the law. It is in the determination of the character of that treatment—the policies to be adopted and the procedures to be employed—that the other two issues arise, and there is considerably less widespread agreement about them. They strike at the heart of the police role with juveniles, for in their resolution they define the nature and extent of police discretion. It is in this area that all so-called reforms in juvenile justice have had their birth.

The initial cries for reform in police techniques for dealing with juveniles were raised against the limited repertory of responses available to the officer. The result was the creation of a juvenile justice system based on a rehabilitative philosophy. Considerable discretion was included for the police officer, giving him or her broad latitude in deciding whether to refer a juvenile to court as well as in deciding what techniques to use in obtaining the information required to make that—or another—dispositional decision. The due process provisions which applied in adult investigations had little effect when the focus of the inquiry was someone destined for the juvenile court. The police had a relatively free hand, since they were not required to invoke criminal proceedings but rather were to seek ways to "help" the juvenile.

In accepting this broad discretionary authority thrust upon them by the juvenile court movement, law enforcement agencies also accepted the need to confront and resolve the latter two issues mentioned above. There could be no participation in a rehabilitative system without some consideration of the extent to which the law enforcement agency itself would assume rehabilitative functions. This was particularly true because the vast majority of referrals to the juvenile court came through the police. The question, then, was how to balance the use of discretion between helping the youngster at the police end of the system and seeking the formal sanctions of the court.

There has not been a definitive resolution of these issues at any point in the history of law enforcement in the United States. It has been agreed generally that the police have a rehabilitative role for at least two reasons. First, they are in a unique position to identify early delinquent behavior and to intervene immediately, counseling youngsters and their families in efforts to deter future wrongdoing. Second, even in those cases in which officers refer young people to other resources, their initial contact sets the stage for subsequent therapeutic intervention. At the same time, serious questions can be raised about an officer's assuming ongoing, in-depth counseling, both in terms of the officer's qualifications and in terms of the proper police role; other individuals and agencies are better suited to such functions.

The most common resolution to the rehabilitative–investigative–prosecutorial issues was to counsel and release minor offenders, to refer more complicated cases to available social agencies for assistance, and to perform detailed investigations of serious offenses with the goal of providing the court with the information necessary to justify ordering wardship and thus obtaining a "conviction" juvenile style. This approach signaled police acceptance of a significant rehabilitative role through the exercise of original discretion and resulted in a major investment by the police in the juvenile court model.

This rather simple characterization of police response to its proper role in a rehabilitative system prevailed for most of this century. It was sanctioned by the court and accepted by the community. Only recently has the situation changed, with the result being a significantly altered role for the police.

The rehabilitative–prosecutorial issue today

Interestingly, the origins of the recent changes were in the court arena and dealt only peripherally with the police. A series of major court decisions involving appeals brought by juveniles who had been the subjects of delinquency proceedings invalidated the concept of *parens patriae* through the application of constitutional guarantees of due process in the juvenile court. The result was a major shift in the judicial proceedings affecting juveniles. Police operations were affected primarily by the requirements of greater caution in obtaining prehearing statements from juveniles and of the preparation of a case that would meet the newly established burden of proof beyond a reasonable doubt.

Such changes, while they may have inconvenienced and angered some police officials because of their investment in the old way of doing business, were easy to effect. The greater impact of the revolution in juvenile court was to alter the police agency's relationship to the other elements of the juvenile justice system. For the first time the police were subject to legal rules of procedure from the point of first contact with the juvenile. The movement of the juvenile court process toward the "battle model"[4] required that the police tighten their investigative procedures as well as formalize their role in the rehabilitative process. Moving the court in the direction of the adult criminal model, and thereby lessening its utility as a referral choice for rehabilitative purposes, has required that greater emphasis than ever be placed upon the development of alternative resources for helping juveniles. As one authoritative text on the subject has put it, "The police must place emphasis on the prevention of delinquency, and, in cooperation with the community, on the development of resources to serve as alternatives to formal court referral."[5]

While judicial action has not created a unitary juvenile justice system, it has forced the constituent subsystems—law enforcement, courts, and corrections—to function more closely and with a greater interdependence. The job of the police juvenile officer thus becomes one of functioning "both as an integral part of his law enforcement agency and as a partner sharing equally with the more clearly definable parts of the juvenile justice system."[6]

The elements of the new police role are emerging gradually, given impetus by court rulings, the availability of federal funds for the establishment and testing of new approaches to dealing with juveniles, and the willingness of many progressive police administrators to participate in such experimentation. Long-established practices are being melded with new approaches. The ultimate configuration of the police role will vary from community to community much as it has in the past, but it is possible to identify a cluster of component functions which appear to characterize the range of police work with juveniles at the present time.

The emergent police role
with juveniles

In the past most discussions of the police role in the juvenile justice process focused on the twin concepts of control and prevention. Control was generally linked to the line functions of patrol and review and/or investigation of cases in which the suspect was a juvenile. Prevention was generally discussed in terms of participation in efforts designed to avert the commission of delinquent acts. While it was conceded that the two were not neatly separable, the concepts did provide a useful means of discriminating between various functions performed by police officers.

The concepts of control and prevention are still important in assessing an agency's juvenile operations, but they no longer categorize the diverse activities which make up the total effort. The tightening of the bonds between the police and other agencies and institutions involved in the control and prevention of delinquency has resulted in the emergence of many new functions which do not fit neatly within either of the earlier categories. It now seems appropriate to examine each function in terms of its focus—namely, whether it is designed primarily to serve internal agency purposes or to meet external needs. Further demarcation of those activities which are directed toward specific programs is also useful. The balance of this chapter, therefore, will cover the internal and external activities of the police department in the juvenile service area and will briefly describe some juvenile service programs.

Internally focused activities

A wide variety of juvenile-oriented activities contribute to the operational objectives of the police agency. Historically, many of them have been regarded primarily as staff functions in the belief that they did not contribute directly to the agency's mission but supported efforts in patrol, traffic, and investigations. However, the significance of the juvenile delinquency problem, which some studies indicate produces from 50 to 75 percent of a police agency's contacts, belies this supportive viewpoint. Rather, it is more appropriate to consider specialized juvenile operations as line functions, both in actual investigation of cases and making dispositional decisions and in efforts to prevent juvenile misbehavior.

Investigation of youth offenses

A major function of the juvenile specialist or unit should be the investigation of offenses committed by juveniles. The National Advisory Commission on Criminal Justice Standards and Goals, through its police subgroup, has said that "the responsibility of the juvenile unit should be to conduct as many juvenile investigations as is practicable, to provide assistance to field officers in matters involving juvenile problems, and to coordinate with other agencies."[7]

This is not to suggest that field officers and general investigators do not have roles to play in dealing with juveniles. The volume of juvenile contacts precludes the assignment of all such matters to specialists. Therefore, it is of the utmost importance that internal policies and procedures be developed to identify those cases which must automatically be investigated by juvenile officers and to provide for their expeditious assignment to such personnel. It is generally agreed that juvenile officers should conduct follow-up investigations in most cases in which there is reason to believe that a juvenile is involved, as well as in such cases as bicycle theft, child abuse and neglect, and school-related offenses.

The vast majority of complaints involving juveniles will be investigated initially by the uniformed officer who responds to the call. In minor cases this officer has the discretion to make an adjustment at the scene by counseling and releasing the juvenile. If the offense is more serious or if circumstances prevent its closure at the scene, the field officer may release the juvenile but must make a full report to the juvenile specialist. Finally, if the offense is of such severity or complexity that the officer believes it is necessary to take the juvenile into custody, he or she should refer the matter immediately to a juvenile officer for further action.

In certain cases—for example, when the perpetrator's age is unknown or when the offense involved is of such a nature that it requires specialized investigative skills—the criminal investigation unit will be responsible. In some agencies, in fact, it is the practice to assign all follow-up investigations to the criminal investigation unit and to involve the juvenile officer only at the point of making the dispositional decision. In either case, it is impossible to avoid some duplication of effort between juvenile and investigation units; therefore, the articulation of guidelines governing areas of responsibility and methods of cooperation and coordination is of paramount importance.

Regardless of who is performing the investigation, scrupulous attention must be paid by all law enforcement personnel to the rights of the juvenile. Even when the officer is trying to support the goals of rehabilitation through his or her investigation, he or she must remember that the initial reason for police involvement is to determine the facts that establish the legal basis for further action. The officer is concerned with behavioral and family factors secondarily as aids to making the disposition decision. Thus, the same procedural regularity that applies in cases involving adults must also apply with juveniles. While the police have the discretion to take action in some juvenile matters which they would not be able to take in adult proceedings, they must not let that fact tempt them into procedural shortcuts.

The primary tool of the investigator is the interview. When interviewing a juvenile, the investigator is attempting:

1. To obtain facts regarding an alleged offense in order to clear up a complaint;
2. To discover whether a particular juvenile was involved in the offense;
3. To learn the significant facts about the juvenile and his total situation;
4. To get the facts about a complaint regarding harmful home conditions or dangerous community conditions; and
5. To obtain information about a child found under questionable circumstances which may indicate a need for help or constitute a menace to the child, his family, and the community.[8]

In elaborating on interviewing and interrogating juveniles, the International Association of Chiefs of Police has suggested several policy guidelines:

During interviews or interrogations, whether of juveniles or adults, officers must scrupulously avoid practices which could be described as being "inherently coercive" and which make it likely that any person would express cooperation or confess to any harmful conduct as a result of induced fear.

During interviews or interrogations, as in all police procedures, officers must be sensitive to and respect the basic legal as well as human rights of all persons, adult and juvenile.

When questioning juveniles, harsh, abusive language, epithets, profanity and other vulgarities must never be used. An officer can learn to communicate with juveniles at their level much the same as he communicates with adult citizens of various cultural and educational backgrounds at their levels.

Consideration should be given to having the parents present during *some* interviews and interrogations and to the advisability of conducting *some* interviews in the home. The decision must be made by the officer in the light of the totality of the circumstances of each specific case.

The initial interview or interrogation of juveniles should be done by the officer who makes the original contact to the same extent that he would initially question an adult. The follow-up investigation, including specific questions regarding the incident, should be conducted by an investigator or juvenile officer. To avoid future court appearances of several officers, the juvenile taken into custody should be turned over to a juvenile officer as soon as possible.[9]

The ultimate purpose of the investigative effort when a juvenile is the suspect is to support the making of a dispositional decision. The adequacy of the investigation, therefore, will be measured in relation to how useful it is in the juvenile specialist's deliberations at this critical stage of the juvenile justice process.

The disposition decision

The discretion which accrues to the law enforcement agency and its officers in deciding how to process a juvenile is indeed great. In most situations the police have the following five dispositional alternatives:

1. Counsel and release in the field
2. Release in the field with the submission of a detailed report to the juvenile specialist
3. Station adjustment or a similar preadjudicative decision, which might include release to the parents with a warning, referral to a youth service agency, or direct referral to a community social service agency

4. Referral to the juvenile court intake unit with no detention
5. Referral to the juvenile court intake unit with detention.[10]

Counsel and release   The first two alternatives are exercised by field officers at the conclusion of their initial investigation of a complaint and represent the resolution of many, if not most, juvenile contacts. While these decisions should be reviewed by juvenile specialists to ascertain their adherence to agency policy and procedure, there is seldom any on-the-scene review or assistance when the decision is made. This is the epitome of the exercise of discretion and demands careful control through: policy statements and procedural guidelines to assist the officer in making the decision; proper training in the use of the guidelines for decision making; and regular supervisory review and counseling to ensure proper application.

Station adjustment   The third alternative normally represents the point at which the juvenile specialist becomes involved. When the field officer determines that the case he or she is investigating demands further attention, the officer refers it to the juvenile specialist in accordance with established departmental practice. Follow-up investigation is then called for, its depth being determined by the severity of the offense and the amount of information required to make the dispositional decision.

In the past, station adjustment most frequently meant a counseling session involving the juvenile officer, the youth, and his parents. Occasionally these sessions resulted in an agreement on the part of the family to seek the services of a community social agency. More recently the concept of direct police diversion into social service agencies has gained favor. In fact, a major result of federal grant-in-aid programs in the past ten years has been the proliferation of a variety of diversion programs.

The National Advisory Commission on Criminal Justice Standards and Goals recommends that the police agency "immediately should divert" any person from the criminal and juvenile justice systems when the process is "inappropriate" or where "other resources would be more effective."[11] The emphasis is on prompt, decisive action and on diversion.

No other agency in the community is in a better position than the police agency to identify young people who might benefit from selected social services.

In making the decision to refer a youngster, the juvenile specialist is subject to many pressures and considerations. The juvenile specialist must be as well informed as possible about the young person's background and family situation, any previous contacts with the law, the nature of the offense that has brought the juvenile to the attention of the police, and the receptivity of the juvenile and his or her family to participation in a voluntary treatment program. The juvenile specialist is influenced by departmental and juvenile court policies, by the availability of referral resources, and by the rights of the complainant or victim. Further constraints include the juvenile specialist's own prejudices, experiences, abilities, and skills. It is no wonder that making a decision on station adjustment is a complicated process. The rewards, however, are worth the trouble if the referral results in no further negative police contacts with the young person.

The process of making the referral decision must be controlled as carefully as possible through the intensive training of the individual who will be making the decision and through the establishment of standards and guidelines against which the juvenile specialist may measure the case at hand.

It is important to distinguish between current desirable referral practices which fall within the definition of station adjustment and the older practice of having juvenile specialists sit as hearing officers in pseudojudicial proceedings. While the police have a legitimate discretionary decision-making role, and while they may realistically participate in matching juveniles with community services, they *do not* have the right to exercise judicial functions.

In making a preadjudicative referral decision, the police juvenile specialist is offering an alternative to the family short of court action. This offer should be made in a helping fashion and should not be cloaked in the guise of a formal proceeding. There is an inherent element of coercion present when the two alternatives presented to the family are participation in a voluntary program or referral to court. Any peripheral practices which heighten that element of coercion are unfair and procedurally unwise.

Referral to the court   The fourth and fifth dispositional alternatives available to the police reflect the belief that either the offense is so severe or the juvenile's record and background are so questionable that delinquency or wardship proceedings are required.

Referral to the court without detection generally involves a citation process. One method includes the issuance of a citation to a juvenile's parents directing them to appear with their child at a specified time. A second method involves a police request to the court intake unit to bring the juvenile before the court. In some states this entails requesting the intake unit to file a petition for court action, which can require further investigation of the offense and related circumstances by court personnel.

When there is reason to believe that the juvenile poses a threat either to himself or herself or to the safety of the community, the juvenile officer may refer the juvenile to the court intake unit with a recommendation that he or she be detained in a secure setting. Officers must communicate fully their reasons for believing that detention is necessary, including sufficient data to allow intake personnel to assess independently the need for detention. That decision is rightfully theirs; although the police should cooperate with the court in formulating detention guidelines, the ultimate decision to apply those guidelines must be the court's.

The juvenile specialist's role in making disposition decisions ranges, then, from aiding in establishing guidelines to be followed by field officers and subsequently reviewing their actions, to deciding whether a juvenile will be allowed to participate in a voluntary treatment program or will be injected into the formal machinery of the court. It cannot be taken lightly.

Development of policies and procedures

The National Advisory Commission on Criminal Justice Standards and Goals recommends that "the chief executive of every police agency immediately should develop written policy governing his agency's involvement in the detection, deterrence, and prevention of delinquent behavior and juvenile crime."[12]

Officers require carefully worded statements of policy and procedure against which to measure their actions. This helps ensure consistent and thoroughly legal handling of cases involving juveniles.

Policies   Given the sensitivity of police work with juveniles, an issue of great community concern, the process of developing and articulating policy can also allow the police administrator to involve a broad spectrum of concerned groups in the identification of relevant policy considerations, making it possible to avoid later charges of narrow and inadequate efforts or insensitive framing of positions.

The juvenile specialist is critical to the development of effective policy statements, for he or she is the person most likely to be familiar with the true nature of the juvenile crime problem in the community, with the functioning of the juvenile justice system from the police point of view, and with trends and practices in the field. Either the individual specialist or the juvenile unit should be responsible for the regular review of existing policies and for recommending modifications or entirely new statements.

Procedures   Equally important to the effective administration of a police agency's juvenile program are procedures which tell how policies are to be implemented. The policy states the goal; the procedure indicates the means by which that goal should be attained.

The agency's policies and procedures should cover at least the following points:

1. Be on the lookout for potential delinquents and for conditions causing delinquent behavior.
2. Work with other agencies on correcting environmental conditions that may foster delinquency.
3. Use preventive police patrol where it has potential for helping to control delinquency.
4. Investigate delinquency problems that lead to juvenile offenses. This includes apprehension and prosecution of adults involved in these cases.
5. Detect and apprehend juvenile offenders.
6. Follow up on juvenile offenders, using referral or other disposition as needed.
7. Maintain prescribed juvenile records as required by law.[13]

Training

Policies and procedures are merely sterile expressions of an agency's ends and means until they are put into effect through the actions of officers.

Juvenile specialists   The juvenile specialist obviously requires the most intensive training of all officers. First, he or she must understand the political and social realities of juvenile delinquency and youth crime. This includes a thorough understanding of the juvenile justice system, its composite agencies, and their modes of operation. Second, he or she must be familiar with the various causal theories advanced to explain delinquent behavior. Virtually all diversionary efforts are predicated upon some theory of causation; while none is sufficient to explain the range of delinquent behavior which the officer encounters, they do provide valuable insights. Third, he or she must understand and be able to apply certain analytical techniques for describing the nature of delinquency in the community. This is increasingly important if there is to be an accurate assessment of the productivity of various preventive and diversionary efforts. Fourth, he or she must become proficient in certain skills in order to survive in the turbulent environment in which he or she applies his or her knowledge. Such skills as interpersonal communication, decision making, conflict resolution, leadership, supervision, investigation, and writing are critical to success.

Some of the training in this knowledge and skill may be obtained on the job. In very large agencies it may be provided through internal training programs. For most new juvenile specialists, however, it is likely that outside resources will be required.

The oldest continuing program offering this range of training is the Delinquency Control Institute (DCI) at the University of Southern California. The DCI conducts eight-week residential programs twice annually, granting university credit for satisfactory completion. It has served officers from all fifty states and more than thirty foreign nations during the past thirty years. The University of Minnesota has offered an eight-week summer program since 1955.

The widespread growth of criminal justice programs in colleges and universities in recent years has also resulted in a variety of valuable educational and training experiences. Many short-term institutes and workshops are conducted annually by such professional groups as the IACP, the National Council of Juvenile Court Judges, and the National District Attorney's Association.

Field officers   Field officers also require some specialized training in juvenile matters. This should be provided through recruit training prior to their assuming full police responsibilities and subsequently through in-service training while they are on the job. Kobetz suggests that the proper subjects for recruit training might include the functions of the juvenile unit; the juvenile court—its purpose, functions, and operation; legal aspects of delinquency control; the responsibility of line officers in dealing with juveniles; laws affecting juveniles; behavioral science background; and treatment of juvenile delinquency problems.[14]

In-service training applies to all departmental personnel who have occasion to deal with juvenile problems. It generally focuses on subjects of demonstrated need, such as gang activity, interviewing techniques, report writing, or orientation to new policies or procedures.

Supervisory and command personnel   Too often, supervisory and command personnel are ignored when the subject of juvenile training is discussed. This is unfortunate, for their leadership positions make them significant actors in determining the effectiveness of the agency's efforts to prevent and control juvenile delinquency and youth crime. Just as they should be basically familiar with the general subjects identified earlier, so also should they receive training specifically relevant to their functions. For example, supervisors and command officers must be able to evaluate the efficacy of departmental programs, to assess the impact of recent legislation or court action on departmental operations, and to coordinate internal and external relationships in the juvenile justice system. These activities require a measure of knowledge and skill that cannot always be obtained on the job.

The juvenile specialist or unit once again occupies a unique position in relation to meeting the department's training needs. A significant share of the responsibility for assessing training needs, designing training programs or identifying outside resources, and providing training rests here.

Internal consultation

Since virtually all line officers in the department must deal occasionally with juveniles and, further, since even the support elements (e.g., records) have a relationship to the juvenile process, the juvenile specialist should be prepared to function as an internal consultant. This is an extremely sensitive role, for it is often based on the tenuous authority of functional expertise and may be regarded as meddling or interference. However, it is necessary given the broadly shared burden of dealing with juveniles, with only the specialist concentrating on it full-time.

The agency's chief executive can do much to facilitate the effective implementation of the consultative role by specifying those areas in which the juvenile specialist or unit will exercise functional supervision (e.g., in reviewing field officers' reports on juvenile contacts and in making certain dispositional decisions) and by encouraging operating units to seek the assistance of juvenile officers when they are confronting issues involving juveniles.

The juvenile unit or specialist is in a key position to identify emergent problems through the regular review of reports, analysis of statistical data, and collection of intelligence from other agencies in the system. The ability to use this accumulated information in solving problems through cooperative, consultative relationships with other departmental units will go far toward creating a viable juvenile delinquency prevention and control program.

Externally focused activities

The administration of juvenile justice is the responsibility of a loosely knit "system" comprising several agencies of government that supposedly espouse the same overarching goals—the prevention and control of delinquency and the protection of the community—while embracing diverse views of how to accomplish those goals.

The formal elements of the juvenile justice system are law enforcement, the courts (occasionally including prosecutors and defense attorneys), and corrections. The informal but nonetheless critical elements include the educational system, public and private social welfare agencies, the religious establishment, and other social institutions which may reasonably be expected to affect youthful behavior.

In the past it was possible for these agencies and institutions to function rather well without a great measure of cooperation. The legalization of the juvenile court process, accompanied by the tremendous growth in diversionary programs, makes such a self-centered approach considerably less viable now. There is a greater awareness that the effectiveness of the system depends on cooperation, joint planning, sharing information, and establishing specific and shared goals. This places an additional burden on the juvenile specialist or unit by requiring the performance of several functions focused outside the agency.

Development of systemic policies and procedures

While each element of the extended juvenile justice system has considerable latitude to establish its own policies and procedures, there are many points of convergence at which cooperative effort can optimize mutual goal attainment. The National Advisory Commission on Criminal Justice Standards and Goals suggests the following:

Every police agency should establish in cooperation with courts written policies and procedures governing agency action in juvenile matters. These policies and procedures should stipulate at least:

1. The specific form of agency cooperation with other governmental agencies concerned with delinquent behavior, abandonment, neglect, and juvenile crime;
2. The specific form of agency cooperation with nongovernmental agencies and organizations where assistance in juvenile matters may be obtained;
3. The procedures for release of juveniles into parental custody; and
4. The procedures for the detention of juveniles.[15]

In addition to formal cooperation in the development of policy and procedure statements, regular liaison with both the justice system and community groups must be the responsibility of juvenile officers or units if the greatest value is to be obtained from their presence in the community.

Training

The interdependency of the agencies affiliated within the extended juvenile justice system has increased to the point where mutual understanding of roles and functions is critical. Breakdowns in communication, which frequently occur and degenerate into dysfunctional relationships, can often be avoided if workers in the various segments of the system understand the circumstances under which their counterparts labor. The IACP recommends that "community juvenile justice systems exchange personnel on an interdisciplinary basis for brief periods of time''[16] to overcome such breakdowns.

It is also important that formal efforts be undertaken to inform related professionals of the police role in the juvenile justice process. The juvenile specialist can provide this information through participation in training efforts conducted by the other agencies.

Consultation

It is no longer possible for any agency in the juvenile justice system to stand alone. There are many opportunities for the sharing of expertise, and there is good reason to believe that the police service juvenile specialist has much to share. The police are the primary source of referrals to all other agencies in the system. The police have the only twenty-four-hour presence in the community. And the police have generally been in the business longer than most other agencies. These and other factors combine to make the juvenile specialist a logical choice for consultation when assistance is required.

These same factors make it highly likely that the police agency will be one of the first in the community to identify emergent problems involving juveniles. If the internal activities of the juvenile specialist or unit are functioning properly, they will encounter the indicators that suggest new problems, such as an increase in the abuse of certain substances or the resurgence of youthful gang activity. This knowledge further enhances the consultative value of the police officer to other community agencies.

Leadership in mobilizing resources

Most citizens regard the police as having primary responsibility for dealing with juvenile delinquency and youth crime. It is the police whom they call when they are victimized, and it is the police whom they see on the street. There is a vague awareness of the other elements of the system, but their functions have low visibility and are little understood by the public.

This salient fact combines with many of those discussed in the preceding section to suggest rather strongly that the police are in a position to fulfill an important leadership role in the juvenile justice system.

Since the debate about juvenile delinquency and youth crime tends to be issue-oriented, usually reacting to crises which demand immediate attention, the solutions that emerge are generally negotiated solutions, hammered out between the relatively independent principals.

Under the circumstances, it is likely that the voice of the police, offering logical suggestions in a reasonable manner, could have considerable impact in mobilizing that range of community resources required to serve young people. This leadership role is too frequently ignored by police administrators, perhaps to their detriment as well as to that of the community.

Programmatic efforts

This chapter opened with the suggestion that police service juvenile operations create certain dilemmas which must be resolved by agency administrators. It identified one of these dilemmas as the need to determine how much responsibility for rehabilitation the police agency has and went on to suggest that this dilemma has plagued modern law enforcement throughout its history.

That dilemma is as troublesome now as ever, perhaps more so given the current emphasis on formal diversion efforts as alternatives to court referral. There is a slightly different slant today, however, with the added issue of programmatic sponsorship. The availability of federal grant-in-aid dollars since the late 1960s has resulted in the formalization of virtually all prevention and treatment efforts into stylized programs with stated goals and objectives, evaluation criteria, and administrative hierarchies. The question facing the police administrator now is not only whether to participate in a program but also whether to initiate and sponsor one.

Again, there are no easy answers. Each decision must be made in light of community and agency needs and systematic consideration of alternative ways of meeting those needs. It is no longer possible to automatically reject the idea of police functioning as counselors or recreation leaders. Instead, it seems reasonable to suggest that the agency should participate in or support those programs sponsored by external agencies which provide services consistent with the police mission and which do not result in an impractical drain on police resources. It further seems reasonable that the agency should initiate and administer programs which are consistent with the police mission, which do not constitute an impractical drain on police resources, which provide measurable benefits to the police agency, and which cannot logically be administered by another agency.

There are a variety of programs in operation today that could elicit some level of police involvement. It is not possible to list them all. However, it is useful to consider a few illustrative efforts, categorized by their target groups.

Juveniles and their families

Most programs aimed at juveniles and their families fall into the diversion category. They include youth service bureaus, which either can be run by the police agency or can exist as independent entities. Youth service bureaus conduct preliminary diagnoses of juveniles to determine what treatment resource in the community appears most compatible with a juvenile's needs.

A police sponsored program aimed specifically at juveniles is the school resource officer program. Actually, this label embraces a multitude of programs, ranging from the placement of an officer in a school setting to function solely as a teacher to the placement of an officer who teaches, counsels, and investigates cases involving students. The orientation of this program is more preventive than diversionary.

Police counselor programs are also found in many agencies. In some, officers function as counselors, providing therapeutic assistance to juveniles and their families. In others, professional civilian counselors are hired to provide assistance under the administrative aegis of the juvenile unit. The intent is to provide the service in the greatest chronological and physical proximity to the initial police contact with the juvenile.

Community groups

The majority of programs which focus on specific community groups are either preventive or public relations in nature. Their intent generally is to improve relationships between the police and the target group.

Police storefront programs typify this effort. Opening police offices in minority communities to provide assistance in solving a multitude of problems, including parent–child disputes, stresses the helping nature of the police presence and may well improve the image and the relationship.

Elements of the juvenile justice system

Some programs are designed to improve the operations of the juvenile justice system or to enhance relationships between its constituent elements. A typical example is the juvenile justice center, in which representatives of all elements of the juvenile justice system are housed together in a single facility to review cases and to expedite the flow of juveniles through the process.

Conclusion

This chapter opened by describing the growth of juvenile services and programs from reform movements of the nineteenth century and posed the pressures for change in terms of three current issues: (1) the extent to which cases involving juveniles should be handled by specialists rather than generalists; (2) the extent to which police officers should be involved in what might loosely be termed "social work" activities instead of investigative activities; and (3) the extent to which police have a responsibility for rehabilitative goals as compared to prosecutorial goals. Instead of dwelling on these issues as either/or questions, the chapter went on to describe juvenile programs as internal and external functions and responsibilities that are no longer neatly categorized. In a word, they are situational, depending on local policies, financial circumstances, and other factors. The chapter then pointed out that each police agency ultimately must determine what juvenile services and programs it will carry that are appropriate to meet the needs of the community it serves.

It is impossible to devise a standardized juvenile program which would suit police agencies in all sections of the nation. It is obvious that the differences in state laws and local conditions call for differences in operational procedures. The differing and changing philosophies of individual judges and juvenile courts produce other program variations. On the police level, the tradition of the department, the personal philosophical orientation of the chief and his command staff, and the recruit and in-service training of officers are factors instrumental in causing other differences. Contemporary social forces within communities are also important. The presence or absence of effective social agencies, both public and private, proper detention facilities, adequate professional services, and so on, all play their part. The net result is that any attempt at defining the role of the police relative to handling programs to combat juvenile delinquency must, of necessity, be phrased in the most general of terms so as to provide broad guidelines and avoid dogmatic policy and procedural recommendations.[17]

1 Richard W. Kobetz, *The Police Role and Juvenile Delinquency* (Gaithersburg, Md.: International Association of Chiefs of Police, 1971), p. 147.
2 Ibid., p. 52.
3 Richard W. Kobetz and Betty B. Bosarge, *Juvenile Justice Administration* (Gaithersburg, Md.: International Association of Chiefs of Police, 1973), p. 155.
4 For an interesting discussion, see: Carl Baar, "Will Urban Trial Courts Survive the War on Crime?" in *The Potential for Reform of Criminal Justice*, ed. Herbert Jacobs, Sage Criminal Justice System Annuals, vol. 3 (Beverly Hills, Calif.: Sage Publications, Inc., 1974).
5 Kobetz, *The Police Role*, p. 103.
6 Thomas M. Frost, "The Juvenile Officer's Role: A Law Enforcement and Corrections Dilemma—Where Does It Fit?" unpublished paper, 1970; quoted in Kobetz, *The Police Role*, p. 104.
7 National Advisory Commission on Criminal Justice Standards and Goals, *Police* [*Report on Police*] (Washington, D.C.: Government Printing Office, 1973), p. 223.
8 John P. Kenney and Dan G. Pursuit, *Police Work with Juveniles and the Administration of Juvenile Justice*, 5th ed. (Springfield, Ill.: Charles C Thomas, 1975), p. 180.
9 Kobetz, *The Police Role*, pp. 132–33.
10 Kenney and Pursuit, *Police Work with Juveniles*, pp. 194–211; and Kobetz and Bosarge, *Juvenile Justice Administration*, p. 143.
11 National Advisory Commission on Criminal Justice Standards and Goals, *Police*, p. 80.
12 Ibid., p. 221.
13 Ibid., p. 223.
14 Kobetz, *The Police Role*, p. 235.
15 National Advisory Commission on Criminal Justice Standards and Goals, *Police*, p. 221.
16 Kobetz and Bosarge, *Juvenile Justice Administration*, p. 161.
17 Ibid., p. 116.

13 Personnel management

The personnel function is a principal concern of management, because it covers every aspect of an organization's human resources.[1] Therefore, the chief executive of any police agency must oversee the recruitment, selection, training, retraining, promotion, and discipline of the personnel within the organization. Since a police department is as good as the quality and utilization of its members, a comprehensive personnel program must be developed that will utilize the human resources to their maximum effectiveness and efficiency. Inasmuch as almost 90 percent of expenditures for police service are devoted to salaries and related personnel matters, it is critical that law enforcement executives consider personnel management a principal concern.[2]

This chapter describes the organization of personnel management within the police agency; personnel recruitment and retention, including (1) the emerging concerns of affirmative action, equal employment opportunity, and women in policing; (2) training, including recruit, in-service, and management training, outside training programs, and educational incentives; (3) personnel development programs and the use of assessment centers; (4) interpersonal relations (the human element in personnel management); and (5) safety and accident prevention.

This chapter concludes with an extensive section for police administrators who must deal with labor–management relations. The section opens with a synopsis of the development of police unions and a description of the characteristics of police unions. It then discusses preparation for unionization and disciplinary procedures. Then several aspects of collective bargaining are treated, including recognition of the bargaining unit, the preelection campaign, preparing for negotiations, negotiation tactics, the scope of bargaining, contract administration, and impasse resolution. The balance of the section treats strikes and strike contingency plans.

The elements of a comprehensive personnel program

A comprehensive police personnel program should include: (1) recruitment and selection of employees on a merit basis; (2) training programs at both recruit and in-service levels; (3) a promotion program; (4) an equitable system of evaluating job performance; (5) job classification; (6) salary plan administration; (7) a comprehensive plan for conditions of service, including fringe benefits; (8) an employee relations program, including grievance procedures; (9) a safety program; (10) medical insurance programs; (11) a retirement program; and (12) a labor–management relations program.

The hallmark of a comprehensive local police personnel program should be an atmosphere of professionalism that pervades the entire force. The chief and division commanders must actively recruit prospective employees for all ranks. These persons should feel the excitement and challenge that police service can offer, regardless of the levels of their positions. The "tone" of the police agency must be positive and exciting for all members.

The chief of police should assume leadership in establishing a personnel system of high quality and seeing that its standards are followed. To do so, the chief must have authority to hire, promote, and discipline within the context of appropriate policies and procedures.

Qualified appointees should be exposed to comprehensive orientation and training programs. All new employees, for example, should become familiar with the structure, operations, and personalities of the department. Beyond this, young employees contemplating careers in police service as administrators should receive additional training in basic administrative techniques, such as budget preparation and administration, organizational practices, space and personnel studies, and procedural analysis.

Beyond training for new employees, there is a pressing need for ongoing development of persons in responsible positions. A program of continuing education and mid-career development—with universities and professional associations playing prominent roles—is crucial to effective administration and executive leadership development in all forces.

Regardless of the size of the city and the strength of its police force, the backbone of an effective personnel program is a citywide position classification plan accompanied by a pay plan that assigns job classifications to proper pay grades or levels and usually provides for step increases. A well-prepared pay plan will properly relate pay to the duties and responsibilities of each job. Employee organizations, more common than ever, are vitally interested in salaries and wages and will closely examine local pay practices. A local pay plan should be updated on the basis of annual salary surveys. These surveys will show how local salaries are keeping pace with salaries paid by other employers for comparable jobs. Pay increases requested by employee groups need to be related to the total pay structure so that proper relationships can be maintained between pay grades.

The police organization and personnel management

Normally, as a police department grows and its employees increase in number, the specialized personnel function evolves. First it is one of the duties of an individual; then it becomes a full-time job; and finally it becomes a highly structured organizational division of the department with skilled technicians and administrators. In medium-sized and large cities there may be a central citywide personnel agency that coordinates personnel administration throughout the jurisdiction.

There are two major types of central personnel agency: the independent civil service commission and the central personnel department (CPD).

The civil service commission

The independent civil service commission is the historic model, dating to the nineteenth century. The commission usually has three or five members appointed by the mayor with long (often six-year) overlapping terms. The most common functions of the independent commission are testing and certification for appointment, but some commissions also have other personnel functions such as job classification, pay plan administration, and other direct personnel management functions. Moreover, the commission may serve an appellate role, hearing employee appeals regarding dismissals, demotions, and, in some cases, suspensions. In these actions the commission constitutes itself as a court and renders what is in effect a final personnel decision.

The central personnel department

In most medium-sized and large cities, authority in the area of personnel management is divided between the police chief and an independent central personnel department. The traditional role of the CPD is to provide technical expertise in the management of personnel resources and to ensure the preservation of the merit system.

A CPD may operate with or without the independent civil service commission. With this organization, the chief executive of the local government (mayor, city manager, or other official) appoints the personnel director, who operates as a municipal department head, just like the police chief, public works director, or controller. This department handles recruitment and examinations, certification, classification and pay plan administration, manpower planning, employee development and training, labor relations, productivity programs, and other elements of the entire personnel program. At the same time, its staff maintains close relations with representatives whose mission is personnel management for the police department.

The CPD assures that there is consistency in personnel practices and no arbitrary treatment of municipal employees. In addition, it is supposed to eliminate duplication of personnel activities among agencies and to provide competent personnel technicians to all agencies, particularly in the areas of personnel testing, position classification, and labor relations. Finally, the CPD is to furnish the public with information concerning job openings and qualifications.

Even though principal responsibility for overall personnel decisions is vested in the CPD, the chief of police should make recommendations and offer assistance as appropriate. In addition, the power to appoint, discipline, and discharge within the police department should be the responsibility of the chief. Coordination and cooperation between the police agency and the CPD are necessary to assure sound personnel decisions affecting the department.

Recruitment and retention

Ideally, a police agency should administer its own recruitment program to attract the "best" employees. Most successful recruiting efforts have two major components: (1) the fact that the entry salary, fringe benefits, and working conditions, as well as the potential for advancement and additional educational opportunities, compare favorably with other occupations in the local labor market; and (2) the intangible benefit of working for an organization characterized by high morale and good esprit de corps. The program should give special emphasis to attracting college educated applicants, including minority group members and females.

One of the most effective methods for recruiting highly qualified individuals, including females and minorities, has been the extensive use of police personnel, either on an individual basis or as members of a special recruitment task force. Experienced officers understand the requirements of the job and are able to explain the department's needs in detail to potential applicants. They also can readily answer questions concerning benefits derived from the police service. Another way to obtain highly qualified personnel is to offer a higher salary for educational attainment.

Beyond salary and fringe benefits, the police personnel recruitment program should offer membership in a modern employee organization, an orderly grievance procedure, and an up-to-date employee handbook. In addition, the opportunity for continuing training after graduation from recruit school is attractive to candidates. There may also be service award programs, safety programs, performance evaluation systems, employee opinion surveys, and an employee newsletter. An effective employee relations program, of which these are important components, can be the basis for an effective police department and a vehicle for inducing quality applicants to seek work with the force.

Once competent employees are recruited and trained, conscientious efforts should be made to retain them. Incompetent recruits should be dismissed. Competence should be determined in a periodic review of all employees by their superiors, with recommendations for tenure, promotion, and salary increases.

Superior personnel should be recognized and praised. Moreover, especially talented young officers and promising lower level supervisors should not be confined within one division or assignment. They should be offered periodic rotation in work assignments for the sake of both career and personal development.

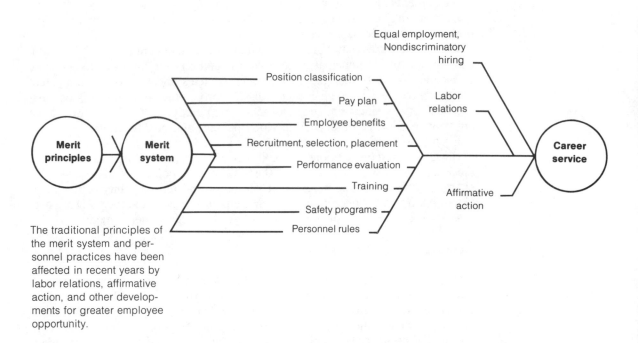

The traditional principles of the merit system and personnel practices have been affected in recent years by labor relations, affirmative action, and other developments for greater employee opportunity.

Affirmative action

The most wanted person in the United States is the well-qualified minority candidate for police work. In fact, police forces across the nation are under a mandate to take affirmative action to ensure the full participation of minorities and females in law enforcement. The attainment of this goal depends on the executive's ability to devise and implement a positive program. Mandate notwithstanding, minority recruitment is among the most vexing challenges facing the modern police administrator. So is the need to eliminate discriminatory promotional practices within the force.[3]

Although police agencies have mounted extensive affirmative action programs in recent years, minority employment has not reached a satisfactory level in many departments, nor has the level of minorities in ranking jobs. Adding to their historical underrepresentation is the fact that entry level educational requirements on a national basis continue to be upgraded. In fact, the National Advisory Commission on Criminal Justice Standards and Goals recommended that every police agency should require as a condition of employment the completion of one year of college education. The same body also recommended the completion of at least four years of college education at entry level by 1982.[4]

It is widely recognized that higher educational standards often create a road-block for minorities who have not had access to educational opportunity. Yet the quest for increased minority representation and the commitment to upgrade the profession are parallel goals.

Another problem is that the federal Equal Employment Opportunity Comission guidelines were not generally applicable in the public sector until 1972, but private employers have been subject to provisions of the 1964 Civil Rights Act since 1965. Thus, private employers, often under intensive judicial pressure, have a significant head start in sophisticated and expensive affirmative action programs. Public and private employers compete for the same minority candidates, sometimes intensely. In the face of such awesome competition, the recruitment of qualified minorities for public service positions will take an imaginative executive and an entire departmental commitment.

Legislation Generally speaking, three pieces of federal legislation are relevant to affirmative action and have been the basis of most challenges to municipal employment practices: (1) section 1981 of the Civil Rights Act of 1866; (2) the Fourteenth Amendment to the Constitution; and (3) most recently, Title VII of the Civil Rights Act of 1964, as amended by the Equal Employment Opportunity Act of 1972.

Three areas of federal law The three pieces of federal law that control employment practices are summarized here.

Section 1981 of the Civil Rights Act of 1866 provides that all persons shall have the same right to make and enforce contracts.

The Fourteenth Amendment protects citizens from unfair procedures by state governments. Until the enactment of the Civil Rights Act of 1964, the Fourteenth Amendment formed the basis for most lawsuits charging discrimination. It provides a right to sue any person who, under state or local law, causes the deprivation of another's rights, privileges, or immunities which are ensured by the Constitution or federal laws.

Title VII of the Civil Rights Act of 1964 as amended by the Equal Employment Opportunity Act of 1972 expanded the number and types of employers who are covered by the original act. As originally enacted, Title VII applied only to private employers. As amended the act removes the exemption for state and local governments, modifies the exemption for educational institutions, and reduces to fifteen the number of employees needed for an employer to be covered.

Title VII also gives courts wide discretion in awarding back pay to employees in order to ensure that victims of unlawful discrimination are compensated for past discrimination and, so far as possible, are restored to positions where they would have been were it not for unlawful discrimination.

Although Title VII is not an exclusive remedy for plaintiffs who allege employer discrimination, it has become the modern civil rights statute. Title VII prohibits any discrimination based on race, color, religion, sex, or national origin in all employment practices to include hiring, promotion, firing, compensation, and other terms, privileges, and conditions of employment for employers with fifteen or more employees. The U.S. Equal Employment Opportunity Commission (EEOC) was established in 1964 to investigate alleged violations of the act. Title VII and its coverage and application are discussed at some length in Appendix B of this book.

Two additional enactments are relevant to affirmative action and public service. The Age Discrimination in Employment Act of 1967 and the revision of 1977 prohibit discrimination in employment against people between the ages of forty and seventy. It is administered by the wage and hour division of the U.S. Department of Labor. And the Crime Control Act of 1976 came about because of ambiguities over the administration of the civil rights provision of the Omnibus Crime Control and Safe Streets Act of 1968. This act amends the 1968 measure to include the phrase "or denied employment" to the prohibitions of discrimination and provides "triggers" that automatically initiate administrative procedures for the cutoff of federal funding. In 1976 federal revenue sharing legislation also was amended to provide the same triggers for the aged and handicapped. While these are not landmark acts, they have had an impact on police personnel management.

The courts Court tests invariably accompany landmark legislation. The Civil Rights Act, as amended, has been no exception. In fact, in an early decision the U.S. Court of Appeals for the Fifth Circuit commented that "the administrative history of Title VII is in such a confused state that it is of minimal value in its explication."[5] This case shows that employment law is constantly developing, and many jurisdictions continue to face apparently conflicting local and federal interpretations of Title VII.

Conflicting interpretations notwithstanding, there is a clearly identifiable trend in court decisions relative to the identification of discriminatory personnel practices and judicial remedies that must be kept in mind when developing a total personnel administration system. Two important U.S. Supreme Court decisions are highly relevant: (1) *Griggs* v. *Duke Power Company*[6] and (2) *Albemarle Paper Co.* v. *Moody*.[7]

The question decided in 1971 by *Griggs* v. *Duke Power Company* was whether an employer legally could require that employees possess a high school education or pass a standardized general intelligence test as a condition of employment or promotion when (1) neither criterion is shown to be significantly related to successful job performance; (2) both requirements operate to disqualify black applicants at a higher rate than whites; and (3) the jobs in question had traditionally been filled only by white applicants.

In deciding the case, the U.S. Supreme Court ruled that the employer bore the burden of showing that any given requirement has a direct relationship to the job itself. Since it was found that neither the high school completion requirement nor the general intelligence test had any demonstrable relationship to successful performance, the Court concluded that any test or procedure used for selecting employees that has an adverse impact on minority hiring is illegal unless it has been validated and is job related.[8]

Two questions were answered in 1975 by the U.S. Supreme Court in its ruling on *Albemarle Paper Co.* v. *Moody*: (1) Should back pay be denied to victims of illegal employment discrimination merely because the employer acted in good faith and did not intend to violate the law? (2) What must an employer show to establish that preemployment tests racially discriminatory in effect though not in intent are sufficiently job related to survive challenge under Title VII?

In response to the first question, the Court ruled back pay should not be denied to victims of illegal discrimination regardless of the employer's good intent not to discriminate. Because the remedies provided by Title VII were designed to "make whole" employees, the Supreme Court declared that trial courts should exercise their discretion to award back pay when it is necessary to compensate workers for injuries suffered owing to unlawful employment discrimination. In answer to the second question, the Court declared that Albemarle's efforts to validate its testing procedures were defective in several respects with regard to proving job relatedness when measured against the Equal Employment Opportunity Commission's guidelines.

The Albemarle case made it incumbent on criminal justice agencies to engage in validation studies, which, admittedly, are often costly and time-consuming.

Refusal to make such studies has resulted in court-imposed quotas at both entry and promotional levels.[9] It seems that the inability to demonstrate empirically a relationship between a standard and its predictability of future job performance constitutes professional and legal proof that the standard is an artificial barrier that serves to impede affirmative action.

LEAA guidelines Successful affirmative action programs are not designed in a vacuum but must be tailored to address the social, economic, and political exigencies unique to individual communities. Stated in its simplest form, affirmative action is a comprehensive effort by an employer to:

1. Identify all barriers in the personnel management system which limit the ability of applicants and employees to reach their full employment potential, without regard to race, sex, religion, national origin, or other extraneous factors.
2. Eliminate all such barriers in a timely coordinated manner.
3. Institute whatever special programs are needed to accelerate the process.[10]

In 1973 the Law Enforcement Assistance Administration (LEAA) promulgated some equal employment opportunity guidelines.[11] These guidelines specifically recognize that full and equal participation of women and minority individuals in employment opportunities in the criminal justice system is a necessary component of the 1968 Safe Streets Act's program to reduce crime and delinquency in the United States. In essence, in order to receive LEAA funds, a criminal justice agency had to develop and implement a utilitarian affirmative action program.

In 1979 LEAA published a booklet that sets out some general recruitment strategies for inducing qualified candidates to accept police positions.[12] Its main point is that criminal justice agencies should be representative of the public they serve. Hence, recruitment strategies can have an impact on the effectiveness of an organization and can widen equal employment opportunities.

Internal challenges to affirmative action Not all police forces have found the notion of affirmative action to be accepted among their personnel. In some there has been substantial bickering and in others there has been a spate of civil suits. Affirmative action hiring proponents won major court suits in Seattle, Cincinnati, and Philadelphia in 1980.

In some places the issue has become frightfully tangled, and officers have splintered into black, Chicano, and white camps. For example, in 1979 a six-year-old lawsuit over alleged discrimination was resolved in Atlanta. Initiated by the Afro-American Patrolmen's League, it charged that blacks were victims of discrimination. In 1976 the Atlanta Fraternal Order of Police countersued, alleging that the recently elected city administration was working against white officers. An out-of-court settlement, a compromise, was reached in November 1979 and was approved by a U.S. district court judge in early 1980.

Women in police work

Since World War II, women have filled a host of roles where they were not welcome earlier. These include work as jockeys, letter carriers, race car drivers, news correspondents, politicians, disc jockeys, commercial airline pilots, and baseball umpires. Increasingly, women are entering precincts once marked "for men only." So it is with police work, but women are not being recruited at an astounding rate. Considering the role women have played in the development of the United States, it is not inconsistent to accept the fact that women, given the opportunity, will contribute substantially to the betterment of the police service at operational, mid-management, and executive levels.

Increasing numbers of women are entering the job market, and well-qualified women are seeking work in law enforcement. Police management must recognize this fact and consider the future with respect to women filling an increasing number of positions in operations and in top management. Thought should be given to current selection, evaluation, and promotional policies and steps taken to eliminate areas where bias or discrimination may be present.

If women are to be accepted as top police managers smoothly and without turmoil, career patterns must be clearly defined for all employees attempting to gain supervisory responsibility through promotion. If there is the slightest hint of preferential treatment for any group, resentment on the part of other parties will negate the validity of any selection procedure. To preclude this, there must be conscious emphasis on nonpreferential and nondiscriminatory treatment for all personnel in any selection or promotion process under consideration.

There may be litigation, too, as in New York City in 1979. A suit filed in federal court by the massive, powerful Patrolmen's Benevolent Association (PBA) alleged that female officers were being promoted to detective ahead of male officers, irrespective of qualifications. The New York police department's Policewomen's Endowment Association was quick to respond, calling the PBA suit a ploy for internal political purposes. In spite of the precipitating factors, a hassle of this nature is clearly divisive and demoralizes the force. It also obscures the larger issue. Such conflicts should be resolved internally, short of the courthouse. This is a major challenge to police leadership.

One of the avenues that promises to help more qualified females into ranking roles is a relatively new approach toward the development of top police service managers. This avenue—the use of assessment centers—has been successful in the business community. The virtues of using assessment centers in the selection, promotion, and development of professional and managerial people are well documented. The assessment center technique, described in a subsequent section of this chapter, might well aid in gaining acceptance for women in top management positions in the police service.

If qualified women are not assimilated in top management roles, the personnel difficulties that may ensue could have a more damaging effect on police administration than did the earlier personnel problems of assimilating females into operational roles. For example, in 1980 one very large city was required by U.S. district court mandate to hire women for 30 percent of its next 2,670 police officer vacancies and to pay $200,000 to ninety-six women who were alleged victims of past sex discrimination in promotions. The court decree also required the city to promote women to the next sixteen detective openings and the next seventeen sergeant vacancies.

Training

The nature of police service imposes unusual intellectual, emotional, and ethical demands on police officers. They must deal with extremely complicated situations and sometimes with remarkably clever criminals. To meet these challenges, officers must be alert, resourceful, decisive, and fully trained.

One means of assuring that recruit training classes fulfill the actual needs of the police service is to examine the role and function of the police officer regularly. This means first making a detailed task analysis of the officer's job in order to identify the knowledge, skills, and attitudes that must be developed if an officer is to perform successfully, and then setting out performance objectives for training courses. This is, in essence, a systems approach to training. It is proactive rather than reactive in nature. Moreover, instructors are tending to shift their emphasis from the traditional lecture method of instruction to "hands on" methods that require student participation in practical situations.

The training process cannot be allowed to become static. Continual reexamination of learning can help make training dynamic and forward-looking, which it must be if the police service is to meet the challenges of the 1980s.

Police managers must be trained, too, particularly to deal with the impact of unionization on police discipline. Police administrators are recognizing the importance of training supervisors to identify the causes of employee misconduct and the type of behavior that leads to potential discipline problems. Police supervisors need to receive training in counseling, human relations, employee motivation, and investigation of charges of misconduct. They also must learn how to deal with employees who have drug, alcohol, emotional, and physical problems and must be in a position to recommend professional psychological and medical assistance.

Recruit training

Nothing has a greater impact on the newly hired police officer than the content and conduct of recruit training. It is critical that a recruit be positively oriented toward the organization and toward police work generally, particularly its service aspect, as officers engage in extensive contacts with all sorts of people. Officers are, really, problem solvers and should be trained as such.

In 1967 the President's Commission on Law Enforcement and Administration of Justice gave notable impetus to the concept of state-mandated standards and training.[13] This thrust has contributed to preparing better-qualified enforcement officers by calling for more hours of training, improved curricula, and the adoption of standards. It was a dramatic breakthrough in the upgrading of police training.

In-service and specialized training

The staff of the President's Commission on Law Enforcement and Administration of Justice spoke directly to the need for in-service training when it observed that:

Much of the existing in-service training is given in brief, daily form. For example, many departments conduct roll call training from 5 to 20 minutes at the beginning of each tour of duty, and utilize excellent training aids such as "Training Keys" or sight/sound film provided by the International Association of Chiefs of Police. While the short, daily training sessions for police officers have great value, these programs should be supplemented by an annual period of intensive in-service training.[14]

In-service training is, or should be, people-oriented and based on the individual or group needs of a department. Training should be continuous, following an officer from basic academy graduation to retirement. Moreover, it is important to be proactive in planning programs. Why wait until an uncontrolled mob destroys public or private property before scheduling an in-service training program on crowd control? Why wait until an officer is injured responding to a domestic complaint before providing officers with courses in family crisis intervention? Must a hostage be killed before officers are trained in hostage negotiation? Roll call sessions are invaluable for keeping officers up-to-date in such areas as state and Supreme Court decisions; new laws and ordinances; changes in county, municipal, or departmental policy; new procedures and programs; and new developments, methods, and techniques in law enforcement.

There are essential in-service training programs designed for everyone in the department. Firearms and first aid refresher courses are two examples. At the same time, however, not all members of the department need exactly the same in-service courses. Each group of officers has individual needs, and police administrators should take all steps necessary to identify these and accommodate them. Then the special groups may be provided appropriate unique training.

Modern instructional delivery systems and new teaching technology may provide opportunities for the training administrator who finds that the lecture method is being overused. Alternative methods for consideration are student participation videotapes, programmed instruction, role playing, case studies, discussion groups, workshops, buzz sessions, and the incident process. An in-service training program, then, should be proactive, people-oriented, based on individual need, and delivered in such a way as to motivate the experienced officer to a higher degree of professionalism.

Management training

Beyond training for new employees, there is a pressing need for continuous development of persons in responsible positions. In fact, management and supervisory training can be a major factor in shaping the future of an agency.

If the budget permits, certain managers and supervisors may be selected to attend outside programs or to participate in regional training and seminars with other departments. Since good street investigators or police officers do not necessarily make good supervisors or managers, an agency needs a screening process and a well-grounded management training program employing the latest technological aids.

There is a host of programs available for training police managers. Some police academies in large cities offer management training programs, often in conjunction with educational institutions. The International Association of Chiefs of Police (IACP), the Federal Bureau of Investigation (FBI), and some state organizations, notably the California Commission on Peace Officer Standards and Training (POST), provide management courses. Educational institutions offer specialized management institutes and semester or quarterly management courses. Private management groups provide seminars, some of which are tailored to government or police needs, and ranking officers may be welcomed.

England has a national police college (Bramshill House) that provides executive training for present and future leaders in the police service, and sometimes managers from the United States are invited to attend. The FBI National Academy at Quantico, Virginia, graduates a thousand police personnel each year who may pass their knowledge on to their respective agencies. The Traffic Institute at Northwestern University, the Southern Police Institute at the University of Louisville, and the University of Southern California's Delinquency Control Institute also have respected programs for the development of police service executive talent.

Outside programs

Police executives should search out education programs in outside institutions for both themselves and their personnel of all ranks. Training is not simply a matter of certifying individuals on the basis of hours spent in a classroom; it is a viable and ongoing process important to each member of any police agency. Such civilian institutions as colleges and universities are readily available to most departments and generally have academic offerings in police-related areas. Many community colleges offer a combination credit toward degree program and police academy basic school. These are excellent examples of police–academic cooperation and represent a significant asset to many smaller departments with limited training budgets. It is also important to know that many colleges and universities offer academic programs leading to the associate, baccalaureate, and graduate degrees. Individual officers can attend classes, establishing good relations for their departments with the academic community, earning credits toward a degree, and improving themselves personally and professionally as police service careerists.

While the advantages of a well-based theoretical foundation of knowledge cannot be questioned, it is essential that specialized and in-service training continue. Police agencies must not assume that a basic academy or college program is sufficient to meet the training needs of their officers. After careful examination of needs, current and future, and identification of promising supervisory, instructional, and executive talent, departmental leaders should be able to select outside programs that will increase the effectiveness of their individual agencies.

Educational incentives

In the past decade the police service has been witness to a societal evolution unparalleled in the history of the United States. No longer can it be assumed that the enforcement of law and selected services can be adequately performed by poorly educated and unmotivated individuals.

Data reflect that overall, national education levels are not static. In fact, citizens are better educated today than they were ten years ago. Therefore, a high school education is an inadequate standard for the police officer, who will be dealing with an increasingly better educated citizenry.

With these facts in mind, a number of police agencies have revised their minimum entry educational requirements. Even more have instituted educational incentive plans to encourage incumbent police officers to upgrade their levels of education. These incentives have ranged from scheduling officers' work shifts to allow them to attend classes to paying salary bonuses for reaching certain levels of academic achievement. Other incentives have included financial assistance for educational expenses, higher starting pay for police recruits, and bonus points on promotional examinations for varying levels of academic success.

Personnel development programs

Professional career development in the police service necessitates the establishment of career ladders and personnel planning for both sworn and nonsworn members. Individuals must be formally apprised of opportunities for enrichment in their current jobs as well as the possibilities and requirements for vertical advancement. Opportunities should be well publicized by the organization, with the added element of career counseling. Career development in a police agency satisfies needs of both the individual and the organization. Planned development for a career-oriented individual provides access to promotional avenues as well as potential job enrichment. It allows the organization to incorporate change into the development programs, thereby improving proficiency and productivity.

Career counseling

Career counseling is necessary to draw together individual and organizational needs. Through professional in-house career counseling, data relating to enrichment or advancement possibilities can be made available to the organization member and be directly related to the member's abilities, skills, and personality. Career counseling is a valid personnel technique for locating and identifying those interested in development and advancement as well as "the best" candidate for a particular position.

Use of nonsworn personnel

Since cost pressures exert extreme influence over any streamlining effort in an organization, appropriate consideration must be given to the use of nonsworn personnel in specialized jobs not requiring the services of sworn officers. There is a need, then, for civilian career paths in the police agency. In order to promote greater efficiency and economy, positions not requiring a police-trained individual should be filled with nonsworn personnel who have appropriate opportunities for job enrichment and promotion. Career counseling should be provided to all personnel, and career opportunities should be publicized for all levels of the organizational structure. Well-formulated career paths will minimize many of the class distinctions currently found in police agencies between sworn and nonsworn personnel.

Job analysis

Job analysis is a systematic process of collecting, processing, analyzing, and interpreting data about work. The data are used to define what is done on the job, how it is done, and why. Job analysis provides the information necessary for recruitment, selection, development, and promotion. However, job analysis is not job classification. Job classification is a method employed to describe the duties performed in a position with a view toward setting salary requirements for that position. Job analysis goes beyond this in that it attempts to differentiate between performances in the same job. A good job analysis is aimed at determining what attributes are necessary for a job to be performed successfully by an individual.

The full impact of job analysis in police agencies has yet to be felt. Spurred on by affirmative action court decisions, police agencies have resorted to job analysis to support the job-relatedness of their testing criteria. Many agencies are using job analysis as the basis of an assessment process in their personnel system. A few agencies are beginning to use job analysis in administrative policy making, too. They are using the job analysis technique to determine the appropriateness of the task to the police role. In other words, there is a movement toward emphasizing not only the *what* and the *how* of the job, but also the *why*.

The increased prominence of budgetary considerations and the search for an alternative to more personnel have made job analysis information essential to provide the following information needed in restructuring or redesigning individual tasks: (1) the "shredding out" of the simpler routine tasks (with an emphasis on more skilled work); (2) the design and establishment of new, lower level, paraprofessional positions to take over simpler (or less frequent) tasks; and (3) the restructuring or redesign of the skilled positions to ensure the most logical grouping of tasks among the skilled positions for maximum effectiveness. Proper job analysis clearly provides needed input for the identification of organizational needs.

The assessment center

Many organizations have incorporated an assessment center as a major personnel practice. This technique provides an excellent measurement of skills and aptitudes for selection purposes as well as creating managerial talent pools within the organization.

An assessment center places the participant in the position of actually performing tasks related to the anticipated position. It identifies the characteristics or dimensions in a person who has applied for a position or is interested in administrative advancement. The participant's behavior is evaluated by trained assessors who use group dynamics in reaching an overall evaluation of the participant. The summary is orally communicated to the participant in a feedback interview.

The assessment center approach incorporates situational techniques in a simulated environment under standardized conditions. The assessment method is a supplement to regular appraisal procedures when it is impossible or impractical to: (1) assess qualities necessary through job performance prior to promotion and (2) compare candidates because of different performance rates and/or different job assignments.

Interpersonal relations

In some quarters, management seems to attach little importance to the individual. Yet managerial techniques must reflect a philosophy of concern for people within the organization. Moreover, management must be "sensitive to their norms, attitudes, values, and motivating forces. Within the organization, management is concerned with the maximization of human and physical resources to effectively fulfill agency goals, as well as providing the climate for individual growth and development."[15]

Understanding, predicting, and influencing human behavior is important if an organization is to be modernized. Streamlining often is brought about by what many professional managers call the "new breed" of employees who make up the work force. One of the most significant changes facing administrators is the shift in individual values of those entering the organizational setting.

Increasingly, the younger, better educated, and more highly trained employee has a great desire to be considered as an individual. These persons place a high premium on autonomy and wish to have greater control over their roles and environment. Regimentation, rigid direction, and simple reward–punishment systems tend to frustrate and restrict initiative and creativity. These are hallmarks of the past. Instead, in a healthy organization most employees wish to be productive and achieve a feeling of identity within the agency. Psychologically, they need an environment in which they can participate and be creative in organizational activities.

This shift in values seems certain to affect the philosophies under which organizations operate. Styles of leadership, administrative policies and procedures, and superior–subordinate relationships are therefore subject to changing viewpoints. Police administrators must develop the ability to manage interpersonal relationships. It has been said that there are few things that managers accomplish as individuals through isolated efforts. They must usually rely on the support, cooperation, loyalty, and approval of a large number of people, including subordinates.

A common weakness of top managers is their failure to recognize the importance of lower level and middle management to the successful functioning of the organization. Lower level and middle managers, more than anyone else, must depend on their ability in the area of interpersonal relationships. Too often these managers are bogged down in paperwork and administrative functions, which in effect take them away from their real job of managing people. They must have frequent face-to-face communication with operational personnel because it is through middle and lower level managers that the plans, policies, and procedures of top management reach operational personnel. If there is a lack of communication between top management and middle and lower level management, programs will suffer and there is a high probability that operational execution will be inconsistent with directives.

Safety and accident prevention

An important but frequently neglected area of personnel management is safety and accident prevention. A concerted effort on the part of management can often bring about a reduction in accidents among personnel. The price to be paid for accidents is readily seen in the spiraling costs of medical and hospital bills, employee salary and disability benefits, and the chance of huge court awards should the police be shown negligent.

A safety program aimed at the reduction of all accidents should include:

1. The intent of management regarding safety and accident prevention set out in a clear statement of policy about the issue.
2. Accountability for safety. The officer in charge of personnel or training is the most logical person to head the effort.
3. The responsibility for safety as a function of operating divisions. It is important for divisional commanders to recognize their responsibility in making the safety program work.
4. Ongoing training and education in safety.

In addition to promotional activities, an annual safety audit should be conducted. A safety inspection can help reduce hazards by ensuring that accidents and violations are identified and analyzed.

Another consideration is the establishment of a safety committee involving employees. Such a committee may assume responsibility for promoting a safety campaign through posters, notices, and other publicity. A combination of the right activities, suitably timed, and the proper acceptance of responsibility will create a safety-conscious attitude throughout a police agency and will contribute to the elimination of accidents.

Labor–management practices

Public employee unions are the fastest growing segment of the American labor movement. For example, in 1978, 263,449 officers were members of some form of employee organization.[16] These persons represented about 55 percent of the almost 480,000 officers working for county or local forces that year, according to the U.S. Bureau of the Census. Very few were affiliated in 1960.

The dramatic upsurge in membership suggests, indeed accurately implies, that there has been a rapid increase in the growth of police employee organizations, with a resultant dramatic impact on the administration and operation of police departments. Other than the office of the chief of police, responsibility for dealing with the employee organization and its membership falls on the staff of the police personnel division.

Police employee organizations are interested in all matters affecting their members. Not only are union leaders concerned with improving wages, hours, and working conditions; they also are vitally interested in many matters that have traditionally been considered administrative prerogatives. Police unions want to bargain over such matters as discipline, job assignments, promotions, patrol techniques, training procedures, the number of officers in a patrol car, and other police policy issues.

Police administrators are recognizing the importance of developing proper management responses to police employee organizations. Labor–management relations necessitate the adoption of new attitudes and philosophies as well as the application of new management techniques. Police administrators must become knowledgeable about the history of labor relations, the organization and function of unions, methods of dealing with organizing efforts, techniques of negotiating, contract administration, and methods of handling disputes and strikes. Police unions are now well entrenched in American public service and will continue to grow in importance.

Historical development of employee organizations

One of the earliest hints that police officers in the United States were inclined to organize for purposes of assuring their well-being was the establishment of the St. Louis, Missouri, Police Relief Association in 1867.[17] Its mission was to provide relief for personnel who became disabled, sick, or incapacitated over long years of service and to help the families of members who had passed away. Before long, police employee organizations were formed elsewhere for similar reasons. Some militance ensued, as in Ithaca, New York, where in 1889 the force of five officers walked off the job because of a pay reduction.[18]

The movement was under way. In 1915 the Fraternal Order of Police (FOP) formed its first local fraternal association. In 1918 Cincinnati police struck over the discharge of four officers who attempted to organize a meeting to discuss job conditions.

A significant event occurred in 1919 when over 1,110 Boston police officers went on strike over the firing of officers who had petitioned the American Federation of Labor to issue a charter to the Boston police. During the four-day strike considerable violence took place and there were a number of deaths. All of the striking officers were dismissed. After the Boston strike, police unionizing efforts suffered a setback because of strong opposition from the public and public employers.

Even in the face of public feeling, the union movement went forward. In 1919 the American Federation of Labor chartered thirty-seven police locals with membership of over 4,000.[19] In 1939 the American Federation of State, County, and Municipal Employees (AFSCME) began to charter police associations and by 1951 had chartered sixty-one.[20] The International Conference of Police Associations (ICPA) was formed in 1953 to serve as an umbrella organization for independent police associations throughout the United States, a role it played until its demise in 1978.

Growth in union membership was only nominal, however, until the 1960s, when membership began to grow rapidly. This growth was related to the adoption of state laws permitting collective bargaining in the public sector and the issuance of President John F. Kennedy's 1962 Executive Order 10988, establishing a system of collective bargaining for federal employees.

The civil rights disturbances and student disorders of the 1960s and the violence surrounding the 1968 Democratic national convention in Chicago aided the rise of police unions by sanctioning the use of militant tactics and damaging the image of the police. Increasing violence against police officers, unpopular court decisions, the rapid growth of police departments, and the formation of civil service systems that resulted in depersonalizing employment relations also contributed to the growth of police unions. Police officers turned to labor organizations as a means of improving their pay, benefits, working conditions, and public image.

Characteristics of police unions

Police employee organizations can be classified into: (1) local independent organizations; (2) organizations affiliated with a larger group at the county, state, or national level; and (3) organizations affiliated with organized labor. The Berkeley, California, Police Association; the Buffalo, New York, Police Benevolent Association; and the El Paso, Texas, Municipal Police Officers Association are classic examples of local independent organizations.

The Honolulu police are affiliated with the State of Hawaii Organization of Police Officers; the Orlando, Florida, police with the Orange County Police Benevolent Association; and San Bernardino, California, officers with the San Bernardino Police Chapter of the citywide Public Employees Association. These are examples of forces affiliated with a larger group.

Some of those linked with organized labor include police in Bridgeport, Connecticut (AFSCME, AFL–CIO); Flint, Michigan (Teamsters); and the District of Columbia (International Brotherhood of Police Officers).

Organizations Local independent associations include police benevolent and peace officer associations. Initially, these associations were formed to provide social and recreational services for their members. Some of the local associations have become loosely federated on a statewide basis for lobbying purposes. Furthermore, the state organizations usually have linkage with a national headquarters for lobbying Congress and, if appropriate, state and local legislative bodies as well.

In 1978 several formerly local associations chose to affiliate with a newly formed body called the International Union of Police Associations (IUPA). These were organizations that had been linked with the ICPA, and their departure contributed to the demise of that association.

In early 1979 the executive council of the AFL–CIO approved chartering the IUPA as an affiliate of organized labor, thereby competing with the International Brotherhood of Teamsters, which also has organized police officers. The IUPA had sixty-seven chapters and more than 40,000 members in 1979. It is an umbrella-type association that provides information, training, and lobbying services to its member organizations.

While not a labor union as such, the Fraternal Order of Police (FOP) is a nationwide professional association. It is a loose federation of autonomous local lodges that engages in all phases of collective bargaining, including work stoppages. In 1980 FOP national headquarters reported 1,350 local lodges in forty-two states representing over 150,000 members. The FOP is particularly strong in the South and North Central states. It publishes the *National Police Journal*.

A relatively new labor organization is the National Troopers Coalition, which was organized in 1977 as a group of state troopers in New England. In 1980 it became national in scope and claims about 17,000 members among its several state associations.

The International Brotherhood of Police Officers (IBPO), formed in 1964, is affiliated with the National Association of Government Employees. The IBPO included about 38,000 members in about 175 chapters in 1977, mostly along the Eastern Seaboard and in New England. It considers itself a police union, is interested in civil service reforms in police departments, and actively seeks to become the bargaining agent for police officers.

Many police forces nationwide are affiliated with an AFL–CIO affiliate, the American Federation of State, County, and Municipal Employees (AFSCME). AFSCME started organizing police in the 1940s and has had notable success in the East and Midwest. At one time the union experienced limited success in expanding its police membership because of its apparent liberal orientation, past suspensions of striking police locals, and the industrial nature of the union.[21]

Another AFL–CIO affiliate organizing police officers is the Service Employees International Union, which in 1972 established the National Union of Police Officers (NUPO) as a separate and autonomous affiliate. The NUPO was first established in 1969 by John Cassese, former president of the New York Patrolmen's Benevolent Association. He had intended the organization to be a national police union and requested a charter from the AFL–CIO, which denied it. Membership in the NUPO was about 10,000 in 1969 and was estimated to be about the same in 1980.

The International Brotherhood of Teamsters has waged a strong drive to unionize police officers nationwide. In 1980 the Teamsters were reportedly negotiating for about 20,000 law enforcement officers in some 250 cities of various sizes. While Teamster police locals are found in many states, its attempts to organize police officers encounter opposition in some forces because of the union's alleged ties to organized crime.

In the late 1960s another type of employee organization surfaced. This was the police association comprised of minority persons who actively sought to protect their interests in police departments. Among the early ones was Chicago's Afro-American Patrolmen's League, founded in 1968. There are other local minority organizations, such as the Guardians, representing the New York City department's blacks, and the Hispanic Caucus, which oversees the interests of the department's Puerto Rican and Cuban officers. Nationally, black officers formed the Black Police Officers Association in 1971 and the National Organization of Black Law Enforcement Executives (NOBLE) in 1976. The former counted over 15,000 members in 1979.

National trends Teamster, FOP, IBPO, IUPA, and AFSCME efforts notwithstanding, a hallmark of police employee groups today is the absence of strong national organizations. Instead, there is a pattern of diversified local organizations that may or may not be affiliated with state or national organizations. In fact, there is a trend toward the formation of county or regional employee organizations whose broader membership base tends to strengthen their bargaining power.

There is some movement toward still greater diversification of affiliations rather than toward one national body. Two happenings are illustrative: (1) In 1979 the Tukwila, Washington, police affiliated with the United Steelworkers of America, a first for that union; and (2) in 1979 three hundred Houston officers withdrew from the local police association and formed a new AFL–CIO-affiliated union called the Houston Police Patrolmen's Association. In contrast, nearly all the nation's fire fighters belong to the powerful International Association of Fire Fighters, an AFL–CIO-affiliated union that has almost 1,800 locals.

On the other hand, there is considerable interest among the rank and file in the establishment of a national police union similar to that of the fire fighters. While police chiefs generally do not support the concept,[22] subordinate personnel believe a national union will promote solidarity among the nation's police and will provide organizing, research, information, and legislative services for its members. Opponents are concerned with the possible misuse of power, the limits such an organization would place on local decision making, and the potential danger of nationwide police strikes and job actions.

Preparing for unionization

The development of an effective employee relations program depends on the quality of personnel administration in the organization. For this reason it is important to review existing personnel policies and practices and to maintain open communications with police employees. Periodic checks should be made to assure that personnel policies are kept current and are being applied uniformly and consistently. Policies covering such matters as hairstyles, residency, discipline, selection methods, and promotion are closely scrutinized by union leaders and may prompt grievances.

Fringe benefits also are of considerable interest to police employees. It is not unusual for present benefits to be taken for granted and overshadowed by requests for new and increased benefits. For this reason management should place a dollar value on such fringe benefits as pensions, holidays, health insurance, vacations, and sick leave.

In preparing for unionization, the police administrator should also be sure that the personnel program includes the following:

1. Sound position classification and pay plans
2. An employee handbook that states personnel policies in writing
3. An orderly procedure for settling grievances
4. Supervisory training in labor relations
5. Managerial pay and benefit plans that distinguish supervisors from rank and file employees

The Policeman's Bill of Rights

Many police employee organizations throughout the country have made determined efforts to achieve more rights for officers during internal investigations. The feeling of these employee organizations is that policemen should not be treated like second-class citizens and should be afforded the same rights as other citizens who are charged with wrongdoing under the criminal law. This philosophy has undoubtedly been the result of the recent extension of many procedural rights to criminal defendants by the United States Supreme Court.

The effort of police employee organizations has been geared toward providing officers with optimum protections during internal investigation interrogations. Police organizations have attempted to achieve this goal by having these protections written into contracts or implemented administratively.

A number of collective bargaining contracts negotiated during 1971 contained the "Policeman's Bill of Rights," a document extending broad protections to police officers during internal investigation interrogations. Included among these contracts were Providence, Rhode Island; New York State Police; and San Francisco, California.

The substance of the Policeman's Bill of Rights was generally the same in all of these contracts. Following is an analysis of the Policeman's Bill of Rights:

1. Time of interrogation
The interrogation of an officer being investigated for a disciplinary violation must be at a reasonable hour, preferably while the officer is on duty and during the daylight hours.

2. Identification of investigating officers
The officer under investigation must be informed of the officer in charge of the investigation and the officer who will be conducting the interrogation.

3. Information about the investigation
The officer must be informed of the nature of the investigation before interrogation commences. The information must be sufficient to reasonably apprise the officer of the nature of the investigation.

4. Length of interrogation
The length of an internal investigation must be reasonable, with rest periods being called periodically for personal necessities, meals, telephone calls and rest.

5. Use of coercion
The officer cannot be threatened with transfer, dismissal or other disciplinary punishment as a means of obtaining information regarding the incident under investigation. Also, the officer cannot be subjected to abusive language or promised a reward as inducement for answering questions.

6. Presence of counsel
The officer under investigation may have counsel or a representative of his employee organization present with him during an interrogation. This representation is usually confined to counseling and not actual participation in the interrogation.

7. Recording of interrogation
The interrogation must be recorded, either mechanically or by a stenographer. There can be no "off the record" questions.

The Policeman's Bill of Rights.

8. Criminal rights warning
If the officer is a suspect in a criminal investigation, he must be advised of his Miranda rights.

9. Furnishing copy of interrogation
The officer under investigation has the discretion to request an exact copy of any written statement he has signed or a copy of the recording of the interrogation.

10. Refusal to answer questions
The refusal of an officer to answer questions concerning *non-criminal* matters may result in disciplinary action.

11. Refusal to answer questions.
An officer cannot be ordered to submit to a polygraph test for any reason unless the officer requests to do so.

6. Service awards, employee opinion surveys, employee newsletters, and other programs that make personnel feel they participate in the organization.

Discipline and unionization

The growth of police employee organizations dramatically affects disciplinary procedures. Police unions provide legal representation to members facing disciplinary charges. Unions are concerned with methods used by police departments in conducting internal investigations of misconduct charges and the importance of impartiality. Police unions have striven to have disciplinary matters covered by negotiated grievance procedures that end in binding arbitration.

The department should have well-defined procedures for disciplining employees, including three or four steps in which progressively severe but well-formulated and well-understood disciplinary action is taken. Forms of discipline can involve oral or written reprimand, suspension, demotion, and discharge. Sanctions must be applied equitably, and the employee should understand the reason for the disciplinary action that is taking place.

Because of their concern for the rights of members during internal investigations, police unions have attempted to have the Policeman's Bill of Rights included in contracts. This document purports to provide protection to the employee involved in an internal investigation and covers such matters as time, place, and length of interrogation, use of coercion during the investigation, and the employee's right to refuse to answer questions. While some of the rights are reasonable, other rights limit the police administrator's ability to conduct an efficient disciplinary investigation.[23]

The collective bargaining process

Prior to 1959 the right of police employees to organize and engage in collective bargaining depended on the approval of local administrative and legislative officials. However, in that year Wisconsin passed a state collective bargaining law. Since then, thirty-four other states have adopted similar legislation authorizing collective bargaining for police employees. In some of the states police are covered by general statutes along with other municipal employees, while in others there are separate statutes for police. The measures have withstood court tests, and it is well affirmed that police and other public employees have a constitutional right to join labor organizations. Public employees, however, do not have a constitutional right to bargain collectively. The courts have held that collective bargaining for public employees cannot take place without legislative authorization.

Stages in the process	Participants in the process			
	Local government officials	Police management	Personnel agencies	Finance agencies
Organization	Restraint	Restraint		
Petition	Review petition	Reviews petition	Review petitions; check lists	
Election	Call for election	Oversees election	Prepare voter list	
Certification and recognition	Formally recognize union as exclusive bargaining representative	Formal recognition of union	Begin authorization of payroll deductions	Payroll deductions
Preparation for negotiations	Determine extent of role in negotiating and establishing bargaining philosophy	Selection of negotiating team	Participate in negotiations	
Beginning phase of negotiations	Analyze labor proposals as a whole and establish guidelines	Analyzes labor proposals as a whole and establishes guidelines	Consider impact of labor proposals on personnel policies	Cost out labor proposals
Intermediate phase of negotiations	Review preliminary budget	Seeks areas of agreement and makes counterproposals	Disclosure of wage and benefit data	Prepare preliminary budget
Final phase of negotiations	Review final budget	Concludes agreement or reaches impasse	Planning and programming for contract changes	Final budget
Resolution of impasse— mediation	Present position to mediator	Presents history of negotiation and position to mediator	Part of negotiation team in mediation	Part of negotiation team in mediation
Resolution of impasse— fact-finding	Determine facts to be presented; may present facts	Selects management advocate; recommends third party; presents facts	Research	Research
Resolution of impasse— arbitration	Selection of arbitrator	Selects management advocate on arbitration panel	Research	Research
Administration of contract	Administer agreement	Educates supervisory personnel in provisions of agreement and labor relations practices	Print and distribute copies of agreement; record-keeping	Implementation of pay practices

Schematic presentation of stages in the collective bargaining process by the principal participants. The major purpose of this figure is to show how other political and administrative forces impinge on labor and management during the collective bargaining process, depending on the stage in the negotiations and the complexity and intensity of the issue.

Some statutes require public employers to bargain, while others permit public employees to present some proposals or to meet and confer with public employers. Under meet-and-confer statutes the relationship is primarily unilateral rather than bilateral. In the fifteen states where legislation does not exist, collective bargaining rights have been extended to police employees through court decisions, by virtue of state attorney general opinions, or through local ordinances.

State collective bargaining statutes recognize the right of police and other public employees to organize and join unions. Some statutes prohibit police and fire employees from joining any group whose membership is not composed of employees doing the same type of work. This restricts membership in police

Stages in the process	Participants in the process			
	State legislature	Union	State mediation service	Electorate
Organization	Legislation	Meets with employees; provides information; solicits membership		Taxation
Petition	Legislation	Submits petition	Reviews petition	Taxation
Election	Legislation	Campaigns; oversees election	Conducts election	Taxation
Certification and recognition	Legislation	Becomes exclusive bargaining representative	Certifies union as exclusive bargaining representative	Taxation
Preparation for negotiations		Meets with membership; develops proposals; chooses negotiating team		Taxation
Beginning phase of negotiations		Receives management proposals; reviews past problems and procedures; establishes guidelines		Taxation
Intermediate phase of negotiations		Seeks areas of agreement; makes counterproposals		Taxation
Final phase of negotiations		Concludes agreement or reaches impasse	Notification of impasse if applicable	Taxation
Resolution of impasse— mediation	Legislation	Presents history of negotiation and position to mediator	Selects mediator; advises to reconcile parties to agreement: advisory authority	Taxation
Resolution of impasse— fact-finding	Legislation	Selects union advocate; recommends third party; presents facts	Selects third party; or labor advocate and management advocate select jointly	Taxation
Resolution of impasse— arbitration	Legislation	Selects labor advocate or arbitration panel	Provides arbitration services if requested; joint selection of third party	Taxation
Administration of contract		Educates officers in provisions of agreement and grievance procedures; on-going representation		Taxation

employee organizations to peace officers. Most statutes establish an agency to administer the legislation and to handle bargaining unit determinations, conduct recognition elections, review charges of unfair labor practices, and in some cases establish dispute resolution machinery. Most state statutes prohibit strikes by police officers. Some statutes provide for compulsory arbitration as a means of settling disputes involving police employees. Many statutes have provisions relating to the scope of bargaining, grievance procedures, union security, and public negotiating sessions.

A glossary of terms used in collective bargaining appears as Appendix C.

The bargaining unit A crucial decision confronting public employers who will soon begin collective bargaining for the first time is the determination of the bargaining unit. A bargaining unit is a group of employees recognized by the employer or designated by an authorized agency as appropriate for representation by an employee organization for purposes of bargaining. The bargaining unit affects which employee organization is recognized, the conduct of negotiations, contract administration, the scope of bargaining, and the resolution of disputes. If there is more than one bargaining unit, considerable strain falls on management because it must negotiate with a number of unions and administer a number of contracts. Fragmentation leads to rivalry among unions and "whipsawing" of the employer over demands.

Administrative agencies must consider a number of criteria, including community of interest, when making a decision regarding the appropriate bargaining unit. Community of interest refers to a similarity of job duties, skills, wages, educational requirements, working conditions, job location, supervision, hours of work, organizational structure, and labor policies. Other factors considered by administrative agencies include the history of collective bargaining, the interests of the employer and employees, effects of overfragmentation, and the extent to which the unit promotes effective dealings between management and the union. Professionals are usually included in a unit with nonprofessionals only if a majority of the professionals vote for inclusion.

In determining a bargaining unit, it is important that management exclude certain positions. Such positions include management officials, supervisors, and confidential, part-time, temporary, probationary, and seasonal employees. The ability to exclude these individuals from the bargaining unit will depend on the facts presented in each case.

The definition of supervisor has created problems in the determination of public safety bargaining units. A supervisor is defined as any individual having authority in the interest of the employer to hire, transfer, suspend, lay off, recall, promote, discharge, assign, reward, or discipline other employees, and having responsibility to direct them or to adjust their grievances or effectively recommend such action if the exercise of such authority is not of a merely routine or clerical nature but requires the use of independent judgment. The National Labor Relations Board policy has been to exclude any employee who has any of the characteristics of a supervisor. Under federal executive order, supervisors are excluded from bargaining units, as they are in the private sector.

Many police unions believe all supervisors should be included in the bargaining unit with patrol officers because their supervisory authority and responsibility are limited. Since many police organizations are under civil service, it is alleged that police supervisors do not have the authority to hire, fire, promote, demote, or suspend. Police union leaders point out that the authority of supervisors is often clearly delineated in department policies and regulations, allowing little discretion. They allege that police supervisors are similar to working foremen and lead workers in the private sector, who are included in bargaining units.

The inclusion of supervisors in the bargaining unit with those they supervise prompts serious management problems associated with the administration of the contract and the handling of grievances because of the inherent potential conflict of interest. It also blurs the line between management and labor. The supervisor problem is complicated in the public safety area because supervisors and subordinates often work under identical conditions and share a community of interest. Most supervisors have come up through the ranks and therefore tend to identify more with those they supervise than with management. And it has not been unusual for supervisors to ride on the coattails of the rank and file with regard to pay and benefits.

The bargaining unit determination should be made in advance of unionization. Police administrators should evaluate the structure and function of the department and levels of supervision. Past and present relationships with employee groups need to be examined carefully. If police administrators have informal discussions with groups consisting of patrol officers and supervisors, it is conceivable that when formalized collective bargaining arrives they will have established a past practice that may result in an administrative agency including supervisors in the bargaining unit. Police administrators should identify positions to be excluded from the unit and should examine the job descriptions of supervisors to assure that they are in fact supervisors.

Police administrators should strive for as few bargaining units as possible and, if necessary, seek expert advice in preparing a unit determination case to be heard by an administrative agency. Unit determination rulings of such agencies are an excellent source of information on the factors considered in the determination of bargaining units. Once a bargaining unit is established, it is extremely difficult to change it without major concessions on the part of management. Therefore, it is incumbent upon management to define the unit carefully as soon as possible.

Recognition   After the bargaining unit is identified, it is necessary to determine how an employee organization is selected to represent the employees in the unit. The most reliable method is by secret ballot election supervised by the state administrative agency or other neutral body such as the American Arbitration Association. Other methods of recognition include the use of dues authorization and membership cards or the use of petitions signed by a majority of the employees in the unit.

Secret ballot elections are preferred because fewer employees usually vote for a union in an election than the number who signed cards before the election. Other methods of recognition seem to encourage group pressure and even coercion and misrepresentation. Many employees will sign cards because of peer pressure but would not necessarily vote for union recognition in a secret ballot election.

The procedure for holding an election is usually established by the administrative or neutral agency. An agreement is reached between the employer and employee organization regarding the notice of election; voter eligibility; time, date, and place of election; kind of ballots; and runoff, tally, and challenged vote procedures. In addition, the ballots should list the organization seeking recognition and also provide for a choice of no representative.

After the ballots are counted, and in the absence of a challenge, the neutral agency certifies the employee organization receiving the majority of votes. Some agreements require that a certain percentage of employees in the bargaining unit vote. The laws usually provide that no election will be held in any unit within which a valid election has been held in the preceding twelve-month period. The certified bargaining representative continues to represent the unit until its status is challenged by a rival union, by the employer, or by the employees in the unit. Provision is then made for another election.

The concept of exclusive recognition is a characteristic of public sector unions. This means that the bargaining agent selected by the employees has the exclusive right, indeed the responsibility, to represent all bargaining unit employees, including those employees not members of the employee organization. The purpose of exclusive recognition is to avoid the problems associated with union rivalry.

Exclusive recognition raises a number of questions relating to union security. The union shop requires employees to become members of the union within a specified period after they are hired and to remain members as a condition of employment. Another union security provision is the closed shop, which is outlawed in the private sector and prevents people from being hired who are not members of the union. An agency shop requires employees not in the union to pay a fee as a condition of employment.

The preelection campaign   After arrangements have been made to conduct a secret ballot election, public employers must decide the extent to which they will participate in the preelection campaign. The employer can remain neutral and take no position for or against recognition. Another approach is to support the request for recognition by permitting the use of official facilities for union meetings and office space, the posting and distribution of union literature, and the use of agency house organs by the unions. Irrespective of stance, it is sound management policy to prohibit organizing activities during working hours and in work areas, including the solicitation of new members or the collection of dues on government time, and to inform employees of their legal rights and election procedures.

A third approach involves a campaign by the employer to defeat a recognition effort. In following this option the employer informs the employees of the implications of union membership, including the requirement to pay dues and possibly fines and assessments, the ramifications of exclusivity, the end of informality and flexibility in dealing with employee needs, and the hardships that are caused by strikes.

Many state statutes establish unfair labor practices that prohibit management and unions from engaging in certain activities during the preelection campaign. Management should be familiar with these restrictions and should be prepared to respond to union actions during the campaign, including the correction of any misrepresentations that may be made.

Preparing for negotiations "Who negotiates?" is the first question to consider in preparing for negotiations. Because of the close association between the police chief and the members of the department, it is generally agreed that the chief should not serve as the chief negotiator. The chief should, however, have a role in mapping prenegotiation strategy and serve as an expert during the negotiations. Only the chief is in a position to determine the impact of the proposals made by the employee representatives.

It is important that elected officials determine allowable limits for the negotiations and give their negotiator authority commensurate with responsibility to bargain. Concurrently, the governing body should be kept informed of the progress of negotiations and should resist efforts by union representatives to "end run" the negotiators and solicit support from elected officials on a political basis.

The negotiating team should include an experienced negotiator, a representative of the operating department that is affected, and someone familiar with personnel, law, and finance. The team should be kept as small as possible, and a single spokesperson should be designated to present the proposals and counterproposals. Various members of the team can be called upon to answer specific questions or to provide advice in the area of their specialties. The team members play an important role in the caucuses that will be called from time to time.

If an agency is entering negotiations for the first time, it would be prudent to retain a labor relations consultant if a staff member is not skilled in negotiations. Many costly and irreparable mistakes may thus be avoided. A consultant offers a short-range means of handling negotiations while at the same time training a member of the management staff to assume this responsibility.

Considerable homework is required in advance of negotiations. Suggestions should be solicited from police supervisors regarding matters to be discussed during the negotiations. An understanding of the structure of the organization, the authority of representatives to make commitments, and information on the union representatives and any internal problems will greatly assist management's negotiators. The negotiating team should be critically objective of existing personnel policies and practices.

Other kinds of information that can be of considerable assistance include a comparative analysis of wages and fringe benefits paid to police officers in other jurisdictions, cost of living information, copies of recent contracts reached by other employers having the same union, recruitment and retention experience, and current budget and revenue information. Information on the distribution of employees by classification, work location, and age also is useful in responding to union requests. So are data on past increases in salaries and benefits, current staffing and work schedules, and other personnel practices. The success of negotiations is, indeed, directly related to the thoroughness of the advance preparations.

Prior to beginning formal negotiations, management and union representatives should agree on ground rules relating to timetable, physical arrangements, and procedures to be followed during the negotiations. Very often state statutes or city ordinances establish the timetable in order to relate the negotiations to budget deadlines. Hence negotiations should be scheduled to begin approximately four to six months before the adoption of the budget.

Another ground rule relates to the location of the negotiating sessions and the physical arrangements. The advantage of conducting sessions in the public employer's facilities is access to staff and information. However, in some instances it is advisable to hold sessions on neutral ground. Negotiating sessions can be more productive if their length is limited, unless considerable progress is being made toward a tentative or final agreement. Sufficient time should be allowed between sessions to gather information and analyze proposals.

Note taking is of key importance during the negotiations. Someone other than the spokesperson should be designated to do this. Verbatim notes and recording equipment are neither necessary nor desirable, because they tend to inhibit discussion and encourage speech making. Notes are useful when the written contract is being prepared and often are used by arbitrators in deciding grievances relating to the interpretation and application of the contract.

Generally, confidentiality is essential to the success of negotiations because it allows for freedom of discussion and flexibility in making proposals and counterproposals. At the same time, handling communications with the public through the media during the negotiations requires forethought. Some state statutes require that negotiations take place at public meetings.

Negotiation tactics   After receiving the union's proposals it is important that police administrators carefully review them in terms of short- and long-range cost and operational and administrative impact. The total cost of each proposal should be computed, including the indirect costs, such as the effect of salary increases on various fringe benefits and pensions. A separation of the proposal into economic and noneconomic items will facilitate review. Every effort should be made to anticipate the priorities placed by the union on its various proposals and to arrange them in terms of management's priorities. The effect of the proposals on personnel policies should be carefully evaluated, too, along with the impact on employees who are not organized.

The negotiations provide an opportunity for police administrators to develop their own proposals directed at improving the operation of the police department and correcting inefficient or unclear policies and practices. Management should not restrict itself to responding to the union's demands. It may submit its own. Management can obtain considerable tactical advantage by directing the discussion to its own proposals rather than the union's.

During the negotiations management representatives should ask questions as a means of clarifying issues. Questions should be carefully worded. Specific illustrations should be used whenever possible. Early in the negotiations both sides must agree that all proposals have been brought forth; an agreement that issues be consolidated and set on the table early avoids piecemeal negotiations.

Throughout the negotiations there are strategic and tactical considerations. The negotiator should listen attentively and give direct answers. Facial expressions can indicate a person's sincerity and feelings. Calmness, the ability to listen, persuasiveness, fairness, honesty, and a sense of humor are traits of a successful negotiator. He or she also needs to understand the organizational, legal, and financial structure of the agency being represented. Management's negotiator should never refuse to consider or discuss a legitimate proposal, but arguments over principles can seriously handicap negotiations and should be avoided. A request for a caucus is advisable if little progress is being made on a proposal, if a deadlock is apparent, or if the negotiators are surprised by a proposal that they knew nothing about beforehand. As tentative agreements are reached on proposals, they should be reduced to writing and initialed. This will facilitate the preparation of the final agreement.

Good faith bargaining does not compel either party to agree to a proposal, nor does it require making concessions. Management's team should remain firm when the situation calls for it and should feel free to disagree in order to reserve certain management prerogatives. As experience is gained and the negotiator is able to profit from past mistakes and omissions, he or she will develop the skills needed to conduct effective negotiations.

The first contract is particularly important because it is very difficult to redress mistakes in later contracts. Clauses requiring special attention include those pertaining to management rights, strikes, union security, grievance procedures, duration of contract, maintenance of benefits, and mutual agreement. Maintenance of benefit clauses are restrictive to management because they continue in effect any existing policies or practices that are not specifically covered by the contract. Mutual agreement or veto clauses require that management obtain the union's agreement before taking action. The importance of the agreement should compel management to consider securing the services of a person experienced in contract drafting and interpretation.

The scope of bargaining In addition to pay benefits, police employee organizations have expressed an interest in police policy areas, including civilian review boards, dress and hairstyles, lateral transfers, undetachable name tags, restrictions on the use of force by officers, guidelines for use of firearms, the employment of civilians to perform certain police duties, and expanded political rights. Police administrators can anticipate that police unions also will be interested in the use of seniority for promotions, vacations, and beat, shift, and job assignments.

As police unions expand their power, police administrators will be confronted with increasing challenges to their authority and discretion. Police unions will continue to press for contract provisions requiring that they be consulted before changes are made in police policies and that they be given the authority to approve such changes. Provisions such as these will have far-reaching effects on police administration. The standards developed by the American Bar Association and the International Association of Chiefs of Police state that law enforcement policy should not be determined by a police union or other police employee organizations.[24] This is an important concept.

Contract administration After the contract has been signed, the task of contract administration begins. The first step is to distribute copies of the contract to all supervisors and to conduct orientation sessions to give them a thorough understanding of each provision and how it affects them. During the review of the contract, management sets forth its expectations regarding implementation and enforcement. Contract review sessions offer an opportunity to explain in simple language the intent of contract clauses, to use case illustrations to explain sections of the contract, and to review procedures that need to be instituted or changed. However, management should not explain contract terms to union membership.

In addition to reviewing the contract, police administrators should ensure that timely steps are taken to implement the terms of the contract. Moreover, contract administration and future negotiations can be aided by encouraging supervisors to maintain accurate records of grievances and of contract provisions that seem unclear, costly, or unduly restrictive.

A major aspect of contract administration is the handling of grievances. Most contracts provide for a grievance procedure relating to the interpretation and application of the terms of the contract. In addition to the procedure outlined in the accord, many public employers have specialized procedures, including civil service appeal procedures allowing employees to appeal allegedly arbitrary and unfair actions.

The handling of grievances is a major service provided by an employee organization. Most unions strive to have binding arbitration as the final step in the grievance procedure. For this reason it is advisable to restrict the negotiated procedure to the interpretation and application of the contract. A broader definition could result in third parties making decisions affecting major management policies.

Suggested steps in processing employee grievances

1. Listen—take notes as necessary.

2. Ask questions; get employee's version of events.

3. Get additional facts from other sources. Verify statements.

4. Check records. Keep all past records.

5. Analyze alternatives.

6. Decide who has authority to act.

7. Make decision.

8. Explain decision.

9. Follow up on decision.

Source: International City Management Association, *Effective Supervisory Practices* (Washington, D.C.: International City Management Association, 1978), p. 148.

Most grievance procedures consist of from three to five steps, including a review by the first line supervisor, the division head, the department head, and a top management official. Some jurisdictions have established grievance committees consisting of management, union, and neutral members. Usually there is a requirement that grievances be put into writing if not resolved at the first step. Employees usually have the right to be represented by a person of their choosing at all steps of the procedure. Careful definition of channels to be followed and definite and reasonable time limits for each step will ensure prompt consideration and adjustment of grievances. Police supervisors should maintain records of all oral and written grievances. A backlog of unconsidered and unresolved grievances creates serious personnel problems.

The skillful handling of complaints by supervisors in the early stages is essential. Contract administration is improved when supervisors receive proper training in grievance handling, techniques of supervision, and counseling. Many grievances result from supervisor antagonism, ridicule, open criticism, lack of consistent and equitable enforcement of rules, failure to comply with contract terms, and poor communications.

Where binding arbitration is the final step for the grievance procedure, clear instructions should be given to the arbitrator regarding the scope of his or her authority and regarding the timetable for submitting a decision. Considerable care should be exercised in preparing the case for arbitration since grievance arbitration can be time-consuming, costly, and divisive. In administering contracts, supervisors need to be cautioned about informal agreements and about allowing modifications and exceptions to personnel rules and contract clauses. These can become past practices which may be used against management in grievance cases and negotiations. Some jurisdictions have found that the joint training of supervisors and union representatives in communication and human relations skills can be a means of improving the level of contract administration.

Impasse resolution   Since not all negotiations end in agreement, it is necessary to develop procedures for resolving impasses. The most common procedures include mediation, fact-finding, and arbitration.

The purpose of mediation is to reopen communications between the parties. The impartial mediator, through informal discussions, helps parties isolate disputed issues and explore areas of settlement. Mediation is voluntary, and the mediator has no authority to impose agreement. Mediators are available from state agencies administering collective bargaining laws, the Federal Mediation and Conciliation Service, and state labor departments, usually at no cost to the parties.

Mediation is the most widely used technique for settling public sector disputes. One variation of mediation is mediation–fact-finding, in which the mediator assumes the role of a fact-finder if mediation efforts are unsuccessful. Another approach is med–arb, where after a period of mediation the mediator becomes the arbitrator of unresolved issues.

In fact-finding an individual or a panel holds hearings in order to identify major issues in the dispute, review the positions of the parties, identify the factual differences, and issue a report with or without recommendations. The recommendations are not binding but usually after a period of time are made public. The publication of the findings tends to put pressure on the parties to settle.

A criticism of fact-finding is that bargaining stops with the appointment of the fact-finder, and on occasion both sides will fail to negotiate in good faith and will depend instead on the recommendations of the fact-finder. Fact-finding is time-consuming and can be costly as well. It is important for public employers engaging in fact-finding to utilize experienced staff to prepare well-documented cases.

Arbitration involves a single arbitrator or a tripartite panel holding hearings on a dispute and issuing a decision. Arbitration may be compulsory or voluntary. Compulsory arbitration may be mandated by state statute or local ordinance and is initiated automatically at a particular stage of the impasse. Voluntary arbitration is initiated upon agreement of the parties.

Arbitration may be binding or advisory. Under binding arbitration the parties must comply with the arbitrator's decision. Advisory arbitration, which is similar to fact-finding, does not require that the parties comply. Reference is often made to interest and rights arbitration. Interest arbitration is the resolution of disputes over new contract terms, while rights or grievance arbitration is resolution of disputes that surface during the term of the contract.

Public managers participating in arbitration proceedings must carefully select an arbitrator and establish guidelines for the arbitrator to follow. Lists of arbitrators are maintained by the American Arbitration Association and the Federal Mediation and Conciliation Service. Before one selects an arbitrator, information should be obtained on previous decisions rendered by the person. Many state statutes establish guidelines for the arbitrator and require the arbitrator to consider the bargaining history, comparable wages and benefits, the public interest, the jurisdiction's ability to pay, and increases in the cost of living. It is advisable to use an experienced individual in preparing and presenting the public employer's case, since very often the proceedings are formal and require the introduction of evidence and the examination of witnesses. Arbitration costs, which may be high, are usually shared by the parties.

Another form of arbitration is final offer arbitration, wherein the arbitrator must choose between the union's and the employer's final packages or must make a selection on an issue-by-issue basis. A virtue of final offer arbitration is that it forces the parties to be more reasonable and realistic.

There is no consensus about the merits of arbitration. Critics contend that it curbs good faith bargaining, is costly and time-consuming, and is no guarantee against strikes. Many public officials complain that the arbitrator is not accountable to the electorate and has no responsibility for implementing awards. Arbitration awards have been criticized on grounds that they upset budget projections, force adjustments of service priorities, and affect assignment and retention of personnel.[25] Arbitration awards may be excessive in cost and may impose serious financial burdens on the municipality and its citizens, especially if the award was made without consideration of the jurisdiction's ability to finance the award. Proponents of arbitration point to its value as a substitute for the strike in the area of public safety.

Labor and management officials are groping for other ways to avoid disruptions stemming from impasses. Binding arbitration, the law in at least twelve states, forces both sides to agree to terms decided on by a third party after negotiations have reached a stalemate. Unions generally feel that binding arbitration results in an equitable settlement, usually somewhere between the last offers by the local government and the workers. Management opposes the concept, asserting that it erodes administrative powers. Political figures believe it guts their executive powers and decreases local control.

On occasion one side (usually labor) may call for a public vote on pay hikes after talks have stalemated. While relatively rare, a referendum of this sort will probably do little more than emotionalize issues and force each side into costly, unnecessary, and perhaps divisive public campaigns.

A similar impasse resolution technique of dubious merit is an ordinance (or worse yet, a charter amendment) that would tie pay hikes for police employees to the average pay of similar employees in nearby localities. This would clearly destroy local control over rates of pay and benefits.

Strikes

In spite of impasse resolution measures, public employees sometimes strike or engage in some other form of work interruption. For example, in 1979 police officers in Birmingham, Alabama; Cincinnati; Hawaii; New Orleans; Salt Lake City; and Santa Barbara County, Burbank, Santa Monica, and Los Angeles County, California, staged some sort of job action ranging from strikes to a sick-out or blue flu.

Why employees strike Underlying reasons: [strikes, blue flu, and slowdowns] represent a failure on the part of both employees and employers to reach a mutual understanding through the collective bargaining process. Union members may strike when there is disagreement on only one issue. That one issue, almost always wages, may only be the precipitating factor. . . . In [one city] the police association went on strike ostensibly over a wage disagreement. Yet a post-strike analysis revealed that there was deep hostility between the younger, more educated, more professional rank and file and the older, more authoritan supervisors who did not allow the former input into decision and policy making. Underlying issues that most often lead to strikes are internal investigation procedures, poor grievance mechanisms, ticket quotas, and/or para-military departmental organization.

Source: This material is excerpted from Bergsman, *Police Unions*, p. 15.

Work interruptions actually are more a political than an economic battle, though economic considerations are what usually politicize the issue. The interruption is a battle to control public opinion, and timing is critical. The employee organization usually can control timing and therefore has an advantage over management. Management isn't helpless, but it must understand the forces at work and, through effective media releases and a defensible posture, appeal to public opinion at the decisive moment.

While citizens recognize the right of government workers to belong to unions, there is an increasingly strong public sense that police officers should not be permitted to strike. This mood was detected in a 1978 Louis Harris poll that asked a representative public sample, "Do you feel that policemen have the right to strike, or not?" Well over 50 percent of the respondents said no. The results of the survey, as well as responses to the same opinion question asked by Louis Harris in three earlier years, are set out in the accompanying table.[26]

Responses to question of whether policemen have the right to strike.

Response	1974 (%)	1975 (%)	1976 (%)	1978 (%)
Have right	47	47	44	41
Don't have right	46	47	49	56
Not sure	7	6	7	3

Police strikes generally are prohibited by statute, court decision, or government policy. Moreover, the courts have held that some classes of public employees have no constitutional right to strike and that government can condition employment on a promise not to withhold labor collectively. Even in states permitting nonessential employees a limited right to strike, there generally is provision for requesting the courts to enjoin a strike if it endangers the health, safety, and welfare of the public.

Strike prohibitions by no means have precluded strikes. In fact, in 1978 there were forty-two work stoppages by police in U.S. cities and states. In all, 5,843 employees were involved. The forty-two stoppages lasted an average of 4.3 days per stoppage.[27] This was a considerable increase over 1974, when the U.S. Bureau of Labor Statistics reported that 1,500 officers engaged in eleven strikes, and 1973, when 600 officers participated in five work stoppages.

Police employee organizations utilize a number of methods other than the strike to underscore their demands. Forms of work interruption include blue flu or sick calls, mass resignations, slowdowns, speedups, working by the book, refusal to wear uniforms, and reporting patrol cars with flat tires or other problems. During slowdowns there may be picketing by friends, relatives, and officers from other jurisdictions. Other techniques may include preventing trucks from making deliveries in cities, sit-in demonstrations at municipal buildings, and mass media campaigns, including leafleteering. The major reasons for strikes and other forms of work interruptions include disputes over wages, benefits, union recognition and security, job security, and working conditions.

Some police employee organizations have joined with other municipal employee groups to gain a more widespread base for an interruption. New York City's 42,000 uniformed employees (police, fire fighters, sanitation workers, and corrections officers) formed an impressive collective bargaining coalition in the summer of 1980. The city's transit and housing police also participated. Uniformed employees citywide in Mobile, Alabama, used the same tactic at about the same time; after an eleven-day strike they settled for amnesty and a 15 percent annual pay increase.

Police unions have not been reluctant to participate in the political process to achieve their goals. They have supported and opposed candidates for office, lobbied for local and state legislation, initiated recall elections and referendums, and blacklisted and censured public officials.

Many state laws provide penalties for public employees who strike. These include fines, jail sentences, loss of pay, dismissal, loss of right to pay raises and tenure, withdrawal of union recognition, and removal of the right to dues deduction. Public employers confronted with strikes have usually sought court injunctions. Another approach has been to file unfair labor practice charges. Experience has shown that when fines or other penalties are imposed they rarely are implemented because of an amnesty agreement negotiated as part of the settlement. Hence, the prospect of jail terms and fines is not a proven deterrent, as in Mobile.

In the past few years, attitudes among public employers regarding strikes have shifted. Some officials believe that strikes are acceptable in preference to exorbitant wage demands and compulsory or binding arbitration. Accordingly, many public employers have mobilized to withstand a strike rather than meet the demands of employee organizations. They have found that with proper planning and with mutual aid pacts it is possible to continue to provide services during a police strike.

Strike contingency plans

A strike contingency plan is essential to provide police service during a work stoppage or other job action, and it may even reduce the possibility of a strike. Police supervisors must participate in the preparation of strike contingency plans, since the department relies on them so heavily in the event of a disruption. The basic components of a strike contingency plan include an operational plan, a security plan, a communications plan, legal and personnel policies, and poststrike procedures.

A strike contingency plan should identify supervisors and other employees who will remain on the job in the event of a strike, as well as others who might be able to provide assistance. It should also identify essential services that must be provided and those that could be extended only in emergencies or discontinued altogether. The operational plan should include provisions for an emergency headquarters and its security and for obtaining necessary supplies and services during the strike. It also should include training sessions to prepare management employees for strike duties and arrangements for backup communication systems.

A security plan is especially important when dealing with police strikes. Arrangements should be made to protect police and other municipal facilities and equipment, to obtain gasoline and vehicle repair service if governmental services are unavailable, and to provide for the security of working personnel. Contact must be made with county and state police officials as well as police departments in surrounding municipalities to work out mutual aid arrangements. The prospective role of the National Guard also should be spelled out. Procedures are needed for handling violence, vandalism, and harassment of and threats to residents and nonparticipating employees, along with bomb threats and the sabotage of governmental facilities and equipment.

In handling media communications during a strike, it is preferable to assign the responsibility to a single individual or office. Extensive use should be made of news conferences and releases and information sheets prepared and distributed by the employer. A rumor center and telephone message equipment can be effective methods of keeping citizens informed.

Prior to a strike, police administrators need to identify personnel policies that will be applied to both nonstriking and striking employees. Arrangements are usually made for nonstriking personnel to work twelve-hour shifts, with all leaves canceled. A determination should be made as to pay and benefits for the working employees. Policies covering the employer's position relating to pay, vacation time, leaves of absence, worker's compensation and health insurance, sick leave, holidays, tuition reimbursement, and other benefits as applied to striking employees are needed. The carrying of guns by striking officers is another problem requiring attention.

Police supervisors need to develop plans for handling all forms of work interruptions. In the case of blue flu, for example, arrangements should be made to require medical examinations for employees reporting sick.

After the strike, police administrators and supervisors need a procedure for recalling employees to work. They must be able to supply information relating to penalties for striking employees, the cost of the strike, and when full service will be restored. Decisions relating to disciplining striking employees must be made. Perhaps most important, measures must be taken to clear out the residue of ill will, dissension, and bitterness between the ranks and those who did not participate. The administration must make clear that it will tolerate no reprisals by either side after a strike. Police supervisors should be trained to deal with these problems, emphasizing the need for reason and rebuilding.

Conclusion

The personnel function encompasses the recruitment, training, promotion, and discipline of employees in the police organization. The chief of police is responsible for setting the tone of the agency and assuring that the personnel functions are carried out efficiently and equitably. Of primary importance in personnel administration are sound position classification and pay plans and an awareness of equal employment opportunity guidelines.

In recent years public employee unions have attracted large numbers of police personnel, and administrators must be prepared to engage in collective bargaining and to respond in case of job actions. Although in many respects collective bargaining can be a traumatic experience for police administrators, it may result in better communication with employees, improvements in personnel management, a reduced level of conflict with employees, and improved departmental performance and service. Police unionization makes it incumbent on police administrators to become acquainted with all phases of collective bargaining, to improve the level of personnel management, to expand training opportunities for police supervisors, and to develop overall labor relations policies and programs directed at building a constructive labor–management relationship.

1 This chapter draws heavily on two chapters in: Bernard L. Garmire, ed., *Local Government Police Management* (Washington, D.C.: International City Management Association, 1977): William M. Mooney and Gerald W. Shanahan, "Personnel Management," pp. 285–309: and John Matzer, Jr., "Labor–Management Practices," pp. 310–33.

2 There are several authoritative texts on law enforcement personnel management. One of particular utility is: Paul B. Weston and P. K. Fraley, *Police Personnel Management* (Englewood Cliffs, N.J.: Prentice-Hall, Inc., 1980).

3 For a selected bibliography, see: U.S., Department of Justice, National Institute of Justice, *Affirmative Action Equal Employment Opportunity in the Criminal Justice System* (Washington, D.C.: Government Printing Office, 1980).

4 National Advisory Commission on Criminal Justice Standards and Goals, *Police [Report on Po-*

lice] (Washington, D.C.: Government Printing Office, 1973), p. 369.

5 *Sanchez* v. *Standard Brands, Inc.,* 431 F.2d 455 (5th Cir. 1970).

6 401 U.S. 424, 431 (1971).

7 422 U.S. 405, 431 (1975).

8 The U.S. Supreme Court decision of *Washington* v. *Davis,* 44 Law Week 4789 (7 June 1976) has caused some confusion relative to the burden of proof question. It should be noted that *Washington* v. *Davis* was concerned solely with a constitutional standard, with the Court holding, "We have never held that the constitutional standard for adjudicating claims of invidious racial discrimination is identical to the standards applicable under Title VII." The Court further held that "the rigorous statutory standards of Title VII involve a more probing judicial review of, and less deference to, the seemingly reasonable act of administrators and executives than is appropriate under the Constitu-

tion." In this light, the above-stated formula still appears to be operative.

9 The federal courts have utilized two sources as a basis for affirmative relief: the equal protection clause of the Fourteenth Amendment, U.S. Constitution; and Title VII, 1964 Civil Rights Act, which has been interpreted as authorizing a federal court upon finding an unlawful practice to order such affirmative action as the court deems appropriate to "make whole the appellant."

10 National Civil Service League, *Models for Affirmative Action* (Washington, D.C.: National Civil Service League, 1973), p. vi.

11 U.S., Department of Justice, *Equal Employment Opportunity Program Development Manual* (Washington, D.C.: Government Printing Office, 1973).

12 National Institute of Law Enforcement and Criminal Justice, *General Recruitment Strategies for Criminal Justice Agencies* (Washington, D.C.: Government Printing Office, 1979).

13 President's Commission on Law Enforcement and Administration of Justice, *The Challenge of Crime in a Free Society* (Washington, D.C.: Government Printing Office, 1967), p. 123. For a far more detailed explanation of the rationale on which the commission's stance was based, see: President's Commission on Law Enforcement and Administration of Justice, *Task Force Report: The Police* (Washington, D.C.: Government Printing Office, 1967), pp. 142–43 and 216–20.

14 President's Commission on Law Enforcement and Administration of Justice, *Task Force Report: The Police,* p. 140.

15 Harry W. More, Jr., *Effective Police Administration* (San Jose, Calif.: Justice Systems Development, Inc., 1975), p. 46.

16 U.S., Department of Commerce and Department of Labor, *Labor-Management Relations in State and Local Governments: 1978,* State and Local Government Special Studies, no. 95 (Washington, D.C.: Government Printing Office, 1980), p. 6.

17 For a more complete, yet concise, description of the history of police employee organizations, see: Tim Bornstein, "Police Unions: Dispelling the Ghost of 1919," *Police Magazine* 1, no. 4 (September 1978): 25–34.

18 Joseph D. Smith, "Police Unions: An Historical Perspective of Causes and Organizations," *The Police Chief,* November 1975, p. 24.

19 Ilene Bergsman, *Police Unions,* Management Information Service Reports, vol. 8 no. 3 (Washington, D.C.: International City Management Association, March 1976), p. 2.

20 M. W. Aussieker, Jr., *Police Collective Bargaining,* Public Employee Relations Library, no. 18 (Chicago: International Personnel Management Association, 1969), p. 2.

21 Ibid., p. 12.

22 John C. Meyer, Jr., "Both Sides Now: Police Opinions of the National Police Union," *The Police Chief,* April 1972, p. 68.

23 John H. Burpo, "The Policeman's Bill of Rights," *The Police Chief,* September 1972, p. 22.

24 American Bar Association Project on Standards for Criminal Justice, *Standards Relating to the Urban Police Function* (Chicago: American Bar Association, 1974), p. 12.

25 Hollis B. Bach, "They Call It Black Jack," *Personnel Letter* (Chicago: International Personnel Management Association), no. 281, December 1975, p. 8.

26 Louis Harris, "The Harris Survey," *The Chicago Tribune,* 30 November 1978, p. 2.

27 U.S., Department of Commerce and Department of Labor, *Labor-Management Relations in State and Local Governments: 1978,* p. 5.

14 Internal controls

The chief of police has the ultimate and irrevocable responsibility for the performance of all the tasks and for the control of all the affairs in the police organization within established policies, guidelines, and procedures. This responsibility provides the basic reason for developing inspection and control as formalized processes of management.

A major goal of the chief of police is to achieve departmental effectiveness and efficiency on the basis of voluntary action. However, failure to achieve this goal may be the result of many factors—ignorance, poor judgment, improper training, lack of equipment and materiel, or deliberate acts of noncompliance, among others. The chief of police must be aware of the levels of compliance within the department in order to take action when needed. The chief can gain this awareness through inspection processes.

This chapter gives primary attention to inspection as the process of obtaining facts relating to persons, things, actions, and conditions by means of observation, inquiry, examination, and analysis. The findings then will show the conditions, if any, that need to be changed and the actions, if any, that need to be taken. Two types of inspection—line and staff—are described. Much more attention is devoted to staff inspection because, being "outside" the organizational unit that is under review, it has the advantage of an independent and objective appraisal.

Other sections of this chapter deal with report review as a means of control, the use of outside audits for appraisal of performance, and the internal control process, including the highly sensitive questions of citizen complaints against the police, citizen review boards, and internal disciplinary processes and the questions of appeals and of union influence.

Two types of inspection may be utilized in all but the smallest of departments. The first, conducted by those in direct command, is called line or authoritative inspection. It is carried out by those who have the authority to act or to demand the immediate action of subordinates.

The second type is staff inspection. It is conducted by persons who have no direct control or authority over the subject of the inspection and who normally report only inspection results and take no corrective action.

Line inspection

Line inspections are made by those who have the authority to require immediate corrective action. These inspections seek to exercise control through the processes of observation and review by those directly responsible for a particular function and activity.

Responsibility

Line inspection, regardless of department size, is always a command responsibility. In the small departments the line inspection process is almost the total responsibility of the chief of police. As the size of the department increases, the responsibility for line inspection is usually shifted to the sergeant, lieutenant, or captain, who has direct command authority to act or to require the immediate response of subordinates. Authoritative inspections are clearly command and supervisory responsibilities throughout every police department. Authoritative inspections are carried out by the command of auxiliary and staff elements units as well as line elements of a department.

The chief or commander may delegate authority to a subordinate to carry out a certain function of the inspection. However, the chief can never delegate ultimate responsibility. The inspection process assists the chief to fulfill his continuing responsibility. More delegation of authority in no way diminishes responsibility. Therefore, the one who issues an order must assure that it has been carried out. This appraisal is made through inspection.

The weaknesses of line inspection

Line inspection is a valuable management tool and often will be the main control mechanism in smaller departments; however, it has its limitations. The inherent weaknesses of this process are a natural protectiveness of one's own operation and personnel from criticism, a lack of objectivity and broad perspective of total departmental responsibility, and, all too often, an unawareness of what proper process should be followed. Consequently, it generally is a more fallible control device than the staff inspection.

Line inspections may be self-serving in simple and somewhat harmless ways, such as tolerance by a supervisor of minimal or halfhearted work efforts on the part of subordinates, sloppy uniforms, casual treatment of citizen complaints, and careless handling of materiel. This complacency or tolerance of apparent nonserious conduct may result in the department failing to achieve its objectives and goals.

The incompetent supervisor can conceal this ineptness by inadequate inspection and also by not fully disclosing the poor performance and conditions of his command. He can even falsify inspection reports to downgrade inadequacies. Even more serious than the inept commander is the case of a commander who falsifies reports and records, accepts gifts and gratuities, and may even participate in criminal acts, yet is responsible for his own line inspection.

It is for these and other reasons that the second type of inspection to be discussed—staff inspection—is a most important control device.

Staff inspection

Staff inspections are conducted for the purpose of providing answers to questions of vital importance to the chief of police; for he has the responsibility for assuring himself and his superiors of compliance of all personnel in the organization with established policies, procedures, and regulations. Another function of the staff inspection process should be to assist operating line units to plan their own inspections. Staff should review formal reports of line inspections to note deficiencies and to help design their own inspection. As an outside auditor bases the audit on the quality of internal auditing and control, so should a staff inspector base his or her inspection on the quality of the line inspection program of the unit he or she intends to inspect.

Just as the exercise of authority is not restricted to, but of necessity permeates, the entire organization, so inspection and quality control are not performed exclusively by any one person but are departmental processes. Staff inspection is a process outside the normal lines of authority and responsibility. It is a detailed observation and analysis of department elements, procedures, and practices designed to inform the chief of police about their performance and effectiveness.

Those involved in the staff inspection process are neither responsible to the commander of the units being inspected nor responsible for the performance of their personnel. Thus, they can conduct their inspections generally with more objectivity and without fear of consequences, working within carefully prescribed guidelines and under general circumstances that are conducive to effective work.

Quality control: the objective of staff inspection

Everything relative to the police department must be subject to control; consequently, inspection should be conducted to include everything in the department and all of its operations. Conditions, situations, and actions that contribute to the success or failure of police operations are exposed by the inspection of administration, personnel, operations, facilities, and equipment.

The broad objectives of staff inspection

The broad objectives of staff inspection have been stated as follows:

1. Are established policies, procedures, and regulations being carried out to the letter and in the spirit for which they were designed?
2. Are these policies, procedures, and regulations adequate to attain the desired goals of the department?
3. Are the resources at the department's disposal, both personnel and materiel, being utilized to the fullest extent?
4. Are the resources adequate to carry out the mission of the department?
5. Does there or could there exist any deficiency in personnel integrity, training, morale, supervision, or policy which should be corrected or improved?[1]

The staff inspection unit should conduct an in-depth inspection at least once a year of all the major elements of the department, such as patrol, auxiliary services, criminal investigation, traffic, and major staff units.

Responsibility for staff inspection

It is recommended that staff inspection always be under the general supervision of the chief. If the department is large enough to have a staff inspection unit, its commander should report directly to the chief of police.

There are general guides which have been proposed for the establishment of a full-time staff inspection unit. Owing to diversity of operations in police agencies of 400 or more employees, a full-time unit outside the operational chain of command can be justified. The police department ranging from 75 to 400 employees may not need a full-time staff inspection unit, but the chief can provide for the function by assigning responsibility to an employee who performs related duties. In agencies with less than 75 employees, the chief of police can use the same criteria as those used in larger departments for temporarily assigning a staff inspection team.[2]

Guide for a staff inspection

Responsibility for staff inspections should be determined by the chief of police and, as mentioned above, should always be under the general supervision of the chief of police. The officer in charge of staff inspection must be a person in whom the chief has complete confidence, and should be mature and experienced and have a high degree of objectivity and good judgment. He or she should thoroughly understand the chief's operating philosophy and should possess the type of personality which will permit him or her to suggest and persuade rather than command. More important than this officer's intellectual ability, even, is his or her morality, which must be impeccable.

For all major inspections the chief inspector (bureau commander/team commanding officer) should have a team to assist him or her. Often, as many as four aides may be necessary on major inspections (e.g., of one of the patrol divisions). A typical makeup of the team for such an inspection would be a member of the planning and research unit, a lieutenant or sergeant assigned to the investigations division, a member of the youth and women's unit, and a records supervisor. Also attached to the team for liaison purposes could be a lieutenant of the patrol division. The aides are temporarily relieved from normal duties for the duration of the inspection and are assigned to the supervision of the chief inspector.

Members of the team should possess the following minimum qualifications:

1. They should have knowledge of, and reasonable experience with, most of the operational problems
2. They should have a completely objective and constructive attitude toward the element being inspected
3. They should have earned the respect of the personnel in the element which is under inspection
4. They should have a high degree of personal and intellectual integrity.

Under most conditions, the element to be inspected should have advance notice of at least one week. A surprise visit by an inspection team is, in reality, only a surprise for a few hours. Those things that a unit can "spruce up" with advance notice are in reality only superficial and should be maintained in top condition with adequate line inspection. A staff inspection, by its very nature, must concern itself with things that are for the most part a matter of record. With even the most rudimentary recording system, alterations are not easily possible.

At about the time notice is given of a major inspection (which is usually done on an annual basis), the chief inspector and the team should meet with the chief of police. At this time, the chief should brief the team on the objectives and process of the inspection. This will establish the chief's support and interest in the inspection program and will help assure its success.

At the beginning of the actual inspection, the chief inspector and the team should meet with the command staff of the element to be inspected. This will set the stage for a cooperative situation.

No matter how large or small the inspection team is or how complex or simple the element to be inspected is, a checklist of items to be covered must be used. It is held that while a good checklist will not ensure a thorough inspection, one carried on without it will surely fall short of its goal.

A patrol division inspection might well include the following elements:

1. Personnel: authorized complement (all ranks); work schedules; vacation schedules; reliefs; special assignments; absences; attrition; morale; integrity; appearance; reports and records; job knowledge (all ranks)
2. Operations: supervision; assignments; utilization of automotive equipment; roll calls; enforcement indices; selectivity of enforcement; utilization of the special operations unit; radio communications policy compliance; accident frequency, police vehicles; citizen interviews
3. Administrative: staff meetings; leadership; supervision; housekeeping; cooperation, other agencies; discipline; personnel development.

The great detail in which an element is examined dictates that considerable time must be spent in the actual inspection. Inspecting the patrol division would normally require a minimum of five days or more.

Following the several days of field work, the team commanding officer should consolidate all the comments of the team into an understandable and useful documentation of the condition of the inspected element. It should be stressed again that a staff inspection is intended to be constructive, and the report, therefore, must be prepared accordingly. It is always important to give sufficient credit to the element and its personnel in any area in which its operation is particularly good. It should be borne in mind that recommended improvements should be made directly to the element's commanding officer in every case where it is within his or her authority to effect the change.

With the exception of commendatory notations, the contents of the report should be kept strictly within the confidence of the chief of police, the inspecting officer, and the element commanding officer. By so doing, the possibility of embarrassment of the commanding officer in the eyes of his or her personnel is prevented. In addition to this, some of the recommendations which might contain highly desirable features are kept from the eyes of personnel until they can be effected. Thus, should budgetary or other considerations dictate the abandonment of the proposed change, no one has great cause for disappointment.

At thirty-, sixty-, and ninety-day intervals after the report has been presented the inspecting officer should be directed to report on the progress of implementation of recommended improvements. It is in this area that the greatest value can be achieved from the inspections service.

Among the chief's responsibilities are (1) locating problems, (2) planning solutions, and (3) putting the latter into action. Inspection, properly directed and honestly used, is a principal administrative tool which will, in fact, locate the problems and assist in developing their solutions. Participation in team inspections by commanding and other officers, temporarily relieved from regular duty, is a significant personnel development process.

There are similarities and differences between line and staff inspections. Both processes are designed to achieve the same objectives and goals and both are valuable tools of management. Both have limitations and shortcomings and, as a consequence, neither can be completely successful without the use of the other to assure good management control.

Report review as a control

Report review is an inspection process whose importance should not be minimized. The report review function may be approached in different ways, depending on the size of the department. The report review process is one of the most basic approaches for analyzing the quality of police service, and it can be carried out by a supervisor, a commander, civilian clerical personnel, or a specialized report review officer.

The report review also includes a random field checking of victims and complaints to establish the accuracy and thoroughness of handling of calls for service which require written reports. This process helps eliminate the problem of inaccurate, misleading reports as well as those instances where serious crime is downgraded or there is a failure to record criminal offenses.

Generally, recommendations are as follows:

1. For departments of all sizes, watch commanders (or desk officers) should perform a general report review function.
2. For all departments, the chief or station commander should conduct a random inspection of routine reports and make a thorough check of all reports of unusual incidents.
3. For all departments, one or more report review officers (according to need) should be assigned to central records for the purpose of spot checking reports for accuracy and completeness (random interviewing of complaints, victims, and witnesses).

4. In departments with specialized functions (criminal investigations, juvenile, vice, etc.), the supervisor should review reports turned in by subordinates. Also, a report review unit in central records should be staffed by specialists who will review reports in their areas of expertise.

Report review procedures will provide for (1) timely and (2) prompt reports which have (3) correct and (4) complete information. The concept of report review is a valuable management tool for internal control.[3]

The outside audit

The management of a police department covers a wide range of services—those provided externally and those necessary for day-to-day internal operation. This diversity requires the officers and administrators of a department to have various degrees of knowledge and skills. However, it is impractical to expect or believe all skills and knowledge necessary can be found internally, even in the largest of departments, nor is it practical to expect that the requisite training or education can be obtained. As a consequence, it should be recognized that outside expertise may be needed and should be requested in areas of the inspectional control process.

The consulting organization

It may be necessary from time to time—and quite often it is desirable—to employ the services of a professional organization which specializes in police management and operations, for example, such organizations as the International Association of Chiefs of Police (IACP), Public Administration Service (PAS), and similar recognized organizations. The use of outside consultants for a "consultant inspection" of a department is particularly valuable when it is recognized that the department has stagnated, has not kept pace with the times, or is in need of major organizational changes. It is also useful when an incumbent chief who has held that position for a long period of time steps down and a new chief takes command. This will provide the new chief and the local government administration an opportunity for a complete management audit or inventory and establish a base from which the new chief of police can clearly show his own management abilities.

Outside help and increased effectiveness

A department should be in a position to identify the types of outside professional skills and knowledge that are likely to be needed for management control. For example, the department may need to call upon other governmental units or a professional accounting firm to audit (inspect) its records of fiscal management. By using such outside fiscal inspection the financial integrity and budgetary soundness of the department's operation can be subject to good management control.

The request of professional assistance in areas of the behavioral sciences and education for inspecting current recruitment, promotion, and training programs, for example, may lend itself well to the inspectional control process. Only the magnitude of need and economic resources would be major considerations limiting this type of outside auditing.

There are many other services, involving business, trade, and craft personnel as well as the professions of medicine and architecture, which may be used on an as-needed basis. This list is a small example of the vast and diverse expertise from which the police chief may request and receive assistance in management control.

The external audit, as conducted by
the St. Louis, Missouri, police department

Since February of 1960 the St. Louis Police Department Bureau of Governmental Research Inspections, with an independent, nonprofit, nonpolitical organization, has jointly conducted crime audits for the purpose of checking the accuracy of crime reporting by the department. The basic purpose of the audit is to determine whether officers are reporting to the department all crimes reported to them by citizens, and whether the reports prepared by the officers are accurate. The audit is conducted on a citywide basis and is made about twice a year.

The outside agency, upon completing the field audit, submits its report to the department and describes the audit by size and type of incidents selected and the results of the audit in terms of the percentage of incidents found to have been improperly reported. It also directs the attention of the department to problem areas revealed by the crime audit—for example, improper valuation of larcenies or improper use of codes in reporting the disposition of a call for police service. Oftentimes, the outside agency offers specific recommendations on how to improve the department's reporting practices.

It is readily apparent that an "external audit" of this type is invaluable to the department in seeking to constantly improve its reporting of crime, and this is best accomplished by having it conducted by an independent organization.

The department also employs the services of a public accounting firm which conducts audits on an annual basis of the Budget and Finance Division and includes payroll procedures, purchasing procedures, supply and equipment inventories, etc.

While these types of external audits are being conducted, an Internal Audit Unit within the Bureau of Inspections has been established for the purpose of making audits on a continuing basis throughout the year and thereby strengthening safeguards over department assets and compliance with the applicable procedures.

With the implementation of the Internal Audit Unit on the first of December, 1975, and with the professional assistance of the public accounting firm, an audit was made of the department's Motor Service Division regarding the inventory and control of automotive equipment and supplies. This audit led to a completely revised system of controls and accounting of its entire operation and will be audited on a continuing basis.

The function of the Internal Audit Unit is a sophisticated one, and it serves as a "watchdog" operation. Since it is a relatively new arm of the inspectional operations of the Bureau of Inspections, its full impact within the auditing processes may not be realized until some time in the future.

The internal control process:
an overview of internal affairs

A specialized function of internal control is that of internal investigations, which generally deals with violation of personnel integrity. This inspectional control is generally referred to as internal affairs. The formation of an internal affairs unit or internal investigations unit should not detract from a commanding officer's responsibility, as the investigation and handling of breaches of integrity or conduct still remain the commanding officer's. However, there are situations which arise that should be investigated by a staff rather than the concerned line unit. There is a clear-cut need for staff-conducted internal affairs investigations, as often the line supervisor or command officer may lack time or expertise to handle these sensitive investigations; but more compelling is the fact that supervisors or commanders may be involved with their subordinates in cases of misconduct, dishonesty, or other breaches of integrity. They are also vulnerable to charges of covering up for self-protection. For these reasons the general public and public officials usually place more confidence in externally controlled investigations.

Establishing an internal affairs unit

The same general guides which were discussed for establishment of staff inspection units can be applied to the establishment of an internal affairs unit. With the diversity of operations in police agencies of 400 or more employees, a full-time unit outside the operational chain of command can be justified. The police department ranging from 75 to 400 employees may not need a full-time internal affairs unit, but the chief can provide for the function by assigning responsibility to an employee who performs related duties.

In agencies of less than 75 employees the chief can temporarily assign an internal affairs investigation, as would be done in a large department, or the chief himself, in the case of very small agencies, might have to conduct the investigation.

Organizationally, the unit or internal affairs investigator should report directly to the chief or a high ranking officer (such as an assistant chief). However, in all situations the unit or investigator must have ready access to the chief.

Unit objectives

The primary objectives of internal affairs investigations are:

Protection of the public. The public has the right to expect efficient, fair, and impartial law enforcement. Therefore, any misconduct by department personnel must be detected, thoroughly investigated and properly adjudicated to assure the maintenance of these qualities.

Protection of the department. The department is often evaluated and judged by the conduct of individual members. It is imperative that the entire organization not be subjected to public censure because of misconduct by a few of its personnel. When an informed public knows that its police department honestly and fairly investigates and adjudicates all allegations of misconduct against its members, this public will be less likely to feel any need to raise a cry of indignation over alleged incidents of misconduct.

Protection of the employee. Employees must be protected against false allegations of misconduct. This can only be accomplished through a consistently thorough investigative process.

Removal of unfit personnel. Personnel who engage in serious acts of misconduct, or who have demonstrated they are unfit for law enforcement work. must be removed for the protection of the public, the department, and the department employees.

Correction of procedural problems. The department is constantly seeking to improve its efficiency and the efficiency of its personnel. Occasionally, personnel investigations disclose faulty procedures that would otherwise have gone undetected. These procedures can then be improved or corrected.[4]

The unit should be responsible for receiving and recording complaints against personnel, for initiating and completing investigations and reporting them to the chief, and for presenting cases to internal disciplinary boards, personnel boards, civil service commissions, or the prosecutor and reporting on case disposition. The reputation of a department may well rest on adequate internal affairs investigations. The chief cannot fail to overlook the importance of this process of internal control. To do so may jeopardize department efficiency, depress morale, undermine public confidence, and destroy interagency confidence and cooperation. Formation of an internal affairs unit requires careful explanation within the department and widespread publicity. It should be emphasized that the unit is a fact-finding body and is as interested in establishing innocence as in establishing guilt.

Selection of personnel

Personnel selected to staff an internal affairs unit is an important factor in the success or failure of the unit. The factors considered essential in the selection process are outlined as follows:

1. All personnel serving in the internal affairs unit must be volunteers. (Because of the nature and sensitivity of the work involved in the internal affairs unit it is believed that it would be unwise and unfair to assign someone to this unit who did not have a genuine desire to serve in it.)
2. The personnel who serve in this unit must have demonstrated in their previous performance that they possess a high degree of investigative skills.
3. The individuals selected to serve in this unit must have excellent reputations both among their peers and supervisors in terms of integrity and overall performance as police officers. Since members of the unit would be called upon to investigate their fellow officers it is deemed important that they themselves not have been found guilty of serious official misconduct in the past. A failure to consider such a factor could later result in charges of administrative hypocrisy.
4. All internal affairs unit personnel must become totally familiar with those state statutes, department policies, and procedures which are related to internal investigations.
5. Members of the internal affairs unit must be proficient in interviewing and interrogation techniques.
6. A knowledge and understanding of the local communities' ethnic minorities is absolutely essential since, for a variety of social, political, and economic reasons, many citizen complaints will initiate from this group of citizens.[5]

It is generally accepted practice to periodically rotate any personnel assigned to any inspectional unit. The assignment of an investigator to an internal affairs unit should not exceed two years in length. This rotation process will assure the advent of new blood and new ideas; it will foster a career development process and allow more employee participation. These factors will also tend to create more understanding and respect for the internal affairs inspection process, which will lessen the alienation of investigators from peers and supervisors.

Citizen complaint processing

The public should be encouraged to report matters of misconduct to the unit, openly and with identification. (Appendix D of this book contains a Guide for Complaint Initiation, Receipt, and Investigation.)

The investigation of anonymous complaints is always a controversial issue. In some states, such as Maryland, Rhode Island, and Florida, it is almost precluded by the Policeman's Bill of Rights laws[6] and in other jurisdictions by union contracts and department policy. However, it is a very valid investigative process to investigate anonymous tips (complaints) about criminal activity, whether the subject of the complaint is a citizen or police officer.

The police chief who fails to investigate these complaints will find his reputation and that of the department in jeopardy. Even if the law precludes formal acceptance of anonymous or unsigned complaints, the department should be able to classify and analyze the number, kinds, and location of complaints, and what actions are being complained about, by whom, and how often.

Complaints from citizens provide the chief of police with valuable information about the operation of the department and with yet another basis for evaluating the performance of the department and identifying potential and existing problems, which then may be corrected. They can also provide information for training programs, inspection programs, and new procedures and policy statements.

The chief of police should guard against departmental procedure that hinders or discourages the citizen from making complaints. Without these complaints, problems may become worse or no action may be taken at all. Thus, the public can provide valuable assistance to the chief in securing internal discipline and reducing officer misconduct.

However, even the best designed complaint procedures can fail because of conditions that discourage the citizen from making complaints. Such conditions are: fear of personal reprisal or harassment, complex and cumbersome complaint filing procedures, and, often, the threat of criminal prosecution for making a false report.

A positive attitude on the part of the chief of police toward a complaint reception process which provides internal discipline will produce officer support and participation that will help curtail employee misconduct. A negative attitude on the part of the chief of police will usually be reflected by the department's officers as well.

The investigation of citizen complaints of alleged officer misconduct must be based on sound investigation processes and formal well-written rules, policies, and procedures. All persons involved in the complaint process must feel that they have been dealt with fairly and have been given an opportunity to participate in the process leading to the final decision of the chief of police.

Citizen review approach

The National Advisory Commission on Criminal Justice Standards and Goals in its report *Police* covers this subject quite thoroughly.[7] The need for review and investigation units has been well documented and advocated by many state and national commissions. The National Advisory Commissions on Civil Disorders and the Causes and Prevention of Violence, and the President's Commission on Law Enforcement and Administration of Justice, have documented the performance of external review boards (usually citizen review boards), and have concluded these external review boards have been of little value and limited success. These commissions have proposed alternatives to external review boards, such as an ombudsman; however, there has been little experience of or documentation on the use of an ombudsman plan.

The civil review board in Washington, D.C., voluntarily ceased operation, giving lack of supportive staff as its reason. The New York City police department had a similar citizen review process, which was voted out of existence after much campaigning against it by the department's officers. However, the New York department hit upon a compromise between the citizen complaint review board and one made up entirely of members of the sworn force. New York City has a Civilian Complaint Review Board made up of civilian members of the police department.

The police chief has the responsibility to run his department, and he cannot abdicate his authority and accountability. The outside review board can provide advice for change. Generally, there has been lack of support from the police, local government, and the general public for the outside review board.

When a citizen makes a complaint against the police it should not be thought of as a confrontation between two people but simply as criticism of the delivery of police services which did not meet the complaining citizen's expectations. Should the chief fail to constantly review and check his department's handling of citizen complaints, he will find that others are ready to do it.

There presently exist many legal external review agencies within government structures, such as the FBI, federal and state court systems, citizen police commissions, the executive administrator of the jurisdiction, the legislative councils, and various prosecutor or district attorney offices. Yet rarely are these legal agencies ever called upon to exercise their review powers over the police.

When the New York City police department was investigated by the Knapp Commission, it was concluded that the governor should simply use the constitutional authority to appoint a special deputy attorney general to investigate police misconduct. The best and most logical solution to reviewing police activities is to use the many governmental agencies already empowered for that purpose.

Disciplinary processes

The police service has traditionally demanded high standards of discipline from its employees. Discipline and accountability are essential to any police department, and only through a well disciplined police department can the integrity of the agency be maintained. Discipline, with both positive and negative sanctions, is vital to the preservation of effective performance and employee morale. Yet the department should not lose sight of the fact that the vast majority of its employees are dedicated and productive and are not cause for concern to the police supervisor and commander. Too great a preoccupation with a few employees who are disciplinary problems may be detrimental to the majority. However, the police department cannot afford to overlook the possibility of employee misconduct and must be in a position to deal with it in a positive and fair manner.

Authority to discipline

The chief of police will find his authority to discipline limited by city ordinances, state statutes, civil service regulations, or policies of the municipal personnel office. Generally, he or his supervisory and command officers will always have the right to reprimand and the authority to immediately suspend a subordinate under specified conditions to prevent further trouble or incidents between the time a particular incident took place and the time a more formal investigation and administrative procedure will be held. A formal hearing in connection with every minor charge of dereliction of duty or officer misconduct is a waste of time and is unnecessary. The immediate commanding officer should have the authority to summarily handle minor matters of misconduct that do not involve corruption, criminal conduct, or insubordination. Prolonged formal procedures and paperwork simply delay the disposition of minor cases and breed contempt for the disciplinary process.

Punishments

The types of punishments usually imposed by police departments against officers who are found guilty of misconduct are (1) reprimand, (2) suspension without pay, (3) forfeiture of vacation or regularly scheduled days off, and (4) dismissal from the department. Cash fines as a form of punishment are seldom used and transfers in assignments are a questionable disciplinary sanction.

Allowing officers who are faced with charges to voluntarily resign or take their retirement is not viewed as an objectionable practice. There is a particularly difficult question to weigh when an officer with many years of service and pension eligibility is dismissed before the pension is secure. Cases do occur where an officer is found guilty of misconduct which would not constitute a crime if committed by a citizen (such as accepting a gratuity of minor proportions) and is dismissed from the department and in consequence loses his right to a pension.

The dilemma of such a situation is recognized. Some police chiefs believe the punishment for a corrupt or dishonest act should be severe and that the possible loss of pension rights is a deterrent to police dishonesty. However, in many cases this punishment can be quite excessive in view of the fact that an officer may have had twenty or thirty years of honest service before committing one transgression.

Employee participation

The chief of police should develop a disciplinary program in which the subordinate employee is encouraged to participate. Employees can participate by drafting rules of conduct, investigating complaints, and sitting in as active members of trial board hearings.

The chief of police who has allowed employees to participate has found that it has strengthened the internal discipline system by increasing employee support and employee observance of the discipline procedures, rules, and policies. The department tends to become self-disciplining, and voluntary compliance is easier to achieve.

Even in very small departments, employee sense of participation is very important. Various boards and committees have been developed as departments recognize the need for greater employee participation.

Some departments have established disciplinary boards comprised solely of top command personnel; others include personnel of various ranks. Some are made up of personnel who may serve over a long period of time, and other boards change personnel frequently. Some boards are formal and legalistic in concept and operation; others tend to be informal and to avoid as much as possible the advocate system.

The internal disciplinary administrative process

Departmental disciplinary board hearings are administrative hearings and should be treated as such. Legal standards such as due process and the degree of proof, hearsay evidence, and exclusionary rules should not be made a part of the administrative hearing. Such hearings serve to seek out the truth: they are more effective without adherence to the technicalities that are present in criminal cases.

Police officers often raise the objection of double jeopardy in administrative board hearings. This view is evident when it is possible for a police employee to receive discipline through an administrative hearing process, to be prosecuted in criminal court, to be investigated about a civil rights violation by the Justice Department, and to be sued in civil court all as the result of the same incident.

Police chiefs should see that their employees are given all the personal safeguards afforded any civilian member of the community. Procedures must be fair and reasonable. Only arbitrary and capricious actions in administrative hearings should be subject to review by a court, and chiefs should never make efforts to protect officers from the consequences of their misconduct.

Boards of inquiry and recommendation

A viable approach may result from having an internal board of inquiry and recommendation hear all cases of a certain level of seriousness. The board would inquire into all cases presented to it by commanding officers, whether initiated by them, their subordinate supervisors, or citizens. Cases developed by an internal affairs unit investigation would be presented to it as well, unless they were of such a serious criminal nature that they were taken directly to the prosecutor for possible criminal action. Even then the chief might wish to convince the board to review the circumstances of the case in order to prevent or correct similar situations.

It would normally be appropriate in many departments to have five members serve on such a board. It is also appropriate to have the chief or the chief's representative serve as an impartial chairman to start the hearings, but this chairman should not participate in the deliberations. Board members should be from all ranks and should serve on a rotating basis. No board member should be of a rank lower than the officer against whom a case is to be presented, but there should be at least one officer of equal rank.

Local circumstances will dictate the degree of formality of the board's operation. The accused officer, though required to be present, may not be required to discuss his or her case. It should be remembered that the board should be advisory in nature and should not be able to independently initiate any direct sanction against the officer appearing before it.

The board should privately and objectively review each case with no other person present, including the chief, and arrive at a decision as to whether the officer did what the allegations charged. If the board decides the officer did what was charged, it should review the officer's personnel file prior to making its recommendation to the chief. The chief is free to accept, modify, or reject the board's recommendation, as their recommendation is only advisory in nature.

Only decisions by the chief of police which are adverse to the officer should be placed in his or her personnel file. In fairness to all officers, the chief must allow them to review their own individual files and the chief should provide a periodic purging of nonessential and out-of-date material from their files.

Internal disciplinary process objectives

A properly established internal disciplinary process should achieve the following objectives:

1. The creation of an esprit de corps based on impartial and just handling of disciplinary cases: the officers will know they are under close supervision but will be held responsible for proper conduct under a program that provides them adequate safeguards
2. A sense of participation on the part of members of the department in the maintenance of discipline
3. A recognition on the part of citizens of the community that their complaints are properly considered, that adequate investigation is made, and that appropriate action will follow the inquiry whether it results in disciplining the officer or clearing the officer of the alleged offense
4. A knowledge on the part of the chief of police and other city officials that there is a well-disciplined agency in which the interests of its members and the public alike are well served.

Appeals from the disciplinary process

To assure equity and to avoid arbitrary and capricious disciplinary actions, a right to appeal must be clearly established and procedures implemented. Normally there are two areas of appeal—internal and external. The internal appeal normally goes through the chain of command to the chief of police, unless the chief is the person prescribing discipline. Except under local statutory prohibitions, there should be a procedure for external appeals. Generally, administrative action taken against an employee while on probation and that taken against an employee who committed a minor infraction are excluded from the appeal process. All other disciplinary actions should be subject to appeal through the administrative process from the chief of police, through the chief administrator's office, to the governing body.

Some cases cannot be or are not resolved during this appeal process, and the appeal must then be made to the courts. Steps should be taken to minimize the incidence of appeals. The most important of these is a sound internal disciplinary process, which has been discussed earlier. Others include: carefully stated policy; carefully written, reasonable rules and regulations; extensive training in personnel management of supervisory and commanding officers; and continued demonstrated administrative integrity.

Unions and internal controls

The police have traditionally had the reputation for extreme group cohesiveness, and this cohesiveness has led easily to officer social and benevolent associations. Some of these organizations have continued through the years pursuing their original purpose and structure. Others have changed to collective bargaining agents.

National labor unions have also organized police departments with mixed success. The subject of police unionization, including its historical background, is discussed in considerable detail in Chapter 13 of this book.

The recent upsurge of unionism has had considerable impact on the chief of police and his department's administration. The police administrator, however, can be very effective in providing an environment which will minimize rash employee union activity. One of the important considerations is fair discipline: this can minimize serious labor trouble.

Discipline and unions

In the police service one of the principal facets of human relationships is discipline.

Negative means have traditionally been used by police departments to invoke discipline; the reprimand, suspension without pay, demotion, and dismissal are universally used. These sanctions are usually imposed by or through the chief of police, who has the authority and responsibility to carry out the disciplinary process.

The advent of the police employee association, with its political and financial strength, has made it feasible and practical to contest disciplinary action; the employee organization assumes this obligation (the investigation and review of discipline) as part of its membership benefits.[8]

The union and the discipline appeal process

Most police departments have some sort of formal grievance or appeal procedure, even without union organization within the department. This fact shows that employee appeal processes and employee organizations are not dependent on each other. However, the presence of a union or employee organization may affect the appeal process. Of significance is the employee organization's role in representing the officer in the appeal process and its attempt to change the procedure.

This chapter has discussed the need for the appeal process and hearing to be formalized but not formal legal trials with all the technical rules of evidence and adversary relationship. Police organizations often provide legal counsel for members at appeal hearings, and are often obligated to defend their members. Other provisions of union contracts often provide that a union steward must be present with an offending officer during the reprimand by the supervisor.

The problem of authority to discipline can be a greater factor affecting morale with supervisors and commanders than with the chief of police, as the former experience the greater difficulty in making the department operate on a day-to-day basis under some union contracts.

Unions and other organizations have created some improvements in discipline, but primarily their influence has been in procedures and the impartial application in an autocratic or paternalistic police department.

Once an employee organization is formed, it will represent its members. The police administrator who faces this fact realistically can ordinarily develop a reasonable accommodation with its representatives. This can be accomplished through open-handed dealing, through an attitude of acceptance—not through fear or deceit, and not by trying to get rid of the organization. The chief of police must remember that the organization's members are still his officers. Prompt and fair procedures are essential to good discipline, officer morale, and public respect and confidence in the police department.

Conclusion

Control methods have been the subject of most of this chapter. Internal control processes have been discussed under line and staff inspection services, under report review as a staff internal control mechanism, and under the outside audit and internal affairs and disciplinary processes. Considerable attention has also been given to citizen complaint processing and citizen review boards. The subject of police misconduct and police discipline are also dealt with, as they have a great effect on the integrity of the department and the public's conception of police integrity. The chapter concludes with a discussion of appeals and the question of unions and internal controls. Both are policy issues on which answers cannot be provided in simplistic terms.

The chief of police must have at his command personnel and materiel in order to attempt to reduce crime, maintain public order, respond to calls for police service, and perform those other tasks determined by local government. A deficiency in either of these resources can limit the chief's ability to move the department effectively toward its objectives. To achieve the department's objectives, the chief of police is responsible for establishing and maintaining a system of inspections to obtain the information he needs to direct and control the police department.

Control has been emphasized as a key management process. Although the ultimate responsibility for inspection and control rests with the chief of police, it should be carried out continually at all levels of supervision and command. The police supervisor and commander should understand both its purpose and complexities, and should utilize the control process to its maximum.

1 Eastman Middleton Associates, Inc., *Police Services in Norman, Oklahoma, 1974: A Status Report and Plans for Improvement* (Kent, Ohio: Eastman Middleton Associates, Inc., 1974), p. 27.

2 National Advisory Commission on Criminal Justice Standards and Goals, *Police* [*Report on Police*] (Washington, D.C.: Government Printing Office, 1973), p. 58.

3 Harry Diamond, "Quality Control in Police Work," *The Police Chief,* February 1968, pp. 43–44.

4 "Excerpts from Manual of the Department of Public Safety, Lakewood, Colorado," unpublished reference material, 1974. (Mimeographed.)

5 Robert L. Smith and Leonard Territo, "The Internal Affairs Unit: The Policeman's Friend or Foe," *The Police Chief,* July 1976, p. 68.

6 See Chapter 13 of this book for a discussion of the Policeman's Bill of Rights and the provisions that are included.

7 National Advisory Commission on Criminal Justice Standards and Goals, *Police,* p. 472.

8 Hervey A. Juris, "Implications of Police Unionism," *Law and Society Review* 6 (November 1971): 28.

Research and planning

Police chief executives routinely make decisions that affect the quality of life of every member of the community, but adequate resources to do the job are seldom available. The complex and demanding job of managing a police agency is receiving increased attention because of the critical importance of the police, the high cost of policing, and the need for cost-effective government services. The complexity of police service and the demands to do more with less require improved decision making. Successful police managers can no longer make decisions on a day-to-day basis, paying little attention to agency goals, unit costs, priorities, and the evaluation of police efforts.

Today, police chiefs must consider short- and long-range goals, effectively utilize resources to meet those goals, and evaluate programs to determine the extent to which goals are being achieved. The wall-to-wall cop theory is giving way to the practice of productivity. The effective use of resources—especially human resources—is a growing concern.

Making effective decisions does not in itself make a good manager, but a good manager is an effective decision maker. Police chiefs can improve their decisions through effective planning. In fact, planning is perhaps the most important of all management functions. Police agencies with a commitment to effective planning will generally have clear directives and policy guidelines, clear goals and objectives to help channel work efforts, standards of performance to improve effectiveness, timely response to problems, and effective utilization of personnel.

Research and planning units appeared in police organization charts in a few agencies during the 1930s and 1940s. By 1962 research and planning units were reported in at least twenty police agencies.[1] Early planning units systematically and intelligently studied problems and recommended solutions. They wrote manuals, developed procedures, evaluated equipment, analyzed crime and traffic data, and conducted deployment studies. In 1967, of the hundreds of pages making up *Task Force Report: The Police* by the President's Commission on Law Enforcement and Administration of Justice, only two pages dealt with police planning,[2] and most of that centered on operational rather than administrative planning. Through the 1960s relatively few police agencies organized for planning.

Today, planning units are becoming increasingly common in large police agencies. Smaller agencies that cannot support a full-time planner are assigning part-time planning duties to agency personnel or, in a few cases, are contracting for planning work. The chiefs in very small agencies are doing more planning themselves.

The presence of a box on an organization chart does not mean that an agency has made a commitment to plan. The fact is that very few police agencies have made such a commitment.[3] Too often, planning has one or more of the following weaknesses: (1) it is attempted without needed research; (2) it is decentralized to the field and to administrative units with little or no coordination; (3) agency planning is attempted in the office of the mayor or other local government administrator; (4) agency planners work on short-range tactical plans for subordinate units and ignore long-range plans; (5) the planning unit is under-staffed or the staff are poorly qualified and trained; or (6) the staff do research but are not allowed to plan.

Although the *concept* of planning has been with policing since the nineteenth century, the *practice* of police planning is only now coming to the fore.[4] Police planning is evolving from an auxiliary function to a critically important task of the police chief executive. It involves gathering information, setting goals, and seeking solutions to help the chief make effective decisions.

This chapter deals with planning vis-à-vis administrative decision making. Unlike most writings on police planning, it is not directed toward operational planning, although the principles of planning for effective decision making have application to every level of the police agency.

The chapter opens with a discussion of information needed for decision making, followed by discussions of research; planning; written policies, procedures, and rules; budgeting; grant planning; and tools for planning and control.

Organizing a planning unit and assembling a planning staff are discussed as important factors in a successful planning effort. Concluding paragraphs challenge police managers to improve their decision making through planning.

Information for decision making

Decisions are influenced by the experience, values, and knowledge a manager brings to a position, and by information received on the job. The importance of a decision and the knowledge possessed by the decision maker govern the amount and kind of information sought. Important decisions are those that involve a serious commitment, cannot be easily changed, or carry a heavy human impact. In such cases, a police chief must be able to make the right decision.

Good decision making often takes time. Police chiefs are not expected to make important decisions on a moment's notice, nor are they expected to delay difficult decisions unreasonably. A police chief who is asked to make a decision or is presented a problem should consider whether a decision really is needed and who should make it. If an important decision is to be made, the decision maker should determine what information is needed and whose opinions should be sought. When a decision is imminent, the chief should consider how it will be communicated and implemented, what results are expected, and what evaluation should take place. A competent chief will not devote five dollars' worth of time to a million-dollar decision, nor will a busy chief devote a thousand dollars' worth of time to a five-dollar decision.

Former Los Angeles Police Chief William H. Parker emphasized reliance on facts and research in decision making when he stated:

If decisions are made without proper analysis of facts, or without regard for standard practices developed as the result of research, the chances are that they will be mediocre decisions—and it is the accumulation of mediocre decisions that produces mediocrity in police administration.[5]

Some information flows naturally to the police chief executive, but it seldom includes all the information necessary for administrative decision making. Police chiefs thus may rely too much on personal interaction with subordinates, obtaining "guesstimates" and opinions rather than facts. Divergent opinions can be of great value in decision making, but without necessary data and research, administrative decisions are likely to be mediocre.

Management information systems

A management information system (MIS) is "an organized method of providing each manager with all the data and only those data which he needs for [a] decision, when he needs them, and in a form which aids his understanding and stimulates his action."[6] In short, an MIS is the systematic collection, indexing, and storage of data and records.[7]

The gathering of data and statistics is costly—even prohibitive—when done manually, but that is rapidly changing. Advances in computer technology have made it possible to process large amounts of information at reasonable cost. In government agencies, automated information systems are used in many jurisdictions, assisting elected officials and criminal justice practitioners. There is a continuing national effort to develop computerized criminal history files. Information on wanted felons and identification numbers of stolen weapons, vehicles, and serial-numbered properties are placed in the National Crime Information Center and in local files. The Offender Based Transaction System is progressing on the state level. In some cases, advances have been made in using computers and analysts to assist in manpower allocation, crime reporting and analysis, dispatching, and budgeting. The subject is explored further in Chapter 16 of the present volume.

Despite these advances, government agencies for the most part lag far behind business and industry. The police use data in computers to manage individual cases, but use of computerized data for police agency management is in its infancy. Police managers continue to manage intuitively in many agencies because data necessary to set and monitor objectives, formulate strategy, decide on alternatives, and evaluate results are no better than they were twenty years ago. The limited amount of information is possibly the greatest obstacle to intermediate and long-range planning.[8]

Uses of an MIS

An MIS can serve several major purposes in a police agency:

1. Records storage and retrieval
2. Budget information and control
3. Decision making (see Figure A)
4. Data processing
5. Program information
6. Internal communications
7. Interdepartmental coordination.[9]

Types of decisions	Decision-making techniques	
	Traditional	Modern

Programmed
Routine, repetitive decisions
(organization develops specific
processes for handling them)
	1. Habit
	2. Clerical routine:
	    standard operating procedures
	3. Organization structure:
	    common expectations, a system of
	    subgoals, well-defined informational
	    channels
		1. Operations research:
		    mathematical analysis,
		    models, computer simulation
		2. Electronic data processing

Nonprogrammed
One-shot, ill-structured,
novel policy decisions
(handled by general problem-
solving processes)
	1. Judgment, intuition, and
	    creativity
	2. Rules of thumb
	3. Selection and training of executives
		Heuristic problem-solving
		technique applied to:
		a) training human decision
		    makers
		b) constructing heuristic
		    computer program

A. Traditional and modern techniques of decision making.

Objective	Hardware	Information system base	Measurement	Mechanism for control	Types of personnel	Organization
Reporting	Mechanical accounting and office machines	Systemized record keeping	Expenditures ($) cost	Line-item budget	Clerks	Department
Measuring	EDP equipment	Work measurement (efficiency)	Expenditures in terms of output (cost≠unit)	Program budget	Cost accountants	Centralized record keeping and analyses
Planning	Computers (2nd generation)	Effectiveness	Production and results related to costs (productivity)	PPBS	Systems analysis, operations research specialists	Program is basis of organization structure
Predicting and controlling	Large time-shared computers plus advanced communications devices and peripheral equipment	Goals and objectives reporting	Event-oriented system with exception impact keyed to modeling and correlation (trend analysis, effectiveness measures)	Inter-governmental analysis to individual analysis	Economists, mathematicians, behavioral scientists	New inter-governmental organizations (data centered)

B. Management information system development and application.

Figure B shows how an MIS can be used to meet several agency objectives.

The kinds of information needed for decision making may vary among police agencies, but they should have some bearing on organizational goals and objectives. Data on reported crimes, traffic accidents, arrests, property recovered, and clearance rates are basic and accessible in every agency. Such data are necessary for effective deployment of personnel. Also, less traditional data may be helpful: victimization studies, utilization of personnel and other resources, and costs of services performed.

The first step in building a management information system is to create a desire for management information. In the past some chiefs were reluctant to centralize information about their agencies for fear that it would fall into the hands of legislators or others and subject the agency to outside scrutiny. Yet the value of having accessible information has outweighed such fears.

In all cases the cost of obtaining data must be weighed against their usefulness. In this era of exploding information, too many data, data in a form not easily used by executives, or untimely data are often worse than no data at all.

Research

Management, perhaps the most inexact of all social sciences, has only recently begun developing a body of knowledge. It is no wonder that research in the field of police work is in its infancy.

Research in police agencies was of little significance prior to the organization of research and planning units in the 1930s and 1940s. In the early 1950s research by police personnel was supplemented by university research. In the

1960s private firms began research in a few specialized police related fields. As federal grant funds became available to police agencies, individuals, firms, and outside agencies descended on police managers in great numbers to engage in research projects. In addition, funding agencies began their own research in criminal justice and law enforcement administration. The resulting body of knowledge has greatly expanded during the past decade, contributing to police professionalism.

In-house research

Research conducted by agency employees is often directed to local problems or potential problems. Such defensive research is, by necessity, unplanned and spontaneous. Unfortunately, some planning units are so busy conducting defensive research that they are unable to develop new policing practices and techniques. Every agency needs some defensive research, but it should not dominate the efforts of the planning staff.

Not all research is—or should be—exhaustive. Pragmatically, the effort should match the importance of the problem. Projects typically assigned to in-house staff take from one to four weeks, although research projects can range in length from minutes to years. (A project that requires one hour or less to determine whether burglaries in a sector of the city have increased during the past month is research as defined here. *Research* includes gathering and analyzing information to investigate and discover facts and report findings. It is not *planning* unless it projects into the future and proposes solutions.)

In-house research can include analysis of paperwork to improve procedures, salary surveys of police agencies to compare wages, comparison of police strength per unit of population among police agencies, or development of deployment formulas to distribute personnel on the basis of need.

Research conducted by agency personnel need not be limited to short surveys. Some agencies have had success in assigning in-depth, aggressive research to agency planners. The chief in one large police agency was concerned about the increasing number of accidental shootings involving his officers. He ordered a study of officer-involved shootings to identify patterns in these incidents. Research revealed that after vehicular pursuits, while taking a suspect into custody, pursuing officers would unholster their revolvers if the circumstances warranted and unconsciously pull the hammer back, cocking the revolver. That was consistent with single-action target practice taught at the police academy. Once the suspect was apprehended, the officer was confronted with the task of handcuffing the suspect while holding a cocked revolver following the excitement of a pursuit. While uncocking the gun, unless the finger was released from the trigger at the proper time, the firing pin could strike the bullet, causing a shot to discharge. Thus, there was a high incidence of accidental discharges at the termination of pursuits.

This study of the problem resulted in corrective action: modification of revolvers to prevent single-action capability, retraining of thousands of officers to fire double-action revolvers, clarification of shooting policy, and development of a written pursuit policy and procedure. In summary, the research pinpointed problem areas, and subsequent planning suggested alternatives to correct the problems.

In another agency the police chief learned that field officers traced the fourth copy of every citation written because the fourth copy was unreadable. Officers were tracing 200,000 citations a year, spending about five minutes for each. Police veterans indicated that this practice had been followed for more than a decade. The planning unit, assigned to make a systems study of the problem, found a way to delete the third copy, allowing the last copy to be legible without tracing. With a slight programming change, the records unit received a computer run of citations rather than receiving and filing the third copy, thereby saving clerical time. Further, printing costs were reduced and the equivalent of nine worker-years of officer time was saved.

In another example of aggressive in-house research, an officer assigned to the planning unit spent nearly a year gathering and analyzing everything in writing over the past fifty years that might reflect policy. His review of city council minutes, police commission files, police annual reports, letters, orders, memoranda, and personal interviews to seek out existing policy statements was a lengthy research task. Statements containing policy were reformatted, organized into a policy manual, adopted, and published for use by several thousand agency employees.

Outside research

Major research projects typically have been conducted by outside researchers with the cooperation of police practitioners. In the past decade there has been more significant law enforcement research than ever before, but the surface has barely been scratched. Whether research is pure or applied, technological or behavioral, operational or administrative, analytical or experimental, the police service should take a more aggressive role in promoting research. Projects initiated and managed by police practitioners, with the advice of scholars and specialists, will be better accepted than research conducted entirely outside. There are increasing numbers of talented, educated police managers who can oversee such research.

One important example of outside research, the Kansas City (Missouri) preventive patrol experiment, began in 1972 at a cost of $560,000 to test the effectiveness of routine preventive patrol on crime and citizen attitudes. Researchers found little value in routine preventive patrol, which involves undirected patrolling between calls for service. This experiment is described in detail in Chapter 7.

A study by the Rand Corporation analyzed questionnaires from 153 detective bureaus in large police agencies and visited twenty-five police departments to find out what detectives did during the investigative process. Included in the findings was a contention that most detective bureaus could be cut in half. Details of this study appear in Chapter 9.

Both these studies challenge traditional law enforcement methods and should stimulate further experimentation. However, neither has been widely accepted by the police. These projects and many additional research efforts, such as those identified in the Law Enforcement Assistance Administration (LEAA) Prescriptive Package series, should lead to improvements in the quality of police service.

While the U.S. police service enjoys a leadership position abroad, we can learn from research taking place in European countries. The Federal Bureau of Criminal Investigation in the Federal Republic of Germany, the Bundeskriminalamt, has made a heavy commitment to forensic science research. That agency is extensively involved in computerized analysis of voiceprints for personal identification, voice-activated video composites for suspect recognition, and computerized handwriting analysis. The Municipal Police Force of The Hague (Netherlands), an agency of 2,200 personnel, is experimenting, in cooperation with the University of Leiden, to bring policing and government closer to the citizens with the *social constable* and generalist *surveillance officer* concepts.

Sources of information

A skilled researcher will know sources of data on the subject being studied. Local libraries, universities, and state planning agencies are valuable sources of information and assistance. The Bureau of Justice Statistics of the U.S. Department of Justice, the International Association of Chiefs of Police, the Police Foundation, and the International City Management Association are among the organizations that have a wealth of resource materials available to assist researchers.

Too often, researchers conduct "armchair research" by limiting their inquiry to what has already been written rather than gaining information by inspections and interviews. A valuable source is the supervisory and command personnel within the agency and in other criminal justice agencies.

Although supervisory and command personnel are often knowledgeable, the people who actually do the work of the organization can provide insights that cannot be gained from the "brass." Patrol officers, clerks, detectives, technicians, and others can help identify agency problems and suggest solutions. Too often, they are never consulted. When management develops policies, procedures, and rules that affect people at the operational level without their input, such directives may not be practical.

Planning

Planning is perhaps the most basic of all management functions since it involves selecting from among alternative courses of action.[10] "Planning is the function by which managers determine (within the constraints of their role) what goals are to be accomplished and how and when they are to be reached."[11] While *research* involves gathering, analyzing, and reporting data, *planning* is projecting into the future those courses of action designed to reach agency goals. Not all planning is based on research; not all research results in a plan.

Agency goals and unit objectives

Comprehensive planning requires the identification of agency goals and the pursuit of those goals by the most effective means. Simply stated, goals are statements of purpose toward which effort is directed. Too often, agency goals are taken for granted and are not put in writing to guide agency employees and to inform the community. Police managers may believe goal statements are unnecessary, referring to the law as their goal. However, legislation rarely serves as an adequate statement of goals. Laws and ordinances creating police agencies and providing enforcement and regulatory power are seldom written to reflect the real goals of the agency, nor are they kept current.

Often distinctions are made between goals and objectives. For discussion here, goals are generalized statements. One of several agency goals may be "to facilitate the safe and expeditious movement of traffic and provide for public safety on the streets and roadways."

Objectives are more specific than goals, stating positions to be attained by divisions of an agency in quantifiable terms and within a given time frame. A traffic division may have an objective "to reduce the rate of accidents (per miles driven) by 15 percent by July 1, 1983." Further, the night traffic detail may have its own objective that supports the division objective: "To reduce DWI accidents by 25 percent by December 31, 1983." Objectives may be set at every level of the agency, establishing a hierarchy of objectives that work toward achievement of agency goals.

In an informal poll in a highway patrol agency, thirty officers and their supervisors were asked what they hoped to accomplish in performing their jobs. Replies included "assisting motorists," "investigating accidents," "supporting local law enforcement," "slowing down traffic," and "protecting property." No one mentioned saving lives or preventing accidents. When questioned further, none believed they could prevent accidents and most said they could do little to save lives. That agency had no written goals or objectives except for a two-word motto inculcated in them from their first day of training. The motto did not include the concept of protection or prevention.

The establishment of goals and objectives gives employees a sense of direction. It tells them what they are expected to accomplish. Efforts of all agency employees should be directed toward achieving agency goals and unit objectives. Planning is a rational approach to accomplishing those ends.

Cost-effectiveness

Business executives, who maximize profits to survive, have to consider costs and revenues in their decision making. Police executives' decisions are much more difficult than those in the private sector. They must consider public safety, fear of crime, and a host of other social factors. Their decisions are subject to public scrutiny and often affect, in one way or another, every member of the community. However, police executives paid only minor attention to costs until recently. Even today, few police chiefs know how much it costs their agency to respond to a call for service, investigate a traffic accident, or recover and release property. Some chiefs do not consider personnel costs because "officers are getting paid no matter what they do." Yet priorities are being set and decisions made with only casual consideration of costs. It is apparent that government must apply business practices to decision making, even when optimum solutions cannot be reduced to dollars or some other specific measure.

To determine effectiveness for decision making where profit and loss do not apply, the U.S. Department of Defense, under Robert McNamara, drew on the work of the Rand Corporation and considered a host of factors. The expenditure of billions of dollars was based on cost-effectiveness analysis. Police executives in many agencies are beginning to apply cost-effectiveness or cost–benefit analysis, as did the Department of Defense, to consider costs in their decision making. The resulting emphasis on productivity is changing modern police practices. Many jurisdictions screen calls for police service: officers do not respond to minor calls; detectives do not investigate certain burglaries in which the profile indicates that solution is unlikely; and paraprofessionals handle tasks that do not require the expertise or authority of officers. These changes are occurring because police executives are considering the relation of cost to benefits in their decision making. Chapter 6 further discusses the framework for productivity in police agencies.

Long-range planning

While all planning involves the selection of alternative courses of future action, long-range planning has an extended time dimension. Some managers incorrectly believe that long-range planning is planning for future decisions. Actually, long-range planning is planning for the future impact of *today's* decisions, incorporating long-term considerations into present decisions. It is making present decisions "with the best possible knowledge of their futurity."[12]

There is no arbitrary length of time that defines long-range planning. In a 1962 study, five years was the norm for long-range planning in business, while in 1973, 86 percent of firms having long-range plans used a time period of three to five years.[13] The oil and tree farming industries understand and practice long-range planning. They make billion-dollar decisions that take up to ninety-nine years to come to fruition.

Police agency planning beyond one or two years may be considered long-range planning. Three to five years may be a norm, but plans involving computerized dispatching and physical plant facilities are examples of plans that may extend beyond that period. Personnel matters, including career development and retirement, may require decisions that project twenty or thirty years into the future.

Resistance to long-range decision making Some police chiefs hesitate to make decisions that require long-term commitments because of the risk. It is true that decisions projecting far into the future carry greater risks than decisions that are short-lived. Long-range planning does not eliminate risk, but it permits the decision maker to choose among risk-taking courses of action. It permits decisions with long-term impact to be made responsibly. Without long-range planning, long-term decisions may have a greater chance of failure.

Decision makers may be reluctant to make long-range plans for fear of future changes. This reluctance should decrease if flexibility is built in. Flexible plans make change less costly and less dislocating, but they may require more complete planning or carry other costs. An illustration is the planning of a new police station. A permanent facility to meet today's needs would be the least expensive to build, but alterations would be very expensive should they be needed. A flexible facility would be more costly to build, but it could be easily and inexpensively altered. Police agencies that have changed from the three-watch to the team policing plan realize that alterations to the police station are required. In anticipation that change will occur, new police stations are being built with interior walls that are not load-bearing, permitting easier reorganization of space. In any long-range plan the cost of flexibility should be weighed against the need.

Environment for long-range planning In a police agency committed to planning, there seldom are enough planners to work on all the assigned projects. The immediate problems are the ones that get attention, and they are often at the crisis stage when assigned to the planning staff. For example, when the supply of a form used by field officers is running low and a revision is required, the planning staff may be assigned to do a systems analysis and paper flow study in time to revise the form, prepare instructions on its use, and get the master form to the printer to permit distribution before the old supply is exhausted. Such reactive planning has caused planning units in some agencies to be called "job shops," "crisis units," or "firemen." In that environment there is little opportunity for long-range planning.

To ensure long-range planning some agencies separate it from their current planning. Some large agencies have separate sections to perform each function. Smaller agencies may assign one person to day-to-day planning while another works on long-range projects. In agencies too small for specialization, chiefs should ensure that some of their own efforts, or the efforts of others, are spent on long-range projects.

Completed staff work

Completed staff work, a concept developed by the military, is defined as "the study of a situation and the statement of recommended action in such a form as to allow the administrator to make a prompt and effective decision."[14] In essence, completed staff work consists of working out all details of a problem, consulting with other staff members, but not consulting with the chief or presenting the chief anything short of the completed project. The completed staff report should be in such form that the chief need only accept or reject the action recommended. Appended to the report should be documents that will be necessary to implement changes.

Planners should be well grounded in the concept of completed staff work. However, few police planners have the experience and knowledge to practice the concept as defined. In addition, some police chiefs, to minimize wasted effort on the part of planners, want greater involvement in planning and, therefore, do not support the concept in its entirety. Where planners lack expertise and/or chiefs want greater involvement, modifications in the concept can be adopted. One suggested modification is not to include derivative plans in an original study until an executive decision is made. A discussion of derivative plans that will be needed for each decision made may suffice. Once a decision is made, derivative plans to implement that decision can be made.

O. W. Wilson and Roy McLaren provide for six steps into which the concept of completed staff work can be distilled and reported.

1. A brief statement of the problem or topic.
2. Elaboration of the problem or topic, containing factual information and detailed explanations, if necessary.
3. Analysis of alternative courses of action and their consequences, taking into account the comments of other staff members and supervisors affected by the work.
4. Final conclusion and recommended action, ready for approval or disapproval.
5. Enabling directives or general orders, ready for signature.
6. Appendix items, if appropriate, consisting of detailed reports having a bearing on the work but not essential to the conclusion; detailed statements of concurrences or objections of staff; exhibits; and examples or mock-ups.[15]

Steps to decision making

It is clear that the key to successful decision making is planning, and the success of any plan is to approach the task systematically and in steps. Many "steps to planning" have been written for use by managers and planners in government, business, and industry, and some of those have been directed specifically toward police planning. Some of the steps for completed staff work are identical with planning steps.

The decision making steps listed below provide for a systems approach to problem solving and encompass the entire range of management functions. Because of the complexity of decision making, it is not possible to place all managerial activities performed at each step neatly into the standard management functions.

All the managerial activities of decision making can be summarized into seven major steps: (1) prepare statement of objectives; (2) consider assumptions; (3) collect and analyze data; (4) identify and evaluate alternatives; (5) make a decision; (6) implement the plan; (7) evaluate the results. Major decision making should include each step to ensure a systems approach to the problem.

Prepare statement of objectives   The first step is to refine the problem into a clear, concise statement of objective. Included in this step should be an interview of the person who initiated the project to ensure that the objective is understood. The initiator may be the police chief, a staff inspector, a division head, or the planning unit. A statement of objective must be formulated, reduced to writing, and agreed upon by the initiator. Once the need for a plan is recognized and the statement of objective is formulated and approved, it should be referred to frequently during the course of the study to keep the planners on track.

Consider assumptions   The second step in decision making is to consider assumptions. Police chiefs and other decision makers often begin with a belief to be tested against reality. The belief may be called an assumption, a premise, a hypothesis, or an opinion. It may be tested in a number of ways, one of which is to seek opinions of police officers, managers, other police chiefs, persons from the private sector, politicians, or others.

Collect and analyze data   The third step is to gather and analyze relevant data. The earlier sections in this chapter on information for decision making and on research can provide some guidance to the planner. If little is known about a subject, the collection of facts will be critically important. In other cases decision makers may require no collection of data other than gathering opinions to test assumptions.

Identify and evaluate alternatives The fourth step in decision making is to search for alternative courses of action and evaluate them. One way to help develop alternatives is to promote discussion of the problem and the objectives. Disagreement can stimulate imagination, which in turn results in creative solutions. A police chief surrounded by ''yes men'' will not have many alternatives from which to choose. A chief who organizes dissent will develop creative alternative solutions and will probably be an effective decision maker.

Because costs are becoming increasingly critical, planners should estimate the cost of each alternative. As indicated earlier, costs should be considered in making the decision. Solutions that involve additional costs may require approval of the funding body.

The rational alternatives should be listed in descending order of priority with the best alternative recommended for approval. In making recommendations, the planning staff should consider the objective of the study, conflicting opinions, conclusions drawn from analysis of data, costs, risks, the impact on personnel, and the degree to which the plan is likely to be accepted. A written report in the form of completed staff work should be submitted to the police chief.

Make a decision The fifth step, the point at which a plan is adopted, is the core of planning. An effective decision is a commitment to action and a desire for results. Decisions that involve agency policy, a major commitment of resources, or a change affecting personnel from more than one division should be made by the police chief.

If a plan is complex or controversial, many chiefs schedule an oral briefing to permit the planners to discuss significant findings or tangential problems and to answer questions. Some planners tactfully present a *proposed* final report before the oral briefing so they can fine-tune the report later to reflect unanticipated management concerns.

Not all plans submitted to the police chief are ready for decision. Those that are not completed staff work may be returned to planners for completion, referred to others for additional input, or laid aside. Planners who seldom see their plans implemented may trace the fault to their own incomplete staff work.

Police chiefs who are uncertain about the recommended action of a staff study may want to evaluate acceptance by ''sending up a trial balloon,'' informing those who will be affected (sometimes indirectly) that the agency is considering a change. The feedback may affect the decision.

Implement the plan Step six, converting the decision into effective action, calls for further planning and communicating to see that the plan is carried out successfully. Effective plans have failed because planners believed their jobs ended when a decision was made. To ensure successful implementation, knowledgeable managers have directed planners to work with operations people to develop plans, and operations people to work with planners to implement plans.

In major planning efforts derivative plans are required to support the basic plan. Fiscal planning may require budget justifications. Personnel may need to be hired and trained. Equipment or buildings may have to be acquired. Changes in state law or local ordinance may have to be initiated. Once a basic plan is approved, turning derivative planning over completely to operational and support units may destroy it.

Acceptance of a plan is extremely valuable to its success, and it is best assured by involving users or people affected by the plan. However, the police have been slow to become involved in participative management, arguing that it weakens the traditional decision making role of managers and replaces it with participant control. Police managers, unlike their predecessors, are slowly adjusting by soliciting some user input before making final decisions on some sensitive issues. In the future, the more astute managerial decision makers "will tend to rely increasingly on greater participative influence, not only from subordinates, but also from the social groups and forces outside" the agency.[16] Employees and concerned citizens who have been left in a cloud of ignorance cannot be expected to support a new program.

Evaluate the results The seventh and last step, evaluating the results of the plan, is a determination of the extent to which the plan has succeeded in achieving an objective. Evaluation involves goal setting, work measurement, analysis of data, and comparison of planned with actual results. Evaluation is used to feed back information to the decision maker, who may modify plans if necessary.

Little attention was given to evaluation in the police field until the Law Enforcement Assistance Administration and other administrators of grant funds required evaluations of some grant-funded projects. During the 1970s some police agencies gained experience in goal setting and work measurement that enabled them to evaluate programs. However, this concept is in its infancy in this field.

The selection of an evaluator can be difficult. To satisfy grant requirements, planners or managers of programs often write evaluations of projects they have planned or managed. While they are in a position to know the strengths and weaknesses of a project from their own point of view, the evaluation may be distorted. An outside evaluator is usually considered more impartial than an agency employee, but often such a person is not knowledgeable about the agency and cannot learn enough in the limited time available to do a thorough evaluation. Some large agencies have resolved this dilemma by assigning agency employees not connected with the project and not under the command of the project director to evaluate the project. The expertise developed in this area can be applied to improving productivity within the agency. Finally, some state planning agencies have evaluators on their staffs to evaluate grant-funded projects for criminal justice agencies.

Written policies, procedures, and rules

The police in the United States exercise considerable discretion, and they receive little guidance in this exercise. As an arm of government, the police must interpret the goals and objectives of the governing authorities and attempt to implement them. If the head of the police agency is silent, others in the agency, even the basic police officer, may exercise their own discretion by setting their own policies. If there is no guidance from the chief of a hundred-person agency, there could be a hundred different policies. The head of every police agency has a responsibility to ensure that policy is formulated and is consistent with the intent of the governing authorities.

If policies are not written, they are often misinterpreted and easily forgotten. Therefore, policies should be reduced to writing and distributed to agency employees. The heads of police agencies are becoming increasingly aware of the need for written guidelines in the form of an agency manual.

Writing an agency manual is a planning function that often requires research. Some large police planning divisions have a manuals and orders unit and assign full-time personnel to prepare orders for the chief and to update the manual. Smaller agencies combine the issuance of directives with other planning duties.

Differences among policies, procedures, and rules

Before an agency undertakes to write a manual, there should be an understanding of what policies are and how they differ from procedures and rules. Policies are the philosophies of management and state the intent of management in broad, general terms. Policies tell departmental personnel how to think about performing their duties; thus they are "attitude forming." Policies tell what is important to the organization. They are guides to action. Every agency has policies that have been formulated over the years, but they are seldom reduced to writing and contained in one place. Policies may be found in letters, notices, position papers, council resolutions, and budget documents.

Policies are flexible in application and permit justifiable exception (justifiable to whoever is responsible for enforcing them). Rules, though, require strict conformance as stated and do not permit deviation. Rules govern behavior while policies guide judgments. With rules, the judgments are already made and conformance is required; thus they are "behavior forming." With policies, judgments are flexible, within broad boundaries, and a "violation" may or may not be deemed justified, depending on the circumstances surrounding the action. Policy alone implies room for discretion, initiative, and the development of judgment in deciding what ought to be done in specific situations. Policies are management's guides to making decisions that will keep the agency on a given course directed at realizing agency goals. Rules tell personnel exactly what to do or not to do.

Policy is subject to change any time a better guideline is discovered. Change can be effected simply by restating the policy and ensuring that concerned personnel are informed of the new policy. Rules are changed much more slowly, simply because it is more difficult to bring about changes in patterns of behavior.

The National Advisory Commission on Criminal Justice Standards and Goals differentiates policy from procedures and rules, stating:

Policy is different from rules and procedures. Policy should be stated in broad terms to guide employees. It sets limits of discretion. A policy statement deals with the principles and values that guide the performance of activities directed toward the achievement of agency objectives. A procedure is a way of proceeding—a routine—to achieve an objective. Rules significantly reduce or eliminate discretion by specifically stating what must and must not be done.[17]

The report clarifies the distinction by further stating:

The difference between policies, procedures, and rules might be illustrated in an agency's decision to identify the true level of crime. That decision would require an agency policy to report crime honestly. A number of procedures might then be established describing how reports are to be completed and approved. Finally, rules might be established to set limits on the conduct of personnel following these procedures. For example, a rule might require a written report each time a radio car is dispatched to a reported crime, whether a crime is found to have been committed or not.[18]

Attitudes toward writing policy

Police chiefs have been reluctant to have policy put in writing. Perhaps the reluctance comes from the advice of attorneys who have difficulty defending the agency or its officers if policy is in writing and subject to discovery. The police chief is torn between the decision to write policy and take the chance of having it used against the agency and the decision not to write policy and take the chance of a lack of uniformity and understanding among agency employees. Despite the risk of lawsuits and bad publicity, police chiefs are recognizing the need to write policy to guide agency employees in the performance of their duties. Written policy that is more stringent than the law itself, in such sensitive areas as the use of force, and specifically on when to shoot, is being implemented in many police agencies. Chiefs who issue policy in these areas realize

302 Local Government Police Management

that employees are less likely to use excessive force if they are guided by sound, written policy.

Some police agencies—for example, those of Los Angeles and Chicago—issue policy in a single document separate from procedures and rules. Most agencies that issue manuals combine policies, procedures, and rules when addressing a specific subject, thereby providing all guidelines for a given topic in one place. Unless each is properly labeled, flexible policy becomes mixed with inflexible rules and, thus, confuses the reader. Therefore, policies, procedures, and rules, if combined, should be clearly labeled.

Budgeting

Budgeting is both an administrative planning function and a control function. A budget expresses the fiscal plans of an agency and is widely used for managerial control of the use of resources. The quality of budget preparation in police agencies ranges from superb to dismal. Some police budgets are of textbook quality, using the most modern budgeting concepts. Others (with no exaggeration) have been prepared on the back of a matchbook cover while the police chief waits in council chambers to address the city council on the agency's fiscal needs.

A common shortcoming of police budget preparation is failure to provide the funding body with a well-planned, well-justified budget. Regardless of the funds anticipated for the police budget, the chief has an obligation to inform the funding body of the fiscal needs for achieving agency objectives. Often, politics prevents the chief from expressing the agency's real needs. Budget programs submitted in priority order will convey to the budget analysts, local government manager, and funding agency the relative importance of programs submitted.

Budget preparation in agencies with more than 150 personnel should be coordinated by a specialized staff member.[19] Fiscal planners who oversee budget preparation are often organizationally separate from the planning unit. Smaller agency budgets are prepared by a manager assigned part time or by the police chief.

Ideally, budget preparation should be a year-round effort that quantifies the approved plans of the agency with cost figures. That is, planning should come first, and the budget should evolve from the plan. Unfortunately, the process seldom works that way. Actually, much of the administrative planning takes place during the annual budget crunch six to eight months prior to the budget adoption date. An item or program is described and justified with a narrative intended to sell the item or program. Then it is submitted through channels to the fiscal planning expert, who costs it out. At some stage the chief is asked whether it should be included in the agency budget. Thus, in the real world, the budget process often forces the agency to do some planning.

Forced planning in response to budget requirements is not *mala in se* as long as administrative planning is ongoing. Agencies that rely solely on the budget process to plan tend to ignore the many problems that can be solved using existing resources.

Close coordination between budget and planning staffs is essential. Planners in some agencies are temporarily assigned to work on some phase of the budget under the supervision of the fiscal planning officer. This helps achieve needed coordination and provides auxiliary staff during the busiest part of the budget year.

Budget preparation is further discussed in Chapter 5.

Grant planning

During the past decade government and private funding agencies have injected staggering sums of money into criminal justice agencies to combat crime and promote safety. Police agencies received the bulk of the action grant funds in the initial years, perhaps because they were better organized, more innovative, and quicker to apply than courts or corrections agencies.

Funding sources

The Law Enforcement Assistance Administration (LEAA), created by Congress in the Omnibus Crime Control and Safe Streets Act of 1968, was for some time the most prominent of the funding agencies. The Police Foundation, the U.S. Department of Transportation (DOT), and the U.S. Department of Health, Education and Welfare (HEW) have also provided appreciable financial assistance to law enforcement agencies. The Police Foundation has sponsored a variety of efforts, including significant research projects, police executive training, and the publication of professional literature.

DOT's National Highway Traffic Safety Administration provides formula grants for a variety of highway related programs designed to reduce traffic accidents, deaths, injuries, and property damage. HEW funds have been received by some police agencies for projects, subgrants, and research contracts to communities implementing emergency medical service systems.

Grants may be sought to support worthwhile planning efforts, demonstration projects, research, and innovative experiments in policing and to implement crime reduction and safety programs. Recipients of grant funds should not expect funding agencies to support long-range, ongoing programs. The recipient jurisdiction should plan to continue successful programs with budgeted funds when outside funding is terminated.

Problems relating to grants

The availability of grant funds has encouraged police chief executives to attempt innovative approaches to policing that could never have been tried if outside funds had not been available. New approaches have brought successes and failures. LEAA's Prescriptive Package series provides information on some of the notable successes. Regrettably, a large number of grant-funded projects have failed to produce the desired results in the time proposed in the grant applications. In most cases the cause has been poor planning or poor management.

Preparation of a grant application does not require expertise in "grantsmanship." It does, however, require an awareness of what types of projects will interest funding agencies, and it requires planning. Many grant applications are poorly written, mainly because the concepts are too general and objectives too hazy. Planners often understate the time needed to complete the tasks or achieve stated objectives. As a result, time extensions are required. Conversely, costs are often overstated; then adjustments are sought to permit enhancement of the project rather than returning funds to the funding agency.

The second common failure of grant-funded projects is poor management. After a grant is approved and funds are received, top management tends to lose interest and relegate the administration of important projects to bottom level employees. In some cases project directors are patrol officers or sergeants; yet they are making important policy decisions that should be made by the agency head. Slippage of timetables most often occurs when the project director lacks control of a portion of a project, such as delivery of a critical item from a vendor. Sometimes the chief, if aware of the problem, could effect a solution. To ensure the involvement of top management, some agencies designate the chief or the chief's immediate subordinate as project director for grant-funded projects.

There really is no appreciable difference in planning and management between grand-funded and agency-funded projects. Both require planning and good management. Despite the benefits police agencies have derived from grants, the injection of large sums of money has called attention to the inability of many police managers to plan and administer new projects.

Tools for planning and control

Program evaluation and review technique (PERT) and critical path method (CPM) are often thought of as controls, but they, along with Gantt charts, also serve as valuable tools of planning and implementation. Henry L. Gantt, early in the twentieth century, developed a simple bar chart showing time relation-

---

CPM and PERT CPM was developed in 1956 for the evaluation of performance time and total cost of projects with well-defined activities. PERT was developed in 1958 for use in

resources in order to ensure that the critical path is kept on schedule and to divert unused resources on float activities (if excessive) to other projects.

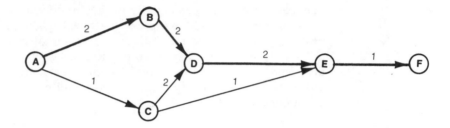

more complicated projects on larger scales, in which degrees of uncertainty were involved.

Both CPM and PERT use a graphic technique called an *arrow network* to describe how *activities* lead to certain *nodes* or *milestones*. In the diagram the arrow network shows that node A is the starting point, with nodes B and C being branches to the next milestones. The arrow from A to B is called an activity and takes 2 units of time to complete. In such a simple network the critical path would be the longest time required to go from the starting point, A, to the completion point, F. This would be A-B-D-E-F, which requires 7 units. Usually in serious applications three time estimates—optimistic, likely, and pessimistic—are used, and a weighted mean time is calculated.

The CPM allows calculations for varying starting and finishing times for activities based on the need for precedence of the nodes. This leads to *float* or leeway. By manipulation of float time, it may be feasible to free

PERT deals with more flexible nodes and activities by manipulating resources and times to reduce the critical path where possible. Thus PERT allows for more complex intelligence to be generated by greater manipulation of time, resources, and personnel for projects with variable requirements.

In order for CPM and PERT to be useful, the project must have a clearly stated set of activities with definable starting and end points. With PERT, especially, it is essential that resources be capable of being shifted between activities. Finally, accurate data and information must be available at prescribed periods to allow the manipulation of the network.

Source: This material is excerpted from Anthony James Catanese, "Information for Planning," in *The Practice of Local Government Planning*, ed. Frank S. So et al. (Washington, D.C.: International City Management Association, 1979), pp. 107–8.

ships among all major work activities. Each activity and event is drawn so the planner and manager of a project can visualize all the components in relation to one another. Events can be scheduled to take place in a logical, systematic fashion. Koontz and O'Donnell note that "the Gantt chart has sometimes been regarded as the most important social invention of the first half of the twentieth century."[20] Its usefulness has not diminished, and it continues to be a valuable tool.

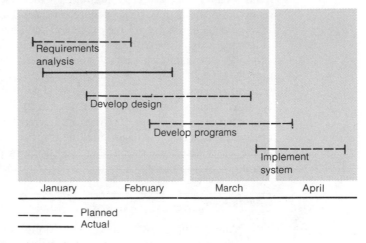

Basic Gantt chart technique.

In 1958 PERT was first applied to the planning and control of the Polaris weapon system by the Special Projects Office of the U.S. Navy. At virtually the same time, engineers at the du Pont Company separately developed CPM. PERT and CPM are extensions of the Gantt chart concept, but events and activities are laid out in a network instead of a bar/time graph.

PERT became widely used, first in government contract work, then throughout the private sector. It permits a project manager, who cannot possibly memorize all the component parts of a project and their time requirements, to perform the management functions necessary to bring the project to a successful conclusion. It has been used in the LEAA-funded Police Task Force for the National Advisory Commission on Criminal Justice Standards and Goals and the LEAA-funded Police Chief Executive Project. Interestingly, law enforcement use has not been limited to planning or staff work. The California Department of Law Enforcement used the PERT/CPM concept to help criminal investigators solve complex cases by tracking suspects and victims, providing a graphic series of lines and symbols showing their time and activities immediately prior to and during the commission of crimes.

One value of PERT/CPM is that it forces planners and managers to plan with greater specificity than they might without this tool. Preparation of a PERT/CPM chart causes them to think through the steps and estimate the time that must be allotted to complete each step of a project. It tells people all down the line how their activities fit into the overall effort and helps them plan to meet the schedule. It also permits the project director to know whether each step of the project is ahead of schedule, on time, or lagging and allows the manager to identify events that can be speeded up, thus assuring that the total program will be on schedule.

A PERT/CPM chart, drawn on paper about three feet high and extending to any width, may be placed on a wall where it can be monitored by personnel on major projects.

A commitment to effective planning

Police chiefs who seek improved decision making and a more effective agency can create a climate for effective planning regardless of the agency size. To create a proper climate for effective planning, one must begin at the top. Police chiefs who see the need for change, want to sharpen their decisions and those of their subordinates, and want to improve the effectiveness of their agencies can create a climate for effective planning. Conversely, chiefs who see a need to preserve the status quo, believe there is no need to improve decisions, and think their agencies are doing all they can will have ineffective planning efforts.

Planning must start with the chief and must permeate the entire agency. Police chiefs who establish agency goals will ask their division chiefs for division objectives. Chiefs who look to improve decisions will ask subordinates to recommend alternative solutions. Chiefs who want improved efficiency will search the entire agency for ways to improve productivity. When subordinates begin developing unit objectives, looking for alternative solutions, and finding ways to improve productivity, decision making improves and subordinates begin bringing the chief solutions rather than solutionless problems. When that occurs, planning is taking place.

Planning units

Early planning units performed tasks quite different from those performed today. Pioneer police planners answered questionnaires, conducted surveys, wrote orders, and gathered data. Except in the most progressive agencies, they did little to help establish agency goals or unit objectives, conduct research, improve productivity, analyze data, or propose alternatives for decision making.

Police agencies that are committed to planning and large enough to specialize will place the planning unit high in the organization, staff it with talented people, and involve it in significant administrative decision making. A few police agencies mistakenly bury the planning unit within the organizational hierarchy, place several layers of supervisors between the planners and the chief, put a low ranking person in charge, or assign unqualified people to the unit.

The planning unit should be placed in a prominent position in the agency to show that it serves the chief of police. Significantly, its position in the hierarchy is an indication of its importance in the agency. There should be no more than one level of supervision between the chief and the planning unit head. In agencies of more than one thousand personnel the head of the planning unit appropriately reports to a deputy or assistant chief and should maintain a close relationship with the chief on planning matters. Planning units in smaller agencies report directly to the chief.

To ensure a position of influence in the agency, the planning unit head should hold a rank or classification equal to that of other major unit heads. Agencies with captains in charge of such functions as training, personnel, records, and communications should not have a patrol officer or sergeant in charge of planning.

The planning function is no less important in a small agency than in a large agency. Some smaller agency chiefs believe they cannot afford to gather data, conduct research, and plan. Some expect to rely on nearby larger agencies that have planning capabilities. Although the sharing of information is vital, much of the planning in one agency has no application in another. A police agency serving an industrial area has different needs from one serving a bedroom community; plans formulated in a rapidly growing city may be of little use to a city with declining population; and urban centers have different needs from rural areas. The administrative planning function needs to be performed in every agency regardless of size.

Agencies with fewer than seventy-five personnel may not require a full-time planning staff unless considerable change is anticipated. An agency undergoing change will need a greater planning effort than a stable agency. Many police agencies with fewer than fifty employees have a full-time planner.[21] In the remaining small agencies that make up the bulk of police agencies in the United States, either some personnel devote a portion of their time to planning, or the chief performs the administrative planning. Alternatively, planning projects may be given to ad hoc committees appointed to deal with specific problems.[22]

The lack of qualified planning personnel may make it impractical to use an in-house, part-time planner. Therefore, the National Advisory Commission on Criminal Justice Standards and Goals proposed that arrangements should be made with another police agency, another governmental agency, or a private consultant if planning needs cannot be satisfied with agency personnel.[23]

Planning staff

Perhaps the most important element in managing people is to place them where their strengths can become productive.[24] In order to match qualified personnel with a planning assignment, it may help to prepare a job description listing the tasks performed, desired qualifications, and minimum requirements for the positions. Through trial and error, police managers have learned that planning personnel need above average ability in reading comprehension and must be able to express themselves clearly and concisely both orally and in writing. Creativity and the ability to reason are also valuable assets. Wilson and McLaren suggest qualifications of planning staff members as follows:

The success of the planning or research and development unit, even in a small department, will be dependent on the qualifications of its staff members. They must have a sound knowledge of police administration bolstered by good judgment, initiative, enthusiasm, and persuasiveness. They must have imagination in order to conceive fresh solutions to problems which may have their roots in traditional, stultified practices. Since a part of their task consists of gaining concurrences on plans, they must be personable and work well with other people.[25]

Planning assignments in some agencies are sought after and attract promotable employees. For example, according to an informal survey conducted in 1974, more than 90 percent of the command officers above the rank of captain in the Los Angeles police department had served in planning and research or advanced planning divisions at some time in their careers. In contrast, some agencies without a commitment to planning attract only the sick, lame, and lazy to planning assignments. The resulting sloppy administrative work is of little value to the police chief.

The demand for high-quality personnel for staff assignments is recognized by Jerry Wilson when he writes that "both police agencies and the public they serve are generally more tolerant of an occasional erroneous arrest and even an erroneous shooting of a citizen than they are of sloppy administrative work by the department."[26] Wilson continues by listing planning as one of the specialized units that have a tendency to draw off high-quality manpower from the patrol division—a problem that no police agency has adequately solved.

Some agencies test potential planners for intelligence, reading comprehension, analytical ability, creativity, or oral and written expression. Other agencies, believing that the best test is demonstrated performance, temporarily assign candidates for thirty to ninety days to judge their ability, and the candidates can judge their own suitability for the position before a long-term commitment is made. Education and experience also have proven valuable. A good academic background, including a baccalaureate degree or other educational qualification, may be required. Candidates should have several years' experience in a variety of field assignments.

The police planner need not be from the ranks of sworn personnel but must have "a thorough understanding of the agency organization, its component parts and interrelationships, and the functions and responsibilities of each."[27] As a practical balance, a planning unit staffed with one-half sworn personnel and one-half civilian planners works well. Sworn officers provide a practical viewpoint, because they know the problems of field officers. Civilian planners often bring a fresh perspective to planning and add stability to the unit by remaining in the assignment while officers rotate in and out. The use of civilians also alleviates the problem of drawing off high quality manpower from the patrol division when the field forces also need talented people.

Analytical ability has proven to be a valuable asset in police agencies as well as in business. The private sector has successfully used trained analysts who investigate and analyze operations. Among other benefits, they have brought significant improvements in efficiency. The use of analysts in specialized police service fields is growing. Narcotics, intelligence, and crime analysts process bits of data to reveal trends and ties that are pursued by officers. Supervisors, managers, and planners who lack analytical ability are at a serious disadvantage, and promotional tests and selection procedures should screen them out.

Once a candidate is selected for a planning position, he or she should attend a training course for planners and be given on-the-job coaching. A two-year commitment to the planning assignment is a desirable minimum.

Conclusion

Research and planning are essential to improve decision making in police agencies. This chapter has dealt with research and planning from the perspective of the head of an agency, but the same principles apply throughout the organization: Patrol officers, detectives, supervisors, and managers at all levels make decisions and plan. Improved planning by any of them will lead to more effective decisions. Planning involves recognizing the need for information, organizing research, projecting the future, establishing goals, and involving others in decision making. Drawing on police experience at all levels, advice from other practitioners, and the literature in planning and decision making, this chapter has provided guidelines to help police administrators improve decision making through research and planning.

1 V. A. Leonard, *Police Organization and Management,* 2d ed. (Brooklyn, N.Y.: Foundation Press, 1964), p. 173.

2 President's Commission on Law Enforcement and Administration of Justice, *Task Force Report: The Police* (Washington, D.C.: Government Printing Office, 1967), pp. 77–78, as cited in: Paul M. Whisenand and R. Fred Ferguson, *The Managing of Police Organizations,* 2d ed. (Englewood Cliffs, N.J.: Prentice-Hall, Inc., 1978), p. 117.

3 National Advisory Commission on Criminal Justice Standards and Goals, *Police [Report on Police]* (Washington, D.C.: Government Printing Office, 1973), p. 117.

4 Whisenand and Ferguson, *The Managing of Police Organizations,* p. 113.

5 William H. Parker, "Practical Aspects of Police Planning" (Paper presented at the 61st annual conference, International Association of Chiefs of Police, New Orleans, 27 September 1954), p. 7, as cited in Whisenand and Ferguson, *The Managing of Police Organizations,* p. 199.

6 Bertram A. Colbert, "The Management Information System," in *Management: A Book of Readings,* 4th ed., ed. Harold Koontz and Cyril O'Donnell (New York: McGraw-Hill Book Company, 1976), p. 554.

7 Thomas P. Murphy, "Management Information Systems," in *Developing the Municipal Organization,* ed. Stanley Piazza Powers, F. Gerald Brown, and David S. Arnold (Washington, D.C.: International City Management Association, 1974), p. 212.

8 National Advisory Commission on Criminal Justice Standards and Goals, *Criminal Justice System* (Washington, D.C.: Government Printing Office, 1973), p. 15.

9 Murphy, "Management Information Systems," pp. 213–14.

10 Harold Koontz and Cyril O'Donnell, *Management: A Systems and Contingency Analysis of Managerial Functions,* 6th ed. (New York: McGraw-Hill Book Company, 1976), p. 125.

11 Koontz and O'Donnell, eds., *Management: A Book of Readings,* p. 91.

12 Peter F. Drucker, *Technology, Management and Society* (New York: Harper & Row, 1970), p. 132.

13 Koontz and O'Donnell, *Management: A Systems and Contingency Analysis,* p. 150.

14 O. W. Wilson and Roy Clinton McLaren, *Police Administration,* 4th ed. (New York: McGraw-Hill Book Company, 1977), p. 160.

15 Ibid., pp. 160–61.

16 Koontz and O'Donnell, *Management: A Systems and Contingency Analysis,* pp. 226–27.

17 National Advisory Commission on Criminal Justice Standards and Goals, *Police* [*Report on Police*], p. 54.

18 Ibid.

19 Ibid., p. 132.

20 Koontz and O'Donnell, *Management: A Systems and Contingency Analysis,* p. 735.

21 National Advisory Commission on Criminal Justice Standards and Goals, *Police* [*Report on Police*], p. 124.

22 Wilson and McLaren, *Police Administration,* p. 100.

23 National Advisory Commission on Criminal Justice Standards and Goals, *Police* [*Report on Police*], p. 117.

24 Peter F. Drucker, *Management: Tasks, Responsibilities, Practices* (New York: Harper & Row, 1974), p. 307.

25 Wilson and McLaren, *Police Administration,* p. 63.

26 Jerry Wilson, *Police Report: A View of Law Enforcement* (Boston: Little, Brown & Company, 1975), p. 142.

27 National Advisory Commission on Criminal Justice Standards and Goals, *Police* [*Report on Police*], p. 120.

16 Information management

The title of this chapter, "Information Management," is a current designation for a subject that used to be referred to as "records and communications." The new designation signals a major change in emphasis. Even a cursory review of the literature on police records shows dozens of texts in which competent and experienced authors have explored the mechanics of records administration. There does not appear to be a need for another detailed review of what information is contained in an ideal offense report form, field interrogation report form, arrest report form, etc. Nor is there a discernible demand for additional detailed listings of all the kinds of reports normally employed in the police establishment. Those who have need for such information should have little difficulty in locating one of the standard texts on the subject. Probably the best is still O. W. Wilson's *Police Records*.[1]

What is more likely to be of interest and value to the police practitioner and the student is a broader analysis of why the police information system is important and how the police administrator might approach the management of the departmental system to obtain the best results. Although this analysis will not provide steps one, two, three, etc., it will provide a set of ideas that may give the police administrator a fresh view of the nature and scope of the information management problem.

Police agencies generally are in a period of transition between isolated manual files in individual departments and the sharing of automated, centralized files by many departments, and it is premature to recommend the ultimate information system for the numerous agencies to whom this book is addressed. It is more productive to explore the pertinent issues, so that the interested administrator can work toward a solution or set of solutions that best answer the unique needs of the individual agency.

Most police administrators in the United States have not thought in terms of a police information system. They appear to have thought, rather, along the traditional lines of "records and communications"—as if this were a single staff function serving overall police operations but not deserving any particular top level involvement.

The effective management of information has seldom been a high priority for chiefs of either large or small departments. In the early 1960s, however, two developments focused extraordinary attention on police information. The first was the development by several computer manufacturers of new capabilities in equipment, which were particularly well suited to the information needs of police (large memory, to handle more complex sets of instructions; direct access, to retrieve a specific record almost instantaneously; and remote terminals, to enter inquiries and receive responses at locations any distance from central computer locations).

The second development was the rise on the national political scene of "law and order" as a significant issue. As a direct result, the President's Commission on Law Enforcement and Administration of Justice was established, with a series of task forces to support it. In their search for better control of the crime problem, the working groups explored many avenues before some members concluded that at least one area of improvement consisted in providing the police with better tools. The search for the kinds of tools that could make the individual police officer a more effective instrument for the prevention of crime and enforcement of the law revealed the fact that technology had more or less passed the police officer by—except for the two-way radio and the squad car (it should be noted that the automobile has no doubt contributed as much to the increase in the police problem as to its solution).

Communication and information

Communication is essentially a social affair involving the sharing of information. Different *systems* of communication make man's social life possible, and human speech and language are, of course, the most prominent of these systems. Other systems may involve formal signs and codes such as highway codes, legal procedures, and machine languages for computers.

The means of transmission, in addition to speech and writing, may be seemingly casual but highly ritualistic both in primitive tribes and formal society in terms of choice of words and oral nuances. Increasingly, however, communication relies on technical means of transmission of information—from the late nineteenth century telephone and telegraph to the latest in radio, camera, and computer.

A third party, technology, increasingly intervenes in the relationship between sender and receiver to make communication depend on precise, quantitative kinds of information that can be handled by magnetic tapes, computer programs, and other hardware and software. Thus current communication in police—and many other fields as well—tends to be centralized, classified, and modular in concept, approach, and methods.

Source: Based in part on Colin Cherry, *On Human Communication: A Review, a Survey, and a Criticism* (Cambridge, Mass.: The M.I.T. Press, 1966), pp. 3–8.

The ultimate conclusion was that the most valuable tool that could be made available to the police officer, on whatever specific assignment, was *information*. Every day that officers report for duty they are confronted with situations in which they need access to information about people or places (specific addresses, general areas), or about things (property, automobiles). This led to a review of how police forces have traditionally made this tool available to officers in the field, and again the results were more than a little discouraging.[2]

In spite of the fact that every available book, paper, or article on police records details the value of a centralized records system and deplores the weaknesses and failures of decentralized records, the common pattern in police departments in the United States, differing from department to department only in minor details, is one of decentralization, as typified in Figure A. While many experienced police officials who are not directly involved in records operations tend to think of all police intelligence as being stored in a central facility (usually called a records division), this is not the case.

In the smallest departments centralization of the records process takes place simply because the physical facility and available staff do not permit decentralization. However, in departments of very modest size, as soon as there is specialization by function the tendency to develop specialized islands of records generally appears. Figure A develops this kind of operation according to the following scenario:

1. *Identification Division*. This is, at least on the surface, a largely self-contained process involving taking, classifying, and filing fingerprints; initiating or updating criminal history records; conducting

fingerprint searches; handling correspondence from outside agencies, etc. It is relatively easy to develop a case for isolating this highly specialized function from the main records operation, particularly where space problems are encountered and the identification staff can locate offices that are separate from central records and adequate for their needs.

2. *Traffic Division.* Again, it is easy to argue that the traffic function has little interdependence with the crime-related activities of the department and that the specialists in this division are better suited to process, file, and analyze traffic-oriented information than are the generalists in central records.

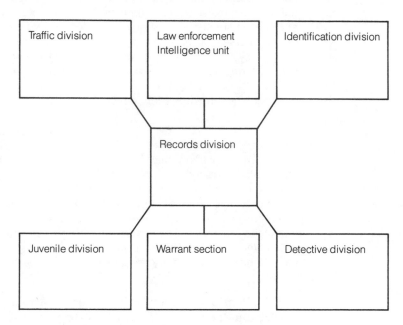

A: Typical decentralization of police records to records division, identification division, traffic division, juvenile division, detective division, warrant section, and law enforcement intelligence unit.

3. *Juvenile Division.* Here the desire to "own" one's files is frequently supported by both law and local judicial decisions bearing on the privileged nature of records dealing with persons under the age of eighteen.

4. *Warrant Section.* Nearly every police agency at some time or other experiences embarrassment or worse as a result of procedural or human failure in the handling of arrest warrants. The common, simple solution to the problem is to establish a separate warrant control section with a staff dedicated to maintaining proper control over warrants. In theory this approach will minimize the problems of lost or misplaced warrants, the service of warrants that have been withdrawn, dismissed, or already served, etc.

5. *Detective Division.* Detectives do not tend to develop as many formal files as they do informal collections of paper that duplicate files kept elsewhere in the department. This is indicative of both their lack of faith in the accuracy and completeness of the official files (and file searches) and their frustration with the time-consuming multiple file search requests they must make as the decentralization progresses.

6. *Law Enforcement Intelligence Unit (LEIU)*. Files relating to persons known or suspected of being involved in organized crime are always maintained separately from other police records, and this is probably the only justifiable deviation from the basic concept of a centralized information system. Data in intelligence files are frequently very sensitive and often unchecked. Improper disclosure could easily result in either an aborted investigation or severe embarrassment, perhaps including civil suit, to the department.

The result of this development of decentralized information systems is that as far as the officer in the field is concerned there is no information system. Or, more properly, there is an information system that is practically available only when a major situation is involved. During routine operations, the moderately well-motivated officer tends to find that asking for many records checks from the field will result in a great deal of time spent waiting for responses; this will gain the officer a very poor reputation with the radio dispatcher who must relay the requests to multiple index locations for a search and then relay the response back. If there is general agreement that information is the most important tool that can be made available to the field officer, then the inevitable conclusion is that overall we have done rather a poor job of making information available.

If practice so often deviates from theory, is the theory of a centralized records system really sound and achievable? The position taken here is that the theory is sound, that decentralized records operations have not served their purpose, and that the reason decentralization continues is because police administrators continue to think of the information system as an auxiliary process that will somehow muddle along while management focuses on more important aspects of police service.

Several conditions have been developing in recent years, however, which, while they may now be causing the police administrator severe headaches, in the long run will produce highly beneficial results for the police service. All of these conditions should focus administrative attention once again on the importance of information and the need for management involvement in this area.

This chapter opens its main discussion with a brief description of information systems technology which will facilitate the centralization of police department records and thus make information management more of a reality. This is followed by a discussion of the issue of information in relation to security and personal privacy. Management policy is then discussed. The mechanics of police reporting are next described with respect to basic reports and report processing. Information management and technology are then brought together in a discussion of local, areawide, state, and national considerations—with examples from several parts of the country. The remaining portions of the chapter show management applications in specific ways, including full index conversion, automated reporting, computer-aided dispatching, on-line management information, crime analysis, query languages, Crime Analysis Support System (CASS), and a concluding section on mobile digital terminals and other specialized techniques.

Information systems technology

In 1965 the first application of computer technology to the police information problem was made for purposes other than the manipulation of numbers and the printing of statistical reports. In that year, in April, the California Highway Patrol implemented the Automated Statewide Auto Theft Inquiry System (AUTOSTATIS), an on-line (inquiry and update instantaneously from remote terminals) computer-based stolen auto system intended to serve the state of California. A short time later, in July, the Police Information Network

(PIN) became operational in the San Francisco Bay Area to provide wanted person and warrant information for some ninety-three police agencies in the nine counties around San Francisco Bay. These two systems were followed by systems in St. Louis and Chicago, and then by nearly every major police agency in the United States. Today most of the populated area of the United States is served, in some degree, by some form of computerized police information system. More will be said about these later in this chapter.

Attention should be drawn to the fact that these very high speed, very flexible, very responsive automated systems have enormous potential, not just for the large center city but for the small outlying department as well. Seventy-five years ago 80 percent of the American population lived in a rural environment, either on ranches or farms or in small isolated communities. Today almost the converse is true, and over 70 percent of our population lives in an urban environment. This condition lends an entire new dimension to the concept of centralized police information systems. Where we used to discuss the need for centralization within a single department, we now need to press hard for centralization throughout a metropolitan area.

Figure B indicates that while the police information problem is still affected adversely by decentralization of records within a given department, the situation is seriously aggravated today by the fact that each department is most often within easy travel distance of a number of other departments—each of which probably has its own decentralized records operation. Add to this the fact

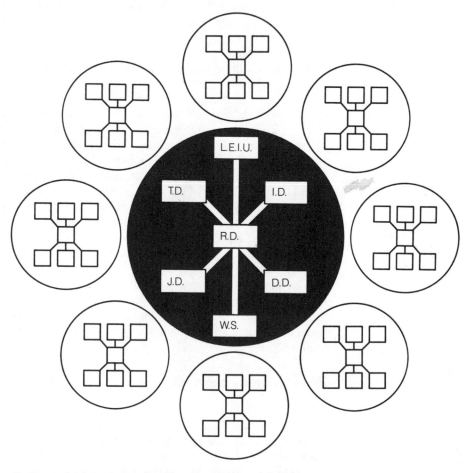

B: The development of metropolitan sprawl has extended
the need for centralization of police information
from a single department to many departments.

that the criminal element in our various communities is not likely to pay much attention to jurisdictional boundaries, and if they recognize the boundaries at all it will be to use them to their own advantage.

The result is that significant effort is wasted as investigators in a half dozen departments each work on a part of what amounts to a single series of criminal acts without knowing that other investigations are ongoing and without the ability to share evidence, descriptions, leads, etc. Individuals are arrested for petty offenses, fined in court and released, while felony warrants remain in files of adjacent jurisdictions. Drivers are stopped and warned or cited for traffic violations and allowed to proceed when perhaps dozens of warrants for their arrest reside in the files of a number of different nearby police agencies. We have not found a way to quantify the dollar cost when a wanted burglar is released after a traffic stop, or when the individual with several outstanding warrants for armed robbery is released with a $25 fine after an arrest for public drunkenness, but it must be significant. Such persons will go on to commit other offenses, which result in physical harm or property loss to honest citizens, which require response by a patrol unit, which require follow-up by an investigative unit, and all of which require additional reports that must be written, typed, indexed, and filed. Perhaps even more costly is the fact that offenders who have so avoided apprehension will be more secure in their belief in the fallibility of enforcement agencies and will communicate this to others of their kind.

While perfection is outside our grasp, many of these failures can be, and are, today, avoided through the application of modern computer communications technology. There are dozens of current examples in the United States in which up to 100 or more local police agencies have on-line access to the centralized information files stored on a computer housed in one of their departments, and where several hundred agencies have on-line access to a state law enforcement system. To date, the ability of most smaller outlying departments has been more or less limited to simple inquiry and update. It is to be hoped that the demonstrated effectiveness of these systems will have the following two results: (1) it will encourage the smaller police agencies to petition for increased service and for the budget to support it; and (2) the administrators of the larger host departments will recognize the fact that their own agencies will benefit by extension of increased information services to smaller neighbors.

It is to be hoped that the complexities of constantly expanding shared operations will encourage the involvement of top police executives, and that information systems management will finally be recognized as the key to effective police operations rather than as a housekeeping function that is required but that does not contribute very much to the accomplishment of the police objective.

Security and privacy

One additional factor that is virtually certain to cause more executive attention to be focused on information management is the emphasis now being given to the individual's right to privacy, and the near certainty that sanctions will be levied against criminal justice agencies that are careless about recognizing this right. Police administrators may feel that much of the furor over invasion of privacy is greatly exaggerated, at least with respect to local government police activity, and that the few instances cited do not at all show any pattern of improper or insensitive behavior. Significant court decisions have been rendered and governmental policy has been set, however, and police records are going to be subjected to far more scrutiny and challenge in the future.

At the time this book was put together, initial guidelines published by the U.S. Department of Justice which defined in considerable detail how local jurisdictions would be required to handle law enforcement records (if these jurisdictions had ever accepted federal funding) had been withdrawn. A new set of guidelines was issued which largely returned control over the collection, processing, and dissemination of criminal justice information to the states. The issue of federal, state, and local control of arrest records and other information in police files and elsewhere in the criminal justice process is one that is far from settled. Several bills were introduced in both houses of Congress in 1975–76 with the intention of protecting individual security and privacy by providing stringent federal controls over local police agencies with respect to investigative, intelligence, and criminal history information.

If the police administrator wants to maintain local control of information, he has to pay attention to information management and how it works in relation to security and privacy. The best way, it would seem, is for the administrator to know precisely what information is maintained in the files of his department, and to know exactly how that information is used, so that he may be sure that both the information and its use are proper. Much of the public (and political) outcry over security and privacy was prompted by clearly outrageous incidents. Making criminal history records available to property owners to be used as the basis for approving applications to rent or buy property was reported as a common practice, for example, in one community. The use of modern computer technology to store and retrieve arrest warrants without adequate procedures to ensure that warrant records are canceled in the file when they become void for any reason has been reported in several instances. Many departments today still routinely record arrest information on criminal history records, with no effort to complete the record with a disposition—even when that disposition is "released after investigation." It is not likely that any police administrator would volunteer to stand up in a public forum and defend any of these practices. They occur only because the administrator has not found the time to ensure that they are eradicated. If that time is not found in the future, the time will soon come when new attacks will be made on the use of police information, and one could not expect that they will be unsuccessful again.

As a final thought on security and privacy, it should be noted that a largely unwarranted proportion of the investigation into the potential for privacy violations by criminal justice agencies has been concerned with the theft of information, or unauthorized access to information, from electronic files. Such potential, of course, does exist, but generally it involves significant difficulty and expense. It is questionable whether the information contained in police files is really worth that much to anyone except in most unusual instances. The real exposure to the department and to the chief of police is the improper dissemination of sensitive information from any files, manual or electronic, by personnel who have authorized access in the first place. This may occur, in very rare instances, with intent to do wrong for money or other considerations. In the overwhelming majority of cases it will occur simply because there are no procedures in place to inhibit it, and no one has ever taken the time or made the effort to impress upon employees who have access to police files how very serious it can be if a federal suit is filed citing both civil and criminal damages.

Management policy on information

Regardless of the size of a police department, several policy considerations relate to information management and, if they cannot be universally accepted, ought at least to be thoroughly discussed. The difference between a department of 50 employees and one of 1,000 is more than merely one of volume. As volume increases, so does the complexity of the task of arranging collected information into meaningful form and getting it back to all the people and units who have need for it. On the other hand, the larger the department, and the jurisdiction it serves, the more resources there are to do the job. In either the 50 employee or 1,000 employee department, the information system will probably be inadequate unless a clear set of policies has been set forth by the administrator and is understood and accepted by the department as a whole. A key set of such policies might be set down as follows in this section.

Information objectives

The total records (or information) system of the department should be designed and operated to further the police objective. This means that both the administration and operations functions should be able to look at the records system for the information they need, when they need it. This also implies that there should be some vehicle for reporting to the chief when needed information cannot be obtained. This is a means of keeping attention focused on the department's information requirements so that these can be met to the degree possible and when resources become available.

Management review

There should be a continuing formal review process to ensure that the departmental records system and its capabilities are both understood and used. In large departments this might be the function of an inspection unit, and in small departments it might be a periodic assignment given to younger supervisors or commanding officers as a form of staff training. In any event, in the absence of machinery to avoid it, police departments tend to learn to live and function with what they have. This leads to stagnation. The information has to be dynamic if it is to serve its purpose. Constant review must also be directed to all report forms and summary reports prepared in the department to ensure that someone does still require them. There appears to be a limitless store of anecdotes about reports or report summaries that were designed for some purpose at some time, and that continue to be collected or compiled although they no longer have a purpose and are wanted or used by no one. This occurs because each person collecting or receiving the information assumes that it must be important to someone, and no one ever calls a halt. This is costly in time and effort, uses resources that can be better used in a productive activity, and tends to discredit the information process.

Information training

Constant attention should be given to training, not merely on what reports are to be filled out in a given circumstance and what information is to go on them, but, more important, on why the reports are filled out and how the reporting officer and his or her unit benefit from the system. Such training is probably best done in depth during in-service training programs, but where department size makes this difficult the necessary training can be accomplished over a period of time at roll call. The key lies in the fact that the individual officer too often sees all of the department's reporting requirements as so much red tape produced by bureaucrats who have been off the street so long that they no longer appreciate the problems of the working police officer. In those departments where the importance of police information is clearly understood and real effort has been made to provide the individual officer with the why of police reporting, the information system is more accurate and productive. It should be noted that if whoever is assigned to provide the training has difficulty determining a sound value of some reporting process to either the individual officer or the department, that report process should clearly be scheduled for early review.

Incident reporting and control

There should be absolute control over all incident reporting. This is best accomplished by numbering all assignment records as an incident is received by the dispatcher, either in the form of a citizen complaint or as an on-view activity reported via radio by an officer in the field. In recent years there has been less of a problem, but there are still departments whose crime statistics are openly questioned from time to time. Where this occurs, there are only two reasonable answers: the department is in fact manipulating its crime statistics, or it cannot demonstrate adequate controls on the reporting system to rebut charges of statistical manipulation. The simple fact is that there are many conditions in society which contribute to crime rates. The effectiveness of police operations is only one of these, and the enlightened police administrator must surely recognize this and make every effort to communicate the fact to the community. The other side of the coin is that when conditions in a community are such that the crime rate is rising, and the department has been resorting to changes of classification or other subterfuges to disguise this fact, the time will surely arrive when department resources are strained to the limit. Where, then, is the basis for requesting an increased budget?

Management analysis

The information system should be designed to support the policy and operational decisions of the chief administrator and his subordinate commanders, and to defend those decisions when they are subjected to attack. The chief and the commanders should rely on the system for such support. The implication is that policy and operational decisions should be formulated on the basis of the soundest possible information and should, therefore, be totally defensible.

The mechanics of police reporting

There are a number of mechanical decisions which need to be made relating to the police reporting process and which, when made, ought to be periodically reviewed. We have seen texts which take a firm position on one side or another on these issues, but experience dictates that what works extremely well for one department may be a disaster in another. The key to good management is to find the solution that best fits the problem being addressed, and then to be willing to change with conditions.

Generalized versus specialized forms

An argument which has gone on for years has to do with the use of a minimum number of generalized reporting forms versus a greater number of specialized forms. The objective, which often gets lost along the way, is not to arrive at an optimum number of forms but rather to develop a system which yields the most complete and accurate information for police use. Many departments have gone from a general form to specialized forms and back several times. Officers in the field tend to equate the number of report forms they have to carry with degree of complexity, and generally resist a move to a number of specialized forms. On the other hand, it is clear that the information gathered on crimes against property varies considerably from that gathered on crimes against persons. Certain other incidents such as auto theft, worthless documents, and missing persons require the officer conducting the preliminary investigation to obtain very specialized pieces of information.

The major shortcoming of the generalized form is that it cannot provide for special information requirements. Specialized forms, on the other hand, can be designed to actually lead the investigating officer through the investigation, so that the chance of failure to gather required information is minimized. During the 1960s the Chicago police department developed a binder to carry specialized forms, with detailed instructions on the divider for each form. While this approach can never take the place of training and supervision, it can help toward reaching the goal of complete and accurate reporting.

Saginaw, Michigan, has developed what might be considered a very acceptable compromise. This department uses a padded book of field report forms which contain the usual boxes (name, address, date, time, reporting officer, etc.) to capture data common to all reports. The cover of the book is a dictation guide for the officer, based on field notes and observations. We would not suggest that any one of these approaches is superior in all situations. What is best is what works best with a given group of officers, a given group of supervisors, a given level of training, etc. The objective is always complete and accurate reporting.

Report processing and distribution

Once police reports are prepared there is always the problem of how to get them from the field into a headquarters location for processing and distribution for follow-up action. Practice seems to vary so widely that it raises the suspicion that this problem has not been subjected to real scrutiny. Most commonly, officers complete their reports at the scene and hold them to the end of the tour of duty. Some departments require that reports of felonies and other serious incidents be delivered to headquarters immediately upon completion of the report. Still others require that all reports of crimes be delivered immediately. While the problem of time away from patrol duty while delivering reports obviously varies with the size of the jurisdiction and the distance of remote patrol areas from headquarters, it is still significant. Delivery of reports at shift end results in large numbers of reports being received at one time, thereby further delaying the processing and assignment operations.

Some years ago a number of departments began to experiment with dictation equipment and had officers dictate their reports over the telephone from the field. Experience varied, but not uncommonly the benefits of a smoother processing work load and less time lost delivering reports appeared to be offset by frustrations encountered with the dictating equipment. Machines would break down in the middle of a report and the reporting officer would continue to dictate. Operators would fail to place new belts or tapes on the equipment. Many of the early attempts to use dictation were determined unsatisfactory and were terminated. This was a proper action, since it would hardly be sound management to pursue a procedure that creates more problems than it solves. Still, sometimes memory can be too long, and this may be such a case. Departments that were late in moving to dictation are now reporting much happier results. The difference appears to be that, as in many areas of technology, dictating equipment has improved significantly in the past few years. Departments that have had problems in this area may wish to reinvestigate.

Another question relating to police report processing has to do with typing or duplicating handwritten reports. In the early 1950s it is probable that nearly all police departments typed all their formal reports. Most moved to color-coded, snap out carbon forms, and this became the accepted standard. Then, by the late 1950s, some police administrators began to look at the cost of forms, the cost of adding typists to meet increasing volumes, and the processing delay involved in getting reports typed. A relatively small number of departments moved to duplicating the officer's handwritten report. Police officers were encouraged to produce legible reports, and, by and large, departments seem to have adopted this practice and to be satisfied with it. Where manual index cards are required they also need not be typed. Innovative departments learned to arrange their report forms so that index data appear in the upper right-hand corner, and the index cards are also copied from the handwritten document.

Report signatures

A minor matter, but one which continues to crop up with some regularity, is the persistence of certain myths in the police reporting field. One of these has to do with the need for officers to sign their police reports. With the exception of traffic citations and certain arrest reports which serve as the formal complaint (simple drunk and certain other ordinances), it is difficult to find any rationale for this requirement. There is certainly nothing wrong with having officers sign their reports, of course, except where this involves excessive loss of time or frustration. It is just that so often suggestions for improvement of records management meet objections on such grounds as, "But if we did that, the officers would not be able to sign their reports." The fact is that the overwhelming majority of departments throughout the United States do not require their officers to sign reports. The argument that the unsigned report is not admissible in court is not comprehensible. Since the report is hearsay and the "best evidence" is the reporting officer's own testimony, we can think of no instances where the report would be admissible to prove the facts stated therein. If the reason for requiring the reporting officer's signature is to require the reporter to attest to the accuracy of his or her report, the chief's problem is far deeper than report accuracy.

Records retention

One other aspect of records management which very often slips into the myth category has to do with records retention. There are, to be sure, both state statutes and local ordinances which deal with retention periods for documents classified as public records. Not infrequently, however, it has been found that the retention of certain files which appear to have no practical use is based on an "understanding" that there is a legal requirement for retention. When a search for the legal requirement is pressed, either it cannot be found or it is not so all-encompassing as it was thought to be. Further, if it is determined that there is an archaic legal information against the destruction of certain records, it probably does not specify *how* they must be retained. Perhaps cardboard storage cases in a warehouse would satisfy the law if satisfy it we must.

The point of this is that over the years too many police chiefs and records commanders have clung to the philosophy that if they ever removed anything from file it might be the very piece needed the next week. Folklore about rigid records retention laws is used to support this uneasiness about clearing files. Where indexes are permitted to grow forever without purging and files to accumulate to the point where work space is limited, there is almost certainly more damage done to the operation through inability to properly benefit from active current data than could ever accrue from the once a year or once in a decade failure to locate a bit of information because aged files have been moved to storage. In the case of index files, especially, the longer they are permitted to build without being purged the greater is the opportunity for islands of misfiles to develop, and therefore the search error rate is likely to increase. While suspect and arrest cards should no doubt be kept for the expected life of the subject, index cards on witnesses, victims, complainants, reporting persons, etc., have no value beyond three years where there is no subsequent entry.

Information management with technology

Throughout most of the careers of currently active chief executives, police information systems remained essentially manual and essentially unchanged. There was the introduction of teletype communication in the 1940s, and, at about that same time, punch card accounting equipment came into fairly widespread use for preparation of statistical summaries. Microfilm has long been used as a storage and retrieval medium. But aside from these modest advances (though they certainly were important), information handling in police agencies remained much the same for many years, which may well explain why "records and communications" came to be viewed as a housekeeping chore and why the literature on dynamic information management techniques is so limited.

Technology and change

As noted early in this chapter, dramatic changes occurred in the mid-1960s when a number of computer manufacturers began to address the police community on the subject of new advances in computer technology. These were, as mentioned earlier: larger internal memory for computers, which made it possible to handle more complex sets of instructions; large direct access files which made it possible to retrieve a specific record almost instantaneously; and typewriter-like terminal devices which made it possible to enter inquiries and retrieve responses at locations any distance from the central computer location.

These capabilities opened up a new world for police information management, and today we are just beginning to appreciate how broad the horizons of that new world are. Essentially, the progress that has been made to date has been in the critical area of centralizing index files for broad population areas and automating these. This advance was in recognition of the fact that our crime problem is not limited by jurisdictional boundaries but is, in fact, a problem that exists in terms of concentrations of people, without regard to the number of political subdivisions involved. Also addressed was the problem of a highly mobile criminal population which tended to further reduce the effectiveness of purely local files. The result of this development is that the picture of police information systems depicted in Figures A and B has been largely replaced by the one shown in Figure C.

The network of systems

This large network of police files has been such an effective addition to the police capability that there is need to comment in some detail on a few of its characteristics which may not be immediately apparent. First of all, it should be clear that this extensive network, which feeds the FBI's National Crime Information Center (NCIC), is not limited to large police departments of several hundred or more personnel. At the end of 1980 there were roughly 12,000 terminal devices located in about 2,500 police departments throughout the United States. Some departments with as few as a half dozen men have found it possible to justify a terminal and the associated costs of data sets, telephone lines, share of the computer, etc. By sharing access to centralized files, these smaller departments are able to increase the safety factor of their own officers and generally improve their effectiveness.

The local government automated information systems indicated in Figure C are by no means standard. In some cases the computerized information system serves only a single large police department, as is the case in New York City, Chicago, and Detroit. More commonly, a center city serves all of the cities in a county. For example, the Los Angeles police system serves the requirements of some seventy-nine agencies in Los Angeles County, and the Bergen

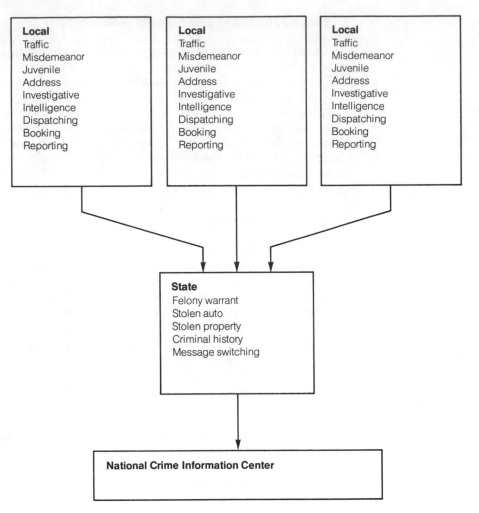

| **Local**
Traffic
Misdemeanor
Juvenile
Address
Investigative
Intelligence
Dispatching
Booking
Reporting | **Local**
Traffic
Misdemeanor
Juvenile
Address
Investigative
Intelligence
Dispatching
Booking
Reporting | **Local**
Traffic
Misdemeanor
Juvenile
Address
Investigative
Intelligence
Dispatching
Booking
Reporting |

State
Felony warrant
Stolen auto
Stolen property
Criminal history
Message switching

National Crime Information Center

C: National network of automated police information systems. The local
systems include a wide variety of intergovernmental networks
below the level of the state government. Each level of government tends to concentrate
on the kinds of information it needs for its area of jurisdiction.

County, New Jersey, data center serves seventy departments in that county. Multicounty systems are also not uncommon. The Police Information Network (PIN) in the San Francisco Bay Area provides service for approximately ninety-three departments in the nine counties surrounding San Francisco Bay. There are even multistate arrangements where the spread of population has ignored state boundaries. The Kansas City police department has terminals in sixty-seven outside agencies in Missouri and Kansas, and a system in Moline, Rock Island County, Illinois, also covers Davenport, Scott County, Iowa.

The importance of this is that it represents a level of cooperation among police executives and police agencies that was considered impossible just a few short years ago. Agreement on standardized formats and procedures, as well as on legal problems dealing with cost sharing and participatory management have not always come easily, but it is a credit to the police service that where the need has become apparent the necessary negotiation has been accomplished and significant results obtained. It is worth considering that while consolidation of police departments has had its proponents for many years and while, from a pure political science point of view, this might be a proper and wise direction, consolidation has only been accomplished in a handful of locations throughout the United States. Consolidation of certain services (information systems, communications, etc.) is proving to be a more practical and realistic approach to improving the effectiveness of police operations without tinkering with the basic structure of local government.

Generally, the local government information systems have limited themselves to the storage of information of interest to the local area served, as indicated in Figure C. Since these local systems are interfaced to state systems by communication lines and therefore inquiries can be switched through to the state system at electronic speeds, there is little justification, for example, for maintaining stolen auto records on the local file. To do so would not improve response time to a noticeable degree, and the problem of maintaining the files would be complicated. On the other hand, there is little justification for maintaining strictly local information in the state files, since a given jurisdiction is not likely to send officers several hundred miles to pick up an individual wanted for nonpayment of a parking ticket or for similar minor offenses. An exception may exist in the Mountain States, where no great population centers exist, or in very small states (Rhode Island), where it is conceivable that, with modern technology, a single police information system might serve the requirements of all of the police departments in the state.

National Crime Information Center

The NCIC is a nationwide computerized information system established to serve all local, state, and federal law enforcement agencies. The purpose of NCIC is to help the law enforcement community better perform its duties by quickly providing current information on criminal activities and offenders. The computer file currently serves approximately 12,000 local police departments in the United States and Canada.

The NCIC comprises ten computerized files: computerized criminal histories, missing persons, wanted persons, stolen securities, stolen license plates, stolen and recovered guns, stolen boats, stolen articles, stolen and felony vehicles, and a criminalistics laboratory information system. The missing persons file is used almost exclusively to help find missing juveniles.

NCIC provides an immediate flow of pertinent data for police officers, prosecutors, judges, and others.

Source: Federal Bureau of Investigation.

For local police departments to participate in this network, it has been necessary for them to agree to certain standards relating to records formats and to comply with procedures established for the entry of new records and the clearance of records when warrants are served, when property is recovered, etc. By and large, the standardization required has not appeared to create any difficulty for local police and in an overall sense has probably been beneficial.

As has been indicated, effort has been made to avoid duplication of files at the local and state levels. Everything that goes into the National Crime Information Center, however, is duplicated at the originating state system. One reason for this is to control the volume of inquiry into NCIC. California police departments, for example, have for several years averaged about 25,000 inquiries each day on license numbers. Since some 99 percent of these are on California license numbers, and since all California records on stolen or wanted vehicles are maintained at the state, these 25,000 inquiries do not have to be switched on to NCIC.

A far more important reason for the state level duplication of files is that it makes it far easier to keep the files properly maintained. During the design of NCIC it was felt that if all the local departments in the country could forward their operational police records to FBI headquarters there would inevitably be a certain amount of carelessness and human error. There have always been errors in police files, of course, and occasionally these have led to false arrest suits or at least to some amount of bad publicity. But, for some reason, the press accepts the idea that some level of error in manual files is to be expected and does not consider it to be newsworthy. An error in an automated file, however, particularly if it leads to a very bad result, is good for national headlines. It was on this basis that the Police Advisory Board, which is comprised of NCIC participants, decided that file discipline should be the responsibility of the states. Under this procedure, if a weakness develops in the procedures of any state and an unreasonable number of errors are detected, access to NCIC files from that state may be limited until appropriate corrective action is taken. This system has worked exceptionally well, and while mistakes do occur they are extremely limited when one considers that NCIC files contain more than 8 million active records and that the system processes more than 300,000 transactions each twenty-four-hour period.

Full index conversion

There are few who would question the fact that the National Crime Information Center network has been an unqualified success, yet there is still a great deal of room for development. The mere existence of NCIC and the thought of having immediate access to the major felony "wanted" files of the nation has encouraged many smaller departments to join the system and thereby truly become a part of the national law enforcement effort. At the same time, it is not only the small terminal-equipped departments that have not taken full advantage of the available capability: the large center cities where the host computers are housed have also not taken full advantage.

Very few of the local government information systems currently operating have gone very far beyond entering wants, warrants, stolen automobiles, stolen guns, identifiable stolen property, stolen negotiable securities, and stolen boats into the automated files available to them. A few agencies are beginning to convert criminal history records, and a fairly large number have added address cross-indexes, so that dispatchers can inquire on addresses as they dispatch a new assignment and relay critical information to the assigned unit if files reflect a history of violence, wanted persons, etc. Most departments, however, even with the computer capability available to them, still maintain large manual index files for witnesses, victims, reporting persons, complainants, etc. It is also common to find large manual indexes in the juvenile divisions and identification divisions, and at other locations, even though the department routinely goes to the computer files for various forms of operational information.

The apparent reason why so many police departments have failed to take advantage of the capability available to them goes back to some studies undertaken when the first on-line police files were established in the mid-1960s. These studies were designed to evaluate the amount of activity against the so-called master alpha files and relate this to the cost of direct access computer storage. The results showed that more than 80 percent of the records going into master alpha files are never accessed, and of those records which are retrieved, all activity is in the first six months after the record goes into file. The conclusion was that police could not justify the relatively expensive luxury of automated files for such limited use.

That was clearly a proper conclusion in 1965. Data entry at that time was generally via punched card, and the combined cost of key punch operators and disk file made conversion of low activity files unattractive. However, by 1975 the picture had changed markedly. Today, data entry is normally called "direct entry," and data are entered via a television-like visual display terminal equipped with a typewriter keyboard. The format is displayed on the screen and the operator merely fills in the blanks, as if filling out a typed form. This is roughly 30 percent faster than keypunching. The cost of direct access storage has also been reduced many times as a result of advancing technology, and while it was quite expensive in 1965, a decade later it cost from $3 to $6 per month to store a million characters of information. It is probably less expensive today to maintain all files on a computer system than to maintain the low access files separately in manual form. This assumes that the computer and necessary programming are already in place.

Automated reporting

While automated techniques are now widely used in the United States for inquiry into operational police files and to update those files, there are only a few departments that have begun to explore other uses of computer technology as a means of improving their overall information management. Where some of these advanced applications have been implemented they are still restricted to the larger departments. Throughout this discussion it should be remembered that these are not just department capabilities, and that virtually anything that can be done at the computer location can also be done via the terminal at a remote location. This is to say that we are on another threshold and that the next major advance in police information management will be in an area called distributed processing.

One of these advanced applications which appears to have great promise and which was first demonstrated by the Indianapolis police department[3] we can call automated reporting. Typically, field reports are received at a district or headquarters location typed on multicopy snap-out carbon forms; index cards are typed; and then the typed data are distributed to file units, action or follow-up units, statistical units, etc. This process has always had many undesirable characteristics. It is slow because reports are usually received in batches by the typists and then batched again for delivery to appropriate action units. It is expensive because reports must be handled several times and the entire process is extremely sensitive to increases in volume. It is inefficient because investigators receive their action copies from the records division and then have to come back to the records division for file checks.

It is entirely feasible today to completely automate this process. As field reports of any kind are received, instead of being recorded on printed forms they may be directly entered into a computer system by calling up the proper form on a visual display terminal and filling in the blanks via the typewriter terminal. The complete report, including narrative, may be entered in this fashion. Through programmed instructions, the computer can automatically update all indexes (names, addresses, property, etc.), and every entry to an index can force an inquiry into the appropriate files of the local agency, the state law enforcement system (including motor vehicle files for driver's license, driver history, and vehicle registration records), and the National Crime Information Center.

When the report is completed the action copy can be printed on a terminal in the appropriate action units so that the flow of work is relatively constant rather than coming in bunches. When investigative units receive their copies a supervisor may make a decision on the need for immediate follow-up, and all possible inquiries and responses are printed at the end of the report so that the investigator need waste no time on records checks. When the investigator is ready to submit a follow-up report, he or she need enter only the report number to call up the original on his or her remote terminal and then add his or her follow-up information.

In the records division itself, the records copies of reports can be machine sorted at the end of the shift, or once a day, and then printed in report number order, so that blocks of reports are simply dropped in the files. It probably would require some study in each department, but it will generally be the case that the complete report need only be retained in computer files for sixty to ninety days, and after that only index data are retained and the report is written off on magnetic tape for permanent storage.

Computer-aided dispatching

The usual nonautomated radio room process is for the complaint to be received by telephone, recorded on a paper form, and transported in some fashion to a dispatcher. The dispatcher makes a selection of a unit or units to dispatch, records this on the form, and broadcasts the assignment. Status of field units (in-service, out-of-service, or not assigned) is most often maintained by a system of lights on a map which are manually operated by the dispatcher. There are, of course, many variations, but the essential elements are the same.

A computer-aided dispatch system would include the following elements:

1. The complaint is received by telephone and the complaint operator enters it on a visual display terminal via the typewriter keyboard.
2. The computer checks on the address against a geo-coded file of the jurisdiction to determine if the address is proper (e.g., if the complainant indicates a location of 6800 Oak Street and the file indicates that Oak Street ends at 6200, the system immediately notifies the complaint operator while the complainant is still on the line). The geographic files normally have not only street address information but intersections and named locations (parks, public buildings, and other places likely to be referred to by name rather than address).
3. The computer checks the active file and notifies the complaint operator if the current incident has already been reported by another source.
4. When the complaint has been recorded, the complaint operator transmits it to the dispatcher and it is displayed instantaneously on the dispatcher's screen.
5. The computer has checked the location address against field

The computer-assisted dispatch system for the Miami, Florida, police department enters calls for service on line to the computer by a complaint taker. The computer sends the incident electronically to a dispatcher who assigns calls to units in the field and keeps track of unit status on line.

assignment locations and displays the best units for the assignment. The dispatcher makes a choice, enters that car number on the keyboard, and broadcasts the assignment. When digital terminals in the police car become more common, the dispatcher will touch a single key and cause the assignment to be displayed or printed in the car.

6. The computer records each step of the dispatch process, including appropriate times, and maintains the status of all units. The status of all active complaints and of all field units can be displayed on demand.

The original basis for the concept of using a computer in the dispatching process was that automation could speed up the activities involved in processing a call for service, selecting the best unit for assignment, and dispatching that unit. This objective is realistic in large departments, but in smaller agencies, where the number of cars on the street is manageable by one or two dispatchers and the volume of calls is comparatively light, it is doubtful that automation will speed the dispatch process.

Police dispatching in the good old days Communication can be highly sophisticated, but the purpose is still the same: to get a message from one point to another or from one person to another. In Flat River, Missouri, in 1960, police radio dispatching was handled by the local cab company. When a call was received, the taxi dis-patcher would turn on a red light on top of the National Hotel. The police officer would then report in to the cab stand for information. He often would be passing the cab stand as part of his regular police patrol, and the system seemed to work reasonably well in this small community.

Departments of modest size are looking at computer-aided dispatching for other reasons, however. If we had to select one record, of all those made by police, as the basis for managing the police operation, it would almost certainly be the radio dispatch record. On this device are recorded all calls for police service and all officers' on-view activity reported from the street, so it gives a reasonably complete record of the measurable police work load, its distribution over time and area, and the amount of time each officer spends on each call; therefore it is possible to determine what part of total police time is available for preventive patrol by area of the jurisdiction. In a computer-aided dispatch system all of this information is captured in machine readable (and processable) form as a by-product of normal dispatching activity, so that basic management information can be available on a far more timely and less costly basis.

Another value of computerizing the dispatching process is just now being recognized in areas where, owing to metropolitan growth, many departments have mutual boundaries and citizens frequently have difficulty determining what jurisdiction they are in when they require police service. Centralized dispatching and a geo-base that covers the entire area can greatly assist in getting the right unit to the scene. Possibly even more important, in emergency situations cover cars can be directed to the scene regardless of jurisdiction.

On-line management information

The executive of any organization must cope with the question of how much he or she should know about the detailed day-to-day operations of the organization. One school of thought has held that the executive should know everything. This philosophy has led to a proliferation of so-called management reports in many organizations, to the point where the administrator is so overburdened with the tools of management that he or she has no time left to manage.

The police executive is by no means immune to this problem. With departmental size limited by both economics and the unavailability of qualified recruits, he still must meet an increasing crime problem. This can be done only through the most effective deployment of available resources and the careful evaluation of enforcement and prevention programs. To achieve these aims with traditional approaches to the development of management information, the police executive is required to absorb tremendous amounts of detail from a mound of daily, weekly, and monthly statistical reports.

The growing complexity of the management task and the speed and the flexibility of modern computer technology have led to the growing acceptance of a new concept of management information. This concept proposes that it is no longer possible for an executive to know and retain everything about the operation of the organization and that the proper amount of information the executive should have is the least amount possible consistent with maintaining the ability to control all phases of the organization. For such a concept to have practical value, the executive must also have the ability to answer almost any question about the operation of the organization on a "right now" basis.

Crime and arrest   The police decision maker of the future should be able to get immediate answers to a vast array of questions about his operation. For example, if a complaint relating to pickpockets and purse snatchers is received from a merchants' association via the city council, the chief should be able to inquire through his terminal for the incidence of such offenses in the subject area for the current time period, selected earlier time periods in the current year, and comparable periods in the previous year. He should also be able to get an immediate display relating to arrests and clearances associated with those offenses. The chief should be able to report back to the council that there is no problem—that there was a rash of offenses some time ago but they have been controlled; or that there is a problem and an appropriate plan will be put into action to correct it.

Such an interactive statistical data base can have huge value. First, it provides the means of making the best possible use of all resources because they can be assigned and directed in terms of the "right now" problem. The decision maker's time is also very much better utilized because he can deal with questions as they arise, rather than having to assign someone to dig through statistical reports (or do it himself) and keep after them until he gets enough information (it is hoped) to take action. It may be noted that the ability to appear on top of every question is certainly not harmful to the image the police administrator conveys to civic groups with which he must deal.

Traffic   There has always been talk about selective enforcement, but the volume of citations and accident reports is usually such that very few departments in the country have really been able to achieve this goal. However, if there is a geo-coded data base, and if accidents are recorded by time, location, and cause, and citations by time, location, and violation, selective enforcement can become a reality with an interactive data base.

Consider, instead of poring over pages of statistics, being able to call up a listing of high accident locations, and then, for each location, the accidents by hour, day, and cause—and then being able to display, next to this, citation data. Where the results seem unsatisfactory, the next step would be to display the individual activity of each officer assigned to the area in question. Experience indicates that once this kind of thing can be done problems are nearly self-correcting.

Personnel   The largest and most important single resource in law enforcement is personnel. Costs for salaries account for up to 90 percent of the total police budget. Yet personnel records management tends to get the least attention of all areas of the overall police information system. In very small departments the problem is not great, but as the department grows in size, if some imagination and attention are not diverted to this area it can get out of hand. It is always surprising to find a department today in which the complete departmental roster is typed every day for timekeeping purposes, showing name, rank, star or serial number, assignment, time on duty, time off duty, and exception data. A far superior procedure is to produce time sheets for two weeks at a time. Then time clerks need only enter exception information (sick, injured, assignment changes, etc.) and return the sheet to payroll for updating of the master record. Where the department is part of a computerized system, the unit roster can be called up on a visual display terminal and changes can be made on-line.

One specific area that generally needs improvement is overtime accounting. Typically, when officers work overtime they complete some kind of paper form. This is approved by a supervisor and forwarded to personnel for processing. If all this is accomplished by means of individual paper transactions, the division commander and chief will usually have very little information on how much overtime is being worked, by whom, and in what part of the jurisdiction. When most overtime was paid with compensatory time off there was often a tendency to treat this problem loosely. Today, with the trend toward paid overtime (and very often paid at time and one-half), the police administrator is forced to be more concerned. If the master personnel file is automated it is not difficult to add a routine that accepts each new overtime entry through a terminal and summarizes the information by the person, the approving supervisor, and the organizational unit, and for the entire department. Such a system stands ready to respond to any inquiry by an authorized person.

Crime analysis

Probably the most important area in which there will be more effective use of police information in the immediate future is in crime analysis. Over the years there has been imaginative use of a variety of techniques to assist the police agency in tracking the development of crime patterns. Some departments still use pin maps very effectively. Colored pins with numbers on the heads can indicate the chronology of a series of related incidents. Connecting pins with rubber bands to indicate the relationship between location of theft and location of recovery for stolen autos has successfully identified patterns and led to clearances. The same technique is used in connection with juvenile activity to relate location of offense with school attended, or location of offense with neighborhood in which the offender lives. This approach can provide early indicators of gang activity or other conditions that can be treated. Other departments have been successful with keeping a second copy of field interrogation reports in location order and relating this to their pin maps.

The problem with all these techniques is that they are only feasible when volumes are quite small. As the department gets larger and volumes increase, it becomes more and more difficult to devote the necessary manpower to what are time-consuming operations. Larger departments can accomplish these activities to some degree with machine listings showing type of offense, location, time, and special characteristics, but these have not really been successful because the reports require much study to yield meaningful results.

For the past thirty or forty years, attempts have been made here and there to develop effective modus operandi (M.O.) files, and periodically a department will report significant success in this area. A check with such departments a few years later will generally reflect that they have discontinued the file. M.O. files do not work very well in the United States, and there are a number of reasons for this. There is a highly mobile population. There is a great deal of opportunistic crime. There are thousands of paperback detective stories and dozens of television crime shows which explain M.O. and associated police procedures in the most minute detail. Given all of these conditions, it is not surprising that M.O. does not prove as good a tool in this country as could be wished. This is not to say that M.O. patterns do not occur. They sometimes do occur and are quite spectacular—but they tend to occur just often enough to keep detectives talking about M.O., and not often enough to justify the maintenance of purely M.O. files. Attempts to automate M.O. files have generally tended to prove that M.O. files do not work much faster on a computer.

Work done in Long Beach and Los Angeles, California, in tne 1970s seems to hold great promise for the effective analysis of crime. These systems were originally developed as "investigative support" systems. The goal was to find a better way to assist the investigator than was possible with the standard M.O./known offender file approach. The results have turned out to have benefit for the uniformed force and the administration as well as the detective. The Los Angeles system is called PATRIC, an acronym for PATtern Recognition and Information Correlation. The information base is data captured from crime reports, field interview reports, investigator follow-up reports, and registered offender files (California law requires persons who have felony convictions for sex or narcotics offenses to register with the police). The system is so constructed that it will be possible to add other information services (traffic citations, pawn shop reports, etc.) if this seems feasible.

The PATRIC system assembles all of the collected information into very large files and then develops a variety of correlations so that a terminal operator is able to enter inquiries to obtain: time patterns; geographic patterns; crime speciality patterns; M.O. patterns; partial description patterns (persons, clothing, automobiles, partial plates, etc.).

This system only became operational in 1976, and so far its use has been limited to the Los Angeles police department. It represents, however, a classic example of a centralized activity in which all of the police agencies in a metropolitan area could participate with major benefit.

There should be, it is hoped, major emphasis in the next few years on the further development of shared systems intended to improve the information management capabilities of all of American law enforcement agencies. The technology is now available to replace the simple inquiry–update terminals with somewhat more complex "intelligent" terminal devices to permit the small surburban or outlying department to enjoy the same level of development and control of information management as the large center cities do. The problems of coordination, development, and funding will be severe, but the precedent already exists. It is quite possible that county and state police chief associations have before them their greatest challenge and their greatest opportunity in police service history.

Query languages

It is timely to mention that, as of 1980, another development in technology has major implications for both management information and crime analysis in police operations. "Query" languages are evolving very rapidly, and for a modest cost they now offer capability that used to be affordable by only the very largest agencies.

These languages are computer programs that construct copies of data files and then so arrange the data in the special files that they can be retrieved in any form desired and immediately displayed. The technique is the same whether the data are required for management or operational (crime analysis) purposes, and the implication is that batch statistical reports, which were always too late to be useful, and which never quite addressed the instant question, are quite obsolete. Police agencies will certainly continue to maintain a variety of printed statistical reports for historical and record keeping purposes, but there can be little doubt that the query techniques will soon be in common use.

The key to successful use of these tools, of course, is clearly in the development of the data base. The automated reporting process discussed earlier becomes even more important because, in addition to providing for automatic indexing, cross-referencing, file search, and real-time distribution of reports, the automated reporting system provides a data base as a by-product of the normal processing of reports.

If these techniques have a drawback, it is that they require rather large amounts of computer memory. The cost of memory has dropped dramatically in recent years, however, and most departments large enough to benefit from this level of sophistication probably spend far more than equivalent amounts in the salaries of officers and clerks developing less complete and timely information by manual means.

Given an adequate data base, the police decision maker (who is not a programmer or technician) can easily learn to use the query languages for an immediate response to almost any question that arises. From personnel files the user can obtain the number of patrol officers by race, by length of service, or by division, or the number of female sergeants by division of assignment, or whatever. From the incident data files he or she can, in a moment, determine the number of armed robberies by reporting district, by day of week, and by shift and can display them in rank order for any subfield. Or the user can display the number of nighttime residential burglaries for several comparable areas for any time period or periods. From the traffic files he or she can look at the number of injury accidents in a given school area for the current month, the previous month, and the same month last year to determine whether complaints of increased hazard are accurate. If it appears that the accident picture is deteriorating for a given area, one can display accidents by cause and citations by violation to determine whether adjustments in coverage are in order.

When a problem of patrol or traffic coverage is identified, the data clearly reflect the need for a change in tactics. Placing a terminal in the roll call area where the officers affected can actually look at the numbers might be worth all the general and special orders and all the roll call lieutenant's pep talks for the previous year. This procedure could have major value in motivating officers by giving them the ability to examine on a daily basis what they are *not* preventing in their areas of responsibility. It might even be possible to reawaken a little competitive spirit that would make the job more fun—and the department more effective.

Crime Analysis Support System (CASS)

The query languages are clearly not for everyone. A great number of police departments in the United States are too small to justify such sophistication but are nonetheless large enough to require greater analytic capability than can be provided by manual methods, and more timely information than can be provided by traditional batch computer techniques. For these, too, there is an answer called CASS, Crime Analysis Support System.

The requirements for CASS were defined by the Law Enforcement Assistance Administration in 1977, and the International Association of Chiefs of Police (IACP) was awarded the contract to develop the system. IACP was awarded a follow-on contract in 1979, and CASS is now available from that organization to run on several small computer systems. The functions that IACP reports and that are addressed by CASS are:

1. *Crime pattern detection.* Identification of related or similar crimes based on geography, trends, common suspects, and method of operation.
2. *Crime suspect correlation.* Identification of potential suspects by physical

descriptors, methods of operation, vehicles, associates, preferred targets, or other known information.

3. *Target profiles*. Development of demographic data that have a direct effect on the community and focus on a community service approach to policing.

4. *Forecast potential*. Capability to predict time and location of future criminal events.

5. *Exception reporting*. Periodic monitoring at fixed intervals of the occurrence of crime, jurisdiction-wide or by geographic area, to identify significant deviations from normal levels of activity.

6. *Forecast of crime trends*. Prediction of crime volume in a time domain (i.e., forecasting by time of day, day of week, etc.), based on the crime data using statistical methodology.

7. *Resource allocation*. Determination of the most efficient and cost-effective method of distributing personnel.

While this "package" approach has less flexibility than the query languages, it is reported to be very adaptable and to provide more ability to retrieve, manipulate, and display data than has normally been available to very modest size departments. A detailed description of the Crime Analysis Support System is available from the International Association of Chiefs of Police.[4]

Specialized techniques

As police administrators are more active in seeking new ways to address ever more complex problems, there are a variety of technologies beginning to evolve that deserve brief discussion here. These are all rapidly developing areas, so detailed analysis will not be attempted. The interested reader should seek current information.

Automated vehicle locator   The concept here is that there would be significant benefit to police command if the precise location of every field unit could be displayed in a command and control center at all times. The benefits suggested are:

1. Constant display of car location would make it possible to dispatch the unit actually closest to the scene of a crime in progress, thereby minimizing response time

2. If status (in-service, out-of-service) as well as location is displayed on an electronic map, the duty commander can observe when a preponderance of the units in a given area of the jurisdiction are out-of-service, and begin to move units from other parts of the jurisdiction, so that response time is kept within reasonable limits if serious offenses continue to occur in the busy area

3. If field units appear to be parked and not moving for extended periods of time, supervisors can be sent to check on them.

Automated vehicle location can be accomplished through several techniques. One method is to transmit a radio signal from each car to several radio towers where the time it takes the signal to reach each tower is measured and this phase shift, as it is called, is forwarded to a computer. The location of the car is then computed on the basis of the difference in the time required for the signal to get from the car to at least three towers. Variations of the technique are known as triangulation, trilateration, parabolation, etc.

Another approach is called signposting and involves locating a low-grade transmitter on signposts or on building walls to emit a location code. A special transceiver in the car picks up this signal as the car moves past the signpost and transmits the location code along with the car identification code to a computer which controls the display. The third technique, generally called dead reckoning, involves a device connected to the car's speedometer and front wheels. It measures speed and change in direction and transmits this data to a computer which can compute location.

All of these techniques, which have been described in the simplest possible terms above, are quite complex, and they have in common one major problem: they are hugely expensive. The question the police administrator must ask himself is whether his operation will really benefit enough from knowing the precise location of all field units to justify what appears to involve a multimillion dollar investment in a jurisdiction large enough to consider this capability. In most police radio systems we have seen, all of the units on a frequency can hear all of the outgoing calls, and we have not found that there is any difficulty in getting the closest car to respond to a crime-in-progress situation even where another car is specifically assigned. Also, imbalances in car availability can be fairly well shown on a simple lighted status board controlled by the dispatcher. Vehicle locator is worth following, however, since, as with most other technology, costs will almost certainly decrease in time.

Mobile digital terminals   Almost certainly there will be more rapid acceptance of mobile digital terminals over the next few years. As more departments develop broader use of automated information techniques, the clear implication is for increased transmission of information between headquarters and field. Over much of the country air time is near saturation point. A most promising solution to this problem may be found in soundly engineered mobile digital terminals which will permit greatly increased volumes of air traffic over existing radio frequencies. The advantages of digital radio transmission are significant:

1. The officer in the field may inquire directly into automated files from his or her digital terminal without going through the dispatcher. This should remove constraints on inquiry that develop when field personnel are aware that dispatchers are abnormally busy, and use of operational files should increase.
2. The digital message is effectively scrambled, and therefore far more secure than voice radio. Burglars, truck hijackers, etc., could no longer depend on relatively inexpensive and readily available radio receivers to intercept police communications. Mobile digital terminals will become a natural extension of computer-aided dispatching.
3. It may even prove practical to move all of the advantages discussed under "automated reporting" out to the car and permit officers to enter their reports directly from the field. This would further speed up the reporting process, minimize the handling of reports, and reduce costs.

Automated fingerprint identification   One long-sought technological advance that has evaded us to date is the ability to read and identify fingerprints with automated techniques and at electronic speeds. As reported offense and arrest volumes have increased over the years, so has the length of time between submission of fingerprints to the state or FBI and receipt of the results. This has meant that investigators, prosecutors, arraignment judges, and even sentencing judges are frequently required to make decisions relating to a particular subject without reference to the subject's prior criminal record.

It is hoped that in the next decade this situation will be much improved. The FBI now has installed a system called Finder which can develop a digital description of fingerprints. When a new set of prints is received, the Finder system can digitize the new set of prints, search against the established file, and display both the new prints and matching prints for a technician who can make the final determination on identification.

The system has the potential to considerably speed up the file search process at the FBI Bureau of Identification. Unfortunately, the fingerprint cards must still be transmitted to the FBI from the assisting agency by mail, and results of the search are normally returned by mail. There have been successful attempts to employ facsimile transmission techniques between the New York City police and the New York State intelligence and identification division and, in Chicago, between police district stations and the headquarters identification division. It appears that adequate resolution can be obtained for identification purposes, but the process is far too slow to accommodate high volumes. These advances provide the basis for some optimism that the near future will bring breakthroughs in this extremely important area. Indeed, the advances in police information management in the past ten years have been very nearly overwhelming, and there is every evidence that this progress will accelerate rather than slow down in future years.

Conclusion

Most police record systems are probably haphazardly organized, disparate, even fragmentary. In many departments they may not even approach a "system." But changes are coming—and rapidly. The introduction to this chapter noted that new kinds of computers are on the market that are particularly well suited to the needs of the police service and that the national issue of "law and order" has put particular pressure on the police service for much better record systems that are integrated with metropolitan and statewide systems.

This chapter has reviewed the developments in technology and the issues of security and privacy to provide the background for developing the basics of information management and the mechanics of police reporting. The chapter has then discussed the interrelationships of information management and technology in the police service and has provided a discussion of the specific applications of full index conversion, automated reporting, computer-aided dispatch, on-line management information, crime analysis, query languages, Crime Analysis Support System (CASS), and the newer and more experimental techniques of the automated vehicle locator, mobile digital terminals, and automated fingerprint identification.

The hardware (computers and ancillary equipment) and the software (programming and related input) are available in highly sophisticated forms and also in much simpler versions to serve police administrators in a wide variety of ways. The police chief now needs to think through his requirements for information in the context of the management issues raised in the earlier portions of this book, especially in Chapters 6, 7, 8, and 9.

1 O. W. Wilson, *Police Records: Their Installation and Use* (Chicago: Public Administration Service, 1951). (Out of print.)

2 For further background to the above discussion, see the following: President's Commission on Law Enforcement and Administration of Justice, *Task Force Report: The Police* (Washington, D.C.: Government Printing Office, 1967).

3 *Indianapolis Police Automated Case Entry and Re-trieval System*, Form no. GK20–0831 (White Plains, N.Y.: IBM Corporation, 1975).

4 National Criminal Justice Information and Statistics Service, Law Enforcement Assistance Administration, *Crime Analysis Support System: Descriptive Report of Manual and Automated Crime Analysis Functions* (Washington, D.C.: Government Printing Office, 1979).

17 Facilities and materiel

Police stations, training facilities, and other real property; the control of departmental property and personal equipment; vehicle specifications, purchase, and maintenance; control of evidence and selection of armament—all are parts of the broad range of considerations in the management of facilities and materiel for the police agency.

This chapter covers the major management responsibilities of the following: building design, including planning, the design considerations for new construction and major alterations, and building maintenance; property control systems, including fund accounting and the design of property control facilities; the development of specifications for the purchase of patrol cars and other automotive equipment, as well as vehicle maintenance and record systems; firearms and other departmental and personal armament; and police uniforms. A brief evaluative summary concludes the chapter.

Building design

Approximately once each half century a community faces the need for a new police building. On a more frequent scale remodeling takes place because of the department's growth or change in organization. Very often the people who must work within the facility are not included in the planning for the new building and must accept a local architect's conception of a police building. The result, in most cases, is a disappointment to the police administrator.

A police building in and of itself is probably one of the most important structures a community will build. The police facility shares responsibility for community services with schools, hospitals, and the city hall. It reflects the image of the community along with the philosophy of the community's commitment to modern police service methods and procedures. Properly planned and designed, the department's building can be a direct influence on the morale and operational efficiency of police officers, clerical employees, and administrative staff. It is a source of pride not only for those who work within it but also for those who must live or work in surrounding areas.

Unfortunately, the majority of police buildings in the United States have been designed around an improper organizational structure or reflect the attitudes of communities towards the police service twenty or thirty years ago. Those departments that must share a building with other city services often find the police portion relegated to lower floors or the basement area. Many police departments have side entrances away from the main thoroughfare of traffic, and, very often, one must go to the rear of the city hall to find the police department. This reflects the attitude of government in the past and to a certain extent of architects today. Very few architects have had the opportunity to design such a structure, and as planners they reflect only what community management directs.

Fortunately, modern government has accepted the police function as a necessary part of its community service and that acceptance is being reflected in the design of modern police structures. Today modern police buildings are attractive to the eye, with entrances opening onto the mainstream of community life.

The interiors of police buildings are no longer dirty and unattractive but present a modern, functional appearance enhanced by an imaginative use of materials.

The building of a modern police facility involves many segments of the community, the police service, and the architectural field. In the next sections a few key elements for police building design and/or renovation will be explored.

The planning process

Police administrators and commanders who will spend hours laboring over plans for operational problems, traffic control, or special events sometimes find it very difficult to become involved in the planning of a police building. An architect or consultant is hired, the administrators provide a list of wants, and then everybody forgets the whole thing until the first set of drawings is produced. Alterations in the plans are made and remade. Eventually a decision is reached and a set of plans is accepted. This lack of departmental involvement will result in a building that is probably unacceptable. The police department, then, must actively participate in the building planning.

Planning begins with the determination that the current structure is no longer capable of serving the needs of the police department. This determination is often made on the basis of structure size versus personnel strength. Police departments have grown over the past few years; thus locker rooms are too small, office space is not available, and records are stored in every nook and cranny. The configurations of modern communication equipment and records retrieval systems require alterations to the building's electrical and other mechanical services. Jail operation and management has altered considerably because of court requirements and demands for more humane treatment for prisoners. Attacks on police buildings have occurred in the United States, and older police facilities are not designed to cope with such threats. Finally, the disproportionate use of personnel required by antiquated facilities is no longer acceptable to the taxpaying public.

Once the determination has been made to proceed to the planning stage for a new police facility, a team should be gathered to plan the project. Composition of this team depends primarily upon the size of the police department and the scope of the project. In a small agency the chief of police will be directly involved as a member of the project team. In larger departments either the departmental planning officer or senior staff members should be assigned.

Size of the team will probably vary depending on the requirements of the project. In addition to police professionals an architect is required. If the project includes an operational jail, then a correctional administrator should be included on the team. (Chapter 19 of this book includes planning criteria for jail facilities.) If the community is charged with court administration then a court specialist must also be included. Finally, members of the community in general should be allowed representation on the team. This ensures that citizen attitudes and desires are fully explored.

Police service members If the department is of sufficient size to appoint a planning officer or senior staff member, this individual should provide leadership to the team in addition to gathering and coordinating the data necessary for the planning effort. In most cases this individual must be relieved of all other duties and allowed to devote his or her total effort to the accomplishment of a proper facility plan. The police administrator in the smaller agency cannot afford this luxury, however, and must provide the guidance to the project along with his other duties.

In addition to the project coordinator, other members of the police department should be involved in the planning process. Although not necessarily members of the planning team, these individuals may be assigned to specific roles during the development of the plan or may be consulted on specific requirements of individualized tasks that will affect the design of the building. It must also be noted that individuals who work within the facility are probably in the best position to identify relevant design problems. These "workers" should also be consulted to create a "shopping list" of needs for the new facility. The basic work force is a valuable resource that cannot be overemphasized or overconsulted.

The specialist Probably no two police buildings in the United States are exactly alike. Even those that have been designed as substations within major police agencies show an evolutionary process in design that meets the specific needs of community or environment. The uniqueness of individual police buildings is the direct result of influences on the agency in the form of community wants, individual law requirements, and departmental operations.

In some states the magistrate system is still in effect. Before police officers may incarcerate an individual they must have a hearing before a magistrate and attain a warrant of arrest. This creates an additional step in the processing of prisoners. In other areas sentenced prisoners are allowed to remain in city jails, whereas in others such prisoners are housed at a county level. These unique problems require individual design and technical help from individuals qualified in prisoner control and treatment.

Other technical areas must be covered in the planning process. Does a department intend to create a crime laboratory? Will data processing equipment be required? Is the department responsible for vehicle maintenance and radio repair? If the answers to these questions are positive a specialist in each technical area must be included on the planning team.

Citizens The idea of citizen involvement in police facility design may meet with some ridicule from police or community administrators who may feel that the task is a technical one. However, a police building is a community structure and as such should reflect community attitudes and desires as closely as possible.

The architect The architect should be selected as early as possible in the planning process. In order to become acquainted with the problems and needs of the police service, one architect in the United States recently took courses in police administration. This gave him a better idea of the operational and administrative problems that could influence the design of a police building. Of course, all architects are not required to go so far, but involvement in the basic planning is a requirement.

The architect should be the technical adviser for the project plan and should provide the backdrop of technical expertise needed by the planning team. A police building is a complex structure—more so than the average school or office building. Electrical, plumbing, and structural requirements create a myriad of special problems. Involvement of the architect at the first stages of planning provides for assistance in functional planning as well as mechanical design.

The planning tasks

The complexity of a police building design plan can stagger the imagination of those who are not familiar with such a project. When large agencies are involved the sheer size of the department creates a formidable planning task. It is necessary to provide guidelines for the planning team. In no special order, the following five basic points must be considered in preparing a good facility plan. While these points are interrelated, each makes its own contribution to the success of the entire plan, and each should be given individual attention by the planning team.

Efficiency   The design of the facility must lend itself to the most efficient work flow possible. Individual segments of the department must be studied to assure their proper placement within the entire structure. Individual work areas must be designed to provide efficient utilization of employee time and job requirements.

Security   Security in a police facility is an intrinsic design element. Protection must be provided against both external and internal forces that might disrupt the operations of the department and destroy vital equipment. However, security must not be allowed to become a dominant force in the design of the police facility. Blockhouses and citadels should not be created within a community; rather, attractive buildings with security features built into them should be the goal.

Flexibility   If there is a truism regarding older police buildings it is that they are inflexible. Architects and designers in bygone years were either unable or unwilling to provide for growth and change within a police department. Thick walls, small individual offices, gloomy halls, and dark staircases are the results. A police department is labor intensive and as such is subject to human whim and desire. Police departments grow, they contract, they alter their appearance, and change their goals. The police facility must be able to breathe with the department and alter its structure with that of the department.

Use of modern design and structural devices provides this flexibility. Partial partitions, movable walls, areas that can be used for dual purposes, all provide flexibility necessary for today's police building. Structures that accommodate expansion either laterally or horizontally provide for the expansion of personnel and functions within the department. Site locations that allow for additional parking, helipads, and building expansion buy tomorrow's world at today's prices.

Aesthetics   The days of the tall gray police structure with forbidding entrances and two glass balls denoting "police" are gone forever. Stark lobbies with straight-back chairs, and the high police sergeant's desk, and a brass rail are things of the past.

There is no reason why a police station cannot present a modern appearance. Attractive façades of brick or stone are not unrealistic. Entranceways that open to clean reception areas provide a feeling of security as well as efficiency. Trees, lawns, and attractive flowerbeds are also possible. Design with an eye for the appearance of the structure provides the community with its image of its police and the outsider with an image of the community.

Costs   Probably the area that will attract the greatest interest, criticism, and frustration is that of the economic constraints of such an undertaking. Economy can be served in many ways. Materials that provide low maintenance of the building in the future serve economic requirements. A design that provides for optimum use of manpower considers future budgets. A plan that allows for growth in the future with minimum cost underwrites economic restraint.

A police building is expensive. Before a community enters into this venture the planning team must decide whether a new building is needed. If the old structure can be expanded, modified, or rearranged to suit the needs and desires of the community at less cost, then strong consideration must be given to that alternative.

Functional design

Certain design concepts must be employed regardless of the nature of the project. These concepts hold true for modifying an existing structure as well as for building a new facility. These concepts are found in two areas of functional design: (1) function: activity related, and (2) function: people related.

Function: activity related Part of the planning effort for the facility must define the relationship of individual activities to each other and to the departmental operation as a whole. Diagrams of these relationships should be developed and reviewed by individuals who work in the specific activity under study to ensure accuracy. Once these diagrams are complete it will become apparent that there are certain hubs of activity within any police organization. The building design should provide the avenues through which identified activities may continue and interrelate.

Although the patrol effort is the major activity of the police organization, the actual hub of a police building is found elsewhere. All police reports, investigative reports, and other areas of reporting come together within the record section. Communications is at both ends of the complaint process and, therefore, has a direct relationship to the record keeping function of a police agency. This functional relationship becomes a center of activity within the building.

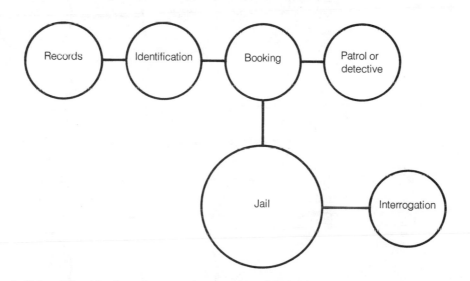

A: This relationship diagram indicates the grouping of activities around one function of the building—the jail. Note that patrol or detective has direct relationship with booking but does not require direct contact with the jail.

Before any sort of functional diagrams can be drawn the police administrator must take a complete look at the organizational structure. Far too often police buildings have been designed around organizations that are functionally disorganized. For instance, many police agencies maintain records as part of the investigative operation rather than as a central record file. Others keep records in separate areas of the department rather than in a central pool. Some agencies staff the communications section as part of the patrol process and communicators are assigned to individual patrol platoons or shifts. If this functional disunity is carried into the building plan a disorganized building will result.

If the planning team discovers such functional improprieties in the organizational structure of the police agency, it must point them out to the chief administrator. An effort must be made to bring the building and the police organization together. If related functional activities are separated, a duplication of personnel is the result. Reorganization that brings related functions together into the same organizational structure and building space will generally result in economies of manpower (Figures A, B, and C).

Function: people related   Once functional activities have been identified and their relationships determined it becomes necessary to look at the clients served by particular activities. In a police facility there are three categories of people utilizing the buildings: personnel, prisoners, and the public.

The term personnel refers to all employees of the police department. Uniformed personnel constitute the bulk of any police department and for the most part their activity is confined to certain areas of the building. The roll call room, report writing center, and shift supervisory office are used primarily by the patrol officer and should be grouped accordingly. On the other hand, the follow-up investigator or detective needs the records center and access to prisoners. Therefore, it is not necessary to have detective and patrol officers in the same area of the building or in close proximity. Finally, administrative officers must have access to supervisors and to records, as well as having a direct relationship to the general public.

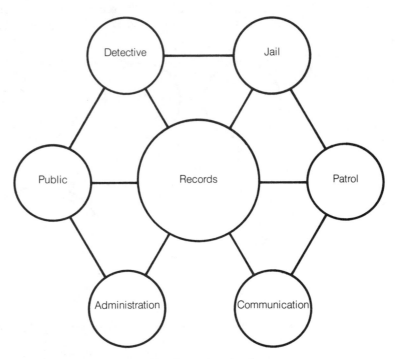

B: This diagram shows the relationship of people using the police building. Note that records is the center of the wheel and thus the center of the building.

The public, on the other hand, will generally deal with investigative personnel and records personnel as opposed to uniformed police officers within the police building. For the most part, functional relationship charts will show heavy overlapping of public, investigators, and records personnel with some shading in the administrators area. Design, then, should ensure that these relationships are maintained within the structure.

Finally, the prisoner presents two problems. His or her involvement with the patrol officer becomes minimal inside the building. After the prisoner is booked either jail or records personnel will be his or her primary contact. In no instances should the prisoner's area of activity touch or overlap that of the general public, nor should the prisoner be allowed to come into contact with the sensitive areas of the police facility (that is, weapons storage, communications, or vehicle control).

Functional relationships are critical to the operation of a police agency and to the design of the police building. The extent of overlapping or contact with each other depends primarily on the size of the agency. In smaller agencies, one individual may perform several functions, therefore the problem becomes less intense on a space relationship basis. In the larger more complicated agencies, relationships overlap but physical separation is required because of the sheer size of the organization. In these instances communication between the segments is mandatory.

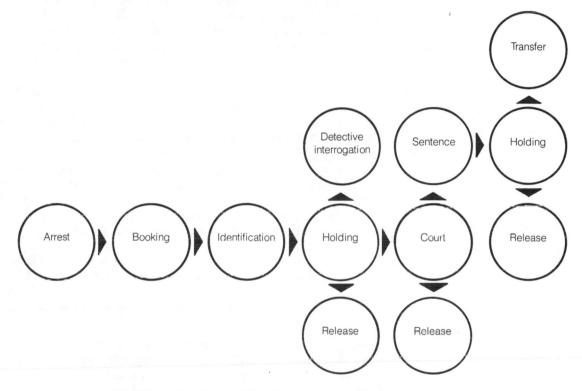

C: Charting functional relationships is a good starting point in highlighting the relationships of major activities.

Once the entire functional approach to design has been fully examined, the "activity" and the "people" processes can be brought together to provide overall guidance to the planning team and to be translated into the building design.

Basic design points

Although it is impossible to cover all basic design points, there are certain elements which should be considered by the planning team.

Location Location of the police facility depends upon several variables. First is availability to the community and the relationship of the site to the community's basic patterns of growth or to planned development consistent with the community's need. In those cities that have reached their maximum growth potential and do not plan expansion, location may be a problem if land is not available and the old site must be used. It must be remembered that in the past police stations were located on the premise of response time. Foot patrol patterns were distributed around the police station. Deployment patterns have changed radically in the last few years. Foot patrol is not necessarily the criterion for planning a station's location. On the other hand, if a precinct or storefront station is anticipated, neighborhood requirements must be involved in the selection of the site. When a central police station for an entire community is being planned, access by the public is a major consideration in the site location. Residents often are best served when all criminal justice components are included in a centralized design concept.

Location of court facilities may be taken into consideration in developing site location. Proximity to the courts will provide economies in manpower, especially for follow-up investigators, crime laboratory personnel, and evidence technicans who spend a large amount of time in court. In addition, if the community is required to house presentenced prisoners, a smaller distance between the court and the police station reduces the risk of escape. Some communities connect courts and police facilities by tunnel to provide the security needed in movement of prisoners.

Police facilities provide a community service and thus generate more traffic. Site location should take into consideration the public services a police facility may provide (i.e., meeting rooms, courts). Well-lighted public parking becomes a prerequisite for a facility such as this.

Police field activity is seldom a criterion for selection of site for a single police facility. It does provide more police coverage because of the comings and goings of police cars throughout the day and evening, but an area of high activity may discourage citizens from using the facility for fear of high crime incidence. On the other hand, when a precinct or community police station is being planned, police activity has a direct relationship to the site, especially if foot patrol units originate from the building.

Finally, site location must provide ingress and egress to police patrol cars on a regular basis. It is unwise to have police cars exiting onto major thoroughfares or divided highways. If conflict with traffic is unavoidable, then provision for traffic signals controlled from within the police building is mandatory.

Security   A police department is probably the most visible of governmental agencies. Because of this visibility it becomes a target for individuals who disagree with the establishment and those who would disrupt governmental operations for their own purposes. John Dillinger attacked a police facility and stole several weapons which he later used in his criminal career. In more recent history, a small police agency in Illinois was actually robbed at gunpoint for money kept in the cash drawer. In Ohio a deranged individual entered a police station, set a bomb, and totally destroyed the building. In Pennsylvania, to cover a bank robbery, a Molotov cocktail was thrown into the desk area of the police station to disrupt the communications activity of the department. This type of attack has become more common in the annals of American police service; therefore, a department cannot afford to be complacent and must protect its personnel, equipment, and operations.

In an effort to provide building protection, certain rules of security should be adhered to by police agencies. These rules should then be translated into design features when a police facility is built or modified. These rules are as follows:

1. The operational areas of the police building must be isolated from public contact.
2. All secondary exits and entrances from the police building should be locked at all times. Personnel may be provided with keys or electronic devices to control the opening and closing of doors.
3. Interior lobby doors must be secured and controlled by reception personnel. No member of the public should be allowed beyond these secure doors without a member of the department as escort.

4. In larger departments, personnel should be required to wear security badges for identification purposes within the police building. In smaller agencies this may not be necessary, except for part-time and maintenance staff who may not be known to members of the department.

5. Public restrooms should be located on exterior walls away from critical operations. If possible, these walls should be nonbearing so that explosions would tend to blow outward rather than into the structure.

6. Police vehicle parking facilities should be fenced or enclosed.

7. External lighting of the police facility must provide illumination for grounds and parking areas.

8. Only one public entrance, clearly lighted and marked, should be provided.

9. A security area or perimeter can be established around a police building and clearly illuminated at night to prevent parking of vehicles adjacent to the building. In some areas this security area could be outlined with a decorative fence which allows visibility but discourages entrance into the security zone.

10. Proper placement of materials and equipment within the police building adds to the security of the structure without amplifying costs. For example, records and communications facilities should be located as close to the center of the building as possible. This prevents the possibility of the destruction of vital records and communications services by explosive charges placed against the exterior of the building.

11. Ventilation shafts, air conditioners, and other mechanical portals to the building should be located in areas inaccessible to the public. Roof installation of such equipment is probably best.

12. Windows are not unacceptable for police facilities but placement of functions vital to the operation of the department in areas of the building with external windows is improper. Administrative units, operational commands, and multipurpose rooms may be provided with windows. Sniper attacks on police facilities are not uncommon, so windows should be provided with nighttime screening devices and tinted for limited interior visibility during the day. Of course, the higher the office is placed within the structure, the fewer security risks a window presents.

13. Prisoners should be brought to a secure portion of the building, where they should remain until transferred or released. Interrogation rooms, lineup rooms, and holding facilities must be separated from the operational areas of the police department. Separate air-conditioning, plumbing, and heating facilities should be designed for the detention complex. The prisoner who sets his bedding on fire can disrupt the entire police operation if common air-conditioning or ventilation facilities are used.

Design concepts A starkly modern police building in the midst of a neighborhood of traditional buildings is likely to be inappropriate. The building should fit in with other public buildings and with the neighborhood character. A precinct station within a small area of the community should conform to the surrounding neighborhood.

Inside, partitions should be kept to a minimum and should be consistent with construction and security requirements. It is not unrealistic to separate areas of the police building with counters, partial partitions, file cabinets and other such devices to lend an air of spaciousness without sacrificing functional separation.

344 Local Government Police Management

The application of color and wood tones to the interior of the police building will not only present a pleasing appearance to the general public but will provide an atmosphere the employee can enjoy. Administrative offices, if carpeted and draped, provide a congenial working space for the administrator and his staff. It is not unrealistic to allow a certain amount of individual taste on the part of the administrator to govern the decor of these facilities.

Extreme importance must be placed on the mechanical portion of a new police facility. Electrical and plumbing facilities should be designed to provide for future expansion of the police facility at minimum cost. The jail and operational portions of the police department should be totally separate in electric and plumbing plants. Each should be independent of the other and both should be provided with emergency power in the form of natural gas generators. These generators should have the ability of operating not only on natural gas but on bottled gas should the natural gas flow be interrupted.

Roll call rooms can be designed to provide the proper facility for roll call and future training programs as the department requires. Locker rooms should be placed at a point in the building most adaptable to external expansion. Growth in a police department is felt in lack of locker room space before it is discernible in the records center or the communications center.

Since records and communications are the center of the police building, counters must be provided for the public as well as for police officers. These counters should be separate and staffed in proportion to demand. In some departments this will result in a full-time receptionist at both police and public counters, whereas in others one individual may serve the entire information needs of the department. If the department is of such size that twenty-four-hour record keeping is not possible, records and communications must be coexistent (see figure on page 345).

Records areas can be designed so that communications personnel may retrieve information as needed. This also assumes that communication personnel will service public and police counters as required. The use of intercom systems and proper placement of partial partitions or file cabinets can provide a measure of security to the communications area under these circumstances. Where the volume of activity warrants, the communications center should be clearly separated from records and isolated in a more secure portion of the building. Placing the communications room adjacent to the records section with the only entrance through the records area provides dual advantages of security and accessibility only for authorized personnel. This design also facilitates the exclusion of uniformed police personnel or follow-up investigators from the communications center or the records center. This protects the integrity of the file system and maintains the quiet of the communications room. In large facilities, communications and records will necessarily be separated because of their size and activity. Design features must provide communication access via telephone, pneumatic tube, and, in some instances, teletype.

Jail facilities Police and jail operations should be separated, if not physically, then through design. Where jail management is part of police responsibilities, careful review of arrest records and case dispositions should be made before any jail design is carried out. The number of maximum security cells, holding tanks, padded cells, and segregated male–female facilities will be directly influenced by the volume of prisoner traffic. Modern durable construction materials should be utilized within the jail facility. Low maintenance wall treatment and cell design, and attractive coloring, add to a manageable, humane jail.

Facilities for booking prisoners must be part of the maximum security portion of the building. If at all possible, a sally port which allows police vehicles to enter the building and discharge their prisoner should be provided. These sally ports provide direct access to the booking area of the jail facility and should be

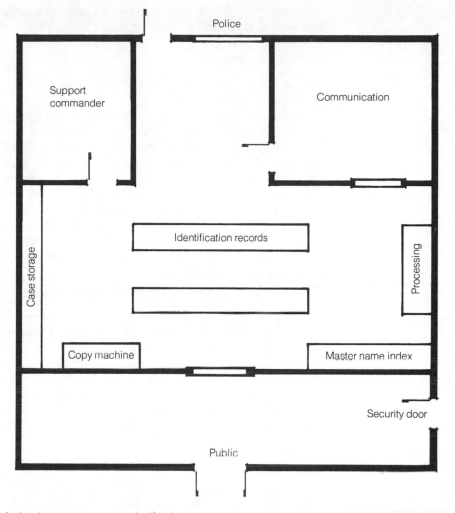

A simple records–communication layout. Note that records area serves
both the public and police officers and that records are located
so that one employee can handle the total operation if necessary.

controlled either by an on-duty jailer or communications room personnel. The
sally port itself can have an external door capable of being closed or opened
from the communications center.

Finally, interrogation rooms, prisoner lavatories, identification processing
rooms, and booking cages may be designed to eliminate external windows or
access to the police complex. In any room in which a prisoner is left alone,
doors should be designed to either slide or open outward to prevent barricading.
Locked receptacles for prisoner property should be provided within the jail
facility and identified by cell and bunk number.

The most difficult portion of jail design is not in the actual structure but in the
control of noise. The very nature of steel and concrete presents sound levels
that may not only disrupt the operation of the police building but antagonize
prisoners into irrational acts. Attempts should be made to dampen noise whenever possible. Finally, jail design must include independent plumbing access.
Service corridors between cell blocks are a necessity to ensure ongoing maintenance and emergency service without moving prisoners or bringing them into
contact with repair people.

Summary Several basic design points have been discussed which include the location of the police facility, its security, and fundamental design concepts.

Attention to detail and strict adherence to planning concepts will develop a police structure that will provide for today's operation and tomorrow's growth.

Building maintenance

One of the more difficult aspects of police administration is in the maintenance of the police building itself. Building maintenance necessarily implies additional personnel. Also, as the facility grows the complexity of the mechanical operation grows proportionately. Elaborate heating and cooling centers, electrical systems, and plumbing facilities require full-time staff to ensure continued operation. The police facility, unlike the normal municipal facility, is operated on a twenty-four-hour day which adds to the maintenance problems.

Proper design of police facilities can reduce many maintenance problems. In larger structures, areas of the building that close down after eight hours of operation can be located adjacent to each other to allow maintenance during the evening hours. Materials used in construction of police facilities must be attractive and provide low maintenance effort. Paneled walls in administrative offices go for years without painting. Low maintenance tile or wall covering in operational or detective offices provides surfaces conducive to cleaning rather than painting. Roll call rooms, locker rooms, and other such facilities can be equipped with low maintenance wall surfaces, acoustic tile, or other covering providing for easy repair and/or painting. Chair rails are a necessity in offices and roll call areas to prevent damage to walls.

Floor coverings should be consistent with the use of the facility. Administrative offices, if carpeted with material that is resistant to soil, can readily be cleaned by vacuuming. Jails, on the other hand, should have bare floors that can be hosed down and cleansed quickly in the event of prisoner illness, etc. Narrow passageways, high use corridors, and offices should be covered with tiles or other wear-resistant flooring.

Maintenance personnel Very often police building maintenance is not the responsibility of the police department but is the function of public works or another city agency. This arrangement may or may not work well. Most often, if the police department is housed in part of the city hall, maintenance services are provided by city government. In these cases, the police administrator has no control over maintenance operations. In larger police buildings it becomes necessary for members of the maintenance staff to be assigned to the police facility on a regular basis. When these individuals are part of another city department, administration becomes difficult.

The police administrator should strive to deploy maintenance personnel in much the same manner as police officers. A police officer is assigned to a task or district on the basis of work load; maintenance personnel should be assigned in the same way. More than one shift is required and should coexist with the time of least activity within the police building. It is unreasonable to expect maintenance personnel to be cleaning administrative offices during the day when the greatest administrative work load occurs. Therefore, an evening shift is desirable. On the other hand, patrol areas of the building are in constant use and, therefore, locker rooms, booking facilities, and operational centers may be cleaned at any point in time during the day.

Prisoner labor Some areas of the United States allow cities or counties to utilize sentenced prisoners as a work force. If the police administrator has this force available, it should be utilized. Prisoners can do the basic maintenance of a police facility with very little training and in most instances with minimum supervision. Minimum security prisoners can be provided with housing facilities within the police facility and can be assigned shifts to provide specific maintenance functions. This presents a savings to the public and, very often, gives a better appearance to the police facility.

Supervision The police administrator should assign a member of his staff to be responsible for the maintenance of the police facility. In larger police agencies this could be a senior staff officer who directs a major division of the department, with part of his or her responsibility being building maintenance. In smaller police agencies the chief may appoint a staff officer or line supervisor to be responsible for this task. This continuity of responsibility will provide for a cleaner building that presents a favorable appearance to the public and employees alike.

Property control

The identification of and accounting for all property that comes under the control of a police agency is an operational requirement and a legal necessity. To meet these needs a property control system designed to govern the reception and distribution of property must be part of the department's basic operation. Once a property control system is established, immediate benefits are realized.

The department knows where assets are located and how they are being used; thus, a reduction in capital expenditures occurs. Specific equipment needs are easier to evaluate and requests for new pieces of equipment may be reviewed to reduce duplication. Property control also provides for proper accounting to provide costs of departmental operations.

Operational efficiency is increased because the system provides for the location of property and the most efficient use of individual pieces of equipment. When the equipment becomes worn or requires service, the property control record provides a basis for maintenance on a regular service schedule. Increased preventive maintenance will result in longer life or in higher trade-in allowances.

A property control system establishes responsibilities for each item of equipment, whether it be personal or departmental. The individual charged with the specific item is therefore held accountable for loss and maintenance. Finally, a property control system will reduce loss. When every item is individually numbered and under an inventory control system, losses or disappearances are controlled.

A property control system includes all property owned or controlled by the police department. Too often, a police agency will provide strict inventory controls on pieces of evidence and neglect its own capital assets. Expendable items such as paper, pencils, and flashlight batteries are often ignored in the control system because they are expendable. It becomes essential that classes of property be established to aid in the control effort.

Classes of property

Capital assets These include chairs, desks, furniture, and other such objects. Vehicles, weapons, and cameras may also be included in this class. Items of personal equipment such as side arms or helmets should not be considered capital assets. However, if the police agency provides each member of the department with an individual hand-held radio, it would be proper to show the radio as a capital asset.

Personal equipment This classification contains items such as uniforms, side arms, batons, and other pieces of police equipment issued to the individual police officer.

Expendable property   Paper, flashlight batteries, pencils and pens, typewriter ribbons, and other such supplies should be categorized as expendable property.

Evidence   This is any piece of property, regardless of its nature, that is confiscated or impounded by the police agency as part of an investigation and that will be used to substantiate the investigation in court.

Recovered property   This is any piece of property that has been identified as having been stolen. In some cases this property may also be classified as evidence.

Found property   This includes any piece of property regardless of its nature that has been found by a citizen or police officer and is being held for safekeeping until the owner can be identified.

Property control system

The foundation of an adequate property control system lies in proper departmental organization. Each department must create a position and unit to be responsible for the custody and disposition of all property coming within the control of the police agency. A property custodian may then be assigned full-time responsibility for administering the property control system. The property custodian need not be a police officer and in the smaller agencies may work only one shift. In the larger departments the property custodian may require several assistants, as well as equipment for transferring property from precinct stations to a central storehouse. Once the position of property custodian has been formalized into the department's organization, then a property control system must be established.

There are two basic elements to a property control system: (1) the proper identification of each item of property and (2) a method that accounts for each item of property. In operation these basic elements resolve themselves into two distinct phases: identification and accounting.

Identification phase   As property comes under the control of the police agency it must first be identified and then formalized within departmental inventory control. A property control number is the best way to identify capital assets. Pre-numbered stickers or metal tags that can be affixed to individual items are the most common form of identification. Those items that are serial numbered may also be issued a property control number. Property or inventory control numbers should then be entered into the departmental inventory control ledger as required by the accounting phase.

Vehicles are generally assigned a separate identification number because of their specific nature and use. Personal equipment such as side arms, helmets, and batons is generally issued directly to the individual officer and may be given the officer's individual employee identification number as an inventory control. On the other hand, items that are classed as expendable property need not be numbered but should be entered in an expendable property control record.

The most sensitive area of property control is in the security of evidence or found or recovered property. The variety of items that fall into this classification do not lend themselves to a normal inventory control system. Therefore, the most logical form of inventory control is to utilize the individual case or complaint number that is connected with the property being held.

Evidence and found or recovered property must be treated in a systematic manner to ensure integrity of evidence and protection of other property. A police officer taking property into police custody must adhere to standard identification techniques when handling evidence, to ensure protection of the evidence for courtroom testimony and identification.

Departmental control should require that each bit of evidence or recovered property be itemized and tagged with a proper police evidence tag. In addition, a complete description of the property should be recorded in the case file on the proper property reports.

Evidence tags must contain the complaint or case number, the name of the officer, the date and time the evidence was taken into police custody, and the name of victims or suspects in the case. The tags should also have a space for the initials of the property custodian receiving the property.

Accounting phase The inventory, or accounting phase, of the property control system need not be complicated, but it must be consistent in capturing all items of property under the control of the police department. The most effective and least complicated method is the use of an inventory control ledger. This ledger provides space to record time of receipt, inventory control number, location and disposition of items, and, in the case of capital assets, vendor from whom the items were obtained.

The ledger format is not adequate for control of individual property which is assigned to members of the department. A form that lists all types of personal property can be completed when property is issued to a specific individual. A copy of the form may be kept in a loose-leaf notebook alphabetically under individual officers' names. The original of the form should be kept in the officer's personnel file as part of the officer's package. This method ensures that both the property control section and the personnel section are aware of what property an individual officer has assigned to him or her when and if he or she leaves the services of the police agency. When a police officer leaves the agency, all personal property should be turned in to the property control section. An endorsement to the personnel department on the personal property record should be made on the form. Formal release of the officer should be contingent on the turning in of all property or repayment to the department for those items which are lost or damaged.

Expendable property may be recorded on a specific inventory control sheet that is reviewed periodically for shortages. This provides immediate indication that supplies must be reordered or that inordinate usage is occurring.

Finally, evidence and recovered and found property should be subject to strict property controls to ensure the chain of evidence and maintain safeguarding of the property. As in the case of capital assets, the simplest and most effective control is in the ledger format. The ledger must indicate the date and time the property was received, the location of the item in the property control room, the officer who took the property into evidence, and the property custodian who received it. Space must also be provided for signing evidence in and out of the property room for court use or laboratory examination. Finally, a space for disposition of the evidence or recovered property must also be made in the ledger.

Fund accounts

Actual cash comes to a police agency in many different ways. Much of it is controlled through normal evidence procedures and is held as part of the evidence process. There are, however, several other ways in which a police agency might find itself in control of substantial amounts of money. Some cash comes to the police department through normal budgetary channels, some comes through fine collections or issuance of permits, and some is donated from grateful citizens. Strict regulatory programs must be instituted to ensure that proper controls and accounting methods are used to protect these funds.

Of course, the ideal situation is to reduce the amount of money or cash that the police department controls to the lowest possible figure. Ideally, police agencies should have no access to cash, nor should they collect money for any reasons. This, of course, is not possible in many cases and therefore special accounts should be set up to handle these special cases. Several types of accounts are possible and a few of the more common are discussed below.

Undercover or "buy" money   Police operations may require the use of cash to purchase narcotics, contraband, or information. Although the police service in the United States does not rely heavily upon paid informants as does the European system, there are occasions when this situation occurs and cash is needed to complete the transaction. The amount of cash may vary and can go as high as thousands of dollars or as low as $5 or $10. Means for obtaining the funds necessary to complete these investigations must be made within the police agency and the financial structure of the community.

The first major control placed on the issuance of such funds should be a file or complaint number that can be referred to. All funds used for case investigation should be recorded within the proper supplementary reports of the individual case or file. If funds are not immediately required, a normal check request or draft may be completed and funds drawn from the finance office. If, on the other hand, funds are needed immediately, arrangements should be made to have a small account in a local bank upon which checks can be drawn. These accounts should not exceed $100 or $200, with strict controls placed on who may sign the check. Again, all checks should be cross-referenced to complaint or file number, and strict accounting methods should be maintained to ensure the proper use of the funds.

Uniform account   Some police agencies maintain a uniform account on which a police officer may draw funds to replenish his or her supply of uniforms. In other cases the officer charges the uniforms and submits the bills for payment. The primary function of these accounts is to ensure that a police officer will have funds available, when needed, to purchase uniforms. Officers are not required to spend their uniform allowance in one calendar year. This allows the officer to replace needed equipment and not purchase unwanted items solely to expend the account.

Each individual officer should have a card account that records the individual purchases and payments. Funds that are to be held over from year to year should be accounted for and regular quarterly reports should be issued to the police officers.

Petty cash   Petty cash accounts are required for unusual office expenses and minor purchases. Normal accounting procedures that require confirmation of expenses should be instituted. A form which indicates all expenses with attached receipts should be completed on a regular basis and submitted to the finance section for approval.

Donations   Many citizens, out of a sense of gratitude, donate funds to a police agency. This type of donation should be returned whenever possible. In some cases, however, donations are made anonymously or for some reason are unreturnable.

Under no circumstances should a police agency set up separate "slush" funds and use the money for departmental purposes. In all cases donations received by a police agency that may not be, or cannot be, returned should be recorded and deposited in the general fund of the community.

Fund control

Several varieties of controls can be instituted on all fund accounts maintained or controlled by the police agency. Strict accounting procedures must be maintained and regular audits instituted to ensure accuracy of bookkeeping methods.

Monies that come to a police agency in the form of permits, fees for report copies, or collection of fines should be recorded in a receipt book and receipts issued for all cash. Receipt books should be audited on a regular basis, and regular deposits of cash into the city treasury should be made. These accounting procedures will ensure the proper handling of money and prevent the possibility of criticism if cash is lost.

Property control room

Design of the property control room is, of course, dependent upon the size and nature of the property function within the police agency. Larger agencies find it necessary to have a quartermaster service function and an evidence control area each staffed with individuals specifically assigned to one of the two functions. In most departments it is not necessary to have police personnel assigned to this task, thus allowing the unit to operate without sacrificing field personnel.

The large department's property control function is unique. Because there are so few large departments in the United States our attention must be directed to the smaller police agency that cannot afford full-time personnel assigned to property control or must operate the property room only on an eight-hour basis.

Design Most police agencies will find it advantageous to design their property control function as one room or center. All departmental property control tasks can be centered in this one area of the police building. The room itself may be segmented into secure areas for evidence and lost or recovered property, and areas dedicated to the quartermaster function of the department. Thus, one individual may provide the total property control staff for the department.

All departmental property should be received at this property control center and entered into the proper control ledger. This requires locating the property room at ground level with access to a loading dock or outside loading door. Main doors to the property room should be large enough to allow for the movement of large pieces of equipment into the remainder of the building. A service counter or window should be provided for normal transactions with police officers, follow-up investigators, and the general public. This prevents unauthorized access to the property room.

Loading doors must be on an exterior wall of the building. This poses a security problem to the property control center. This weakness can be strengthened through the use of double loading dock doors equipped with an alarm device that sounds in the communications center. Metal doors should be provided on all property room interior corridor doors and should also be equipped with an alarm device.

The size of the room is dependent on the number of transactions and amount of property that will be stored in it. The secure portion of the room, for evidence and found and recovered property, can be achieved in several ways. Chain link fence or wire mesh from floor to ceiling with a standard chain link type of gate is a simple, effective method of partitioning. Solid walls and doors may also be used. The method of securing evidence and found and recovered property is immaterial as long as it is maintained separately from departmental property.

Inside the secure portion, individual bins or shelves should be built to accommodate evidence and other property. Each bin should be numbered or lettered so that property placed in it can be readily located. Bins may also be designated

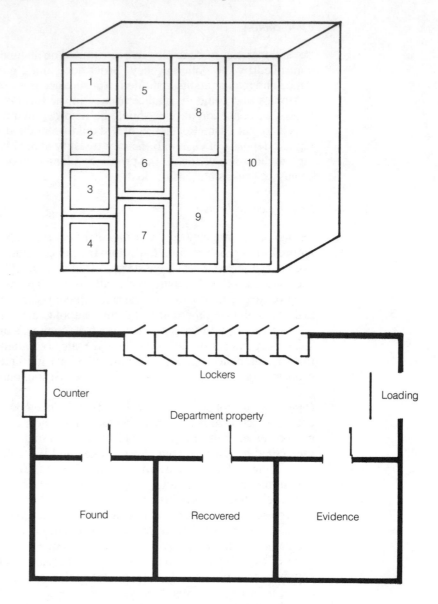

Simple property room design with evidence lockers built into the wall for night storage of property.

by letter and year to allow for automatic removal of property that has been held for a long period of time.

A safe, within the secure portion of the property room, allows for storage of highly valuable items and money. A refrigerator is needed for storing blood and other evidence. Lockers that are capable of being secured provide for the storage of weapons and narcotics. Again, a numbering system for each locker must be established so that property can be located quickly.

Nighttime property control Many departments cannot staff a property control center on a twenty-four-hour basis, thus police officers who impound evidence or recover property during evening hours find it difficult to secure the property. In many cases evidence is stored in personal lockers, desks, or closets in the assembly room. This method of property control is unsatisfactory because the integrity of the evidence may be challenged in court. Twenty-four-hour security for evidence and recovered property must be provided.

The simplest and probably the most widespread method of providing complete security is the property control locker system. The locker system is based on the principle of the railway or bus lockers that have numbered keys. The police officer who impounds property or evidence brings it to the station, completes the necessary paperwork, and places the item in an individual property locker. He or she locks the locker and retains the key. When the case is called for court or the property is to be transferred he or she removes it and takes it to its proper place.

This system has some basic restrictions, because the police officer may be responsible for several items of evidence in several different lockers. In addition, the number of lockers required to provide the service may be prohibitive. A simpler and more popular method is to provide lockers that have keys available only to a property control clerk. Under normal conditions, when empty the locker is unlocked and is available to receive property. Once the officer has completed the property forms he or she places the item into the property locker, locks the lock, and has no further access. The property control clerk then has the necessary key, opens the locker, and records the evidence or recovered property in the property center control ledger, as if the officer had given it to him or her personally. This method frees the locker almost immediately and does not require police officers to be responsible for several locker keys. If the police officer needs the evidence for court he or she notifies the property control officer a day or two before court and picks the evidence up on the way to court.

These two systems have proved highly successful, because they reduce the risk of tainting evidence, ensure continuity of control, and provide safekeeping. In addition, a minimum of personnel are required to operate them.

Property disposition

Property that comes within the control of the police department is used up, passes through the hands of the agency to its rightful owner, or is destroyed under court order. Thus, a system of recording disposition of property is a necessary part of the property control process.

Capital assets The disposition of used or worn capital assets is a matter of individual municipal law or policy. Some municipalities auction used property on a regular basis, whereas others are required by law to submit it for competitive sealed bidding. Whatever the individual municipal requirements are, a system of determining that property is being disposed of properly is mandatory.

The determination that property is no longer useful to the department is a decision that should be made after careful review of the item's ability to perform the task it is designed for. A method of certifying the property for disposal ensures that proper disposition will be made at the proper time. Once final approval for disposition has been authorized it should be recorded in the inventory control ledger.

If a piece of property is transferred from the police department to another municipal unit, then the transfer should be recorded in the inventory control ledger.

Evidence The police officer or investigator charged with the follow-up of a case involving a particular piece of evidence should be queried on a regular basis to ascertain the status of the evidence. The property control unit should be notified in writing as to the need to retain evidence or dispose of it through return to owner or destruction. If evidence is to be destroyed, this should be done on court order or because of its nature. Once the authorization has been returned to the property custodian disposal should occur as authorized by law. Many jurisdictions allow for sale of unclaimed evidence or property held for safekeeping. This should be done in conformance with state or local law and, if possible, at public auction. Many departments find themselves without enough property to auction and may wish to combine disposal of property with other community equipment in a once-a-year auction or sale. In any event, the disposition of property should be recorded in the property control ledger as a matter of permanent record.

Summary Property control is a major part of a department's operations. It ensures the proper safeguarding of evidence and recovered and found property. It provides control of capital assets, personal property, and expendable items that are owned by the community. Proper design of the property control center will ensure that all controls are effective and are carried out with the minimum number of personnel.

Automotive equipment

A significant number of automobiles are purchased each year by police agencies in the United States; their combined cost amounts to hundreds of millions of dollars. Regardless of size, each police agency will probably find that its major capital equipment purchase each year is in its vehicle fleet.

The modern police vehicle provides many services and functions. It is a carrier of equipment and provides space for the necessary tools, radios, and miscellaneous equipment common to modern law enforcement. It is an office for the patrol officer and provides the officer with shelter for completing forms, writing reports, and interviewing people. It may also suffice as a tactical or operational center for a supervisor in multiunit operations. When necessary, the police patrol vehicle serves as a jail in which persons are temporarily detained while being transported to detention facilities. During inclement weather the patrol car serves to protect police officers from the elements, and occasionally it is used as a shield to protect officers from attack. Finally, and probably most apparent, the police vehicle serves as transportation for police officers in the performance of their duties. It is also used to transport other personnel, prisoners, and, at times, citizens.

Types of vehicles

There are basically four types of vehicles that a police agency will employ: patrol vehicles, supervisory vehicles, administrative vehicles, and support vehicles.

Patrol vehicles The general patrol vehicle that is operated in a city or a town provides the basic police transportation unit. It must have stability and good handling qualities because of the amount of traffic in which it will normally operate. Since it is operating in a community atmosphere with narrow streets or dense traffic, high speed performance characteristics are not really required. The highway patrol or traffic patrol unit must have all the qualifications of the basic patrol vehicle but should be heavier to provide greater stability at higher speeds.

Supervisory vehicles Field supervisory vehicles provide the transportation and operational center for the first-line supervisors. These vehicles may take the form of a van or station wagon and may be equipped with additional pieces of field equipment or tactical supplies. Performance requirements should not be the same as for the patrol unit; however, durability is desirable.

Administrative vehicles This general classification contains both follow-up investigative vehicles and those vehicles used for administrative personnel of the department. Performance requirements for these vehicles may be somewhat lower than for standard patrol cars, since their primary function is to transport administrative and detective personnel only.

Support vehicles   Into this catagory fit the remaining vehicles a police agency may require: pickup trucks, rescue vehicles, mobile command centers, mobile supply centers, canteens, prisoner transportation vans, etc. The specific need for the support function must be reviewed and the performance requirements for the individual vehicle established.

Vehicle specifications

The two basic approaches to establishing motor vehicle specifications are use and design.

When establishing specifications by use, questions such as these are raised: What kind of seating should be provided for the police officer? How many persons should the vehicle carry? What type of climate will the vehicle operate in? What are the topography and altitude? What types of streets and traffic congestion will be encountered? These and other questions related to use will help determine the function of the patrol car and are directed toward the persons using the car.

The second approach is aimed toward design characteristics and the mechanics of the police vehicle. The engineering and construction features are given more emphasis. This is the more traditional approach, with the vehicle considered more in isolation. Design is much more generalized and tries to meet the needs of all anticipated users. This generally results in a standard passenger vehicle that is modified to accommodate police needs.

Neither of these approaches, in isolation, is of course completely adequate; they must be combined in establishing police vehicle specifications. Most of the standard vehicles manufactured in the United States in the past have not performed well in police service. The automotive industry has not attempted to design vehicles for the American police market, although it has attempted to develop police packages that could be attached to standard vehicles so as to provide vehicles for police service needs. Careful scrutiny of these packages, however, shows only vehicles that have been modified by a limited design approach.

In purchasing police vehicles, the police administrator, working closely with the finance officer and the purchasing agent of the local government, should develop specifications on a performance basis that will meet the needs of the service. While it may not be possible to find a vehicle that will meet every departmental requirement, the effort should be made. The National Bureau of Standards has conducted tests and developed publications that can offer some useful guidelines. Their publications should be consulted, as well as the research findings of independent consumer groups. To put it as succinctly as possible, police vehicle specifications should be drawn on the basis of the types of officers using the vehicles, the functions of the vehicles, and the design characteristics needed.

The following guidelines are offered as a starting point in the development of specifications, so that the administrator, the departmental purchasing agent, and others with an immediate concern can be better prepared for this assignment.

Speed and acceleration   A basic decision needs to be made on engine size, depending on type of patrol. If freeway patrol is required then acceleration speed and cruising performance are mandatory and a larger engine is needed. For town and residential patrol, however, a smaller engine may have definite advantages.

Handling and maneuverability The police vehicle must be controllable on any road surface at high speeds. On congested streets it must be able to make turns at higher than normal speeds without loss of control.

Reliable brakes The brakes on a police vehicle get heavy use and should be as large as possible.

Interior design This includes a number of small items that add up to a large measure of safety and avoidance of driver fatigue. The seat belt/shoulder strap combination should not tangle up on the officer's equipment. If officers don't use the equipment because they fear entanglement then the safety feature is lost.

Split or bucket seats will be required if male and female teams are assigned to vehicles. This will allow for differential positioning of the seats for the driver and passenger. In addition, the seat construction must be sufficiently firm to prevent breaking down under constant use; the upholstery material should be porous to allow for maximum ventilation and should be capable of easy cleaning.

Finally, the instrumentation should be grouped in front of the driver and designed so that it can be installed and removed from the vehicle.

The suspension system Stiffer suspension systems than those that are standard on passenger cars are needed for the maneuverability and handling qualities that are required for police use.

Electrical and cooling systems A police vehicle may run for hours while traveling only a few miles. Severe stress, therefore, is placed on many of the components, including the cooling system, radios, and air-conditioning. This will require heavy duty radiators, a fan with additional blades, transmission oil coolers, high capacity alternators, battery heat shields, and other special equipment.

Tires The automotive tires on the market are grouped into three generic types: bias ply, bias belted, and radials. They generally go up in that order in price. The current trend is toward the police radial tire which, although it costs more initially, will provide better performance handling characteristics and lower long-term operating costs.

Emergency vehicle accessories

Although not part of the specifications for police vehicles, specifications for emergency vehicle accessories are necessary. These accessories can generally be divided into three categories: lights, sirens, and miscellaneous.

Emergency lighting The type of emergency lighting used by a police department will necessarily be governed by individual state law. There is a trend in the United States to adopt either blue lights or a combination of red and blue. A recent study pointed out that a blue lamp is not a good substitute for red during daylight but is a good deal brighter than amber. The same study indicated that a combination of one red and one blue strobe light is probably the most effective.

The argument for blue indicates that the eyes are more sensitive to blue wavelengths than to red or yellow, and blue is also a distinctive warning color. In addition, Europe uses blue lights and the adoption of blue in the United States will promote uniformity. The argument against blue lights is that they are not widely recognized in the United States as a warning of danger or emergency. Blue requires more luminous energy and therefore more powerful lamps drawing more electricity. Finally, because red and yellow are standard in most communities the conversion to blue becomes expensive.

In addition to the emergency lighting, a method must be provided to allow for illumination of dark areas. It has become extremely difficult to mount spotlights on the modern vehicle. The body design does not permit post mounting and thus requires spotlights to be mounted on fenders or through the dash system. Many police agencies have discontinued the exterior mounting of spotlights in favor of an interior hand-held unit.

All external lights must be capable of being controlled by the vehicle operator. During certain operations it is necessary to operate the vehicle in a darkened condition. Switches should be installed to enable the operator to extinguish brake lights which are not controlled through the normal light switch system.

Emergency vehicle sirens Audible warning devices are required on all operational police vehicles. The state of development of such devices has progressed to a point where an electronic reproduction of a siren sound is transmitted through a speaker system and projected to the front of the vehicle. This sound can be altered to produce several effects that are intended to attract the attention of motorists. Most police agencies favor the use of the electronic siren over the manual or mechanical siren which is air driven.

An additional advantage of the electronic siren is that it allows for a dual use of the speaker as a public address unit or external radio monitor.

Miscellaneous equipment Several items of accessories that are required in a police vehicle fall into this general category. Shotgun racks are a necessity. If shotguns are carried in the trunk of the vehicle, availability is reduced. This becomes a serious problem if the officers are under attack. Several varieties of shotgun racks are available: some are key operated and others are electrically controlled by a switch on the vehicle dashboard. The disadvantages of the electrical shotgun rack very often outweigh its advantages. In most cases the vehicle must be turned on before the lock can be operated and, should an electrical failure occur, the shotgun cannot be removed from the rack. The manually operated shotgun lock probably provides the least disadvantage in obtaining the shotgun.

Rear seat partitions should be designed to provide maximum movement of the front seat without sacrificing leg room in the rear of the vehicle. These devices, while protective in nature, seriously limit the use of the rear seat of a patrol car. The solid Plexiglas divider is probably more desirable than is the wire mesh one.

Finally, miscellaneous holders and racks for police equipment may be installed as needed by the department's operations. These include baton holders, flashlight holders, and small writing desks that are illuminated.

Vehicle maintenance

Great emphasis must be placed on the police vehicle maintenance program. This program not only ensures the safe operation of the equipment but in the long run will pay off in higher turn-in allowances and lower cost of operation.

Preventive maintenance Because the police vehicle operates on a basis of hours rather than miles, a preventive maintenance program should be instituted that provides for regular hourly checks of the vehicle. After a given number of hours of operation the vehicle should be inspected for brake wear, fluid levels, and other first-line maintenance problems. Tires should also be inspected on the basis of wear and miles driven.

The establishment of a preventive maintenance program will ensure that as minor maintenance problems arise they are identified and corrected. This prevents the development of major problems and ensures the longer life of the police vehicle.

Regular inspection sheets should be designed and maintained on each vehicle throughout its life. On the basis of these inspection sheets, the department should set up an optimum operational cost per vehicle mile. Once this has been discerned, then any vehicle that exceeds that cost should be removed from the fleet and sold. This procedure keeps maintenance costs within certain limits and controls major expenditures in repair.

On-duty inspection   Prior to each tour of duty the police officer assigned to the vehicle should inspect the unit to ensure that visible defects are identified. Lights should be checked, tires should be inspected, and the body of the vehicle scrutinized for needed repairs. If a discrepancy is found it should be noted on the officer's daily inspection sheet and forwarded to the vehicle maintenance section for correction. If minor corrections are required, they should be accomplished immediately.

Washing   Washing and waxing of police vehicles not only creates a good image of the police department but ensures the long life of the vehicle paint and chrome. Those departments that are not capable of providing their own vehicle washing should contract with local vehicle washers.

Summary   The police vehicle is probably the most expensive item any police department will buy during a budget year. It is fundamental to the operation of the police department and requires high specification and performance levels to perform that function. The maintenance of the vehicle is an ongoing fact and must be reviewed constantly to ensure that maintenance costs do not exceed vehicle worth.

Armament

Police departments, because of the nature of their unique mission, must provide unique equipment to ensure that the mission can be carried out. Items of weaponry and personal protective equipment fall into the general classification of armament. It is necessary that police departments pay specific attention to the requirements of their individual community in determining the type of armament best suited for their operation. Some suburban police agencies still equip individual police vehicles with Thompson submachine guns that have little use in today's police operations and, in light of modern weaponry, border on the archaic. Many agencies fail to specify the types of weapons that are carried by individual officers and thus create a profusion of guns that does not allow for interchangeable ammunition. The planning and equipping of the department's basic armory require some effort, but the benefits will have long-range effects on the department's operation.

The equipment needed to make up basic armament requirements of a police agency can be divided into two distinct areas: individual armament and departmental armament.

Individual armament

Individual equipment can be defined as those pieces of armament assigned to the individual and used in day-to-day operations. Generally, these items include handguns, batons, handcuffs, and Mace. Some items of personal equipment are issued to the individual and maintained for special operations. These include helmets, riot sticks, and gas masks. Specifications for all such items of equipment are as necessary to the department's operation as are specifications for police vehicles. In recent years, not only police agencies, but federal agencies, in their law enforcement standards program, have given deep consideration to the specifications for basic equipment.

Handguns   The side arm carried by the police officer as part of his or her regular duty uniform must have rigid specifications to ensure uniformity of weaponry within the department and to provide for interchange of ammunition. Basic specifications should call for a .38 caliber revolver with a swing-out cylinder load rather than the break-top. Barrel length should be a minimum of four inches and the revolver should be capable of carrying at least six shots. Standard blue finish with a heavy barrel and open fixed sites is considered the most serviceable weapon for police officers. Departments should discourage the use of pearl or plastic white grips and require standard wood finish.

For urban areas the .357 magnum revolver should not be encouraged. This weapon provides too much fire power and can penetrate walls as well as vehicles. This becomes a hazard to innocent persons when police have to fire on suspects.

Ammunition for the police handgun can be an extremely sensitive issue. The trend is towards semijacketed hollow point bullets which provide high shocking power upon impact. Full-jacketed ammunition, although highly capable of deep penetration, is not practical for police use since it endangers not only the suspects but innocent bystanders. The new ammunition begins to disintegrate upon impact and thus creates less ricochet or bounce. Tests have also shown that, upon impact, although great trauma is caused to the impact area, there is less likelihood of deep penetration to the more vital parts of the body and thus more likelihood that someone shot by the newer police ammunition would survive.

Batons   Most agencies in the United States require police officers to carry a baton or nightstick. Generally speaking, a baton should be approximately twenty-four to twenty-six inches in length and equipped with a leather thong. The modern polyethylene batons are more desirable than the former wood material. Wood tends to nick and will splinter, whereas nicks in the plastic baton can be easily repaired.

Handcuffs   The police handcuff is designed to restrict the movement of a person under arrest and thus provides a certain measure of protection to the arresting officer, as well as preventing the individual from inflicting self-injury. Police handcuffs should meet the law enforcement standards program NILECJ–STD–0307.00 for metallic handcuffs. Eleven models of police handcuffs were tested in this study and only three passed the test. When a department purchases handcuffs or specifies the type to be used by their personnel, care should be taken to ensure that all handcuff keys are of the same type and thus interchangeable. This allows one police officer to utilize the handcuffs of another or to remove handcuffs when the arresting officer is not present.

Chemical Mace   Chemical Mace is probably the newest innovation in the police armament category. Initially designed to provide a nonlethal and nontraumatic method of subduing violent persons, chemical Mace is generally the size of a small hair spray can and is worn upon the belt of the police officer. Several other variations of this type of equipment are found in small pocket units that resemble a fountain pen or in cannisters that fit into the end of a police baton. Strict specifications should be drawn when purchasing such equipment and sufficient replacement should be kept on hand.

Helmets Police helmets are worn in some areas of the country as part of the normal duty uniform, whereas in other areas helmets are for specialized operations such as riot and crowd control. The ballistic helmet will normally be heavier than the uniform helmet and specifications should be drawn to conform with use required by the police agency. If ballistic helmets are required, the law enforcement standards program NILECJ–STD–0106.00 should be conformed to.

Departmental equipment

Those items that are commonly required to fill the needs of special operations or to supplement the individual equipment issued to a police officer fall into the category of departmental equipment. The heavier weapons, specialized riot equipment, and individualized pieces of protective equipment that are used for special functions generally make up the departmental armory.

Shotguns The police shotgun is a versatile weapon and provides the field police officer with an extra measure of support when dealing with armed or potentially armed criminals. The shotgun should be a slide action four shot 12-gauge with a barrel length of about eighteen inches. It should have a standard sighting device and be equipped with a wood forestock and a pistol grip type rear stock. Rubberized shoulder pads are desirable. Standard 00 buckshot is most commonly used as the ammunition for shotguns.

Sniper rifles If the police agency is of sufficient size to employ the use of an antisniper team, then a rifle for that purpose must be provided. Because most shots will be between 50 and 100 yards, the weapon should be equipped with a free floating bull barrel and a glass bedded action. Highly recommended is the .222 caliber weapon with a fixed power scope.

Automatic weapons As pointed out, many police departments still utilize the ancient .45 caliber Thompson submachine gun as their standard automatic weapon. Highly sophisticated foreign designs have also been employed. Fully automatic weapons are not really desirable for modern police work. Very seldom will the police officer be in a situation that requires fully automatic weapons. A semiautomatic .223 caliber rifle will provide the necessary fire power without the hazards of a fully automatic weapon.

Gas guns The most common gas gun in use today is the .37 millimeter. Several sophisticated changes have been made in the launching of gas, and smaller agencies will probably find these more desirable than the older more cumbersome weapons. A new 12-gauge gas shell that can be fired through a shotgun is now commercially available and will provide many of the same features formerly found in the older, heavier units. There are also adapters for the .38 caliber pistol which will launch small grenades. Gas must also be checked on a regular basis as it loses its potency.

Protective vests Antisniper or hostage retrieval work requires protective vests with fifteen to sixteen layers of protective material that will protect the upper torso front, back, and sides. Individual vests with fewer layers provide some protection to handguns and are more flexible. Ceramic vests are also available that will protect against high-powered weapons. These have little flexibility, however.

Gas masks Standard military gas masks that are rated for tear gas are recommended for police armories.

Maintenance

A police armory houses several pieces of delicate and expensive equipment; thus, scheduled preventive maintenance is necessary. Each police department should set aside regular days for weapons cleaning and equipment maintenance. Those weapons that are normally stored in the armory may require only a once-a-month inspection and cleaning. Shotguns should be cleaned on a weekly basis, as should all weapons carried in command cars.

Periodically, departmental inspections should be conducted by command or administrative officers to ensure that proper maintenance is being carried out on armament and other equipment of this nature. At frequent intervals, inspections of individual equipment should be conducted by shift commanders to ensure that handguns, handcuffs, and other items of personal equipment are being cared for by the individual charged with the equipment. On an infrequent basis, command officers should conduct spot checks of individual equipment to enforce the need for preventive maintenance.

Personal equipment

Every police agency provides some items of personal equipment to members of the department. Some provide only expendable items such as flashlights, batteries, and pencils, while others issue all equipment necessary for police operations. In recent years the trend has been towards complete outfitting of the police officer. Regardless of how the police department provides for the personal equipment that a police officer will need, it is necessary that controls be placed on the type of equipment used. There are two methods of accomplishing these controls: uniform allowances and uniform specifications.

Uniform allowances

The common trend today is to provide individual police officers with a uniform allowance. This allowance provides the officer with funds to purchase necessary pieces of equipment as required. Some departments place no controls on the use of this allowance and issue the officer a check for the necessary items. Others control the amount of money the police officer may spend through a special fund that requires invoices to substantiate the cost of replacement. A few departments purchase uniforms in bulk and the police officer draws the required item as needed from a quartermaster unit of the department.

Probably the most desirable method is for the department to totally control the issuance and purchase of uniforms. If the department buys in bulk, better prices can be obtained and a police officer can draw equipment when he or she needs it rather than waiting for an individual vendor to deliver items that have been ordered. The smaller departments may, however, be unable to support a quartermaster function and, therefore, must seek different alternatives. One alternative that has been successful in some departments is to allow the police officer to draw on an account that is controlled by the department. In this way, when a police officer needs a new item of clothing or equipment he or she presents a purchase order to the uniform vendor, who supplies the equipment and bills the uniform account. This system allows strict controls on the expenditure of funds and ensures that worn equipment will be replaced.

Uniform specifications

Small police agencies find the establishment of uniform specifications a difficult problem. Without quantity buying it is impossible for vendors to create specific dye lots and uniform weights. The small police agency, then, must rely on the larger department to establish specifications for color and type of fabric used in police uniforms. This often results in small police agencies emulating their larger counterparts in uniform and equipment design. It is not uncommon to see small agencies dressed as mirror images of state police.

Uniform specifications are required to ensure that all uniformed individuals dress alike and that variations in uniform color do not occur.

Uniform specifications become more meaningful if the department provides a manual of uniform requirements. The type of equipment that may be worn with the uniform, the control of items that will be worn on the uniform, the placement of patches and insignia of rank, all should be covered in the uniform manual. Once this has been done, a consistent appearance will be achieved.

Maintenance

The maintenance of pieces of individual equipment is primarily the responsibility of the person to whom that equipment is assigned. Departmental responsibility takes the form of inspections on a regular basis and of making available equipment for cleaning various items.

Conclusion

The management of facilities and materiel for the police department includes the management of buildings (design and construction as well as maintenance), as well as administrative and financial management for police department property, automotive equipment, personal and departmental armament, and other personal property. This chapter has provided an introduction to the subject that highlights management responsibilities in planning, design, preparation of specifications, accounting, and control.

The chapter opened with a review of design of police buildings and other structures, including planning, design, and maintenance; it proceeded to the subject of property control, including fund accounting and property disposition; it then covered briefly automotive equipment, including a set of guidelines for specifications to be considered; and concluded with a discussion of personal and departmental armament and uniforms.

The facilities and materiel provided a police agency will affect its overall operational efficiency. The police building reflects the community's philosophy towards the accomplishment of police service goals. A police building that is functionally sound will eliminate duplication in personnel and economic waste and will thus reflect a sound police organization. If planned properly, the building can serve the community for years and can provide for changes in organizational structure and growth of the department.

In addition to the police building, police vehicles will provide a major capital outlay each year. Proper specifications that are achieved through adequate design and functional considerations will provide a comfortable office for the police officer and an economic savings to the community.

Finally, police armament has been somewhat overemphasized in the past but is still a necessary part of the police agency. Careful consideration should be given to the types of weapons and protective equipment utilized by a police department and specifications should be drawn to ensure quality of equipment. All of these items should be controlled through a property control system that allows for identification and accounting for all pieces of equipment or property that come within the control of the police department.

18 Criminalistics

With rising crime rates and tighter restrictions on how evidence and convictions may be obtained, the reliance on the development of scientific evidence is greater now than at any other time in recorded history. Physical evidence can stand on its own in criminal and civil courts, or it can help corroborate or contradict the testimony of witnesses, persons with vested interests, or investigative agents. When properly examined and with correct emphasis placed upon its meaning, this type of evidence can be an "unbiased witness" in judicial and other legal proceedings.

This chapter introduces the subject of criminalistics by giving a brief review of its scope and its limitations. Almost half of the chapter is then devoted to the basic concepts of physical evidence—with particular emphasis on the elusive term "identity." In this part of the chapter various sections describe associative evidence, circumstantial evidence, and probability, while other sections deal with class characteristics and similarity, comparisons, individuality, rarity, and exchange. All of these are terms that are used for methodological approaches to identification.

The remaining portions of the chapter describe the advances in technology that have revolutionized criminalistics in recent years, the methods of collecting evidence, the personnel and equipment used in evidence collection, and laboratory needs. An evaluative summary concludes the chapter.

The scope and the limitations of criminalistics

The Criminalistics Laboratory is concerned with the processing of physical evidence in the furtherance of criminal justice. As such it is devoted to the recognition, identification, individualization and evaluation of physical evidence. Results of analysis are presented and defended in a court of law.[1]

The criminalistics laboratory is staffed by skilled professionals who may hold a variety of titles such as chemist, criminalist, forensic scientist, analyst, firearms examiner, etc. Regardless of title, these individuals will closely follow the definition of criminalist as set out in the Assessment Projects of the Forensic Sciences Foundation:

A Criminalist is an individual trained in the scientific and professional discipline of criminalistics, a science directed towards the recognition, identification, individualization and evaluation of physical evidence in the reconstruction of events related to a crime and in the connection of or elimination of a suspect with that crime. Criminalistics involves the application of the natural sciences and scientifically based techniques to the analysis of such items of evidence as alcohol, blood, body fluids, cloth, drugs, explosives, firearms evidence, glass, hair and fiber, paints, etc.[2]

Scope

The criminalistics laboratory functions in three main categories: reconstruction, corpus delicti, and connective–disconnective.

Reconstruction   The skilled criminalist can often add his or her expertise to that of the police investigator to reconstruct the events leading up to, taking place during, and sometimes preceding a felonious act. The gathering of parts from an exploded device and the subsequent reconstruction of these parts may be the only way to determine what the explosive was, how it was packaged, and how it was detonated. Evidence of forced entry into the explosion scene may establish how the bomb was brought to the scene, and the finding of tire impressions leading up to and leaving the scene may establish the route and means of travel of the felon(s). Much can be learned by reconstruction of events through physical evidence. The presence or absence of gunshot residue on the hands of a gunshot victim, along with the evaluation of blood splatter patterns on the surroundings and the victim, may aid in determining whether the individual was the victim of a homicide, suicide, or accidental discharge. These are prime examples of reconstruction.

Corpus delicti   Corpus delicti can be established, for example, when the laboratory conducts analysis on samples submitted as suspect as to the presence of dangerous drugs or narcotics. Should the criminalist find the presence of heroin in a sample, then the crime has been established (corpus delicti). If the sample contains no controlled substance, no crime has been committed.

Connective–disconnective   One of the major roles of the criminalistics laboratory is tied directly to the adage that a criminal always leaves something behind at the crime scene and takes something away from it. By recognition, collection, and analysis of those physical items recovered from a scene and from a suspect it is often possible to offer dramatic proof that the individual was connected to the victim and the scene. It is also as important—and as dramatic—to show a negative relationship or to disconnect a suspect from the scene and the victim.

Because many of the types of physical evidence examined by the criminalistics laboratory do not by themselves achieve an identification, there is sometimes an inclination to consider them worthless. Nothing could be further from the truth. Each piece of physical evidence that links the perpetrator to the crime, even though not by itself conclusive, does at the same time add to the process of eliminating other persons. And if there are enough pairs of evidence that eliminate other persons while including the suspect, a point is reached which justifies the "trier of fact" in judging the suspect as being the only individual who could reasonably fit all the established points of comparison. Thus, a reliable verdict of guilt can evolve from sufficient connecting evidence, though no one pair of evidence would be sufficient or would offer a positive identification.

A suspect's shoe print found at the scene, a hair matching the suspect's head hair clutched in the victim's hand, a bloodstain on the suspect's shirt matching that of the victim—all these are connective. A suspect's shoe size differing from the shoe print at the scene, his or her hair differing in color from that found with the victim, and the red substance on the suspect's shirt being identified as paint—all tend to be disconnective. Each set of circumstances has great value. Each points in an important direction.

Limitations

The criminalistics laboratory, though staffed by highly trained specialists and equipped with today's sophisticated instrumentation, is limited in two ways: first, since few types of physical evidence can by themselves identify an individual, it is necessary to attempt to identify multiple evidence types when possible and to always integrate laboratory findings into the entire web of direct and circumstantial evidence available to the investigators; second, the scientist must rely on the investigators to recognize, collect, and submit the proper evidence. In other words, the criminalist is dependent. It is incumbent upon every element within the justice system, but primarily upon the police, to see that a full awareness of the importance of proper gathering of physical evidence permeates each echelon and operational element of the organization.

Numerous studies at the federal, state, and local levels have strongly emphasized the need for crime scene searches on a broad scale. These studies have shown that few police agencies seem prepared to select, train, and dedicate adequate manpower to this task. Although most admit awareness of the need, it can be stated, with a fair level of confidence, that adequate crime scene processing and physical evidence development are nevertheless neglected. Perhaps the need for a better understanding by the police administrator of the role and value of the criminalistics laboratory has not been properly appreciated. This, then, is the challenge of today and the concern of those dedicated to making available to the police service every tool for the apprehension of the felon and the protection of the innocent.

Basic concepts of physical evidence[3]

The problem of identity

The primary objective of law enforcement is to prevent crime. When the prevention phase breaks down and a crime is committed, the investigation phase of law enforcement begins.

The entire objective of the investigative phase is to identify the person or persons who committed the crime, arrest them, and bring them before a court of law. In accomplishing this mission, the identity of the victim will have to be established and the identity of an object or the source of an object may have to be determined.

In collecting the materials to establish this identity, the legal and scientific requirements must always be kept in mind. No matter how good a latent may have been, if too much powder is used to develop it its value will be lost. In the same way, no matter how well the latent was developed and lifted, if it was not properly marked by the investigating officer it will never be seen by the jury deciding the case in a court of law.

Methods of direct identification of an individual

There are at present few scientific methods available to directly identify an individual. Modern investigators are limited to the use of fingerprints, photographs, and handwriting in marking individual identifications.

Fingerprints are the most frequently used means of identification. Even this "exact science" has certain limitations. For a fingerprint to be identified, it must be compared with known prints on file or taken at a later date. No matter how many latent lifts were made at the crime scene, if the person depositing the prints is never fingerprinted the latents will never be identified.

Photographs are extremely useful to the investigator in searching for the suspect of a crime that has been witnessed by others. It should be remembered, however, that even the best photography is two dimensional and can be deceptive for identifying a particular individual. Most "mug shots" available to the police today are black-and-white prints showing the front and the profile of a person the last time that person was arrested. These may be quite old and the features of the person may have changed. Some agencies are now developing "mug files" in color on thirty-five millimeter film for more detail as to skin tone, hair color, etc.

Handwriting is probably the least frequently used method of establishing an identity. Its use is almost as exacting as the use of fingerprints. There are two main reasons why handwriting is not used more often: first, there are very few qualified document examiners available, and second, there are very few handwriting standards available in police files. Again, as with fingerprints, the unknown sample of handwriting must be compared with a known standard if an identification is to be established.

Sometimes eyewitnesses are used to identify an individual. When this occurs, every effort should be made to use other means to corroborate such identification, as eyewitnesses are frequently unreliable. Suggestion by others as well as by the police officer can have a strong influence on an eyewitness.

While the means available to the technical investigator for making direct identifications are rather limited today, the future may be quite different owing to recent technical advances. The use of neutron activation analysis, soft X ray and the laser probe may expand the possibilities of identification. Already, much work is being done in an effort to individualize blood, semen, and hair as well as to identify firearms residue. The final outcome of the extensive research in these areas remains to be seen.

Definition of identity

Identification is the process of placing an entity in a predefined restricted class. An example of predefined restricted class may be the fingerprint pattern called the whorl. The whorl is a pattern in which the ridges form at least one complete circuit, and it has two deltas. All fingerprint patterns with these characteristics may be identified as whorls. The arch and the loop are restricted from this class. While a great number of fingerprints are excluded in this way, a great many still remain. To establish identity, further details must be examined.

By describing a particular whorl as having an oval shape, having an inside tracing between the deltas, and having certain relationships between the ridge details of the pattern, we are able to reduce the identification of whorls to the specific identity of only one whorl.

Identification, then, would be establishing that an object is one of a rather large group (class), but identity is establishing that the object is the only one (individual) of its kind in that group.

The number of details required and the similarity between them necessary to establish an identity cannot be stated with certainty. Statistical considerations, related experiences, and the like are the guidelines governing the formation of an opinion after evaluation of the details.

It follows that the unique details which go together to make like appearing items different are the real basis for identity. The fact that they may or may not be there in the first place, and the scientific requirement in developing them, set the limit on identities.

Practical versus absolute identity

It has been said that no two things are exactly alike. In the most precise terms this is absolutely true if methods are available for the full disclosure of ultramicroscopic details.

Two tool marks will never be completely alike, and are likely to show readily apparent differences even when the same tool is applied in as nearly the same way as possible. From a practical standpoint, however, it can be stated definitely that two marks were or were not made with the same tool. Thus, while in the former case they are not alike in the absolute sense, from the practical standpoint they may be alike and may have the same cause or source.

In all matters involved in the examination and the interpretation of physical evidence, the term identity must be understood to mean practical and determinable identity only. The technical investigator must be willing to admit that he or she cannot ever establish absolute identity, and, in fact, there is no such thing when the concept is applied to tangible objects.

Since absolute identity is impossible to establish, great care must be taken in establishing identities in a practical sense. Identities should be based on adequate knowledge of the material being studied as well as adequate knowledge of the nature of identity itself. This knowledge must be backed up by both the experience and the technical facilities necessary for observing all practical details.

Most identities are based on statistical probabilities of the uniqueness of the details observed.

Associative evidence: indirect identity

If the direct methods of fingerprints, photographs, handwriting, and eyewitnesses fail to identify the person or persons who committed the crime, indirect methods may be used.

The value of indirect evidence arises through association or exchange. As an example, during the investigation of a crime scene a shell casing is recovered from the floor, tool marks are collected from the point of entry, a small fragment of cloth is taken which was discovered on the striker plate of the door, and a cigarette lighter is reported missing. A suspect is arrested in the area of the crime. At the time of arrest the suspect carries a firearm and also a small assortment of pry tools. A small area on the coattail and the right sleeve are damaged. A cigarette lighter found in the suspect's pocket matches the description of the one taken from the scene of the crime. All these facts associate the suspect with the items found at the crime scene. If, then, the items recovered from the suspect can be associated with the crime, an indirect identification may be established. Both association and exchange would have been used in establishing the identification, as the suspect left behind part of his coat and took with him an object associated with the crime scene.

Since the major function of the crime laboratory is to link the criminal and the crime scene through physical evidence, it is necessary that materials be recovered from both. When working with associative evidence, the best crime scene examination in the world will be of no avail if the comparison materials recovered are not associated with a suspect. The same would hold true for a weapon found in a sewer, a torn coat found in the street, etc.

Relation of probability to physical evidence

It has already been stated that absolute identity is not possible to establish. The courts have taken this into consideration by requiring that the defendant in a criminal case be proven guilty beyond a "reasonable doubt" or by the "preponderance of the evidence." No scientific definition may be given for the term reasonable doubt. It seems to be merely a state of mind of those hearing the evidence rather than a tangible rule.

In associative evidence The role of the scientific investigator, the laboratory, and the prosecutor in a criminal case is to produce a chain of facts—each of which taken alone could leave reasonable doubt but which taken together make it unreasonable to believe that any other person could have committed the crime. This requires quality of evidence as well as quantity.

Quality of evidence is determined by the statistical concept of probability. Probability should be taken to mean the likelihood of the occurrence of any particular form of an event, estimated as the ratio of the number of ways in which that form might occur to the entire number of ways in which the event might occur in any form.

A familiar example of probability is the flip of a coin. There are two forms or events which may occur. The coin may land tails or it may land heads. The likelihood of the coin landing heads is taken as 50–50 or, more simply stated, 1:1.

An example of the use of probability to determine the quality of a particular type of physical evidence is the use of fingerprints to establish a positive identification. When the following are considered: the type of pattern, the ridge count of loops, the tracings of whorls, and the relationship of the ridge details of the pattern, the likelihood of two patterns being the same with no dissimilarities is set as high by some as $1:10^{60}$ (one chance in 10 followed by 59 zeros). Certainly, this exceeds the population of the world, and leaves very little room for doubt.

Almost any visible bloodstain may be grouped into one of four major types of human blood: O, A, B, and AB. Statistical data indicate that blood grouping is a matter of heredity and has the following frequency of distribution:

O	40%	8:20
A	40%	8:20
B	15%	3:20
AB	5%	1:20.

This tells us that type AB blood is eight times better physical evidence than either type O or type A and three times better than type B. Thus, the statistical distribution of the different blood types enables us to estimate the likelihood of a particular blood type occurring in a ratio with the occurrence of all other possible blood types.

It should be obvious that blood grouping alone will not establish guilt beyond a reasonable doubt, but taken with a number of other events similarly arrived at, the preponderance of the evidence could lead to a certain belief.

While blood grouping alone will not establish guilt, then, it is well to point out that it can establish innocence. If blood from the scene of the crime believed to be that of the suspect is found to be type A blood and the suspect has type B, it may be concluded with certainty that the blood found is not the suspect's.

Probability, then, becomes important in estimating the quality or value of nearly all types of physical evidence. The exceptions to this are the direct application of an exact science such as physics or chemistry to the study of some particular property of the evidence. Whether a particular object is iron or copper is not a matter of chance but rather a matter of certain identifiable physical and chemical properties. These properties can be determined with certainty.

Many forms of physical evidence used today do not lend themselves readily to statistical evaluation. There are no statistical data showing the frequency of a particular characteristic of a tool mark occurring a particular distance from one edge of the total mark or, for that matter, of it appearing at all. The value of this type of evidence must be estimated from experience alone. Even though we have no statistical data on which to base our opinion, we know through experience that the unique interrelationships of the microscopic details of a tool mark are the signature of only one tool. It can be said with the same certainty that is understood in fingerprints that a tool did or did not make a particular mark.

It is here that the greatest caution should be exercised. Experience must be based on *quality* as well as *quantity*. (For example, many typists have used the same typewriter for years and do not know whether the capital *W* has a full wedge or a half wedge in the center.) What one observes about the uniqueness of certain characteristics is every bit as important as how many observations were made. The basis of any opinion of identity or nonidentity must be adequate experience in the examination of a particular type of evidence, a complete understanding of the details of that particular type of evidence, and a thorough understanding of the nature of identity itself.

Probability, then, whether arrived at by statistical calculations or deduced from experience, is the basis used to evaluate physical evidence. The term probability is generally considered poor psychology if used by a witness on the witness stand. Taken out of the scientific context it has a large element of chance attached to it and therefore is not very convincing and does not fall into the concept of beyond reasonable doubt to the layman. The word itself may establish reasonable doubt in the minds of the parties hearing the evidence. It is usually better to understand the concept but to avoid the term itself if at all possible.

In investigative leads This discussion of probability or statistical calculations up to this point has been limited to items of direct or associative evidence. Statistical calculations also enable us to make certain correlations. These correlations are often referred to as investigative leads.

As an example, we may subject data concerning a particular type of crime, the location or area in which the crime was committed, and the time of day that the crime was committed to statistical calculations. Since the data are random in nature and have some of the elements of chance, we might notice that there is a tendency for the data to group around some particular time as well as some particular area. The data would then indicate that prevention of this type of crime might best be attained by increased patrol in the area during the time of greatest occurrence. This does not mean that one event causes the other. The area or time of occurrence does not cause the crime. Certainly, these crimes occur in other areas at the same time and at other times, but the data tell us where these are most likely to occur and at what time. Data concerning traffic accidents are frequently used in this way in traffic control.

Another example of a generally accepted correlation is the relation of sex to a particular crime, such as burglary. Generally, when a burglary is committed a male is involved. This does not mean that only men commit the crime of burglary, but statistics show that more burglaries are committed by males than by females. (It must be remembered that correlations are not intended to prove or disprove any fact but merely to assist in giving direction to the investigation.)

As more and more data become available through the use of the modern computer, more and more correlations may be drawn to assist the investigator. These are investigative leads based on statistical probabilities. As more events are added to the data the problem of multiple correlations becomes more and more complex and the danger of misuse through the lack of understanding becomes greater.

The criterion that separates direct or associative evidence from investigative leads is clearly one of probabilities. With direct and associative evidence the probability of all the events occurring again is small enough to lead to the belief that it would be unreasonable for this to happen. The probabilities of the investigative lead are great enough to allow for some doubt in this belief, but they are too small to overlook as assistance to the investigation.

Class characteristics and similarity

Identification, as has been mentioned above, is the process of placing an entity in a predefined restricted class. It is the class characteristics that make it possible to define this restricted class. These characteristics are common to all the objects in the group. For example, a bullet recovered from a crime scene is found to be .38 caliber, with five grooves inclined to the right. Only weapons having these class characteristics could have fired the bullet. While a great number of weapons are excluded, there remain many weapons which could have fired it, in other words, which can be identified as belonging to this class. Class characteristics, then, are what make like things similar.

Class characteristics give us a means of screening objects before a comparison is made between two objects to determine their individual characteristics, for if we are to establish identity we must find details which make like appearing (class) objects different (individual).

Comparison

In the search for identity, two pieces of physical evidence that have the same class characteristics are compared in greater detail. The items may be placed together in the manner of a jigsaw puzzle. They may be examined side by side in photographs or by the use of a comparison microscope, or they may be examined with some sensitive instrument to determine chemical content or certain physical properties.

Regardless of the means of comparison, the first consideration is to search for differences in the details. If no differences are found and sufficient details are present for an opinion, the investigator may conclude that the two objects have a common origin or came from the same place.

The limit to identity is set by the number of details that can be developed or observed. If the detail is not greater than the class characteristics an identity cannot be established. If only the class characteristics can be observed the investigator must conclude that the two objects could have had the same origin but not to the exclusion of all other similar objects. It is important, then, that the detail includes some individual characteristics not common to other items in that particular class.

A comparison is made by finding a sufficient number of similarities in the detail and the absence of any differences that cannot be explained. (Some of the differences that can be explained are missing parts, rocks in a plaster cast of a footprint, or a typewriter that has been cleaned and repaired after a document has been prepared with it.)

The best type of comparison is when two objects can be fitted together. This is an impressive type of evidence, as it can be shown in court if the items are large enough. If the items are too small, large photographs are used instead of the actual items.

Individuality

After the criminalist has established the fact that two items being compared are similar, he or she then looks for individuality, or that which makes one thing different from all the others like it. The criminalist looks for something uncommon or unusual, some imperfection or peculiarity. If the criminalist can show that this unusual thing is present in both items, he or she has established a practical identity.

With some forms of physical evidence it is not now possible to establish an identity. Blood, hair, and semen are examples of this type evidence. Since each person is biologically different there are great possibilities in these areas. Advanced technology is working with these items at the present time.

Firearms and tools, on the other hand, can be identified with a very high degree of probability because the machines that make them leave uncommon and unusual markings on them.

Some forms of physical evidence gain individuality as a result of use, wear, and accidental damage. Examples would be automobile tires, shoes, and typewriters. The greater the wear or accidental damage from use is, the more individual the item becomes.

Paint and glass become individual by the very nature of the mixing and manufacture of these materials. Glass in the molten state is very difficult to mix; also, it is composed mostly of sand, the mineral content of which will vary from load to load. With paint the trace elements present as a result of the chemicals mixed serve as identification.

Errors in manufacture may serve to individualize some types of physical evidence. Cotton string is manufactured in 20 and 24 strand. If, as a result of a manufacturing error, a length of 23-strand cotton string is found, that length of cotton string has individuality.

Rarity

Rare means hard to find or seldom met with. This term is applied to physical evidence that is unusual or uncommon. Location has much to do with rarity. A hat on a suspect's head has no value as evidence. Found at the scene of a crime it becomes important.

The value of physical evidence increases as it is found closer to the center of the crime. A footprint on the outside of a building is not as strong physical evidence as one that is found next to a dead body or near a forced safe.

There are three kinds of rarity associated with physical evidence: (1) a common thing found in an unusual place; (2) an unusual thing found in a common place; (3) a common thing that has some unusual quality. An example of each is given below:

1. *A common thing found in an unusual place.* For example, there is a burglary of a sugar warehouse. A suspect is arrested. He is a carpenter by trade. Sugar is found in his automobile, on his clothing, and adhering to his shoes. We would expect to find sawdust but not sugar.
2. *An unusual thing found in a common place.* For example, there is a burglary of a mining company and gold bars are stolen. A suspect is arrested. He is a plumber by trade. Fine gold dust is found in his automobile, on his clothing, and adhering to his shoes. We would expect to find lead and copper but not gold.
3. *A common thing found that has some unusual quality.* For example, a murder is committed in which the victim was struck with a beer bottle. The victim has type B blood. A suspect is arrested. The suspect has type A blood. Fragments of a broken beer bottle are found in the suspect's car. Type B blood is found on these fragments. An ordinary glass beer bottle is not valuable as evidence because it is common, but, with type B blood on it, this broken bottle now has individuality.

Exchange

When two objects come into contact with each other, more often than not there will be a transfer of material from one to the other. When a suspect comes into contact with the victim and the crime scene the suspect leaves traces of himself or herself behind and takes away traces of both the victim and the crime scene. These traces are generally very small and the suspect and the investigator may overlook them.

The investigator and the laboratory wish to place the suspect at the scene of the crime. This is possible by the examination of the trace materials resulting from exchange.

For example, the suspect approaches the back door of a residence and crossing the back porch he steps on a brown paper bag on the floor. To gain entry he breaks a small glass window in the back door and reaches in to unlock the door. After gaining entry he is surprised by the victim and a struggle follows. During the struggle the victim's nose begins to bleed. The suspect flees the scene. The following exchanges may have taken place by the contact of the suspect with the victim and the crime scene:

1. The suspect's shoe print may be on the brown paper bag on the back porch

2. Fibers from the suspect's clothing may be on the broken rear window glass
3. Fingerprints may be on the broken glass of the rear door
4. Fibers from the suspect's clothing may have been transferred to the victim.

The following transfer evidence may be found on or in possession of the suspect:

1. Glass fragments from the broken back door glass may be on the suspect's clothing and shoes
2. Paint may be on his upper garment from the back door window frame
3. Fibers from the victim's clothing may have transferred to the suspect during the struggle
4. Blood from the victim's nose may be on the suspect
5. The suspect may bear bruises or lacerations from the struggle with the victim
6. Fibers from the rug or furniture at the crime scene may have transferred to the suspect
7. Hairs from the victim or a pet at the crime scene may have transferred to the suspect.

Even though the above is an ideal case intended only to illustrate the possibilities of exchange, if we excluded the shoe print and the fingerprint and include the other exchanges there would be little doubt that the suspect was at the crime scene.

Finding a fingerprint at the crime scene is the best type of contact evidence because if the print is there the suspect was there. With other types of trace evidence the investigator has an additional problem of connecting the traces to the suspect (associative evidence).

Advancing technology

New instruments, advanced techniques, and constant research into scientific advances are no longer a promise but a reality.

Probably the best example of the expanding capabilities in the criminalistics field is in the area of serology. In the past, a color and a crystal test for identification, an antihuman precipitin examination for species origin, and a direct agglutination or absorption-inhibition test for ABO grouping were considered a complete examination of a dried bloodstain.

A complete dried bloodstain examination now is limited only by the techniques available to the examiners and the amount of bloodstain present. Some of the tests on bloodstains now being used include: antigen systems, A, B, O; subgroups of A, MN, and Rh; and isoenzyme systems, such as erythrocyte acid phosphatase (EAP), phosphoglucomutase (PGM), adenylate kinase (AK), and adenosine deaminase (ADA).

An example of the use of these new techniques would be the following. A spot of blood is found on a suspect's clothing. The blood is determined to be human blood of type O. The victim's blood is also type O. The criminalist now reports these facts to the police, prosecutor, and jury.

The probability of the suspect also being type O or this sample coming from another source is high because approximately 40 percent of the population has type O blood. However, if other tests are run and the blood found on the suspect is typed as O, M Pos, R,r, PGM 2–1, ADA 2–1, EAP–CB, and H_p 2–1, and is the same type as that of the victim, the probability of the blood coming from another source is low, because the population frequency of this combination is 0.04 percent, or one person out of every 2,500.

Other technological contributions include the use of live closed circuit television by criminalists to testify at a distant court during actual trial proceedings. In addition, color slides showing composite pictures of murder victims before and after have been shown to juries during trials. Experiments utilizing scanning electron microscopes and dispersive X-ray analysis are being conducted across the nation. Computers are being used to handle qualitative and quantitative data on large numbers of complex evidence materials. Worldwide statistics are now being collected on population frequencies of blood variants and other materials.

Finally, the Federal Bureau of Investigation has been given authority to develop a nationwide computer system to tie every laboratory in the nation together by computer terminal using existing lines of transfer to form a crime laboratory information system (CLIS).

In an age of advanced technology, then, the criminalistics laboratory has finally become adjusted to the use of the so-called "space age" technology.

Evidence collection

The question of which came first the chicken or the egg does not properly apply to the use of criminalistics evidence. No matter how sophisticated the criminalistics laboratory may be, it is useless unless a system is established for the proper recognition and collection of physical evidence at the crime scene. The importance of this mode of operation is best stated by Clarence M. Kelley, then director of the Federal Bureau of Investigation and former Kansas City, Missouri, chief of police:

The crime laboratory is one part of the scientific and technological organization that supports the police and the courts in the furtherance of criminal justice. Just as important, the laboratory is often able to produce evidence that clears the innocent person from suspicion. One result of the process of social change that has occurred in the United States in recent years has been legal decisions that greatly increase the value of physical evidence in the solution of crime and the conviction of offenders. The crime laboratory therefore represents an important potential extension of the investigating officer's abilities. However, the potential can only be realized if physical evidence is properly collected and transmitted to the laboratory for analysis.[4]

In addition, it is worth taking note of the comments of Justice Arthur Goldberg, speaking for the majority of the Supreme Court in *Escobedo* v. *Illinois*:

We have learned the lesson in history, ancient and modern, that a system of criminal law enforcement which comes to depend on "confession" will, in the long run, be less reliable than a system which depends on extrinsic evidence independently secured through skillful investigation.[5]

Processing the crime scene

Accordingly, every police administrator should see that his department has the capability of processing the scenes of all crimes which take place within the jurisdiction. Many concepts have worked exceptionally well. However, whether a specialized group of evidence technicians is formed, or whether the expertise of trained personnel working outside the police service is utilized, the emphasis must always be on complete and professional crime scene investigation. Ideally, each patrol officer should be trained to fully process his or her own crime scenes, and even in those larger agencies in which specialized evidence technicians are utilized, the training of the individual patrol officer should in no way be reduced.

One of the most pervasive concepts by far among police administrators is that the evidence technician be a trained police officer assigned to the crime laboratory. The laboratory in turn is assigned as a service element in the police organization with a direct link to the chief administrator of the department. Another organizational concept treats the evidence technicians as a separate element of the patrol function, a specified task of all patrol or operations personnel, or a specialized task under operational control of the patrol function. The latter concept has been adopted by some agencies in order to maintain an identity with the patrol function and to prevent crime scene processing from becoming the sole domain of the investigative element and thus being utilized only in large crime scene investigations such as homicides.

Regardless of the organizational concept utilized, it is mandatory that the group be thoroughly trained by practitioners. Consequently, the scientific arm of the agency or members of that crime laboratory utilized by the agency must have responsibility for the direction of a training program for these individuals. A good portion of the training necessarily must be conducted by criminalistics personnel. Instructors should also be provided by the coroner's or medical examiner's office, the training academy, the prosecutor's office, the fire department, and the investigation bureau.

The degree of emphasis on the various techniques must be made the responsibility of those doing the training. Consideration should also be given to ongoing in-service training programs. Where feasible, the crime scene specialist should spend time in the laboratory for in-service training. The purpose of this training is twofold: to give the field technician a thorough understanding of the reasons for certain requirements in processing of crime scenes and of how results are obtained and factors which may influence the results; and to establish a rapport between the bench and the field. Essentially, the evidence technician is the producer of the raw material and the bench develops the raw material into a final product. This final product is used by the prosecutor to indict a suspect, by either the defense or the prosecution to convict or exculpate a defendant, and in some cases by environmental and health authorities to identify a potentially hazardous situation so that the community may be alerted.

Protection of the crime scene

More lip service is paid to "protection of the crime scene" than to almost any other concept in the police service. However, the subject ranks as a major problem in the process of physical evidence development.

While it is recognized by most police administrators and operational personnel that the crime scene should be recorded in as near the condition as it was when discovered, the emphasis on keeping unnecessary personnel away from the scene is often lacking. In many instances a rope is put up to keep onlookers and media personnel outside of an established perimeter, but an army of police personnel "jumps into the rope."

There is no guarantee that every crime scene will yield useful evidence, but it is a demonstrated fact that unless the scene is processed without unnecessary contamination good evidence is lost.

From an operational viewpoint only those responsible for the actual gathering and documenting of the evidence along with one investigator or individual responsible for the investigation should be considered inside personnel (this may also include patrol). An outside link should be available to pass information. It is of great importance that the scene be protected from the outside to assure that no one enters while the scene personnel are busy. It is also too often the case that during the long hours of crime scene processing the entire contingent on the outside drifts away to other assignments leaving those on the inside not only without informational contact pertinent to the ongoing investigation but also subject to the peril of criminal or belligerent persons surreptitiously entering the scene.

Pressure should be placed on all echelons of the agency to ensure proper crime scene protection. It should be borne in mind that usually those doing the actual processing are of lower rank than most of those with little reason to enter the scene. Without proper support from the top, the scene personnel can be helpless—should tact and diplomacy fail—in dealing with those superior officers who do appear on the scene. The key to proper crime scene processing is "slow down," and, when involved with a major crime which will receive considerable attention from the media and in the community, then it is "slow, slow down," and "protect, protect, protect."

The scene personnel

Duties of the evidence technician
(personnel responsible for collection)

The duties of the evidence technician encompass a wide range of responsibilities, mainly directed at the recognition, collection, and preservation of evidence at the scene of a crime. To fulfill these crime scene investigative requirements the evidence technician should be proficient with many individual pieces of equipment and should be knowledgeable in their application to a given crime scene. In addition, he or she should have the following qualifications:

1. The evidence technician should be able to determine, from discussions with police personnel at the scene and witnesses, items most likely to be of evidentiary value and the chain of events of the crime.
2. The evidence technician should be proficient in the use of several pieces of camera equipment and their attachments, for overall scene and close-up photography. He or she should be competent in the various collection techniques for blood, fluids, and any item which by its composition is subject to being broken, distorted, or decomposed. He or she should be able to use available casting techniques (silicone or plaster) on pry marks, tire or shoe impressions, or any other impressions of an evidentiary nature.
3. He or she should be able to collect minute items of trace evidence, hairs, fibers, threads, etc.
4. He or she should be able to mark and recover various items of firearms evidence, handguns, rifles, bullets, cartridge cases, etc., and should be able to mark these items so as to not destroy the areas used for laboratory examination.
5. He or she should be able to collect and package any evidence in such a way as to prevent contamination, destruction, or loss during transportation.
6. He or she should be able to locate, develop, and lift latent fingerprints and, if circumstances dictate, photograph such latent prints prior to the application of fingerprint tape.
7. He or she should be able to examine the bodies of deceased persons and chart and photograph all wounds and pertinent scars or identifying marks and should be proficient in the fingerprinting of such persons. He or she must also be able to utilize any of several techniques available in the fingerprinting of partially decomposed, burned, or mutilated bodies.
8. The evidence technician should be able to examine the bodies of living persons, suspects, or victims, for the purpose of collecting trace evidence, foreign material, blood, dirt, fibers, hair strands, fingernail scrapings, or fingernails.

9. He or she should be able to prepare a crime scene sketch showing all relevant details of the crime such as the location of weapons, furniture, height and width of these various items, and their relationship to each other. This sketch should be proportionate.
10. He or she should be able to maintain notes during the initial crime scene investigation and then prepare a written report, in chronological order, from these notes, detailing his or her observations and actions, and the disposition of all evidence recovered, and fill out property forms listing all this evidence to further maintain the chain of custody.
11. He or she should be able to appear in a courtroom and give testimony concerning his or her involvement in a scene which he or she investigated with a minimum use of report forms or notes and to do so in a professional manner.

It is required of the evidence gathering specialist that his or her sum total of training and experience represent a blend of technical skills, legal knowledge, imagination, initiative, tact, specialization, generalist knowledge, and the ability, above all, to grow with ideas, resist preconceived notions, and adapt to the irregular, the unorthodox, and the improbable.

Equipment for field operations

Equipping an evidence technician can be very costly if not properly investigated and kept at a practical level.

Specialized units will need a vehicle with sufficient size and storage space to carry equipment to the scene and added space for removal of evidence from the scene. A crime laboratory mobile unit should be clearly differentiated from a crime scene evidence unit. Unless the agency plans to do actual analysis in the field, which in most instances is not the mode of choice, then the large trailer type vehicle is unnecessary. It is recommended that a full-size passenger vehicle (police car) or a medium-size van be utilized. Electrical generation capability is needed and may be generated by the vehicle itself, but a dedicated generator is more reliable and in the long run more economical.

Multiple kits which are product lines of commercial distributors are quite expensive, both initially and for restocking. Technicians may not like to carry multiple kits to and from a scene because of limited or difficult accessibility. It is more reasonable to build an evidence kit that is stocked only with those items routinely used. This kit should be complete, but one should avoid building a kit that contains so much that it is overloaded and unworkable. Each police agency will want to work out its own requirements, but typical items will include large and small scissors, several sizes of scalpels, a screwdriver and other small tools, pillboxes in several sizes, several sizes of evidence bags, fingerprint powder, several types of tape, pens, tongue depressors, twine, etc.

As far as photographic equipment is concerned, this is a matter of personal preference. In considering this subject all agencies should work along with the prosecutor's office to establish acceptance of color photographs and slides in lieu of black-and-white photographs. In an arbitrary situation, a black-and-white print can always be made from a color negative.

In considering the particular brand of camera, thought should be given to cost, feasibility of local repair, ease of operation, durability, and versatility.

Protective clothing should be obtained and, although it is not yet applicable directly to local government agencies, consideration should be given to the requirement of the Occupational Safety and Health Act of 1970. Wearing protective headgear and footwear at the scene of fires and bombings, using a filter mask when there is considerable fingerprinting to be done, and adopting a utility uniform as a duty uniform are some areas to consider.

Relationship between the investigator[6] and the laboratory

Modern analytical techniques and legal scrutiny of physical evidence have dictated renewed burdens on the roles of the laboratory and the investigator. These burdens can only be carried out by total professionalism and cooperation on the part of both factions.

The investigator's ability to recognize evidence is the critical starting point to the fragile physical evidence chain. Prerequisite to any object becoming evidence, it must be recognized by someone as having potential information concerning the crime. The ability to recognize valuable physical evidence is cultivated by on-the-job experience and by broadening one's technical investigative background. This technical background is a melting pot of many disciplines.

The investigator must have an ability to recreate imaginatively the events transpiring before, during, and after the commission of the crime. He or she must have a knowledge of the legal aspects of physical evidence so as to render that evidence admissible to court proceedings. The investigator must also have a working knowledge of the scientific arsenal available to him or her from a full-range criminalistics laboratory.

New analytical procedures and techniques performed on physical evidence are constantly being discovered and refined. The interpretations of the results of the analyses are providing increasing information to the investigator.

The investigator–laboratory relationship can be nothing less than professional. The science of criminalistics is a dynamic one to the investigator as well as in the laboratory. Both entities must direct their efforts toward the same goal—the factual solution of the crime. It is incumbent upon the investigator–laboratory that they serve to supplement each other, not to compete.

It is incumbent upon the investigator that he or she does not send packages of evidence to the laboratory without indicating what examinations he or she thinks are appropriate. The laboratory scientist cannot be expected to guess at what the investigator had in mind when he or she secured certain evidence.

A national priority

Three national studies have paid specific attention to the need for crime scene search and physical evidence development. The report by the President's Commission on Law Enforcement and Administration of Justice found that police were "not making the most of their opportunities to obtain and analyze physical evidence."[7] The commission recommended that each police department develop "the capacity to make a thorough search of the scene of every serious crime and to analyze evidence so discovered."[8]

The National Advisory Commission on Criminal Justice Standards and Goals stated the following:

Every state and every police agency should acknowledge the importance of efficient identification, collection, and preservation of physical evidence; its accurate and speedy analysis; and its proper presentation in criminal court proceedings. These are essential to professional criminal investigation, increased clearance of criminal cases, and ultimately, the reduction of crime. Every agency shall insure the deployment of specially trained personnel to gather physical evidence 24 hours a day.[9]

The Forensic Sciences Foundation, in a survey conducted in the early 1970s,[10] found that evidence technicians are most likely to be found in the police departments employing fifty or more officers, are likely to have had four years or more of experience, and are likely to have entered the field from other duties as police officers. Most evidence technicians spend the largest amount of their time at the crime scene in such tasks as: searching for physical evidence, fingerprint work, photography, and measuring and sketching. Evidence technicians testify most often as expert witnesses in homicide, burglary, and rape cases. They are predominantly male with an associate of arts degree from a community college. The survey also provided other findings relative to educational and demographic background; experience and training; duties; career expectations; and educational, working, and professional criteria that they would like to change and upgrade.

On the basis of these findings, the survey developed a number of recommendations for criminal justice administrators, including: development of model entry qualifications for evidence technicians; development of model job titles and descriptions; a study of the possibility of making the evidence technician concept a career program; development of formal courses, workshops, and other types of continuing education; and development of educational curricula at the associate's and bachelor's levels.

These three studies, especially that of the Forensic Sciences Foundation, are cited to encourage police administrators and others in criminal justice administration and the criminal justice process to consider the evidence technician and his or her role in investigation and criminalistics.

Determining laboratory needs

Several of the most widely accepted studies pertaining to the criminalistics laboratory have been cited herein. It must be noted, however, that numerous studies are not in good repute with the practitioner, and, because of the misdirected use of systems groups and the reliance on high cost studies by nonexperts, many of the planning studies in the police service have been anything but progressive.

The use of a systems group to review local needs often presents two problems: either the group has had little experience in the area or the group uses so much material from other studies that its report is simply another report to set on a shelf.

Such approaches which give detailed floor areas for various units of activity, equipment costs, and salary schedules usually ignore local precedents, preexisting equipment, direction of technology growth, and the existence of a floor plan where the new facility will be in a renovated space.

It is recommended that planners and administrators interested in a criminalistics laboratory approach those practitioners who are well respected by their peers and who hold the collective expertise necessary to aid the decision maker. These experts have made themselves available for such activity through the American Society of Crime Laboratory Directors (ASCLD). In 1974 the crime laboratory directors of almost every criminalistics laboratory in the United States and Canada formed this organization, which has as one of its basic tenets the desire to aid local, regional, state, and federal planners with deliberations pertinent to crime laboratory development.[11]

In addition to ASCLD the Forensic Sciences Foundation, Inc., located in Rockville, Maryland, working closely with such organizations as ASCLD and the American Academy of Forensic Sciences, has developed into a positive force in forensic sciences administration and research.[12]

Conclusion

This chapter has provided an overview of the criminalistics function in police services, with particular emphasis on the basic concepts of physical evidence: methods of direct identification; definitions of identity; practical versus absolute identity; associative evidence, probability, class characteristics; and the more detailed factors of comparision, individuality, rarity, and exchange. The balance of the chapter has reviewed technological advances, the procedures for evidence collection, and the role of evidence personnel, particularly the evidence technician. All of the material discussed herein is shaped by the broader framework of criminalistics and the criminalistics laboratory.

As the clamor for additional physical evidence production has continued to rise from the nation's courts, prosecutors, police, and defense communities, the criminalistics laboratory has been catapulted into the "space age." Today, a respected profession has begun to emerge from the back room where the occupants were once titled "the lab boys."

The criminalistics laboratory uses science and scientific methods to establish the service related to its mission of "aiding in the process of criminal justice." The police administrator can and should expect answers to the vital questions: Has a crime been committed? How? When? And by whom? Equally important is the question: Who could *not* have committed the crime?

Since each criminalistics laboratory is different from another, it is important that police administrators familiarize themselves with the capabilities of the laboratory supporting their own investigations. Regardless of variances in capability, the mission of eliminating uncertainty and supplementing fact for supposition is common to all criminalistics laboratories. Should the laboratory in a particular jurisdiction lack expertise in an area of importance it is incumbent upon police officials in that jurisdiction to question the laboratory administrators on the subject. Often the laboratory administrators recognize the deficiency but need the support of others within the system to obtain the priority, staff, and/or funds in order to grow in a particular area of expertise. If this is the case, a concerted effort will be needed to arrive at success. If it can be shown that the laboratory is deficient because of poor administration, then the laboratory administrator must be provided with additional management or scientific training or, possibly, in some extreme cases, be replaced by a more knowledgeable manager.

The criminalistics laboratory is by no means a panacea for the solution to crime, nor is it able to replace or supplant good investigative personnel. It does, however, offer an excellent tool in the quest for truth and in the establishment of the public good.

1 Forensic Sciences Foundation, "Assessment of the Personnel of the Forensic Sciences Profession," survey undertaken by the Forensic Sciences Foundation in the early 1970s, unpublished at this date. LEAA Grant 73–Ni–99–0052G.

2 Ibid.

3 This section is partially excerpted from the author's unpublished lecture series. The general body of literature on criminalistics and crime scene search was drawn upon in preparing these lectures. The following sources were of particular benefit: Richard H. Fox and Carl Cunningham, *Crime Scene Search and Physical Evidence Handbook* (Washington, D.C.: Government Printing Office, 1973); Lorenzo A. Sunico and Elliott B. Hensel, *Elements of Criminalistics* (Manila: The Police Commission, 1968); James W. Osterburg, *The Crime Laboratory* (Bloomington: Indiana University Press, 1971); Charles E. O'Hara and James W. Osterburg, *An Introduction to Criminalistics* (New York: The Macmillan Company, 1949); Paul L. Kirk. *Crime Investigation: Physical Evidence and the Police Laboratory* (New York: Interscience Publishers, 1960); Charles R. Kingston, "The Law of Probabilities and the Credibility of Witnesses and Evidence," *Journal of Forensic Science* 15 (January 1970): 18–27. The interested reader is referred to these texts. Additional material appears in the Selected Bibliography to this book.

4 Fox and Cunningham, *Crime Scene Search and Physical Evidence Handbook,* p. iii.

5 *Escobedo* v. *Illinois,* 378 U.S. 478 (1964), pp. 128, 129.

6 The term investigator is used here interchangeably with patrol officer, detective, investigator, evidence technician, etc. From the laboratory standpoint, dealing with large and small departments alike, the important thing is that all police personnel involved in any level of criminal investigation must relate to the evidence and the laboratory personnel what they see, collect, and submit, and why.

7 President's Commission on Law Enforcement and Administration of Justice, *The Challenge of Crime in a Free Society* (Washington, D.C.: Government Printing Office, 1967), p. 118.

8 Ibid.

9 National Advisory Commission on Criminal Justice Standards and Goals, *Police* [Report on Police] (Washington, D.C.: Government Printing Office, 1973), p. 295.

10 Forensic Sciences Foundation, "Assessment of the Personnel of the Forensic Sciences Profession."

11 American Society of Crime Laboratory Directors, P.O. Box 1456, Atlanta, Georgia 30301.

12 Forensic Sciences Foundation, 11400 Rockville Pike, Rockville, Maryland 20852. The American Academy of Forensic Sciences is also at this address.

19 Jail management

One of the responsibilities of police agencies is the detention of prisoners for circumscribed periods ranging from a few hours to as long as a year or more. Usually considered as holding points until persons are brought to trial, detention facilities are also used for short-term offenders. The operation of these facilities, usually known as jails, is a police department responsibility in many parts of the country. Handling this responsibility is the subject of this chapter.

The chapter opens with a brief survey of the historical development of jails and a description of the special relationship of the police agency to jail management. This is followed by discussions of the courts and jail management and the numerical scope of the facility. The philosophical issue of the police agency role in jail management as compared with the desirability of regional operation of jails is next discussed. The regional concepts of jail operations are then explored; this is followed by a brief discussion of custody and rehabilitation.

The balance of the chapter covers five major aspects of jail planning, management, and operations that are of direct concern to the police administrator: planning for a new construction or the renovation of an existing jail; search, admissions, property inventory, and other steps in prisoner intake procedure; prisoner discipline, visitation privileges, and other aspects of jail operations; head count, control of medications, prohibition of weapons, and other security measures; prisoner release procedures; personnel selection and training, jail records, and other aspects of staff services. There is also a brief discussion of special programs.

The historical background

Historically, the "local jail" is one of the oldest components of the criminal justice system. In 1166, Henry III of England had the Parliament pass an act providing for construction of jails at the assize of Clarendon. Their purpose was to provide a detention capability for suspected or accused persons until such time as they could be brought before the proper court. These facilities were inadequately heated and improperly ventilated and provided little or no ancillary services.

When the English colonists came to the New World, "gaols, lockups, and stockades," which doubled as warehouses, were among the very first structures built in many of the new settlements. These were conceived as places of confinement for those who broke the law. Coercion and correction were added as a religious requirement. These structures also housed the insane, the poor, vagrants, orphans, and sometimes the ill. These persons were thrown into confinement without regard to sex, age, or history, usually under the most squalid conditions. Today we can still find in Massachusetts and Virginia buildings that were used as community jails prior to 1700.

The jail in the United States was eventually to give birth to the American innovation of the penitentiary, many of which were built and designed during the nineteenth century. But while this development was being instituted at the state level local institutions at both the county and municipal levels continued to pose major problems to police executives throughout the country. One need only pick up the newspaper on any day to read of the problems that a police department can have concerning detained persons. These problems involve escapes, riots, dangerous contraband material being introduced into secured areas of the jail, physical and sexual assaults upon inmates by other inmates, suicides, and even murders. In addition, many facilities are badly overcrowded, which adds to the tension of a prisoner population. It can be safely said that the successful operation of a jail will not win any accolades for the police administrator, but let there be any problems and any good public relations existing between the police and the community will quickly be jeopardized.

Special relationships and problems

The police–jail relationship

The relationship that the jail has to the police is obviously one of accommodation and cooperation. It has the responsibility to accept any prisoner who is legally detained and who can be legally received. It cannot say who may enter, how long they will stay, and who will be released. If a community is concerned with drunks or vagrants, then its detention facility will generally hold a large number of persons charged with these offenses, since the arrest policy of many police agencies is usually a reflection of the community attitude and governmental policy. The point to be made is that the jail feels the effect of the community and its police policies because it is not an independent governmental unit. It is a component of a much larger system and it is strongly affected by the acts of that system and the events that go on around it.

When an accused person is detained, coordination between the police and jail personnel may be required. There is generally an exchange of information between these personnel, particularly where there is a need to keep accomplices separated. When a long-term investigation is under way, police and jail personnel may need to schedule and coordinate their efforts for interviews and lineups. In some instances a material witness may be detained as an additional service for the police function.

The court–jail relationship

The jail and the courts must cooperate and work very closely with each other. In this regard, the jail has the specific responsibility of detaining accused

Squalid facilities that are typical of many jails still found in the United States.

persons until they can be brought before the court for processing and adjudication. Its personnel must be aware of those judicial procedures which require the presence of defendants, and must also adhere to all court orders directed to it. Because of these functions, the jail may appear to be an agency of the court. If there is a lack of judicial manpower or if the courts do not process their dockets quickly, the inmate population will increase. Finally, the need for close coordination between the court and the jail has, in most areas of the country, led to their close physical proximity. In most instances they are located in the same building or immediately adjacent to each other.

The numerical scope of concern

Historically, jails have been the responsibility of local law enforcement officials.[1] For purposes of clarification, a jail is defined here as a facility (1) in which persons are held until such time as they are brought before the court, and (2) for the detention of prisoners sentenced for a term not to exceed one year.

Many of the police departments in this country have some form of holding facility for minimal, temporary detention, and some departments operate large, full-scale institutions. The National Advisory Commission on Criminal Justice Standards and Goals states:

Although larger urban areas have built some facilities for special groups of offenders, in most parts of the country a single local institution today retains the dual purposes of custodial confinement and misdemeanant punishment. . . . Thus jails are the catchall for social and law enforcement problems.

Jails are the intake point for our entire criminal justice system. There are more jails than any other type of "correctional" institution.[2]

In 1970 a national jail census conducted by the U.S. Bureau of the Census under agreement with the Law Enforcement Assistance Administration (LEAA) showed that there were 4,037 locally administered jails with authority to detain adult offenders for forty-eight hours or longer.[3] Many of these jails were overcrowded and overused and a large percentage were in the process of deterioration. According to the same study, more than 25 percent were built before 1920.[4] The jail census did not include the many drunk tanks, lockups, and other types of facilities which are used to detain persons for less than forty-eight hours. In counties and cities with populations in excess of 25,000, some 85 to 90 percent of the jails offered no educational or recreational facilities, 50 percent provided no medical facilities, and 25 percent had no provisions for visitation.

Owing to their multiple uses, local jails contain a population more varied than that of any other type of correctional institution. The jail census found that "of 160,863 persons held on the census date, 27,460 had not been arraigned, 8,688 were awaiting some postconviction legal action, 69,096 were serving sentences (10,496 for more than a year), and 7,800 were juveniles."[5] In many cases, then, accused felons, misdemeanants, and juveniles were found improperly thrown together while awaiting trial.

It is easy to see from the above that a large number of people come into contact with detention facilities; these people can be greatly affected by the confinement experience. But because it has not caused much concern among the general public, the jail has tended to evolve more by default than by plan.

Operation arrangements

The philosophical issue: police in jailing

As has been pointed out, the operation of any jail can be a problem to the police administrator. This is not to say that a police department should not operate its own jail where the facts warrant it, but two federal fact-finding commissions give some philosophical and reasonable arguments against it (President's Commission on Law Enforcement and Administration of Justice, 1967, and National Advisory Commission on Criminal Justice Standards and Goals, 1973). Both commissions point out that there are major distinctions between the enforcement activity that policing requires and the correctional activity which, in some instances, requires rehabilitative and detention capability. In addition, both commissions raise valid arguments which are difficult to overcome concerning the use of highly paid and trained police personnel to maintain and operate the jail. The President's Commission on Law Enforcement and Administration of Justice went so far as to say that municipal police departments should not operate jail facilities (apart from perhaps maintaining immediate and short-term detention facilities—and even these should be run by a separate agency). The commission further recommended that "state governments should establish a jail administration agency with responsibility for the operation and management of all local detention facilities."[6]

The National Advisory Commission on Criminal Justice Standards and Goals was more specific in recommending that a police department not operate a jail. They advised the following:

Every police agency currently operating a detention facility should immediately insure professionalism in its jail management and provide adequate detention services. Every municipal police agency should, by 1982, turn over all its detention and correctional facilities to an appropriate county, regional, or State agency, and should continue to maintain only those facilities necessary for short term processing of prisoners immediately following arrest.

1. Every police agency that anticipates the need for full-time detention employees after 1975 should immediately hire and train civilian personnel to perform its jail functions.
2. Every municipal police agency currently operating its own detention facility should immediately consider using an easily accessible State or county facility for all detention except that required for initial processing of arrestees. Every agency should also consider using State or county facilities for the transfer of arrestees from initial processing detention to arraignment detention.[7]

These recommendations are predicated upon the philosophical issue of a police agency making arrests and placing persons in jail and then having to be concerned with the care and custody of the accused. The prevalent view concerning this matter is that it is better to have a "neutral custodian" that would ensure the rights of individuals awaiting trial and at the same time provide the necessary services for the police department. The police administrator, then, should consider carefully the necessity of maintaining and operating his own facility. He should also take into consideration court decisions which indicate that jails at all levels of government must be properly maintained and adequately staffed with trained personnel in the area of corrections, and that the inmates should be provided with adequate food, exercise, recreation, sanitation, and medical services.

Because of the increasing costs in operations, the shortage of physical and personnel resources, and the role of the detention function, the use of a regional facility may provide some worthwhile advantages.

Regional concepts of jails

The regional sharing of facilities, equipment, and personnel is not new to the police services in this country. There are both a formal and an informal approach to cooperation and coordination between various governmental entities concerned with police services. An entire chapter of the task force report on the police of the President's Commission on Law Enforcement and Administration of

Justice deals with the topic of coordination and consolidation of police services.[8] It includes, among other things, a discussion of crime laboratories, communications, records, training programs, and related activities that could be merged or regionalized.

With regard to jails, this chapter recommends that "a number of local jurisdictions should join in the operation of detention facilities, sharing physical facilities under contractual agreements, eliminating duplicate facilities, or establishing jail districts."[9]

This concept is also put forward in the National Advisory Commission on Criminal Justice Standards and Goals report entitled *Corrections,* wherein the recommendation is made that governmental entities might well consider the pooling of resources for the purpose of establishing regional detention facilities.[10] This concept has merit where there are limited local resources and only a small number of arrests made by the policing agency. Because of these factors, it may be difficult to justify separate detention facilities and other related programs. Under this concept several police jurisdictions may pool their financial and human resources and elect to create a regional arrangement for a detention facility. This plan would allow the police administrator to make use of a detention facility at a minimal cost while at the same time making use of a wide variety of specialized services that such a facility could provide. A regional facility could obviously then contribute to the effectiveness of the local police department by releasing funds and personnel that might otherwise be required for an individual jail operation. In addition, this arrangement can improve the management of detention and thereby create a more favorable public attitude regarding jails and police agencies. It can foster sound correctional training procedures with greater attention given to achieving and maintaining accepted penological standards and a more efficient organization and administration.

An outgrowth of the pooling arrangement may well be an integrated "satellite" jail program. It is obviously good practice to have the major detention facility immediately adjacent to the courts. This facility would house only pretrial detainees and would serve as the hub of the satellite program. Located at strategic sites would be smaller facilities which, depending upon physical requirements, would have a capacity of not less than twenty-five but not more than a hundred prisoners. Each would be linked to the main jail via land line capability or, in some instances, through closed circuit television, so that booking and other record keeping requirements could be rapidly transmitted.

Such a program would lend itself to uniform construction methods in which the same standard plans, modules, and specifications could be used as new facilities were built. It would reduce construction costs and, since each facility would have the same floor plan, would permit the implementation of uniform operating procedures. These facilities could process newly arrested offenders and release those who were eligible for bonding or other types of release programs close to their neighborhoods. They could also house those persons who cannot be released but for whom there is no space available in the main jail. As a last resort, if there were no other alternative available, they could house sentenced prisoners. While small in size, these satellite facilities could have built into them the capability of providing the same services that the main detention facility might have related to education, recreation, religion, or other such programs. The ability to transport prisoners to a nearby facility would also reduce police operational costs and increase patrol time.

For this concept to be developed, a cooperative, interagency planning process is needed that takes into consideration, among other things: location of the courts; distances to be traveled by police, prosecutors, defense attorneys, and other interested parties; population centers; types of offenders to be detained; and services to be provided to inmates. The actual cost of establishing such a jail can be easily determined and assessed among its users. With new construction, the pooling approach makes it possible for the cooperating jurisdictions to pay a pro rata share of the actual building costs, or to pay a predetermined amount per inmate per day. In jurisdictions where it is appropriate, new city–county buildings could include detention facilities in which each has its own jail, but kitchen, laundry, commissary, and other similar services are operated jointly. This also provides the possibility of using different facilities to house different categories of offenders (e.g., male prisoners in one section and female prisoners in another). In this type of arrangement neither jurisdiction has to provide the total range of jail facilities or services.

Another concept that the police administrator might well consider is contractual services. Since many municipal jails duplicate their services, especially in the holding of sentenced prisoners, the contractual agreement offers some merit in cost saving. Under the terms of a contract, cities can pay a major city or county jurisdiction for each prisoner detained in its jail, and it is possible that a county could provide complete jail services on a contractual basis for all cities within it. Such an arrangement exists in Los Angeles County, California, where the sheriff's office provides a bus service to pick up prisoners from the various municipalities and transport them to the county jail.

While regionalization is not the complete answer to eliminating the serious problems of local jails, it can relieve the progressive police administrator by removal of this function from the police operation and can, in addition, improve service to the community and to arrestees through professional correctional administration.

Regional jailing will require that the police administrator take into account all the variables in, and present alternative approaches to, new jail construction as well as modification of existing facilities. The role and function of the jail facility and its ability to meet inmate and community needs must be explored in full. The police administrator will have to determine initially whether or not his department will maintain and operate its own detention facility and whether, through mutual agreements, a cooperative effort for a regional jail can be arranged.

A great deal of technical assistance and guidance for this approach can be obtained at no cost from the National Clearinghouse for Criminal Justice Planning and Architecture.[11] This clearinghouse is a Law Enforcement Assistance Administration project designed to assist governmental entities in design, equipment, and related matters concerning jail facilities. Planning for the jail is discussed in detail later in this chapter.

Custody and rehabilitation

The role of the jail is changing. New ideas, new programs and new methods are modifying present practices. In spite of these influences, the basic goals of the jail remain unchanged: the safekeeping and welfare of prisoners; the protection of society by prevention of escapes; and the safety of jail personnel. If these three goals cannot be achieved it will not be possible to introduce new plans, programs or procedures into the jail. An additional requirement is the need to maintain a balance between security and correctional objectives. It is no longer sufficient that a jail merely be safe and secure; it must also correct.

This balance must be maintained under pressure of a diverse prisoner population with a wide range of security and correctional needs. Within this population are found the drunk, the aggressive homosexual, the first offender, and the sophisticated criminal. The escape risk must be identified and procedures applied that will hold him securely; the assaultive prisoner must be kept from harming others; and the suicide risk must be supervised so that he does not harm himself. The emotional needs of the prisoners result in a tremendous number of problems that must be met by a variety of correctional programs—but within the framework of security.[12]

It is obvious from this statement that some form of balance is needed between the matters of custody and rehabilitation. Again, it is important to point out that custody and rehabilitative programs are not within the scope of a true law enforcement concept. While the jail itself may be a part of a county or municipal police department, its primary objective is criminal detention.

Custody carries with it security. Whether the prisoners are awaiting trial or have been sentenced, the jailer's role becomes most important. He must forever be on the alert for security breaches, and yet his custodial duties must be balanced by the rights of the inmates. The jailer must treat all inmates evenhandedly and must not allow his own emotional responses to enter into his work. Discipline is necessary and must be carried out at all times, but care must be taken in absolute unyielding disciplinary situations, for these can foster unrest and create antagonism between the inmate population and the jailers. The primary consideration of the jail, then, is to confine the prisoners held in a secure and safe environment. Once that is achieved, the rehabilitative process can be applied.

Rehabilitation carries with it the ability to return the arrested person to the community as a useful and productive member of society. Whether we are discussing a large or small facility, the conditions that exist there can and do affect its inmate population, both sentenced and unsentenced. The emotional atmosphere in dealing with tension and anxiety is greatly increased where overcrowding and few constructive activities exist.

All persons who are arrested and detained in a jail are subject to its influences. This is especially true for the person who is arrested for the first time. The local jail, then, should be viewed as the first opportunity for the taking of initial corrective action. As one authority has put it, "More can be done to redeem . . . [a] man in the first three days after his arrest than can be done in six months after he has been . . . sentenced."[13] Therefore, it is imperative that the rehabilitative processes begin as soon as the person is taken into custody.

Major aspects of jail management

The present section covers the major considerations of planning the facility, intake procedures, jail operations, security, prisoner release, and staff services. There is also a brief section on special programs.

Planning for the jail

Planning for the jail is a necessary and vital step, whether the facility is to be a new construction or the renovation of an existing jail. The facility should serve numerous functions in addition to its primary function, custody. The types of functions to be served must be identified and planned for on the basis of particular community needs. It is this role that the police administrator should bear in mind throughout the planning processes, regardless of the size of the facility in question.

Steps in planning   Listed immediately below are the major steps to be considered in planning for the jail facility:

1. The definition of the problem—collection of data and information that will help in the assessment of needs.
2. Reviewing existing information about present and future needs, including the physical plant and its existing or proposed programs.
3. Coordinating the various study efforts that will develop the information.
4. Defining the role and objectives of the jail.
5. Seeing to it that the plans developed integrate and harmonize with the other segments of the criminal justice system, such as the courts, other police departments, other correctional facilities and agencies, as well as services that may be available from both the public and private sector for the facility.

The assessment of needs of the jail [mentioned in 1, above] should be evaluated from the following viewpoints:

1. The jail as a humane shelter. It must meet the physical needs of prisoners by providing housing that is safe, adequate, and sanitary. It must be possible to keep clean, not be overcrowded, and ventilation and lighting should be adequate. Also, the prisoners should be protected from each other.
2. The jail as an adequate plant. The physical condition of the jail must be evaluated to determine the structural and functional conditions of floors, walls, plumbing, wiring, locks, and various heavy equipment. The evaluation must provide an estimate of the cost of renovation and of the continued costs of maintenance and repairs. These evaluations and estimates must be made by specialists such as architects and plant maintenance engineers.
3. The jail as a security system. The areas to be reviewed here are:
   a) The adequacy of the physical plant to provide safekeeping of prisoners in cells, in visiting rooms, and in other parts of the facility
   b) The existence of security devices
   c) The use and effectiveness of security procedures.

Renovation may be a reasonable alternative to new construction and this should [also] be considered in the evaluation. The cost of making a deficient jail into an adequate one must be carefully compared to the cost of constructing a new and even more adequate jail.[14]

The police administrator should call upon experts in the correctional field with institutional experience who can provide valuable assistance in evaluating security and programs. There are some variables that must also be considered in this type of planning process which deal with inmate population studies and forecasting as well as with court sentencing practices. The average daily count, the high and low booking rates, the seasonal factors, age, and sex are some of the factors that affect the capacity of a jail and its ability to safely and adequately house prisoners. In addition, community population trends, present and projected arrest rates, and overall crime rates must also be taken into consideration.

The speed at which the courts handle the pretrial proceedings (i.e., bond hearings, release on recognizance [ROR]) is a factor that will affect the jail population's size. Finally, the number of persons sentenced by the courts and the alternatives to sentencing will also affect the population size (i.e., pretrial intervention, work release, probation and parole).

The jail cannot function, then, as an independent unit where these types of variables will affect the population to be served. These variables are a major factor to be considered in the planning for design and construction.

Design and construction As has been mentioned earlier, the National Clearinghouse for Criminal Justice Planning and Architecture can be of invaluable help in jail design and construction. The clearinghouse can provide technical assistance through the auspices of the various state planning agencies. This can include a review of architectural renditions, construction costs, building and construction materials, design and physical settings, and various related aspects. While flexibility in design can be afforded in the police facility through use of movable walls and partitions, the same flexibility cannot be afforded in the jail area.

Design also plays a major role in a functional jail. Listed below are some important factors to be considered in designing a functional facility:

1. Simplicity of layout of cells and patrol corridors
2. Location of plumbing and electrical wiring
3. Provision of rehabilitative programs
4. Number of jail personnel necessary to properly control and maintain the facility

5. Ancillary services to be performed by the personnel (e.g., radio communications; booking and fingerprinting; dealing with bondsmen, attorneys, and other interested visitors)
6. Ease with which a prisoner can be brought to a secure visiting area and can be observed under conditions which still permit the assigned personnel the opportunity to perform their ancillary duties
7. Provisions for easy removal of inmates, with a minimum of confusion, in the event of a fire
8. Procedures that the jail personnel will be required to implement in the event of fire evacuation
9. Alternative exits from the jail that can be secure and yet meet fire department regulation standards
10. Width of all doors in the event stretchers or other emergency equipment are required to enter the cell block
11. Keeping to a minimum the distances that inmates must travel for purposes of court hearings, visitation, and similar activities
12. Emergencies and contingencies that may pose future problems such as riots, sudden overcrowding, and natural disasters.

Simplicity in construction is an important factor in light of ever increasing costs. For example, a new wide range of clear, tough plastic materials can, in many instances, be used as a replacement for steel bars and doors. This type of material can provide cost reduction in construction where properly used and, at the same time, can add to the security capability by providing direct visual observation of the cell areas by jail personnel. Such material can also play a major factor in letting outside natural light and environment into the jail, thus improving many of the forbidding and oppressive aspects of the jail itself.

Finally, no discussion on the type of detention facility to be constructed or renovated would be complete without some consideration of the more subtle psychological factors that affect not only the inmate population but the correctional staff as well. These include the use of air-conditioning, heating, and lighting, and the correct use of colors within the jail. Here, again, the National Clearinghouse for Criminal Justice Planning and Architecture can be of great assistance.

Location and type of facility　The planning process must also take into consideration the location and type of facility to be designed and constructed. Many jails are an integral part of existing police buildings, while others have a separate location. If new construction is being considered, then site location is a most important factor.

There is a tendency in the congested urban areas to build large multistoried or "high-rise" jails. These are the most expensive to build as well as to maintain. In addition, they pose major operational problems to the staff. The movement of prisoners by elevators, their feedings, visitations, court appearances, and recreational activities can become a nightmare of control situations. Fire, riots, and related problems are also compounded in direct proportion to the number of floors. Such buildings also require many additional jail personnel—the single most expensive item in a jail budget. If, because of lack of suitable sites, a multistory facility must be built, it should be developed as a short-term detention facility only, and its design requirements should include a total activity component for the inmates.

Where new construction is planned, the addition of a jail to a governmental complex or the construction of the jail alone can pose problems with the surrounding citizenry. Care and patience must be taken to diminish the concern of the citizens in having "a jail in their midst." This can, to some extent, be accomplished by encouraging the community to become involved in meaningful programs within the facility.

Intake procedures

The first steps in dealing with those persons who are to be booked into a jail can and do affect new prisoners and their immediate and future behavior while in a jail. The officer assigned to the task of booking the prisoner must be made to recognize that he or she asserts a great deal of influence upon the attitude of prisoners. It is possible that hostile prisoners may quickly transfer their hostility from the arresting officer to the booking officer. Therefore, the booking officer should be trained to present a calm and understanding appearance to the arrested person, even under the most trying conditions. He or she should not personally be affronted by the remarks that many prisoners will make at the time of their booking. Officers who exhibit short tempers or other forms of hostility in processing prisoners can cause difficulty for other staff members who must later deal with the prisoners.

There are some essential steps that must be taken in the intake processes. These are described below under the following headings: search, admissions, inventory of property, strip search, bathing and grooming, clothing, personal history, identification, medical screening, and classification.

Search Every prisoner who enters the jail is potentially dangerous, to the personnel as well as other prisoners. Therefore, the first step in the intake procedure should be a careful search of the prisoner and his or her personal effects.

Admissions A prisoner can only be admitted or "booked" into a jail on legal criminal charges, court commitments, or confinement orders. Where prisoners are brought to the jail by the police, they must be accompanied by either an appropriate arrest form or a citation signed by the arresting officer. The charges should be predicated upon law and prisoners should not be booked where the forms contain only a "hold" for the police personnel or agency. Unless the jail is adequately staffed with a medical facility and attending personnel, injured, sick, or unconscious prisoners should not be admitted. Instead, every effort should be made to transport them to a medical facility, preferably one with some detention capability. It should be remembered that once a jail accepts this type of prisoner it becomes legally responsible for his or her medical care.

Inventory of property All personal property should be taken from the prisoner. Each item should be carefully listed on a proper receipt form. This should include a sufficiently detailed description to identify each item. Money should never be permitted to remain with the prisoner, as this may lead to gambling, robbery, and related incidents among the jail population. All personal items should be placed in a sealed bag or envelope, signed by the prisoner and the booking officer or property room clerk, with a copy of the receipt given to the prisoner.

Strip search Next, a thorough and systematic search should be made of the prisoner, outside the presence of other prisoners. All clothing should be removed. This type of search must be concerned with weapons, drugs, and other contraband that can be hidden on the human body. The prisoner should also be examined for lice and any infectious type sores; if such are detected, proper treatment should be administered.

Bathing and grooming If possible, each prisoner should be given a bath after the strip search, and periodic bathing should be encouraged while the prisoner remains in the jail. The length of hair and beards, if not a health hazard (lice), cannot be regulated by jail rules as various courts have ruled that such regulation is a violation of the prisoner's civil rights.

Clothing   Although some jails permit prisoners to retain their own clothing, it is generally agreed that prisoners who will be placed in the general population should be provided with jail clothing. This can be an inexpensive T-shirt and washable trousers.

Personal history   Some personal history is necessary, both for identification and in the event that emergency notifications are required.

Identification   All prisoners should be fingerprinted and photographed with copies of their prints forwarded to the FBI. Photographs of the prisoner are necessary in many large jails to ensure that the right person is being released, receiving medication, or retrieving personal property.

Medical screening   This is a most important step in the screening process. A physical examination at admission is essential to identify and, where necessary, treat illness, injury, or communicable disease. In small facilities there may not be a medical screening capability or procedure. If not, a contractual agreement with a local physician, hospital, or public health program can be arranged. Special medical problems such as epilepsy, narcotic addiction, and diabetes should be noted during the admission process and the appropriate medical treatment arranged. The booking officer should be instructed that, when there is doubt as to the physical condition of a prisoner, a doctor should be called in. This is particularly true in the case of prisoners seemingly under the influence of alcohol. In many instances, what is thought to be drunkenness can turn out to be diabetes, a heart attack, or a head injury. In some instances a prisoner may exhibit cuts, bruises, or scratches. These should be properly noted in the event they result in a future legal action. Such injuries may also be the basis of "police brutality" suits, and by the recording and photographing of the physical condition of the prisoner, claims of mistreatment can be minimized.

Classification   The purpose of classification is to: (1) determine which prisoners may be escape risks; (2) protect the prisoner from himself or other prisoners; (3) protect the other inmates and jail personnel from a potentially violent new prisoner.

It is classification which may determine where a prisoner may be assigned and with whom. The governmental entity may be held legally responsible should an incident occur through its failure to provide some form of classification. Regardless of the size of the facility, all prisoners should be classified to determine what, if any, special needs will have to be provided for. A program that can provide some help to the prisoner with mental or emotional problems can add to the safety and security of any jail.

For purposes of administrative simplicity, three security designations are recommended in the jail: maximum, for the person who needs close supervision and control; medium, for the prisoner who needs routine control in the jail; and minimum, for those who need very little supervision and who are not escape risks.[15]

Jail operations

Operational considerations are subject to a delicate balancing process: on one hand, there is the security of the facility; on the other, there are the rights of the prisoners housed in the facility. At times these considerations may appear to be in direct conflict. The material in this section may be of assistance in helping the administrator make decisions.

Rights of inmates   The rights of confined prisoners in this country have substantially increased owing to a large number of judicial decisions handed down during the last several years. These have expanded the constitutional guarantees that prisoners in a detention status have. These rights include: (1) protection from other, hostile, prisoners and abusive correctional personnel; (2) adequate and wholesome food; (3) adequate clothing; (4) prompt and adequate medical treatment when necessary.

Discipline of prisoners The entire disciplinary process of prisoners has come under a great deal of court scrutiny in recent years, and there are definite trends in decisions that indicate that due process applies to disciplinary procedures. To meet this requirement, written rules should be established that are clear and are available to each prisoner. These should establish the norms of behavior expected of the prisoner and the consequences of violating them. If an infraction occurs, the violation should be documented and become a part of the disciplinary hearing process which the courts now require. The prisoner must be given an opportunity to present his or her side in the deliberation, and a written report of the incident, hearing, and action taken should be filed in the event that legal questions are raised later. If punishment is to be meted out it generally falls into three categories: (1) loss of privileges, (2) loss of ''good time,'' and (3) segregation from the main population. Loss of good time is applied to sentenced prisoners only. Care should be taken to ensure that all of a prisoner's good time is not taken at once, as this may leave the prisoner with a ''nothing to lose'' attitude.

Visitation This falls into three categories: professional, general, and special. Each should be planned and supervised.

Professional visits include attorneys, members of the clergy, and psychiatrists. These are usually of a confidential nature and space should be provided accordingly. This does not mean the visit should be totally unsupervised, as precautions must be taken to ensure that no contraband will be given to the prisoner. A simple method of ensuring this is to search the prisoner before and immediately after such visits.

General visits include family and friends. These can help reduce the prisoner's tension. Again, adequate security precautions should be taken to prevent the entry of contraband into the facility, and the prisoner should be searched before and immediately after the visit.

Finally, plans should be provided to take into account court ordered or emergency visits that may involve serious illnesses, accident, or death of a family member.

Feeding The jail administrator must be aware of what the prisoners think of the food served. Nothing will cause an incident or riot more quickly than food. While some prisoners will always complain as to all aspects of jail surroundings, most will be willing to give an honest evaluation of the food. In some jails a cafeteria style of feeding is used, while in others, feeding occurs in the cells. In either situation the serving and feeding can pose problems.

In the cafeteria, care and thought must be given to control and supervision of feeding large numbers of prisoners at one time or in shifts. Jail personnel must be placed in strategic locations in the eating area. If prisoners are used in the kitchen area to prepare or dispense the food, they should be clean and well-groomed. Sex offenders should be avoided for this type of work assignment since most prisoners seem to resent being served by them.

In cell feeding, food carts are used to transport the food from the kitchen to the cell areas. Every effort should be made to keep the food hot while it is being dispensed. In addition, portion control should be constantly adhered to so that there will be enough food to go around and to prevent some prisoners who know the feed crew from getting extra helpings. This type of favoritism can cause numerous fights among the prisoners.

In both situations all utensils should be accounted for at the conclusion of the

392 Local Government Police Management

meal. If this is not done, prisoners will attempt to hold back utensils for a variety of reasons. An immediate search should be conducted for any missing utensils. Many jails have adopted tough new plastic utensils to replace the metal type. This plastic type cannot be sharpened and will break if too much pressure is applied.

Commissary Many jails provide a service whereby prisoners can purchase needed articles. This service provides the prisoner with some items that add to his or her comfort and convenience at a minimal cost. Most commissaries operate on small margin of profit and the profits are usually used to further the prisoners' welfare. Newspapers, magazines, books, recreational and sporting equipment, clothing for indigent prisoners who must go to court or to funerals are some of the items that come under this heading. In some instances salaries of those working in the commissary are paid from the profits, and prisoners may be used as stock men. The total amount of purchases that can be made by each prisoner may vary with the institution. In small jails, arrangements can be made with a local vendor to provide the basic requirements of the prisoners and establish minimal items to be purchased. The prisoner should be given receipts (via the jail) by the vendor. These should be limited to miscellaneous toilet articles. (The new cartridge type plastic blade can safely be used in a jail without concern that it may be used as a cutting weapon.)

Recreation and exercise Recreation is another activity that jails must provide for. The objective of recreation is to provide an outlet for energy, to eliminate monotony, and to allow pent up emotions to be released. It also provides prisoners with a choice in an environment in which they do not have many choices available. Space will obviously be a factor for security considerations; games, sports, and athletics are the most common activities of recreation, while hobbies and crafts, art, and other hand skills may be considered. There is a series of court cases that state that prisoners should be brought out of their cells for purposes of exercise. It appears to be a factor that jail administrators must now consider in their operations. Thought must be given to security, control, and personnel factors if this is to be provided.

Use of trusties The use of trusties must be carefully weighed, both from a security and from a custody point of view. The designation of a prisoner as a trusty means that the prisoner has been evaluated and screened for work in and around the jail. Such a designation should take into consideration whether the prisoner is sentenced or unsentenced, the charges against the prisoner, the possibility of escape, the need for minimum supervision, the lack of prior disciplinary problems, and the type of work he or she will perform. Under no circumstances should a trusty be given authority to supervise other prisoners. He or she should not be permitted to work or come into contact with jail finances or records, or the property of other inmates, as this could lead to serious problems of security and trust, no matter how closely supervised the trusty might be. The jobs assigned to the trusty should be under the constant supervision of jail personnel. Trusties should always be thoroughly searched before returning to the cells if they have been working outside the confines of the jail. Their cell area should, from time to time, also be searched.

Sanitation Another major operational consideration is sanitation. The U.S. Bureau of Prisons provides excellent guidelines for this activity.

Any relaxation of control over waste, refuse, or personal filth may permit the spread of vermin. "Cleanliness, construction, and chemistry" are key words in vermin control. Cleanliness, including the proper handling and disposal of garbage, creates an unfavorable environment for vermin by limiting their food supply and breeding places. Construction involves exclusion of vermin through screening and rat-proofing. . . .

Vermin control requires constant effort, as the potential for new infestation is always present. All incoming shipments of food should be thoroughly inspected for vermin.[16]

Key control   No element of security is more important to a jail than its key control. This procedure requires that a central point exist where all keys are checked in and out to jail personnel. It must be totally secure from prisoners. Each key should be placed on a control panel board and when a key is checked out by an officer a small metal tag should be hung on the hook as a receipt. It should be established procedure that no officer carry outside keys into the cell block under any circumstances. Under no conditions should keys ever be left lying around, nor should a trusty be allowed to carry or handle keys.

Emergency plans   This most important phase of operations must be predicated upon good planning procedures. Emergency plans should be complete, should be simple to understand and implement, and should be communicated to all personnel who will be involved or concerned with them. They include planning for riots, civil disturbances, escapes, and fires.

Riots   The causes of riots may vary widely, but once a riot occurs the major consideration must be to confine the riot to a small area and not permit it to spread. Since each riot is different, the decision on how to deal with it may also vary, but every effort should be made to establish control as quickly as possible. Only that force necessary to subdue the rioters should be used. If necessary and additional manpower is needed, other police agencies should be contacted. The use of gas should be very carefully weighed and the type and amount to be used may be determined by whether the riot is taking place indoors or outdoors. Many times water can be utilized in place of gas to disperse and subdue rioters. An alarm system should be installed to alert the personnel that a riot is taking place, and when it goes off the jail should be sealed off until the rioters are subdued.

Civil disturbances   Some communities may be faced with mass arrests as a result of civil disturbances. The entire operating procedure may have to be modified to meet the influx of mixed populations, which can include both women and juveniles. Attention in the plan should be given to court appearances, special contacts with bondsmen and attorneys, and related problems of feeding and visitation. If the jail is too small to house all of the arrestees, then an alternative should be considered as a backup.

Escapes   An alarm system similar to that mentioned in the riot plan can also be utilized to alert the jail that an escape has occurred or may be in progress. Again, the jail should be immediately sealed when such an event takes place. Notification of other police agencies may be necessary at the same time that the escape is being investigated or being curtailed.

Fire   The fire department can be of valuable assistance in helping to develop the fire plan. The major emphasis of the plan should be on prevention, and, while most of the construction materials used in jails are not flammable, fires can and do occur. This is one of the heaviest responsibilities that the jail administrator has because many times not all of the prisoners can leave the jail in the event of a fire. Fire plans can help avert major tragedies with resulting loss of life. Plans should include location of fire extinguishers, hoses, and other firefighting apparatus, together with the training of personnel in fire prevention and control. This latter should include the use of air breathing devices which may be necessary for the personnel to wear when they enter cell areas filled with smoke. The evacuation path must obviously be another part of the fire plan and should include where the prisoners will be taken and guarded while the fire is being dealt with. Fire exits should be clearly marked and the doors leading to them should be kept free of all obstructions.

Transportation   It should be borne in mind that escapes, deaths, and injuries are more likely to occur during the transportation of a prisoner than at any other time. When a prisoner is to be transported, two officers should be utilized where possible, one armed and the other unarmed so that he or she may approach the prisoner without fear of losing his or her weapon. Prisoners should always be handcuffed, and other types of restraining equipment, such as wrist chains and leg manacles, should be used when necessary. Jail personnel must be trained to understand that these devices are not foolproof and that there is no substitute for alertness. The prisoner should never be left out of the sight of the transporting officers, and, should an escape occur, the nearest police agency should be notified immediately.

Maintenance   The key to maintaining a jail in fairly good condition is preventive maintenance. Jails that are permitted to deteriorate represent a danger to the community, the staff, and the prisoners. Locks, wiring, plumbing, and electrical switches are only some of the items that can deteriorate and wear out, but with a good preventive maintenance program these items can be replaced before they become major problems. All personnel should be trained and instructed to make certain that preventive maintenance is a viable and ongoing process. A systematic inspection should be carried out at least once a week to note items that must be repaired or replaced. Many jails combine security inspections with maintenance. This is particularly true with regard to the examination of bars and locks. Where these items are felt to have been tampered with, or where they begin to show signs of wear, they should be replaced immediately.

Special considerations   Thus far, this discussion of jail operations has been concerned generally with adult male prisoners. Two groups of prisoners, however, require some special planning for their needs and supervision. These are women and juveniles.

Women   It is generally agreed that correctional objectives and methodology are the same for women and men. However, it is essential that women prisoners be separated from men prisoners. Female personnel should be used in the majority of dealings with women prisoners; however, from time to time it may be necessary for male personnel to assist with certain unruly or hard to handle female prisoners.

Juveniles   While most jails do not admit juveniles as a matter of practice, there may be times when courts order juveniles detained in adult facilities. When this occurs it sometimes poses problems for the jail administrator. Juveniles should never be placed among the adult population. Constant supervision is necessary among juvenile offenders, since they are frequently destructive, mischievous, and restless, and many times they will act without thinking. All of the other security problems that apply to adults are also applicable to the juvenile offender.

Religious services   Many jails provide religious services within their facility. These are conducted either by full-time ministers or local religious leaders. Bibles and hymnbooks, as well as other religious literature, are often donated, and, in many cases, church groups can provide meaningful programs to assist prisoners during their time of incarceration.

Security

Security of the local jail is predicated on historical practice, custom, law, and, most important, public opinion. The normal citizen views his or her local jail as a place where arrested persons are held humanely but securely. Control of contraband, security inspections, control of firearms, head count, control of medications and drugs, and tool and utensil control are all related to security.

Control of contraband   The U.S. Bureau of Prisons, in discussing control of contraband, states:

Any item that is not issued or not authorized in the jail is contraband. Control of contraband is necessary for several reasons:

1. To control the introduction of articles that can be used for trading or gambling;
2. To control the collecting of junk and the accumulation of items that make housekeeping difficult; and
3. To identify medications and drugs and items that can be used as weapons and escape implements.[17]

It is obvious that the most effective method of controlling contraband within a jail is proper searching, not only of the prisoners but of the physical facility itself. All searches should be conducted in a systematic and orderly manner and done at irregular intervals. The prisoners' personal effects, as well as the remainder of the cell, should be left in their original condition, and whenever contraband material is discovered a written report should be made describing the items and location.

Security inspections   Security inspections may be conducted at the time that the cell searches for contraband are being carried out, although this is not necessary. The major objective is to examine the bars and locks to determine if they have been tampered with. In addition, bolts, locking plugs, ventilator covers, glass panels, and protective screening should be a part of the inspection. As with searches, these inspections should be made at irregular intervals. All personnel must be made aware of security requirements and should be constantly on the alert for breakdowns. In jail situations nothing should be considered routine, as laxity on the part of personnel is a contributing factor to breakdowns in security.

Firearms   Under no circumstances should any type of weapon be permitted into a jail. This is particularly true of firearms. If a firearm is carried into a jail and taken from an officer, for example, its use in the hands of a prisoner can be fatal. Police officers should be instructed to leave their weapons at the major entries to the jail. If a prisoner is with an officer, the former should be admitted into the facility first, before the officer turns over his or her weapon, unloaded, to jail personnel. Jails should provide for the secure storage of firearms and the officer who receives the weapon should request that it be unloaded before he or she takes it and hands back a receipt. If the jail is a part of a police building, the armory should be located as far away from the jail as possible.

Head count   Head count is universally performed in all jails, regardless of their size. In large jails this may be done at the beginning of each shift in accordance with the prisoner records. Usually this type of record shows the number of prisoners in any given cell block, which prisoners are in court, and which prisoners may be assigned to work details. In smaller facilities head count may be taken by simply counting the number of prisoners and comparing the count to the number shown in the booking log. No interruptions should be permitted during the count. The officer performing the count should be required to sign the head count sheet when he or she has completed the count.

Control of medications and drugs In jails that store medications and drugs, it is essential that they be securely locked in a proper container such as a safe or cabinet. The medical personnel should keep detailed records showing the amounts of medications and drugs received and the amounts dispensed and the inventory on hand. Where decrepancies arise, they should be called to the jail administrator's attention for proper investigation.

Tool and utensil control Nearly all jails have some tools on hand which may be used by the maintenance people or by the jail personnel themselves. These should be numbered and inventoried and kept within a secure area.

Prisoner release procedures

This section has discussed how prisoners are admitted into jails and has reviewed the operations and security aspects of a jail; it will now consider how prisoners are to be released.

Following are the means by which prisoners are released: posting of monetary bail; release on recognizance; custody release; dismissal, nolle prosse, and not guilty dispositions; completion of sentence; transfer to a hospital; transfer to another facility; temporary release; and detainer.

It is extremely important that jail personnel verify, either through photographs or, if these are questionable, through fingerprints, which prisoner is being released. If the wrong prisoner is released through error, it is extremely embarrassing to the department and dangerous to the community.

The prisoner, upon release, should have all of his or her property returned. If good admission procedures were followed, this step should be fairly easy to administer. The prisoner's copy of the inventory slip should be compared to the property room's copy, the bag or envelopes containing his or her property should then be opened by the prisoner in the presence of the property room officer and verification of contents made. If there is agreement by the prisoner as to the contents, he or she should be made to sign and date the receipt indicating acceptance. If there is disagreement, then a full report should be made together with a claim by the prisoner for the missing property. The jail administrator should then attempt to prove or disprove the claim. Where the claim is correct, financial remuneration for the loss should be made.

Staff services

Without the proper supporting services no jail could function adequately, if at all. The police administrator should see that the jail budget and all of its attendant processes are clearly identifiable and separate from the overall police budget. This section reviews personnel management, record keeping, budgeting, and rules and policy that affect jail management.

Selection and training of personnel While it is true that a physically deficient jail is difficult to operate, a jail whose staff is deficient will certainly not only be difficult to operate but potentially dangerous. Many police personnel view an assignment to work in the jail as a form of punishment or as a reflection upon their ability to work "out on the street." If it is the decision of the police administrator to continue the operation of his jail, he might very well wish to consider another job category for assignment to the jail. If the jail is to be used only as a short-term detention center, then the requirements for the persons to be employed there will differ considerably from those of personnel who will be employed in a community correctional complex. It may not be necessary to provide any correctional programs in the short-term facility. In the community correctional complex, however, programs and services should be provided. Once this decision has been made the requirements for staffing the institution can be determined. In either case, the use of correctional job descriptions and titles would be more appropriate than police job descriptions and titles.

Selection The potential employee should be screened as any other applicant within the police service with regard to his or her character, criminal history, and related factors. Both the testing and the oral interview panel processes should be aimed at seeking personnel who will be able to function within the confines of a jail setting.

Training Since very few employees have been prepared for jail work, a training program should be provided for the correctional officer with the emphasis on the knowledge, skills, and philosophy necessary to perform the job. Large departments may make use of their own academies or training institutes. Small departments may make use of the U.S. Bureau of Prisons' correspondence course on jail operations and management. Both can and should make use of educational institutions that have the necessary expertise to assist in correctional officer training.

Promotions Promotions for jail personnel should be modeled along the same lines as police promotions and, if a local civil service system concerning promotional processes already exists, it can and should be adopted for jail operations. Some communities have found it expedient to offer police personnel a one- or two-step pay increase as an option for remaining with the jail and giving up their police rank for a correctional title rank. This type of procedure frees budgeted positions for police operations and, at the same time, provides an incentive for experienced personnel.

Record keeping It is essential, regardless of the size of the facility, that accurate records relating to jail activity be kept. These should include not only personnel records for salary, overtime, transfers, shift changes, etc., but also fiscal records relating to the prisoner, admission and release records, drug use and medical records, records of food and supplies, machinery, and population, as well as incident reports and disciplinary records. These types of records should be kept in such a way that their retrieval can be assured and so that they do not pose major administrative problems. Only those records and reports that have a purpose or achieve an objective are necessary. Obviously, each jail will determine its own record and reporting needs.

Budgeting The jail should have a separate and distinct budget. The type of budgetary process used by the police department can be used by the jail (e.g., line item budgeting, program budgeting, and performance budgeting). In light of the fact that jails must compete for a shrinking tax dollar, a separate budget is an excellent device to maintain parity and, in some instances, increase the jail budget. Some 80 to 90 percent of the police budget is earmarked for personnel salaries. This same salary ratio applies also to the jail's operation. The jail budget also includes many items that are not a traditional part of the police budget and that tend to give the appearance of inflation to the police budget, for example, food, bedding, inmate clothing, and repairs. However, where a separate budget can be presented it may help the decision-making bodies recognize the peculiar needs of a jail and supply the necessary funding. The costs should be measured against the average daily inmate population, so that some standard of adequacy and quality can be established as a major step toward good systematic analysis.

Rules and policies The jail may use the same set of rules and policies that are used for police personnel. In some departments this may work quite well, particularly if the job titles have no relationship to specific tasks. However, in the event that correctional titles are implemented as a part of the jail's revamping, the rules and policies issued by the department should be carefully reviewed to determine their feasibility. For example, many police departments that employ the term "correctional officer" as a job description provide that such personnel should not have arrest authority and should not carry firearms when off duty. In such cases both rules and policy statements should be reduced to writing and conveyed to all affected personnel.

Special programs

Municipal and county jails can adopt several correctional programs that will benefit not only the community but the prisoner and the prisoner's family as well. In addition, they may be the first useful steps that can divert a prisoner from the "revolving door" concept as it pertains to criminal justice. Their operation and maintenance can be assumed by other agencies, both public and private, and yet can be integrated into the jail operation. They are community-oriented activities that can bring the jail and the community closer together in matters of mutual interest. These programs are: work release; halfway houses; and educational and vocational training.

Conclusion

This chapter has provided an overview and synthesis of jail management, beginning with the historical development and the relationship of jail operations to police and to the courts, then exploring the issue of the appropriateness of jail operations as a part of police services. The desirability of jail operations on a regional basis were then discussed. Custody and rehabilitation of prisoners were briefly described. The balance of the chapter was devoted to the major aspects of jail management: planning for the construction and alteration of jail facilities; intake procedures, management of jail operations; jail security and prisoner release procedures; personnel, budgeting, records, etc.; and special programs that can be undertaken.

There is little doubt that the role and scope of the local jail are undergoing a dramatic change. Whether by evolution, court decision, or legislative action, the jail's role in the criminal justice system is being questioned and examined in the wake of its many shortcomings.

It now appears that a movement is under way to create regional, full service jails at the local level, operated by nonpolice ranks. How this will be accomplished is not yet clear, but the police administrator should be making plans now as to what type of jail he will need in the future and the services he expects it to provide for the community, for the prisoner, and, finally, for the police department itself.

If the impact of corrections is to be felt on the crime situation in the United States today, it should be felt first of all in the basic segment of corrections—the local jail.

1 President's Commission on Law Enforcement and Administration of Justice, *Task Force Report: Corrections* (Washington, D.C.: Government Printing Office, 1967), p. 79.

2 National Advisory Commission on Criminal Justice Standards and Goals, *Corrections* (Washington, D.C.: Government Printing Office, 1973), pp. 273–74.

3 U.S., Department of Justice, Law Enforcement Assistance Administration, *1970 National Jail Census* (Washington, D.C.: Government Printing Office, 1971), p. 1.

4 Ibid., p. 2.

5 Ibid., pp. 10–11.

6 President's Commission on Law Enforcement and Administration of Justice, *Task Force Report: The*

Police (Washington, D.C.: Government Printing Office, 1967), p. 90.

7 National Advisory Commission on Criminal Justice Standards and Goals: *Police [Report on Police]* (Washington, D.C.: Government Printing Office, 1973), p. 313.

8 President's Commission on Law Enforcement and Administration of Justice, *Task Force Report: The Police,* Chapter 4, "Coordination and Consolidation of Police Service," pp. 68–119.

9 Ibid., p. 90.

10 National Advisory Commission on Criminal Justice Standards and Goals, *Corrections,* p. 281.

11 National Clearinghouse for Criminal Justice Planning and Architecture, University of Illinois at Urbana–Champaign, 505 East Green, Suite 210, Champaign, Illinois 61820.

12 Nick Pappas, ed., *The Jail: Its Operation and Management* (Washington, D.C.: U.S. Bureau of Prisons, 1970), p. 16.

13 Hastings H. Hart, "Do These Conditions Exist in Your Local Police Station, County Jail, or Work House?" *The American City,* October 1929, p. 111.

14 Pappas, *The Jail,* p. 176.

15 Ibid., p. 130.

16 Ibid., p. 145.

17 Ibid., p. 23.

Appendix A

**Five presidential and
national commissions
and their reports**

Throughout this book, frequent reference is made to the reports of five commissions that have had considerable influence on police services and specific aspects of law enforcement and the criminal justice process. The first of these commissions, the President's Commission on Law Enforcement and Administration of Justice, was established in July 1965 and issued its overall report, *The Challenge of Crime in a Free Society,* in 1967. This was followed in 1968 by the *Report of the National Advisory Commission on Civil Disorders* (this commission was popularly known as the Kerner Commission). The National Commission on the Causes and Prevention of Violence (the Eisenhower Commission) issued its overall report, *To Establish Justice, To Insure Domestic Tranquility,* in 1969; next followed the President's Commission on Campus Unrest, which issued its report, *Campus Unrest,* in 1970 following the deaths at Kent State and Jackson State. The last of these five reports was the overall report of the National Advisory Commission on Criminal Justice Standards and Goals, issued in seven volumes in 1973. Citations for these reports are shown in the Selected Bibliography. A brief description of each of these reports is given below.

President's Commission on Law Enforcement and Administration of Justice

The Challenge of Crime in a Free Society: A Report by the President's Commission on Law Enforcement and Administration of Justice. Washington, D.C.: Government Printing Office, 1967. The commission report, over 300 pages in length, contains more than 200 specific recommendations and outlines seven major objectives: preventing crime; providing new ways of dealing with offenders; eliminating unfairness in the criminal justice system; providing higher personnel standards in the criminal justice system; developing research standards for criminal justice; investing substantially more money in the criminal justice system; and establishing responsibility for change with citizens, so-

cial service agencies, universities, and those involved in the criminal justice system.

The commission report was extremely influential in the adoption of the Safe Streets Act of 1968 and has been influential in police training. The commission also issued nine task force reports, on police work, drug abuse, corrections, and other subjects.

National Advisory Commission on Civil Disorders

Report of the National Advisory Commission on Civil Disorders. Washington, D.C.: Government Printing Office, 1968. This commission was appointed in the summer of 1967 following racial disorders in American cities, especially in Newark, Detroit, and Atlanta. The report provides profiles and patterns of disorder; a historic review going back into the Depression years; an extensive sociological and economic review of life in racial ghettos; and prescriptive measures, including governmental, economic, and criminal justice responses, as well as police department measures. The report looks at the future of cities and includes recommendations for national actions.

National Commission on the Causes and Prevention of Violence

To Establish Justice, To Insure Domestic Tranquility: Final Report of the National Commission on the Causes and Prevention of Violence. Washington, D.C.: Government Printing Office, 1969. This report deals with some unusual aspects of violence that the police may encounter, including assassinations; campus disorders and student violence; civil disobedience; group violence; and the perennial question of firearms. Thirteen task force and investigative reports were prepared on appropriate and relevant backup subjects including historical background; violence in America; crimes of violence; the politics of protest and violent aspects of confrontation; assassinations;

firearms and violence; mass media and violence; and campus disorders.

**President's Commission
on Campus Unrest**

Campus Unrest: The Report of the President's Commission on Campus Unrest.
Washington, D.C.: Government Printing Office, 1970. This report describes college and university campuses of the 1960s in terms of student protests; the black student movement; the response from university administrations; and the law enforcement response. The report is more than a historical document, particularly on police response and the use of the National Guard. The reports on Kent State and Jackson State are of special interest.

**National Advisory Commission
on Criminal Justice
Standards and Goals**

Report of the National Advisory Commission on Criminal Justice Standards and Goals. Washington, D.C.: Government Printing Office, 1973. The six reports of the National Advisory Commission set forth national goals and priorities with major recommendations in the areas of: *A National Strategy to Reduce Crime; Criminal Justice System; Police; Courts; Corrections; and Community Crime Prevention;* there is also a volume of proceedings. One of the distinguishing characteristics of the report is the effort to develop standards and recommendations that are keyed to a national strategy to reduce crime.

Appendix B

**Equal opportunity as defined
by Title VII of the
Civil Rights Act of 1964**

The U.S. Equal Employment Opportunity Commission (EEOC) was established to ensure compliance with Title VII of the Civil Rights Act of 1964, as amended by the Equal Employment Opportunity Act of 1972. Title VII prohibits discrimination in employment because of race, color, religion, sex, or national origin and covers all private employers, state and local governments, educational institutions, labor organizations, joint labor–management apprenticeship programs, and public and private employment agencies with fifteen or more employees or members. Through its Technical Guidance Division, EEOC furnishes technical assistance to aid voluntary compliance with the law.

Pre-employment inquiries
Employment application forms and pre-employment interviews have traditionally been instruments for eliminating, at an early stage, "unsuited" or "unqualified" persons from consideration for employment and often have been used in such a way as to restrict or deny employment opportunities for women and members of minority groups.

The law, interpreted through court rulings and EEOC decisions, prohibits the use of all pre-employment inquiries and qualifying factors which disproportionately screen out members of minority groups or members of one sex and are not valid predictors of successful job performance or cannot be justified by "business necessity."

In devising or reviewing application forms or in seeking information from job applicants, employers should ask themselves: (1) Will the answers to this question, if used in making a selection, have a disparate effect in screening out minorities and/or members of one sex (i.e., disqualify a significantly larger percentage of members of a particular group than others)? (2) Is this information really needed to judge an applicant's competence or qualification for the job in question?

Business necessity and job relatedness
The concept of business necessity has been narrowly defined by the courts. When a practice is found to have discriminatory effects, it can be justified only by showing that it is necessary to the safe and efficient operation of the business, that it effectively carries out the purpose it is supposed to serve, and that there are no alternative policies or practices which would better or equally well serve the same purpose with less discriminatory impact.

An employer should be able to demonstrate through statistical evidence that any selection procedure, which has a "disparate effect" on groups protected by the law, is job related (i.e., validly predicts successful performance in the type of job in question). If this cannot be shown or if the employer cannot or does not wish to perform a technical validation study, the use of that procedure should be discontinued or altered in such a way that there is no longer a discriminatory effect. Even when a procedure having an adverse impact can be validated, it may not be used if there are other procedures which would accomplish the same goal and have a less discriminatory effect.

Race, color, religion, sex, or national origin
Under Title VII, pre-employment inquiries concerning race, color, religion, sex, or national origin are not considered violations of the law in and of themselves. However, inquiries which either directly or indirectly disclose such information, unless otherwise explained, may constitute evidence of discrimination prohibited by Title VII.

Some state fair employment practice laws expressly prohibit inquiries on employment applications concerning the applicant's race, color, religion, sex, or national origin. In some states it may also be considered illegal to seek related data (e.g., former name, past residence, names of relatives, place of birth, citizenship, education, organizational activities, photographs, and color of eyes and hair) which could indirectly reveal similar information.

Denial of equal opportunity to individuals because of marriage to or association with persons of a specific national, ethnic, or racial origin, or because of attendance at schools or churches, or membership in organizations identified with particular racial or ethnic groups, is considered a violation of Title VII.

An employer may justifiably and legitimately seek and obtain information needed for implementation of affirmative action programs, court-ordered or other government reporting or record keeping requirements, and for studies to identify and resolve possible problems in the recruitment and testing of members of minority groups and/or women to ensure equal employment for all persons.

However, the employer must be able to demonstrate that such data were collected for legitimate business purposes. Such information should be kept separate from the regular permanent employee records to ensure that it is not used to discriminate in making personnel decisions.

Height and weight
EEOC and the courts have ruled minimum height and weight requirements to be illegal if they screen out a disproportionate number of minority group individuals (e.g., Spanish-surnamed or Asian Americans) or women, and the employer cannot show that these standards are essential to the safe performance of the job in question.

Marital status, number of children, and provision for child care
Questions about marital status, pregnancy, future child-bearing plans, and number and age of children are frequently used to discriminate against women and may be a violation of Title VII if used to deny or limit employment opportunities for female applicants. Employers are cautioned against use of such non-job-related questions. Information needed for tax, insurance or Social Security purposes may be obtained after employment.

It is a violation of Title VII for employers to require pre-employment information about child-care arrangements from female applicants only. The U.S. Supreme Court has ruled that an employer may not have different hiring policies for men and women with preschool children.

Educational requirements
The U.S. Supreme Court has found an employer's requirement of a high school education discriminatory where statistics showed such a requirement operated to disqualify blacks at a substantially higher rate than whites and there was no evidence that the requirement was significantly related to successful job performance. This standard applies to all groups protected under Title VII

and is relevant to all questions relating to educational attainment, where no direct job-related requirement or business necessity can be proven.

English language skill
Testing or scoring an individual in English language proficiency when English language skill is not a requirement of the work to be performed obviously has a disparate effect upon certain minority groups and is a violation of Title VII.

Friends or relatives working for the employer
Information about friends or relatives working for an employer is not relevant to an applicant's competence. Requesting such information may be unlawful if it indicates a preference for friends or relatives of present employees and the composition of the present workforce is such that this preference would reduce or eliminate opportunities for women or minority group members. However, a "nepotism" policy which prohibits or limits employment opportunity of a spouse or other relative may also be illegal if it has an adverse impact on job opportunities for either women or men as a group.

Arrest records
Because members of some minority groups are arrested substantially more often than whites in proportion to their numbers in the population, making personnel decisions on the basis of arrest records involving no subsequent convictions has a disproportionate effect on the employment opportunities of members of these groups. The courts and the commission accordingly have held that without proof of business necessity an employer's use of arrest records to disqualify job applicants is unlawful discrimination. EEOC has ruled that even if an employer does not consider arrest information, the mere request for such information tends to discourage minority applicants and is therefore illegal.

Conviction records
Federal courts have held that a conviction for a felony or misdemeanor may not by itself lawfully constitute an absolute bar to employment, but that an employer may give fair consideration to the relationship between a conviction and the applicant's fitness for a particular job. These decisions indicate that conviction records should be cause for rejection only if their number, nature, and recentness would cause the applicant to be unsuitable for the position. If such inquiries are made, they should be accompanied by a statement that a conviction record will not necessarily be a bar to employment, and that

factors such as age and time of the offense, seriousness and nature of the violation, and rehabilitation will be taken into account.

Discharge from military service

Employers should not, as a matter of policy, reject applicants with less than honorable discharges from military service. According to a Department of Defense study, minority service members receive a higher proportion of general and undesirable discharges than nonminority members of similar aptitude and education.

Thus, an employer's requirement that to be eligible for employment, ex-members of the armed services must have been honorably discharged has a disparate effect upon minorities and may be a violation of Title VII.

One federal district court has held that an employer may inquire into an applicant's military service record if information regarding discharge status is used not in making a hiring decision but in deciding whether further investigations should be made into the applicant's background and qualifications. If further inquiry reveals nondiscriminatory grounds for denying employment, the employer may then refuse to hire the applicant.

Since a request for this information may discourage minority workers from applying and therefore be grounds for a discrimination charge, employers should avoid such questions unless "business necessity" can be shown. As in the case of conviction records discussed above, questions regarding military service should be accompanied by a statement that a dishonorable or general discharge is not an absolute bar to employment and that other factors will affect a final decision to hire or not to hire.

Age

The Age Discrimination in Employment Act of 1967 prohibits discrimination on the basis of age with respect to individuals who are between forty and seventy years of age. The law does not apply if an age requirement or limit is: (1) a *bona fide* job qualification (e.g., actors required for youthful roles); (2) part of a *bona fide* seniority system or employee benefit plan (except that mandatory retirement based on age is prohibited); or (3) based on reasonable factors other than age. An exception is also made when the discharge or discipline of an employee is for good cause.

Citizenship

The EEOC *Guidelines on Discrimination Because of National Origin* indicate that consideration of an applicant's citizenship may constitute evidence of discrimination on the basis of national origin.

The law clearly protects all individuals, both citizens and noncitizens domiciled or residing in the United States, against discrimination on the basis of race, color, religion, sex, or national origin.

Where consideration of citizenship has the purpose or effect of discriminating against persons of a particular national origin, a person who is a lawfully immigrated alien, legally eligible to work, may not be discriminated against on the basis of his/her citizenship, except in the interests of national security or determined under a United States statute or presidential executive order respecting the particular position or premises in question.

Where states have enacted laws prohibiting the employment of noncitizens, they are in conflict with and therefore are superseded by Title VII of the Civil Rights Act of 1964, as amended, if they have the purpose or effect of discriminating on the basis of national origin.

The U.S. Supreme Court has found that a state civil service law which restricted state employment to U.S. citizens was unconstitutional and a denial of equal protection and benefit of the laws. A flat ban on employment of aliens without regard to the type of position or to the characteristics of the applicant involved was not justifiable on grounds of public interest.

Economic status

Rejection of applicants because of poor credit ratings has a disparate impact on minority groups and hence has been found unlawful by the commission, unless business necessity can be shown.

Inquiries as to an applicant's financial status, such as bankruptcy, car ownership, rental or ownership of a house, length of residence at an address, or past garnishment of wages, if utilized to make employment decisions, may likewise violate Title VII.

Availability for work on weekends or holidays

While questions relating to availability for work on Friday evenings, Saturdays, Sundays, or holidays are not automatically considered violations of the law, employers and unions have an obligation to accommodate the religious beliefs of employees and/or applicants, unless to do so would cause undue economic hardship. If such questions are asked, it is advisable to indicate that reasonable efforts will be made to accommodate employees' religious needs.

**Data required for
legitimate business purposes**
Data on such matters as marital status, number and age of children, and similar issues, which could be used in a discriminatory manner in making employment decisions but which are necessary for insurance, reporting requirements, or other business purposes, can and should be obtained after a person has been employed, not by means of an application form or pre-employment interview.

Conclusion
It is reasonable to assume that all questions on an application form or in a pre-employment interview are for some purpose and that selection or hiring decisions are made on the basis of the answers given. In an investigation of charges of discrimination, the burden of proof is on the employer to show that answers

to all questions on application forms or in oral interviews are not used in making hiring and placement decisions in a discriminatory manner prohibited by the law.

To seek information other than that which is essential to effectively evaluate a person's qualifications for employment is to make oneself vulnerable to charges of discrimination and consequent legal proceedings.

It is therefore in an employer's own self-interest to carefully review all procedures used in screening applicants for employment, eliminating or altering any not justified by business necessity.

Source: Reproduced from material furnished by the U.S. Equal Employment Opportunity Commission. Information current as of May 1981.

Appendix C

Glossary of terms used in municipal collective bargaining

Administrative and supervisory employees: See *Managerial employees.*

Agency shop (agency service fee): See *Union security.*

Agreement: A written contract between an employer and an employee organization, usually for a definite term, defining conditions of employment (wages, hours, vacations, holidays, overtime payments, working conditions, etc.), and procedures to be followed in settling disputes or handling issues that arise during the life of the agreement. See *Collective bargaining.*

American Arbitration Association (AAA): A private non-profit organization established to promote arbitration as a method of settling commercial and labor disputes. The AAA provides lists of qualified arbitrators to employee organizations and employers on request, and also rules of procedure for the conduct of arbitration.

American Federation of Labor–Congress of Industrial Organizations (AFL–CIO): A federation of autonomous national and international unions created by the merger of the American Federation of Labor (AFL) and the Congress of Industrial Organizations (CIO) in December, 1955. The initials AFL–CIO after the name of a union indicate that the union is an affiliate.

Annualized cost: Cost during any twelve month period, usually calendar year, fiscal year, or twelve month period commencing with the effective date of an agreement or the effective date of the implementation of a wage increase or other economic item.

Appropriate bargaining unit: See *Bargaining unit; Community of interest.*

Arbitrability: The question whether an employer is obligated by contract to arbitrate a particular grievance or dispute. The answer is usually determined either by an arbitrator or by a court.

Arbitration: A method of settling disputes through recourse to an impartial third party. Grievance-arbitration involves the interpretation of terms of an existing contract and is usually *final and binding* but occasionally is advisory. Impasse arbitration involves disputes over what the contract terms ought to be. Arbitration may be *compulsory,* i.e., required by law, or may be voluntary. Compulsory arbitration may require the arbitrator to choose the final offer of either party on the whole package or on individual issues.

Arbitrator (impartial chairman): An impartial third party to whom disputing parties submit their differences for decision (award). An *ad hoc* arbitrator is one selected to act in a specific case or a limited group of cases. A permanent arbitrator is one selected to serve for the life of the agreement or a stipulated term, hearing all disputes that arise during this period.

Authorization card: A statement signed by an employee authorizing an organization to act as his representative in dealings with the employer, or authorizing the employer to deduct union dues from his pay (check-off). See *Card check; Check-off.*

Automatic increment (automatic step increase): Automatic wage increase based on length of service in a job classification, which employee continues to receive until he reaches maximum pay specified for such job classification.

Award: The final decision of an arbitrator in settlement of a dispute.

Bargaining agent: The employee organization designated by an appropriate government agency or recognized voluntarily by the employer as the representative of all employees in the bargaining unit for purposes of collective bargaining. Such representation is usually exclusive of any other employee organization.

Bargaining unit: Group of employees recognized by the employer or designated by an authorized agency as appropriate for representation by an organization for purposes of collective negotiations. Appropriateness is usually determined by community of interest among the employees sought to be included. See *Community of interest*.

Business agent (union representative): Generally a full-time paid employee or official of a local union whose duties include day-to-day dealing with employers and workers, adjustment of grievances, negotiation and enforcement of agreements, and similar activities. See *International representative*.

Call-in pay (callback pay): Amount of pay guaranteed to a worker recalled to work after having completed his regular work shift.

Card check: Procedure whereby signed authorization cards are checked against a list of employees in a prospective bargaining unit to determine if the organization has majority status. The employer may recognize the organization on the basis of this check without a formal election. Card checks are often conducted by any outside party, e.g., a respected member of the community. See *Authorization card*.

Catch-up money: Description of a salary increase or part thereof which is designed to erase a long-term lag behind salaries of comparable positions, often in the private sector, or in recognition that a position has historically been underpaid.

Certification: Formal designation by a government agency of the organization selected by the majority of the employees in a supervised election to act as exclusive representative for all employees in the bargaining unit.

Check-off (payroll deduction of union dues): Practice whereby the employer, by agreement with the employee organization (upon written authorization from each employee where required by law or agreement), regularly withholds organizational dues from employees' salary payments and transmits these funds to the organization. This arrangement may also provide for deductions of initiation fees and assessments. See *Union security*.

Collective bargaining (collective negotiations): A process by which an employee organization negotiates with an employer in good faith with a view toward reaching agreement on wages, hours and conditions of employment. The process does not require either party to agree to any particular proposal nor does it require the making of a concession.

Community of interest: A description of the criteria employed by a government agency to determine whether a group of employees sought to be represented by an employee organization constitutes an appropriate bargaining unit. Criteria may include similarity of skills and duties, common supervision, common hours, wages, and working conditions.

Compensation grade: See *Labor grade*.

Compulsory arbitration: See *Arbitration*.

Conciliation: See *Mediation*.

Confidential employee: One whose responsibility or knowledge relating to issues involved in municipal employee relations would make his being represented by a particular union for collective bargaining incompatible with his official duties.

Consultation (discussion): An obligation of the employer to consult with a union on particular issues before taking action. The obligation of consultation or discussion is more extensive than notification which may amount simply to providing the union with information, but is less extensive than the obligation to negotiate, which requires full and complete bargaining resulting either in agreement by the employee organization or a genuine impasse before the action can be taken by the employer. See *Meet and confer*.

Contract: See *Agreement*.

Contract bar: A denial of a request for a representation election by Union B based on the existence of a written, signed collective bargaining agreement with Union A, which meets certain technical requirements as to content.

Contracting out: Practice of a municipal employer using outside contractors with their own employees to perform work previously performed by municipal employees.

Cooling off period: A required period of delay fixed by law during which there can be neither a strike nor a lockout. Normally refers to the National Emergency Disputes provision of the Taft–Hartley Act, which authorizes the President, in the event he feels the nation's health or safety is imperiled by a strike or lockout, to take steps resulting in an 80-day "cooling off" period.

Craft unit: A bargaining unit composed solely of workers having a recognized skill, for example, electricians, machinists, plumbers, or printers.

Credited service: Years of employment counted for retirement, severance pay, seniority. See *Seniority*.

Decertification: Withdrawal by a government agency of an employee organization's official designation as exclusive negotiating representative, usually as a result of employee disaffection.

Discussion: See *Consultation; Meet and confer*.

Dispute: Any disagreement between an employer and the employee organization which requires resolution in one way or another; e.g. inability to agree on contract terms or unsettled grievances involving the interpretation of contract terms. See *Impasse*.

Dues deduction: See *Check-off*.

Election: See *Representation election*.

Exclusive representative: The employee organization designated as the only organization to bargain collectively for all employees, including nonmembers, in a bargaining unit.

Fact-finding: Investigation of a labor dispute or bargaining impasse by an individual, panel, or board. The fact-finder assembles and reports the facts, after a hearing, and may make recommendations for settlement.

"Favored nations" clause: A provision in an agreement indicating that one party to the agreement (employer or union) shall have the opportunity to share in more favorable terms negotiated by the other party with any other employer or union.

Federal Mediation and Conciliation Service (FMCS): An independent federal agency which provides mediators to assist the parties involved in negotiations, or in a labor dispute, in reaching a settlement; provides lists of suitable arbitrators on request; and engages in various types of "preventive mediation." Mediation services are also provided by several state agencies.

Feeler: An exploratory attempt to find a basis of setting a bargaining issue without making a formal proposal.

Front-end load: Increasing the cost of a multi-stage wage increase by making all or the greater part of it effective in one lump sum at the outset. For example, instead of giving $100 at the outset for the first six months and an additional $100 for the second six months, an employer agrees to give $200 at the outset to be effective for the full year.

Grievance: Usually a complaint by an employee or employee organization concerning the interpretation or application of a collective bargaining agreement. Occasionally defined as any dispute over wages, hours, or working conditions.

Grievance procedure: Typically a formal plan, specified in a collective bargaining agreement, which provides for the adjustment of grievances through discussions at progressively higher levels of authority in management and the employee organization, usually culminating in arbitration if unresolved.

Halo effect: A description of favored treatment of one employee out of a group of employees doing equal work.

Impartial chairman (umpire): An arbitrator employed jointly by an employee organization and an employer, usually on a long-term basis, to serve as the impartial party on a tripartite arbitration board and to decide all disputes or specific kinds of disputes arising during the life of the contract. The functions of an impartial chairman often expand with experience and the growing confidence of the parties, and he alone may constitute the arbitration board in practice.

Impasse: A situation in collective bargaining which occurs when the employer and the union, both negotiating in good faith, fail to reach agreement. See *Dispute*.

Increment: One of a series of rate steps in a range between the minimum salary and the maximum salary specified for a job classification or for a labor grade.

Incumbent-only rate: See *Red circle rate*.

Inequity of compensation grade: A claim that a job should be placed in a higher labor grade, usually based on a comparison of the duties of such job with other jobs covered under the salary schedule, or on changes in job content or work load.

Injunction: A court order restraining individuals, groups, or employee organizations from committing unlawful acts or acts which, in the court's opinion, will cause irreparable harm or endanger public health, safety, or welfare.

International representative (national representative; field representative; business agent): Generally, a full-time employee of a national or international union whose duties include assisting in the formation of local unions, dealing with affiliated local unions on union business, assisting in negotiations and grievance settlements, settling disputes within and between locals, etc.

International union: A union claiming jurisdiction both within and outside the United States (usually in Canada). Sometimes the term is loosely applied to all national unions; that is, "international" and "national" are used interchangeably.

Job description: A detailed written description of the duties constituting a particular job or position; may also include a description of the required qualifications for the job or position.

Job evaluation system: A method of analyzing jobs so that jobs of relatively equal "value" or "worth" are grouped together for pay purposes.

Job upgrading: Reclassifying a job from a lower labor grade to a higher labor grade, usually to reflect a change in job duties or to cure an inequity. This differs from promotion, where an employee is moved from one job in a lower grade to a different job in a higher labor grade.

Jurisdictional dispute: Conflict between two or more employee organizations over organizing or representing workers or whether a certain type of work should be performed by members of one organization or another. For example, maintenance work on fire trucks may be a bone of contention between a firefighting union and a union representing maintenance mechanics.

Labor grades: One of a series of rate steps (single rates or ranges of rates) in a wage plan. Labor grades are typically the outcome of some form of job evaluation, or of wage-rate negotiations, by which different jobs are grouped, so that jobs of approximately equal "value" or "worth" fall into the same grade and, thus, command the same rate of pay.

Labor Management Relations Act of 1947 (Taft–Hartley Act): Federal law, amending the National Labor Relations Act of 1935 (Wagner Act), which, among other changes, defined and made illegal a number of unfair labor practices by unions.

Labor–Management Reporting and Disclosure Act of 1959 (Landrum–Griffin Act): A federal law designed "to eliminate or prevent improper practices on the part of labor organizations, employers," etc. Its seven titles include a bill of rights to protect members in their relations with unions; regulations of trusteeships; standards for elections; and fiduciary responsibility of union officers. The Labor Management Relations Act of 1947 was amended in certain respects by this act. Unions representing municipal employees are excluded.

Leap-frogging: Attempt by rival unions to demonstrate their effectiveness by forcing an employer to make greater concessions in successive negotiations. See *Whipsawing*.

Maintenance-of-membership clause: See *Union security*.

Management prerogatives: Rights of a municipal employer which may be expressly reserved in a collective bargaining agreement or which may be removed from the scope of municipal collective bargaining by state law.

Managerial employees: Administrative and supervisory employees whose primary duties involve the exercise of discretion and independent judgment to make, execute, or effectively recommend management policy to accomplish the mission of a public agency, and to direct and control employee activity in furtherance thereof.

Mandatory subject of bargaining: See *Scope of bargaining*.

Master agreement: A single labor agreement covering employees in multiple bargaining units of one employer or covering employees of a group of employers in one bargaining unit.

Mediation (conciliation): An attempt by an impartial third party to help in collective negotiations or in the settlement of an employment dispute through suggestion, advice, persuasion, or other ways of stimulating agreement, short of dictating its provisions (a characteristic of arbitration). Mediation in the United States is undertaken through federal and state mediation agencies, or by a person selected by the parties to act as mediator.

Meet-and-confer: A process of determining wages, hours, and conditions of public employment through discussions between representatives of the employer and employee organization with a view toward reaching a nonbinding agreement to be presented to the employer's governing body or statutory representative for final determination. See *Consultation.*

Merit increase: An increase in employee compensation given on the basis of individual efficiency and performance.

Moonlighting: The simultaneous holding of more than one paid employment by an employee, e.g., a full-time job and a supplementary job with another employer, or self-employment.

Multi-employer bargaining: Collective bargaining in the private sector between a union or unions and a group of employers, usually represented by an employer association, resulting in a master agreement. Experiments in the public sector may involve a group of cities negotiating jointly with a union.

Multi-unit bargaining: Collective bargaining between a union which represent(s) many bargaining units and an employer or group of employers.

National Labor Relations Act of 1935 (Wagner Act): Basic federal act guaranteeing employees in the private sector the right to organize and bargain collectively through representatives of their own choosing.

Parity: Equality in weekly base salary for two or more categories of employees. This most often arises in relation to police and firefighters. In some states, insistence to impasse on parity may be an unfair labor practice.

Permissive subject of bargaining: See *Scope of bargaining.*

Picketing: Patrolling by employees near the place of employment to gain public support for a union in a labor dispute with an employer.

Probationary period: Usually a stipulated period of time (e.g., 30 days up to six months) during which a newly hired employee is on trial prior to establishing seniority or otherwise becoming a regular employee. During his probationary period an employee may ordinarily be discharged without recourse to a grievance procedure, and may not be entitled to certain benefits received by regular employees.

Prohibited practice: See *Unfair labor practice.*

Raiding (no-raiding agreement): Term applied to an organization's attempt to enroll members belonging to another organization or employees already covered by a collective agreement negotiated by another organization, with the intent to usurp the latter's bargaining relationship. A no-raiding agreement is a written pledge signed by two or more employee organizations to abstain from raiding and is applicable only to signatory organizations.

Ratification: Formal approval of a newly negotiated agreement by vote of the organization members affected.

Recognition: Formal acknowledgment by a public employer that a particular employee organization has the right to represent employees in an appropriate bargaining unit.

Red-circle rate (incumbent only rate): A wage rate paid to individual job incumbents which is higher than the maximum rate specified for the job. The red-circle rate ceases to exist when the employment of the particular incumbent in the job classification is terminated.

Regional collective bargaining: See *Multi-employer bargaining.*

Reopening clause: Clause in a collective agreement stating the time or the circumstances under which negotiations can be requested, prior to the expiration of the contract, on specific subjects, as, for example, weekly salary.

Representation election (election): Election conducted to determine whether the employees in an appropriate unit (See *Bargaining unit*) desire a labor organization to act as their exclusive representative.

Right-to-work law: Legislation which prohibits any contractual requirement that an employee join a labor organization in order to get or keep a job.

Ripple effect: Impact of a negotiated salary increase or other economic benefit on employees of the same employer who are not in the bargaining unit.

Runoff election: A second representation election conducted after the first produces no winner according to the rules. The runoff may be limited to the two unions receiving the most votes in the first election. See *Representation election.*

Scope of bargaining: The subjects of bargaining are usually defined as mandatory, permissive, and prohibited. The parties must bargain over mandatory subjects, may bargain over permissive subjects, may not bargain over prohibited subjects. Determinations are made by state labor relations agencies, neutrals, and courts.

Seniority: Term used to designate an employee's status relative to other employees, as in determining order of promotion, layoff, vacation, etc. *Straight seniority* describes seniority acquired solely through length of service. *Qualified seniority*—other factors such as ability considered with length of service. *Departmental or unit seniority*—seniority applicable in a particular department or agency of a city, rather than in the entire establishment. *Seniority list*—individual workers ranked in order of seniority. See *Superseniority.*

Standard agreement (form agreement): Collective bargaining agreement prepared by a national or international union for use by, or guidance of, its local unions, designed to produce standardization of practices within the union's bargaining relationships.

Strike (wildcat; quickie; slowdown; sympathy; sitdown; general): Temporary stoppage of work by a group of employees (not necessarily members of a union) to express a grievance, enforce a demand for changes in the conditions of employment, obtain recognition, or resolve a dispute with management. *Wildcat strike*—a strike not sanctioned by union and one which violates a collective agreement. *Quickie strike*—a spontaneous or unannounced strike. *Slowdown*—a deliberate reduction of output without an actual strike in order to force concessions from an employer. *Sympathy strike*—strike of employees not directly involved in a dispute, but who wish to demonstrate employee solidarity or bring additional pressure upon employer involved. *Sitdown strike*—strike during which employees remain in the workplace, but refuse to work or allow others to do so. *General strike*—strike involving all organized employees in a community or country (rare in the United States). *Walkout*—same as strike.

Strike vote: Vote conducted among members of an employee organization to determine whether or not a strike should be authorized.

Superseniority: A position on the seniority list ahead of what the employee would ac-quire solely on the basis of length of service or other general seniority factors. Usually such favored treatment is reserved to union stewards, or other workers entitled to special consideration in connection with layoff and recall to work. Not prevalent in the public sector.

Supervisor: See *Managerial employee.*

Sweetheart agreement: A collective bargaining agreement exceptionally favorable to a particular employer, achieved through improper means. Such arrangements usually imply that employees covered under any such agreement receive less favorable conditions of employment than could be obtained under a legitimate collective bargaining relationship.

Taft-Hartley Act: See *Labor Management Relations Act of 1947.*

Unfair labor practice (prohibited practice): Action by either an employer or employee organization which violates certain provisions of national, state, or local labor relations acts.

Union security: Protection of a union's status by a provision in the collective bargaining agreement establishing a union shop, agency shop, or maintenance-of-membership agreement.

Union shop: The employer may hire anyone, but all employees must join the union within a specified time period after hire, often after 30 days, and must remain members as a condition of employment. A *modified union shop* may exempt those already employed at the time the provision was negotiated but who had, until then, not joined the union.

Agency shop (agency service fee): Requires all employees who do not join the union to pay a fixed amount, usually the equivalent of union dues to the union treasury as a condition of employment, to help defray the union's expenses as bargaining agent. Some clauses provide for payments to be allocated to the union's welfare fund or a charity rather than to the union's treasury.

Maintenance-of-membership provision: Employees who are union members at the time the provision is negotiated, or who thereafter voluntarily join the union, must maintain their union membership for the duration of the agreement as a condition of employment.

Union steward: A union representative of a group of fellow workers who carries out union duties, e.g., handles grievances, collects dues, recruits new members. He is elected by fellow employees or appointed by union officials. The steward usually continues to work at his regular job.

Wagner Act: See *National Labor Relations Act of 1935.*

Whipsawing: The tactic of negotiating with one employer at a time, using each negotiated gain as a level against the next employer. See *Leap-frogging.*

Zipper clause: An agreement provision specifically stating that the written agreement is the complete agreement of the parties and that anything not contained therein is not agreed to unless in writing and signed by both parties subsequent to the date of the agreement. See *Reopening clause.*

Source: Allan W. Drachman, *Municipal Negotiations: From Differences to Agreement* (Washington, D.C.: Labor Management Relations Service of the U.S. Conference of Mayors, 1970), pp. 42–47.
See text discussion, Chapter 13.

Sources for glossary

National Governors' Conference, 1967 Executive Committee, *Report of Task Force on State and Local Government Labor Relations,* Chapter 6, pp. 65–69.
Advisory Commission on Intergovernmental Relations, 1969 Commission Report, *Labor–Management Policies for State and Local Government,* Chapter 1, pp. 2–4.
Glossary of Current Industrial Relations and Wage Terms, U.S. Department of Labor, Bulletin No. 1438, as selected by the Center for Labor Education and Research, University of Colorado, Boulder, Colorado.
Glossary of Labor Relations Terms, Excerpts from Information Bulletin No. 112, Michigan Municipal League, as printed in *The ABC's of Collective Bargaining,* by Chester Beisen, Executive Director, Association of Washington Cities, Information Bulletin No. 306, 1968.

Appendix D

Complaint initiation, receipt, and investigation

Procedural instruction

Subject: *Complaint initiation, receipt, and investigation*

I. **Purpose**

The purpose of this order is to establish departmental procedure for initiation, receipt, and investigation of complaints against employees of the police department.

II. **Policy**

It shall be the policy of the police department to investigate all complaints against or allegations of misconduct committed by police department employees, whether initiated by employees of this department or by citizens.

III. **Procedure**

All complaints against police department employees will be referred to the employees' immediate supervisor whenever possible; should the immediate supervisor be unavailable, the next level of supervision will be assigned the investigations, unless otherwise determined by the chief of police. Cases initiated by immediate supervisory officers normally will be investigated by those supervisors.

A. Telephone complaints will be accepted as will all other methods of complaint receipt.

1. If the complaint is received by either a telephone operator or a dispatcher, the complaining party shall immediately be referred to:

   a) The commander in charge of the unit to which the subject employee is assigned, if known, and, if between the hours of 08:00 and 17:00, or

   b) The on-duty watch commander if the call is received between 17:00 and 08:00 or on weekends and holidays.

2. If the complaint is received by a field officer or field supervisor who is not responsible for the subject employee, the complainant shall be referred to either the on-duty watch commander or to the commander in charge of the unit to which the subject employee is assigned, as noted in 1 a) and b) above.

3. Upon receipt of the complaint, either the appropriate unit commander or the on-duty watch commander shall complete the appropriate report form, and forward the completed form to the subject employee's immediate supervisor through the regular chain of command, assuring proper notification of supervisory personnel of an impending investigation.

4. A copy of the complaint form shall be forwarded immediately to the chief of police by the officer completing the form.

5. The investigating supervisor shall inform the subject employee of the investigation as soon as possible, and complete a thorough and comprehensive investigation without delay.

6. The subject employee may request the investigating supervisor to provide a copy of the complaint form.

7. After the investigation is complete, the findings and all other supportive materials including a recommendation for disciplinary action, if appropriate and if desired, will be forwarded to the chief of police for his review.

8. The chief of police shall, at his discretion, and after careful review of the material and the subject employee's work record, determine whether any or what action should be taken, whether the investigating supervisor's recommendations are appropriate, or whether the materials presented and the circumstances of the complaint warrant the activation of the board of inquiry and recommendation.

9. In all cases, both the subject officer and the complainant (if

known) shall be notified in writing of the findings and action taken or not taken.

IV. **Investigative reporting procedure**

All supervisory personnel shall intensely investigate all personnel complaints initiated by them or assigned to them, gathering all available information from all known sources.

A. Upon receipt of a complaint, the commander completing the complaint form shall obtain a case report number for a confidential personnel investigation and include it on the form.

B. A case report shall be completed for the records files and shall include:

   1. The fact that a confidential investigation is being conducted,
   2. By a particular investigating supervisor,
   3. Who will maintain all materials of the investigation,
   4. Until the materials are finally filed with the chief of police.
   5. No other information should appear on the case report.

C. The supervisor assigned to investigate the complaint shall include a reference to the case report number on all materials related to the investigation and, upon completion, submit all materials to the chief of police for his review and consideration.

V. **Appeals**

The subject employee has alternative appeal processes to consider.

A. If the subject employee is a civilian, the appeal for a reprimand, suspension, or other action shall be the citywide grievance procedure.

B. If the subject employee is an officer, and no board of inquiry and recommendation has been called, the officer may request the chief to call one. Should the request be denied, the city's grievance procedure is available. If a board had heard the complaint and the subject officer was not satisfied, the city's grievance procedure is still available.

VI. **Filing unfounded complaints**

No unfounded complaints shall be filed in an employee's personnel file. A copy, however, of all reports of investigation shall be retained by the chief of police, whether founded or unfounded.

VII. **Effective date**

This order is effective immediately.

See text discussion, Chapter 14.

Selected bibliography

The following bibliography is highly selective and includes basic readings in the field of the police service and its administration. For additional sources, see the endnotes following each chapter.

1 Emerging Police Issues

Banton, Michael. *The Policeman in the Community*. New York: Basic Books, Inc., 1964.

Bittner, Egon. *The Functions of the Police in Modern Society*. Cambridge, Mass.: Oelgeschlager, Gunn & Hain Publishers, Inc., 1980.

Black, Donald. *The Manners and Customs of the Police*. New York: Academic Press, 1980.

Chevigny, Paul. *Police Power*. New York: Pantheon Books, 1969.

Conklin, John E. *Robbery and the Criminal Justice System*. Philadelphia: J. B. Lippincott Company, 1972.

Fogelson, Robert M. *Big-City Police*. Cambridge, Mass.: Harvard University Press, 1977.

Gardiner, John A. *Traffic and the Police*. Cambridge, Mass.: Harvard University Press, 1969.

Goldstein, Herman. *Policing a Free Society*. Cambridge, Mass.: Ballinger Publishing Company, 1977.

Greenwood, Peter W.; Chaiken, Jan M.; and Petersilia, Joan. *The Criminal Investigation Process*. Lexington, Mass.: D. C. Heath & Company, 1977.

LaFave, Wayne R. *Arrest: The Decision to Take a Suspect into Custody*. Boston: Little, Brown & Company, 1965.

Manning, Peter K. *Police Work*. Cambridge, Mass.: MIT Press, 1977.

Ostrom, Elinor, and Parks, Roger B. *Patterns of Metropolitan Policing*. Cambridge, Mass.: Ballinger Publishing Company, 1978.

Packer, Herbert L. *The Limits of the Criminal Sanction*. Stanford, Calif.: Stanford University Press, 1968.

Platt, Anthony, ed. *The Politics of Riot Commissions*. New York: Macmillan Publishing Company, 1971.

Reiss, Albert J., Jr. *The Police and the Public*. New Haven: Yale University Press, 1971.

Sherman, Lawrence W. *Scandal and Reform*. Berkeley: University of California Press, 1978.

Skolnick, Jerome H. *Justice without Trial*. 2d ed. New York: John Wiley & Sons, Inc., 1975.

Smith, Bruce. *Police Systems in the United States*. New York: Harper & Brothers, 1940.

Wilson, James Q. *Varieties of Police Behavior: The Management of Law and Order in Eight Communities*. Cambridge, Mass.: Harvard University Press, 1968.

2 The Evolution of Contemporary Police Service

Brown, Michael K. *Working the Street: Police Discretion and the Dilemmas of Reform*. New York: Russell Sage Foundation, 1981.

Chang, Dae H., ed. *Introduction to Criminal Justice: Theory and Application*. Dubuque, Iowa: Kendall/Hunt Publishing Company, 1979.

Freed, Leonard. *Police Work*. New York: Simon & Schuster, Inc., 1980.

Inciardi, James A., and Faupel, Charles A. *History and Crime*. Springfield, Ill.: Charles C Thomas, 1980.

Martin, Julian A., and Astone, Nicholas A. *Criminal Justice Vocabulary*. Springfield, Ill.: Charles C Thomas, 1980.

O'Brien, J. T., and Marcus, M., eds. *Crime and Justice in America*. New York: Pergamon Press, 1979.

Pelfrey, William V. *The Evolution of Criminology*. Cincinnati: Anderson Publishing Company, 1980.

Staufenberger, Richard A., ed. *Progress in Policing: Essays on Change*. Cambridge, Mass.: Ballinger Publishing Company, 1980.

U.S. Department of Justice. *Attorney General's Task Force on Violent Crime: Final Report*. Washington, D.C.: Government Printing Office, 1981.

Walker, Samuel. *Popular Justice: A History of*

American Criminal Justice. New York: Oxford University Press, 1980.

Wright, Kevin N. *Crime and Criminal Justice in a Declining Economy.* Cambridge, Mass.: Oelgeschlager, Gunn & Hain Publishers, Inc., 1981.

3 The Governmental Setting

American Bar Association Project on Standards for Criminal Justice. *Standards Relating to the Urban Police Function.* Chicago: American Bar Association, 1974.

Bittner, Egon. *The Functions of the Police in Modern Society.* Cambridge, Mass.: Oelgeschlager, Gunn & Hain Publishers, Inc., 1980.

Bollens, John C., and Schmandt, Henry J. *The Metropolis: Its People, Politics, and Economic Life.* 3d ed. New York: Harper & Row, 1975.

Dunham, David M., and Hilhorst, Joseph G., eds. *Issues in Regional Planning.* The Hague: Mouton, 1971.

Freeman, Linton C. *Patterns of Local Community Leadership.* Indianapolis: Bobbs-Merrill Co., Inc., 1968.

Goldstein, Herman. *Policing a Free Society.* Cambridge, Mass.: Ballinger Publishing Company, 1977.

Hale, Charles D. *Fundamentals of Police Administration.* Boston: Holbrook Press, 1977.

Kelly, Michael J. *Police Chief Selection: A Handbook for Local Government.* Washington, D.C.: Police Foundation and International City Management Association, 1975.

Kenney, John Paul. *Police Administration.* Rev. ed. Springfield, Ill.: Charles C Thomas, 1975.

McNichols, Thomas F. *Policy Making and Executive Action.* 4th ed. New York: McGraw-Hill Book Company, 1972.

National Advisory Commission on Criminal Justice Standards and Goals. *Police* [*Report on Police*]. Washington, D.C.: Government Printing Office, 1973.

National Sheriffs' Association. *Mutual Aid Planning.* Washington, D.C.: National Sheriffs' Association, 1973.

Norrgard, David L. *Regional Law Enforcement: A Study of Intergovernmental Cooperation and Coordination.* Chicago: Public Administration Service, 1969.

President's Commission on Law Enforcement and Administration of Justice. *Task Force Report: The Police.* Washington, D.C.: Government Printing Office, 1967.

Skolnick, Jerome H. *Justice without Trial: Law Enforcement in Democratic Society.* 2d ed. New York: John Wiley & Sons, Inc., 1975.

Smith, George Albert, Jr. *Policy Formation and Administration.* 5th ed. Homewood, Ill.: Richard D. Irwin, 1968.

U.S. Advisory Commission on Intergovernmental Relations. *State–Local Relations in the Criminal Justice System.* Washington, D.C.: Government Printing Office, 1971.

Wilson, Orlando W., and McLaren, Roy C. *Police Administration.* 4th ed. New York: McGraw-Hill Book Company, 1976.

4 Corruptive Influences

Barefoot, J. Kirk. *Employee Theft Investigation.* Woburn, Mass.: Butterworth, 1979.

Fishman, Janet E. *Measuring Police Corruption.* New York: John Jay Press, 1978.

National Institute of Law Enforcement and Criminal Justice. *An Anticorruption Strategy for Local Governments.* Washington, D.C.: Government Printing Office, 1979.

———. *Prevention, Detection, and Correction of Corruption in Local Government: A Presentation of Potential Models.* Washington, D.C.: Government Printing Office, 1978.

Sherman, Lawrence W. *Scandal and Reform: Controlling Police Corruption.* Berkeley: University of California Press, 1978.

Simpson, Antony E. *The Literature of Police Corruption.* New York: John Jay Press, 1979.

Ward, Richard H. *An Anti-Corruption Manual for Administrators in Law Enforcement.* New York: John Jay Press, 1979.

5 Police Organization and Management

American Bar Association Project on Standards for Criminal Justice. *Standards Relating to the Urban Police Function.* Chicago: American Bar Association, 1974.

Athos, Anthony G. *Behavior in Organizations.* Englewood Cliffs, N.J.: Prentice-Hall, Inc., 1968.

Banovetz, James M., ed. *Managing the Modern City.* Washington, D.C.: International City Management Association, 1971.

Berenbaum, Esai. *Municipal Public Safety: A Guide for the Implementation of Consolidated Police–Fire Services.* Springfield, Ill.: Charles C Thomas, 1977.

Bristow, Allen P., ed. *Police Supervision Readings.* Springfield, Ill.: Charles C Thomas, 1971.

Dale, Ernest, and Urwick, Lyndall. *Staff in Organization*. New York: McGraw-Hill Book Company, 1960.

Davis, Edward M. *Staff One: A Perspective on Effective Police Management*. Englewood Cliffs, N.J.: Prentice-Hall, Inc., 1978.

Etzioni, Amitai. *Modern Organization*. Englewood Cliffs, N.J.: Prentice-Hall, Inc., 1964.

Gellerman, Saul W. *Management by Motivation*. New York: American Management Association, 1968.

Iannone, Nathan F. *Supervision of Police Personnel*. 3d ed. Englewood Cliffs, N.J.: Prentice-Hall, Inc., 1980.

Jay, Anthony. *Corporation Man*. New York: Random House, 1971.

Katz, Daniel, and Kahn, Robert L. *The Social Psychology of Organizations*. New York: John Wiley & Sons, Inc., 1966.

Kenney, John P., and Williams, John B. *Police Operations: Policies and Procedures*. 2d ed. Springfield, Ill.: Charles C Thomas, 1973.

Kuykendall, Jack L., and Unsinger, Peter C. *Community Police Administration*. Chicago: Nelson-Hall Company, 1975.

Lawrence, Paul R., and Lorsch, Jay W. *Organization and Environment: Managing Differentiation and Integration*. Homewood, Ill.: Richard D. Irwin, 1967.

Leonard, Vivian A., and More, Harry W. *Police Organization and Management*. 4th ed. Mineola, N.Y.: The Foundation Press, Inc., 1974.

McGregor, Douglas. *The Human Side of Enterprise*. New York: McGraw-Hill Book Company, 1960.

Mintzberg, Henry. *The Nature of Managerial Work*. New York: Harper & Row, 1973.

Morrisey, George L. *Management by Objectives and Results*. Reading, Mass.: Addison-Wesley Publishing Co., Inc., 1970.

Munro, Jim L. *Administrative Behavior and Police Organization*. Cincinnati: The W. H. Anderson Company, 1973–74.

Nigro, Felix A., and Nigro, Lloyd G. *Modern Public Administration*. New York: Harper & Row, 1973.

Odiorne, George S. *Management by Objectives: A System of Managerial Leadership*. New York: Pitman Publishing Corp., 1965.

Powers, Stanley Piazza; Brown, F. Gerald; and Arnold, David S. *Developing the Municipal Organization*. Washington, D.C.: International City Management Association, 1974.

Reber, Ralph W., and Terry, Gloria E. *Behavioral Insights for Supervision*. Englewood Cliffs, N.J.: Prentice-Hall, Inc., 1975.

Toch, Hans; Grant, J. Douglas; and Galvin, Raymond T. *Agents of Change: A Study of Police Reform*. New York: John Wiley & Sons, Inc., 1975.

Vroom, Victor H., and Yetton, Philip W. *Leadership and Decision-Making*. Pittsburgh: University of Pittsburgh Press, 1973.

Weston, Paul B. *Police Organization and Management*. Pacific Palisades, Calif.: Goodyear Publishing Company, 1976.

Whisenand, Paul M. *The Effective Police Manager*. Englewood Cliffs, N.J.: Prentice-Hall, 1981.

Whisenand, Paul M., and Ferguson, R. Fred. *The Managing of Police Organizations*. Englewood Cliffs, N.J.: Prentice-Hall, Inc., 1973.

6 Police Productivity

Bouza, A. V. *Police Administration: Organization and Performance*. New York: Pergamon Press, 1978.

Greenwood, Peter W.; Chaiken, Jan M.; and Petersilia, Joan. *The Criminal Investigation Process*. Lexington, Mass.: D. C. Heath & Company, 1977.

International City Management Association and The Urban Institute. *Measuring the Effectiveness of Basic Municipal Services: Initial Report*. Washington, D.C.: International City Management Association and The Urban Institute, 1974.

Nardulli, Peter F., and Stonecash, Jeffrey M. *Politics, Professionalism and Urban Services*. Cambridge, Mass.: Oelgeschlager, Gunn & Hain, Inc., 1981.

Petersen, David M., ed. *Police Work: Strategies and Outcomes in Law Enforcement*. Beverly Hills, Calif.: Sage Publications, 1979.

Savas, E. S., ed. *Alternatives for Delivering Public Services: Toward Improved Performance*. Boulder, Colo.: Westview Press, 1977.

Stevens, John M., and Webster, Thomas C. *Report on Productivity Improvement in the Bridgeport Police Department*. University Park, Pa.: Institute of Public Administration, 1977.

Washnis, George J., and Esser, George H. *Productivity Improvement: Handbook for State and Local Government*. New York: John Wiley & Sons, 1979.

7 Patrol Administration

Aaron, Thomas F. *Control of Police Discretion: The Danish Experience*. Springfield, Ill.: Charles C Thomas, 1966.

Adams, Thomas F. *Police Patrol: Tactics and Techniques*. Englewood Cliffs, N.J.: Prentice-Hall, Inc., 1971.

Banton, Michael. *The Policeman in the Community*. New York: Basic Books, Inc., 1964.

Elliot, James F. *Interception Patrol*. Springfield, Ill.: Charles C Thomas, 1973.

Felkenes, George T. *Police Patrol Operations*. Berkeley, Calif.: McCutchan Publishing Corp., 1972.

Fisk, James M. *The Police Officer's Exercise of Discretion in the Decision To Arrest: Relationship to Organizational Goals and Societal Values*. Los Angeles: Institute of Government and Public Affairs, University of California, Los Angeles, 1974.

Gourley, Gerald D. *Patrol Administration*. 2d ed. Springfield, Ill.: Charles C Thomas, 1974.

Greenwood, Peter W.; Chaiken, Jan M.; and Petersilia, Joan. *The Criminal Investigation Process*. Lexington, Mass.: D. C. Heath & Company, 1977.

Hale, Charles D. *Police Patrol: Operations and Management*. New York: John Wiley & Sons, 1981.

International Association of Chiefs of Police. *The Patrol Operation*. 2d ed. Gaithersburg, Md.: International Association of Chiefs of Police, 1970.

Kelling, George L.; Pate, Tony; Dieckman, Duane; and Brown, Charles E. *The Kansas City Preventive Patrol Experiment: A Summary Report*. Washington, D.C.: Police Foundation, 1974.

President's Commission on Law Enforcement and Administration of Justice. *Task Force Report: The Police*. Washington, D.C.: Government Printing Office, 1967.

Schell, Theodore H., et al. *National Evaluation Program, Phase I Summary Report: Traditional Preventive Patrol*. Washington, D.C.: National Institute of Law Enforcement and Criminal Justice, 1976.

Schultz, Donald O., and Norton, L. A. *Police Operational Intelligence*. Springfield, Ill.: Charles C Thomas, 1973.

Sherman, Lawrence W., et al. *Team Policing: Seven Case Studies*. Washington, D.C.: Police Foundation, 1973.

Wilson, James Q. *Varieties of Police Behavior: The Management of Law and Order in Eight Communities*. Cambridge, Mass.: Harvard University Press, 1968.

8 Traffic Supervision

Baker, James Stannard. *Traffic Accident Investigation*. Evanston, Ill.: Traffic Institute, Northwestern University, 1975.

Baker, Robert Fulton. *The Highway Risk Problem*. New York: Wiley-Interscience, 1971.

Drew, Donald R. *Traffic Flow Theory and Control*. New York: McGraw-Hill Book Company, 1968.

Fisher, Edward C., and Reeder, Robert H. *Vehicle Traffic Law*. Evanston, Ill.: Traffic Institute, Northwestern University, 1974.

Gardiner, John A. *Traffic and the Police*. Cambridge, Mass.: Harvard University Press, 1969.

International Association of Chiefs of Police, Highway Safety Division. *Selective Traffic Law Enforcement Manual*. Gaithersburg, Md.: International Association of Chiefs of Police, 1972.

Leonard, Vivian A. *Police Traffic Control*. Springfield, Ill.: Charles C Thomas, 1971.

Vanderbosch, Charles G. *Traffic Supervision*. Gaithersburg, Md.: International Association of Chiefs of Police, 1969.

9 Criminal Investigation

Aubry, Arthur S., and Caputo, Rudolph R. *Criminal Interrogation*. 3d ed. Springfield, Ill.: Charles C Thomas, 1980.

Dowling, Jerry L. *Criminal Investigation*. New York: Harcourt Brace Jovanovich, 1979.

Gilbert, James N. *Criminal Investigation*. Columbus, Ohio: Charles E. Merrill Publishing Company, 1980.

Johnson, Edwin S. *Research Methods in Criminology and Criminal Justice*. Englewood Cliffs, N.J.: Prentice-Hall, Inc., 1981.

O'Hara, Charles E. *Fundamentals of Criminal Investigation*. 5th ed. Springfield, Ill.: Charles C Thomas, 1980.

Rutledge, Devallis. *The Search and Seizure Handbook*. Flagstone, Ariz.: Flage Publishing Company, 1980.

Svensson, Arne; Wendell, Otto; and Fisher, Barry. *Techniques of Crime Scene Investigation*. 3d ed. New York: Elsevier North Holland, 1981.

U.S. Department of Justice. *Proving Federal Crimes*. Washington, D.C.: Government Printing Office, 1980.

10 Organized Crime

Abadinsky, Howard. *Organized Crime*. Boston: Allyn & Bacon, Inc., 1981.

Bequai, August. *Organized Crime: The Fifth Estate*. Lexington, Mass.: Lexington Books, 1979.

Chambliss, William J. *On the Take, from Petty Crooks to Presidents*. Bloomington: Indiana University Press, 1978.

Dorman, Michael. *Payoff: The Role of Organized Crime in American Politics*. New York: David McKay Co., Inc., 1972.

Forer, Lois G. *Criminals and Victims*. New York: W. W. Norton, 1980.

Harney, Malachi L. *The Narcotic Officer's Notebook*. 2d ed. Springfield, Ill.: Charles C Thomas, 1973.

Ianni, Francis A. *Black Mafia: Ethnic Succession in Organized Crime*. New York: Simon & Schuster, Inc., 1974.

Lester, David. *Gambling Today*. Springfield, Ill.: Charles C Thomas, 1979.

Manning, Peter K. *The Narcs' Game: Organizational and Information Limits on Drug Law Enforcement*. Cambridge, Mass.: MIT Press, 1980.

Pace, Denny F. *Handbook of Vice Control*. Englewood Cliffs, N.J.: Prentice-Hall, Inc., 1971.

Pace, Denny F., and Styles, Jimmie E. *Handbook of Narcotics Control*. Englewood Cliffs, N.J.: Prentice-Hall, Inc., 1972.

President's Commission on Law Enforcement and Administration of Justice. *Task Force Report: Organized Crime*. Washington, D.C.: Government Printing Office, 1967.

Reid, Ed. *The Anatomy of Organized Crime in America: The Grim Reapers*. Chicago: Henry Regnery Company, 1969.

Schur, Edwin M., and Bedau, Hugo A. *Victimless Crimes: Two Sides of a Controversy*. Englewood Cliffs, N.J.: Prentice-Hall, Inc., 1974.

Yablonsky, Lewis. *The Violent Gang*. Rev. ed. New York: Penguin Books, 1971.

11 Crime Prevention and the Community

Banton, Michael. *Police–Community Relations*. London: William Collins Sons & Co., Ltd., 1973.

Bard, Morton. *The Function of the Police in Crisis Intervention and Conflict Management*. Washington, D.C.: Law Enforcement Assistance Administration, 1975.

Belson, William A. *The Public and the Police*. New York: Harper & Row, 1975.

Bent, Alan E., and Rossum, Ralph A. *Police, Criminal Justice, and the Community*. New York: Harper & Row, 1976.

Brandstatter, A. F., and Radelet, Louis A. *Police and Community Relations: A Source Book*. Beverly Hills, Calif.: Glencoe Press, 1968.

Clark, Ramsey. *Crime in America: Its Nature, Causes, Control, and Correction*. New York: Simon & Schuster, Inc., 1970.

Clinard, Marshall B. *Cities with Little Crime*. New York: Cambridge University Press, 1978.

Coffey, Alan, et al. *Human Relations: Law Enforcement in a Changing Community*. 2d ed. Englewood Cliffs, N.J.: Prentice-Hall, Inc., 1976.

Cole, Richard L. *Citizen Participation, Democratic Theory, and the Urban Policy Process*. Lexington, Mass.: Lexington Books, 1974.

Conklin, John E. *The Impact of Crime*. New York: The Macmillan Company, 1975.

Earle, Howard H. *Police–Community Relations: Crisis in Our Time*. 3d ed. Springfield, Ill.: Charles C Thomas, 1980.

Gibbons, Don C. *Society, Crime, and Criminal Careers*. 3d ed. Englewood Cliffs, N.J.: Prentice-Hall, Inc., 1976.

Jeffery, Clarence R. *Crime Prevention through Environmental Design*. Beverly Hills, Calif.: Sage Publications, 1976.

Kobetz, Richard W., ed. *Crisis Intervention and the Police: Selected Readings*. Gaithersburg, Md.: International Association of Chiefs of Police, 1974.

Larson, Richard C. *Police Accountability*. Lexington, Mass.: Lexington Books, 1978.

Lipman, Ira A. *How to Protect Yourself from Crime*. New York: Atheneum, 1975.

McDowell, Charles P. *Police in the Community*. Cincinnati: The W. H. Anderson Company, 1975.

Moolman, Valerie. *Practical Ways To Prevent Burglary and Illegal Entry*. New York: Cornerstone Library, 1970.

National Institute of Law Enforcement and Criminal Justice. *Police Burglary Control Programs*. Washington, D.C.: Government Printing Office, 1975.

Niederhoffer, Arthur, and Smith, Alexander B. *New Directions in Police Community Relations*. Madeira, Calif.: Reinhart Press, 1974.

Robinson, Robert L. *How to Burglar-Proof Your Home*. Chicago: Nelson-Hall Company, 1977.

Rosefsky, Robert S. *Frauds, Swindles and Rackets: Alert for Today's Consumers*. Chicago: Follett Publishing Company, 1973.

Schwartz, Alfred I., et al. *Employing Civilians for Police Work*. Washington, D.C.: The Urban Institute, 1975.

Trojanowicz, John M., and Moss, Forrest M. *Community Based Crime Prevention*. Pacific Palisades, Calif.: Goodyear Publishing Company, 1975.

Washnis, George J. *Citizen Involvement in Crime Prevention*. Lexington, Mass.: Lexington Books, 1976.

Wasserman, Robert; Gardner, Michael Paul; and Cohen, Alana S. *Improving Police–Community Relations*. Prescriptive Package, LEAA.

Washington, D.C.: Government Printing Office, 1973.

Whisenand, Paul M. *Crime Prevention.* Boston: Holbrook Press, 1977.

Whisenand, Paul M.; Cline, James L.; and Felkenes, George T., eds. *Police–Community Relations.* Pacific Palisades, Calif.: Goodyear Publishing Company, 1974.

12 Juvenile Programs

Altman, Michael. *Standards Relating to Juvenile Records and Information.* Cambridge, Mass.: Ballinger Publishing Company, 1980.

Bittner, Egon, and Krantz, Sheldon. *Standards Relating to Police Handling of Juvenile Problems.* Cambridge, Mass.: Ballinger Publishing Company, 1980.

Hahn, Paul H. *The Juvenile Offender and the Law.* 2d ed. Cincinnati: Anderson Publishing Company, 1978.

Hindelang, Michael, et al. *Measuring Delinquency.* Cambridge, Mass.: Ballinger Publishing Company, 1981.

Jankovic, Joanne. *Juvenile Justice in Rural America.* Washington, D.C.: Government Printing Office, 1980.

Kenney, John P., and Pursuit, Dan G. *Police Work with Juveniles and the Administration of Juvenile Justice.* 5th ed. Springfield, Ill.: Charles C Thomas, 1978.

Mayers, Michael O. *The Hard-Core Delinquent.* Lexington, Mass.: Lexington Books, 1980.

National Advisory Committee for Juvenile Justice and Delinquency Prevention. *Standards for the Administration of Juvenile Justice.* Washington, D.C.: Government Printing Office, 1980.

Shichor, David, and Kelly, Delos H., eds. *Critical Issues in Juvenile Delinquency.* Lexington, Mass.: Lexington Books, 1980.

Trojanowicz, Robert C. *Juvenile Delinquency Concepts and Controls.* 2d ed. Englewood Cliffs, N.J.: Prentice-Hall, Inc., 1978.

13 Personnel Management

Ayres, Richard M., and Wheelen, Thomas L., eds. *Collective Bargaining in the Public Sector: Selected Readings in Law Enforcement.* Gaithersburg, Md.: International Association of Chiefs of Police, 1977.

Bopp, William J., and Whisenand, Paul. *Police Personnel Administration.* 2d ed. Boston: Allyn & Bacon, Inc., 1980.

Boyer, J. K., and Griggs, Edward. *Equal Employment Opportunity Program Development*

Manual. Washington, D.C.: Law Enforcement Assistance Administration, 1974.

Burpo, John H. *Labor Relations Guidelines for the Police Executive.* Evanston, Ill.: Traffic Institute, Northwestern University, 1976.

———. *Police Unions in the Civil Service Setting.* Washington, D.C.: Government Printing Office, 1979.

Calvert, Robert, Jr., *Affirmative Action: A Comprehensive Recruitment Manual.* Garrett Park, Md.: Garrett Park Press, 1979.

Crouch, Winston W., ed. *Local Government Personnel Administration.* Washington, D.C.: International City Management Association, 1976.

Drucker, Peter F. *Managing in Turbulent Times.* New York: Harper & Row, 1980.

Eisenberg, Terry; Kent, Deborah Ann; and Wall, Charles. *Survey of Police Personnel Practices in State and Local Government.* Washington, D.C.: Police Foundation, International Association of Chiefs of Police, and Educational Testing Service, 1973.

Feinman, Clarice. *Women in the Criminal Justice System.* New York: Praeger, 1980.

Fullinwider, Robert K. *The Reverse Discrimination Controversy: A Moral and Legal Analysis.* Totowa, N.J.: Rowman & Littlefield, 1980.

Gentel, William D., and Handman, Martha L. *Police Strikes: Causes and Prevention.* Gaithersburg, Md.: International Association of Chiefs of Police, 1979.

Glazer, Nathan. *Affirmative Discrimination: Ethnic Inequality and Public Policy.* New York: Basic Books, Inc., 1976.

Horne, Peter. *Women in Law Enforcement.* Springfield, Ill.: Charles C Thomas, 1975.

Iannone, N. F. *Supervision of Police Personnel.* 3d ed. Englewood Cliffs, N.J.: Prentice-Hall, Inc., 1980.

Larson, Richard C. *Police Accountability: Performance Measures and Unionism.* Lexington, Mass.: Lexington Books, 1978.

Levi, Margaret. *Bureaucratic Insurgency: The Case of Police Unions.* Lexington, Mass.: Lexington Books, 1977.

Melnicoe, William B., and Mennig, Jan C. *Elements of Police Supervision.* 2d ed. Encino, Calif.: Glencoe Publishing Co., Inc., 1978.

Milton, Katherine Higgs, et al. *Women in Policing: A Manual.* Washington, D.C.: Police Foundation, 1974.

Police Foundation, International Association of Chiefs of Police, and Labor–Management Relations Service. *Guidelines and Papers from the National Symposium on Police Labor Re-*

lations. Washington, D.C.: Police Foundation, 1974.

Runecki, S., and Cairns, D. A. *Police Collective Bargaining: A National Management Study.* Washington, D.C.: National League of Cities, 1978.

Showalter, R., and Dart, R. F. *Potentials for Police Union Management Relations in American Towns: A Guide for Police Administrators and Police Union Leaders.* Bethesda, Md.: Social Development Corporation, 1976.

Territo, Leonard; Swanson, Charles R., Jr.; and Chamelin, Neil C. *Police Personnel Selection Process.* Indianapolis: Bobbs-Merrill Publishing Company, 1977.

Trojanowicz, Robert C. *The Environment of the First-Line Police Supervisor.* Englewood Cliffs, N.J.: Prentice-Hall, Inc., 1980.

U.S. Department of Justice. *Police Unions in the Civil Service Setting.* Washington, D.C.: Government Printing Office, 1979.

Weston, Paul B., and Fraley, Philip K. *Police Personnel Management.* Englewood Cliffs, N.J.: Prentice-Hall, Inc., 1980.

14 Internal Controls

Brink, Victor Z., et al. *Modern Internal Auditing.* New York: The Ronald Press Company, 1973.

Hewitt, William H. *Police Records and Administration.* Rochester, N.Y.: Lawyers Co-Operative Publishing Company, 1968.

International Association of Chiefs of Police. *Model Police Rules of Conduct.* Gaithersburg, Md.: International Association of Chiefs of Police, 1972.

Leonard, V. A. *The New Police Technology: Impact of the Computer and Automation on Police and Line Performance.* Springfield, Ill.: Charles C Thomas, 1980.

Smith, Alexander C. *Internal Control and Audit.* London: Pitman, 1968.

Wilson, O. W. *Police Planning.* 2d ed. Springfield, Ill.: Charles C Thomas, 1977.

15 Research and Planning

Cohn, Alvin W., ed. *Criminal Justice Planning and Development.* Beverly Hills, Calif.: Sage Publications, 1977.

Drucker, Peter F. *The Effective Executive.* New York: Harper & Row, 1967.

————. *Management: Tasks, Responsibilities, Practices.* New York: Harper & Row, 1974.

————. *Technology, Management and Society.* New York: Harper & Row, 1970.

Koontz, Harold, and O'Connell, Cyril, eds. *Management: A Book of Readings.* 4th ed. New York: McGraw-Hill Book Company, 1976.

————. *Management: A Systems and Contingency Analysis of Managerial Functions.* 6th ed. New York: McGraw-Hill Book Company, 1976.

Lynch, R. G. *The Police Manager.* Boston: Holbrook Press, 1975.

National Advisory Commission on Criminal Justice Standards and Goals. *Police* [*Report on Police*]. Washington, D.C.: Government Printing Office, 1973.

————. *Police Chief Executive.* Washington, D.C.: Government Printing Office, 1976.

Whisenand, Paul M., and Ferguson, R. Fred. *The Managing of Police Organizations.* 2d ed. Englewood Cliffs, N.J.: Prentice-Hall, Inc., 1978.

Wilson, Jerry. *Police Report: A View of Law Enforcement.* Boston: Little, Brown & Company, 1975.

Wilson, O. W. *Police Planning.* 2d ed. Springfield, Ill.: Charles C Thomas, 1977.

Wilson, O. W., and McLaren, Roy Clinton. *Police Administration.* 4th ed. New York: McGraw-Hill Book Company, 1977.

16 Information Management

Armstrong, J. Scott. *Long-Range Forecasting: From Crystal Ball to Computer.* New York: John Wiley & Sons, 1978.

Fielding, J. E., et al. *State Criminal Justice Telecommunications (STACOM).* Final Report. 2 vols. Washington, D.C.: Government Printing Office, 1978.

Klein, Carol, compiler. *Criminal Justice Information Systems: A Selected Bibliography.* Washington, D.C.: Government Printing Office, 1980.

Leonard, V. A. *The New Police Technology: Impact of the Computer and Automation on Police and Line Performance.* Springfield, Ill.: Charles C Thomas, 1980.

Levine, Emil H. *Information Science: Law Enforcement Applications.* Cincinnati: Anderson Publishing Company, 1979.

Megargee, Edwin I., and Bohn, Martine. *Classifying Criminal Offenders: A New System Based on MMPI.* Beverly Hills, Calif.: Sage Publications, 1979.

Standardized Crime Reporting System. An Assessment of SCRS: Implementation Case Studies. Sacramento: Search Group, Inc., 1980.

U.S. Department of Justice. Bureau of Justice Statistics. *Expenditure and Employment Data* for the Criminal Justice System. Washington, D.C.: Government Printing Office, 1981.

U.S. Parole Commission. *Using Court Records for Policy Analysis: PROMIS: Prosecutor's Management Information System.* Washington, D.C.: U.S. Parole Commission, 1980.

17 Facilities and Materiel

Bureau of Alcohol, Tobacco and Firearms. *State Laws and Published Ordinances: Firearms.* Washington, D.C.: Government Printing Office, 1980.

Downey, Robert J. *Weapon Retention Techniques for Officer Survival.* Springfield, Ill.: Charles C Thomas, 1981.

Greenberg, Allan M. *Standards Relating to Architectural Facilities.* Cambridge, Mass.: Ballinger Publishing Company, 1980.

Law Enforcement Standards Laboratory, National Bureau of Standards. *Guide to High Speed Patrol Car Tires.* Washington, D.C.: Government Printing Office, 1980.

Page, Harry Robert. *Public Purchasing and Materials Management.* Lexington, Mass.: Lexington Books, 1980.

Ruegg, Rosalie T. *The Police Patrol Car: Economic Efficiency in Acquisition, Operation and Disposition.* NBS Special Pub. 480-15. Washington, D.C.: Government Printing Office, 1978.

Williams, Mason. *The Law Enforcement Book of Weapons, Ammunition, and Training Procedures.* Springfield, Ill.: Charles C Thomas, 1977.

18 Criminalistics

Block, Eugene. *Science vs Crime: The Evolution of the Police Lab.* San Francisco: Cragmont Publications, 1980.

Califana, Anthony L., and Levkov, Jerome S. *Criminalistics for the Law Enforcement Officer.* New York: McGraw-Hill Book Company, 1978.

Collins, James C. *Accident Reconstruction.* Springfield, Ill.: Charles C Thomas, 1979.

DeAngelis, Joseph. *Criminalistics for the Investigator.* Encino, Calif.: Glencoe Publishing Company, 1980.

Ferguson, Robert W., and Stokke, Allan H. *Legal Aspects of Evidence.* New York: Harcourt Brace Jovanovich, 1979.

Goddard, Kenneth W. *Crime Scene Investiga-*

tion. Englewood Cliffs, N.J.: Prentice-Hall, Inc., 1977.

Matte, James Allan. *The Art and Science of Polygraph Techniques.* Springfield, Ill.: Charles C Thomas, 1980.

Saferstein, Richard. *Criminalistics: An Introduction to Forensic Science.* 2d ed. Englewood Cliffs, N.J.: Prentice-Hall, Inc., 1981.

Schlesinger, Steven R. *Exclusionary Injustice: The Problem of Illegally Obtained Evidence.* New York: Marcel Dekker, Inc., 1977.

Siljander, Raymond P. *Fundamentals of Physical Surveillance.* Springfield, Ill.: Charles C Thomas, 1977.

Spitz, Werner U., and Fisher, Russell S. *Medicolegal Investigation of Death: Guidelines for the Application of Pathology to Crime Investigation.* 2d ed. Springfield, Ill.: Charles C Thomas, 1980.

Wilbur, Charles G. *Forensic Toxicology for the Law Enforcement Officer.* Springfield, Ill.: Charles C Thomas, 1980.

Yarmey, A. Daniel. *The Psychology of Eyewitness Testimony.* New York: Free Press, 1979.

19 Jail Management

Antonio, Octavio. *Behind Jail Bars.* New York: Philosophical Library, Inc., 1979.

Clute, Penelope D. *The Legal Aspects of Prisons and Jails.* Springfield, Ill.: Charles C Thomas, 1980.

Jansen, Francis O., and Johns, Ruth. *Management and Supervision of Small Jails.* Springfield, Ill.: Charles C Thomas, 1978.

Kalinich, David B., and Postill, Frederick J. *Principles of County Jail Administration and Management.* Springfield, Ill.: Charles C Thomas, 1981.

Miller, E. Eugene. *Jail Management.* Lexington, Mass.: Lexington Books, 1978.

Moynahan, J. M., and Stewart, Earle K. *The American Jail: Its Development and Growth.* Chicago: Nelson-Hall Company, 1980.

Mullen, Joan. *American Prisons and Jails.* 5 vols. Washington, D.C.: Government Printing Office, 1980.

U.S. Department of Justice. *Jail Operation: A Training Course for Officers, Programmed Instruction.* 6 vols. Washington, D.C.: Government Printing Office, 1979.

List of contributors

Persons who have contributed to this book are listed below with the editor first and the authors following in alphabetical order. A brief review of experience and training is presented for each. Since many of the contributors have published extensively, books, monographs, articles, and other publications are omitted.

Bernard L. Garmire (Editor) has had thirty-eight years in the police service. He was Chief of Police for Miami, Florida, from 1969 to 1975, for Tucson, Arizona, from 1957 to 1969, and for Eau Claire, Wisconsin, from 1950 to 1957. Previously he was with the Fort Wayne, Indiana, police and the Indiana State Police. He has served as consultant to the President's Commission on Campus Unrest (Scranton Commission), and to Attorneys General Ramsey Clark and John Mitchell, and has been a member of the White House Conference on Youth and the Task Force on Race Relations and Minority Groups. He has been a member of the faculty at the University of Arizona, the University of Louisville Southern Police Institute, and the FBI National Academy, and has been a lecturer from time to time at many other university police institutes. Mr. Garmire is a member of a number of professional organizations; he has authored numerous journal articles pertaining to police science and police administration; and he has served as police management consultant to many of the nation's police departments.

Egon Bittner (Chapter 1) is Harry Coplan Professor in the Social Sciences at Brandeis University. He received his Ph.D. degree from the University of California at Los Angeles in 1961 and is a member of the Commission on Accreditation for Law Enforcement Agencies.

Noel C. Bufe (Chapter 8) has been Director of the Traffic Institute, Northwestern University, since July 1978. Dr. Bufe is also a professor at Northwestern's Kellogg Graduate School of Management. He previously served as Deputy Administrator of the U.S. Department of Transportation's National Highway Traffic Safety Administration, Executive Director of Highway Safety Planning for the Michigan State Police, and a management consultant to the International Association of Chiefs of Police. He has

also served with the Michigan Crime Commission Traffic Safety Committee, the National Conference of State Criminal Justice Planning Agencies, and the National Conference of Governors' Highway Safety Representatives. He is a graduate of Michigan State University with a Ph.D. from the Department of Education, and is a recipient of the U.S. Department of Transportation Secretary's Award of Appreciation.

Samuel G. Chapman (Chapter 13) is Professor of Political Science at the University of Oklahoma. Earlier, he served as a police officer in Berkeley, California; as a police consultant for the Public Administration Service, Chicago; as Chief of Police of the Multnomah County (Portland), Oregon, Sheriff's Office; and as Assistant Director of the President's Commission on Law Enforcement and Administration of Justice. In local politics he has served as an elected member of the Norman (Oklahoma) City Council since 1972 and as mayor pro-tem in 1975–76 and 1979–80. He holds undergraduate and graduate degrees in criminology from the University of California at Berkeley.

Monte R. Davis (Chapter 5) has been with the Garden Grove (California) Police Department since 1959 and has been a police captain for the past ten years. He has a bachelor of arts degree from the University of Redlands and is a graduate of the FBI National Academy.

Richard H. Fox (Chapter 18) is a private consultant in the area of criminalistics. He is former Director of the Ventura County Criminalistics Laboratory and former Director of the Regional Criminalistics Laboratory for the Metropolitan Kansas City, Missouri, Region. He is former Assistant Director of the Pittsburgh and Allegheny County Crime Laboratory and instructor of forensic chemistry at the University of Pittsburgh Graduate School of Chemistry, and has served as research associate to the Department of Neurology at the Emory University School of Medicine and the University of Pittsburgh School of Medicine. He is past Chairman of the Board of Directors of the American Society of Crime Laboratory Directors, Inc., a fellow of the American Acad-

426 Local Government Police Management

emy of Forensic Sciences, and President of the Forensic Sciences Foundation, Inc. Mr. Fox is a 1970 recipient of the International Chiefs of Police and American Express Award for Scientific Advancements to International Police Science Technology. He holds a B.S. from the University of Pittsburgh.

Charles D. Hale (Chapter 7) heads his own consulting organization, providing general management consulting to local government, including police organization and management studies and police chief selection projects. He was formerly a Principal Associate with the Public Administration Service, Chicago, where he was responsible for the direction and supervision of local law enforcement studies. Mr. Hale was involved in more than fifty law enforcement studies during his employment with PAS, and he served as Assistant Director of a federally funded study of the factors involved in assaults on police officers. He began his career with the El Segundo (California) Police Department, where he served as a patrol officer, field supervisor, and detective.

Thomas F. Hastings (Chapter 9) is the former Chief of Police of Rochester, New York. He was a career police officer and joined the Rochester Police Department in 1947. He attended Monroe Community College. He has designed and implemented a great number of innovative investigative concepts in his former police agency and has wide experience as a consultant to public and private bodies. Mr. Hastings currently is the Executive Director of Rochester Jobs, Inc., a privately funded organization that develops and implements training programs for the underskilled to prepare them for industry.

Vernon L. Hoy (Chapter 15) is past Director of the Arizona Department of Public Safety, having served in that position from 1976 to 1980. He joined the Los Angeles Police Department in 1950 and served there in all ranks from police officer to Deputy Chief until his retirement in 1976. During 1972 Chief Hoy served as Executive Director of the Police Task Force of the National Advisory Commission on Criminal Justice Standards and Goals. In 1975 he was the Executive Director of the Police Chief Executive Project. He has served as Chairman of the California Crime Control Committee and Vice-President of the FBI National Academy Associates, California Chapter. Chief Hoy holds an M.S. in public administration from the University of Southern California.

Norman C. Kassoff (Chapter 19) is an Assistant Director with the Dade County (Florida) Corrections and Rehabilitation Department. He was a police lieutenant for ten years with the Dade County Public Safety Department and was later an Assistant Director for the

Professional Standards Division of the International Association of Chiefs of Police. He has authored several books and has served as a consultant for two presidential commissions.

Francis R. Kessler (Chapter 5) is Chief of Police of the Garden Grove (California) Police Department. He has B.S. and M.A. degrees in public administration from the University of Arizona, and in 1972–73 he was a Ford Fellow at the Harvard University Law School. Prior to joining the Garden Grove Police Department in 1976 he retired from the Tucson Police Department after twenty years of service.

Hubert G. Locke (Chapter 2) is Professor, Graduate School of Public Affairs, and Vice Provost for Academic Affairs at the University of Washington. He served as Administrative Assistant to the Commissioner of Police in Detroit, on the State Commissions for Law Enforcement and Criminal Justice in Michigan, Nebraska, and Washington, and on the Twentieth Century Fund Task Force on the Law Enforcement Assistance Administration. He has taught at Wayne State University and the University of Nebraska at Omaha, and is a member of the Board of Directors of the Police Foundation, the Institute for the Study of Contemporary Social Problems, and the Public Administration Service.

Richard E. McDonell (Chapter 16) is Manager, Law Enforcement and Criminal Justice Activities, with IBM in Bethesda, Maryland. He has been Director of Planning with the Chicago Police Department (1960–63), and Commanding Officer of the Planning and Research Division, Oakland, California, Police Department (1954–59). He was an agent with the Criminal Investigation Division of the Department of the Army in Europe (1946–49). He attended the Graduate School of Criminology, University of California.

Patrick V. Murphy (Chapter 4) is President of the Police Foundation. He has served as the chief police executive in New York City, Detroit, Washington, D.C., and Syracuse, New York, and was appointed by President Johnson as Administrator of the Law Enforcement Assistance Administration. He holds a B.A. and a master's degree in public administration and is a former Dean of Administration and Police Science, College of Police Science, City University of New York.

James M. Slavin (Chapter 8) was Director of the Traffic Institute, Northwestern University, from 1963 to 1976. He joined the staff of the Traffic Institute in 1948 as Assistant Director of Training in Police Administration. Mr. Slavin has served as Chief of Police in Kalamazoo, Michigan, and Denver, Colorado. He has been a guest lecturer at the FBI National Academy for over seven years. He is a graduate of the Traffic Institute's Police Administration Program, and has attended the Salmon P. Chase School of Law in Cincinnati, the University of Cincinnati, and Northwestern University. He currently serves as a special consultant to the Director of the Traffic Institute.

James P. Morgan, Jr. (Chapter 6) is Associate Professor, Department of Administration of Justice, and Director of Public Safety, Virginia Commonwealth University. He has served as Chairman of the Law Enforcement Advisory Group of the National Commission on Productivity. His law enforcement experience includes positions with the New York City Police Department and the FBI, and he has served as Director of Public Safety for St. Petersburg, Florida. He holds a bachelor's degree from Manhattan College and a master's in public administration from the Baruch School of Public Administration, City University of New York.

Donald D. Pomerleau (Chapter 11) is Police Commissioner of Baltimore, Maryland. He has served in that capacity since 1966. Previously, Commissioner Pomerleau served on the professional staff of the International Association of Chiefs of Police and as the Director of Public Safety for the Cities of Miami, Florida, and Kingsport, Tennessee. He retired from the United States Marine Corps in 1958 after having served over twenty years. He is a former patrol inspector of the United States Border Patrol.

Charles H. Rogovin (Chapter 10) is Professor of Law, Temple University School of Law, where he has also served as Visiting Professor and Associate Dean. He has been President of Criminal Justice Associates, Inc., a Massachusetts based consulting organization, and Toor Lecturer in Legal Studies at Brandeis University. He is a member of the Massachusetts Organized Crime Control Council by appointment of the governor. He has held many posts, including those of: Consultant, Senate Select Committee on Presidential Campaign Activities (1973–74); President, Police Foundation (1970–72); Administrator, LEAA (1969–70); and Assistant Director, President's Commission on Law Enforcement and Administration of Justice (Director, Organized Crime Task Force) (1966–67). Mr. Rogovin is a consultant to the Joint Public Safety Committee of the Massachusetts legislature. He holds a B.A. in history from Wesleyan University and an LL.B. from Columbia University Law School.

John K. Swan (Chapter 14) has been the Chief of Police of Lynchburg, Virginia, since 1973. Prior to this appointment he served for fifteen years with the Kansas City, Missouri, Police Department, where he worked in patrol, criminal investigations, and planning and research, and as a commanding officer of the Tactical Unit and also of the Staff Inspections Unit. He served on two presidential commissions (Task Force on Police Standards and Goals and National Commission on Productivity). He has a bachelor's degree from the University of Missouri and a master's degree in criminal justice administration from Nova University, and he attended the Southern Police Institute, University of Louisville.

David A. Varrelman (Chapter 17) is Chief of Police, Mt. Lebanon, Pennsylvania. From 1969 to 1972 he was on the staff of the International Association of Chiefs of Police as a police management consultant specializing in police building design. From 1956 to 1969 he served as a member of the Los Angeles County Sheriff's Department. He has taught in California, Maryland, and Pennsylvania and is currently a lecturer for the IACP and an instructor in the local police management course for the International City Management Association. He holds a bachelor's degree in police science and administration from California State University at Long Beach and an advanced POST certificate.

Steven M. Ward (Chapter 12) holds joint appointments as the Chief of Security of the University of Southern California, Program Director of the National Sheriffs' Institute, and Senior Associate with the Delinquency Control Institute in the USC School of Public Administration. He has served as a law enforcement officer and as a professional staff associate with Public Administration Service. He directed the Attorney General's Advisory Commission on Community–Police Relations for the California Department of Justice. A former Director of the Delinquency Control Institute, he has wide experience as a consultant and trainer in the fields of organization design, community mobilization, juvenile programs, and career development. He has consulted nationally with public and private agencies. He holds a bachelor's degree from California State University and a master's degree from the University of Southern California.

Robert Wasserman (Chapter 3) is President of the Public Executive Institutes. He was formerly Assistant to the Police Commissioner, Boston Police Department, where he also served as Director of Training and Education. His prior experience includes heading a State Police Crisis Intervention Team in Massachusetts and serving as Administrative Assistant to the Chief of Police in Dayton, Ohio. He has broad experience as a consultant in training, management, and crisis intervention to police agencies throughout the country. He did his undergraduate work in sociology at Antioch College and his graduate work in police administration at Michigan State University.

Acknowledgments

Numerous individuals have contributed to this and the first edition of *Local Government Police Management.* ICMA particularly acknowledges the fine work of Bernard L. Garmire, who has served as editor of both editions.

Valuable service was rendered by the editorial committee that met in Washington, D.C., in the early spring of 1976 to help in drafting the final outline for the first edition. Committee members also participated actively in reviewing chapter drafts and providing critical commentaries. In addition to Bernard L. Garmire, who served as chairman, the committee membership included the following persons (with their affiliations at that time): Allen H. Andrews, Jr., Superintendent of Police, Peoria, Illinois; Lee S. Ayres, City Manager, Sunnyvale, California; Esai Berenbaum, former Public Safety Director, Durham, North Carolina; Keith R. Bergstrom, Assistant City Manager, Miami, Florida; G. Curtis Branscome, City Manager, Decatur, Georgia; Gerald Caplan, Director, National Institute of Law Enforcement and Criminal Justice; C. E. Dixon, Chief Administrator, San Joaquin County, California; Glen D. King, Executive Director, International Association of Chiefs of Police; William H. Mooney, former Training Director, FBI Academy; Robert J. Schiedler, Town Manager, Barrington, Rhode Island; William H. T. Smith, the Police Foundation; Charles Wall, Chief of Police, Rockville, Maryland; William H. Walls, Business Administrator, Newark, New Jersey; George Washnis, Washington, D.C.; Hubert Williams, Public Safety Director, Newark, New Jersey; and Frank Dyson, Chief of Police, Austin, Texas.

Acknowledgment is due to several other persons who reviewed one or more chapter drafts, including Robert B. Angrisani, Assistant Director, Administrative Services Division, International Association of Chiefs of Police; Chet Dettlinger, Jr., Loss Prevention International; Herman Goldstein, University of Wisconsin Law School; Professor Elinor Ostrom, Workshop in Political Theory and Policy Analysis, Department of Political Science, Indiana University; and Eric Wilson, Systems Development Manager, Miami Police Department, Miami, Florida.

Recognition is due also to Mary Lou Knobbe, who prepared the Bibliography; to Herbert Slobin for graphic design and preparation of many of the illustrations; to Barbara H. Moore, who was responsible for the final editing of the book; and to Emily Evershed, who prepared the index. Two ICMA staff members, Marie Hayman and Mary Od'Neal, assisted, respectively, on research and illustrations, and on documentation for the editing of the chapters. David S. Arnold, Senior Editor, Publications and Policy Center, ICMA, provided general editorial supervision for the book and worked closely with Mr. Garmire in all stages of planning, manuscript review, and subsequent stages in the development of the book.

Finally, the lineage that binds this book to the earlier volumes should be recognized. Over the years many distinguished persons have worked on *Municipal Police Administration,* beginning with the late Lyman S. Moore, who supervised preparation of the 1938 edition. The late O. W. Wilson, Dean of the School of Criminology, University of California, and later Superintendent of Police, Chicago, Illinois, edited the 1943, 1950, and 1954 editions. Richard L. Holcombe, Director, Bureau of Police Science, University of Iowa, was editor of the 1961 edition. George D. Eastman and Esther M. Eastman, Kent State University, served, respectively, as Editor and Associate Editor for the 1969 and 1971 editions.

Illustration credits

Chapter 2   p. 19: Education and Training Division, Baltimore (Maryland) Police Department; p. 24: Adapted from: U.S. Advisory Commission on Intergovernmental Relations, *State–Local Relations in the Criminal Justice System* (Washington, D.C.: Government Printing Office, 1971), pp. 68–69.

Chapter 3   p. 37: National Sheriffs' Association, *Mutual Aid Planning* (Washington, D.C.: National Sheriffs' Association, 1973), p. 87.

Chapter 5   p. 83: Notes drawn from classroom discussion at fellowship program, Harvard Center for Criminal Justice, 1973.

Chapter 7   p. 125: Based on: Stanley Vanagunas and James F. Elliott, *Administration of Police Organizations* (Boston: Allyn and Bacon, Inc., 1980); and Joan L. Wolfe and John F. Heaphy, *Readings on Productivity in Policing* (Washington, D.C.: Police Foundation, 1975).

Chapter 8   p. 137: District of Columbia Department of Highways and Traffic, *Highway and Traffic Safety Improvement Program for the District of Columbia* (Washington, D.C.: District of Columbia Department of Highways and Traffic, n.d.), p. 20.

Chapter 10   p. 186: President's Commission on Law Enforcement and Administration of Justice, *The Challenge of Crime in a Free Society* (Washington, D.C.: Government Printing Office, 1967), p. 194.

Chapter 13   p. 244: International City Management Association, *Personnel Administration*, unit 3 of *Small Cities Management Training Program* (Washington, D.C.: International City Management Association, 1975), p. 13; pp. 258–59. *Public Safety Labor Reporter*, published by Public Safety Labor Relations Center, Research Division, International Association of Chiefs of Police, April 1972; pp. 260–61: Prepared by Cabot J. Dow and Pat Sisco, and reproduced from Cabot J. Dow, "Labor Relations," in *Local Government Personnel Administration*, ed. Winston W. Crouch (Washington, D.C.: International City Management Association, 1976), pp. 222–23.

Chapter 15   p. 291: Stanley Piazza Powers, F. Gerald Brown, and David S. Arnold, eds., *Developing the Municipal Organization* (Washington, D.C.: International City Management Association, 1974), p. 202; p. 292: *Developing the Municipal Organization*, p. 214; p. 305: *Developing the Municipal Organization*, p. 202.

Index

Page numbers in italics refer to illustrations.

434 *Local Government Police Management*

Building inspections as crime deterrent,
208, 211, 212
Buildings. *See* Facilities
Burglary control programs, 212–13
Business
affiliations with organized crime, 56, 59,
181, 182, 183, 185, 187, 189–90,
192, 196, *186*
crime prevention, 214–17

California Commission on Peace Officer
Standards and Training, police management courses, 250
California Council on Criminal Justice, and
premises survey programs, 212
California Highway Patrol, Automated Statewide Auto Theft Inquiry System
(AUTOSTATIS), 313
CAO. *See* Chief administrative officer (municipal)
Caplan, Gerald M., on crime reporting
delays, 99
Career criminals, 160, 174–75
CASS. *See* Crime Analysis Support System
Central personnel agency
central personnel department, 242, 243
description, 242–43
independent civil service commission,
242
types, 242–43
Challenge of Crime in a Free Society (President's Commission on Law Enforce-
ment and Administration of Justice), 14,
20, 27, 28, 401
Chicago, Illinois, early policing efforts, 17
Chief administrative officer (municipal)
relations with police administrator, 30, 43,
45–50, *32, 46*
role regarding police function, 30, 31, 34,
45–50, 51, *46*
Child abuse programs, 222
Cincinnati, Ohio, early policing efforts, 16,
17
Citizen complaint bureaus, 25
Citizen complaint processing, 274, 282–83,
288, 415–16
Citizen involvement
in crime control, 22, 25–26, 197, 203,
204, 205–6, 209, 210–11, 212–19,
222–23
in facility design, 337
Citizen review boards, 274, 283–84, 288
Citizens
aid in combating police corruption, 66
connivance in police corruption, 57–59,
60–61, *59*
effects of police corruption on, 53–54
Civil disorders, 14, 20, 34, 35, 39, 401
Civil Rights Act of 1866, 245
Civil Rights Act of 1964
as amended 1972, 245, 246
and private employers, 245
Title VII (as amended 1972), 245, 246,
272–73 nn. 8–9, 403–6

see also Equal Employment Opportunity
Act of 1972
Civil rights movement, 14
Civil service movement, effect on policing,
33–34, 45
Civilian employees, 251–52
in clerical work, 103
patrol use, 120–21
in police service, 120–21, 144
in traffic control, 103, 143–44, 153
in traffic law enforcement, 143–44
Collective bargaining, 13–14, 259–69, 272,
260–61, 267
bargaining unit, 261–63
contract administration, 266–68
established for federal employees, 255
glossary of terms, 407–13
grievance procedure, 267, *267*
impasse resolution, 268–69
negotiation tactics, 265–66
preelection campaign, 263–64
preparing for negotiations, 264–65
process, 259–69, 272, *260–61, 267*
scope of bargaining, 266
see also Labor–management relations;
Police unions
Commercial theft prevention programs, 212,
215–17
Commission form of government, 33
Communication, definition of, 311
Communications. *See* Information management; Information systems
Community relations. *See* Police–community relations
Community relations concepts, 198
Community service officers, 120, 205
Community standards and police corruption, 60–61
Computer use. *See* Information manage-
ment; Information systems
Conflict management programs, 18, 220
Consolidation of police services. *See* Unification of police services
Consultant services, for police department
audit, 279–80
Council-manager government, 33
Courts
as contributors to police corruption, 60, 65
court–jail relationship, 380, 381–82
and discriminatory hiring, 246–47,
272–73 nn. 8–9
and traffic supervision, 140
see also Legal cases; U.S. Supreme
Court; individual cases
CPM. *See* Critical path method
Crime
common crime, 4–5, 6
definitions of, 4–5, 168
victimless crimes, 5, 56–57
white collar crime, 4–5, 6, 181, 192–93,
196
see also Crime control; Crime prevention;
Crime syndicates; Organized crime
Crime Analysis Support System (CASS),
331–32

Municipal Management Series

**Local Government
Police Management**

Text type
Times Roman, Helvetica

Composition
Progressive Typographers, Inc.
Emigsville, Pennsylvania

Printing and binding
Kingsport Press
Kingsport, Tennessee

Paper
Unisource Offset, 60#

Design
Herbert Slobin